THE SPAIN OF
FERNANDO DE ROJAS

El nacimiento de la novela y drama modernos en las páginas *La Celestina* no fué un fenómeno divertido. La auténica novela surgió de un sentimiento trágico de la vida.

—Américo Castro

The Spain of Fernando de Rojas

THE INTELLECTUAL AND SOCIAL LANDSCAPE OF
La Celestina

BY STEPHEN GILMAN

PRINCETON UNIVERSITY PRESS

Publication of this book has been aided by the
Whitney Darrow Publication Reserve Fund
of Princeton University Press.

This book has been composed in Linotype Granjon
Printed in the United States of America
by Princeton University Press at Princeton, N.J.

CONTENTS

CONTENTS

PREFACE

The pages of *La Celestina* are a venerable meeting place. In them as in the pages of every work of its magnitude, whether of fiction or non-fiction, the minds of generations of readers have encountered with ever-refreshened wonder the mind of the author. But it is not just because Rojas' waiting mind is unique, sensitive, or intelligent that marvel and secret exhilaration are engendered. The sense that something mysterious, wholly new, and immensely important is transpiring is also due to an intuition of timelessness. Here is a mind which has discovered how to free itself from the tiresome limitations of day-to-day perseverance, a mind at the pinnacle of creative power, ranging like a hound, soaring like a hawk, and converting "moments stolen from study" into forever. Such minds and such liberation are the very substance of the quality called—by those who experience it at second hand—artistic greatness.

Our notion of what authorship means is often illustrated with anecdotic reminiscence of these timeless intervals. Berceo in his darkening portal, Cervantes in his prison, Stendhal in hiding at 8 rue Caumartin remind us that what seems beyond human capacity begins in human liberation. But Fernando de Rojas has no such familiar myth—even though he tried to provide one in his prefatory letter. Readers have been so entranced with the voices he recorded and which concealed his own that they have generally overlooked the circumstances of his transcendence. The very autonomy of the speakers provides an almost intoxicating sense of freedom from self, with the result that when readers meet Rojas' mind they fail fully to realize it is a mind—that is to say, the mind of a living author, beset with biography, writing feverishly in a student's room during a fortnight's vacation from classes.

It is this that the present book will try to remedy. By putting Fernando de Rojas back into his Spain, back into historical and biographical circumstances called the Puebla de Montalbán, Salamanca, and Talavera de la Reina, it may be possible to meet him again and to appreciate better the experience. By the very nature of the records at their disposal, most biographers attempt to reveal their human subjects by an examination of their life-long captivity. Yet they need not apologize. Only through knowledge of specific bars, chains, fetters, walls, and wardens, can the miracle of escape be recognized and admired.

I recall the moment when I first became aware of meeting Fernando de Rojas. It happened in Columbus, Ohio, on a spring morning in 1954. I was sitting in my study trying to revise a manuscript entitled "The Art of *La Celestina*"—that is to say, a manuscript premised on the tacit notion that the text in some way was its own artist. I was thinking about that interpolation in Act XII in which Sempronio mentions his boyhood fears in the service of "Mollejas el ortelano," when suddenly I remembered having read in one of the three biographical documents then published that Rojas himself had owned a property in the Puebla de Montalbán called "la huerta de Mollejas." The irony and cunning of his provision of Sempronio (of all interlocutors!) with a boyhood memory of his own communicated a sudden and vivid sense of the man behind the dialogue, a presence of which theretofore I had been only dimly aware. Much later I was to learn that Rojas' descendant, the late don Fernando del Valle Lersundi, had published the document in question (a transcript of testimony concerning Rojas' status as an *hidalgo* conserved in his private archives) with the idea of making this very point. But at the time I was dumbfounded both by the fact that *I* had made such a discovery and by the unexpected appearance on the page of an artist whom I had previously thought of as a kind of necessary assumption.

At that time I had no idea of the danger I was in, and perhaps, if I had possessed more foresight, I would resolutely have dismissed the resemblance as coincidental. However, in the blindness of my excitement, I decided to check certain paleographical doubts (several witnesses give different versions of the name Mollejas) in the original document, which is to be found (as my colleague, the late Claude Anibal told me it would be) in the archives of the Royal Chancery in Valladolid. Upon so doing, I was further amazed to find that I had discovered a substantial amount of unknown testimony concerning Rojas, testimony printed here for the first time according to the transcription of that most eminent of paleographers, don Agustín Millares Carlo (see Appendix III). At that point my scholarly future was determined. One document led to another and that to still another in a continuing chain that has resembled nothing so much as the game we used to play as children called "Treasure Hunt." Indeed, I have often felt that it was not I who was engaged in writing this book but rather that the book itself—like the Ancient Mariner and the Wedding Guest—had chosen me as its human instrument for coming into being. Why this should be so, given my professional and temperamental unsuitability for the task, it would be hard for me to say. I can only ask for the reader's indulgence when he encounters signs of disarray and discouragement here and there in the course of his reading.

Before turning from personal reminiscence to expression of gratitude to the people who have helped me, I should like to speak of my relations with the man who contributed the most to making *The Spain of Fernando de Rojas* possible: don Fernando de Valle Lersundi. When I realized that the testimony he had published in 1925 had not come directly from the Chancery (in which case all of it would have come to light) but from a partial transcription (made centuries before in an effort to establish the doubtful "nobility" of the Rojas) which he must have found in his family papers, it occurred to me that he might also possess other items of interest. I then wrote to him and arranged for a meeting in Madrid. When he appeared on the terrace of the Café Gijón, carrying a leather case full of sixteenth-century documents, I realized I was in the presence of a wholly remarkable person. I say this not because of his commanding appearance, his extraordinary energy (already in his late seventies, he left me panting when he ran up the stairs of the steeple of San Miguel in the Puebla two at a time), or his phenomenally quick mind. What seemed to me even more impressive was the fact that, as the descendant ("por línea recta de varón," as they say in Spanish) of the author of *La Celestina,* he was as aware of the full significance of the papers he showed me as I was and certainly far better prepared to exploit them.

As a young man, don Fernando had been fascinated with the extensive archives (the some eighty documents having to do with Rojas and his lineage are only a small portion of the whole) that are conserved in the family mansion or *solar* in Deva. As a result, he trained himself in paleography and, taking advantage of a library collected over ancestral generations (actually containing a

few of the books owned by Rojas!), went on to become a professional genealogist. It was, therefore, not a question of my using his
documents but rather of helping him publish material that he already knew and understood. And for that he needed what I, as a
professor in a North American university, could in some measure
provide: time and money. Our agreement was as follows: we
would share whatever grants I might obtain in the United States
(as it turned out at different times we were assisted by Harvard
University, the American Council of Learned Societies, and the
American Philosophical Society); he would allow me to do spadework in his Deva library and would help me with difficult transcriptions; and I would prepare an article or résumé to be signed
by both of us which would present in direct quotation information
pertinent to Fernando de Rojas and his immediate family. This task
took me two years to complete, it being necessary to relate the mass
of new facts to what was already known and to others that I was
at the same time bringing to light. It was also necessary to consult
a number of scholars, including my master, Américo Castro.

I also arranged with don Fernando that when my work was
finished I would submit it to him for review and approval. His professional reputation was going to be involved as well as mine, and
he was the only expert in a position to correct the amateurish
errors or misreadings for which I might be responsible. Unfortunately (for reasons it is unnecessary to explain here) the final
scrutiny was never made, although as late as 1969 I continued my
efforts to persuade don Fernando to undertake it. In my last letter
to him I told him that, since my only real interest in the matter was
the availability of information for this biography, I would be quite
willing for him to publish a corrected version under his name
alone. He answered me that he hoped to bring out transcriptions
of his own in the future—and then a few months later I learned of
his death.

As a result, in writing *The Spain of Fernando de Rojas,* I am
in the awkward situation of those government officials who
attempt publicly to justify their policies on the basis of classified
information. A solution which I have more than once contem-
plated would be to include my résumé here as an appendix. My
personal obligation to don Fernando no longer exists, and my professional obligation to his ancestor is overriding. All available facts

about such an enigmatic and important figure as the author of *La Celestina* should be brought to light. On second thought, however, I have decided to let the matter rest as it is. Although I am confident that my factual interpretations are correct, there is no doubt but that the transcriptions should be thoroughly checked by an expert with access to the original documents before publication. In case any individual scholar should question my statements, I will be glad to provide him with a copy of the evidence at my disposal. In most instances this could be a microfilm. Another possibility is private recourse to the archives in Deva, archives which, I personally hope, will eventually be acquired by the Biblioteca Nacional. At some point everything concerning Rojas will have to be printed, but, in the meantime, it is of importance to me—and I hope and believe to *La Celestina*—that this book should appear as soon as possible.

Aside from those already named, the list of scholars and friends who have been generous with their time and knowledge is lengthy. Indeed so much indispensable help has been given to me by so many people that, as I begin to compile this list, my one fear is that I may forget to include someone deserving of much gratitude. To begin with, my student research assistants—Margery Resnick, Peter Goldman, Nora Weinerth, and above all Michael Ruggerio— have not only devoted many hours to spade work but also have made many helpful suggestions for improvement. And the same thing can be said for other guest readers inside and outside the profession: Francisco Márquez Villanueva, Francis Rogers, Roy Harvey Pearce, Morton Bloomfield, Raimundo Lida, Claudio Guillén, Dorothy Severin, and Jorge Guillén. All of these saw one chapter or another at different stages of development, some of them so long ago they may not remember their individual contributions. But I do. The only scholar I know who has seen the whole in more or less its final form is Edmund L. King. To him and to the other anonymous reader selected by Princeton University Press special thanks must be given for their thorough scrutiny and essential suggestions. Without their knowledge and sense of style many egregious mistakes and obscurities of expression would never have been caught. As usual, for the many that remain the fault is mine.

Many others have responded to my appeals for help with a generosity which the course of the text will acknowledge. These include: Luis G. de Valdeavellano, Ernest Grey, Ricardo Espinosa Maeso, M. J. Benardete, Almiro Robledo, the late Antonio Rodríguez Moñino, Angela Selke de Sánchez, Harry Levin, George Williams, Isadore Twersky, Rafael Lapesa, Carmen Castro de Zubiri, Edith Hellman, and the archivists; Fathers Gerardo Maza of the Royal Chancery in Valladolid, José López de Toro of the Biblioteca Nacional, Ramón Gonzálvez of the Cathedral of Toledo, and Gregorio Sánchez Doncel of the Cathedral of Sigüenza. To all of them I wish to express my most profound gratitude.

But, aside from don Fernando, there are two people who did more than anyone else to bring this book to its conclusion and to whom it is lovingly dedicated: my master, don Américo, and my wife, Teresa.

Cambridge, Mass.   S.G.
November 1971

LIST OF ABBREVIATIONS

AHN   Archivo Histórico Nacional

Ajo   C. M. Ajo and G. Sainz de Zúñiga, *Historia de las universidades hispánicas*, 2 vols., Madrid, 1957

Amador de los Ríos   J. Amador de los Ríos, *Historia social, política y religiosa de los judíos de España y Portugal*, Madrid, 1960

The Art   Stephen Gilman, *The Art of "La Celestina,"* Madison, 1956

Artes   Raimundo González de Montes, *Artes de la Inquisizión Española*, edited and translated from the original Latin edition (Heidelberg, 1567) by L. Usoz y Río, n.p., 1851

BAE   Biblioteca de Autores Españoles

Baer   Yitzhak Baer, *History of the Jews in Christian Spain*, 2 vols., Philadelphia, 1961, 1966 (also: Fritz Baer, *Die Juden im Christlichen Spanien*, 2 vols., Berlin, 1929, 1936, source book for the same author's later *History*)

BAH   Boletín de la Academia de la Historia

Bataillon   Marcel Bataillon, *"La Célestine" selon Fernando de Rojas*, Paris, 1961

Bell   Aubrey Bell, *Luis de León*, Oxford, 1925

Bethencourt   F. Fernández de Bethencourt, *Historia genealógica y heráldica de la monarquía española, casa real y grandes de España*, 10 vols., Madrid, 1897-1920

BH   Bulletin Hispanique

BHS   Bulletin of Hispanic Studies

BN   Biblioteca Nacional

BNM   (citation for a manuscript in the Biblioteca Nacional)

BRAE   Boletín de la Real Academia Española

BRAH   Boletín de la Real Academia de la Historia

Caro Baroja   Julio Caro Baroja, *Los judíos en la España moderna y contemporánea*, 3 vols., Madrid, 1961

Caro Lynn   Caro Lynn, *A College Professor of the Renaissance* (Lucio Marineo), Chicago, 1937

Catálogo de pasajeros   Catálogo de pasajeros a Indias, ed. C. Bermúdez Plata, 3 vols., Seville, 1946

Domínguez Ortiz Antonio Domínguez Ortiz, *La clase social de los conversos en la edad modernos*, Madrid, 1955

Dumont Louis Dumont, *Homo hierarchicus*, Paris 1966

Epistolario Peter Martyr, *Epistolario*, in *Documentos inéditos para la historia de España*, nueva serie, vols. IX-XII, edited by J. López de Toro, Madrid, 1955-57

Erasmo Marcel Bataillon, *Erasmo y Espana,* Madrid, 1950

Esperabé Arteaga E. Esperabé Arteaga, *Historia pragmática e interna de la Universidad de Salamanca*, Salamanca, 1914

FELS Fondo de Expediente de Limpieza de Sangre

Gilman-Gonzálvez Stephen Gilman and Ramón Gonzálvez, "The Family of Fernando de Rojas," *Romanische Forschungen,* LXXVIII (1966), 1-26.

HR *Hispanic Review*

Inquisición de Toledo (documents in the Archivo Histórico Nacional relating to the Inquisition in Toledo; since the reference numbers have been changed manually in the catalogue compiled by Vincent Vignau, Madrid, 1903, the documents are cited in this book by page number only)

Investigaciones Francisco Márquez, *Investigaciones sobre Juan Alvarez Gato*, Madrid, 1960

Judaizantes Francisco Cantera Burgos and P. León Tello, *Judaizantes del arzobispado de Toledo habilitados por la Inquisición en 1495 y 1497*, Madrid, 1969

Lea H. C. Lea, *The Inquisition of Spain*, 3 vols., New York, 1907

Llorente Juan Antonio Llorente, *Historia crítica de la Inquisición en España*, 10 vols., Madrid, 1822

MLN *Modern Language Notes*

NBAE Nueva Biblioteca de Autores Españoles

NRFH *Nueva Revista de Fililogía Hispánica* (México)

Orígenes Marcelino Menéndez Pelayo, *Orígenes de la novela*, edición nacional, Santander, 1943 (orig. 1905)

La originalidad María Rosa Lida de Malkiel, *La originalidad artística de "La Celestina,"* Buenos Aires, 1962

Propalladia J. E. Gillet, *Propalladia*, Philadelphia, 1961

RABM *Revista de Archivos, Bibliotecas y Museos*

Realidad, edn. I / edn. II Américo Castro, *La realidad histórica de España*, edition I, México, 1954; edition II, México, 1962 (Quotations in English from *Realidad*, edn. I, are the translations of Edmund L. King as they appear in *The Structure of Spanish History*, Princeton, 1954.)

Relaciones *Relaciones de los pueblos de España, Reino de Toledo*, edited by C. Viñas and R. Paz, Madrid, 1951

Reynier Gustave Reynier, *La Vie universitaire dans l'ancien Espagne*, Paris, 1902

RF *Romanische Forschungen*

RFE *Revista de Filología Española* (Madrid)

RH *Revue Hispanique*

RHM *Revista Hispánica Moderna* (New York)

Riva A. Basanta de la Riva, *Sala de los hijosdalgo, catálogo de todos sus pleitos*, 4 vols., Valladolid, 1922

RO *Revista de Occidente*

Salazar y Castro Salazar y Castro archives in the Academia de la Historia, published *Indice* edited by B. Cuartero y Huerta and A. de Vargas-Zúñiga, Madrid, 1956

Serrano y Sanz Manuel Serrano y Sanz, "Noticias biográficas de Fernando de Rojas," *Revista de Archivos, Bibliotecas y Museos*, vi (1902), 245-298

Sicroff Albert A. Sicroff, *Les Controverses des statuts de "pureté de sang" en Espagne du XVe au XVIIe siècle*, Paris, 1960

VLA Valle Lersundi Archives

VL I VLA 35, published by Valle Lersundi as "Documentos referentes a Fernando de Rojas," *Revista de Filología Española*, xii (1925), 385-396

VL II VLA 17 and 33, Rojas' testament and the inventory made after his death, published by Valle Lersundi as "Testamento de Fernando de Rojas," *Revista de Filología Española*, xvi (1929), 367-388

CHAPTER I

The Reality of Fernando de Rojas

No quiere mi pluma ni manda razón
Que quede la fama de aqueste gran hombre
Ni su digna fama ni su claro nombre
Cubierto de olvido . . .

—Alonso de Proaza

❧ The Testimony of the Text

Not long ago a distinguished American humanist proposed to the present generation of scholar-critics a radical and disconcerting query as specially appropriate for changing the course of our meditations. The question he asked, and urges us to answer, was simply: "How is literature possible?"[1] And, as far as I am concerned, the troubled critical reception of a book of mine entitled *The Art of "La Celestina"*[2] justifies the proposition. Labeled by reviewers either as an "Existentialist" or as a "New Critical" interpretation, its close textual analysis of *La Celestina* seemed to them anachronistic. In my opinion, the labels are contradictory and the accusation of anachronism is unfounded. Yet at the same time I must admit that the misunderstandings are my responsibility. Captivated by the vitality of speech and speakers, I failed to consider the preliminary historical question: "How was the completely unprecedented, immensely original art of its author, Fernando de Rojas, possible?" By which is meant primarily: "How could a man living at the end of the fifteenth century in Spain have written a book so significant to us and our concerns?" And, secondarily: "What can be found out about him and his life which may help provide an answer?"

The question just set forth is manifestly identical to that presented by every time-traveling masterpiece—by *Don Quijote,* by *Oedipus Rex,* by *Hamlet,* and by their limited number of peers. The only difference is that in these cases the would-be answerer may take advantage of a great deal of previous historical and biographical spadework, whereas in the case of *La Celestina* he has very little, neither a known life nor an adequate understanding of the times, upon which to support his insights. As a result of this lack of foundation, *Celestina* interpretation has gone in two directions. On the one hand, there are those who attempt to supply historical comprehension of an archaeological sort from their own stores of erudition. *La Celestina* is a creation of fifteenth-century rhetoric, a mirror of medieval morality, or an allegory of the seven

---

[1] Roy Harvey Pearce, "Historicism Once More," title essay in *Historicism Once More: Problems and Occasions for the American Scholar,* Princeton, 1969.
[2] Madison, Wis., 1956 (hereafter referred to as *The Art*).

deadly sins—which is to say, it is interesting but dead. On the other hand, there are a few of us who have been so concerned with the bursting life of Rojas' dialogue that we are open to the charge of ignoring what *La Celestina* was historically speaking. A new approach, therefore, is not only appropriate but urgent. Having tried to show how the work lives, we must now try to provide the background necessary for understanding how the book came alive so immortally. Evaluation of *La Celestina* as one of man's major creations, I now see, requires more than textual analysis of style, structure, or theme. A sustained effort to comprehend the historical agonies of its birth is also necessary. We cannot, in other words, really know what *La Celestina* is without speculating as rigorously and as learnedly as possible both on how it came to be and on the broader query of how it could come to be. It is to nothing less than this that the present book is dedicated.

Such a statement of purpose confronts both writer and reader with theoretical problems of the sort for which confessions of commitment are more proper than attempted solutions. To begin with, interrogation in terms of possibility was designed to eliminate positivistic search for historical causation. *La Celestina* was not written by its "race" (Judeo-Spanish), "milieu" (Salamanca), or "moment" (the Isabeline Renaissance). Instead, it was written (setting aside for the time being the excruciating problem of Act I) by a man called Fernando de Rojas, who encountered and experienced these three determinants, who lived within—and through!—his historical climate. Not out of history, but from deep inside individual awareness of history, masterpieces make their way up into the light. Which is to proclaim the obvious: that history shapes art only insofar as it works through the whole of the artist's life. There are no short cuts or short circuits. *La Celestina* may perhaps be conceived of as a historical possibility realized by a Fernando de Rojas *de carne y hueso*. But it cannot be conceived of as a historical necessity.

Thus our commitment and thus our program. If literature is, as Jean-Pierre Richard would have it, "an adventure in being human,"[3] we must accordingly view the "times" of a work from the

---

[3] "On a donc vu dans l'écriture une activité positive et créatrice à l'intérieur de laquelle certains êtres parviennent a coincider pleinement avec eux-mêmes. . . . L'élaboration d'une grande oeuvre littéraire n'est rien d'autre en effet

point of view of their impingement on and assimilation to the biography of a "human being." We shall not be concerned with what happened in history but with history as we may relive with Diltheyesque reverence its immediate presence for a man alive and super-sentient within limited carnal, rural, and urban circumstances. Domesticity in the broad sense will above all be decisive. Furthermore, since our only significant knowledge of the man who concerns us is his work, it is through the prism of our reading that we shall have primarily to look. In this sense it can be maintained without paradox that *La Celestina* creates its times rather than the other way around. What it has to say to us is our only possible measurement of the historical and biographical meaning of whatever facts, old and new, we may present. The work does not select the facts (such license when so few are available would be grossly improper), but it does evaluate them and arrange them in an inevitable hierarchy. Only by allowing *La Celestina* to perform this essential function may we hope to avoid the critical fallacy against which we are warned by José F. Montesinos, the fallacy "according to which the real life of a poet conditions comprehension of his art, when the truth of the matter is just the opposite."[4]

A second and perhaps more vulnerable flank separates us from those who are discouraged by the perils of relating historical and biographical information to literature. In spite of all precautions, certain critics feel, approximation of the two is at worst noxious and at best nonsensical, a foolishly complacent mixture of irreconcilable criteria. Against such beliefs, two separate lines of defense may be erected. The first is that of my master, Américo Castro: comprehension of history itself as a dominion of value within which literature rather than being alien is indigenous—and among the most respected inhabitants. Characteristic of Castro's valiant and unceasing effort to recapture history for the humanities is the following unpublished judgment: "The literature of an epoch and the epoch of that literature are indivisible phenomena. Without the

---

que la découverte d'une perspective vraie sur soi-même, la vie, les hommes. Et la littérature est une aventure d'être" (*Littérature et sensation*, Paris, 1954, p. 14).

4 ". . . la aberración inconcebible . . . según la cual la vida real de un poeta condiciona la comprensión de su arte, cuando lo cierto es justamente lo contrario . . ." (*Estudios sobre Lope de Vega*, México, 1951, p. 71).

light cast by literature and art, the 'historiability' of a given period of the past cannot be determined."[5] I have translated Castro's "dimensión historiable" with the neologism "historiability," since by it he means a period's worthiness of an historian's attention. Among other reasons, the life and times of Fernando de Rojas are important insofar as they constituted the human soil in which *La Celestina* could be, and, in effect, was, grown. We must understand literature historically and biographically, Castro would maintain, if only in order to save biography and history from triviality.

It is easy to accept this commitment for a work of the inherent significance and immortality of *La Celestina*. As far as my own efforts are concerned, Castro's denial of disparity between literature and history provides at least preliminary justification for writing about the Spain of Fernando de Rojas. And afterwards, although the proof, as usual, will be in the pudding, with such ingredients the risk is not grave. If an essay on Rojas' life and times can bring to light even one hitherto unknown fact, even one hitherto unperceived condition of creation, the essayist—whatever his sins of omission and commission—has nothing to fear. All of which leads to the second line of defense: the situation of *La Celestina* at the headwaters of a genre, the novel, which has traditionally been composed of great chunks of raw, unprocessed experience, much of it experience of historical circumstance. What the author feels about the historical world into which he has been thrust has been expressed in every important novel from *Lazarillo de Tormes* to *Finnegans Wake* and beyond. Precisely for this reason those opposed to biographical and historical criticism have generally preferred to treat other more formally elaborated varieties of literature. The student of *La Celestina*, however, cannot allow himself to be so fastidious. As I hope to demonstrate in the course of the many pages to follow, its dialogue cannot rightly be understood if we eliminate from it Fernando de Rojas' profound experience and sardonic judgement of the Spain in which he lived.

These assertions should not be taken to mean a Romantic equation of what happens in *La Celestina* with presumed events in Rojas' biography. As contrasted with a Stendhal who left us every possible facility for observing the transformation of his life into art

[5] For further development of these ideas see his *Dos ensayos*, Mexico, 1956.

(apparently conceiving of such observation as a necessary component of the kind of appreciation he sought), Rojas offers us nothing at all—not even the few playful hints of a Cervantes! Although he is willing on occasion to let us glimpse his sources, his models (and surely they existed, since no creation of *La Celestina*'s magnitude can be grown only from sources) are quite deliberately hidden from our view. He is even reluctant to indicate in any way the name of the city which is the scene of his tragicomic "argument." Every artist imposes the acceptance of the terms of an implicit compact, and since these are evidently Rojas' own conditions, we must live with them. Which was my answer to a well-intentioned person who once asked me how I could possibly write about Rojas' life without knowing the identity of Melibea. Obviously, if we were in a position to identify Rojas' models or to relive his personal experiences of love and death, the temptation would be irresistible. So that in a very real sense it may be fortunate for *La Celestina* that this first attempt to describe Rojas' life has been made more than four centuries after his death.

Like most qualifications, this one needs to be qualified further. Assertion of the undesirability (not merely the impossibility) of revealing the anecdotic incubation of *La Celestina* is not intended to cast doubt on the living and breathing reality of its maker (or of its makers). It is historical, as we said, precisely because it is autobiographical—autobiographical in a far deeper sense than that of mere narrated reminiscence. "How to write a novel? Rather, why write a novel?" Unamuno asks and goes on to answer: "In order that the novelist may create himself. And why should the novelist create himself? To create the reader, to create himself in the reader. And only by becoming one can the novelist and the reader of the novel be saved from their radical solitude."[6] We shall have occasion in a later chapter to meditate at greater length on *La Celestina* as such an "autobiography," concluding, with the collaboration of Kenneth Burke, that Rojas sought in his writing not so much to *create* himself as, by a process of transmutation of his most intimate burdens, to *save* himself. But for now it is sufficient to confess belief in the Unamunian "weight on the ground" of the fifteenth-century man whose experiences are about to haunt us.

[6] "Cómo se hace una novela," *Obras completas*, ed. M. García Blanco, vol. x, Madrid, 1958, p. 922

Those unfamiliar with the body of criticism which adheres to *La Celestina* may not realize the unprecedented nature of these commitments. For Fernando de Rojas from the very beginning has been surely the least recognized of the major authors of the Western world. Lope de Vega, whose admiration of *La Celestina* yields to no man's, failed to mention him in the company of Jorge de Montemayor, Fray Luis de León, and other earlier writers in his *Laurel de Apolo*. Even more telling is the brief mention of him by the proto-historian of Spanish letters, Nicolás Antonio. Rojas' name, as we remember, only appears in passing in a paragraph devoted to Rodrigo de Cota, whom most readers of the time supposed (not unreasonably) to have been the author of Act I. More anonymous during the "Siglo de Oro" than his fully anonymous predecessor, Rojas has not fared better since then. Not only is there no street in Madrid named after him, not only is he confused by careless scholars with Francisco de Rojas Zorrilla, but, even when he is mentioned, it is usually as a nonentity, an empty human label. Blanco White's remark that "no author has enjoyed less the glory of his achievement than he of the famous tragicomedy"[7] still holds good.

The most distinguished exception of this generalization was, of course, don Marcelino Menéndez Pelayo, the virtual founder of Hispanism. But in spite of his valiant efforts at the beginning of this century to establish Rojas as a major, though admittedly enigmatic, writer,[8] few of his successors have cared to assert so much. Those aware of the history of the problem will understand why. Both for Blanco White and for Menéndez Pelayo, Rojas needed to be re-invented in order to fortify a critical perception of *La Celestina*'s organic unity. For them it could have only been the child of a single father, a father whose virtual disappearance made critical assertiveness all the more necessary. But now that Rojas' statement that Act I was written by a predecessor is generally accepted, his reality as an author seems even more doubtful and uninteresting than before.

Thus, Menéndez Pidal refers to *La Celestina* as "semi-anony-

---

[7] *Variedades o el Mensajero de Londres*, London, 1824. Cited by Bataillon (see n. 12), p. 21.

[8] *Orígenes de la novela*, Edición nacional, Santander, 1943 (orig., 1905; hereafter referred to as *Orígenes*).

mous,"[9] while Claudio Sánchez Albornoz, inexcusably ignoring unequivocal documentary evidence, doubts whether it was really
"Fernando de Rojas, the *converso* and not another Castilian of the
same name" who was referred to in the acrostic verses.[10] Others,
admitting that Rojas probably did exist, de-emphasize his role as
an author. Carmelo Samonà, for example, sees him as a "non-
crystallized personality," gathering and reflecting the commonplaces and the rhetoric of the age.[11] Less baldly stated, this seems
to be somewhat the same position as that of Marcel Bataillon. Not
only because, at least by implication, Bataillon seems to consider
Rojas merely as a talented imitator of the "primitive *Celestina*,"
but also because his thesis that the dialogue is a mirror of medieval morality leaves little room for personal creation.[12] But perhaps the most devastating judgment of all is that of the editors of
the most recent scholarly edition: "Replacing former belief in a
single author (a belief which represented the idealistic approach
and the great authority of don Marcelino Menéndez Pelayo) is the
conviction that diverse epochs and authors are superimposed in the
text. According to our present concept, *La Celestina,* far from being an improvised and personal creation, is the result of a long and
varied elaboration in the course of which an extensive quantity of
medieval and Renaissance elements were brought together."[13]
Rojas' friend and editor, Alonso de Proaza, showed singular insight
when in the concluding verses cited in the epigraph to this chapter

[9] "La lengua en tiempo de los reyes católicos," *Cuadernos Hispanoamericanos* (Madrid), no. 40, 1950, p. 15.

[10] *España, un enigma histórico*, 2 vols., Buenos Aires, 1962, II, 280.

[11] *Aspetti del retoricismo nella "Celestina,"* Rome, 1953, p. 11.

[12] Marcel Bataillon, *"La Célestine" selon Fernando de Rojas*, Paris, 1961
(hereafter referred to as Bataillon).

[13] G. D. Trotter and M. Criado de Val, *Tragicomedia*, Madrid, 1958, pp.
vi-vii. In a sense, this is in accord with María Rosa Lida de Malkiel's belief
(see below, n. 14) not only in an original author and Rojas but also in a
"cenáculo" of friends who together composed the additions of 1502. There is
no evidence whatsoever supporting this last opinion, an opinion which seems
to have emerged from her distaste for or disagreement with certain sentences
and phrases in the additions. An example would be Calisto's tenderly mocking
"el que quiere comer el aue, quita primero las plumas." However, it seems
to me better scholarly procedure to accept Rojas' direct and stated assumption
of responsibility than to follow Cejador and Foulché Delbosc in imposing
subjective preferences on the text.

he expressed the fear that "the fame of this great man" along with his "clear name" might remain "covered with forgetfulness."

In the presence of such a chorus of authoritative voices, the reader may well ask, "Why bother to argue?" There is only one equally brief answer to be given: "For *La Celestina*'s sake." As Menéndez Pelayo knew, the peculiar character of this literary orphan makes discovery of a parent imperative. By which I mean specifically: to think of it as spontaneously generated, or, even worse, as the offspring of an indefinite number of characterless progenitors, leads to the kind of misinterpretation that is implicit in many of the above remarks. Unlike, say, the *Poema del Cid* or the "Romancero," *La Celestina* (Proaza was absolutely right!) is ill-suited for anonymity. To eliminate its presiding mind tends necessarily to convert it into a bundle of sources, a sampler of styles, a "breviary" of fifteenth-century doctrine, or a congregation of "medieval and Renaissance elements"—whatever these last may be.

There is, of course, a story which, like all stories, can be read as if the author didn't matter. But taken by itself, it is a derivative and slapdash affair that is properly described by Rojas as a dry and fleshless skeleton. There are also speakers—all of them fascinating, but in so many guises, intonations, and levels of expression that their fixed and independent characterization often seems ambiguous. Only Celestina, herself, as an autonomous and consequential voice, remains to confer on the work the unified meaning that eventually resulted in her conquest of the title. At best *La Celestina*, once the author is discounted, becomes the property of an ancient procuress whose combination of sensual awareness ("May I so enjoy the sinfulness of my soul!"), epic valor ("Twice now I have put my life at stake on the gaming board"), and Stoic self-assertion ("I am an old woman just the way God made me") has entranced generations of readers. But, as readers, they may be excused. When scholars, and they are far more dangerous, decide to dispense with Rojas, they often convert *La Celestina* into little more than a receptacle for their individual collections of learning.

Admittedly neither the impressionable reader nor the myopic scholar is entirely to blame for the eclipse of Fernando de Rojas. As we shall see, he himself, as a designer of the prologue material,

10

must share a portion of the responsibility. By owning up so humbly to the prior existence of Act I (somewhat less than a fifth of the whole) and by revealing so deviously (in an easy acrostic) his own authorship of the rest, he invited both dispersed elements of his creation ("fontezicas de filosofía") and the most conspicuous of his created lives to cast their shadows over him. Indeed he even seemed to welcome the darkness. The very fact that he never afterwards exercised his genius for dialogue can without unfairness be interpreted as demonstrating a lack of interest in personal publicity. Later we shall consider in more detail some of the problems presented by Rojas' confession of continuation, by his curious prefatory behavior, and by his failure to establish his claim to fame with a second work. But for now all three may be dismissed as relevant but hardly crucial factors in the disappearance of the author. Granting the explosive originality of *La Celestina*, an originality documented in over 700 pages of passionate erudition by the late María Rosa Lida de Malkiel,[14] it would seem that the corresponding need to conceive of an originator renders inconsequential such external sources of doubt. The creative posture of the Archpriest of Hita is at least as ambiguous as that of Rojas, yet few critics would for that reason describe him as a nonentity or erase his name from the history of literature in Castilian.

For a more profound understanding of what happened to Fernando de Rojas on the way to Parnassus we must look inside the text. It was in what James Fitzmaurice-Kelly (one of the few scholars aside from Menéndez Pelayo to recognize *La Celestina*'s crying need of parentage) called the "high accomplishment" of his art and not in his "furtive" self-presentation that his fate was decided. Precisely because the altitude of Rojas' accomplishment was attained through the creation of seemingly autonomous voices, his own dwindles and recedes. The speakers and particularly that grandmistress of speech, Celestina, take over *La Celestina* seeming—in a kind of Pirandellian apotheosis—to be its authors. However, recognition of this phenomenon need not imply its acceptance. I am as fervent as anyone else in my admiration of the existential reality of Celestina, but I think it is about time we stopped listening to her

---

[14] *La originalidad artística de "La Celestina,"* Buenos Aires, 1962 (hereafter referred to as *La originalidad*).

11

voice as if it actually were made of sound. That is, as if she were recorded on tape instead of being printed in a book. The root problem is how this appearance of auditory autonomy could be achieved. Who was, we ask again, Celestina's creator? And how could he, a silent nobody in the opinion of most readers, have captured her on paper?

If these questions seem to return us to our point of departure—to the problem of the possibility of literature—they also sharpen the interrogation: how was this particularly mysterious kind of literature possible? In search of a preliminary answer to a question which at this point is obviously premature, we may turn for guidance to three well-known authorities. The first is Stephen Daedalus: "The personality of the artist, at first a cry or cadence of mood and then a fluid and lambent narrative, impersonalizes itself so to speak. The esthetic image in the dramatic form is life purified and reprojected from the human imagination. The mystery of esthetic is accomplished. The artist like the God of creation remains within, behind, or beyond or above his handiwork, invisible, refined out of existence, indifferent, paring his fingernails."[15] To this much-quoted assertion two comments may be appended. In the first place, to refine oneself out of existence is neither a factual situation nor a possibility but, as was to be expected of the young scholastic who formulated the notion, a paradox. Someone has to do the refining, someone who is all the more himself by the act of self-refinement. The mystery has been restated with juvenile verve, but it has not been solved. In the second place, if recourse to dialogue were in itself capable of producing such results, all playwrights would be equal in their ability to liberate human life in their manuscripts—which, of course, is absurd on the face of it. Genius aside, we shall see in a moment that it is in part precisely because Rojas was not a dramatist and not subject to the prior expectations (more or less rigid characterizations, calculated timing of dialogue for best effect, and the rest) of a theater full of people, that his voices sound so self-generating.

Let us try again with a formula offered by Giuseppe Borgese: "Romantic writers identify art with its source or root inspiration,

[15] James Joyce, *A Portrait of the Artist as a Young Man*, New York, 1928, p. 252.

while classical writers identify it with its realization or flowering in achieved form."[16] The phrasing of this antithesis is particularly interesting to readers of *La Celestina* in that it reminds us of an image from the Prologue. The word of the wise man, Rojas says, is like a seed swollen and full of virtue which "aspires to burst, throwing out from itself such flourishing leaves and branches that from the slightest bud discreet persons may later pluck abundant fruit." Commonplace origins aside, the writer, it is implied here, is less a god than a gardener. As words grow from each other blossoming into situations and arranging themselves into acts, his solicitous horticultural hand and mind are never manifest. The flow of voices across the pages with its constant generation of meaning seems spontaneously autonomous—and to such an extent that readers not only forget the human source but even come to doubt its existence. It is thus that in the best of planted gardens artifice is absorbed into the overall effect. Should we accept Borgese's two categories, then, we would conclude that "classical self-effacement" attains its ultimate realization in *La Celestina*. But only if we are willing to accept the formal monstrosity, the fierce wildness of Rojas' landscape! As in the case of Stephen Daedalus' generic distinctions, the simplicity of the classification cannot encompass the uniqueness of the work we would describe. There is a boundless oral fertility here that we instinctively know to be closer to Shakespeare than to Racine.

This comparison leads us to a third critic preoccupied specifically with the problem of autonomy in *La Celestina*. Although Shakespeare has often served as a yardstick for measuring Rojas' art (particularly because of the resemblance of the plot to that of *Romeo and Juliet*), their rapport has been most extensively and cogently discussed by Mrs. Malkiel. The "rich individuality of the characters," like their creator's "integral vision" and "avidity" for human reality, could not, she knew, be captured by literary formulae. Only comparison with the greatest—with a Shakespeare or a Sophocles—would suffice. Thus, for example, when Rojas "penetrated" the souls of speakers of whom he obviously disapproved (into Areusa's sterile rebellion, Celestina's upside-down sense of

---

[16] Cited by Francis Fergusson, "D. H. Lawrence's Sensibility," *Forms of Modern Fiction*, ed. W. V. O'Connor, Minneapolis, 1948, p. 77.

13

honor, or Pleberio's blind solicitude), only Shakespeare's at once objective and intimate presentation of Shylock could equal him.[17] Lovers of *La Celestina* cannot fail to applaud Mrs. Malkiel insofar as such comparisons honor its author. But her clear implication that Rojas *is* a great dramatist like Shakespeare is, I would maintain, itself oversimplified and ultimately misleading.

The view of Shakespeare's art expressed by Mrs. Malkiel goes at least as far back as Hazlitt, and, in its inception, tended towards the same sort of bemused obliteration of the poet that has been the critical fate of Rojas; "Shakespeare . . . was the least of an egotist that it was possible to be. He was nothing in himself, but he was all that others were or that they could become. He not only had in himself the germs of every faculty and feeling, but he could follow them by anticipation. . . . His characters are real beings of flesh and blood; they speak like men, not like authors. One might suppose that he had stood by at the time and overheard what passed."[18] There is room for doubt whether such obeisance to the Shakespearean mystery has been of much help to readers or theatergoers. But one thing is sure: transferral of this Protean view of the artist to Fernando de Rojas can only aggravate his state of historical and biographical evanescence. Which, in turn, will inevitably impede appreciation of the very *originalidad* that Mrs. Malkiel has taken such pains to demonstrate.

Partisans of Shakespeare, when confronted by such, to them, impudent claims, might respond by pointing out the disparity in the magnitude of the two achievements. After all, Hazlitt continues exultantly, Shakespeare "had 'a mind reflecting ages past' and present: all the people that ever lived are there . . . 'All corners of the earth, kings, queens, and states, maids, matrons, nay the secrets of the grave' are hardly hid from his searching glance." How can Rojas' mere fourteen voices divided only among men and women, youths and the aged, rich and poor, all living within walking distance of each other in a single unidentified urban milieu be compared with such universality? It might be argued, of course, that mere scope does not affect deep similarities of artistic procedure. But ultimately, I think, Mrs. Malkiel would have been willing to

[17] *La originalidad*, p. 310.

[18] *Hazlitt's Works*, London, 1902, ed. A. R. Waller and A. Glover, vol. v, "Lectures on the English Poets," p. 47.

admit that limitation of the number and variety of speakers in *La Celestina* (in this sense, it might well be considered classical) was indispensable to its creation. Insofar as the work is a mosaic of carefully juxtaposed encounters or situations (for example, Celestina's seduction of Areusa as a repetition in caricature of the earlier seduction of Melibea), the relevance of the comparisons and contrasts to be drawn necessarily restrained and channeled Rojas' creative *élan*. The nascent Rabelaisian verve of Act I has been harnessed but not diminished. Which is to say, Rojas' "amplification" in savagely intense detail of successive units of dialogue by its very nature rules out Shakespearean freedom of character creation.

In view of Mrs. Malkiel's stress on the characterization of the inhabitants of *La Celestina* as the basis for comparison with those of Shakespeare's plays, it would be well to clarify further the distinction just made. She is, of course, right when she states that, when we look back on the reading experience offered by the *Tragicomedia* as a whole, it is legitimate finally to characterize not just Celestina but even such vacillating voices as those of Pármeno and Areusa. By Act XXI they have all revealed themselves as fully as they are ever going to and, in that sense, do possess a "third person," a being to be judged as a whole from the outside. But this is not at all the same thing as saying that Rojas as an artist was primarily concerned with individual characterization. What mattered to him, as I maintained in *The Art of "La Celestina,"* was dialogue conceived of as the interaction of consciousnesses, which is to say consciousnesses involved with each other and changing with every change of interlocutor. To characterize is to stress elements of stability in behavior and reaction, elements which interested Rojas far less than momentary or lasting mutation. As he himself indicates in the Prologue, he is less intent on portraying his two lovers as individuals than in tracing to its end the "process of their delight." This was surely the first time such an intention had been expressed in Castilian, and it is therefore a personal innovation necessarily to be considered in later chapters of this "biography."

Ultimately my disagreement with Mrs. Malkiel—or perhaps it would be more accurate to say hers with me[19]—comes down to the

---

[19] Mrs. Malkiel is, I think, unnecessarily critical of my approach to the inhabitants of *La Celestina* as conscious lives not only known exclusively through dialogue but living in function of dialogue. The statement that no

basic question of how *La Celestina* should be read. If the reader approaches it with expectations derived from the theater, a theater virtually nonexistent in Rojas' time, its unprecedented number of acts, designed scene by scene to illustrate the onflowing of consciousness, will not be fully comprehensible. We will understand about as much about the work as have its recent Madrid audiences. Only by reading as Rojas wanted us to read—which is to say, by observing the things he wanted to show us—can the ever-repeated juxtaposition of speakers and encounters (described perceptively by Mrs. Malkiel as "geminación," the process of "twinning" usually thought of as novelistic) be related to the human structure of the whole. This is not to say that Shakespeare, as a master of dialogue, did not know how to employ similar techniques (for example, Polonius' advice to his son and to his daughter) but that they are hardly the fundamental unit of his art. Speech as self-expression, I dare propose, took dramatic precedence over speech as self-betrayal.

Accepting for a moment the old-fashioned generalizations of A. C. Bradley, we might go on to say that in the five acts of a Shakespearean play character visible and oversized meditates desperately upon the mutability (usually a single sequence) to which it is submitted, while in *La Celestina* character is the end product of a thousand and one major and minor transformations overheard in relentless detail. As for tragic anguish, it can only emerge in the forms of death and solitude when dialogue finally subsides. *The Tempest* is seen and heard; it presents a world of magnified characters who fill its stage in figure and voice only to melt like the dreams they are at the end of Act V. But Rojas, whose art (as we shall see in a later chapter) is entirely oral, whose stage is limitless,

---

fixed third persons can be found is obviously extreme, but it is still true that the reader who devotes his major effort to characterizing the speakers in his mind will upon conclusion either have oversimplified Rojas' art or remain puzzled by its almost infinite number of unexpected human changes. It is, for example, possible to explain Pármeno's reversion to virtue in Act II, but readers who thought Act I had provided sufficient characterization are always nonplussed when they first encounter it. Just as they are by the lack of physical description on which to center their notions of what exactly the speakers look like. Even in the case of Celestina, for whom the typical portrait of a witch would seem eminently suitable, it is surprising that her scary presence does not seem to bother Melibea.

16

and who purposely prevents us from imagining the faces and bodies of his speakers, listens at greater length and closer range to the most momentary inflections of conscious life. Both created seemingly independent human beings but by different means and to differing ends.

Objection to these three answers to the question of possibility does not mean rejection. Each of the critics just cited has set forth a fundamental condition to be met by the author of autonomous life. He must, as Stephen Daedalus discerned, place himself at a distance and observe dispassionately the destinies he traces. But at the same time, as Borgese reminds us, instead of paring his finger-nails, he must be a consummate artificer, an invisible yet ever-present and solicitous gardener capable of training growth into cunning arrangement. Finally—Mrs. Malkiel's condition is surely the most important—he must be nothing less than a genius, a genius gifted with insight into life and capable of penetrating to its roots as well as arranging its branches. That Fernando de Rojas fully complied with these requirements is attested to by the exist-ence of *La Celestina*. Critics and readers to the contrary notwith-standing, he is all the more real as a man and as an artist precisely because Celestina seems to speak for herself. As Galdós, who lik-ened his own art of dialogue to that of Rojas, knew, although an author "may be more or less hidden, he cannot disappear." Or in the words of Eliot, "The world of a great poetic dramatist is a world in which the creator is everywhere present and everywhere hidden."[20]

From the biographical point of view the first two conditions are more important because more accessible. Genius—whether of Shakespeare, Rojas, or any one else—is by definition more to be re-vered than explained, while distance and artistry may more hope-fully be related to personal experience. To begin with, Rojas' dis-tance was at once ironical and intellectual, both adjectives corre-sponding, as we shall see, to portions of his life. Walter Kaiser in his recent *Praisers of Folly* has proposed Rojas' contemporary, Erasmus, as the first professional ironist of European literature. But Rojas, whose precocious *Celestina* antedated Erasmus' earliest publication, presents (professionalism aside, since he is a self-

---

[20] Galdós, prologue to *El abuelo*. The quotation from Eliot is from "The Three Voices of Poetry," *On Poetry and Poets*, London, 1947, p. 102.

confessed amateur) as convincing a claim. As I tried to show in my previous book and as we shall see again here, *La Celestina* is an immensely complex structure of irony, and its dialogue is properly read only when the author's everpresence is sensed between the lines. It was this that Stephen Daedalus failed to consider. Irony by its very nature implies an ironist who searches for us and who, according to Vladimir Jankélévitch, above all wants to be "understood."[21] There exist here, as in any work created ironically, two opposed lines of communication: the sonorous dialogue of the speakers and, crossing it vertically, the silent quest of the author for our company and (as José Ferrater Mora, in agreement with Jankélévitch, expresses it) "participation."[22] Which serves to confirm my initial judgment: an authorless *Celestina* is as puzzling, foreshortened, and likely to be misunderstood as would be, let us say, the *Chartreuse de Parme* cut adrift from Stendhal.

Kaiser's advocacy of Erasmus as the founding father of European irony indicates both the difficulty and the importance of understanding Rojas' claim to a share of the title. It will be my contention that Rojas could be an ironist not only because of personal temperament or because he was a Renaissance man but also because he was what was called in his Spain a *converso*. This is not an entirely new contention. Both Menéndez Pelayo and Ramiro de Maeztu have explained certain attitudes expressed in *La Celestina* —metaphysical pessimism and hedonism—in terms of the fact (established in 1902 as firmly as any historical fact can be established)[23] that its author was a Christian of Jewish origin—that is to say, a person who might well have abandoned one faith without gaining another, a potentially lost soul skeptical of traditional dogma and morality. To my mind, this explanation is well founded

[21] *L'Ironie ou la bonne conscience*, Paris, 1950, p. 51 (quoted by Victor Brombert in his *Stendhal et la voie oblique*, Paris and New Haven, 1954: "L'ironie ne veut pas être *crue*; elle veut être *comprise*.")

[22] *Cuestiones disputadas*, Madrid, 1955, pp. 31-32.

[23] Manuel Serrano y Sanz, "Noticias biográficas de Fernando de Rojas," *RABM*, vi (1902), 245-298 (hereafter referred to as Serrano y Sanz). In the trial of Rojas' father-in-law there reproduced, the accused states specifically: first, that his son-in-law wrote *La Celestina*; and, second, that "he is a *converso*." Accepting this—as well he might—Menéndez Pelayo used it as a basis for the biographical sketch in his *Orígenes*. Maeztu's discussion of Rojas' "hedonistic" theme is to be found in *Don Quijote, Don Juan y La Celestina*, Madrid, 1926.

but insufficient. It is impossible to demonstrate to those who, like Marcel Bataillon and Gaspar von Barth, read *La Celestina* from other points of view. And, by supposing that Rojas sought primarily to express personal sentiments and opinions, it over-simplifies the relationship of biography to creation.

More recently, however, Américo Castro, in an epoch-making series of books and monographs (initiated in 1948 with the publi-cation of *España en su historia*), has transferred the *converso* dilemma from the realm of the isolated individual, with his uncer-tainty and psychological dislocation, to that of society. To be a *con-verso* is not just a way of being to oneself; it is more importantly a way of being with others. Rojas was not alone, although he may have been lonely. Biographically speaking, he was a member of a caste subject to intense scorn and suspicion, forced into a marginal position, and reacting to persecution in a number of characteristic ways. Among them, as we shall see at length, were cultivation of the intellect and its métiers (Rojas' Salamancan experience will be the subject of a later chapter) and irony. One can philosophize alone, but to be ironical, as Jankélévitch and Ferrater Mora indi-cate, there must exist potential companionship, potential under-standing. The ironist needs a society—or perhaps it would be bet-ter to say a counter-society, a "Happy" or, as in this case, "Unhappy Few." Hence, the insufficiency of the equation: *La Celestina* equals *converso* product. Rather, following the thought of Castro, I shall interpret the ironical and intellectual distance necessary for *La Celestina*'s creation as made possible by the *converso* situation.

Such an interpretation will eventually lead us out beyond the frontiers of Rojas' private life and personal art into broader reaches of literary history. If we can come to understand how ironical cre-ation was first possible—which is to say, how an ironical relation-ship among author, character, and reader was first achieved—we shall have prepared ourselves to meditate on its later exploitation. By learning how Rojas could be ironically distant, we may also learn how the novel—Spain's major generic contribution to Euro-pean letters—became increasingly possible during the century fol-lowing *La Celestina*. In one way or another, a wide variety of narratives and dialogues (imitations of *La Celestina*, *Lazarillo de Tormes* and its continuations, *Guzmán de Alfarache*, *Viaje de Turquía*, *Crotalón*, *Lozana andaluza,* and numerous others) con-

19

tinued to exploit ironical potentialities of the *converso* situation into which their authors were born. A corollary effect evident in some of these works was the immediate popularity of Erasmus with members of Rojas' caste, not only because of his proposals for religious reform but also because of his mastery of ironical expression. Indicative is the merging of the two traditions in the *Quixote*, the product of a mind that was educated by an Erasmist and was almost surely aware of remote *converso* origin.[24] The pitilessly mordant (inhuman, Cervantes implies) irony of the half-converted has become in more gentle and complex form a way of exploring artistically the dubious relation of modern man to the devaluated society in which he lives. What we shall describe later as *converso* alienation was a harshly imposed forerunner of the more general alienation which has become a way of life for all of us and which found its first full novelistic expression in the pages of the *Quixote*.

Mention of the novel that was to come leads us back to the condition suggested by Borgese's definition of classicism. Lacking the generic advantages of a Cervantes—lacking a narrative voice and the possibility of manipulating narrative style—how could Rojas bring to flower what Ortega would have called his ironical "posture towards life"? Or, to put it more simply: how can autonomous voices carry ironical implications? One example is that of Greek tragedians, and there is unquestionably in *La Celestina* an overall dramatic irony as grim in its way as that of *Oedipus Rex*. However, as I suggested in reply to Mrs. Malkiel, Rojas was ultimately less interested in a dramatic portrayal of man's fate than in what he calls in the Prologue the "aceleramientos e mouimientos . . . afectos

---

[24] Salvador de Madariaga was first to give printed expression to a suspicion that those readers who had perceived Cervantes' constant mockery of pretensions to lineage (not only in the *Retablo de las maravillas* but also in the *Persiles* and the *Quijote*) had fleetingly entertained. See "Cervantes y su tiempo," *Cuadernos*, 1960. Since then Castro in his *Cervantes y los casticismos*, Madrid, 1966, has brought additional indications to the fore and corrected Madariaga's tendency to view Cervantes as somehow non-Spanish because of his origins. As we shall insist ourselves, nothing could be further from the existential truth of the matter. In any case, interpretation aside, facts are facts, and the presence of no less than five physicians in Cervantes' immediate family will seem highly significant to those familiar with the social history of the time. Another, although far less conclusive, fact is that first noticed by Esténaga (see n. 38) that one of the Salazars of Esquívias married a grandson of Rojas.

20

diuersos e variedades . . . desta nuestra flaca humanidad." That is to say, in the immediate and momentary mutability of consciousness, the comic texture of the larger tragedy. How was it possible to communicate ironically—not only to fellow students and fellow *conversos* but also to future generations of readers—his unequaled comprehension of such ephemeral stuff as this?

It is necessary to ask this question with such repeated emphasis, if only in order to avoid the danger of trying to explain *La Celestina* sociologically. It is all very well to describe Rojas—as I shall do at length in chapters to follow—as belonging to a marginal caste and as judging the society around him from a sardonic distance. But, in order to relate the dialogue of *La Celestina* to this biographical situation, we must take equal pains to describe him as an artist. In addition to understanding the possibility of absence from society ("de sus tierras ausentes"), we must also try to understand the possibility of creative presence in every speech and every nuance of conscious change. As Mrs. Malkiel, herself fervently concerned with Rojas' Judaic background, states, "It cannot serve as a panacea which will solve all at once the problems presented by *La Celestina*."[25] In particular it will not elucidate the possibility of Rojas' peculiar art. In other and cruder words, although he may well have been as self-conscious, as ironic, and as embittered as his fellow *converso*, the poet, Antón de Montoro, their techniques of expression and communication were antithetical. Juxtaposition of the unique artist and the man of his time is a major problem for any literary biographer. In my case, given the inaccessibility of Rojas as a person, it will be a central preoccupation until the end of the last chapter.

For the time being, however, there is the consolation of a preliminary answer, an answer derived only from close reading of the text. Rojas, it was pointed out, is present in *La Celestina* in the same fashion that a gardener is present in his garden. We sense him through his meticulous arrangement, through his calculated twinnings, and through his cunning conversion of the living flow of dialogue into malicious displays of self-betrayal. As the speakers confront each other in their multitude of parallel and antithetical situations (for a work with so few characters *La Celestina* is a sur-

[25] *La originalidad*, p. 24.

prisingly intricate human garden), their questions and answers, their exclamations and rationalizations, are set forth in such a way as to communicate their constant inconstancy. Even when they attempt to maintain a firm character (Pármeno's transparent and fragile mask of virtue in Act II) or to give acceptable reasons for inner changes and tides of feeling (Celestina's explanation in Act V of a revised strategy for handling Calisto when she is really bursting with her good news), Rojas knows exactly how to let us hear what they are attempting to hide. His is the presiding mind and ear, and it is our appalling and delightful task to listen with him, to share in his horticultural eavesdropping. Ultimately, of course, I shall have to supplement this textually derived sense of Rojas' real presence with historical understanding. It is precisely then—upon attempting to convert a critical point of departure into a biography—that trouble awaits.

Before resting my case in defense of the reality of Rojas as an author, I must recognize the obvious objection. The notion of a writer as a presiding consciousness listening to, judging, and arranging the voiced consciousnesses of his speakers is on the face of it as paradoxical as Stephen Daedalus' portrait of the artist as a ghost. "Where do these voices come from, if not out of their author's mind?" the reader may well ask. And it will not do to put him off by suggesting the possibility of oral models of the sort Galdós is known to have used. Although such models surely existed, Rojas' art, as I have described it, has little to do with stenography. The real truth, I think, is that Rojas was less interested in his individual speakers than in Castilian—as he lived and breathed it—as a means of communication. That is to say, in spite of our inevitable tendency to read *La Celestina* dramatically or novelistically, Rojas himself was only secondarily concerned with exposing the individual passions, weaknesses, hypocrisies, and rationalizations of his lovers and servants. Along with listening to one voice after another, the phenomenon of language itself was the source of his ironical fascination. The human depths and discoveries of *La Celestina* were for Rojas in a sense an unexpected by-product.

Along with the primacy of language went a corresponding view of human life. However much Rojas may have felt gleefully complacent at the writhings and evolutions of each of his speakers, we should not interpret his achievement as a collection of psychological or moral case histories. Such a pitiful rogues' gallery can, of course, be abstracted from the dialogue, but to do so is to destroy it. Rojas' deepest originality, his most profound relevance to us and our concerns is his presentation of human life as a mutual affair, as a continuing interaction. In simultaneous separation and company (like all who share verbally the interval between birth and death), the inhabitants of *La Celestina* are to be understood in terms of their inextricable involvement with each other. Even at the end, when Pleberio is totally abandoned, he still searches vainly for interlocutors, (a "tú" or "vosotros") who are not dead or alien. So, too, the other soliloquies habitually recollect past interchange or imagine feverishly those which are to come. In these twenty-one acts men and women are often lonely, but they are never really alone. Their being alive is radically an involvement with other lives in an ever-changing—because ever-speaking—flux of mutual consciousness.

I have already mentioned the most conspicuous example: Calisto and Melibea overheard by their author during the "process" of their love. And what applies to them applies to the cast as a whole. Rojas presents the cast not as an aggregation of characters or types (the exception which proves the rule is Centurio) but as a unit, as a complex and dynamic togetherness which interdependently evolves towards its own destruction. It is not without significance that all of its members seem to know or know about each other prior to the first meeting of the lovers. Celestina was Calisto's midwife; Sempronio and Pármeno are well aware of the bellicose reputation of Pleberio's servants; Melibea has a curious memory of Celestina as "hermosa" (flashily gotten up fifteen years before?); and so on. The nameless city is small, and its most representative citizens have little need to waste dialogue making each other's acquaintance. Even when they momentarily forget each other (Celestina's failure to recognize Pármeno as an adolescent and Alisa's possibly hypocritical reluctance to remember Celestina), the point is further reinforced. Rojas listens to each individual insofar as he is a part of the chorus of the whole. His irony and his artistry embrace a texture of relationships, and, in so doing, present a vision (or an audition) intentionally relevant to the society and history in which he lived.

This repetition of my view that *La Celestina* must first of all be

23

understood in terms of Fernando de Rojas' profound experience and sardonic judgment of the Spain of the Catholic monarchs does not mean that its four households constitute a world in miniature. Although a precursor of the novel, Rojas' dialogue is anti-novelistic if we think of the novel in Balzacian or Galdosian terms. Rather than presenting a descriptive diorama of representative individuals and roles, he arranges for us what might be called a social care or matrix, a horticultural exhibit of interpersonal relations reduced to their oral essence. The least common denominator of any society lies in the communication or failure of communication among its members, and it is this that Rojas proposes to display to the "conterráneos" of "nuestra común patria." How life was lived and expressed, what was felt and what was understood by all who spoke or listened (not "who was who" in Castile as in the *Generaciones y semblanzas*) was to be the subject of his ironical attention. Hence his unparalleled ability to record in dialogue minimal details of conscious behavior.

It is hardly surprising to observe that this social core as recorded in *La Celestina* was manifestly rotten. Rojas—like many of his caste and classmates whose views will appear in later chapters—was acutely conscious of what would be called by Ezra Pound the breakdown of "right relationships." Men and women, masters and servants, parents and children (society's three basic inner divisions) were not only opaque to each other but in a state of undeclared warfare. As in the *Lazarillo* and its picaresque descendants, every sentence and indeed every word of self-betrayal projects awareness of inrooted social decay. As I shall try to show, the perennial medieval theme of disorder (the best known example is the introductory frame of the *Decameron*) became an anguished "theme of the time," a communal form of historical awareness for Rojas and his fellow *conversos* during the first decades of Inquisitional onslaught. But having said as much, we must avoid oversimplification. In *La Celestina*, as in other works sharing its view of society, the infinitely disrupting effects of the new institution on interpersonal relations were not, and indeed could not be, directly presented.[26] Yet what might be called a generational reaction to

---

[26] An exception is Torres Naharro's *Comedia Jacinta* with its cast of fugitive *conversos* barely concealed under flimsy pastoral disguise. See my "Retratos de conversos en la *Comedia Jacinta*," NRFH, XVII (1963-64), 20-39. Somewhat

experienced history is everywhere implicit. What the Revolution and Napoleonic wars were for Stendhal (not as a subject but as providing a new perception of the way people are related to each other) the Inquisition, I shall maintain, was for Rojas.

The core of the social core is that genius of persuasion, Celestina, whose verbal putrefaction attracts and infects all who listen to her. Not just the cast but the whole tacit population of the city—clergy and nobility, doxies and debutantes, ambassadors and valets— cluster around her like flies on carrion. As in her initial conversation with Pármeno, she provides—in addition to the sheer delight of her mastery of the mother tongue—the sophistry necessary to their lives. Sinfulness aside, sensual freedom exists here in function of exaggeration, prevarication, rationalization, lamentation, trivialization, and every other sort of communicative misbehavior. Which is to say, for both Rojas and Celestina (the one deploring ironically and the other celebrating fiercely) men are animals who speak and who therefore inevitably pervert rational discourse. The result is the unending and fatal warfare of their reasonless *razonar*.[27] Marcel Bataillon, in stressing Rojas' didacticism (as opposed to irony) misses this essential distinction. By reading the lesson in terms of traditional morality, he not only, as we have remarked, tends to depersonalize the author but also fails to see that the "right relations" so conspicuously absent in *La Celestina* are those of reason and speech rather than of revelation. Rojas, as he listens to his creature Celestina, aspires to be a "great philosopher" in both the Stoic and Aristotelian senses and not, as I shall try to show, a preacher.

Hence the overt hopelessness and sarcasm which come to the surface in Act XXI and which are implicit all along the course of

---

less transparent are the speakers and characters of Núñez de Reinoso's poetry and prose. See Constance Rose, *Life and Works of Alonso Núñez de Reinoso,* Rutherford N.J., 1971.

[27] *Razonar* is synonymous with dialogue in the oral world inhabited by Rojas. And so it appears both in his *argumentos* and those of the printers. See *The Art*, Appendix B. Rojas' skill at reproducing speech in such a way as to make irrationality evident indicates his ironical awareness of its betrayal of reason—which is to say of its own ideal possibilities. Rojas' bellicose imagery for language as such (the "cutting" of his critics and other examples to be referred to later) indicates full awareness (at this point we verge on the thematic core of *La Celestina*) that words which betray reason generate disharmony, warfare, and inevitable perdition.

25

the dialogue. A moralist, however discouraged, may not despair of man or of the ultimate fruition of history; but the ironically distant "philosopher," the gardener of minds and voices as skilled as he is implacable, has no such commitments. The full implications both of transient comedy and ultimate tragedy are clear to him. It is, thus, at the end that the text most explicitly testifies to the reality of Fernando de Rojas. When he takes leave of irony (or perhaps it would be better to say when irony along with dialogue is no longer possible), and in the voice of Pleberio he speaks directly about man's life on earth, his own existence as a man is confirmed. Or, translated into theological terms, when Pleberio realizes that the impossibility of rational harmony among men entails the impossibility (or perversity) of God, he has unknowingly proved the existence of another author, Fernando de Rojas. Speaking as one person, they are both provided by final solitude with self-knowledge as well as desperation: "I alone know the fullness of my anguish; I alone am completely aware; I alone am rational in an irrational society, history, and universe; therefore I am." So the presiding mind—if not in these words, in their clear equivalents—comes at last to define itself. And if this once again be interpreted as Existentialist, I would beg the interpreter carefully to reread Act XXI in the light of its analysis in Chapter VII before passing final judgment.

The Testimony of the Archives

Documentary information about Fernando de Rojas is scanty, but hardly to the extent that the critical opinion discussed previously might lead us to believe. We may not know the exact date of Rojas' birth, the identity of his first love, or possess samples of his epistolary style; yet, on the other hand, I imagine Shakespearean scholars would be jubilant were they to discover records similar to those we do possess: an inventory of their bard's private library or extensive testimony as to his social status from the old men of Stratford-on-Avon. Committed for the most part to the notion of semi-anonymity, students of *La Celestina* have conspicuously failed to meditate on biographical facts that have long been known. It is distressing to point out, for example, that the first detailed discussion of Rojas' collection of books is that attempted—I fear rather amateurishly—in Chapter VIII of this book. But what is even more regrettable is the existence in the archives of relevant and easily obtainable documents that nobody has taken the trouble to look for. Given his connection with a masterpiece of such central historical and literary importance, I cannot avoid the suspicion that Rojas has been the victim of an erudite conspiracy of silence.

In addition to the inhibitions for which Rojas' peculiar artistry and evasive self-presentation may have been responsible, apparently his long known membership in the caste of Spanish *conversos* has also discouraged those best prepared from further consideration of his biography. The dismay and distaste which in certain circles have greeted the findings of Américo Castro in this connection reveal the depths of the problem.[28] The Jewish origins of many important Spaniards of the past are first of all denied (in the case of Rojas, as recently as 1967[29]); and then, if the denial cannot stand up in the face of the evidence, they are ignored. There is no better indication of the miseries endured by individuals in the sixteenth and seventeenth centuries whose "stains" were publicly known than the reluctance of many twentieth-century scholars to take their situations and experiences into account. The belief that only the caste of Old Christians was truly Spanish and truly honorable was so inrooted that it has endured over four centuries. There even seems to prevail among some of our colleagues, peninsular and otherwise, the tacit notion that to bring to light the background of a Rojas or a Diego de San Pedro (not to speak of a Saint Teresa of Avila) is an unpatriotic act, a virtual deletion of their works from the national Honor Roll. Hence, unlike Cervantes (whose probable *converso* origins fortunately lack documentary proof), Fernando de Rojas has had to wait for a most improbable biographer: a North American disciple of Américo Castro.

We should not, of course, overreact against such attitudes. As Mrs. Malkiel has warned us, the category of *converso* should be used only with great caution to characterize adjectivally a given author or work. There is, for example, an enormous difference be-

---

[28] Typical of the polemic are the two tomes of Sánchez Albornoz cited previously (above, n. 10) and more recently Eugenio Asensio, "Reflexiones sobre *La realidad histórica de España*," *MLN*, LXXXI (1966). Each in his own way expresses both nationalistic resentment and intellectual incomprehension of Castro's approach.

[29] J. Caro Baroja, *Vidas mágicas e Inquisición*, Madrid, 1967, I, 119.

tween a Rojas who belonged to a more or less unassimilated family at the end of the fifteenth century and whose father and father-in-law were both condemned by the Inquisition and a Cervantes (or a Rojas Zorrilla, if documents be insisted upon), who a hundred years later was harassed by awareness of remotely suspicious origins. Yet those who accept unthinkingly the prejudices of the past are hardly in a position to meditate on such distinctions. For my part, I have no hesitation in accepting Castro's view that, as far as Spanishness is concerned, each is as Spanish as the other—and as their persecutors, too. In different terms (depending on generation, caste, and place of residence, among other factors) and with varying degrees of intensity, suspicion, and anguish every soul born in the peninsula shared a common dilemma: having to represent a social role and to exist at the same time.

If the dilemma so expressed seems less Spanish than human, it may be added that in the Spain of Rojas and Cervantes roles were both far more rigid and far fewer than our own experience of life in society enables us to comprehend. Conversely, consciousness so constricted became all the more passionate and embittered, exalted and deranged. Or, using the terms of Castilian grammar, human *ser* and human *estar* were pitted against one another. The outrageous honor of Celestina and the trampled heroism of don Quijote—although satirical reflections of contemporary values and behavior—both indicate the profound Spanishness of authors deeply concerned with the insurmountable difficulties of so being. When Rojas referred to "nuestra común patria" he was speaking as sincerely—and perhaps as wryly—as he knew how. As we shall see, resentful *converso* alienation and self-righteous Old Christian "integration" are two sides of the same coin.

To return to the documents, those long available and those here made public for the first time, their scarcity is less troublesome than their paucity of anecdote. The life of Fernando de Rojas by dint of patient assembly may be encaged by a fair number of facts, but almost nothing that the documents tell us about him serves to reveal him as a person. The corrosively ironical mind in which the dialogue of *La Celestina* germinated and burgeoned has little apparent relation to the human entity attested to by surviving records. I shall establish beyond any doubt that Rojas was a *converso*, that he wrote twenty acts of *La Celestina*, and that, for decades prior to 1541, he lived a reasonably prosperous and successful life in Talavera. And by adding strong probabilities to certainties, it is possible to conclude a good deal more. But it is Rojas' intimacy that is hopelessly beyond our reach—perhaps with the one small exception of a moment of reminiscence of childhood. This is a situation which may be fortunate for *La Celestina* (insofar as its art is premised on self-concealment) but which is disheartening to a would-be narrator of its author's life.

How to proceed then? Intuition and imaginative embroidery being out of the question, the only alternative has been what might be called a process of amalgamation. I have, very simply, tried to gather as many details as are available and seem at all relevant concerning the lives of his neighbors, relatives, and acquaintances as well as those concerning the places he lived in and institutions to which he belonged. Indeed, had I chosen to pattern my title after Ortega y Gasset instead of Menéndez Pidal, this book might well have been called *The Circumstance of Fernando de Rojas*. Although documents reveal little about the man, they do point to an abundance of people, events, and places falling within the domain of his point of view. These then have been arranged as appropriately as possible around the leached out biographical shell formerly inhabited by the composer of the acrostic. It goes without saying that such a method is both unsatisfactory and, what is worse, repetitive. Chapters on the case of Alvaro de Montalbán, Rojas' *converso* family, life in the Puebla, and the rest often seem to involve more a change in perspective than a change in subject matter. But, since nothing less than the historical possibility of *La Celestina* and the reality of its author are at stake, I felt it necessary to proceed—to proceed, even though the resulting mosaic of what is called in Spanish, *convivencia* or shared living, may amount to less than a single instant of Rojas' lost experience. For this disparity there is no consolation; I have had to do the best I could with the copious insignificance at my disposal.

One reason for dissatisfaction with what Siegfried Giedeon has called these "voices which come to us out of the fortunes or misfortunes of an age"[30] is that they are for the most part legal voices. We hear about the Bachelor of Civil Law Fernando de Rojas and those who knew him (or knew of him) in wills, in carefully prepared and

[30] *Space, Time, and Architecture*, Cambridge, Mass., 1959, p. 18.

deceitful depositions of status, in bills of sale, in books of accounts, in contracts for division of property, and even in the receipt for his funeral expenses. As a result, all that we are told refers to a Rojas in statutory relation to others, not the person of the author but a legal entity defined in terms of social position, ownership, and obligations. The testimony of the archives and the testimony of the text seem divided by an unbridgeable chasm, and only from time to time, cautiously reading between the lines of one document or another, shall we glimpse possibilities of relationship.

It may be objected that our sources of information are hardly unique in the case of Rojas and that these remarks do little justice to the enormous biographical value of sixteenth-century legal archives. It is indeed true that much of what is known about the lives of Rojas' contemporaries has emerged from just such documentation. Latter-day scholarship has put to good use what the late Agustín G. de Amezúa has called the "furia legal" and the "frenesí en papel" of the period.[31] In the sixteenth-century social and legal relationships which had previously been determined by oral tradition were in the process of being transferred onto paper. Everything had to be recorded—fixed, it was assumed, forever—or lawsuits rendered interminable by conflicting testimony might develop. Political change, social tension, and a loss of confidence in the truth of the spoken word, all taken together, often deposited veins of concentrated historical ore in these mines of parchment.

In the case of Rojas, however, there is a decisive circumstance still to be considered. Most of the documents relating to him more or less directly were those collected and preserved in family archives by his grandson of the same name, the Licentiate Fernando de Rojas. These archives, miraculously preserved and now in the possession of Rojas' direct descendant, don Fernando del Valle Lersundi, were accumulated in response to two fundamental interests, neither of them literary or sentimental. Their catalogue indicates the exclusive conservation, first, of financial and legal records and, second, of what are called therein "papeles de nobleza." Even though the grandson, like many others among Rojas' descendants, on occasion refers proudly to his grandfather's authorship of La Celestina, he discarded whatever papers might have

---

[31] For his eloquent defense of the historical and literary value of such archives see La vida privada española en el protocolo notarial, Madrid, 1950.

been related to it. The only personal letter in the whole collection (from one of Rojas' daughters living in Madrid to his eldest son in Talavera) contains an acknowledgment of a payment from an inheritance.

The Licentiate Fernando, it should further be pointed out, in addition to being highly intelligent was, like his grandfather, sensitive to history. Upon graduating from Salamanca in 1565, he was admitted to the bar of the Court of Chancery in Valladolid: "I went to Valladolid in the middle of January, 1566, and two months later I passed the examination which accredited me as a lawyer of the Royal Chancery, of which the president at that time was Santillana."[32] And there, as we shall see, he proceeded to amass a small fortune. Among other things, a kind of supreme court of social privilege and exemption, the Chancery was empowered to decide who was an *hidalgo* and who a *villano* or *pechero* (those obligated to pay the "breast" or head tax). So it was that the young lawyer made a career of catering to the snowballing importance of lineage and status in the Spain of his time and of the foreseeable future. Gossipers might murmur (as we shall see them doing in his own case), but façades of nobility had become a marketable commodity. Wealth, however acquired, could not be fully enjoyed without blazonry, and it would pay heavily for the professional counsel necessary to obtain it.

Although bourgeois vanity obviously played a great part in this acute awareness of status, the Licentiate Fernando's clients had another and more excusable motivation. As we shall see, three generations after the establishment of the Inquisition, the descendants of Jews (either because they considered themselves assimilated or because they had had time enough to practice their roles) were less in danger of persecution than of being harassed by implacable discrimination. Unable to impugn the religious observance or acculturation of *conversos*, society seemed determined to punish them for their lineage by means of "edicts of exclusion" from desirable professions, posts, and organizations. And against such injustice one of the most frequent remedies was that supplied by the Licentiate Fernando: a fabricated and official new lineage as an

[32] Valle Lersundi Archive, document 25, "Libro de memorias del licenciado Fernando de Rojas." Hereafter information obtained from these archives will be identified as VLA followed by the appropriate document number.

31

hidalgo. Although a later chapter will probe deeper into this area of social conflict, for now what concerns me is the light it throws on the nature of many of the available documents. That is to say, the fact that the original archivist who first selected and arranged the family papers was a professionally adept manipulator of the past, a person experienced in concealing precisely those things which might have been most interesting, must be taken into account. Even more, as will be shown in a moment, the Licentiate Fernando's skill at his peculiar specialty meant knowledge of just how far it was safe to go in ancestor substitution. More than one twentieth-century scholar has, as a result, been hoodwinked by his artistic blurring and falsification of the family past. The profession of the Licentiate Fernando fully justifies the observation of Marcel Bataillon: "The burning desire to be an Old Christian has falsified many things about Spanish history."[33]

While lamenting the loss of all that perhaps might have been saved, we should nevertheless be grateful to the archivist. Without his care, neither the will nor the inventory would have survived. The catalogue of some eighty items lists documents ranging from the beginning of the fifteenth century to the beginning of the eighteenth, and, among them, a sizeable fraction refer to Rojas and his children. There is, for example, a copy of a contract between the Bachelor and a member of his wife's family for the purchase of a "censo perpetuo" (permanent mortgage or lien) on property in the Puebla. There are the wills of his wife (1546, followed as was his own by a complex division of property among the heirs) and of an unmarried daughter, Juana (1557). There are the "Libros de memorias" (personal record books) of the Licentiate Fernando and his son, both of which refer to their education and their ancestry: "My great-grandparents were the Bachelor Fernando de Rojas, who composed Celestina, and Leonor Alvarez." There are copies of two separate *probanzas* (depositions), one of *hidalguía* and the other of *hidalguía* and *limpieza* (cleanliness of blood).[34]

---

[33] Cited from a personal letter reproduced in Américo Castro's *España en su historia*, Buenos Aires, 1948, pp. 615-616. He comments further on the historical problem posed by many cases of successful self-camouflage in the *Avant-propos* to the French translation of *De la edad conflictiva: Le Drame de l'honneur dans la vie et dans la littérature espagnoles du XVme siècle*, Paris, 1965.

[34] VLA 34-8. This is a seventeenth-century transcript of a portion of the

In both, the family is traced back as far as the Bachelor's supposed father, Garcí Gonçález Ponce de Rojas, who, it is asserted, emigrated to the Puebla de Montalbán from Asturias. There are, as will shortly become apparent, strong reasons for disregarding some of the evidence, but, whether true in all details or not, testimony by witnesses who had known the author of *La Celestina* personally cannot fail to be interesting. Many other items of lesser or nonexistent relevance complete the list.

It would be, I further surmise, anachronistic to expect a lawyer grandson in the sixteenth century to have preserved literary records for our benefit. The notion of his grandfather as a possible subject of literary biography, if it had been proposed to him, would surely have seemed both risky and pointless. Interest in authors as individuals did not really come into existence until such later sixteenth- and seventeenth-century *ingenios* as Montemayor, Lope, and Cervantes began to celebrate and denigrate each other's fame for the benefit of the new national public. Hence my sincere gratitude to the Licentiate Fernando as well as to his descendant and namesake, don Fernando del Valle Lersundi. Without the solicitude of the one and the generosity and learning of the other even the unpretentious amalgamation here attempted would have been impossible.

Documents have the fortunate—if at times wearisome—habit of leading to other documents. A card file of all the individual names mentioned in the Valle Lersundi collection as well as in those published by Serrano y Sanz indicated the existence of a motley collection of testaments, depositions of *hidalguía,* Inquisitional proceedings against friends, relatives, and acquaintances, baptismal records, investigations of *limpieza,* genealogies, and other items. All of these—in fact, considerably more than those actually cited— had to be found, transcribed, and examined often with only the most trifling profit. Here and there a few pebbles of significance would be uncovered and fitted as appropriately as possible into the developing mosaic. These documents in their turn would point to others and in such abundance that *The Spain of Fernando de Rojas* (and what an exceedingly queer and unofficial Spain it

---

original *probanza* (still in the Archivo de la Real Chancillería in Valladolid) and was published by Valle Lersundi in the *RFE*, xii (1925). Hitherto unpublished testimony appears here as Appendix III.

33

has turned out to be!) comes now to an end less because of the exhaustion of its source material than because of that of its chronicler. When initially promising leads more and more frequently produced information often fascinating in itself (for example, the curious trial and strange escape of the Toledan Licentiate Diego Alonso mentioned briefly in Chapter V) but irrelevant to the author of *La Celestina*, it seemed time to abandon the task. As I write this, I still have hope that Almiro Robledo will uncover in time for inclusion more material in the Talaveran archives on Rojas' activities as a lawyer in the service of the municipality.[35] But I can wait no longer.

A mosaic by definition must have a pattern as well as a texture, an overall design as well as individual pieces. That which will become apparent here was drawn, as was indicated previously, by my interpretation of *La Celestina* as a masterpiece of ironic agnosticism, or perhaps it would be better to say agnostic irony. This in turn conferred extreme significance on two sets of documents revealing the author's suspicious and marginal status as a *converso*. As we shall see, the Licentiate Fernando knew of the existence of both sets, and we may surmise that under the circumstances he would have sacrificed a great deal to have them destroyed. But fortunately for us and unfortunately for him there was no way he could get his hands on them. They were Inquisition records which, in accord with the inherent secrecy of the institution, were available only to the Inquisitors and their staff of initiates. Guarded with extraordinary care in strongly locked chests or massive vaults ("el secreto" was the bureaucratic term), Inquisition files were unreachable: "No prisoner or accused person has ever seen the record of his own trial much less that of anyone else." These words and their almost audible tone of wonder and horror were written by Father Juan Antonio Llorente,[36] who was a *secretario* when history in the shape of Napoleon's armies broke the locks, and who afterwards became the most completely informed and one of the

---

[35] His little-noted articles in *Municipalia*, nos. 161 and 170 (1967), "La Muy Noble y Leal Ciudad de Talavera de la Reina" and "Alcalde que dejó grandiosa huella," contain references to and excerpts from documents in the municipal archives.

[36] *Historia crítica de la Inquisición en España*, 10 vols., Madrid, 1822, I, 6 (hereafter referred to as Llorente).

most reliable historians of the suddenly illuminated area of past darkness.[37]

The first of these two sets of documents, principally Manuel Serrano y Sanz' transcript of the 1525 trial of Rojas' father-in-law, Alvaro de Montalbán, need not be discussed now. It has long been known, and some of its implications will be explored in detail in the chapter to follow. But the second set, because of its recent availability and its crucial importance to the reality of Fernando de Rojas, must be introduced at this point.[38] The original documents—those which the Licentiate Fernando could never hope to see or be free of—have disappeared. But we know their dates, nature, and purport, due to a curious series of historical coincidences and malevolences.

It all began with a desperate and grievously mistaken decision. In 1606 a distant cousin of the Rojas, Hernán Suárez Franco, pressed to final judgment legal proceedings intended to establish his family's claim to *hidalguía*. The Licentiate Fernando who had originally been in charge of the litigation (in conjunction with that

---

[37] Llorente was still under violent attack as late as 1956 by Bernardino Llorca (in "Problemas religiosos y eclesiásticos de los Reyes Católicos," *Estudios*, vol. II, Quinto Congreso de Historia de la Corona de Aragón) and in 1961 by Miguel de la Pinta Llorente (in *Aspectos históricos del sentimiento religioso en España*, Madrid, 1961). The latter calls him typically an "hombre sin conciencia moral e histórica," "desleal y traidor," etc. (pp. 51-52). However, as Francisco Márquez remarks, ". . . hemos podido verificar en muchas ocasiones la exactitud de sus datos contrastándolos con otras fuentes, y . . . en este punto nos agrada encontrarnos en la compañía de aquel gran científico que fue el P. Fidel Fita, S.I., autor de expresivos juicios sobre la probedad de Llorente" (*Investigaciones sobre Juan Alvarez Gato*, Madrid, 1960, p. 82; hereafter referred to as *Investigaciones*). I would like to add that I too have found Llorente's summaries and conclusions to be entirely in accord with the evidence of the documents— in the cases which I re-examined.

[38] The documents (summarizing information taken from the files of the Inquisition) were first brought to light years ago by Narciso de Esténaga, archivist and canon of the Cathedral of Toledo in his "Sobre el Bachiller Hernando de Rojas y otros varones toledanos del mismo apellido," *Boletín de la Real Academia de Bellas Artes y Ciencias Históricas de Toledo*, IV (1923), 78-91. But they were presented by him both incompletely and with no comprehension of their true significance. The usual desire to deny Rojas' *converso* origins as well as failure to take the Serrano y Sanz material into account seem to have been responsible. A full reporting on these documents may be found in *Romanische Forschungen*, LXXVIII (1966), 255-290: Stephen Gilman and Ramón Gonzálvez, "The Family of Fernando de Rojas" (hereafter referred to as Gilman-Gonzálvez).

35

of his own immediate family) had probably advised against push-ing matters so far.[39] He knew the family background, and he knew that to request an *ejecutoria* (a certificate of status granted by the Chancery court) would involve a risky investigation. In his own case, as will become apparent, he abandoned the suit after taking depositions only from prearranged friendly witnesses, thereby de-priving us of a mine of information.[40] The Francos, however, felt that an *ejecutoria* was indispensable.[41] Not only were they reck-

---

[39] As we shall see, in 1606 he was described by an opposing attorney as an "abogado que fue de Valladolid, letrado de Hernán Suárez." His name also appears from time to time as the attorney in charge in the records of the favorable testimony of witnesses convoked by Hernán Suárez' cousin, Pedro Franco, who had also in 1578 and again in 1579 attempted to establish *hidalguía*. See A. Basanta de la Riva, *Sala de los hijosdalgo, Catálogo de todos sus pleitos*, Valladolid, 1922, I, 424 (hereafter referred to as Riva). A witness from the Puebla de Montalbán (testifying in the Toledo "expediente de limpieza" referred to above) confirms what we have said and provides further identification: "the Licentiate Hernando de Rojas, . . . grandson of the Licentiate [*sic*] Hernando de Rojas who composed the *Celestina*, acted as a relative of the Francos in their petition of *hidalguía*." It is not clear if the witness refers to the case of Pedro Franco or to the later case of Hernán Suárez Franco, or both.

[40] A partial transcript of this favorable testimony (the one still possessed by Valle Lersundi—see n. 34) was requested of the Court and was included in the file entitled "Papeles de nobleza" as evidence of the family's status. The actual text of the petition for the transcript precedes the original in the Archivo. It is interesting to note therein that the Licentiate Fernando simul-taneously requested a *traslado* both of his own incomplete *probanza* and of that of his distant cousin, Pedro Franco. It would seem that he conducted the cases concurrently and planned that Pedro Franco should content himself (as were his own intentions) with this safe half-measure. *Ejecutorias* for either branch of the family—he obviously and correctly felt—were dangerously beyond reach.

[41] Failure to be able to display an *ejecutoria* was eventually to prove em-barrassing to the Rojas as well. When investigators (working on the Toledo *expediente*) asked the Bachelor's grandson, Fray García de Rojas, about the family's reputation, he replied that a cousin would be glad to show them the family *ejecutoria*. However, the latter (a great-grandson, Juan de Rojas, secretary to the Count of Lodosa), when asked to do so, had to confess that none was available: the witness says "that he doesn't have any more proofs of *hidalguía* other than those already mentioned and that he doesn't need an *ejecutoria* because his ancestors were always recognized as well-known *hidalgos* wherever they resided" (Gilman-Gonzálvez, p. 11). The "proofs" which had been mentioned included the two *probanza* transcripts, an exemp-tion from the *pecho* tax recognized by the village of Crespos where the Rojas owned property (all still in the VLA), and the fact, hitherto unrecorded, that the Licentiate Fernando had wangled membership in the restricted "Cofradía

lessly ambitious for municipal offices and honors, but also they had to cope with an urban atmosphere polluted with gossip and hatred. Toledo, among all Spanish cities, seems to have offered the most vicious example of what might be called the sociology of a "pannier de crabbes." In its hotbed of bitter inter-family rivalries, fabricated genealogies, calumny, and counter-calumny such a definitive document would serve as a valuable shield. The Francos knew of other *converso* families who had survived the full investigation which might be required for an *ejecutoria* (the Cepedas in Avila were only one of many such cases); they were wealthy enough to pay for as much favorable testimony as might be necessary; and more than 120 years had passed since their ancestors had been suspected. Why not go ahead?

The consequences of this decision were as disastrous as the Licentiate Fernando (dead twelve years earlier) had apparently feared. The *ejecutoria* was denied; the Francos were sentenced to pay all court costs; and they were further shamed by being publicly forbidden ever to pursue their aspirations again ("les pusieron perpetuo silencio"). What had happened was that the *fiscal* (state's attorney) instead of being swayed, as was usually the case, by the influence and wealth of the Francos (of which we shall see details in a later chapter) was urged on to full performance of his duty by a powerful enemy of the family. That individual, one don Antonio de Rojas, seems to have been a particularly ferocious *linajudo*, a standard social type of the time dedicated to critical scrutiny of others' lineages. But whatever his motivations, don Antonio's participation in the suit as an interested party was clearly decisive.[42]

---

de los Abades junto al ospital de Esgueva." An *ejecutoria*, as we shall see, might also testify to a lie, but it would have done so more convincingly.

[42] An *expediente* witness later testifies that he had heard about a number of strategy sessions in which various individuals "por orden del dicho don Antonio" gathered to discuss ways and means of frustrating the hated Francos (Gilman-Gonzálvez, p. 18). One motive for don Antonio's persistent persecution may have been his own remotely Jewish origins as a member of a collateral branch of the Téllez Girón family (see Chap. V, n. 33). That is to say, at the top of the heap (two brothers were canons and another, "el señor de Mora y Layos") and yet not entirely exempt from the odious gossip which permeated the city, it was to be expected that he and his family would try to squelch social climbers of far more recent and obvious *converso* origins. Intragroup or intracaste discrimination is both a well-known sociological phenomenon and a historical fact about the Spain of Fernando de Rojas (see Chap. IV,

Had the *fiscal* conducted the affair in a routine manner, the result would most likely have been one more facile metamorphosis of *converso* into *hidalgo*, categories which were not always antagonistic. But he did not. At the behest and with the help of don Antonio he won his case by obtaining damning information about the family background from Inquisition archives.

There, in those archives—as everyone knew—could be found the truth in a world of false appearances, social camouflage, and well-remunerated perjury. There, as I have said, lay the danger which, for all his cunning and skill, the Licentiate Fernando could not allay. When we think about the Inquisition as a historical institution, we naturally tend to stress its grim flamboyance (burning at the stake, torture, penitential garb, the ritual of the *auto de fe,* and the rest), its corruption, and its suppression of religious and intellectual freedom. But perhaps just as important as these to those who lived in fear of it was its bureaucratic routine. Dossiers conserved for centuries were secret weapons never before possessed by any society—and indeed hardly conceivable today in our own age of change. The *secreto* (and the wretched affair just described is only one minuscule example) was nothing less than a device for the petrifaction of social history.

But we still have not got to the end of the story. Although records of the vain attempts of another desperate Franco to become an *hidalgo* are still intact in the Chancery archives,[43] our information concerning the Inquisitional history of Rojas' family does not come directly from Hernán Suárez's fatal *probanza*. Like the original dossier in the *secreto*, it too has disappeared—and quite likely at the hands or the behest of one of the Rojas. However, once again chance and ill-will acted together to prevent complete obliteration.

---

n. 67). Just as likely a reason, however, might have been envy of the Francos' considerable wealth and of the municipal honors and local subservience which it purchased. In any case, don Antonio's hatred was so bitter that, according to the title—*delator desta causa*—of the *árbol* (as reproduced in Appendix II) he found a way to participate officially in opposition to the suit.

[43] See n. 39. Pedro Franco (unlisted in the *árbol*) is identified therein as the son of Juan Sánchez Franco (no. 22) a brother of the Gaspar Sánchez Franco (no. 19) who was the father of the second and finally defeated litigant, Hernán Suárez (no. 25). Certain witnesses mention knowing all four and go on to explain the details of their relationship. In the petition (see n. 40), Pedro Franco is associated with an Alonso Franco who may have been no. 26 on the *árbol*.

In an effort to put the contradictory testimony about Hernán Suárez and his relatives into some sort of order, the Chancery Court prepared an *árbol* (family tree) displaying for each disputed ancestor the allegations that had been made by both sides. This was then printed, an unusual procedure which not only provided copies for those concerned but also—inevitably—for unauthorized gossip-mongers as well. It was because of their malicious interest that a single copy of the tell-tale *árbol* still exists today.

The second series of events is even more complex than the intrigue which was fatal to the Francos. In 1616, some ten years after their final "silencing," a candidate for a canonry in the Cathedral of Toledo named Juan Francisco Palavesín y Rojas submitted to the customary genealogical examination of his qualifications. This involved full consideration of all adverse testimony, a requirement which tempted an enemy of the aspiring canon's family to accuse him of blood relationship with "the Rojas of the Puebla de Montalbán and Talavera." Even a suspicion of *converso* lineage could be fatal to candidates for this most wealthy and exclusive of posts; and, if he could not prove beyond all doubt that his ancestors shared no blood with the author of *La Celestina,* the smear would stick. As it turned out, after 227 witnesses from Toledo, the Puebla, Talavera, Valladolid, and elsewhere had been questioned and after over 800 folios had been filled with their testimony (such was the social insanity of the time!),[44] the charge was proved to be false. The aspirant, ironically enough, was not related to the Bachelor but rather, through an illegitimate liaison, to the vindictive don Antonio, the self-righteous nemesis of the Francos.[45] But I am now

[44] Now catalogued by one of the present archivists, Ramón Gonzálvez, who collaborated with me in bringing its information to light as FELS (Fondo de Expediente de Limpieza de Sangre) 7-122. Father Gonzálvez at present is preparing a catalogue of the Cathedral collection of such *expedientes*.

[45] The candidate's grandfather, the Licentiate Martín de Rojas, was the illegitimate son of a Fernando de Rojas, Abad de Santa Coloma, who seems to have been a relative of don Antonio's (Gilman-Gonzálvez, p. 18). The Licentiate Martín's bad temper and vindictive behavior (he was involved in lengthy suits and altercations both with the Francos and with another Toledan family of wealthy *conversos* known as the "Madrides") seem to have motivated the later denunciation of his ambitious grandson. As the latter's *expediente* reveals vividly, families under a cloud frequently would initiate a campaign of counter-calumny against their persecutors (*ibid.*, p. 6). In any case, the Licentiate Martín, perhaps in part because of his own particularly shameful

less interested in this particular display of bureaucratic and social perversity for its own sake than in two small portions of the record which the investigators themselves probably did not think at all important—except in a negative sense. The first is the testimony of Rojas' descendants and of those who knew the family, and the second is the copy of the printed genealogy of Hernán Suárez that had been bound into the manuscript as an exhibit. In his original accusation, the enemy of the Palevesín y Rojas family had mentioned having seen it, and the investigators, if only to prove there was nothing significant therein, thought it worthwhile to conserve a copy. All the Licentiate Fernando's caution and all the ravages of time were in vain. The hidden facts found their own circuitous and peculiar path to survival.

Before going into the genealogical heart of the matter, let us see briefly what the respondents to the immense ecclesiastical questionnaire had to say about Fernando de Rojas. He had, of course, died too long before (three quarters of a century) for any of them to remember him personally. It is therefore all the more worth emphasizing that time after time he is identified spontaneously as the author of *La Celestina*. Not only the two surviving grandchildren (Fray García de Rojas, an official of the Calced Carmelites, and Garcí Ponce de Rojas, a solicitor of the Court of Chancery[46]) and great-grandchildren but many others as well habitually add to Rojas' name the epithet: "que compuso a Celestina."[47] Unlike latter-

---

illegitimacy (as son of a priest), was noted for being contentious even within the standards of his ingrown and infected society. He is described by witnesses as full of "ojeriza y mala voluntad," as being "de tan áspera condición que estrellaba con todo el mundo," and as cherishing implacable hatred for all *conversos* (*ibid.*, p. 5). One wonders if he was aware of the origins of the Téllez Girones to whom (as we have seen in n. 42) he was distantly related.

[46] A brother of the Licentiate Fernando (the Friar being a first cousin), it was he who married one of the Salazars of Esquívias (see n. 24). His kindness in supplying board and lodging and a clerical position for a cousin of the aspiring canon was used by slanderers to lend credence to the charge of relationship (Gilman-Gonzálvez, pp. 9-10).

[47] Eight such identifications are cited in Gilman-Gonzálvez, but in the Palevesín *expediente* (as Esténaga noted) there are many more: ¿Se puede deducir de las informaciones testificales . . . que el Bachiller Hernando de Rojas fue autor de *La Celestina*? Así lo declaran Martín de Avila, familiar del Santo Oficio . . . de la Puebla . . . el 13 de Octubre de 1616, Don Antonio de Meneses y Padilla, vecino y natural de Talavera de la Reina y familiar del

day critics, this society of gossips and *linajudos* had no doubts about the authorship problem. Lacking the benefits of literary scholarship, their own personalistic variety kept them abreast of who was who among past authors and other more or less prominent members of society.

Along with awareness of literary achievement, all the witnesses who knew anything about the Rojas family were equally aware of its tainted origins. This was, of course, never admitted by those belonging to it (as we shall see, they spent much time and effort trying to maintain their status as *hidalgos* and to conceal the identities of their condemned ancestors), but everybody else was quite certain. The enemy of the future canon states, for example, "that he had heard it publicly said that the Rojas of the Puebla, those of Talavera, and those remaining in Toledo were unclean" ("no era gente limpia"). But even more revealing is the testimony of the favorable witnesses in that they had no personal axes to grind. When asked if their candidate was related "to the Francos of this city or to the Rojas who left it to go to the Puebla de Montalbán and Talavera," they react with indignation and disgust. One calls it "a false accusation originating in a grudge"; another says he is "nauseated" by the question ("abomina y hace ascos de la pregunta"); and still a third terms it an "evil and offensive charge" ("muy grande maldad y agravio").[48] Even a remote relationship to the author of *La Celestina* was a grave matter in sixteenth- and seventeenth-century Spain. In spite of more than a hundred years of scrupulously Christian behavior, two depositions of *hidalguía*,

---

Santo Oficio en ella, y don Alonso Fernández Aceituno, el 14 del mismo mes y año . . . y varios más. Cuando se nombra el autor de la famosa tragedia y son muchísimas las veces, se le llama 'el Bachiller Hernando de Rojas que compuso a Celestina la vieja,' sin que ni en las preguntas ni en las respuestas jamás se ponga en duda, refiriéndose siempre los testigos a lo que tienen oído a sus padres y es público y notorio en sus lugares" (p. 81).

[48] Gilman-Gonzálvez, pp. 6-7. In another portion of the testimony, an independent witness has no doubt about the Rojas' background: "He has heard it publicly said that the Rojas were not clean, and his father heard it said in Valladolid and Escalona, and this has always been their public reputation . . ." (*ibid.* pp. 6-7). The only Rojas from Escalona that I have been able to uncover are the family which provided tutors and *mayordomos* for the Téllez Girones in the Puebla. However, as we shall see in Chapter V, there are some indications that they may have been at least distantly related to the Bachelor.

and three changes of residence,[49] the family reputation was hope-lessly clouded.

What was it that these witnesses knew that we do not—or at least that we did not know until the official genealogy of Hernán Suárez came to light? It was not merely that Rojas was of *converso* origin, a misfortune for which wealth or fortune could at least partially compensate. It was lamentable, but hardly enough so to justify such vehemence. No, Toledan society remembered and took pains not to forget something far more shameful: at least five of the Bachelor's cousins were forced to undergo the ceremony of volun-tary public penitence and humiliation that was called *reconcil-iación* in the "Newspeak" of the time. Since this amounted to open admission of false conversion and secret Jewish practices, it con-stituted a far blacker family stain than those of other *conversos* who, confident in their innocence or precautions, did not submit themselves to the Inquisition.

The full details of Rojas' relationship to the dishonored family of the Francos appear in the transcription of the *árbol* (Appen-dix II).[50] For now, a brief list of the names and occupations of those whose admitted guilt was uncovered in the files of the "secreto" by the "fiscal" and the jubilant don Antonio will suffice. The oldest was Marí Alvarez, the wife of Pedro Franco, an old clothes dealer and tax farmer ("arrendador y trapero") who was a first cousin of Rojas' father. Of their six children, four joined their mother (Pedro Franco having died before the Inquisition was established) on the harrowing day of "reconciliation" in 1485. They were: Mencía Alvarez accompanied by her husband, a cloth mer-

---

[49] From Toledo to the Puebla, from the Puebla to Talavera, and from Talavera to Valladolid.

[50] To satisfy any remaining doubts that the *árbol* does indeed indicate the blood relationship of the Rojas to the Francos, we may begin by pointing to the Licentiate Fernando's joint handling of their *hidalguía* litigation "as a relative" (see n. 39). However, another independent witness remembers something far more specific and conclusive: two years after his departure from Salamanca the aforesaid Licentiate "Fernando de Rojas came to this city of Toledo and lodged in the house of a Fulano Franco near the buildings of the 'correo mayor.'" In that house, the witness goes on to say, he and the future Licentiate studied for their final exercises. Then, after graduation, "this Fer-nando de Rojas went to the town of Valladolid where he became a lawyer 'en materia de hidalguía' and earned many ducats . . ." (Gilman-Gonzálvez, p. 24). Information regarding the fortune amassed by the Licentiate from his prominent clientele may be found in Chap. VIII, n. 186.

chant named Alonso de San Pedro; Catalina Alvarez, wife of a *trapero*; and Juan and Alonso Franco whose occupations are unspecified. As we shall see, such means of making a living were typical of the caste of *conversos*.

This fine catch of delinquents from the century before last became even more useful to the two avid investigators when they found in addition a record of the interrogation of a great-grandson under arrest as a *"judaizante"* (a "Judaizer" or person secretly following Jewish law and customs). His entry on the *árbol* reads as follows: "Luis Alvarez Franco (one of the unreconciled children), warden of the mint. His son, Juan Franco was imprisoned as a *judaizante*. There was no sentence, because he went mad. He names as brothers and sisters of his father Hernán Franco and Alonso Franco and Mencía Alvarez."[51] From these records, then, we may fairly conclude that Fernando de Rojas was a member of that group of *converso* artisans, professional men, merchants, and city officials which between 1485 and 1501 (the total number is usually estimated at between seven and eight thousand)[52] was permanently dishonored (publicly reconciled, jailed, or executed) by the Toledo Inquisition. A verifiable blood-tie with any of these was enough to deny claims to *hidalguía* and, had it not been fully disproved, would have been a bar to admission to the college of canons. Years, decades, and even centuries had done nothing to mitigate such a fatal stain.

Since Fernando de Rojas was alive in 1485 and probably old enough to have witnessed the ceremonial downfall of his family (or at least to have participated in a childlike manner in the accompanying alarm and anguish), let us consider for a moment the nature of the ordeal imposed on the Francos. When the Inquisition

---

[51] The shift of tenses here and elsewhere in the *árbol* ("se volvió loco" followed by "nombra por hermanos") indicates that certain phrases, particularly those in which relationships are explained were copied from the original interrogation records. That is to say, Juan Franco *names* his uncles or brothers for the Inquisitors, while the later compiler of the *árbol* sums up the final result of his case in the past: "he *went* mad."

[52] This estimate (first proposed by Llorente) is broken down into categories in H. C. Lea, *The Inquisition of Spain*, New York, 1907, IV, 518 (hereafter referred to as Lea). For a catalogue and discussion of their occupations, see F. Cantera Burgos and P. León Tello, *Judaizantes del arzobispado de Toledo habilitados por la Inquisición en 1495 y 1497*, Madrid, 1969 (hereafter referred to as *Judaizantes*).

was established in Toledo in 1484, its first step was as usual to issue an Edict proclaiming a Period of Grace.[53] Those guilty of careless disobedience of Christian precepts or of having in a clandestine manner followed the religion of their forefathers might during these days confess, publicly repent, and be restored to the Church. Their reconciliation would be accepted without expropriation, imprisonment, or other penalties. If at first glance this may seem merciful, a closer look reveals a more perversely efficient intention. One had not only to confess in order to obtain forgiveness but also to denounce, to denounce anyone, whether close relative or distant acquaintance, whom one suspected of similar transgressions. And it was well to be thorough, for, if the Inquisitors later should discover through someone else's confession that information had been withheld, the reconciliation was considered null and void. After which the overdiscreet individual would be classified as "relapsed" and would be subject to rigorous penalties. The result was that those who worshiped together had later to conspire together (in order to decide on how much to reveal) and finally (as in the case of the Francos) to atone together. Still, as far as can be told from the *árbol*, the Francos were comparatively lucky. We shall see cases among Rojas' wife's relatives in which weak or malicious members of the family broke under interrogation and exposed them all to further persecution.

The atmosphere of shared consternation and mutual suspicion which surrounded Fernando de Rojas' childhood was not dispersed rapidly. After the Period of Grace, it took about a year to record and cross-check the large number of confessions, denunciations, interrogations, and declarations of genealogy (precisely the documents later furnished to the opponents of Hernan Suárez) that were involved. Then in 1485 came the carefully prepared day of public penance—marking by its climax of spiritual pain the watershed between excruciating uncertainty and the lasting dishonor which followed. In Chapter II there is included a contemporary description of a reconciliation en masse which took place a year

[53] For more detailed discussion of Edicts of Grace and "reconciliation," see Amador de los Ríos, *Historia social, política y religiosa de los judíos de España y Portugal*, Madrid, 1960, p. 689 (hereafter referred to as Amador de los Ríos), Lea, I, 165, and III, 146-147, and J. Caro Baroja, *Los judíos en la España moderna y contemporánea*, Madrid, 1961, I, 318 (hereafter referred to as Caro Baroja).

later, and one is struck therein by the calculated shaming of the participants: the barefoot procession through the streets of 900 more or less prominent citizens (hooted and laughed at by their more humble neighbors), the sermon and mass in front of the gallows, the unlighted candles, and the chanted recantations. Everything was designed to remain etched in the memories of both penitents and spectators—as well as of the children whose families were implicated.

The intuition of the reality of Fernando de Rojas that emerges from the *árbol* of the Francos may seem hypothetical. Living in the Puebla de Montalbán, five leagues away from Toledo, Rojas might well have been ignorant or only vaguely aware of the ordeal of his cousins. It is natural to keep family scandals away from children. There is, however, another entry on the *árbol* which concerns him directly and which indicates that, before childhood was over, he became fully conscious of the fate of his family and his kind. It reads as follows: "The Bachelor Rojas who composed Celestina la vieja. The *fiscal* contends that he was a son of Hernando de Rojas condemned as a *judaizante* in the year '88 and that from him descends the Licentiate Rojas, a lawyer who was from Valladolid and attorney for Hernán Suárez, for whom they also contrived an Asturian great-grandfather." In other words, in order to demolish the Francos' case for certification as *hidalgos*, the *fiscal* went so far as to look up whatever Inquisitional information was available about their second cousin, the "Bachiller Rojas que compuso a Celestina la vieja." And what he found out was that he was the son of a *judaizante* condemned in the year 1488, a fact which he then had included on the printed *árbol* in the form just reproduced.

Here is documentary evidence, then, to the effect that when Rojas was perhaps twelve years old[54] his father was arrested, imprisoned, tried, found guilty, and in all likelihood (in that initial period of Inquisitional rigor) executed by fire in an *auto de fe*. The horror of the fact needs little imaginative decoration. The "Medieval and Renaissance elements," which according to extreme historicists created *La Celestina*, have no father whose carnal vulnerability is the precondition of one's own. Or to say the same thing in the terms of Spain's greatest "realist," Benito Pérez Galdós,

---

[54] A tentative effort to establish Rojas' year of birth may be found at the beginning of Chapter V.

if one's reality is first intuited through pain, such a death in the family led the son to a more vivid discovery of what it meant and how it felt to be himself than most of us ever make.

Those who are familiar with the few published documents relating to the author of *La Celestina* may wonder why I consider the *fiscal*'s statement of his parentage infinitely more credible than that made by the Licentiate Fernando. The two *probanzas* of the family's *hidalguía* (which we mentioned the Licentiate's having arranged), the genealogy furnished by Hernán Suárez Franco, and the two "Libros de memorias" in the Valle Lersundi archives, all agree that Rojas' father was not a condemned *judaizante* also called Hernando or Fernando but rather one "Garcí Gonçález de Rojas who came from the town of Tineo in Asturias to the Puebla de Montalbán."[55] Why not accept this reiterated assertion of his progeniture instead of the prejudiced accusation of a family enemy? One good reason is implicit in the *fiscal*'s added remark "the Licentiate Rojas . . . for whom they also contrived an Asturian great-grandfather." This seems clearly to refer to the family's assertion that Garcí Gonçález came from Tineo in Asturias, an assertion that is suspicious per se. It was a well-known practice for *conversos*, struggling to integrate into an inimical and status-conscious society, to claim Asturias, "la Montaña" of Castile, or the Basque country as their place of ancestral origin. These were what North Americans might term the "tidewater" regions of the reconquest, the starting point in the northern mountains from which the original Old Christian survivors of the Moorish invasion began their centuries-long push to the South. As such, their inhabitants claimed racial cleanliness by historical and geographical definition. So that, if a *converso* could make his neighbors believe that his forefathers were Asturians or Basques, he might at long last live in peace and enjoy whatever prosperity he possessed.

This may seem a very obvious deception. And indeed there were many contemporary jokes about, and ironical references to, such standard camouflage. Maritornes, for example, is among other things a mocking portrait of a grotesque Asturian with absurd pretensions to *hidalguía*. And it is easy to imagine the counter-jibes of Old Christian busybodies at new announcements of Northern

---

[55] No. 4 on the *árbol*.

provenance.[56] Nevertheless, in spite of its obviousness, the Hernán Suárez *árbol* makes it quite clear that this was the remedy proposed by the Licentiate Fernando both for the Francos and (as the *fiscal* remarks with an almost audible sneer) himself. It also indicates the elaborate and calculated pains he found it necessary to take in order to make the deception more convincing: an actual journey to Asturias and the bribery of an indigent *hidalgo* in return for his complicity. Such were the lengths to which extreme social pressure forced him to go.

The results of the Licentiate Fernando's efforts were reported as follows in the first entry on the *árbol*: "Pedro Gonçález Notario was married in 1420 to his wife, Mayor Fernández. The present suitor, Hernán Suárez Franco, claims that he (Pedro Gonçález Notario) left three sons: Aluar Pérez who remained in Asturias, Garcí Gonçález de Rojas who went to the Puebla de Montalbán, and Pedro Franco who went to Toledo. And it is from this latter that Hernán Suárez is descended. . . ." From another entry we learn that the "head of the house in 1584 at the time the *probanza* was initiated" was one Juan de Rojas Francos—so that it was presumably he who sold his birthright.[57] In any case, whether or not this

[56] See Caro Baroja, II, 298-299, 347, and 364. For typical jokes, see J. Silverman, "Judíos y conversos en el *Libro de Chistes* de Luis de Pinedo," *Papeles de Son Armadans* (Mallorca), no. 69, 1961, pp. 289-301. Castro comments on a similar example to be found in the *Guzmán de Alfarache* in *La realidad histórica de España*, Mexico, 1962, p. 223 (hereafter referred to as *Realidad,* edn. II; the earlier edition, Mexico, 1954, will be referred to as *Realidad*, edn. I). Aubrey Bell points out that one of Fray Luis de León's forebears similarly claimed that the family originated in "La Montaña" (*Luis de León*, Oxford, 1925, p. 87). Alonso de Ercilla's vaunted Basque origins appear to represent a similar case.

[57] In the 1578 Franco *probanza* (see n. 39) the regional origin of the family is identified more vaguely as "la Montaña." Particularly in the testimony taken in Valladolid, witness after well-coached witness repeats with almost identical wording: "A Pedro Franco, visagüelo del que litiga"—that is, the "arrendador y trapero" who was founder of the family and who is number 3 on the *árbol* —"no le conoció mas de aver oydo dezir del a ombres viejos e ancianos que a muchos años que son fallescidos, los quales dezían que hera natural de las montañas e hijodalgo e que abía venido a bivir e morar a Toledo." Similarly in the 1584 testimony in the Rojas *probanza* initial witnesses continue to mention "la Montaña" as the place of family origin (see Appendix III), but toward the end we find Tineo in Asturias named for the first time (Appendix III, p. 528). From which I conclude that it was precisely at this point that the Licentiate Fernando decided to switch provinces and to lay claim to a specific

supposition be admitted, the fact that the *árbol* effectively disproves the Old Christianity of Pedro Franco (the "arrendador y trapero" who died just in time) indicates that the statements about Garcí Gonçález' origins were also invented. There is, I think, every reason to believe that both the Rojas and the Francos were of Toledan origin.

However, there is still another doubt to be satisfied. Granting that the Rojas' Asturian blood is a deception, why conclude therefrom that the condemned Hernando and not Garcí Gonçález was

---

locality and known family. In connection with the timing of the change in strategy, it is also worth noting that in the 1571 "probanza de Indias," also organized by the Licentiate Fernando for himself and his two brothers, no mention of the origins of the Rojas (not even the Puebla de Montalbán!) is made and that afterwards Tineo is insisted on proudly in his "Libro de memorias" (1593). In order to learn what really happened in 1584, the testimony of a witness alive at the time will be helpful: "The family tree of the Francos, he informs the Palavesín investigators, was a fabrication prepared in connection with a very long lasting suit for *hidalguía* in which they were involved. When they saw they were getting nowhere, they decided to go to Asturias and to return with the tree proving that they were of the blood of Juan de Rojas Francos which in that province is very noble (*hidalga*) and esteemed" (Gilman-Gonzálvez, p. 26). That this gossip was not inaccurate is demonstrated by the fact that the witness was able to identify the same Juan de Rojas Francos named on the *árbol* as "head of the house at the time the *provanza* was initiated in 1584." It is thus evident that the Licentiate Fernando went up to Cangas de Tineo, a properly Northern town, because he had been told about a family there whose two surnames resembled both his and his cousins'. How he then managed to obtain the indispensable compliance of the "head of the house" for the merger of the two families cannot, of course, be determined. But I would venture to guess that the latter (like such fellow *hidalgos* as Alonso Quijano and Lazarillo's third master) may have been land poor and so susceptible to an offer of cash. In this connection we may further note that in the Valle Lersundi Archives (34-10) there are filed together two curious documents (significantly catalogued among the "papeles de nobleza") which the Licentiate Fernando appears to have obtained from his new relative. Written in archaic and dialectal Asturian, they are, first, the will of one doña Sancha de Arrojas (a variant of the surname, Rojas, both of them appearing in a 1588 *ejecutoria* issued to one Gonçalo García de Rojas of Tineo, Archivo de la Real Chancillería, Leg. 819) and, second, the record of an equally old lawsuit brought by an Alonso Francos of Tineo against a neighbor. These were needed, I assume, in order to give increased verisimilitude to the deception. Additional information about the Rojas of Tineo may be found in the 1651 investigation of the genealogy of one Alonso Flórez de Valdés y Rojas undertaken in connection with his candidacy for the Order of Santiago. See the section of "Pruebas de Santiago," no. 3108, in the Archivo Histórico Nacional (hereafter referred to as AHN).

the Bachelor's father? Again why not accept the family's reiterated statement rather than the probably prejudiced contentions of their enemies? Not only is Garcí Gonçález named in several documents but also a number of witnesses (asked to testity to his *hidalguía* in 1584) remember by name his wife, Catalina de Rojas. And one even goes so far as to mention his honorable sepulchre covered by a "large brown stone" in the parish church in the Puebla.[58] Here is a statement too easily verifiable to be dismissed as perjured. Against these arguments, I would reply, first, that verifiable existence is far from being the same thing as proved parentage. And, second, that a relevant case in point is provided by another stratagem of the harassed Rojas: the substitution in the family tree of a more acceptable relative for Alvaro de Montalbán.

Those who have worked closely with the Rojas papers have surely found it striking (whether they wish to admit it or not) that, aside from the trial transcript, in no other document (those under family control) is any mention made of Leonor Alvarez' male parent. In accordance with a strategy (probably agreed upon in 1616), whenever his descendants had to account for his branch of the family tree, they provided a more acceptable substitute. Rojas' wife—they maintain in unison—"was the daughter of the physician, Dr. Juan Alvarez."[59] And who was Dr. Juan Alvarez? As a glance at

[58] VLA 35, published by the owner in *RFE*, XII, 1925, as "Documentos referentes a Fernando de Rojas," p. 395 (hereafter referred to as VL I). Rojas' testament and the inventory made after his death (VLA 17 and 23) were published in *RFE*, XVI, 1929, as "Testamento de Fernando de Rojas" and will be referred to hereafter as VL II.

[59] In the 1621 "Libro de memorias" of Rojas' great-grandson, Juan (see n. 41) Leonor Alvarez is identified specifically as the "hija del doctor Juan Alvarez de San Pedro y de Ynés Dávila, hija de Gonçalo Dávila." Here he is in disagreement with his father, the Licentiate Fernando, who in his own "Libro" (1594) correctly identifies the Doctor and his wife as "abuelos de parte de madre." Leonor Alvarez' parents are simply not mentioned. From this and from the fact that all the Rojas who testified in the Palavesín *expediente* maintain in unison that, "the Bachelor Hernando de Rojas who composed 'Celestina la vieja' . . . married Leonor Alvarez, the daughter of Doctor Juan Alvarez, physician, both of them natives of the city of Toledo," I conclude that the lie was agreed on in 1616 when the family became uncomfortably aware that their whole background was going to be scrutinized. In the 1584 *probanza de hidalguía* it had not been necessary (because of the nature of the document) to introduce maternal lineage. But now, since a canonry with its requirements of total cleanliness was at stake, it would have to be accounted for. What to do? The decision taken was that alluded in the

the chart (Appendix II) will show, he was actually her son-in-law who had been moved back two generations to a spot where he was more needed.[60]

Even an introductory glimpse of the society into which Rojas' grandchildren and great-grandchildren were born enables us to comprehend the necessity of such falsification. But at this point we are less concerned with the perils and maneuverings of the Licentiate Fernando and those close to him than with the light this documented deception throws on the Bachelor's true parentage. The erasure of Alvaro de Montalbán indicates—by behavioral analogy —that a similar operation was performed on Hernando de Rojas "condemned as a *judaizante* in the year '88." Rojas' father, like his father-in-law, was obliterated, and a relative suitable because of his honorable church burial was displayed instead. The *árbol*—given its digested and unverifiable nature—is open to question. But to dismiss it on the basis of what a family such as the Rojas have to say about themselves would be naive. The more they tell the same story and the more they flaunt their Asturian cleanliness, the more reliable the *fiscal* and don Antonio appear.

By way of conclusion let us abandon for a moment the documentary reality of Fernando de Rojas and permit ourselves a para-

---

text: to move their maternal grandfather back two generations. Which is to say, they replaced their condemned great-grandfather, Alvaro de Montalbán, with their mother's father. The principal advantage of this arrangement, one imagines, was that, if challenged or accused of perjury, they could claim that they were confused. In any case, the lie is patent. Not only the Licentiate Fernando's "Libro," but also two other Valle Lersundi documents (the "probanza de Indias," no. 32, and the division of Ynés de Avila's estate among her children, no. 31) state unequivocally the true relationship of the family to the physician. Before the Rojas had found it necessary to hide only one condemned ancestor (the Bachelor's father); now there were two, and the family tree, accordingly, had once more to be rearranged.

[60] In a 1565 *expediente de limpieza* obtained by a maternal uncle of the Licentiate Fernando, Francisco de Avila, for the purpose of being admitted to a canonry in Sigüenza, there is a comparable shifting around of branches. Instead of listing his true parents, Ynés de Avila and our friend the Doctor (as shown both in VLA 31 as well as in the Palavesín testimony), for some reason he substitutes the names of his brother and sister. The only salvation for such a restrictive social order seems to have been the willingness of many witnesses to swear to anything. I am indebted to Father Gregorio Sánchez Doncel, for a transcription of the document: Archivo de la Catedral de Sigüenza, Expedientes de limpieza, Leg. 5.

graph of biographical speculation. In view of the affirmation (often repeated and never denied in the Palavesín testimony) that the Rojas family left Toledo for the Puebla, we may further guess that they did so under a cloud. Perhaps the move was made in 1485 after the "reconciliation" of their relatives, perhaps in 1488 after the condemnation of the Bachelor's father. If this were the case, the author of *La Celestina* would not have been born in the Puebla after all but in Toledo. He most probably grew up in the Puebla (perhaps in the home of a charitable relative named Garcí Gonçález), since, as we shall see, he maintained close ties with the place until his death. But he was a native of Toledo. The one clear biographical statement of the acrostic verses—"and he was born in the Puebla de Montalbán"—would accordingly have to be considered an initial concealment of inconfessable origins. And from this first step, the Licentiate Fernando and his family would three generations later weave their further elaborations.

❧ The Testimony of the Author

Our supposition that the veracity of the acrostic may be challenged results not only from the testimony of the *árbol* but from a lack of confidence in Fernando de Rojas when he assumes the role of *autor*. Critics have with good reason generally suspected that the information provided by the prologue material taken as a whole was designed more to mislead than to inform them about the intentions and the reality of the man who wrote *La Celestina*. In part this seems to have been due to his single-minded effort to "conceal his life" (as Stendhal later was to phrase it) both inside and outside the frontiers of creation. As has been remarked, in the course of writing the writer cunningly and determinedly covered his personal tracks and to such an extent that the dialogue that was produced may be considered a supreme example of creative self-effacement. And, as we shall go on to see in chapters to follow, the Bachelor Rojas who went to Salamanca and who afterwards settled down to modest domesticity and legal practice in Talavera seems equally determined to betray nothing about himself, to make sure that every step of his uneventful pilgrimage to death was in time with those of his neighbors. Jean-Paul Sartre points out how lives, once personal, become more and more generic

51

as they recede into the past,[61] but Rojas appears to have taken good care to make his life as generic as possible while still living it. Which is to say, by so dedicating himself to his "être-pour-autrui" he chose a comfortable form of death—unreality—as a form of life. As a result, when suddenly and unexpectedly he stands up, identifies himself, and tells us about his intentions and feelings as an author, we are justifiably suspicious. Is prefatory *Wahrheit* conceivable for such a *Dichter*?

But lack of confidence aside, we may also sympathize with Rojas at this exceedingly difficult moment of his existence. He was, after all, face to face with a problem identical to that which now concerns me: how to account in personal terms for such an ostensibly impersonal work of art? *La Celestina* has achieved its sixteen-act completion; Pleberio has pronounced his last word; and now in the act of verbal baptism Rojas must at least briefly speak with his own voice. He must directly as well as by implication explain who he was and what he had meant to say. The creative writer had now, in other words, to present himself as an *auctor* and to convert his intuitions into acceptable *auctoritas*. And to do so involved a self-distortion and a public presumption that may well have been painful. It is a discomfort familiar to all who write, and it may have been partly responsible for the conventionality of the solution: self-exhibition not as a man but as a mask, self-attribution of the most commonplace intentions, self-depiction in the most standard of literary postures. The result is a counterfeit portrait of the artist as a young man which, however explicable, is both unconvincing and poverty stricken. Celestina, as a mistress of using the truth and richly detailed facsimiles of the truth to deceive, would have spurned it. But for all its haste, barrenness, and lack of originality, the prologue material is worthy of close examination. It is both the first attempt to bring life and work into meaningful relationship and the only one to be made by a "critic" with access to the facts. Read with care, therefore, it may betray some of the things it tries to conceal.

[61] *L'Etre et le néant*, Paris, 1943, p. 626: "Etre oublié, c'est en fait, être appréhendé résolument et pour toujours comme élément fondu dans une masse (les 'grands féodaux du XIIIᵉ siècle,' les 'bourgeois whigs' du XVIIIᵉ, les 'fonctionnaires soviétiques,' etc.), ce n'est nullement *s'anéantir*, mais c'est perdre son existence personelle pour être constituée avec d'autres en existence collective."

Rojas seems himself to be dissatisfied with his mask as author. He sensed its unconvincing awkwardness, and in three successive versions he sought to improve it, to bring it—like his lovers' "process of delight"—to ripeness. In the earliest known edition (1499) the mask had no features at all; it was the ultimate mask called anonymity. But there was a title,[62] a long title as was the custom of the century, and in it Rojas (or his predecessor) suggests indirectly his own claims to authority: "The Comedy of Calisto and Melibea with its 'arguments' newly added which contains, in addition to its agreeable and sweet style, many philosophical maxims and warnings very necessary to young men who are shown the deceits practiced by servants and go-betweens." The author proclaims first of all his professional skill, his consciousness of possessing an uncommon mastery of Castilian prose style ("agradable y dulce estilo"). There then follows an assertion of learning: the anonymous author has read a great deal and has collected in his commonplace book (according to the approved fashion of our ancestors) a great store of "sentencias filosofales." Finally, he is wise. He has seen life and knows from experience the perils of the deceptive world. In the word "mancebos" there is a possible implication of maturity, an implication to be abandoned later on. Thus, in so describing his book, the writer of the title has to all intents and purposes described himself. Its skill, its learning, and its wisdom are his. They are the generic traits of a mask of authority that is still primitive and tacit.

A year or so later the writer made up his mind to give himself an identity, which is to say a name and a capsule biography. The implied self-characterization of the title seemed insufficient, if only because such an unheard of work needed a more satisfactory and explicit human introduction. Readers all over Spain must have been asking themselves what it really meant, who wrote it, and how it came to be written. Then, too, it is not unfair to suspect Rojas— for all his evasiveness—of a natural wish to claim credit now that *La Celestina* was a success and he had been asked to prepare a second edition. As Proaza (in justifying the announcement in appended verses) remarks, it was now time to associate the "digna fama" with a "claro nombre," phrases to be discussed in detail in a later chapter.

---

[62] It has often been surmised that this title was the one heading the original fragment.

But, however natural and reasonable Rojas' decision may seem to us, he apparently felt it would be inadvisable merely to add his name to the title ("acabada por el bachiller Fernando de Rojas") and let it go at that. The self-revelation had to be carefully and strategically prepared. Hence, using the standard device of a prefatory "Letter to a friend," he explicitly justifies an anonymity which he declares he is going to maintain: "don't blame me if I don't express my name." His new mask, unlike the old, is one of inexperience, modesty, and timidity, and he pretends that he doesn't dare make his name public. Yet at the same time, as he himself says ("offrezco los siguientes metros"), he was engaged in composing eleven stanzas of acrostic verses designed to give away the secret. And his friend Proaza, with whom he must have consulted at length about the stratagem, undertook (in the closing poem just mentioned) to provide the curious reader with a key to Rojas' hidden message—"put together the first letter of each line and they will reveal in a cunning manner his name"—along with the heroic accessories of lineage ("clara nación") and birthplace ("tierra"). The reader who follows these instructions is quickly rewarded for his effort with the well-known declaration: "The Bachelor Fernando de Rojas finished the Comedia of Calisto and Melibea, and he was born in the Puebla de Montalbán."

We may well wonder whom Rojas expected to deceive or impress with such a transparent device. How could a mind endowed with the insight that is manifest in *La Celestina* have invented such an unconvincing game of hide and seek? Scholars refer us to similar acrostics used by other uncomfortable authors of the time. But we may seek a more illuminating answer in the nascent state of the relationship between author and public. In the first decades of the new era of Gutenberg there was no ready-made, habitual form of contact between them. Neither knew what to expect of the other, a situation which often resulted (as readers of Guevara or Juan del Encina also know)[63] in complex and even desperate struggles with the inherited commonplaces of prefatory self-presentation. That is to say, authors attempted to make prologues say things and express feelings for which the age-old topics of humility and exemplary didacticism were unfitted.

[63] See my "Sequel to the *Villano del Danubio*," *RHM*, xxxi, 1965, and J. R. Andrews, *Juan del Encina*, Berkeley, 1959.

Along with the deeply felt need to find a new relationship with an unknown reader (a need not fully satisfied until Cervantes broke the spell of the past in the prologue to the *Quijote* of 1605), fifteenth- and early sixteenth-century authors were alternately fascinated with and afraid of their newly-massive clientele. One senses in writers like Rojas and Guevara (of whose reactions more later) a veritable terror of public opinion, as alien to the accepted *ingenios* of the seventeenth century (who often made fun of the *vulgo* they served) as to the isolated and defiant artists of more recent times. In other words, Rojas, aware in his own terms of the originality and importance of what he had done, desiring a share of the resultant glory, but fearing the unpredictable consequences, simply had no traditional way to behave. No tried and true public posture or protective word magic was available. He was forced to experiment.

Finally, in the very act of painting the oversimplified and purposefully misleading self-portrait of the Letter, Rojas may well have learned about the nature of masks: that they function as something not only to hide behind but also to flirt with. He had learned how to brag while pretending to do the opposite, how to allude to the truth in the act of camouflaging it. These lessons derived from the Letter were then applied to the acrostic which followed, an acrostic which was a complementary exercise in flirtation and feigned humility. By this I mean specifically that, once having decided to come to the center of the stage and to pose for a moment under the spotlight of "fame" as a "great man," Rojas had first to arrange to be pushed there against his will by a friend. Astute readers might see through the deception and into the calculation, but no matter. More important than fooling everybody was to be able to reveal his identity without openly contradicting the false modesty of the Letter. Thus, he invented a way to be announced without losing all the strategic protection of his earlier anonymity. And the sad proof of his success is the state of his reputation today.

The details of the fabricated self revealed in the Letter and the acrostic verses are too well known to require lengthy exposition. But, briefly, the author deposes as follows: he is a lawyer and proud of his profession. While preparing for his career at Salamanca he "found" an uncompleted act of dialogue, a fragment

55

so artistically and morally excellent, that during a fortnight's vacation when his fellow students ("socios") had gone home he completed it with fifteen more acts. He undertook this unfamiliar and uncongenial task, he says, both out of admiration for the first act and out of disapproval of love's fatal dominion over all varieties of his fellow countrymen: "damas, matronas, mancebos, casados." Morality, national preoccupation, and aesthetic judgment join together in a fashion not unfamiliar to readers of literature in Spanish. He is, of course, well aware of the inferiority of his continuation, and he draws an apologetic contrast between it and the dialogue of his predecessor. Only his good intentions and exemplary motivation may serve to justify him.

Although we may dismiss this elementary strategy (Rojas obviously knew by this time how successful he had been), we feel that the author is sincere when he goes on to comment on his intellectual distance. That is, when he presents himself as an observer who, as if he were "absent from his own country," can see clearly and judge impartially. Unlike the cases of Cervantes or Vicente Espinel who had returned from abroad and viewed their country with new eyes, the physical distance of the traveller is here only a comparison. Although in making it he may have betrayed (as I shall suggest later) a frustrated desire for farther horizons, at this point, the author's apartness is solely of the mind: "I have on various occasions withdrawn to my chamber and there meditated chin in hand, my senses ranging out like hunting dogs, my judgment soaring." Soaring—we wonder—like the hawk whose chance flight through space gave rise to *La Celestina?*

The horizontal and vertical spatial images, ranging dog and soaring hawk, just cited combine with others[64] to introduce the thematically central role of space as a determinant of the dialogue that is to follow. And yet at the same time we also sense in them the possibility that Rojas' temporary isolation might have accentuated his acute awareness of space at the very period of most intense creation. A mind withdrawn and alone tends naturally to brood on the four corners of the room and on the farther space beyond the windows. Vacancy and solidity exist for it far more intensely than when blurred (or even erased) by human company. Time, too, as readers of Machado know, ticks off more emphatically in solitude,

[64] See *The Art*, Chap. V, sect. 2, "From Thesis to Theme—Fortune."

and we may surmise that the remarks on "stolen moments" and hours carefully measured out "for recreation" as well as the inexorable two weeks are indicative of a writer of extreme temporal awareness. Rather than mere professional apologies, do they not betray the state of a mind overhearing with attentive irony the temporal anxieties and complacencies of his speakers?

In any case, there alone in his room, when not meditating on the sad state of Eros in Spain nor idly measuring dimensions against the self, our author has something marvelous to do. He is a reader. And in telling us so, he points to a real Rojas who belonged (as we shall see) to the first generation to grow up in a world of book availability. He is a reader, and he reads with that almost vicious surrender to the printed page which those of us who grew up before the advent of television will remember. As he himself says, when he looked at the fragment which was later to become Act I, "I read it three or four times. And the oftener I read it, the more I seemed to need to read it again. I enjoyed it more and more." He goes on to pretend that what really pleased him were the sententious maxims and "little fountains of philosophy" which men of his time thought of as the only valid reason for opening a book, but between the lines we sense a reader fully submerged in what Albert Thibaudet has called one of the two varieties of "voluptuousness" denied to the ancients.[65] The other, tobacco, could conceivably have been discovered by Rojas before he died. In any case, we may conclude that Rojas' meditative distance was achieved not only in terms of the solitary Vaucluse of the sage but also through continuous perusal, the intimate literate companionship which provides what Cervantes was to call "a new kind of life" to the modern addict. Like Montaigne, he had found another world of words in which both to submerge his reality of pain and to judge his circumstance.

The Prologue added two years later (as an introduction to the expanded twenty-one-act *Tragicomedia* of 1502) re-emphasizes and reinforces the earlier self-portrait. And, in doing so, it augments the reader's already strong suspicion that a counterfeit has been foisted on him. There is patent hypocrisy in the initial self-deprecation: "My poor learning is insufficient even to gnaw the dry

[65] See *Le Liseur de Romans*, Paris, 1925, p. ii. Pierre Louys had suggested tobacco as our only progress in the field—up to that time!

crusts of the wise sayings of the . . . clear minded geniuses of the past. . . ." What follows naturally is a display of learning designed to impress the reader with the untruth of the pretense of ignorance that was just announced. The strategy is almost insultingly elementary. We are supposed to wonder at the modesty of a savant who, knowing so much, has such a low opinion of himself. But this is not all. There is a second level of hypocrisy as fatal to our respect for the author as his pretended anonymity. All the erudition is cribbed, and, what is worse, from a source available and probably well known to his better educated readers. Rojas' prologue, aside from a few personal remarks, is nothing more than a careful reorganization and ruthless condensation of the essay introducing Petrarch's remedies for adverse fortune (the second part of the *De remediis utriusque fortunae*). All the examples, including even the opening citation from Heraclitus, were copied, and the only acknowledgement is that of the cheating schoolboy who mentions with assumed casualness the origin of a single sentence. If accused of plagiarism by the teacher (or in Rojas' case by a reader acquainted with him), he can always claim he meant to refer to his source.

We must, I think, judge this all too apparent insincerity in the same terms used for comprehending the recourse to an acrostic. Once again Rojas in the role of author is confronted with the puzzling and painful task of trying to account for the work in the context of himself and his life. And once again he finds no ready-made or even satisfactory solution. All he can do is repeat and underline his feigned humility and afterwards feign erudition to be humble about.[66] It is a double deception which does him little credit but which also brings out the insurmountable difficulties he found in taking his place at the head of *La Celestina*. Rojas clearly did not know how to comport himself as an author—how to put on for his public an unfamiliar mask of modern authority.

There is one feature of the Prologue which, insofar as it betrays

[66] One of the really extraordinary things about *La Celestina* is the paucity of its author's learning. As we shall see, in the century of humanism Rojas' personal culture amounted to that of a reader of printed best sellers. His direct sources are not those proposed by Castro Guisasola (*Observaciones sobre las fuentes literarias*, Madrid, 1924), but rather in great measure correspond to enthusiastic reading of the literary *nouveautés* of the decade as well as the rudimentary and neo-medieval Latin learning (Seneca, Terence, Cicero, etc.) of a "Bachiller."

the man behind the role, deserves special attention. It is the curious description of the conflicting reactions of the reading public to the earlier sixteen-act version, a version already at least three years old. After expressing his second-hand amazement at the universality of struggle in nature and society, the author concludes: "I am not surprised that the present work has been a cause of dissension and battle among its readers, for everyone judges it as he lists. Some have said it was diffuse; others, too short; some, agreeable; others, unclear; so that to please them all would be a task that only God could successfully accomplish." Yet it is precisely this that Rojas would like to do: to find a way "to please" everybody. There is no better example than his solution to the argument over the proper generic designation. Using the same device resorted to by Sancho Panza when he placated the partisans of both basin and helmet, he finds a middle path between those of comedy and tragedy and calls his new version a "tragicomedia."

Identical prudence and an identically supine desire to please accompany the justification of the five added acts:

> I was concerned to find out what the majority felt about it [miré donde la mayor parte acostaba] and learned that most people wanted me to extend the process of the lovers' delight, and to this end I was much importuned. And so, although against my will, I agreed once again to apply my pen to a task unfamiliar and foreign to my profession, stealing spare moments from my work along with other hours ordinarily devoted to recreation—since the new version will not lack for new detractors.

This last clause, so illogically and revealingly appended, is a clear indication of timorousness. The circumstantial reality of Fernando de Rojas—as he sees it—is not unlike that to which the inhabitants of *La Celestina* are subjected. Both were worlds of verbal warfare where tongues were as sharp and deadly as swords ("reproches, revistas y tachas me están cortando") and against which the only defense was a "shield of silence." In a later chapter we shall add other examples, but for now it will suffice to have remarked on the fear hiding beneath the mask of a modest young lawyer-author earnestly preaching morality and parcelling out his hours. Clinging almost desperately to the middle path, he will go to any length

to placate majority opinion. Just as in the case of Sempronio suddenly confronted with the explosive and menacing passion of his
master, every decision to act is accompanied by anguish and
hesitation.

The portrait of the author which emerges from the prologue
material in its finally completed form—title, Letter, acrostic verses,
Prologue, and his and Proaza's concluding verses—is patently
spurious. So much so that we have every right to suspect that instead of being moral in his intentions and modest in his self-estima-
tion, the man who was hiding behind his prefatory role, was in
reality both cynical and proud. Those who place Rojas in the tradition of Cervantes, Stendhal, and the anonymous author of
Lazarillo de Tormes (all masters of the art of writing ironical prologues) may be disappointed by this inept performance. It would
indeed seem that the awkwardness and feebleness of the several
deceptions just exposed correspond to a genuine inability to face
the public as an author. Rojas, in other words, for reasons probably having as much to do with personal temperament as with the
printed metamorphosis of the authorial role, seems both to want to
tell the truth and to lie at the same time. Hence, the legitimacy of
reading between the lines a sense of intellectual alienation, a delight in the refuge of reading, and a morbid fearfulness. The
testimony of the author may be both perjured and commonplace,
but it is also a betrayal—indeed the only remnant—of the lost intimacy of Fernando de Rojas.

I would further surmise that an even more favorable judgment
may be made of the facts which are given us. Although insistence
on birth in the Puebla de Montalbán may have been a first
desperate effort to conceal his parentage, Rojas had no particular
reason that I can imagine to lie to his public about the genesis of
La Celestina. The student readers and auditors when they returned
from their vacation would certainly be in a position to check up on
gross distortions. And indeed the truth of the separate origin of Act
I, long passionately denied and recently confirmed beyond reasonable doubt by Martín de Riquer,[67] indicates a possibility of equal
truth for other introductory statements. The rhetorical pose may
be transparently fraudulent, but the information imparted is not
for that reason necessarily suspect.

[67] "Fernando de Rojas y el primer acto de *La Celestina*," *RFE*, XLII (1958).

We should, therefore, begin by believing most of what the author says about Fernando de Rojas. He was a law student at Salamanca. He did find a fragment of dialogue probably already entitled the *Comedia de Calisto y Melibea,* and he did perceive in it a literary quality attributable only to the greatest writers in Castilian. Indeed, he read it and reread it with such mounting excitement that he could not resist trying to finish it during a period of recess from classes.[68] There in the rose-tan university town suddenly silenced, emptied overnight of its turbulent and transient student population, one student remained. But no more in a state of boredom or homesickness than Columbus himself on his lonely way to San Salvador five or six years earlier. At high creative pitch, he was engaged in one of the most memorable and decisive journeys of discovery of the world within man ever to be made in Spanish.

Then, when the university filled again, the just-completed *Comedia* was read aloud to its author's classmates, among whom it created a great stir. The product of a lonely vacation, the fifteen added acts were now the center of vehement public discussion. And since that public was primarily one of students, the new book was subjected to all the dispute, debate, and intellectual passion to which the university milieu can at its best give rise. A year or two passed; the manuscript, which had been sent (perhaps at the urging of some of its first auditors) with its title as its only prologue to a German printer recently established in Burgos, became known to a far wider national public.[69] Success led to another edition, and the student author decided to reveal his identity in the strange way we have seen. It is even possible that the idea originated with his friend and older mentor Proaza, who was clearly an excited and enthusiastic reader. Also between 1497 and 1500 (in a later chapter the reasoning behind these assumptions will be made clear) something else of great importance happened to the author. He graduated, and, now on his way to the higher degree of Licentiate,

---

[68] I don't think it necessary to revive the tired argument about the human possibility of writing the fifteen acts in a fortnight. According to the *carta,* Rojas expected that the claim might be disputed and shrugs his shoulders: "aún más tiempo e menos acepto." But even though he may not have had it finished when classes reopened, there is no reason not to believe that he began his continuation in the circumstances claimed.

[69] One should not rule out the possibility of an earlier Salamanca edition.

he could proudly identify himself in the acrostic as "Bachiller." At any rate while still in Salamanca, he again acceded to the urging of his comrades and brought *La Celestina* to its full twenty-one-act ripeness. In "moments stolen" from his legal pursuits, he would musingly reread a printed copy of his own earlier creation and musingly write careful interpolations along its margins.[70]

The author's story, retold in this way, allows us better to understand both the indications of fearfulness and the sense of isolation which we detected beneath the authoritative mask. That is, the very fact that Rojas was a continuing author, surely the greatest continuing author ever to exist, suggests the special quality of these feelings. Instead of as a lonely, shut-in academic hermit, let us rather think of Rojas as a man of supreme empathy, as a man who could penetrate within, and create from, another's work and another's point of view with a genius comparable only to that of a Lope de Vega. His was a sense for "otherness" which places him—in spite of the attitude of irony they shared—at the human antipodes of a Stendhal. If the latter, as León Blum has suggested, plays all the roles in his novels, the former writes dialogue which not only captures the alien selves of his speakers but also—and more astoundingly—continues and grows from an alien creative vision. On these terms it was only to be expected that Rojas should, by his own confession, have been so vulnerable to the pressure of others or so anxious to please them.

This is not necessarily to say that Rojas was unsure of himself or unaware that his own achievement was at least as remarkable as that of his predecessor, an awareness expressed obliquely in his praise for Act I. But in spite of whatever self-confidence we may attribute to him, he still portrays himself as feeling almost fatally compelled to cater to the minds and the opinions of everyone around him. His extreme sensitivity, his compulsive use of his senses to sniff winds of incoming thought ("echando mis sentidos por ventores") converted him into a vulnerable subject of admirers and detractors. The word "cowardice" is inexact and unfair, but Rojas' keen interest in cowards and derisive understanding of their feelings indicates that, in his own world of intellectual and physical

---

[70] See J. Homer Herriott, *Towards a Critical Edition of the "Celestina,"* Madison, Wis., 1964, p. 283.

warfare, he shared their exacerbated form of consciousness. Like a man sitting by a wilderness fire surrounded by luminous eyes, he felt other points of view converging on him, transfixing him.

As for solitude and distance, the being capable of continuing Act I necessarily combined his enjoyment of them with a need for close companionship. As my teacher Augusto Centeno has phrased it, Rojas, like all artists of his magnitude, was at once "separated" and "inseparable" from the human realities which were his stock in trade. But what seems peculiar about the self revealed in the prologue material is its acute awareness of present apartness and approaching reunion. During those two intense weeks when Rojas' "socios" (the use of this expression may itself be significant) were absent, he lived in uneasy expectation of their return. Although as an author he portrays himself in the topical pose of the lonely thinker "withdrawn to my chamber with chin in hand," his thoughts were not of himself but of others: those others whose voices he was transcribing and those others who would soon listen to them. Only a mind able so "to refine itself out of existence" could have completed the truncated fragment it had absorbed with so much ardor.

It should be noted in conclusion that the others Rojas was waiting for and on whom he depended were not representatives of the dangers and hostilities of society in general. Nor were they exclusively a pack of rivals, hidden antagonists, and dissembling enemies. Acting to compensate for Rojas' wary realization of dangerous exposure (with corresponding stress on protective armor and commonplace camouflage) was the comfort of belonging. Those who discuss *La Celestina*, the author tells us, are of one age, "la alegre juventud e mancebía." Which is to say in our contemporary terms, Rojas thought of himself as a member of a generation. He might have been a controversial and at times "withdrawn" member, but obviously there were also at Salamanca friends to whom he could turn for advice and with whom he could slake the raging thirst for companionship which perhaps he shared with the inhabitants of his creation.

Let us, then, balance the initial portrait of the author alone in his room acutely aware of space and time with another. Let us also envision him—as Proaza indirectly describes him—at the center of

63

a group of ten companions reading *La Celestina* aloud with appropriate elocution. The first of these oral performances was indeed a "generational moment" as clear-cut and significant to the history of Spanish literature as the funeral of Larra. And it was at that moment that author and man coincided in full reality.

CHAPTER II

❧ The Case of Alvaro de Montalbán

> ... this rumor had got abroad upon
> the gun-decks and in the tops, the
> people of a great warship being in one
> respect like villagers, taking micro-
> scopic note of every outward
> movement or non-movement going on.
>
> —*Billy Budd, Foretopman*

෨ The Arrest

Early in June in 1525, Fernando de Rojas' father-in-law, Alvaro de Montalbán, was arrested by the *alguaciles* of the Holy Office.[1] The action was sudden and unexpected. He had been left alone by the Inquisition since his first confession and "reconciliation" some forty years before, that is, during the same initial epoch of community disgrace referred to in the *árbol* of the Francos. And now he was charged with an offense he could neither imagine nor remember: an unfortunate slip of the tongue made many months before while staying with relatives in Madrid. Nor did the Inquisitors modify their usual practice of attempting to obtain a prior confession while keeping the prisoner in the dark concerning the specific accusation. Although they often obtained all sorts of unexpected information from such fishing expeditions, the procedure did not work in the case of Alvaro de Montalbán. Try as hard as he might, he could come up with no idea of what he was supposed to have done. All he knew was that his worldly goods had been impounded and his person consigned to the Inquisition prison in Toledo.[2]

[1] The entire transcript of the trial is contained in Serrano y Sanz.

[2] The presiding Inquisitors were Baltasar de Castro, Antonio González Francés, and the Licentiate Alonso de Mariana, a canon of Toledo and Father Superior of San Vicente. These same Inquisitors acted in the case of Alvaro de Montalbán's nephew, Bartolomé Gallego, "tried" in the same year, as we shall see at the end of the present chapter. As for the prosecutor, the Bachelor Diego Ortiz de Angulo, he was implacably active in a large number of Inquisition trials including those of Leonor Alvarez' cousin, Teresa de Lucena (Serrano y Sanz, p. 292), the Talaveran, Francisco López Cortidor (see Chap. VIII), the Bachelor Sanabria (discussed above), Antonio Medrano (see Angela Selke de Sánchez, "El caso Medrano," *BH*, LIX, 1957), and the witch, Catalina de Tapia (see Caro Baroja, *Vidas mágicas*, II, 24). But our best insight into the perverse stupidity and relentlessness of his professional behavior emerges from Angela Selke de Sánchez' excellent study, *El Santo Oficio de la Inquisición, Proceso de Fray Francisco Ortiz*, Madrid, 1968. See also Lea, II, 14. Among those who witnessed Alvaro de Montalbán's formal "abjuration" were Pero López de Ayala, Count of Fuensalida, Juan de Ribera, and the Licentiate Blas Ortiz (Serrano y Sanz, p. 297) The last, a canon in the cathedral, is referred to as a professional witness for Inquisitional procedures by Lea (II, 15). Later on he appears as an Inquisitor in Valencia (Lea, I, 384 and IV, 97).

Later, after the formal accusation had been read to him, the new prisoner was asked if he wished a lawyer for his defense. He replied that he did not wish to be defended and that he hoped the Inquisitors would decide his case quickly and charitably. Only after a few more day's meditation did he emerge from his despairing passivity. When asked a second time, "he said he would appoint as his lawyer the Bachelor Fernando de Rojas, his son-in-law, who is a *converso*."[3] The presiding Inquisitor replied that such a representative would be inappropriate and that someone beyond suspicion ("sin sospecha") must be found. It was a refusal which was not surprising. As Llorente indicates, the Inquisition generally insisted that the accused choose from its own list of approved lawyers.[4] Such a one was the Licentiate de Bonillo who was substituted for Rojas at this critical moment and whose only advice to his client was to plead for mercy.[5]

Publication of the trial of Alvaro de Montalbán at the beginning of this century was a first revelation of Fernando de Rojas' social status. In view of scholarly reluctance to credit the document, we may be grateful that it has since been amply confirmed. But, in itself, Alvaro de Montalbán's direct statement should have been definitive. Precisely at a moment of maximum pressure on mind and heart, at a moment when a lie could prove fatal, at a moment when an "Old Christian" would have been the most convenient variety of son-in-law, Fernando de Rojas was identified as a *converso* by his wife's father. Nor is there any possibility of mistaken identity. Earlier, when questioned about his family, Alvaro de Montalbán had mentioned his daughter, Leonor Alvarez, "wife of the Bachelor Rojas who wrote *Melibea*, an inhabitant of Talavera."[6] As so many times in the Palavesín *expediente,* the Rojas who was a *converso* and the Rojas who "composed" *La Celestina* are named as incontrovertibly one and the same.

This should not be taken to mean that Rojas himself ever had to submit to conversion, that, in the language of the time, he was compelled to "walk to the baptismal font." We need not imagine him

---

[3] Serrano y Sanz p. 269. [4] Llorente, ii, 180.

[5] Bonillo was also Diego de Oropesa's lawyer in a 1517 trial in which Rojas himself gave testimony (see Chap. VIII). A Bachelor de Bonillo acted for the Talaveran bookseller, Luis (Abraham) García in a 1514 trial also to be considered in Chap. VIII.

[6] Serrano y Sanz, p. 263.

in his early adolescence facing the enforced choice of Spanish Jews in 1492: exile or apostasy.[7] As it was used most commonly, the word *"converso"* (like the even more derogatory *"marrano"* or "swine," probably first used by Jews scornful of those who violated the dietary laws and afterwards adopted by Christians) could signify anyone of converted lineage. Although, as we shall see, at least one and perhaps more of the Montalbáns were forced to become Christians at the last hour, the very fact that Rojas' father was condemned (along with the use of Castilian names in the Franco *árbol*) indicates a family that had long been nominally Christian. The date of 1420 for Pedro Gonçález Notario's marriage[8] leads me to believe that Rojas' great-grandparents probably crossed the frontiers of faith during the tidal wave of conversions that followed the massacres of 1391. Yet, though he may well have been three or four generations removed from his last Jewish ancestor, Rojas was still a member of a caste that was "suspect" by definition. Hence the genealogical zeal which characterizes not only this interrogation but virtually all Inquisitional records concerned with *conversos* and *judaizantes*.

Mere identification of Rojas' lineage signifies very little in and of itself. However, carefully read, the trial transcript will reveal more than social status or the touching confidence—human as well as professional—of Alvaro de Montalbán in his daughter's husband. To begin with, we deduce from its contents a time of maximum consternation in the family. Not only were Leonor Alvarez and her husband worried about Alvaro's present hardships and eventual fate; with good reason they were also (like Sempronio trying to avoid being burnt by sparks from his master's flame) concerned with the possible effects of the affair upon themselves. The very least that could happen, a punitive confiscation of part of the dowry, actually occurred—although, as we shall see in Chapter VIII, Rojas seems ultimately to have recovered it. But what was even more dangerous was Alvaro's known weakness under pres-

[7] Menéndez Pelayo maintains the contrary. If Rojas had not himself been converted, he thinks, Alvaro de Montalbán would have used the standard formula, "de linaje de conversos" (*Orígenes*, p. 238). However, given the laxity of usage at the time (familiar to anyone who has worked with the documents) and the Christian names in the *árbol*, the distinction seems too fine to carry much weight.

[8] See Appendix II.

sure. As he stated to his Inquisitors, when he had been "reconciled" four decades earlier, he had had no scruples about implicating his relatives and acquaintances. Accusation of others was demanded as a proof of good faith, and, against the advice of his Toledan friend, Hernando de Husillo, by telling all he knew he had managed to escape public penance.[9] Those who were forced so to humiliate themselves (and this included a brother, two sisters and their husbands, and a first cousin) noticed, he remembers, his immunity and drew the obvious conclusions. Scenting the truth of his behavior, they had despised him and called him a *perdido* (no-good).[10] Then he was in his mid-thirties; now he was close to

---

[9] Casting about desperately for a possible transgression (under questioning prior to the reading of the charges), Alvaro de Montalbán remembered a conversation he had omitted to include in the confession made forty years before: "He said he remembers that, when he confessed, he first sought the advice of Hernando Usillo, a resident of Toledo, who told him that, even though his sisters might have confessed the things they had done against the Holy Catholic Faith, he himself should not bring these things up no matter what he might have seen or suspected. . . . He had previously asked Usillo if he should tell all he had seen and suspected about his sisters . . . and if he erred in this or anything else, he asks for mercy." (Serrano y Sanz, pp. 265-66) The particular "Hernán Usillo" consulted by Alvaro de Montalbán is difficult to identify. There seem to have been at least three or four Fernando Husillos in the *converso* community of Toledo. One of them, a municipal *jurado*, was forced to testify against his own wife in a posthumous trial which took place in 1487 (AHN, Inquisición de Toledo, p. 219; since the reference numbers have been changed manually in the catalogue compiled by Vicente Vignau, Madrid, 1903, hereafter we shall refer to documents from these archives as Inquisición de Toledo, followed only by the page number.) In this trial other witnesses are another Fernando Husillo, son of Diego Husillo, and Maior Rodríguez, "wife of the Fernando Husillo who was burned." The Fernando Husillo identified as a *"jurado,"* we learn from another trial, was the son of one Fernán González Husillo acquitted in 1489. The latter was a rich and well-known merchant who sold both Jewish and Christian religious garb. The record of his trial indicates clearly that, at a very early age, he both wrote and spoke Hebrew and that his second name was David Abengonçalen. The most effective factor in his defense seems to have been the fact that his person and goods were respected in the two great fifteenth-century anti-*converso* riots in Toledo (Inquisición de Toledo, p. 194). For further information concerning these and other Husillos, see *Judaizantes*, pp. xlviii-xlix.

[10] Serrano y Sanz, p. 265. The list of relatives in the Puebla forced to pay for "rehabilitation" (see n. 11) as given in *Judaizantes* includes many names which we shall meet again in chapters to follow. They are with certainty: "Alonso de Montalbán hijo de Fernán Alvarez, 8,000 mrs.," a brother; Gonçalo de Avila, Elvira Gomes su muger, 10,500 mrs.," a sister and brother-in-law; "Pedro Gonçales de Oropesa, Leonor Alvares su muger, 5,000 mrs.,"

seventy-five. How, in his weakened age and after long decades of witnessing burnings at the stake, would he react? What was happening to him? What was he saying? These were the questions which must have inevitably occurred to anyone who knew Alvaro de Montalbán—and above all to his immediate family.

In the second place, when in 1526 (presumably after a substantial payment had been made by his relatives)[11] the sentence of perpetual imprisonment was commuted to house arrest, there were unavoidable after-effects. Alvaro de Montalbán's story of fear and anguish, discomfort and despair, and above all loss of honor became common gossip. As late as 1537 his case was still referred to in testimony given at the trial of Diego de Pisa, a Puebla neighbor. What was worse, since family relationships are matters of acute concern in small towns, Alvaro de Montalbán's humiliation was one in which Rojas and his wife (though residing in Talavera some leagues way) had their full share. When he attended enforced Mass in his conical hat and yellow *sambenito* (penitential garb) shamefully emblazoned with the cross of Saint Andrew, the dishonor of the family entered with him and sat down beside him. When the congregation looked at him and others in the same plight, its members saw (and were meant to see) a web of tainted relationships. Uncertainty, shame, dishonor, increased dread of those "fierce lions of the will,"[12] the Inquisitors, were the residue of such a catastrophe within a family.

---

another sister and brother-in-law; and "Francisco de Montalvan e Elvira Alvares su muger e Pedro e Aldonça sus hijos, 4,000 mrs.," the son of his uncle, Pero Alvarez de Montalbán. A third brother-in-law and a distant cousin are less certain but probable. The sums they had to pay are among the highest assessed in the Puebla. See *Judaizantes*, pp. 130-131.

[11] For a discussion of "rehabilitation" (payment of fines to the Crown for commutation of sentences and for permission to resume normal dress, to ride on horseback, etc.), see Lea, II, 402-408 and more recently M. Bataillon, "Les nouveaux chrétiens de Ségovie en 1510," *BH*, LVIII (1956) and *Judaizantes*. The price, according to Montes (p. 181; see below), varied with the severity of the sentence, running from removal of clothing restrictions to liberation from "cárcel perpetua irremisible." In each case, the Inquisitors and *escribanos* who had originally been involved with the case received a cut! (Raimundo González de Montes, *Artes de la Inquisizión Española*, edited and translated from the original Latin edition, Heidelberg, 1567, by L. Usoz y Río, n.p., 1851; hereafter referred to as *Artes*.)

[12] Amador de los Ríos, *Etudes sur les Juifs d'Espagne*, Paris, 1861, p. 470. David Abenatar Melo praises God after his release in 1611 as follows: Nel

71

Finally, and most important of all, such a trial exposes the living soul of a person very close to Fernando de Rojas, a person who shared with him not only the *converso* situation but years of common biography. What we can see Alvaro de Montalbán going through is at once typical and at the same time radically personal, intimately relevant to the lives and minds of his family. Possession of this document is, in fact, the one real advantage we have in our struggle to bring the author of *La Celestina* out of the darkness of self-imposed anonymity. Safe, as we have seen it to be, from the determination of the Licentiate Fernando to whitewash the family background, the transcript reveals experience as well as facts. It behooves us, therefore, to reflect on it at length and with sympathy. Of the documents we know to have been lost, perhaps only the manuscript of *La Celestina* or the trial of Hernando de Rojas "condemned as a *judaizante* in the year 88" would have been of more importance.

A Curriculum Vitae

When Alvaro de Montalbán was brought before the Inquisitors, he was asked for the customary genealogy, a genealogy which further questioning expanded into a rudimentary autobiography. Back in the 70's of the fifteenth century Alvaro de Montalbán and his eight brothers and sisters, although grandchildren of a baptized Christian, Garcí Alvarez de Montalbán, lived in a milieu which was to a great extent still Jewish in its customs, attitudes, relationships, and reactions. It was a world in which the *conversos* were only nominally different from their Jewish fellow townsmen. Alvaro de Montalbán's first love affair was with a Jewess well known in the Puebla as an "errant and disreputable woman"; his bread was unleavened; his family purchased meat from the Jewish butcher ("la carnicería de los judíos"); and, most telling of all, the annual cycle of his behavior was more Jewish than Christian. He admits, for example, failure to observe Lenten restrictions on his diet: "I sinned in that sometimes I ate bread and cheese and eggs and milk during Lent and on days when such things are forbidden by our Holy

---

infierno metido / de la Inquisición dura / entre fieros leones de alvedrío, / de allí me has redimido. . . ." Elsewhere he prays that God may break their "colmillos de leones" (p. 473). See also Chap. IV, n. 22.

Mother Church." His only "law" seems to have been that of his Jewish ancestors and companions: "At times I would go into the synagogue of the Jews and into their tabernacles ("*cabañuelas*")."[13]

When the Inquisitors question Alvaro de Montalbán about the meaning of this behavior, his answers seem significantly ambiguous. He was a foolish "youth of little age," he says, and without thinking followed the example of his fellows. At times the only meat available in the Puebla was that slaughtered in the Jewish fashion. Even observance of Jewish rites hardly corresponded to a conscious program of deception: when he and other Christians went into the *cabañuelas* or tabernacles, it was only in order to have a good time with the Jews ("a jugar él y otros cristianos con los judíos").[14] Since all this was such a long time ago, he doesn't remember if he entered with the intention of worshipping as a Jew ("con yntincion de judaizar"). On the other hand, since he has already confessed that he ate the unleavened bread with the intention of obeying the law of Moses, maybe he did enter the aforesaid *cabañuelas* with the same intention, but he doesn't remember. One senses genuine puzzlement in the old man as he looks back on the *temps perdu* of his youth—before the coming of the Inquisition.

Alvaro de Montalbán's memory of playful foregathering with his Jewish neighbors in a Puebla free from fear may be illustrated by the beginning of an anecdote told in Solomon ben Verga's *Chebet Jehuda* (The Staff of Judah). Ben Verga, too, from exile looks back on life in Spain in the years before the Catholic monarchs but less with puzzlement than as a moral historian attempting to explain the fate of his people in terms of sin and imprudence. Nevertheless, there are also notes of nostalgia and reminiscence, as in the following portrayal of the Jews of Monzón going out into the country to enjoy themselves on the day of Passover: "And they played

---

[13] Fray Hernando de Talavera defines "*cabañuelas*" (used during the September feast of Tabernacles) as "those cabins or huts in which the people were to remain for seven days; they represent the length of time that they spent in huts in the desert when they left Egypt; they also represent the pleasure and greenness of the earthly paradise" ("De como se ha de ordenar el tiempo," NBAE, vol. 16, p. 99).

[14] Serrano y Sanz, p. 267. Yitzhak Baer in his *History of the Jews in Christian Spain* (Philadelphia, 1961, 1966; hereafter referred to as Baer) interprets "*jugar*" to mean specifically gambling (II, 345).

together there the same game that children play, which consists of putting a blindfolded person in the middle of a circle while the others run around him. And the one he succeeds in catching takes his turn in the middle."[15] There is here a pastoral innocence and glee that is strikingly in contrast with the bitter times of which we now speak.

In general it can be said that Alvaro de Montalbán's initial difficulties sprang from his Inquisitors' determination to interpret a traditional way of life as a conscious, intentionally perpetrated crime. The emphasis on food habits in both the confession and the questions was typical of such investigations. Literally thousands of *conversos* were condemned and even burned for dietary reasons: avoidance of pork, baking of unleavened bread, removal of the leg tendons from lamb,[16] and other such practices. The rest, as the *converso* poet, Antón de Montoro (familiarly known as "The Old Clothes Dealer from Córdoba") phrased it in embittered verses, forced themselves to "worship/ fat pork stew"[17] along with more spiritual objects of religious adoration.[18] A contemporary anthropologist, Dorothy Lee, has remarked on the deeply rooted and central role of dietary habits, particularly the relation of certain foods to a yearly cycle of myth or belief, in any culture. And in the tenacious neo-Judaic culture of Spain her thesis is strikingly upheld.[19]

[15] Solomon ben Verga, *Chebet Jehuda*, Granada, 1927, tr. F. Cantera Burgos, p. 117.

[16] See Genesis 32.32: "Therefore the children of Israel eat not of the sinew which shrank, which is upon the hollow of the thigh, unto this day: because he touched the hollow of Jacob's thigh in the sinew that shrank." To this sinew are attached certain lymph glands. A characteristic defense against accusations of having prepared lamb in this manner (usually made by spying Old Christian servants) was to claim that the gland was cut out merely as a matter of custom and not "con anima de judayzar." This typical phrase is from the trial of Fernando González Husillo; see n. 9 above.

[17] *Cancionero*, Madrid, 1900, pp. 99-100.

[18] The necessity of eating pork in ostentatious quantities is underlined by the anonymous author of the anti-Jewish satire *Diálogo entre Laín Calvo y Nuño Rasura* (*RH*, x, 1903), when he remarks that *conversos* can recognize each other by their peculiar odor of "tocino añejo puesto al fuego" (p. 174). Despite the cruel exaggeration, there is revealed the *marrano* (this is a frequently proposed etymology) nutritional predicament in all its enforced disgust.

[19] "Cultural Factors in Dietary Choice," *Freedom and Culture*, Englewood Cliffs, N.J., 1959, pp. 154 ff. Her point is strikingly confirmed by Solomon ben

What one ate, and when, was the principal holdover from the past, and to change demanded a conscious effort of the most strenuous sort. Even the sight of pork could make sensitive *conversos* sick in soul and body, while its consumption often induced painful allergic reactions.[20] How could it have been expected of Alvaro de Montalbán and his friends in the years before the Inquisition made conformance imperative that they should dine like Christians? Even afterwards, when *conversos* lived under the strictest vigilance, in many cases it took several generations before conversion became a reasonable facsimile of acculturation.[21]

Alvaro de Montalbán's education amounted to a kind of commercial apprenticeship: "When the accused was nine or ten years old his father sent him to the Parish of Saint Vincent in this city of Toledo to learn to read [*le puso a leer*] in the establishment of some relatives of his who were traders in spice and, having studied for three or four years, he returned home. . . . At the age of 15 or 16 he used to accompany Diego de Dueñas and Martín Sorja, both merchants of this city, to the fairs at Zafra . . . and to the Mancha

---

Verga: "All food to which man is not accustomed is rejected when it is presented to him, and his natural inclination is to detest it. If one were to tell a Christian to eat dog or cat meat, he would vomit and flee from it the way a Jew flees from pork or lard" (*Chebet Jehuda*, p. 62). Ben Verga goes on to point out that, in addition to the enmity felt by Christians arising from the Jewish practice of usury, "I think there exists still another reason for such hate: the great difference that separates the two peoples in their eating and drinking. For there is nothing that endears people to one another more than the custom of eating intimately together" (p. 66).

[20] The large number of individuals persecuted by the Inquisition for dietary deviations evidently included many who had no particular intention of backsliding but rather were sickened physically by the food they were forced to eat. Lea translates the gruesome stenographic record of the torture of a woman accused of "not eating pork" and who finally confesses that the charge was true because "pork made me sick" (III, 24).

[21] That Alvaro de Montalbán's problems were far from unique is confirmed by Caro Baroja's comments on the general difficulties encountered by *conversos* in trying to adjust to their new historical situation: "The *judaizantes* condemned even in the first three decades of the sixteenth century show a constant individual inadaptability or incomprehension toward the regime of force which the Holy Office implies and which makes them act at times differently and more imprudently than their descendants. They criticize the Inquisition in public, defend liberty of conscience, ironize or 'Judaize' without fear" (I, 433).

75

and other places to purchase cloth. . . . He lived this life more on the road than at home for almost a decade."[22] Then, his father's death when he was about twenty-four years old brought him back to the Puebla where, along with a widowed sister and another unmarried brother, he took care of his mother. The opportunity to assist a brother-in-law, Gonzalo de Torrijos, in the collection of rents for the Bishop of Astorga and León later came his way and was too good to miss, but he did try to return as often as he could to stay a day or two with his mother. His care for her is further shown by his sad remark to the Inquisitors that she died while he was away in Galicia.

Even from these sparse recollections we may draw some tentative conclusions. As he tells about himself, it becomes clear that Alvaro de Montalbán's sense of his own life involves two separate sets of values: those measurable by money *and* the immeasurable ties of family affection and obligation. One sets out on the road or goes to the city to earn and to learn, but one also returns to the family home whenever he can and whenever he is needed. Only after his mother's death, when he was about 30, was Alvaro de Montalbán able to accept the responsibility of marrying Mari Núñez to whom he had become engaged years before. But money was involved here, too. The dowry of 50,000 maravedís which Mari Núñez brought with her, he says, helped to make up for the slimness of his mother's estate, "su poquilla hacienda," divided up into many portions. To give an account of oneself—according to Claudio Guillén, the most ominous responsibility of sixteenth-cen-

---

[22] Serrano y Sanz, p. 276. A Martín Sorja, "*mercader*," is listed by Cantera as a "*condenado*" from the parish of San Ginés (*Judaizantes*, p. 24). For *converso* domination of the cloth trade (already noticed in the case of the Francos), see Caro Baroja, 1, 73. In an "Indice alfabético de personas vecinas de los pueblos del distrito de la Inquisición de Toledo al parecer acusados o culpables de delitos contra la fe" (undated but apparently compiled in the late 1490's or early 1500's) we find the name "Alvaro de Montalván, gujetero." That is to say a seller of *agujetas* or laces. This would correspond to the commercial autobiography given above, but the identification seems slightly doubtful because his listing is followed by two others: "*su muger*" and "*su madre*." Alvaro states clearly that his marriage followed his mother's death. On the other hand, it might be argued that the Holy Office was noted for keeping its files for the dead active. The list is catalogued Leg. 262, no. 1. I am indebted to Angela Selke de Sánchez for telling me of its existence.

tury Spaniards[23]—was to give both a financial statement and a sentimental genealogy.

The coming of the Inquisition to the Puebla in 1486[24] (when Alvaro de Montalbán was about 37 and the future Bachelor still a child) deeply affected both sets of values. As such standard authorities as Lea explain in detail, a typical campaign would begin with a hair-raising sermon informing the community that to conceal one's own or anyone else's heretical behavior was not only a mortal sin but a crime which would be punished with all possible rigor. Denunciation was the order of the day. Then, a Period of Grace would be announced during which, as we have seen, information would be gathered from terrified informers until the files were bursting. The knowledge that one was vulnerable to accusations created a kind of chain reaction in which the hapless candidates for "reconciliation" were induced to tell all they knew or suspected about their relatives. The fact that Alvaro de Montalbán's collapse under this pressure was so abject that he managed to avoid public shame did not make those years any less painful. He could not avoid witnessing—or at least hearing about—the humiliating ceremonies in which his family had to participate, at least partly as a result of his own declarations. And even more distressing must have been the public burning of the remains of his mother and father,[25] an act accompanied (as it almost invariably was) by expropriation of their worldly goods from their heirs. Another result was the imposition of clothing restrictions, restrictions for the removal of which Alvaro de Montalbán had to pay 2,400 maravedís in the Puebla as well as 600 in Toledo where he may have maintained a second residence.[26] Financial loss, personal humiliation, and disruption of families followed the Inquisition as the night the day.[27]

[23] "La disposición temporal de *Lazarillo de Tormes*," HR, xxv (1957), 264-279.

[24] As we saw in the case of the Francos, the Inquisition was established in Toledo in 1485, but it apparently took another year before the *reconciliados* of the Puebla could be processed. See Lea, I, 166.

[25] Serrano y Sanz, p. 262.

[26] For general discussion of such expropriation, see Lea, II, 327. For Alvaro de Montalbán's rehabilitation in the Puebla and Toledo, see *Judaizantes*, pp. 8 and 131.

[27] As the inevitable result of this disruption, denunciation within families

Because of our contemporary familiarity with many of the same Inquisitorial techniques on a much larger, electronically amplified scale, we must keep in mind the peculiarly local nature of the ordeal of the Montalbanes. These were people living a small town existence, shaped by the eyes of their neighbors, subjected to the opinion of others, and, like Celestina herself, constantly aware of their duty to "maintain honor." And their ceremonial recantation and humiliation was prepared on precisely these terms. A contemporary witness describes an *auto* of this sort which took place at just this time (in 1486, a year after the similar reconciliation of the Francos):

On Sunday, December 10, the Holy Inquisition conducted an *auto*; and all of the *reconçiliados* of the *arcedianazgo* of Toledo came out in procession. And 900 people—both men and women—left the Monastery of St. Peter the Martyr; and the men wore no shoes nor hats; both men and women walked with their faces uncovered and the men had no hats nor belts; and with unlighted candles they went where the previous processions had gone as far as the main church. And having arrived at the gallows where the Inquisitors were, they listened to a sermon and heard Mass; they were standing on the stone pavement ["*losas*"] and were afflicted by the cold. And after the sermon a notary got up and announced how those people had practiced the Jewish religion ["*avía judaizado*"], and then [the *conversos*] replied that from that time forth they would like to live and die in the Faith of Jesus Christ; and they were told the articles of the Faith, and to each article they said aloud: *Yes, I believe*; and I do not know whether or not they sincerely meant this. And they took a book of the New Testament and a cross; and all, their hands raised, swore never again to practice the Jewish religion, and that if they discovered anyone who did practice it, they would report it, and they would always be in favor of the Holy Inquisition and contribute to the exaltation of the Holy Catholic Faith."[28]

---

was frequent. In addition to Alvaro de Montalbán, other persons whom we shall have occasion to mention and who suffered the same misfortune were Diego de Pisa, the Bachelor Sanabria, and the Lucena sisters.

[28] Frequently cited since publication in 1887 by Fidel Fita in *BRAH*, xi

Whether or not the relatives of Alvaro de Montalbán (or the children of Pedro Franco *"arrendador y trapero"*) participated in this particular ceremony cannot be determined. But we do know that, after their initial exposure in Toledo, they were forced to parade over and over again through the streets of the Puebla where their shame—insofar as it was local—was even greater. As we learn from contemporary testimony, "the *reconciliados* of the Puebla de Montalbán . . . walked in sorrow and disgrace, and some of their neighbors tormented them so much that they were on the verge of suicide."[29] The world of Fernando de Rojas' childhood was no longer one in which converted Christians and Jews could foregather in the tabernacles to enjoy each other's company. It was instead a world of high social tension undergoing an organized and spectacular form of agony. Rigid self-righteousness and concealed resentment—not the careless glee of blind man's buff—were the salient attitudes of those who played its unprecedented games.

⅏ The Trial

The record of Alvaro de Montalbán's trial suggests more than it tells of his life in the new historical circumstance. Although he seems to have been able to continue his commercial activities, he was limited in other ways. For a time he was the *mayordomo* (hired superintendent or administrator) of the Puebla town council, but, when the Inquisitors "came again," they fined him a

---

(p. 302). When confronted with such an alien and, to us, repugnant spectacle, we may wonder about the character of the plastic imagination behind it. An indication may be found in a contemporary remark cited by Menéndez Pelayo (*Historia de los heterodoxos*, Madrid, 1956, I, 1070) concerning a 1559 *auto de fe* in Valladolid: "It looked like a general congregation of the world . . . the very portrait of the Day of Judgement."

[29] Pedro Serrano, Inquisición de Toledo, p. 229: "andovieron su pena y andavan avergonçados e algunos los corrían de manera que pudieran venir a desesperaçión . . ." This was probably on the occasion of the secondary parades in the Puebla. Indication that they took place is contained in the document just cited, p. 302: "E luego, otro día lunes salieron en procession de Sant pedro mártir, e fueron a sant francisco disciplinándose en la forma susodicha. E les mandaron que anduviessen siete viernes disciplina; e después todo un año, de cada mes el primer viernes, y más que viniessen el dia de santa maría de agosto a esta ciudad a fazer una procession, y el jueves de la cena otra en dicha ciudad; e todas las otras processiones fuesen en sus tierras, que se juntassen en las villas más principales de su tierra."

79

thousand maravedís, and he "never held public office afterwards."[30] In later years he spent a great deal of time with his children's families; in Valencia with his daughter Ysobel Núñez, in Madrid where another daughter, Constança Núñez, had married a prosperous and well-placed cousin, Pero de Montalbán, the royal *aposentador* (master of lodgings), and probably with Leonor Alvarez and her lawyer husband—although he doesn't say so explicitly. It would seem that he was more at ease away from his native soil.

These visits would last for periods of three or four months to a year at a time, and, while he was away, Alvaro de Montalbán was less careful about attending mass and presenting a proper appearance of orthodoxy than in the Puebla. One of the sentences in his rather pitiful effort at defense implies that he found reverence among his neighbors to be uncomfortable: "It is a fact that he went to Mass every day when he was in the town of the Puebla, and, if sometimes he was absent, it was because he was away from home . . . and that he and his household continually confessed and received communion. . . ."[31] In Madrid, according to the testimony of the priest who had denounced him, he never submitted himself either to confession or communion. Whether as a result of resentment, distaste for Christian rituals, the feeling of being constantly observed, or of all three, Alvaro de Montalbán clearly seems to have preferred to have the semi-anonymity of Valencia or Madrid to parish life in the town whose name he bore.

In the 1494 trial in which the brutal harassment of the Puebla *reconciliados* was described (and which we shall have occasion to cite at length in Chapter V), there is further evidence of the dubious local reputation of the Montalbanes and of the kind of slurs and slights to which they were subjected. The defendant was a well-situated *converso*, the *mayordomo* of Alonso Téllez Girón, the Lord of the Puebla, and, following the usual procedure, the Inquisitors gave him a chance to try to guess the identities of his accusers and to prove their bias. Accordingly, he composed a somewhat frantic list of every disagreeable incident, quarrel, and personal encounter that he could remember. As we shall see, it amounts to a very revealing sociological report on the way life was lived in the Puebla de Montalbán during Rojas' boyhood. But what

[30] Serrano y Sanz, p. 266. [31] *Ibid.*, p. 274.

concerns us now is that among the names and events he mentions are the following: "Pero González Oropesa and his wife hate me and are my enemies. Fray Andrés, who used to lodge with them, came to me with the proposal that I marry their daughter, and I answered him saying that [I would have nothing to do] with people who were still *ajudiada* [Jewish in aspect and habits]. On account of this they conceived a great hatred for me, and they sent a crazy woman out to say dishonorable things about me. My witness is Fray Miguel de la Puente."[32] The point is that Pero González Oropesa and wife here mentioned were none other than Alvaro de Montalbán's sister, Leonor Alvarez (for whom Rojas' wife was named) and his brother-in-law.[33] Both of these were on the list of those "reconciled" and "rehabilitated" (see note 10), but this evidence is even more decisive. Even among other *conversos* the Montalbanes of the Puebla were spurned for their personal proximity to what was called the "Old Law."

It is not surprising, then, that Alvaro de Montalbán made the fatal slip which led to his arrest at a time when he was away from home and presumably somewhat less wary than he otherwise might have been. The Puebla, in the words of one of the witnesses testifying in the later *probanza*, was "a small place where every one is known as being who he is in particular," a place where one had to walk and speak with the greatest of care. The story behind the arrest is best told in the words of the principal accuser, one Yñigo de Monçón,[34] probably (and very appropriately) a relative by marriage[35]:

[32] "Tienele odio e enemiga Pedro Gonsales de Oropesa e su mujer, porque tratando Frey Andrés, que en su casa posaba, dixo al dicho Pedro Serrano que se casase con su fija, que le respondió, que no '¡con gente tanto ajudiada!' De ay le tomaron grande odio e echaron una loca que lo desonrase. Testigos Frey Miguel de la Puente." For problems of translation and editing, see Chap. V, n. 85.

[33] Serrano y Sanz, p. 275.

[34] Llorente (II, 155-156) describes the process of accusation as follows: "Trials commence with an accusation. . . When the accusation is signed, the informer's sworn testimony is received in which there are made manifest all the persons whom the accuser knows to possess relevant information or whom he presumes may possess it. These persons are interrogated, and their declarations along with that of the accuser form what is called '*información sumaria*.'"

[35] An Iñigo de Monçón is listed in the 1506 *padrón* of the Parish of San Ginés in Madrid as an *hidalgo* exempt from the *pecho* tax. This document

One day in the month of May or June last year (1524), Alvaro de Montalbán, a man of some seventy years more or less, the father-in-law of Pedro de Montalbán, the Royal Master of Lodgings and a resident of this town of Madrid, having come to visit his daughter, went with his son-in-law and daughter (whom the present witness believes to be named Constança) and Alonso Ruyz, parish priest of San Ginés and the present witness to a country property of the aforesaid Pedro de Montalbán which is not far from the gardens of Leganés . . . to enjoy themselves and take their ease. After midday when they had eaten and passed time pleasurably and were returning to town, the present witness remarked, "You see how the pleasures of this world pass by; for we have enjoyed ourselves, and it's all over. Everything except winning life eternal is foolish and illusory [*Todo es burla syno ganar para la vida eterna*]." At this the aforesaid Alvaro de Montalbán replied saying: "Let me be well off down here, since I don't know if there's anything beyond [*Acá toviese yo bien, que allá no sé si ay nada*]." And, replying to this, the present witness said to him: "Don't you know that according to our faith he who is righteous shall

is quoted in part of the 1548 *probanza de hidalguía* of Alonso Montalbán, the son of Pero de Montalbán, the Royal Master of Lodgings with whom Alvaro was staying at the time of his arrest. Iñigo de Monçón's name is next on the list after that of Alonso de Montalbán, the grandfather (see Riva, II, 420). The Monçones and the Montalbanes were related in a number of ways. A Fernando de Monçón (there is no specific indication of his relationship to Iñigo) was the father of Ysabel Hurtado de Monçón, the first wife (Alvaro's daughter, Constança Núñez, was of course the second) of Pero de Montalbán. A Diego de Monçón, "*escribano público*," was a godfather at the baptism of that Alonso de Montalbán who instituted the *probanza* proceedings; see Serrano y Sanz, pp. 297-298. Gonçalo de Monçón, "*vecino de Getafe*," was a *probanza* witness for Alonso, identifying himself as "pariente deste que litiga de parte de su madre y este que litiga es sobrino deste testigo, hijo de una prima hermana deste testigo" (p. 89). Further information about Iñigo de Monçón himself is provided by a 1540 entry in the *Catálogo de pasajeros a Indias*, ed. C. Bermúdez Plata, Seville, 1946, vol. III, no. 1081: "Alonso de Gutiérrez de Gibaja hijo de Iñigo de Monçón y de Ysabel de Gibaja vecinos de Madrid a Nueva España, 30 enero." That a relative and close connection of Alvaro should have denounced him will not surprise anyone familiar with Inquisitional matters. It is curious to note that one of the *padrinos* of the *converso* author of La Araucana, Alonso de Ercilla, at his baptism (1533) in Madrid was a Licenciado Monzón (see José Toribio Medina, *Vida de Ercilla*, Mexico, 1948, p. 284).

have eternal life?" And the aforesaid Alvaro de Montalbán replied and said, "Here let me be well off, since I know nothing about what lies beyond." All of this was heard as well by the aforesaid priest. And the present witness, having winked at him, tugged at his sleeve, and the aforesaid priest said to him, "I wish I hadn't heard it, because I shall have to report it, for it is heresy."[36] And afterwards they drew apart and talked together about denouncing him, since a letter of the Edict of the Inquisition had been issued. . . .[37]

In thinking about this fatal fragment of sixteenth-century conversation, we should in the first place take into account its attendant circumstances. Alvaro de Montalbán had eaten, drunk, and taken his ease with friends on a spring day in the country. He was a man off guard, a man who had for a moment stripped himself of his armor of self-vigilance, a man lulled into forgetting that he must never be himself. And in this relaxed condition he made the single slip that the Inquisition had waited almost forty years to hear.

The records of the Holy Office are full of similar instances of momentary verbal carelessness; its nets were finely meshed, and they were cast with the expectation of catching just such tiny fish.[38] Let us listen, for example, to one Gonzalo de Torrijos, a cloth shearer (*tundidor*) from Toledo who one day in 1538 had several drinks too many and, while in church, remarked to the wife of a

---

[36] Alonso Ruiz, the parish priest of San Ginés, seems to have been somewhat reluctant to accuse a relative of the influential parish family of the Montalbanes. His testimony, in general, is less malicious and extensive than that of Iñigo de Monçón, the real instigator of the affair. We may notice that the Madrid Montalbanes continued long after Alvaro's trial to be prominent in parish affairs. Pero de Montalbán was buried in his family's private chapel in San Ginés (the so-called "capilla del lagarto" containing a stuffed alligator, still on view today, which, according to Valle Lersundi, was brought back by a member of the family from one of Columbus's voyages). In 1528 an unnamed "cura de San Ginés" was named as executor by the deceased (Serrano y Sanz, p. 298).

[37] *Ibid.*, p. 272.

[38] In the so-called *Libro verde de Aragón* (a kind of "confidential guide" to Inquisitional activity or "Who's who among the condemned," apparently compiled by a malicious *converso* official), there is recorded a veritable harvest of such phrases as these. (Reproduced in *Revista de España*, 1885, vols. 105-106; see also Lea, II, 563-564.) Later on we shall see something of the historical background of *converso* skepticism, but for now it is better to concentrate on reactions to immediate situations.

colleague "that God did exist and the Moors were right when they said they could be saved within their law as well as the Christians in theirs."[39] The remark was picked up by bystanders and, after a year's time, reached the ears of an Inquisitor. The Bachelor Sanabria (a Salmantine lawyer, mayor of Almagro, and possible author of the *Auto de Traso*) was betrayed in 1555 by a different sort of carelessness. In a public conversation he indulged himself in a jocose outburst against the hypocrisy of his own situation: "¡Boto a Dios, que soy judío, boto a Dios! (I swear to God I'm a Jew!)"[40]

Or, instead of drunkenness or jesting, the heat of an argument often led to self-betrayal. Llorente had access to a transcript which

[39] Inquisición de Toledo, p. 54. Torrijo's actual words ("dios era verdad e los moros dezian verdad que se salvaban tambien los moros en su ley como los cristianos en la suya") represented another commonplace opinion quite different from that expressed by Alvaro de Montalbán. In contrast to his skepticism about the whole notion of the after life, we find here a tolerance equally reprehensible from the point of view of the Inquisition. For acceptance of this opinion among *conversos*, see Sicroff's fascinating "Clandestine Judaism in the Hieronymite Monastery of . . . Guadalupe," *Studies in Honor of M.J. Benardete* (New York, 1965) and A. Castro's "Saladino en las literaturas románicas," *Semblanzas y estudios españoles* (Princeton, 1956) as well as in *Realidad*, edn. II, p. 200. Ernst Cassirer, in his *The Individual and the Cosmos in Renaissance Philosophy* (New York, 1963), discusses Nicholas of Cusa's advocacy of a similar doctrine. The attribution of Torrijo's imprudence to drunkenness emerges from the testimony of a witness who was afraid of getting into trouble for not having denounced his friend much earlier. Intoxication seemed to the witness, if not to the Holy Office, a good reason for overlooking the slip.

[40] Inquisición de Toledo, p. 227. The so-called *Auto de Traso* is a one-act fragment of a lost early continuation ("la comedia que ordenó Sanabria") appended to *La Celestina* in three editions after 1526. It is interesting in that its author seems to have tried to employ Rojas' own technique of continuing Act I. That is, without interval of time, it departs from a situation of the original on its new direction. My attribution of the *comedia* to this Bachelor Sanabria is purely a guess. It is somewhat strengthened by the anti-Inquisitional tenor of some of the dialogue of the *Auto* and by an indication (mentioned above) of his relationship to a family of *conversos* in the Puebla de Montalbán. Sanabria was later freed as a result of favorable testimony on the part of Old Christian clients and protégés in Almagro. In the course of the investigation it became clear that the principal denouncer (as in the case of Iñigo de Monçón, a relative) was motivated by greed and a past quarrel. From the trial it would appear that Sanabria was born in the first decade of the century. If he was the author of the *comedia* from which the *Auto* was taken, it must have been a production of early youth, like *La Celestina*, written while its author was attending Salamanca.

recounts how a physician was defending a diagnosis against the contrary opinion of a colleague not only with pagan authorities but with the four Evangelists. At which the colleague shouted back imprudently: "They lied too, just like the others." Later, when he had calmed down, he hastened to disavow the remark to the attentive bystanders ("Look what a stupid thing I said!"), but it was too late.[41] Even lesser offenses could at times bring equally disproportionate results. A distant relative of the family, Juan de Lucena, who for a time, as we shall see, printed Hebrew books in the Puebla, is described by a hostile witness as an "hombre leydo y tenía grandes yrronías en la santa fe" (a well-read man given to extreme irony about the Holy Faith). The example given is absurdly trivial but was nonetheless recorded with all gravity: "I talked to him, and I said, 'Sir, will Vuestra Merced do thus and so?' and he answered, 'Don't call me *merced*; I'm only a *judío azino*.' "[42]

For our purposes the most significant aspect of cases such as these is not to be found in the individual psychological circumstances—confidence, euphoria, anger, intoxication, despair—which lead to their trivial yet perilous revelations. It is rather the light that, taken together, they cast on the potential explosiveness of *converso* existence. Rigid masking of the inner self, calculated conformity,[43] unremitting self-observation induced in these first

---

[41] Llorente, III, 174-180.

[42] Serrano y Sanz, p. 282. The words *"judío azino"* may be translated as "wretched Jew" (*azino* apparently coming from the Arabic *hazin*). More specific and less trivial "yrronías en la santa fe" are cited by Caro Baroja from the 1608 trial of the Bachelor Felipe de Nájera (*Los judíos*, II, 201-206). Unlike blasphemy with its direct and angry aggression, such "yrronías" play humorously with accepted beliefs—as, for example, when Nájera calls the Virgin a "buena vieja" or when one Martín de Santa Clara recalls his grandfather remarking, "There is no paradise other than the market in Calatayud" (J. Cabezudo Astrana, "Los conversos aragoneses según los procesos de la Inquisición," *Sefarad*, XVIII (1958), 282). At times the Old Christians—although most sixteenth- and seventeenth-century antisemitism was violent and bitter to an extreme degree—returned *converso* irony in kind. Thus, in a mock *probanza* conferring *marrano* status on a poor *hidalgo* and the right to share in *marrano* prosperity, we find that the applicant is officially allowed to believe "that there is no other world than that which exists between birth and death." See the "Respuesta del Capitán Salazar" in A. Paz y Melia, *Sales españolas*, Madrid, 1890, I, 95.

[43] It is obvious that this enforced situation was in the early sixteenth century far too immediate and tense for intellectual generalization or moral reflection. Even the notion of "dissimulation," defended by the seventeenth-

dwellers in the shadow of the Inquisition states of extreme tension and instability.[44] Later on, hypocrisy was to become a second nature, but in the lifetime of Fernando de Rojas it had to be maintained purposefully and precariously. It would, of course, be far-fetched to try to explain *La Celestina* in these terms—that is to say, as a maximum expression or explosion of inwardness which, once having spent itself, allowed its author to accept the inauthenticity of all the rest of his life. On the other hand, without some insight into the way it felt to be a *converso* in the 1490's, a *converso* determined not to follow his father's doomed footsteps, the possibility of the most important qualities of the work—its mordant irony, its implicit attack on God, its almost epic destruction of meaning and value—cannot be understood.

I am, of course, well aware of the infinite distance separating a masterpiece such as *La Celestina* from a few thoughtless words which suddenly could no longer be bitten back. At the same time, I would emphasize strongly that, unless we can achieve some understanding of the immediate human situation, the potentially

---

century philosopher, exile, and former prisoner of the Inquisition, Isaac Orobio de Castro (in a Latin dialogue with a protestant theologian discussed by Caro Baroja at some length, II, 282) seems too abstract and easy for such anguished masking.

[44] Angela Selke de Sánchez in her fascinating "Un ateo español," (*Archivum*, VII, 1957) presents the case of a physician whose own routine prayers suggested to him the recurrent phrase, "Deus non est." The commonplace assertion, even when made by oneself, seems to suggest its opposite. She concludes (pp. 22-23): "We believe that the fact that Illescas was from *converso* stock is pertinent to those doubts and to that anguish. Although he had been born and had lived in a completely Catholic world, as the descendant of Jews he doubtlessly was very different from the Old Christians. Christians never felt obligated to ask themselves whether or not they believed what the Church taught. The *conversos* on the other hand, and leaving aside the great number of forced conversions, conversions only in appearance, had to begin by becoming believers through an act of will, through an interior acceptance of the creeds and practices of the Church. And it would be too much to suppose that they or their children or even their grandchildren could always feel themselves identified totally with the world of those who were Catholics through the mere fact of being born. In the trial against Illescas we find some indications of how precarious in reality the integration of certain *conversos* in Christian society was, even when they believed, as did the doctor of Yepes, that they had embraced firmly the Catholic faith; and still other indications of how, at the most unexpected moment, ideas and feelings which they had repressed could come to the surface."

eruptive human soil in which Rojas' work was grown, we shall fail to appreciate its almost incredible uniqueness as a work of art. We are likely, instead, to try to explain its possibility merely in terms of the literary tradition from which it came or to which it gave rise. Both points of reference, the biographical and the literary, are necessary and useful, but unthinking dependence on either as a basis for interpretation leads to distortion. As I shall try to show, the sometimes moralizing, sometimes jocose continuations offer a particularly dangerous temptation to the historical critic. To read *La Celestina* only in their light, and in so doing to deny the brooding and compressed life that lies behind its dialogue, is just about as valid as reading the *Quijote* in the light of Avellaneda.

But to return to the case of Alvaro de Montalbán, aside from the immediate circumstances, what was it that provoked him to this sudden, obviously uncalculated expression of agnosticism? We may surmise from the transcript that he was impelled less by a desire to argue seriously against Yñigo de Monçón's beliefs than by an irrepressible reaction against the pious, self-consciously moral style of their utterance. It was the prating of the commonplace, the repetition of doctrine heard a thousand and one times before and pronounced as solemnly as if the speaker had just invented it, that without warning penetrated into the raw flesh beneath the armor of prudence. When a *converso* accepted Christianity in the fourteenth and fifteenth centuries, he had to accept not only an alien dogma, not only a revolution in his most intimate daily and yearly patterns of existence (the new "Law"), but also a whole body of commonplace assertions which had become less and less original and more and more insistent during the course of the Middle Ages. God's immediate presence was underlined over and over again; every event was treated as a parable; moral behavior was sententiously praised on all occasions—with the inevitable result that the tradition of ascetic meditation, a tradition within which a Saint Bernard or an Innocent III had attained greatness, became as commonplace and stale as the language of newspapers today. Yet not to give at least lip service to these pieties was dangerous to an extreme degree. The priest, Alonso Ruyz, who confirmed Yñigo de Monçón's denunciation, remembered the conversation in this way: "Speaking with Yñigo de Monçón about the trials and misfortunes of this world and other things of like nature, the present witness

87

said that, if he were not absolutely certain that he would find rest in a better world, the trials he had to undergo in this one would make him wretched, and he then began to praise God and His works, and the aforesaid Alvaro de Montalbán replied saying, 'We can see the here and now; what lies beyond we cannot know (lo de acá vemos, que lo de allá no sabemos qué es).' "[45]

It is easy to imagine how such pat reflections as these could become first boring and then intolerable even to *conversos* who lived their faith with a fervor lacking in Alvaro de Montalbán. A Saint Teresa, for example, knew well how to cut through false piety with salty good sense, while rejection of platitudes and mellifluous sermonizing was a common characteristic of the impatient Erasmists. Raimundo Montes, celebrated for his escape from the Inquisition, described his intellectual master, the fervently heterodox Dr. Constantino de la Fuente, as a wit who "above all used to mock foolish preachers, the vilest of all races of men and one which abounds everywhere."[46] And, if irritating to these people, off-the-cuff sermonizing seems to have been intolerable to an Alvaro de Montalbán and to those of his fellows who reacted skeptically to the situation of being a *converso*. So much standardized daily emphasis on the existence of God, on our good fortune in having Him on our side, on the bounties of Providence, on automatically rewarded virtue in the life to come, could only produce an inner attitude of violent rejection. The endangered authenticity of one's own existence, indeed the very sense that one was a victim of organized injustice, led inevitably to passionate and abrupt denials of the sort we have just witnessed.

A pattern of reaction identical to that of Alvaro de Montalbán, is to be found in the case of one Ysabel Rodrígues of San Martín de Valdeiglesias not far from Talavera. Imprisoned during her lifetime (1506), she was finally convicted after death (to the financial

---

[45] Serrano y Sanz, p. 272.

[46] Dr. Constantino de la Fuente is described by his disciple in terms which indicate that his frequent verbal slips were due to "un injenio sumamente festivo" which led him to "perder, alguna vez, con la libertad de sus chistes aun en la edad mas provecta, sus aprobadas costumbres." His favorite targets were, as indicated above, "clérigos hipócritas" and "predicadores necios, raza vilísima de hombres" (*Artes*, pp. 305-306). Solemnly mouthed commonplaces led him, as they led so many other *conversos*, into attitudes of comic non-participation. Irony and wit were weapons of oral defense and offense in the stifling world of loudly pious assertion in which they lived.

detriment of her heirs) for having interrupted violently a conversation of a group of "Catholic persons . . . on the subject of death and how those who died would have to suffer in the other world for the sins they committed." To which she cried out: "A man is no more than his breath and his blood." But an even more extreme example is that furnished by Diego de Pisa, a resentful adolescent from the Puebla and cousin of the imprudent Bachelor Sanabria mentioned above. During his (1537) trial a quarrel with his mother is described: "On one occasion the aforesaid mother was scolding Diego de Pisa, her son, because of some mischief he had done . . . and, threatening her son with God in order that he might reform himself, Diego de Pisa answered, 'There is no God' or something very similar."[47] As we shall see elsewhere, agnosticism and even atheism had both a historical tradition and a kind of sociological inevitability among certain *conversos*, but for now we are less interested in the history of ideas than in the immediate reactions of individuals to the situation in which they are forced to live.[48]

I would maintain, then, that the commonplace faith of the priest

[47] The Inquisitional clerk sums up the charge against Ysabel Rodrígues as follows: ". . . hablando en cosas de la muerte e de los que murían e de commo por las culpas que acá cometían avían de penar en el otro mundo, diziéndolo otras personas cathólicas, la dicha Ysabel dixo que el ombre no tenía mas que huelgo e sangre." She was also accused of remarking (with an irony that would have delighted Voltaire) that this was the best of all possible purgatories: "no avia syno tres purgatorios y que este era el mejor deste mundo y que ella acá querría biuir mill annos. . ." (Inquisición de Toledo, p. 221). As for Diego de Pisa, the original reads: "Una bez riñendo ella a diego de Pisa, su hijo, algunas travesuras suyas . . . poniendo ella a Dios delante y amonestando al dicho su hijo con Dios para que se enmendase, el dicho su hijo, Diego de Pisa, rrespondió, no ay Dios, o cosa semejante" (*ibid.*, p. 45).

[48] The 1517 trial of Diego de Oropesa in which Rojas himself was called as a witness (and which we shall consider in Chap. VIII) records a number of irritated and careless outbursts similar to those considered above. One of them, in particular, indicates a touchy reaction to pious speech making: "Porque cierta persona reprendía a ciertas personas que no quebrantasen las fiestas, el dicho Diego de Oropesa dijo: 'Mira que majadero; déles él de comer y no quebrantarán las fiestas" (Inquisición de Toledo, p. 215). The point is that to characterize Diego de Pisa, Diego de Oropesa, Alvaro de Montalbán, and their fellows as atheists or agnostics on the basis of such remarks is to take them out of context. It seems quite plausible that Alvaro de Montalbán had little or no faith in an afterlife arranged for by a benevolent divinity, but the abrupt disbelief expressed in "Acá toviera yo bien . . ." must first be understood as a reaction to the maddeningly emphatic world of belief on the margin of which he lived.

and Yñigo de Monçón created, or at least gave clear definition to, the suddenly expressed skepticism of Alvaro de Montalbán. That he himself partly understood the way he had been led to his fatal indiscretion emerges from his defense. Once he had read the accusation and had had time to think about it, he pathetically alleged his own fondness for commonplaces:

> "He said that he had thought over the accusation that he had stated that he was well off down here and that he didn't know if there was a life to come. He doesn't remember having said any such thing; rather he had always maintained the contrary. He always used to say when speaking of the things of this world that worldly goods are worth nothing because they are perishable. With one coat to wear he was as happy as a rich man with twenty in his trunk [because only one could be worn at a time]. And if he had a tiny portion of meat, he was as satisfied as another who was served twenty fowl and only could eat one. And if a boy brought him a glass of wine, he was as well served as by twenty pages. And once he had these few things, he had no regard for any other worldly goods. He has said phrases like this to many people and he can prove it. He believes that whoever it was that overheard him must have been confused and gotten things backwards; they must have mistaken what he meant to say about this world and applied it to the other world. . . ."[49]

Aside from the unintentional revelation of Alvaro de Montalbán's fondness for warm clothes, good food, and wine, it is interesting to overhear him attempting to prove his citizenship in the commonwealth of clichés. But it was in vain. Once the verbal camouflage that was indispensable to a peaceful fifteenth- and sixteenth-century existence had been broken through, no further hiding was possible. Alvaro de Montalbán had failed to master the marvelous ironical ambiguity with which his son-in-law was able at once to affirm and to undermine the commonplace tradition of his time. Rather, much like certain characters in *La Celestina,* he managed to betray himself in almost every word he uttered. "Why," he asks wistfully a little later on, "if he believed what these witnesses say he believes, should he have purchased indulgences, as he has done

---

[49] Serrano y Sanz, pp. 268-269.

many times ever since the Catholic Monarchs first called for a Crusade some forty-two years ago more or less, and they cost him six reales apiece?"[50]

Another curious indication of the daily battle of the individual *converso* with the ready-made religious assertions which beset him during all his waking hours was the invention and wide circulation of a counter-commonplace, a commonplace of skepticism and resigned disbelief. I refer to a proverbial sentence appearing in several forms of which the earliest recorded (in the *Fortalitium fidei* of Fray Alonso de Espina, 1460) was: "En este mundo no me veas mal pasar; en el otro no me verás penar" (Let me not be seen having a hard time in this world; and in the next I shall not be seen being punished).[51] Just as in the case of Alvaro de Montalbán's imprudent remark, the meaning here clearly is that we should get along as well as we can in this life, since that which is to come—if any—will take care of itself. The rhyme appears in such a surprising number of later Inquisition trials, including those of the

[50] Although Alvaro de Montalbán's son, Juan del Castillo, along with his brother-in-law, Pedro de Montalbán, and a third partner "cobraba la bula en los obispados de Mallorca, Orihuela, y Córdoba" (Serrano y Sanz, p. 298), the social pressure which enforced the purchase of dispensations was a particular source of annoyance to defenseless *conversos*. It was all right (even a picaresque pleasure as in the case of Lazarillo's cunning *buldero*) to sell nothing for something, but to be forced by circumstances and with full awareness to buy on these terms was intolerable. In the testimony fabricated to obtain the conviction of the poor wretches who were supposed to have crucified the "Santo Niño de la Guardia," the following obviously apocryphal dialogue is attributed to two of the accused: " 'Fi de Puta sea quien blanca gastare en tomar tales bullas.' E el dicho García Franco dixiera: 'Non es de faser así; e destas cosas semejantes nunca nos apartemos por el desir de las gentes; e por tanto non dexemos de entrar y estar en algunas cofradías y cabildos, o tomar algunas vezes bullas, solamente por dar color a la gente.' " (F. Fita, "La verdad sobre el martirio del Santo Niño de la Guardia . . . ," *BRAH*, xi, 1887, p. 45.) What better indication of widespread *converso* resentment against "las bullas" than this primitive effort at verisimilitude! One of the many accusations against the Talaveran *librero*, Abraham García (see Chap. VIII), was his reply to a pious neighbor who on one occasion said emphatically "que a los labradores les era penoso pagar las bulas de la Santa Cruzada pero que [él] gracias a Dios nunca había dejado de adquirirlas." Hearing this, he, like Alvaro de Montalbán, could no longer repress his feelings and cried out "que eran burlas esas bulas" (Inquisición de Toledo, p. 184).

[51] Baer, ii, 286. The phrase was also attributed, according to Baer (ii, 369), to the Aragonese conspirator against the establishment of the Inquisition, Jaime de Montesa.

Bachelor Sanabria and Diego de Pisa previously cited,[52] that one comes to suspect that it was a standard accusation made against suspicious *conversos* by their enemies or their Old Christian neighbors.

What is particularly significant from our point of view is the fact that in the course of the Diego de Pisa trial a witness specifically relates the cynical commonplace to the case of Alvaro de Montalbán. A housemaid in Diego de Pisa's residence in the Puebla is reported as saying, "En este mundo no me veas mal caer, que en el otro no me verás arder." Although susceptible in this form to a pious interpretation ("Let me not sin in this world, and I shall not burn in the other"), the reporting witness perceived the resonance of the skeptical version and remembered warning the talkative housemaid ". . . que por otro tanto como esto que ella dezía llevaron a la Ynquisición a Alvaro de Montalbán" (that for something resembling the thing she had said they handed Alvaro de Montalbán over to the Inquisition).[53] A second incident involving a member of the Montalbán family is the self-denunciation in 1536 of one Isabel López, a cousin of Rojas' wife, for the sin of having uttered the same phrase. She apparently feared that someone else might denounce her, and her very reasonable excuse was that she had said it carelessly "as one might repeat a proverb" without realizing the heretical implications.[54] Trials and punishments of the sort alluded to here had by 1536 created an atmosphere of acute oral anxiety, an atmosphere which may not be unfamiliar to students of contemporary history.

As readers of *La Celestina* are aware, Rojas was far more concerned with utilizing and undercutting the commonplaces of neo-

---

[52] For other cases see Caro Baroja, I, 371 (the case of one Francisco de Madrid accused of having said not only this proverb but also another similar one, "yo despues de muerto ni viña ni huerto") and II, 366. At the moment of correcting these notes, I have encountered by chance the same expression in the trial of Francisco Alvares (Inquisición de Toledo, p. 162), one of Alvaro de Montalbán's fellow prisoners.

[53] Serrano y Sanz, p. 261.

[54] "Yo Ysabel López, muger que soy de Francisco Pérez, digo que no mirando lo que dezía ni creyendo que errava dixe las palabras siguientes, 'en este mundo no me veas mal pasar que en el otro no me verás penar,' y esto digo que lo dixe por manera de refrán que se suele dezir." Afterwards she informs the Inquisitors that "a su padre llamaron Francisco de Montalbán y a su madre Ana López de Toledo los quales eran convertidos de judíos." Francisco de Montalbán was a first cousin of Alvaro: see Appendix II.

Stoicism than with responding to the pious phrases of his Christian friends and neighbors. Only the fully anonymous author of the *Lazarillo de Tormes* was to dare, fifty years later, to give literary form to his "grandes yrronías" against topical religious language.[55] However, in one key passage from Act VII (significantly imitated at the beginning of the *Lazarillo*) Rojas does display both his irritation at standard formulae of metaphysical consolation and his skill at ironical rebuttal. I refer, of course, to Celestina's use of Matthew V.10 in order to predict the salvation of her companion in sorcery, Claudina. The fact that her friend was tried by the Inquisition and sentenced to shameful public exposure in the town square will, according to Celestina, serve her as a passport into Heaven: ". . . the priest, may he rest in peace, when he came to console her, said that Holy Scriptures teach us that 'Blessed are those who are persecuted for righteousness' sake for they shall inherit the kingdom of Heaven.' Consider, if it is not worthwhile to exchange the sufferings of this world for the glories of the other. . . . So, since your good mother had these troubles down here, we should believe that God will give her a good recompense up there, if it is true what our priest told us, and with that I am consoled."

It will be impossible for English readers to understand how Celestina manages to include the arch-sinner and notorious witch, Claudina, in the company of those "persecuted for righteousness' sake"—which is to say, the company of Christian martyrs. However, in the Spanish version cited by Celestina "los que padecían persecución por la justicia," the word *justicia* can be taken to mean either the value of justice (the just cause or "righteousness" which brings on persecution) or the forces of justice (the institutions of law enforcement, as in our "Department of Justice"). What Celestina has done, then, is to have substituted perversely one meaning for the other. As a result, the martyrs whom Christ intended to bless are forgotten, and anyone, Claudina included, who has been punished by the law now qualifies for salvation.

To have Celestina quote Scripture in order to get Claudina into Heaven is at once a monstrous *reductio ad absurdum* and an expression of extreme annoyance at those who blithely speak of the life to come. But Rojas, unlike his far more candid and imprudent

[55] See my "The Death of Lazarillo de Tormes," *PMLA*, LXXXI (1966), 149-166.

father-in-law, does not burst out in indignant denial; instead he prefers to parody the complacent oral pieties and commonplace phraseology of his neighbors. This interpretation is supported by a fact which will be documented in an article of mine entitled "Matthew V.10 in Castilian Jest and Earnest" (to appear in the forthcoming *Homenaje a Rafael Lapesa*). It is that this same verse was frequently repeated by sincere converts to Christianity who were nonetheless persecuted by the Inquisition. Feeling themselves to be authentic martyrs, they found in Matthew V.10 and its promise of reward a source of consolation. One example from many occurs in the same trial which described the suicidal "desperation" of those who had been "reconciled" in the Puebla. In their travails the belief that "those who suffered in this fashion would be blessed" offered surcease. But for Rojas the application of delayed celestial balm to infernal circumstances of immediate persecution was like treating a cancer with patent medicine. It was, I think, significant that it should have been the naïveté of fellow *conversos* who did not share his skepticism that triggered Rojas' half-concealed riposte. Perhaps he is even reacting against his memory of the living model of Celestina's priest.

To return to Alvaro de Montalbán, a subsidiary accusation illustrates the central agony of *converso* existence: suspicion. He and his fellows were condemned to life under constant observation, a life during which every change of expression or unthinking gesture was closely scrutinized for signs of self-betrayal. Readers of *La Celestina* (and of its imitations)[56] have been prepared to understand their torment, since it too makes use of unremitting observation of human exteriority. That is to say, *La Celestina* may be thought of as reflecting in its own way a Spain described by another *converso* as a nation of tell-tales and spies ("moscas y azechadores").[57] Every minute of the day was dangerous, but the

---

[56] For example, Sancho de Muñón's *Lisandro y Roselia*, ed. J. López Barbadillo, Madrid, 1918. Caro Baroja concludes, "The Inquisition was like an eye which scrutinized everything, a marvellously penetrating eye as thousands and thousands of witnesses reveal" (1, 359). See also 1, 308.

[57] *Artes*, p. 105. Technically the "*mosca*" refers to the police spy who, pretending to be a prisoner, reports on the conversation of his fellows; the "*azechador*," on the other hand, often a "familiar" of the Inquisition, operated outside, keeping an eye out on neighbors and friends. Castro describes

watchers were particularly attentive during church services. At moments of ritual intensity, in prayer, or when the chalice was raised, the pressure of alien eyes could become unbearable. A pertinent example is mentioned by the accused *mayordomo* in the trial just referred to: "I always inclined my head whenever they named the name of our saviour, Jesus Christ, and of our Lady, the Virgin Saint Mary, and at the *Gloria Patri,* and those who observed me maliciously from their point of view (los que malamente miraron desde donde vieron) said with great hatred and capital enmity that I was bowing like a Jew."[58]

---

the situation of the typical *converso* as subject to a "sociedad enloquecida, que fisgaba en sus actos" (*Realidad*, edn. I, p. 543; *Structure*, p. 569). Later on he quotes Luis Vives referring to *conversos* who remained in Spain as if they were in exile: "Y allí creen tener su destierro donde el ciudadano molesta al ciudadano o al advenedizo; donde el vecino curioso o turbulento causa enojo al vecino; donde inquiete el ánimo el pariente, el amigo, el conocido a medias, el perfecto desconocido, y le arranque de aquel reposo" (p. 552).

[58] Similar cases of closely observed and maliciously interpreted religious gestures abound in Inquisition annals. From the records of persons arrested or investigated in Talavera and vicinity I have selected four more typical examples. First, a peasant employee of Rojas' friend, Diego de Oropesa, testifies: "antes veía este testigo al dicho Diego de Oropesa y tañendo al Ave María que no humillaba ni rezaba la oración e que algunas vezes este testigo y el dicho su marido e madre se dejaban de humillar porque el dicho Diego de Oropesa no lo hazía." Second, in 1557 accusations against the wife of the Licentiate Montenegro, Doña Marina de Rojas (apparently not a relative of the Bachelor), by a crazed and malicious *beata*, we find the following: "porque de diez vezes que doña Marina entrava en la dicha iglesia una vez tomaba agua bendita y esa vez la tomava con un dedo como cosa que yba poco en ello" (*Inquisición de Toledo*, p. 95). Third, and perhaps the most frightening case of all is that of Martín Fernández Rubio of the neighboring town of Halía (where Rojas held mortgages on a considerable amount of property). His parents and his wife had all been "burned," and he was, as a result, under constant inspection by every parishioner while in church. Some reported that they never saw him pray when the Host was raised, but his doom was sealed when, in 1522 or thereabouts, two neighbors reported that instead of folding his hands in the proper manner, he inserted his thumb through his fingers thereby making a disrespectful gesture known as *higas* both at the Virgin and the Holy Sacrament. As he said later, the place was full of "mala gente," and he should have sold his property and left long before. After his execution, his *sambenito* was hung in the church, but there was no family left alive to shame. Some 70 years later, the parish priest wrote to the Inquisition to find out who he was and what he had done! (*Inquisición de Toledo*, p. 182). Finally, there is all sorts of contradictory testimony about Abraham García's physical behavior. Certain witnesses claim that they never saw him

II. THE CASE OF ALVARO DE MONTALBÁN

Again in the record of another trial held in 1525, that of the Erasmist and "*alumbrada*" (illuminata), María Cazalla, we find a series of witnesses who had watched closely her behavior during Mass. The following is typical of the abundant testimony: "When the time came to raise the host or chalice, I looked at María *with curiosity*, and I saw she was on her knees holding her cloak closely around her. She was dressed plainly and held herself straight, but, instead of looking at the Holy Sacrament, she kept her eyes fixed on the ground. I considered this an unwonted innovation (cosa que tomé por nueva), and I was amazed." María Cazalla denied these charges, claiming to have "practiced while listening to Mass the exterior actions to which we Catholics are accustomed such as crossing myself with holy water, beating my breast when the Holy Sacrament is raised, getting up at the reading of the Evangels, bowing and praying aloud." Nevertheless, she is supposed to have told a witness that sometimes during Mass she felt so anguished that "she would rather be beaten in public by two torturers and that she went to church because of what people might say."[59] Her special feelings clearly reflect the rejection not only of ostensive religiosity but also of many forms of ritualistic exteriority on the part of the Erasmists and the *alumbrados*.[60] But at the same time

---

pray, bow, or kneel while others—also carefully watching—state that he was most scrupulous in so doing. Albert Sicroff, in the article on the Monastery of Guadalupe previously cited (n. 39 above), demonstrates that its Hieronymites (composed of Old Christians, sincere yet often more or less unorthodox *conversos*, and outright *judaizantes*) spent a great deal of time observing each other's expressions and gestures, particularly during Mass and other ceremonies. One Fray Alonso de Nogales was, like Pedro Serrano, accused of "encorbándose y encogiéndose" during Mass in a fashion resembling Jewish prayer (p. 103).

[59] J. Melgares Marín, *Procedimientos de la Inquisición*, Madrid, 1888, II, 8 and 117.

[60] The authoritative study of Erasmistic religiosity in Spain is Marcel Bataillon's lucid and sensitive *Erasme et l'Espagne*, Paris, 1937. More recent amplified versions in Spanish appeared in Mexico in 1950 and 1966 (*Erasmo y España*). Although not primarily concerned with racial origins, Bataillon reveals the predominance of *conversos* among enthusiastic Erasmists. They seem to have found in his teachings a variety of spiritual Christianity more meaningful and more comfortable than that which could be watched from without. Fray Hernando de Talavera, a *converso* pre-Erasmist and saintly confessor to Queen Isabel, recognizes in a rather ambiguous way the importance of external behavior in instructions entitled "Como se ha de haver

96

it is curious to see the skeptical Alvaro de Montalbán and the deeply religious María Cazalla existing week after week in the same situation and reacting to it with comparable discomfort. The enthusiastic reception of Erasmus' *Enchiridion* on the part of many *conversos* is a phenomenon more complex and far reaching than such anecdotic experiences. Nevertheless, one cannot help speculating on the extent to which shared Sunday martyrdom may have affected the history of sixteenth-century ideas.

That Alvaro de Montalbán underwent a similar ordeal during his weekly public exposure (daily while in the Puebla!) emerges from the testimony of his *azechadores*: "The present witness never saw him attend Mass on Sundays or holidays except once in a while with his daughter, and then, after entering the church, he would sit on a bench with his head down, and he would stay there without kneeling or taking off his hat. . . . Many women used to gossip when they saw him sit there with so little devotion, without praying or even moving his lips. At other times he would go into a chapel and stay there sitting down until the service was finished. . . ."[61] Alvaro's defense has the same tone of utter weariness and submission that we sensed before: "To the charge that he sat in church with his head down and showing little devotion, he replies he doesn't remember, but he might have done so, because he is old and deaf . . . but he always felt devotion; he always prayed; he always kneeled and uncovered himself when they raised the host; and above all he asks that mercy be shown him."

Rojas' father-in-law is a man who has been observed so long and so intensely that he seems numbed. He can no longer keep up the necessary pretenses—which is to say, in the language of our century, he can no longer control his image. The opposite case would be that of the son-in-law's creation, Celestina, who, like Lazarillo's blind master,[62] could give a perfect imitation of a *"beata"* (more or

---

al momento de comulgar" (How to comport oneself at the moment of communion). He says, for example, "Moreover the communicant should bemoan and weep, *at least in his heart*, for the ingratitude to our good Lord" (*Breve forma de confesar*, NBAE, vol. 16, p. 39). Fray Hernando, in other words, recognizes that proper comportment is indispensable for survival and insufficient for salvation.

[61] Serrano y Sanz, p. 271.

[62] In the *Lazarillo* there are at least two other past masters of the art of

less hypocritical devotee) and at the same time keep her inner life to herself. As Sempronio says, "When she goes to church with her rosary in her hand, it's because there isn't much left to eat in the house. . . . When she tells her beads, what she's really telling are the virgins she has in charge, the number of lovers in the city, and all the girls she has working for her. When she moves her lips, it is really to prepare lies and to invent deceits in order to obtain money: 'I'll approach him first saying this; then he'll reply saying that, but I will be ready for him with my own answer.' "[63] Alvaro de Montalbán, however, had been drained by numberless piercing eyes of the vitality which pulses in Celestina. He is a sieve, a man so tunneled through by alien observation that he can no longer present a firm appearance of being (a *"ser quien es"* in the language of the time) to the world. He has become in a sense the person his watchers interpret him to be. They have captured him so effectively that his actual incarceration by the Inquisition seems almost anticlimatic.

✐ Self-effacement and Self-assertion

Comprehension of the ordeal of Alvaro de Montalbán as representing the way many *conversos* were forced to live may help explain Fernando de Rojas' own thirst for self-effacement. It would be as gross an oversimplification to assert that Rojas spent his life trying to hide from the Inquisition as it would be to claim that *La Celestina* hides a subversive message under a moral smoke screen. The thing is more subtle and deeply rooted. Besieged by a multitude of inquiring eyes, anonymity was rest, Nirvana, life without image. As Sartre says about Jews living in a Gentile society: "The Jew is not bothered about being loved for his money; the respect, the adulation which his riches procure for him are addressed to the anonymous being who possesses so much purchasing power; indeed it is precisely this anonymity which he seeks: in a paradoxical way he wants to be rich in order to live unseen." The monetary

---

public prayer, the extravagant but effective *buldero* and the irreproachably tranquil *escudero*. See my "Death of Lazarillo," previously cited, n. 55 above.

[63] Act IX. Far more interesting for us than the doubtful hypothesis that Celestina may be a successful *conversa* (See Chap. VII) is the relevance of the theme of external and hypocritical piety to Celestina's way of life and to the world in which *conversos* were forced to live.

image, in other words, deflects and bedazzles the eyes of the observers.[64]

Although this particular path to anonymity was inadvisable in a world dominated by avaricious Inquisitors and envious Old Christians, the need for self-erasure was far more intense. And it was perhaps Fernando de Rojas who was the greatest genius of his time at meeting it. By moving to another town and there mimicking Christian behavior to apparent perfection, as well as by "refining himself out of existence" in a work of art built of uninterrupted dialogue, Rojas succeeded where his father-in-law had failed.[65] At the end of *La Celestina*, after all the characters have finished speaking, there are some verses entitled "Concluye el autor" which (as Marcel Bataillon notes)[66] have been usually overlooked by critics. The reason is clear. In these verses, the so-called "author" immerses himself in the point of view of the collectivity, of the watchers surrounding him. He castigates the lovers morally, bids the reader to avoid their fatal transgression, and "concludes" with one of the two explicit references to Christ (the other is in the initial verses) in the entire work:[67] "Since we now see how those lovers / Perished

---

[64] Jean-Paul Sartre, *Réflexions sur la question juive*, Paris, 1954, p. 157. Lope de Vega makes the same point about *converso* wealth as Sartre in a conversation in *El galán de la membrilla*. In Act I, two characters discuss the qualifications of a suitor whose blood, it turns out, has a slight stain: TELLO: "Ramiro es rico y galán; / no le está mal a Leonor." BENITO: "Tiene no sé qué, señor; / mas son cosas que ya están / cubiertas con el dinero / en el mundo." TELLO: "Bien sé yo / lo que el dinero doró, / que fué el dorador primero. / Si dora una guarnición / de espada un pobre, echarán / de oro un pan, y sólo un pan, / que a la primera ocasión / que se trae, se desdora / y luego el hierro se ve; pero si de rico fué, / con tantos panes se dora. / Que nunca el hierro descubre; / y tales las faltas son, / que en la menor ocasión / la del pobre se descubre, / y la del rico jamás, / porque tiene a las riquezas / respeto el mundo."

[65] As we shall see, the Rojas family may be thought of as belonging to an epoch posterior to the anguished and imprudent contemporaries of Alvaro de Montalbán. Unlike these maladjusted and surprised individuals (discussed by Caro Baroja, see n. 21), the Bachelor and his children and grandchildren made, as far as we can tell, every possible effort to conform. For contemporary documentation of this pattern of behavior see Antonio Domínguez Ortiz, *La clase social de los conversos en la edad moderna*, Madrid, 1955, p. 223 and elsewhere (hereafter referred to as Domínguez Ortiz).

[66] Bataillon, p. 215.

[67] This does not take into consideration the expletive *jesú* used on several occasions. In Chap. VII we shall discuss *converso* reluctance to pronounce the name of Christ.

so fearfully, / Let us flee from their dance. / Let us rather love Him whose blood was spilled / By thorns, lance, lashes, and nails. / The false Jews spat in His face; / Vinegar and gall were His drink. / May he take us to His bosom / Like the good thief / Of the two who were placed / In His holy company." In the words "falsos judíos," Fernando de Rojas, with all the dexterity of a stage magician, completes his disappearance.[68] It is the ultimate irony of *La Celestina*, the appropriate parting flourish of an author who has communicated all he has to communicate and is about to take up a new life as a lawyer.[69]

The fact that other *conversos* reacted in a very different way, that, like the Bachelor Sanabria, they shamelessly exhibited their personal condition to the world with variations on his half-jesting, half-anguished cry, "¡Boto a Dios que soy judío, boto a Dios!" is not a valid objection. Human reactions like human values—Erik Erikson teaches us—are polar in nature, and the very need for anonymity often led to attitudes of humorous and aggressive self-display. A champion of this dangerous game was Rojas' classmate at Salamanca, the physician, Francisco de Villalobos, who all his life long played bitter charades with his own image.[70] A typical anecdote still current at the end of the century is recalled by Luis de Pineda in his anthology of witty remarks, the *Libro de chistes*.[71] Villalobos is in church in the embarrassing situation of being pub-

---

[68] As Mrs. Malkiel observes, Rojas added the deprecatory description "falsos judíos" only in 1502 as one more of the changes which converted the "comedia" into the "tragicomedia." The very fact that it was a second thought indicates—in my opinion—Rojas' conscious desire to appear to conform.

[69] There is possible ambiguity in the adjective *falsos*. It could conceivably be interpreted as separating the treacherous Jews responsible for the crucifixion from those who had nothing to do with it. *Conversos* frequently tried to limit the guilt of their ancestors in this way, just as they frequently insisted on the Jewishness of the Holy Family and the apostles. See Caro Baroja for a discussion of the "memorial" of Torreblanca Villalpando defending Spanish Jewry against the charge of deicide (II, 313-314).

[70] *Childhood and Society*, New York, 1963, particularly Chap. VII. That Villalobos was perfectly conscious of his choice and of the antithetical terms built into it is expressed in these revealing verses: "Escrivo burlas de veras, / Padezco veras burlando, / Y Çufro dissimilando / Mil angustias lastimeras, / Que me hieren lastimando / Y con risa simulada / Dissimulo el llanto cierto . . ." *Algunas Obras*, Madrid, 1886, p. 21.

[71] *Sales españolas*, I, 225 ff.

licly denounced as a quack by the widow of a patient. A young man approaches him and urges him to come quickly to his father's bedside. Villalobos replies: "Brother, don't you see that lady yonder cursing me and calling me a Jew because I killed her husband? And there above the altar can't you see another lady crying and holding her head in her hands because—she says—I killed her son? And now you want me to come and kill your father!" Or again in a direct self-portrait (written in dialogue form) he even whispers his doubts about the existence of the Holy Ghost.[72]

In comprehending such strange behavior from within, Sartre is relevant, insofar as he is not concerned with Jewishness per se but with the "vital situation" of the Jew in an alien society. For it is precisely that situation (a situation independent of discrepancy in belief) which was grievously intensified for Rojas and his fellows. Sartre writes as follows: "The root of Jewish restlessness is the necessity of the individual Jew to question himself unceasingly, and eventually to adopt a definite attitude towards that phantom personage, unknown yet close by, who haunts him and is none other than himself, himself as he is for others."[73] Which means—interpreted for our purposes—that the watchers create another self, a self which can either be evaded by retreating into anonymity or be dominated and directed through clowning. One was either camouflaged or else became a persistent *chocarrero*, a familiar human category of the time, the wit who specializes in shocking remarks and who thereby converts his watchers into an audience.[74]

If Rojas, after writing *La Celestina,* seems to have taken the first course, Villalobos clearly took the second. Accentuating his Jewishness, embroidering on *converso* characteristics, playing his role to the hilt, he entertained his noble clientele at the same time that he

[72] See *Curiosidades bibliográficas*, BAE, vol. 36, p. 444.

[73] *Réflexions*, p. 101.

[74] The Bachelor Sanabria defended himself against various charges of oral carelessness by saying that he was an "hombre de muchas chocarrerías y burlas con los amigos." On the other hand, for the fanatical Juan de Padilla, known as "el Cartuxano," the excuse, had he heard it, would have been as reprehensible as the offense. In his *Retablo de la vida de Cristo* he specifically sends *chocarreros* to Hell along with other *converso* Judases who make a practice of "selling their saviour." See Chap. VIII, n. 120. Similarly but more gently Fray Hernando de Talavera in his *Breve forma de confesar*, p. 30, discusses at some length "el pecado de la ironía o de disimulación."

acted as its physician. To cite only one from his extensively recorded store of such comments, speaking of his own cowardice, he
says, "Yo que era el mayor judihuelo de mi pueblo. . . ."[75] And yet,
at the same time, we can sense in his writings his profound distaste
for himself, his disgust even with the laughter he knew so well how
to provoke.[76] Both he and Rojas wrote their first books in the last
years of the fifteenth century while at Salamanca, but at that point
their lives diverged into opposite but not unrelated channels. One
chose anonymity, and the other, a restless and ultimately disappointed quest for personal advancement by flaunting both his professional skill and his "phantom personage" before the most powerful men of his time.

Having proposed this schematic contrast between the attitudes
and biographies of Rojas and Villalobos, I would hasten to add that
a significant factor therein is the quality and depth of creative self-
expression in each case. *La Celestina* is, among other and more important things, a coherent and profound revelation of the *converso*
view of life—an assertion based not merely on my own interpretation but also, as we shall see, on those of its contemporary readers.[77] Once having said what *La Celestina* says, Rojas could in a
sense make peace with himself; he could, as it were, accept his own
acceptance of his condition during the long years through which
he still had to live. But a Villalobos, contriving one fragmentary

---

[75] For many *conversos*—the poets Rodrigo de Cota and Antón de Montoro
are familiar examples—the discomfort of their situation could only be relieved
by such exhibition. Villalobos' letters are rich in comments often too painful
to be humorous. In 1518 he writes, for example: "I cannot deny my accursed
lineage derived from a nation so dirty that all Jordan could not wash it
off even with the help of the Holy Ghost" (*Algunas obras*, p. 21). The hidden
critique is of Christians who do not believe in the effectiveness of their own
sacrament of baptism, but at the same time there is also a note of perverse self-
flagellation. For further discussion and examples, see Caro Baroja, i, 284-292.

[76] In his *Tratado de la gran risa* Villalobos describes the circumstance of a
humorist at court in the following pre-Quevedesque way: "Laughter is the
passion and the property of the beast called the court. The court is a peculiar
animal which continually laughs without any real desire to do so; it has two
or three thousand mouths all of which die laughing. Some of them have no
teeth like the mouths of masks, others are as big as the mouths of skulls
which open from ear to ear, others are all pursed up like button-holes; some
are bearded, others shaven; some are masculine, others feminine; some are
penetrating in tone, others hoarse and growly . . ." (*Curiosidades*, p. 454).

[77] See Chap. VII, nn. 16-21.

variation after another on his two dimensional image (he even includes himself playing the role of Sempronio in the experimental fragment of Celestinesque dialogue just mentioned),[78] could never find satisfaction.[79]

I hasten also to admit that the contrast is not absolute. Rojas, unlike the author of the *Lazarillo de Tormes*, did not choose total anonymity.[80] Not only was there the acrostic and self-portrait as a preoccupied intellectual and timorous author in the prologue material (if he had to make an image, this conventional yet not misleading mask would serve), but also, as we have seen, he was well known as "el que compuso a Celestina" for three and four generations after his death. The fact of writing *La Celestina,* we can only conclude, carried with it a bare minimum of self-assertion: "I am the author, and this is who I am." But, at the same time, the way of its writing and the way of living of its writer reflect an extraordinary talent for both creative and biographical self-effacement, a talent which at least in part must be related to Alvaro de Montalbán's statement: "He said he would appoint as his lawyer the Bachelor Fernando de Rojas who is a *converso.*"

Consideration of the life and final ordeal of Alvaro de Montalbán, has, thus, served us as an entryway into the human situation within which *La Celestina* was created. This was possible less because the victim was Rojas' father-in-law than because his existence was typical of that of many *conversos* of the period.[81] The funda-

---

[78] After a series of jocular interchanges, some of which remind us of the style of Act I, we find the following half-overheard aside:

"*Duque.* . . . en mi seso me estoy de haceros mercedes, como os las he hecho, mas por vuestra buena razón que por la física.

Doctor. Tal salud os dé Dios como vos me habeis hecho las mercedes, y aun como me las haréis.

Duque. ¿Qué estáis gruñendo entre dientes?

Doctor. Digo, Señor, que Dios dé mucha salud á vuestra señoría por las mercedes que me ha hecho y me hará." (*Curiosidades*, p. 446)

[79] For perceptive and detailed discussion of an author tormented by a succession of roles unsatisfactory to the consciousness, see J. R. Andrews, *Juan del Encina*, Berkeley, 1959.

[80] See my "Death of Lazarillo," previously cited (n. 55 above).

[81] I refer particularly to those maladjusted, surprised, and imprudent individuals whose various indiscretions supplied the Inquisition with business during the early decades of its existence (see n. 21). However, as we have seen, all members of this generational category were not necessarily participants in Alvaro's skepticism. Contemporary with him, many others were

103

mental attribute of that existence is revealed to us in the words of the Inquisitors themselves: the almost literally recorded statement that they would only accept a lawyer "sin sospecha." The malaise of the numberless lives which almost cry out to us from the archives of the Inquisition emerges not only from a feeling of difference (of the sort described by Sartre) but even more from the clouds of mortal suspicion which surrounded them. Suspicious of each other, suspected by everybody else, the *conversos* lived in a world in which no human relationship could be counted on, in which a single unpremediated sentence could bring unutterable humiliation and unbearable torture. It was a world in which one had constantly to observe oneself from an alien point of view, that of the watchers from without. It was a world of simulation and camouflage interrupted by outbursts of irrepressible authenticity, of commonplace repetition broken by sudden "originality," of neutral masks removed to reveal grimacing faces and harsh voices of dissent. An expressive and oft-repeated symbol for this repression was used by Raimundo Montes (in his partly autobiographical *Artes*): the gags and iron muzzles which impenitent victims wore to the stake in order to keep them from addressing the multitude. These, he tells us, are only the physical counterpart "of those other gags stronger than iron with which the Inquisition assures its tyranny."[82]

Twentieth-century readers may be tempted to comprehend the existences of Alvaro de Montalbán and his fellows in terms of the characters of Franz Kafka. However, the former felt no uncertainty about the kinds of transgression which might lead to trouble, nor was there any vagueness about the nature of the ultimate authority to which they were subjected. The physical and mental torment of these men, women, and children, rather than emerging from half-comprehended *angst*, was clear and perfectly definable. Like Calisto's amorous agony, its white heat was longer lasting and more painful than that of any flame.

---

suspect because of a fervor antithetical to his "Acá toviera bien": intellectual Erasmists, sensual *alumbrados*, ignorant followers of a variety of unlikely prophets, including a 15-year-old girl who claimed to have visited Heaven and seen the martyrs of the Inquisition on golden thrones, and others. As we shall see, it is far more difficult to categorize reactions than it is to describe the common situation of the caste.

[82] *Artes*, p. 5.

On the other hand, the enormous disparity of strength between those who suspected professionally and those under suspicion is familiar to our own historical experience as foretold by Kafka. Lea, the most sober and thorough student of the subject, writing at a time when it appeared that such institutions belonged to the past, describes the Inquisition in this way: "Such a concentration of secular power and spiritual authority guarded by so little limitation and responsibility has never, under any system, been entrusted to fallible human nature."[83] As a result, according to a contemporary description: "These badly baptized ones walk along the streets so full of fear that they tremble like the leaves of a tree. If someone jostles them, they turn their eyes, and, with uncertain and astonished hearts, they stop, fearing that someone will grab hold of them."[84]

Against this bureaucratic monster and against the infinite number of amateur and professional eyes and ears which served as its organs of sense,[85] the individual *converso*'s only defense was to merge with the crowd, to wear at all times his frail and acutely uncomfortable armor of conformity. Standardized phrases of piety, ritual gestures, calculated facial expressions, and elaborate exhibition of Christian dietary habits, all constituted a kind of non-self—dependent on unrelenting self-inspection—within which one might

---

[83] Lea, II, 233.

[84] Samuel Usque, *Consolaçam as tribulaçoens de Ysrael*, cited by Caro Baroja, II, 440. Usque was actually speaking about Portugal, but the situation in Castille in the early decades of the sixteenth century was entirely comparable. The Talaveran *librero*, Abraham García, declared to the Inquisitors that a relative of his, one Martín Enrique, the Royal Physician in Portugal, had repeatedly urged him to seek safety in that kingdom, expressing his surprise that a *converso* could sleep peacefully in Castile since "no estaba en más su vida de cuanto su mozo quisiese."

[85] Llorente in his *Memoria histórica* and Castro in *La realidad* cite the cautiously expressed statement of the Jesuit historian Father Juan de Mariana to the effect that the most objectionable feature of the Inquisition was not the visiting of the sins of the fathers upon the children, not secret denunciation, and not the death penalty for minor infractions. Worse than this ascending list of institutional iniquities was that "people were deprived of the liberty of listening and talking to one another, for there were in the cities, towns, and villages special persons to give warning of what was happening, a practice which some regarded as like a servitude most onerous and on a par with death." *Realidad*, edn. I, p. 509; *The Structure of Spanish History*, tr. Edmund L. King, Princeton, 1954, p. 534. Future quotations in English from *Realidad*, edn. I, will be taken from the King translation.

hope to live unnoticed. But inside this shell consciousness burned all the brighter, kindled by enforced alienation and stoked by fear, shame, pride, and, above all, resentment. Villalobos, who knew his *conversos* as well as anybody in his time, expresses their feelings with a typical stylistic flourish. Commenting on a letter from a French friend, he writes: "I said to myself [with surprise], 'This noble lord talks to me; he even seems to be answering me; his language is pure Castilian; his rhetoric, Tuscan; his prolixity, Sicilian; his vengefulness, that of a Marrano (*la venganza, de marrano*); and his nonsense, his own.' "[86]

Resentment or vengefulness is not a feeling we associate with the helplessly tormented creatures of Kafka, but, as we shall see, it does seem to underlie certain deeply malicious speeches in *La Celestina*. Granting that such a reaction to life and the world is, by definition, negative, lonely, disagreeable, and in most cases unproductive, let us nevertheless offer it sympathy and comprehension. Let us begin by accepting Francisco Marquez' invitation to meditate "on the non-life (*sin vivir*) of those existences held up by an initial lie and collapsible like a house of cards at the breath of a single accusation—often a trivial accusation and probably resulting from some hidden feeling of envy or injury."[87] If we do so, and, if we are able across the centuries to catch a reflection of those blazing consciousnesses in our own, we may then learn something else. And it is this something else that matters: we may learn how it was possible for Fernando de Rojas to utilize his situation creatively and positively, to convert, in other words, his resentment into irony. Or, as the Spanish philosopher, José Ferrater Mora remarks, "Irony emerges only when human life exists—whether individually or collectively—in a state of crisis. . . . If at the bottom of all human crises there is desperation, we may further admit that irony, whatever its form, is a mode of escape, or of trying to escape, from desperation."[88] If we can come to understand Ferrater's meaning not just with our minds but in our lives, if we can come to participate imaginatively in Rojas' desperation, we shall at long last have begun to answer our guiding question: "How was *La Celestina* possible?"

[86] *Algunas obras*, p. 9.   [87] *Investigaciones*, p. 79.
[88] *Tres mundos*, Barcelona, 1963, p. 137.

✌ The Prison

By way of epilogue we may glance briefly within the impenetrable walls of the Inquisitional prison in Toledo. In 1525 when Alvaro de Montalbán took up enforced residence therein, there was a substantial number of other prisoners whose individual cases —in spite of senile resignation and solitary confinement—may well have come to his horrified attention. From trial records and from the reports they include, either by inmates trying to curry favor with their Inquisitors or by professional *moscas,* it would seem that the entire institution was involved in note passing, wall tapping, shouting, surreptitious whispering, and signalling from windows.[89] In agony and uncertainty, the collection of accused individuals found in themselves an irresistible impulse towards community. Advice from those who had experienced interrogation or torture, news from the outside world and from families brought in by new arrivals, warnings against treacherous testimony, and above all the sheer solace of dialogue for its own sake were indispensable and gave the grim lodging more the resemblance of an infernal club than of an impersonal hotel. In any case, whether or not Alvaro de Montalbán made full use of his oral membership, there were others there with him, and their individually unique predicaments deserve examination. However distinct from his, they may provide perspectives complementary to his own case and history.

Two of the prisoners were surely well known both to Rojas worriedly waiting in Talavera and to his father-in-law waiting with pathetic despondence inside the walls. One was a relative of uncertain degree, Bartolomé Gallego, who had been arrested a month

[89] The trials of Abraham García (1514) and of the physician Bachelor Francisco de San Martín (1537, Inquisición de Toledo, p. 229) reveal more than any others I have read this aspect of prison existence. Aside from the original denunciations (San Martín had refused to eat a lamprey stew in a tavern in Valladolid), both men were injured gravely by dutiful reporting of their outraged conversations in prison (see Chaps. IV, n. 22, and III, n. 49). Since they were not *judaizantes,* they could hardly bring themselves to believe what was happening to them or that such a regime was possible. In any case, since everything they said was reported by *moscas* and fellow prisoners, their cases offer a fascinating transcription of the dialogue of prison society. In the former trial it is reported that "every night the prisoners shout to each other the questions asked by your Reverences during the interrogations."

before and whose case we shall examine in more detail in Chapter VIII. For now, it is enough to say that under interrogation he identified his mother as an aunt of Leonor Alvarez and himself as a Jew who had accompanied his father into exile in 1492. Before returning first to his birthplace in the Puebla and afterwards to Talavera, he had lived in Morocco and Algiers, and it was, in fact, because of his careless praise of Mohammedan ritual cleanliness that he had been denounced.[90] The other was a witch from the hamlet of El Carpio in the immediate vicinity of the Puebla. Her name was Inés Alonso, "la Manjirona," and since, at the time of her arrest the year before, she was some 90 years old, her reputation in the region and her knowledge of the seamy side of local community life were presumably great. Again we shall have to wait until later (Chapter V) for further discussion of her rather primitive professional activities (far beneath the level attained by Celestina).[91] What concerns us now is to suggest that both of them must have seemed very uncomfortable companions to Alvaro de Montalbán. Presumably he steered as clear of them as he could, hoping desperately not to become involved with them in any way. To have his name come up in their interrogations could only make things worse. As we know, the Inquisitors often suggested possible leniency to prisoners who knew details of the past of their fellows and were willing to report on them.

A prisoner from Toledo, whose principal offense was not unlike Alvaro's own, was one Francisco Alvarez further described as "*portugués*."[92] Imprisoned for the first time in 1522, he later told an acquaintance that he had been held for three years with only a chair to sleep in. Further exaggerating Inquisitional iniquity, the resentful and imprudent ex-prisoner went on to say that his only offense was having worn clean shirts on Saturdays and that the hostile witnesses were all scared *conversos* carefully coached by the Inquisitors. It was for this crime of violating "*el secreto*" (that is, speaking to others of one's experience with the institution) that in 1531 he was rearrested and eventually condemned, although a number of other charges were resurrected from the files.[93] Among

[90] Serrano y Sanz, pp. 252-255.
[91] Caro Baroja, *Vidas mágicas*, II, 12-16.
[92] Inquisición de Toledo, p. 162.
[93] He was condemned in 1537, although the nature of the penalty is not

them and apparently what started his troubles was an unthinking indiscretion of the sort examined earlier. The occasion was a dispute over the authenticity of a personal note (*"carta de pago"*) which Alvarez had not signed but which someone else attributed to him. After examining it in the presence of the *alcalde*, he exploded: "I swear to God, it's as false as faith in God!" And then (like the hapless physician who had shouted that the Evangelists were liars) he hastily corrected himself: "I mean it's as false as the devil himself."[94] Whether the carelessness of a moment of anger can be blamed for this fatal oath or whether the word "God" in the initial "I swear to God" triggered a Freudian slip, it is hard to say. But, as in the case of Alvaro, once the words were out and entered in his dossier, Francisco Alvarez could never unsay them or forget them.

Finally, according to documents seen by Lea, no less a personage than Francisca Hernández, whose powers of physical and spiritual seduction were the scandal of the epoch, spent one of her several periods of incarceration in the same prison in 1525.[95] Since later on we shall have occasion to mention the fervent cult (particularly among more or less heterodox believers) which she encouraged and exploited, further comments at this point are unnecessary. What is important is that even this chance sampling of the prison population (extant records are hopelessly fragmentary) illustrates the wide variety of kinds of delinquency represented by Alvaro de Montalbán's fellow sufferers. Witches, returned exiles who had sampled all three religions, angry skeptics, and those who knew how to make a career out of contemporary religious exaltation, were all accumulated behind the bars of what can be called literally his penitentiary.

---

specified in the record. Among other charges are violations of Friday and Lenten dietary restrictions, failure to attend Mass, and having remarked as follows: "Que alabando a uno por muy agudíssimo dixo, queréis ver quan agudíssimo era que había dicho que en la ley de Moyssen moría y también en la de Christo."

[94] "Que mostrándole una carta de pago que otro dijo tener del reo, dijo este reo: juro a Dios tan falsa es como la fe de Dios. E luego tornó a decir: tan falsa es como el diablo."

[95] *Chapters from the Religious History of Spain*, 1890, p. 261. Cited by Angela Selke in *El Santo Oficio*, p. 53. She states that she has not seen any documents confirming imprisonment on this date.

CHAPTER III

❧ *Converso* Families

"Los claros ingenios de doctos
varones castellanos"

—Fernando de Rojas

"No sé yo por cierto, señor, cómo
esto se pueda proporcionar:
desecharnos por parientes y
escogernos por señores."

—Fernando del Pulgar

✒ The Caste of *Conversos*

The ordeal of Alvaro de Montalbán at the hands of Baltasar de Castro, Antonio González Francés, and the redoubtable Alonso de Mariana was solitary. No matter how much surreptitious cell-to-cell communication he may have had with his errant relative, Bartolomé Gallego, or with his aged neighbor, Inés Alonso, when confronting his Inquisitors he was as alone as a man can be. Only at the point of death are we likely to participate in a comparable situation. And, what was even more anguishing, the interrogation by its very nature sought from him memories of company: an adolescent love affair, games in "las cabañuelas," excruciating days in church, a picnic in the country, partnerships in business, and, above all, the family relationships he had cherished and betrayed. During those hours of radical solitude when dialogue itself took the shape of a hopeless battle, there was raised the phantom of another, accompanied life, a life dedicated—at times with moderate success and at others with painful failure—to love and livelihood. It is this second life with which we shall be concerned in the present chapter. Instead of continuing to meditate on Alvaro de Montalbán, Francisco de Villalobos, or the all but vanished Fernando de Rojas as individuals reacting to a circumstance of suspicion, we shall now glance at them as a group, as members of what Américo Castro has termed (recapturing the significance of the language of the time) "la casta de los *conversos*." Born together into a common historical predicament, how did they live and how did they view themselves as a social entity?

The concept of caste implies first of all the maintenance—either by choice or by inability to do otherwise—of a common genetic line through intermarriage among the members.[1] And so it was with the

[1] The word *casta* as used then (and now) meant roughly "breed" and could be used for other living things—as when Lazarillo ironically compares his third master to a *"galgo de buena casta."* The same significance is attached to the Hindu *jati*, according to Louis Dumont in his *Homo hierarchicus*, Paris, 1966, p. 63. Dumont, however, seems to attach little importance to this meaning, nor does he pay much attention to the Iberian origin of the word "caste" itself (as has long been known, Portuguese explorers fell back on their familiar word when they tried to explain to themselves the nature of the strange society they had discovered) so significantly surprising to Castro (see

Rojas and the Montalbanes. The marriage of Fernando de Rojas to Leonor Alvarez was by no means the only link between the two families. As an examination of the appended genealogies will show, the Bachelor's daughter Catalina married Luis Hurtado who was both a distant cousin of Alvaro de Montalbán and a step-grandson. The first relationship arose from the fact that Luis Hurtado's grandfather (Alonso de Montalbán who founded the Madrid branch of the family) was Alvaro's first cousin; and the second, from the fact that his father (Pero de Montalbán who went with Alvaro on the fatal picnic) took as his second wife Constança Núñez, a sister of Leonor Alvarez.[2] A third intermarriage was that of Rojas' eldest son, the Licentiate Francisco, to "doña" (as she is referred to in the *probanzas*) Catalina Alvarez de Avila, the granddaughter of Elvira Gómez (one of those younger sisters of Alvaro's who had been "reconciled as children"). In addition to these documented matches, the two families apparently had a further history of consanguinity—a history not surprising in a small town such as the Puebla. In the 1571 "probanza de hidalguía y limpieza" (mentioned previously as arranged for by Rojas' grandchildren in order to qualify for emigration to the Indies)[3] one of the Puebla witnesses, Alfonsina de Avila, admits "that she is related to the aforesaid doña Catalina Alvarez de Avila but doesn't know to what degree and also a bit to the aforesaid Licentiate Rojas." As such a relative she had been present at their "desposorios," a ceremony which probably took place in the Puebla.[4]

Realidad, edn. II, p. 30). Spanish *castas* and Indian castes are not identical in one important characteristic (the lack of accepted and recognized hierarchical status among Moors, Jews, and Christians, each whom believed themselves superior), but, as we shall see, a number of other key resemblances do credit to these unsung amateur sociologists from Portugal.

[2] Serrano y Sanz, p. 263, and Appendix II.

[3] VLA 32.

[4] See Chap. V, n. 130. Another indication of relationship between the two families is contained in the will of Inés Dávila, the Licentiate Francisco's mother-in-law (VLA 31). Dated in 1558, the will leaves her worldly goods to "Alvaro Dávila, neighbor of the city of Granada, Melchor de Rojas, neighbor of Talavera, and Francisco Dávila." Since the two Dávilas are her male children (Francisco being the Sigüenza canon who falsified his genealogy, Chap. I, n. 60), so also must have been the mysterious Melchor de Rojas (no other document refers to him), whose surname perhaps reflects further consanguinity. Another son, Antonio, is listed as a passenger to the Indies in 1534

Intermarriage among *converso* families was indeed frequent during the decades which concern us.[5] If in the fifteenth-century reigns of John II and Henry IV certain wealthy *conversos* had been pleased to marry their well-dowried daughters to land-poor Christian nobles and if later many *converso* families were to disguise their origins and merge with the society around them, during the lives of Alvaro de Montalbán, of Fernando de Rojas, and of his children, exogamy was harder to arrange. This was both a time of suspicion and a time when the past was still more or less clearly remembered. A second factor—although perhaps operative only in individual cases—was the age-old Jewish repugnance to such alliances. In the trial record of a distant cousin of the Montalbanes, Teresa de Lucena, there is evidence of the persistence of this feeling among the *conversos* of the Puebla: "The present witness said that he saw the aforesaid Juan de Lucena, the father of the accused, rise suddenly and violently from his seat and go to the house in the aforesaid Puebla de Montalbán of a cousin of his called Fernán Gómez. This witness followed Juan de Lucena and found him at table where supper was just finished, and he heard Juan de Lucena say to Fernán Gómez: 'What do you think, cousin, about our cousin, Dr. Mosén Fernando de Lucena who has abandoned his god and his law for a whore?' And he said it, because he had married a Christian woman of clean blood" (mujer cristiana linda).[6] Whether or not the accusation be true, the mere fact it was made indicates the strong persistence in given persons of postbaptismal caste consciousness.

Other reasons undoubtedly had to do with the interaction of the two sets of values that were implicit in Alvaro de Montalbán's autobiography: that is to say, with the desire to keep money and property in the family. This was a charge frequently made—and not

---

(*Catálogo de pasajeros*, i, 4663). He probably died there, since he is not mentioned in the will.

[5] See *Investigaciones*, p. 63. For the similar behavior of the family of Luis Vives, see *Realidad*, edn. I, p. 551. Caro Baroja (i, 395-403) attributes *converso* intermarriage only to a desire to practice secret Judaism. This would seem to be an unacceptable overgeneralization.

[6] Serrano y Sanz, pp. 284-85. A Fernando de Lucena of the parish of San Ginés in Toledo paid 2,000 maravedís for his "rehabilitation" according to *Judaizantes* (p. 29). Fernán Gómez cannot be identified.

without justification—by Old Christian neighbors and debtors. As the carefully arranged betrothals moved to and from the church, gossip and financial analysis among the spectators were inevitable. But just as decisive as any of these possible motives, in my opinion, was the desire for a domesticity in which one could be oneself, in which self-imposed masks and muzzles might at last be laid aside. Only a Villalobos could perversely enjoy the contrary situation. As he writes to a friend after his May and December marriage to a Christian girl, "She is always speaking badly of the *conversos,* and I tell her that she is right, that they are as Jewish today as they were the day they were born."[7]

As interesting as the complex of motives behind these three inter-marriages is their revelation of the economic and social milieu in which the Bachelor of Law who married Leonor Alvarez lived. We have already taken note of the various occupations pursued by the Francos (cloth merchants, dealers in old clothes, municipal offi-cials, and one Warden of the Mint); and about the Montalbán family—thanks again to the Inquisition—we are even better in-formed. As a group, the Rojas, Francos, and Montalbanes are representative of a *casta* or *nación* which was of decisive impor-tance in the history of the time. If previously we observed the misery of individual "conversos" as mirrored in the fate of Alvaro de Montalbán, it is now time to consider the grandeur of the caste in making possible Spain's almost incredible political and cultural Renaissance. As the author of *La Celestina* and as the son of his father, Fernando de Rojas' full participation in both the misery and grandeur into which he was born cannot be doubted.

Recent studies of *converso* participation in Spanish society by such historians as Francisco Márquez, Antonio Domínguez Ortiz, Albert Sicroff, and Julio Caro Baroja[8] reveal that conventional re-

[7] *Algunas obras,* p. 138. The phrase is, of course, intentionally and com-ically ambiguous.

[8] Márquez' *Investigaciones* and Domínguez Ortiz have already been cited. Sicroff's fundamental study is entitled, *Les Controverses des statuts de "pureté de sang" en Espagne du XVᵉ au XVIIᵉ siècle,* Paris, 1960 (hereafter referred to as Sicroff). Caro Baroja's chapters entitled "El 'cristiano nuevo' en lucha: capitalismo incipiente" and "El 'cristiano nuevo' en lucha: la realidad eco-nómica" (*Los judíos,* II, 9-50) contain a detailed discussion of *converso* occupations and economic power. He concludes that many members of the caste come to constitute a new nobility, the "nobility of money."

striction of *converso* activities to medicine, finance, and administration (one unreconstructed social historian describes *conversos* merely as a "sub-aristocracy of capitalists, businessmen, and government officials")[9] is so limited as to be grudging. Continuing dislike of Jews as money grubbers and pencil pushers, or what Sartre calls more politely "anti-official" prejudice, would seem to be manifest here. In any case, Márquez corrects this limited view in a paragraph summing up the widely varying fields of activities in which peninsular *conversos* excelled: "Not only were the most decisive religious thinkers of the period *conversos* but also the lawyers, physicians, merchants, financiers, diplomats, and poets." And to that impressive list he might well have added skilled manual workers (surveyors, cloth shearers, tailors, weavers, shoemakers),[10] professors of astrology, mathematics, and grammar, and even "conquistadores." As Francesco Guicciardini remarked crossly, "The whole kingdom was full of Jews and heretics, and the greater part of the towns were spotted with this infection, and they had in their hands all the country's principal posts . . . and they had so much power and were so numerous that they could be observed with no trouble at all."[11] If his conclusions are accurate—and the historical evidence supporting them is overwhelming—we cannot help but wonder at the paradoxical situation of a caste at once at the center

[9] G. Céspedes del Castillo. See volume II, p. 410 of the *Historia social y económica de España y América* (ed. J. Vicens Vives, Barcelona, 1957) in which the *converso* presence is scandalously reduced to a few passing references.

[10] The citation from Márquez is from the "Estudio preliminar" to Fray Hernando de Talavera's *Católica impugnación*, Barcelona, 1961, p. 43. The introduction to *Judaizantes* makes it clear that quantitatively the great majority of *conversos* were manual workers. However, from among their number individuals (such as the tailor Juan de Baena, who became a "Comendador de Santiago" with the help of the Grand Master, don Juan Pacheco) seem to have enjoyed exceptional "upward mobility"—as it is called now.

[11] *Viajes por España*, Libros de antaño, VIII, ed. A. M. Fabié, Madrid, 1879, p. 208. Another traveler, Hieronymus Münzer, traveling through Valencia about five years before *La Celestina* was written remarks that when one *converso* would say to another, " 'Today we shall go to the Parish of Santa Cruz,' everyone knew that it meant they were gathering in the synagogue." He concludes that the *conversos* "had been, and to a certain extent still were, the masters of Spain, because they held all the principal offices." *Viajes de extranjeros por España y Portugal*, ed. J. García Mercadal, vol. I, Madrid, 1952, p. 342.

and on the margin of society. It is a paradox of central importance to which we shall have occasion to return repeatedly.

Although a great deal had been said about *conversos* in previous studies of the Jews in Spain, of the Inquisition, and of the Erasmistic movement, it remained for Américo Castro in his epoch-making *España en su historia* (1948) to grasp their full significance to Spanish history. Castro, as one of the great humanists of this or any century, did not begin by tabulating social categories or occupational fields. Rather, he perceived with sudden astonishment the numerous great individuals, creators of values, who were of *converso* origin. In literature, aside from Rojas, we shall observe that the founders of three of the four pre-Cervantine varieties of the novel (sentimental, pastoral, and picaresque) were *ex illis*. Among philosophers and humanists, Luis Vives, Arias Montano (the editor of the first polyglot Bible), and Fray Luis de León (also a major poet) were among the most outstanding in a field abounding with *conversos*. But even more than literature, philosophy, or scholarship, the crucible of values was religion, and there again *conversos* were in the vanguard. Reformers and mystics such as Fray Hernando de Talavera, Saint Teresa, the Blessed Juan de Avila, theologians such as Vitoria and Suárez, and (if we admit value destroyers along with value creators) such Inquisitors as Fray Diego de Deza (Columbus's protector) and Torquemada all share the same blood. There is hardly need to add to this roster the names of all the well-known lawyers, physicians, scientists, noblemen, and statesmen whose Jewish ancestry is beyond question.[12] We should not conclude the list, however, without mentioning the, to us, surprising fact that (as everyone knew at the time) the man whom Gracián was to call "The Politician," Ferdinand the Catholic himself, had a *converso* quartering.[13] Discarding coincidence, here was, Castro felt, a phenomenon deserving serious meditation.

[12] Among the many names frequently listed are the royal physician and professor of medicine at Salamanca, Dr. Fernando Alvarez de la Reina, the legal theorist and reformer, Alfonso Díaz de Montalvo, the natural scientist from the Puebla de Montalbán, Francisco Hernández, as well as the lineages of Alba, Puñonrostro, Pozas, Osuna, and many others.

[13] Ferdinand's grandmother, Juana Henríquez, was of the family of the Almirantes (admirals) de Castilla. Her mother was a known *conversa*. The interesting thing about this taint in the royal blood, however, was the awareness that both the King and his subjects had of it. An anecdote of the time

As a result of this axiological approach to the matter, Castro's comprehension of the grandeur and misery of the *conversos* has deepened and become ever more complex in a series of major studies appearing since 1948.[14] Admitting oversimplification, his method can be described as essentially double in nature. On the one hand—as we have done in the case of Alvaro de Montalbán—Castro has been concerned with the confrontation of the individual *converso* with society. He examines selected individuals (particularly authors) insofar as he or she expresses reactions to social pressure. Shameful concealment and flaunting pretension, reason and fanaticism, ambition and abnegation, diligence and desperation, self-expression and self-destruction, all contribute to the offensive and defensive postures of individuals "harried by a mad society." Which is to say, by a mass of Old Christians who, in their determination to maintain Medieval values in a world of historical change, were becoming ever more frustrated, passionate, bitter, and obsessed with honor.

On the other hand, Castro also views the *conversos* collectively as a continuation of the obliterated caste of the Jews, a converted caste which at the very least had lost nothing of its traditional importance to the functioning of society. Although sliced by history into disunited and hostile segments (the rich against the poor, the sincere Christians against the *judaizantes,* and even the noble against the plebeian), the *conversos* must nevertheless, he believes, be considered as a discrete social entity. That is, as a "caste" united not only by its genetic origin (maintained by intermarriage), not only by the indiscriminate hostility of non-members, but also by preferred or mandatory occupations. As we know, the notion of caste as derived from Indian practice and sociological theory requires, in addition to common descent, limitation to a customary

---

portrays him teasing his cousin, one don Sancho de Rojas, about being a *converso.* The cousin is supposed to have replied: "Hablome aquel morico en algarabía como aquel que bien la sabe" (Paz y Melia, *Sales,* 1, 279). The use of a popular phrase from the *romancero* insinuates that the King and his interlocutor spoke the same caste "language." Other examples of jocular racial self-consciousness on the part of the Henríquez are referred to by Villalobos.

[14] Particularly *De la edad conflictiva,* Madrid, 1961; *"La Celestina" como contienda literaria,* Madrid, 1965; and *Cervantes y los casticismos españoles,* Madrid, 1966.

economic sphere.[15] As such a caste, then, the *conversos* dedicated themselves to thinking, making, and arranging: the indispensable production, administration, and distribution that enabled Spain to transform itself almost overnight from a collection of divided and anarchically feudal kingdoms into the first modern nation-state. Individual *conversos* might excel under pressure in all the unique ways noticed previously, but, viewed as a social whole, they dominated an enormous (far larger than that of any Indian caste) yet clearly delimited vocational area.

Between the *conquistadores* on the new frontiers of the Empire and the peasants rooted into the plains and mountains of the peninsula, the *conversos* spent their time making Spain possible. The two extremes (at this point my historical overgeneralization becomes so blatant as to need no apology) of warrior and peasant centered their activities in the realm of belief: in the epic harvest of new souls for God, and in the traditionally sacred harvest of wheat, wheat which in the Eucharist could become God Himself.[16] Living in a Medieval context in which all things were potentially sacra-

---

[15] Dumont, *Homo hierarchicus*, Chap. IV. The third, and for Dumont decisive, characteristic of caste division is preoccupation with purity and impurity, each caste regulating its behavior (meat eating, willingness to engage in certain suspect occupations, etc.) according to the degree of purity which corresponds to it. Here is the major difference between this social phenomenon in West and East. In India a more or less definable sense of the impure is accepted by all, while in medieval Spain each *ley* proposed its own distinct *limpieza*. In a sense it can be said that the conflicts of the 16th century arose from the efforts of the caste of Old Christians to impose hierarchy (with themselves as Brahmins and the *conversos* as unclean Untouchables) upon groups which in the Middle Ages had been separate and unrelated. Once converted and in the same fold the problem of superiority and inferiority, previously non-existent, became acute.

[16] In his essay on Berceo (*Lenguaje y poesía*, Madrid, 1962) Jorge Guillén comments on this central poetic tradition, a tradition which was still vigorous in the Golden Century as readers of the "autos sacramentales" will recognize (see, for example, Lope's *La siega*). In this connection it is curious to note that *conversos* were thought of as tainting wheat by touching it (a superstition typical of the caste mentality). In a section of the Palavesín *expediente* having nothing to do with the Rojas or Francos we find reference to an individual whose *limpieza* is questioned because others refuse to purchase his wheat. Father Gonzálvez informs me that such accusations are numerous in the Cathedral archives. As we remember, Lazarillo's Squire is reluctant to accept the bread begged for him because he doesn't know whether it was "amasado de manos limpias."

mental, their minds and wills were centered on what both Castro and Alvaro de Montalbán call the "más allá," the world which lies beyond—but never far from—this one. Between these two extremes, Castro shows us (and once shown, how many facts fit themselves into place!) Spain was administered by converted Jews and their descendants of pure and mixed blood.

It was, thus, the honor and dishonor of the *converso* caste to understand and to manipulate human affairs—and divine as well, insofar as some of its members brought reason to theology and effective bureaucracy to the Church. At once the continuation of its Medieval frontier experience and a newborn state involved in multiple national and international enterprises, the Spain of Fernando de Rojas was contradictorily the most traditional and the most modern in Western Europe. As such it had to be reformed, managed, financed, and its parts adequately coordinated. Such functions had been performed during the Middle Ages in a more limited way by the Jews; now the mutated caste they left behind them found itself in charge of a far larger and more demanding territory: the "más acá" (the rational and tangible "down here" which consoled Alvaro de Montalbán) of a sudden Empire. Indeed, the extreme tension of relations between Old Christians and *conversos* resulted less from the desire of the former to take over the latter's functions (although envy of *converso* wealth was inevitable and bitter) than from resentment against the greatly increased rationalization of national life.[17] The Empire was an expression of what was felt to be the historical mission of the Spanish

---

[17] On one level this expresses itself in an angry conviction that *conversos* were in some mysterious way peculiarly fitted for such offices. They are "*agudos*"; they infiltrate in a way that is impossible to prevent. Cardinal Silíceo in his successful effort to exclude *conversos* from the chapter of canons in the Cathedral of Toledo (the exclusion which made the Palavesín *expediente* necessary), cites an apocryphal letter which purports to be from the Jews of Constantinople to the Jews of Spain and which expresses this feeling: "Pues os quitan la hazienda, hazéd a vros. hijos mercaderes, y pues os quitan las vidas sean vros. hijos médicos y boticarios, y pues os destruyen vras, synagogas hazed a vros. hijos clerigos, y enquanto a las demas exaçiones, procurad que vros. hijos tengan officios publicos y de gouiernos . . ." (cited by M. Méndez Bejarano, *Histoire de la juiverie de Séville*, Madrid, 1922, pp. 266-267). On a deeper level there is resentment against the office itself as expressed in the satire of *escribanos* or in the phrase "¡Del rey abajo ninguno!" For *converso* predominance in such posts see Amador de los Ríos, p. 563.

people and, at the level of the individual, of what Castro calls "the imperative dimension of the Spanish person,"[18] and yet its very existence made necessary a kind of organization that was felt to be alien to both, an organization manned by canny entrepreneurs of cause and effect.

❧ The Montalbanes, Avilas, Rojas, Torrijos, Lucenas, and Francos

However schematic the above résumé of Castro's meditations, it may help us to understand the vocations and activities of the Montalbanes and the principal families with which they intermarried: the Rojas, the Avilas,[19] the Torrijos, and the Lucenas. As a group, taken along with the Francos, they may be considered as a demonstration in miniature of the accuracy of the historical intuition first expressed in *España en su historia*. Not only do they follow the vocations of their caste, but, in Fernando de Rojas, their seed produced a great individual creator of values.

The first member of the family referred to by Alvaro de Montalbán was Garçí Alvarez de Montalbán "who was neither investigated by the Inquisition nor burnt after death." Since his grandson was born around 1450, it is chronologically probable that Garçí Alvarez, like the patriarch of the Rojas and Francos, Pedro González Notario, was one of the innumerable Jews who crossed the frontiers of faith in the aftermath of the violence of 1391. It was precisely then—although previously individual conversions were not infrequent—that the *converso* caste was born. Furthermore, his name indicates that his enforced baptism took place in the Puebla.

---

[18] *Origen, ser y existir de los españoles*, Madrid, 1959, p. 87ff. Castro there refers to the projection of one's being (*ser*) out into the world, a world subject not to rational manipulation but to domination by the will. His major example of such successful Quixotism is the peculiar character of the conquest of America.

[19] The Avila family had been living in the Puebla as early as 1417. F. Cantera Burgos in his *Alvar García de Santa María* (Madrid, 1952) refers to Ferrant Gómez de Avila, a "*procurador* and neighbor of the Puebla de Montalbán" who granted on that date a lease to certain houses in Toledo (p. 65). In the *Registro General del Sello* (Simancas), vol. VI, item 2391 we find mention of Gonzalo de Avila el Viejo (the grandfather of Catalina Alvarez de Avila, Rojas' daughter-in-law and "reconciled" brother-in-law of Alvaro) as receiving in 1489 an "*amparo*" (a form of legal intervention) in his efforts to take possession of property in the Puebla.

It was usual at the time to attribute Jewish forebearers to any family whose surname was that of a town or locality, since it was a common practice to christen topographically. Where one was baptized became who one was.[20] There is no indication of his profession, but we do know that his son Fernando Alvarez de Montalbán (Alvaro's father who, as we remember, was burnt after death) was an "escribano" or notary. And since the necessity of maintaining legal records over generations and centuries tended to give the profession a hereditary quality, it is not unlikely that the father occupied the same typically *converso* post.[21] This is at best a reasonable supposition, but what can be affirmed is that Garçí Alvarez founded a family which either directly or by marriage was involved in almost all the occupations familiar to his kind.

In the first place, there were those engaged in handling money on a whole or part time basis. We remember Alvaro de Montalbán describing to his Inquisitors as the most natural thing in the world how he helped his brother-in-law, Gonçalo de Torrijos, collect ecclesiastical rents in Galicia. Similarly his son, Juan del Castillo, only two years after Alvaro's condemnation accompanied his cousin and brother-in-law (Pero de Montalbán, the royal *aposentador*) to Majorca, Orihuela, and Córdoba in order to collect the proceeds of indulgences.[22] Among the Lucenas (one of

---

[20] This habit is satirized by the author of the *Diálogo entre Laín Calvo y Nuño Rasura*. The latter explains a sarcastic jest to the former by stating that these "mercadercillos caualleros" that they observe coming and going all bear the names of cities or saints (that is names derived from the place or day of baptism)—except when they disguise themselves with aristocratic and pseudo-medieval designations such as Diego Arias. Similarly when a certain Alonso de Avila denied having *converso* lineage, the *librero*, Abraham García, is reported to have stated that "debía de serlo o bien de baja condición, pues solo en estos casos toman su apellido del lugar." As far as saints' names are concerned, we remember that Quevedo indicated don Pablos' origins by attributing to him ancestors of pious nomenclature.

[21] See *Investigaciones*, p. 52. Among the *escribanos* in this complex of families was one Rodrigo de Avila who in 1496 recorded documents for Gonzalo de Avila el Viejo (VLA 1 and 2). Rojas' son Alvaro also followed this profession as did by apparent inheritance his son García in his turn. See Luis Careaga, "Investigaciones referentes a Fernando de Rojas en Talavera de la Reina," *RHM*, 1938, p. 15.

[22] The Spanish "para cobrar la bula" seems to indicate administration of the accounts and collection of the proceeds from retailers rather than actual sales, in the manner of Lazarillo's master, the "*buldero.*" Juan del Castillo (Rojas' brother-in-law as indicated above) was about 30 years old in 1525

whom was married to a Montalbán) were two *arrendadores*, the same traditionally Jewish profession of tax farmer followed by the original Pedro Franco when he wasn't dealing in rags. Closely related to such activities were those discharged by *mayordomos*, professional stewards or managers of noble estates, municipalities, ecclesiastical organizations, and other such entities. Alvaro de Montalbán mentions having acted in this capacity for the town council of the Puebla. And he seems to take some pride in the fact that two other members of the family had held similar positions of honor and trust. One of them, his brother-in-law, Diego López,[23] had been the *mayordomo* of no less a personage than Arias de Silva, a noble leader of the *converso* faction in the fifteenth-century Toledo uprisings.[24] As Marcel Bataillon has observed, "When one studies the genealogies furnished in Inquisition trials, one is astonished to see so many members of these *converso* families serving the grandees, particularly as administrators, mayordomos, or secretaries."[25]

Another profession that was represented in these families was medicine. As is well known, in the Middle Ages physicians had been traditionally Jewish, and now *conversos* were carrying on. According to a frequently cited anecdote, on one occasion Francis I asked his colleague Charles V to lend him a good Jewish

---

(Serrano y Sanz, pp. 263 and 298). In 1548 he (or a person of identical name) appeared as a witness in the *probanza de hidalguía* initiated by his nephew, Alonso de Montalbán, to be discussed later on in this chapter. He states that he is a "neighbor of the village of Huente."

[23] This is confirmed by *Judaizantes* (p. 40): "Diego López, mayordomo de Arias de Sylva. Catalina Alvares, su muger 1,500 maravedís." The other was Alvaro's maternal grandfather, Francisco Rodríguez de Dueñas, a Toledan *escribano* and *mayordomo* of the convent of Santo Domingo el Real.

[24] Regarding Arias de Silva, co-leader of the *converso* faction along with Fernando de la Torre, later executed, see E. Benito Ruano, *Toledo en el siglo XV*, Madrid, 1961, pp. 114 ff. For the family's turbulent proclivities see Amador de los Ríos, p. 633.

[25] Bataillon, *Erasmo y España*, México, 1950, I, 212. This edition (hereafter referred to as *Erasmo*) was the most recent at the time of writing. See also *Investigaciones*, pp. 68-69, and Domínguez Ortiz, p. 146. The duties of the *mayordomo* are set forth in detail by Fray Hernando de Talavera in his *Instrucción* for the functionaries of his Archepiscopal palace in Granada (ed. J. Domínguez Bordona, *BRAH*, xcvi, 1930, pp. 785-835). The *mayordomo* acted as a general manager, auditor, purchasing agent, disbursement officer, and steward.

physician. There was, of course, none available, and when a *converso* was substituted Francis dismissed him, apparently feeling that the change of faith might have diminished his skill.[26] This was certainly not the case of "el doctor maestre" Martín, the patriarch of the Lucenas who, far more than Rojas, was recognized as the most distinguished member of our cluster of families. Amador de los Ríos mentions him as the court physician for Juan II,[27] and in the *Chebet Jehudah* he is referred to as a "great scholar of our race."[28] His son, Doctor Francisco de Lucena, as well as his grandson, the Papal physician, Luis de Lucena, followed the same profession. Aside from these very distant connections, we have already mentioned Doctor Juan Alvarez de San Pedro, the Bachelor's *consuegro*. Of his professional reputation little can be said, but that he was respectable is attested to by his grandchildren's use of his name in their family tree as a substitute for that of Alvaro de Montalbán. Numerically, Cervantes with no less than five medical men

[26] *Realidad*, edn. I, p. 449; *Structure*, p. 472.

[27] Alvaro de Luna "entrusted the King's health to the science and to the care of Doctors, Diego Rodríguez and maestre Martín, distinguished physicians who inherited the doctrine of the Aben-Zarzales and Mayres" (Amador de los Ríos, p. 573). In a note he comments on the charge made against both, to the effect that they "did not discharge properly their duties with regard to the examination of '*físicos e çerujanos*' and that they approved those who lacked sufficient skill and knowledge."

[28] The reference is contained in an anecdote concerning an unnamed Castilian queen who, at the urging of a fanatical friar, persuaded her husband to decree mandatory conversion. "A certain prince then advised the Jews: 'The Queen likes gold and silver very much; therefore, gather quickly 50,000 escudos and place them in a house which I shall point out to you near her palace. I'll have the Queen walk by there, and I will tell her what I think to be appropriate in your favor.' The Jews did this, and the aforementioned prince had her pass by that house and said to her: 'My lady, is it right to pull up the vine that has given such fruit?'

"That very same day there also passed by the place a great scholar of our race called Maese Martín de Lucena, and he advised the Jews that they need not obey the order to submit to conversion, because on the following day they would hang the friar, and it is customary for rulers to annul the sentence when they kill the individual whose intrigue brought about the sentence. That night the servants of the King bore witness to the fact that the friar had directed shameless words to the Queen; they called the Queen who affirmed that this was so, and the King ordered the friar to be hanged from a tree" (pp. 203-204). The meaning of all this seems to be that Maese Martín as a member of the Royal household was able to tip the Jews off that their bribe had been accepted and that a scheme to get rid of the friar was being put into effect.

125

in his immediate family was far more closely involved with the profession than Rojas. However, even a remote kinship with such distinguished physicians as "el doctor maestre" Martín and his descendants indicates the status of these families within their caste.

The law and local government were two related fields in which the Rojas side of the family seemed to specialize.[29] In addition to the two *regidores* and the *jurado* in the Franco family tree, we learn from one of the *probanzas* that the Bachelor's brother, Juan, was a *regidor* in the Puebla. But, most important of all, it has long been one of the few known facts about Fernando de Rojas (a fact provided by the only person of the time who thought it worthwhile to refer in writing to his biography) that "on several occasions he held the office of Alcalde Mayor in Talavera."[30] As we shall see, incomplete municipal records confirm this only for the period between 15 February and 23 March 1538, but the point is that in a society premised on honor and having a great regard for official distinctions the appointment—whether unique or repeated—is an indication of the Bachelor's high standing in his adopted community.

But this is not all. The Valle Lersundi archives further reveal that Rojas' eldest son continued the tradition. Not only did the Licentiate Francisco follow his father's biographical path to read law at Salamanca; not only did he return to the Puebla to find a bride from his mother's family; but in his turn he also acted as the Lord Mayor (Alcalde Mayor) of Talavera and went on to such appointments as judge in Llerena.[31] Recent historical studies have brought out the considerable extent of *converso* participation in municipal government during this period.[32] Political management,

---

[29] The only lawyer on the Montalbán side of the family was the Bachelor García de Montalbán, a brother of Alonso, the first *"aposentador real."* It was he who was referred to previously (Chap. II, n. 10) as the probable distant cousin of Alvaro's who was "reconciled" and "rehabilitated" according to the list in *Judaizantes.*

[30] Cosme Gómez Tejada de los Reyes, *Historia de Talavera,* BN MS 8396. Cited in *Orígenes,* p. 244.

[31] VLA 32 (the *probanza* obtained for passage to the Indies in which a witness states that both father and son had been mayor). For the judgeship in Llerena (1546) see VLA 25, the "Libro de memorias" of the Licentiate Fernando.

[32] See particularly Francisco Márquez, "Conversos y cargos concejiles en el siglo XV," RABM, LXIII (1957), 503-540.

it would seem, like economic management was attractive to members of the caste. And if its practice was on occasion spectacular, as in the case of Antonio Pérez, or arbitrary, as in that of Mateo Alemán,[33] more often it was exercised moderately and responsibly as seems to have been done by the Rojas, father and son.[34]

In addition to financial, medical, legal, and administrative occupations (involving the rationalization of human existence and co-existence), the Montalbanes were related to at least one merchant, the Toledan *especiero* in whose service Alvaro de Montalbán passed his apprenticeship.[35] It was the Francos, however, who constituted a spectacularly successful family of businessmen. Related to the Montalbanes only indirectly through the Rojas, they form a separate group the wealth of which was primarily commercial. In the *árbol* we noticed a number of references to trade in first- and second-hand cloth, beginning with Pedro Franco, "*trapero*," dead in 1485. Three generations and almost a hundred years later when members of the family employed the Licentiate Fernando (presumably because he was at once a relative and a specialist) in their suit for *hidalguía*, one branch owned a chain of three permanent

---

[33] See Claudio Guillén, "Los pleitos extremeños de Mateo Alemán," *Archivo hispalense*, 103-104 (1960), 1-21.

[34] In addition to the office of mayor, they also, according to two witnesses, held such municipal posts as "alcaldes de la hermandad, jurados y procuradores generales" (see Appendix III). Another son, Garçi Ponce, is identified by a *probanza* witness as "procurador sindio en esta villa de Talavera" (VLA 25). "Sindio" is undoubtedly "síndico."

[35] A Toledan branch of the Montalbanes (of uncertain relationship to those mentioned by Alvaro in his genealogy) was that founded by an Alonso de Montalbán who married Mari Núñez de la Torre and was buried in the Capilla de la Piedad in the church of San Nicolás. A son, Rodrigo López de Montalbán (d. 1569), is described as an "insigne predicador." Other children intermarried with the Fuentes of the Puebla. These descended from Diego de la Fuente who "tubo casas en la Puebla" and "casó en Toledo con Guiomar Hurtado." See doc. 24,404 of the Luis de Salazar y Castro archives in the Academia de la Historia. (Hereafter reference to the *Indice*, ed. B. Cuartero y Huerta and A. de Vargas-Zúñiga, Madrid, 1956 will be Salazar y Castro.) Diego's son Rodrigo "vecino de la ciudad de Toledo" had dealings with Alvaro de Montalbán in 1500 (VLA 3) and is identified in the Serrano trial as owner of a "lagar." It was probably a grandson, also named Rodrigo, "vecino de Toledo morador en la Puebla," who 37 years later denounced his own stepson, Diego de Pisa (Chap. II, n. 47). There were several inter-marriages with the Montalbanes, but five generations later among their descendants were the Marquises de Peñaloza, canons in the Cathedral of Toledo, and knights of Santiago.

outlets for drygoods in Andalusia along with "substantial capital and much property." As a result they could ride "fine horses," choose among several "luxurious residences," and "represent themselves as *hidalgos*." They were in fact much admired and envied by their favorable witnesses, many of whom were small-time traders and peddlers working local fairs—just as had Alvaro de Montalbán in his young manhood.[36]

Another vocational outlet for Castilian *conversos* was that chosen by Saint Teresa's seven brothers: emigration to the Indies where administrative talents were even more needed than at home. And once there, they frequently (as in the case of an Ercilla) became in being and behavior indistinguishable from the rest of the *conquistadores*.[37] Indeed, aside from abundant opportunities to make a fortune, the Indies seem to have offered escape from the pressures of life in home localities. Although the Inquisition, too, eventually made the transatlantic voyage (1528), it was great solace to find that in the New World everyone was a newcomer. In any case, from the families which now concern us no fewer than five individuals (including Rojas' son Juan de Montemayor just after his father's death) are on emigrant lists.[38] I am inclined to doubt, however, that the Licentiate Francisco's children actually intended to

[36] See Chap. I, n. 39.

[37] Although Lucía García de Proodian gathers much useful material in her *Los judíos en América*, Madrid, 1966, her primary interest is in clandestine Jews rather than in *conversos*. The full history of the conquest as a *converso* enterprise remains to be written. Castro provides a suggestive point of departure with his views on the Semitic tradition behind "La guerra divinal."

[38] VLA 26. He was dead in 1555, since his share of his mother's property was divided among his brothers and sisters on that date (VLA 28 and 29). The record of his departure is to be found in the *Catálogo de pasajeros*, III, 1658: "Juan de Rojas, hijo del Bachiller Hernando de Rojas y de Leonor Alvarez, vecinos de Tenerife, a Nombre de Dios. —12 Agosto." Tenerife is obviously a faulty transcription of Talavera. The other family emigrants were: Antonio de Avila (a brother of Catalina Alvarez de Avila mentioned in n. 4); Alonso de Montalbán (a son of Pero, the first "aposentador"), who departed in 1538 with a retinue of servants (*Catálogo*, II, 4563); Francisco de Montalbán, a brother of Pero, who left as early as 1512 (*Catálogo*, I, 670); and that Montalbán who, according to Valle Lersundi (I have been able to find no record of him), acted as physician on one of Columbus' voyages and brought back the stuffed alligator to the Capilla del Lagarto in San Ginés. Another possible relative who departed in 1535 for the same haven was one Mateo Ramírez, the son of "Aldonza de Rojas, natural de la Puebla" (*Catálogo*, II, 2129).

leave when they arranged for the *probanza de limpieza* that was a preliminary requirement. As we shall see (Appendix I), these particular *probanzas* were among the easiest to obtain, and it is probable that the Licentiate Fernando arranged it as a first step in his campaign to achieve family respectability.

The humblest occupations to which we find reference are those of silk weaver (Alfonso de Torrijos, one of Alvaro de Montalbán's brothers-in-law) and tailor (his errant nephew and prison mate).[39] Another artisan—and, aside from Rojas himself, surely the most interesting member of our Puebla families—was Juan de Lucena whose "grandes yrronías en la santa fe" have already been mentioned. Partly as the result of denunciation by a feeble-minded nephew (how many cases resemble that of Alvaro de Montalbán!), his story and that of his family are preserved in Inquisitional archives. The second son of the "doctor maestre" Martín de Lucena, Juan, in the 1480's set up a printing shop in the Puebla where, with the help of his daughters, Teresa and Catalina (of whom more later), he produced and sold the first books in Hebrew to be printed in Spain.[40] Although only remotely connected to the author of *La Celestina* (as far as we can determine from the documents), Juan's activities provide significant evidence that at the time of Rojas' childhood there was still a robust tradition of Hebraic learning among the Jews and *conversos* of Toledo and the Puebla. We remember Cervantes' hints that as late as 1605 it would not be hard to find in Toledo a linguist versed in "a better and more antique language" than Arabic.

Perhaps because of this continuing tradition or perhaps because the skeptical antagonism of Alvaro de Montalbán to all things religious was shared by his relatives, the families produced no churchmen until the generation of Rojas' children. We have al-

---

[39] For discussion of the lower social and occupational strata occupied by the *converso* caste (shoemakers, weavers, potters, etc.), see Caro Baroja, II, 26 ff., and Domínguez Ortiz, pp. 145 ff. Before 1492, it would seem that these less desirable vocations were followed by Jews (see Chap. V, n. 75). Afterwards they were naturally held by those converted at the last moment.

[40] Serrano y Sanz, pp. 256-260 and 282-295. The data there provided have been used by J. Bloch, "Early Hebrew Printing in Spain and Portugal," *Bulletin of The New York Public Library*, XLII (1938); Baer (II, 345 ff); and Bernhard Friedburg, *History of Hebrew Typography*, Antwerp, 1934 (see Chap. V, n. 55).

ready mentioned Catalina Alvarez de Avila's brother, Francisco de
Avila (the Sigüenza canon who rearranged his family tree), and
in the same generation among the Francos there was a Franciscan
Friar, Alonso de Villareal, and a Francisca de los Arenales, only
identified as a "*monja*." The following generation produced Rojas'
grandson Fray García, that official of the Calced Carmelites (and
possible antagonist of Saint Teresa) who was sure the family must
possess an *ejecutoria*. But the roster of family occupations comes to
its fitting conclusion in 1616 when a witness testifying in the
Palavesín *expediente* identifies himself as "Martín de Avila, familiar
de la Santa Inquisición de la Puebla de Montalbán."[41] As we remember, the duties of a *familiar* (lay member) included spying on
neighbors and friends and reporting all suspicious behavior!

"My principal studies"

My justification for stressing to this extent the economic and
professional solidity of Fernando de Rojas' family background is
the need to correct and amplify the grim portrait of *converso* existence which emerged from our reading the ordeal of Alvaro de
Montalbán. Anguished and vulnerable subjectivity and outward
girding of social armor constitute a very incomplete picture of
what *conversos* felt and were. Such a limited view may help us
understand certain aspects of *La Celestina*. But the man who lived
in Talavera for some thirty-three years as an "honrado bachiller,"
who brought up a successful family, and who ended his career with
the honor of appointment as "Alcalde Mayor" surely possessed an
inner firmness, a bedrock of identity, which neither a genius for
creative anonymity nor fear of non-conformance can explain. It is
precisely here that our survey of his family background is of service. Rojas alludes to this aspect of himself in the one-sentence autobiography of the acrostics when he prefers to invent nine
additional verses rather than omit his title of "bachiller." Like his
relatives and other educated *conversos*, he had a strong sense of

---

[41] Another probable relative, Gutierre de Avila, witnessed two transactions
for Gonzalo de Avila el Viejo in 1496 and 1498 (VLA 1 and 2). He may
possibly be identified with the "comendador de Santiago" and "mayordomo
del Cardenal de España" of the same name who in 1514 testified in the trial
of Abraham García concerning the proceeds of the "alcabala" collected by
the latter.

130

personal vocation, of identification with what he calls his "principal estudio."[42]

Without doubt, the several phrases in the prefatory Letter and the Prologue in which Rojas deprecates his literary achievement as compared to his status as a lawyer involve a certain amount of false modesty. Yet, at the same time, if read from the other point of view, they also reveal a genuine sense of professional pride: "Do not blame me . . . for not expressing my name. Above all since I am a lawyer; although this is a discreet work, it is foreign to my profession, and whoever identified me by name would say that I wrote it, not as a recreation from my principal studies of which I am more proud, but as a person gone astray from the law." We are reminded of another lawyer-author, Henry Fielding, who, although he lived in a society which may have been less suspicious of fiction, had similar doubts about the compatibility of the two occupations: ". . . it [the fact that a certain novel had been attributed to him] may have a Tendency to injure me in a Profession, to which I have applied with so arduous an intent a Diligence that I have had no Leisure, if I had Inclination, to compose any thing of this kind."[43] In Rojas' case the vocation and the title of Bachelor of Law both maintained and sustained him for decades after the writing of *La Celestina* had become a youthful memory. His epitaph may seem grotesquely inappropriate to the literary biographer, but it surely was as he wanted it to be: "Aquí yace el honrado bachiller Fernando de Rojas."[44]

In addition to the self-portrait in the prologue material and the inscription on the tombstone, Rojas' intense vocational feeling also appears within the frontiers of *La Celestina*'s dialogue. One indirect expression of resentment and thinly veiled outrage against the legal irregularity of Inquisitional procedures has frequently been

[42] Caro Baroja in his useful, dispassionate, and curiously arbitrary study on one occasion grossly oversimplifies ultimate *converso* motivations. Despite the fact that one aspect of *converso* consciousness was financial (that is, as we have seen in the case of Alvaro de Montalbán, money was not just purchasing power or an object of collection but a way of thinking in rational terms about life), it is misleading and unjust to attribute the vocational dedication of the caste to "gold fever . . . in the last analysis" (II, 50).

[43] Introduction to Sarah Fielding's *The Adventures of David Simple*, London, 1744, p. iv.

[44] VLA, final unnumbered document, "Libro de memorias" of Juan de Rojas.

mentioned. When Celestina describes Claudina's persecution by the Inquisition (that same persecution which was supposed to guarantee salvation), she also remarks that her friend was not guilty of the charges for which she was convicted: ". . . according to what everybody said, on that occasion false witnesses and harsh torture forced her to confess against all reason and justice things she hadn't done." Civil justice, she concludes, when compared to such procedures is far preferable.[45] In an ironical context it is always risky to attribute any opinion or statement to the author, but I would be willing to surmise that in matters related to his own profession Rojas allows his characters to speak for him. The just and efficient municipal judge who condemns and executes Pármeno and Sempronio with laudable dispatch and without deferring to Calisto's influence (Act XVI), thus, stands in sharp contrast to Claudina's (and his father's) Inquisitors. It would seem that the one field of human activity in which Rojas fully believed was that to which his life was to be dedicated: the study and practice of civil law.

It was only to be expected that other members of Rojas' caste, particularly those who emigrated to America, should be infected with the exaltation of the century. An Alonso de Ercilla,[46] arriving at an Antarctic extremity of Chile, asserts in a fashion as alien to the *chocarrero* Villalobos as to the self-effacing Rojas: "Aquí llegué donde nadie ha llegado" (Here I have come where none other has been before me). And he went on to rest his claim to lasting fame on an epic creation, *La Araucana*, which in its celebration of values is antithetical to *La Celestina*. It is typical that Ercilla should leave

---

[45] "Calla, bobo!"—Celestina exclaims to Pármeno—"Poco sabes de achaque de iglesia y cuanto es mejor por manos de justicia que de otra manera." For the context of these remarks and their relationship to Celestina's perverse interpretation of "Blessed are those who are persecuted for righteousness' sake . . ." see my "Matthew V:10 in Castilian Jest and Earnest" to appear in the forthcoming homage to Rafael Lapesa. When in *La Thebayda*, a "rufián gracioso" boasts that through bribery he has been able to obtain the freedom of a criminal at the foot of the gallows, the author's attitude towards civil justice seems antithetical to that of a Rojas. In a world bereft of reason on every level from that of our final destiny to our most rudimentary conversations, civil law, for all its possible flaws, offered firm refuge.

[46] For details of the falsification of the Ercilla *probanza* see notes 3, 4, and 5 of Medina's *Vida de Ercilla* (cited Chap. II, n. 35), as well as Castro, *Realidad*, edn. I, p. 540.

behind elaborately bound volumes of his work and that Rojas' will should mention only one "Libro de Calisto" assessed at ten maravedís. But Ercilla is in many ways an exception. For the most part individual vocations were rooted into the small towns and cities of Spain where the ancestors of the *conversos* had occupied their *aljamas* (ghettos) and lined the *calles de judíos* with their houses. There, conscientiously, methodically, and proudly, they carried on the unheroic business which the same century needed: collecting, accounting, recording, managing, curing, judging, thinking, writing, and making. Or if they left home, they did so less as adventurers than as men following specific careers of learning, administration, or service.

In the *relaciones* given by every locality to Philip II (Spain's first effort at a census), Torrijos, a small agricultural community of some 750 *vecinos* about seventeen kilometers north of the Puebla de Montalbán, lists proudly the graduates of its grammar school. From this one institution, the local reporters assert, there emerged over 50 professors, doctors, lawyers, judges, theologians, bishops and bureaucrats—most of them apparently of *converso* origin. Included are Alonso de Torres, the professor of Greek at Alcalá; Doctor Diego López, the Royal Physician; the Licentiate Busto de Villegas, Governor of the Archbishophric of Toledo; and a Doctor Covarrubias, Judge of the Royal Council. All were students of one Bachelor Francisco de Torrijos (perhaps related to the two Torrijos who married Alvaro de Montalbán's sisters), a creator of vocations long forgotten but as remarkable in his way as any *institucionista* in the nineteenth century.[47] Although the school in

[47] *Relaciones de los pueblos de España, Reino de Toledo,* ed. C. Viñas and R. Paz, Madrid, 1951, III, 624-625 (hereafter referred to as *Relaciones*). As ben Verga notes (p. 206), all the Jews in Torrijos had been converted in the 1390's with the result that "de Torrijos" was a not infrequent name among *conversos.* See, for example, the *Libro verde de Aragón,* p. 271. It is also worth noting that Francisco Hernández, the natural scientist from the Puebla, served as a physician in Torrijos for the Duke of Maqueda around 1530. See his *Obras completas,* ed. G. Somolinos D'Ardois, México, 1960, I, 116. It is impossible to determine whether or not this school had any relation to the charitable institution founded in Torrijos by doña Teresa Enríquez, the Duchess of Maqueda, known as "la loca del Sacramento," sometime prior to her death in 1503: "Instituyó en su mismo palacio un Recogimiento con destino a niños de todas edades, las cuales vivían en comunidad y bajo la dirección de un eclesiástico a fin de que, por medio de una educación prudente

133

Torrijos was apparently founded after the future Bachelor received his pre-university education, its record of success illustrates the vocational talents that the population of the Tormes valley between Toledo and Talavera was capable of producing in the sixteenth century.

The strong identification of such individuals as these with their "callings" may have resulted in self-respect and even in a certain amount of deference from others. But at the same time such positions carried with them all the dangers which could result from latent popular resentment. Undoubtedly most of the above were known *conversos* whose power, official presumption, and wealth might well lead them to destruction. The popular phrase and title of a play, "Del rey abajo ninguno" (Nobody between me and the King), is tacitly directed against the intermediate situation of the caste and confirms Sartre's perception of the profoundly "anti-official" nature of anti-Semitism. Or, as he puts it elsewhere, "Let us affirm that anti-Semitism is a passionate effort to realize national unity *against* the division of society into classes."[48] Castro, with an anthology of convincing examples, has demonstrated the identity of the strange peasant honor that is peculiar to the Spanish seventeenth-century theater with the myth of "limpieza de sangre," a myth of equality in blood that is antagonistic to presumptions of superiority based on class or vocational positions. As for wealth, it was both despised and envied, an invitation first to mob violence and later to Inquisitional rapacity.

With this situation in mind, we may begin to grasp the profound difference between the circumstances and self-vision of our sixteenth-century *conversos* and those of the seventeenth- and eighteenth-century Protestants as described by Max Weber. Justifica-

---

y cristiana, lograsen el alivio a sus necesidades y el camino por donde alcanzar el inapreciable tesoro de la sana moral y letras. . . . Vistió a todos los niños con un traje decente y uniforme . . . les servía de almorzar con sus propias manos. . . . Despues acudían a la escuela para aprender las primeras letras, y los proficientes se dedicaban a estudiar gramática latina y filosofía con el padre Contreras (el primer superior de dicho asilo)" (M.A. Alarcón, *Biografía compendiada de la Excma. Sra. Doña Teresa Enríquez*, Valencia, 1895, pp. 43-44). The Duchess, we might add in passing, as the daughter of the third "Admiral of Castile," belonged to a well-known family of *converso* nobility.

[48] *Réflexions*, p. 193.

tion of one's life in terms of financial success and attainment of salvation through faithfulness to one's mundane calling were simply not admitted by the society which the *conversos* served. As Castro puts it (speaking of medieval Spanish Jews):

> It is a serious affair when the services we lend or are lent to us do not mesh with a system of mutual loyalties or common values, as they did when the feudal organization was an authentic reality. In important areas of Spanish life, loyalty and esteem were replaced by the tyranny of the lord and the flattering servility of the Jews, forced to pay this price to subsist. This false situation was fatal, and equally so was the situation in which the common people had to accept a group whom they hated and despised as their superiors, legally entitled to prey regularly through collection of taxes on their meager resources. And the more evident the superiority of Jews turned out to be, the worse it became.[49]

The roots of hostility were, thus, centuries deep, the natural and simple resentment of the oppressed *villano* having by the time of Rojas evolved into a complex system of negative estimations and automatic social reactions. The *converso,* in other words, not only lived under suspicion; he lived under disesteem as well. And only among his fellows, within his own "counter-society," could he come to respect himself and at times assert with either violence or irony his damaged sense of superiority.

Abundant examples of hierarchical strife between the two castes will emerge in later chapters. For now it will suffice to listen to one insignificant yet representative altercation between the bookseller, Luis (Abraham) García, and a guard in the prison of the Inquisition. The date, as we remember, was 1514, and the spark which kindled their passions was a lack of water in the jug with which the cell was provided:

> Luis García insisted on saying that this witness and the Licentiate Mariana [the same Inquisitor that was to fall to the lot of Alvaro de Montalbán] wanted to kill him because they had a grudge against him. This witness replied: "¡Mejor os sería

[49] *Realidad,* edn. I, p. 473; *Structure,* pp. 496-497.

135

perder esos cojones que tenéis!" [a very profane way of saying, "You'd be better off if you didn't try to be so tough!"] At this, Luis García replied with insults, and after that words gave way to deeds, this witness throwing a plate at the prisoner which missed him. Again they fell to with insults and blows, both emerging from the fight torn and bruised, but Luis García still continued to say that a New Christian was far better than an Old one, since the new one sprang from the lineage of Christ and the old ones from Gentiles. "You lie like a knavish rogue," this witness replied, "for the sole of the shoe of the most humble Christian peasant is worth more than all of you in your big houses."[50]

The social history of Rojas' Spain was a texture of just such forgotten clashes between castes.

In order to comprehend the disdain that the mass of Old Christians felt for the *converso* caste and for its typical vocations, we must be careful not to think in terms of contemporary prejudice or of our own minority groups. The American sociologist Everett Stonequist significantly chose the adjective "marginal" to describe the individual who is "condemned to live in two worlds" and compelled "to assume in relation to the worlds he lives in the role of a cosmopolitan and a stranger."[51] The negro, the gypsy, the acculturated Indian, and, in some cases, the Jew, according to Stonequist, exist marginally within the United States in that they at once belong and are treated as not belonging. This, as we suggested, was not the case of the *conversos*. Although the Montalbanes might be called marginal insofar as they were members of a self-conscious minority, the

[50] The original text reads as follows: "Insistió Luis García en decir que si tenían ganas de matarlo este testigo y el licenciado Mariana por malquerencia que le tienen y que le respondió este testigo: '¡Mejor os sería perder esos cojones que tenéis!' A esto respondió Luis García con insultos y de allí pasaron a los hechos, arrojándole este testigo un plato que no le acertó. Trabáronse de nuevo en insultos y golpes, saliendo ambos de la pelea maltrechos y desgarrados, y no sin que todavía Luis García dijese que *más valía un cristiano nuevo que uno viejo* ya que ellos, los nuevos venían del linaje de Cristo y los viejos de los gentiles. 'Mientes como un bellaco,' respondióle este testigo, 'que *más vale el más pequeñito labrador cristiano en la suela del zapato que vosotros* en la casa. . . .' "

[51] Everett V. Stonequist, *The Marginal Man*, New York, 1937 (intro. by R. E. Park), pp. xvii-xviii.

136

lives they led and the vocations they pursued were hardly on the margin. Instead they were at the very heart of things, essential functionaries at once honored and suspected, trusted and resented. Indeed, it might almost be said that the embittered and suspicious society they served was marginal to them. In an anti-Semitic tract of the time, the *Diálogo entre Laín Calvo y Nuño Rasura,*[52] the statues of two medieval warrior heroes engage in shocked and envious conversation as they look from a cathedral perch at the modern world. In their view it is a world dedicated to alien and repugnant occupations, a world in the hands of the *conversos* who ride back and forth on fine horses and dress in decadent finery. It is these two petrified traditionalists who find themselves on the margin, a position from which their only possible means of regaining control is Inquisitional intervention.

Thus, we observe again from a different perspective the paradox noted previously. It was the sociologically singular situation of this caste to be at once wholly inside and wholly outside the society in which it lived,[53] at once empowered to make the most crucial and delicate decisions and yet subject to the arbitrary power of the Inquisitors and to the vilification of the "miserable stupid masses who worshiped them."[54] Or as Albert Sicroff concludes from a different point of view, "Terrible indeed was the irony of Spain's efforts to purify her Christian society which, despite mass riots, enforced baptisms, discriminatory pure blood statutes, inquisitions, and ultimately the Edict of Expulsion, only seemed to drive the 'impure' Jewish element ever deeper into the controlling nerve-centers of her civil and ecclesiastical life."[55]

---

[52] See Chap. II, n. 18. In addition to gross sexual details, the two noble statues criticize principally the reduction of all values to monetary terms. Marriages are arranged to keep fortunes in the family, titles are bought and sold on the Royal market, and so on. For the "Celestinista" it is curious to note that the writer seemed to consider "mal de madre" a *converso* expression (p. 166).

[53] Caro Baroja, in passing, refers to the *converso* situation as "contradictory and unique" because of this paradox (II, 37). His failure to go on to meditate at length on this essential anomaly is to my mind a major weakness of the book, a book which sorts out an admirable abundance of facts without conferring on them a consistent sociological structure.

[54] *Artes,* p. 156.

[55] "Clandestine Judaism" (see Chap. II, n. 39), p. 125.

✒ Freedom and Dissent

As Caro Baroja points out, there were surely as many different shades of sentimental reaction to the anomalous situation of the
caste as there were individuals forced to live together within it:[56]

> It is when one finishes presenting the whole gamut of attitudes
> and thoughts which can be observed in the *conversos* and
> their descendants that one can realize better how false the his-
> tories are that present them to us with homogeneous char-
> acteristics. No, the human soul, however much it is coerced
> (or perhaps the more it is coerced), can react in a thousand
> different ways, and this is the only guaranteee that we have in
> a world like the present one, in which we are again subject to
> countless coercive procedures, . . . that man is free in essence;
> at least in relation to other men, if not in the face of blind and
> imperious Nature. He is free to be a Christian mystic, like the
> Blessed Juan de Avila, or a Jewish mystic like Abraham Car-
> doso; to be a heretic from Catholicism like Doctor Cazalla or
> to separate himself from Judaism like Spinoza; to be a skeptic
> like Montaigne or to deny the immortality of the soul like
> Uriel; to burn at the stake or to apostatize. And no desire for
> unity, whether it be that of the Church or the Synagogue, the
> State or the Inquisition, will prevent this liberty from mani-
> festing itself as the most precious gift at his disposal.[57]

The debate on freedom versus determinism to which Caro Baroja
has just invited us by its very nature envisions the caste (or the two
separated but genetically related castes) as made up of a con-
glomeration of independent consciousnesses. And while seen in this
way such is indeed the case, for our purposes it is indispensable to
meditate for a moment on reactions at another level, a level somewhere in between the monad and the collectivity. By this I mean

[56] Francisco Márquez in his *Investigaciones* (p. 44) poses this problem
with his customary precision: "If we can succeed in establishing the Jewish
origins of a particular person, it is probable that, far from having solved a
problem, we have only reached the threshold of the really decisive questions:
In what forms and ways does this Jewishness manifest itself? Does it reveal
itself by mere chance? In short it is necessary to pose afterwards the problem,
always difficult, of the isolated, concrete person with its multiple and profound implications."

[57] II, 244.

specifically that we must try to classify not conscious choices but rather kinds of more or less spontaneous reactions to the imposed historical and social situation. Within the caste as a whole can we not perceive patterns of response, typical ways of being a *converso*?[58]

I have three to offer: first, the aggressive resentment proposed by Francisco de Villalobos ("la venganza de un marrano"); second, ironical withdrawal and camouflage; and, third, acceptance, partial or complete. Sociologists pursuing other ends and with professional preparation would surely insist on a more truthfully complex scheme, while literary critics are taught to believe that what really matters are the infinite individual shades of feeling and self-expression. I defer to both of them, but the desperateness of our present enterprise—our pursuit of a man who has all but disappeared—demands some sort of rudimentary categorization. Like a police artist sketching simplified criminal features, in attempting to re-invent the person suggested by our reading of *La Celestina*, we have no choice but to employ this means of circumscribing the missing life.

Aggressive resentment (along with its sentimental companions, scorn and hatred) is perhaps most directly expressed in the *De vita felici* of Juan de Lucena. Lucena was a Royal Chronicler for the Catholic Monarchs, the father of Luis de Lucena (with whom we shall be concerned as a classmate and fellow author of Rojas at Salamanca), and probably a relative of the printer in Hebrew of the same name. In any case, whereas Alvaro de Montalbán repressed his feelings as well as he could and Villalobos projected his into the self-made role of *chocarrero*, Lucena apparently in a position of power, displayed his sentiments without inhibition or transformation. When he discusses lineage, for example, he points out that descent from the Romans "who sinned in bestial ways" or from the Goths or the twelve peers of France, "each more bestial than the other," is highly esteemed. Such a person is a "gentil hombre," "hardly less than an Apollo," but if a man be of Hebrew descent,

[58] Márquez goes on to say: "The fact that one was a New Christian in the fifteenth century presupposed, for the majority, being framed within a panorama of acute and vital urgencies towards which it was necessary to adopt given intellectual attitudes and, what was even more serious, a norm of conduct" (p. 44). These, in effect, unlike the individual, free consciousness, may be subject to classification.

139

no matter how virtuous and wise he may be, they call him a *"marrano* which is less than the dust." And he goes on to exclaim: "Oh ungrateful Christians who say such things, may their eyes be blinded!" (¡Marrados tengan los ojos!).[59] Against the disesteem of society, here is verbally relentless *venganza*.

But what about Rojas? If in the preceding chapter we observed him effacing himself while under suspicion, we may now dicuss the ironically indirect counterattack which he and others—less daring than a Lucena—mounted against their hostile society. Actually, I would propose, the possibility of *La Celestina* depended on the mutual interaction of both attitudes, on both prudent withdrawal and mordant self-expression. The clearest example of Rojas' ironical undermining of accepted values occurs in a speech in Act III, a speech surely better understood by his family and *socios* than by those who today see in it only an indication of the date of composition. As we remember, Celestina has remarked on the danger to the servants which might result from Calisto's passion. Sempronio, alarmed, replies, "To the devil with his love affair! . . . He may be suffering now, but time will take care of that." After which he rather unnecessarily goes on to expand upon the everlasting war of time with values:

> Good and evil, prosperity and adversity, glory and grief, all lose the strength they start out with. Wondrous events awaited with high hopes are forgotten as soon as they're over. Every day we see new things happen or hear about them, and then we pass them by and leave them behind. Time makes them small, even makes them doubtful. Would you be so awestruck if you were told there had been an earthquake or something

[59] *Libro de la vida beata,* ed. A. Paz y Melia, Madrid, 1892, *Opúsculos literarios,* p. 148. Rafael Lapesa has recently commented on Lucena's style and on his unorthodox defense of the immortality of the soul in his "Sobre Juan de Lucena," *Collected Studies in Honour of Américo Castro's Eightieth Year,* ed. M.P. Hornik, Oxford, 1965. In another article seen since writing the above, Angel Alcalá offers the fascinating hypothesis (based on a number of surprising factual coincidences) that the printer and the chronicler-author are one and the same person. However, until further facts appear, this is only an hypothesis. In the trial printed in part (along with that of Alvaro de Montalbán) by Serrano y Sanz, the latter's activities at the Royal court are completely ignored in a situation which might well have resulted in their being mentioned. See "Juan de Lucena y el pre-erasmismo español," *RHM,* xxxiv (1968), 108-131. Both scholars provide abundant additional bibliography.

like that, that you would not soon forget it? I mean things like: the river is frozen over, the blind man can see again, your father just died, a lightning bolt has struck, Granada has been taken, the King is coming today, he has won a battle against the Turks, the bridge has been washed away, so and so has become a bishop, Pedro has been robbed, Inés has hanged herself, Cristobal got drunk. You can't tell me that three days later or the second time he hears about it, anyone will still be amazed. Everything is like that; everything passes on in the same way; everything is forgotten; everything stays behind as we go on.[60]

To have included the Conquest of Granada, the great epic event of the age and the historical climax to all of Spain's past, as an example of the fragility of human meaning comparable to "Cristobal got drunk" is a really extraordinary denial of the estimations of the time. To have treated it merely as one more news item in the senseless course of daily history has a kind of ironic glee about it that clearly corresponds to a feeling of *venganza*.

As for the statement in the Letter that the author's intention is to provide the "conterráneos . . . de nuestra común patria" with armor against Love, the reader when he emerges from the full twenty-one-act experience will find it hard to believe that Rojas thought love could—or even should!—be defeated. Not only is there implicit tenderness in his contemplation of the end of the "process" (as we shall see in Chapter VII), but also all along love serves his ironical purpose. Rather than being castigated as a vice, it is used as an acid of concentrated biological strength which (like the hunger of Lazarillo) etches out the manifold pretenses and hypocrisies of life in urban company. It is a surgeon's knife which in Rojas' skilled hands slices into the rotten core of society and lays it open for our inspection.

How Rojas himself might have explained the ultimate nature of what was wrong, who was responsible, and what could be done about it is not our present concern. What matters is to understand how he, like the fully anonymous author of the *Lazarillo*, created from a distance at once serene and corrosive. These were ironists, not satirists—if we think of satire in terms of John Middleton

[60] The translation was made for me by Edmund L. King.

141

Murry's definition[61] and Pero López de Ayala's practice as criticism of "society by reference to an ideal." Neither author really proposes social health as a possible or desirable state. Only suicide—physical in the case of Melibea, spiritual in that of Lazarillo—provides a possibility of escape from a world in which no values are left. Lineage, honor, flaunted piety, social eminence, once shattered by the creative counterattack, turn out to have been masks over nothing at all. Erasure of the self both by authors and characters is concomitant with an erasure of meaning.[62]

The third category of reaction illustrates Stonequist's notion that the mind of a "marginal man is a crucible in which two different and refractory cultures may be said to melt and, either wholly or in part, fuse."[63] Resentful rejection and ironical devaluation of the surrounding society was inevitably accompanied by partial assimilation of the points of view of the dominant caste. I do not refer only to those *conversos* who, like Bishop Pablo de Santa María or Micer Pedro de la Caballería, became fanatics in the new faith and proceeded to attack their own kind.[64] Self-redefinition into a rigid and aggressive mold, although a phenomenon not unfamiliar among those who submit to conversion of any sort, hardly characterized the Montalbanes and their kindred families. The only

[61] *The Problem of Style*, Oxford, 1960. p. 159.

[62] Everett Stonequist in the book previously cited (n. 51) remarks as follows on the aggressive social criticism of "marginal men": "Because of his in-between situation, the marginal man may become an acute and able critic of the dominant group and its culture. This is because he combines the knowledge and insight of the insider with the critical attitude of the outsider. . . . He is skillful in noting the contradictions and the hypocrisies of the dominant culture. The gap between moral pretensions and actual achievements jumps to his eye" (pp. 154-155). If this is true of marginal men in general, how much more applicable such a statement must be to minds thrust into the paradoxical social situation of the Spanish *conversos* in the early 16th century! From which we might further conclude that the much discussed problem of Rojas' maturity or immaturity is really irrelevant. To be what Rojas was and to exist as he had to exist was to be more mature than most of us ever get to be.

[63] Park, in introduction to Stonequist, *Marginal Man*, p. xv.

[64] As Castro maintains (although the point has caused great antagonism among scholars committed to a morally absolute history), many of the Inquisitors were themselves of *converso* origin. The whole concept of *limpieza* and the concomitant notion of *castas* central to Spain's historical peculiarity are, he suggests, Jewish.

possible exception visible in the documents is Iñigo de Monçón. The reaction which now matters more to us is something quite different: acceptance by *conversos*—at times half-unwittingly, at times half-hypocritically—of the values and ways of behavior of their Old Christian neighbors and oppressors.

Aside from enforced living together and enforced striving—often with alien ways and means—towards the same national goals, surely the central channel of axiological osmosis between the two castes was a common language. For *conversos* the built-in meanings and values of the words and idioms which formed the very pattern of their consciousness necessarily brought about at least partial acceptance of the culture in which they had grown up. Even for antagonistic individuals, linguistic community involved the speaker or writer in tacit dialogue with much that he rejected, a dialogue depending upon agreed on terms and evaluations. In this sense the *converso* caste (and particularly *converso* writers in their acute grandeur and misery) resembled the members of that literary generation which produced the Irish Renaissance. When Rojas speaks of his predecessors (the several possible authors of Act I) as "learned Castilians" he is acknowledging the community which on another level (that of the Conquest of Granada) he rejects. It is more than a coincidence, I would propose, that at least three well-known *converso* intellectuals, Juan de Valdés, Mateo Alemán, and Juan de Luna, all in the tradition of Nebrija, were as concerned with the nature and improvement of Castilian as had been their Jewish forefathers who had defended and illustrated it four centuries earlier at the court of Alfonso el Sabio.[65]

Hence, the conservation of the Spanish language and its oral literature in the form of ballads (some of them on themes from the Christian epic poems of Castile) for centuries among Sephardic colonies all over the world. Hence, the works of Quevedo in the

---

[65] Alonso de Proaza in his closing verses states that no famous Roman or Greek dramatist equalled "this poet in his Castilian." The three books referred to are Mateo Alemán's *Ortografía española*, Juan de Valdés' *Diálogo de la lengua*, and Juan de Luna's *Arte breve y compendiosa para aprender a leer, escribir, pronunciar y hablar la lengua española*, London, 1623. For an account of Jewish cultivation of Castilian at the court of Alphonse the Wise, see *Realidad*, edn. I, pp. 460 ff. Castro believes (although there is no direct evidence) that Nebrija, characteristically named after the town of his birth, was of *converso* origin.

library of Spinoza and the sixteenth- and seventeenth-century flourishing of Judeo-Spanish literature. And hence, above all, the laments for Spain as a lost homeland, a *común patria*, by those whom the Edict of Expulsion or Inquisitional pressure afterwards sent into exile. The possibility of violently negative (Juan de Lucena) or ironically creative (Fernando de Rojas) dissent and self-separation was open to all who lived within the *converso* situation. But, at the same time, one had to dissent in a language which gave inherent value to much that one wanted to reject, to take the offensive against values which were not only "theirs" but at the same time linguistically "ours." The almost limitless stylistic complexity of *La Celestina* and the *Lazarillo*, the tiered layers of significance lying beneath their verbal signs, can only be understood as suddenly possible in terms of this dilemma. Ambiguity is here not an abstraction for critics or a strategy for poets but a way of existence.

"Because I am an *hidalgo* ..."

A principal area of acceptance and fusion (and one well exemplified among our families) was the value of nobility. Within the paradoxical *converso* situation—that is to say, the situation of being simultaneously central and marginal—it was natural that the estimations most readily taken over were those that adhered to the surface of being. By which I mean values relating to confrontation of the self with others: honor, rank, dress, presumption, position, posture. Against surrounding disesteem, in case after case, a façade of nobility was erected, defended, and after a while believed in. "They treat themselves as *hidalgos* ..." and "They represent themselves as *hidalgos* ..." are phrases which anyone reading *probanza* testimony encounters again and again. And from there to feeling themselves actually to be *hidalgos* was a short step. Thus, a Diagarias (Diego Arias de Avila, the immensely wealthy treasurer of Henry IV) may have had himself baptized with a name from the epic tradition with a certain cynicism; and, when his grandson purchased the castle of Puñonrostro along with the right to entitle himself its count, he was surely aware of his own brashness. But after a generation or so, the holders of the title (descendants not only of his but also, through a much discussed marriage, relatives of the

Marquis of Santillana)[66] were convinced of their own nobility.[67] They and everybody else knew the origin of their lineage, but the earlier assertion had with the years gained acceptance.

Even more striking is the well-known fact that Jews and *conversos* who later fled Spain because they could not bring themselves to live within their new faith took with them a strong sense of *hidalguía.* Sephardic claims to aristocracy are proverbial, and it is therefore only momentarily surprising that (as M. J. Benardete informs us) a large number of tombstones in the Jewish cemetery in Salonica should display elaborate Spanish blazonry.[68] We can only conclude that, while the estrangement of one's soul and the intimacy of one's dietary habits could not be transformed short of complete assimilation, social self-presentation was more easily modified. Once Jewish dress and ghetto living had been discarded, confrontation with a hostile and suspicious society created new defensive roles which were soon so genuine and such a matter of pride that they were not abandoned even when no longer needed.

Another aspect of the same fusion is the exaltation in Christian terms of Hebrew ancestry. Those who refused to camouflage their lineage (in the years before the Inquisition and the discriminatory edicts of exclusion made such action indispensable) often took the opposite path and boasted of it as the oldest and least contaminated. Castro discusses at length the many proud references to *"linaje"* and *"alcurnia"* among Jews and known *conversos,* references which gave Spanish terms and connotations to a racial pride that was originally Hebraic. Thus, Rabbi Mosé Arragel in the pro-

---

[66] Rodrigo Cota, the author of the Celestinesque *Diálogo entre el amor y un viejo* and, on that account, a leading candidate for the authorship of Act I, immortalized in a caustic poem this marriage of a son (or perhaps nephew) of Diagarias to a relative of Cardinal don Pero González de Mendoza. He had not been invited to the wedding. See the "Epitalamio satírico," ed. Foulché-Delbosc, *RH,* 1894, pp. 69-72.

[67] Among those scandalized by a later Cardinal Mendoza's debunking of the genealogical pretensions of the nobility in his *Tizón de la nobleza,* Barcelona, 1880 (written in 1560 because a close relative had been denied admission to a restricted military order), was one Bachelor Camándulas (obviously a pseudonym), who accused the Cardinal in a satirical ballad of being a second Judas who had "betrayed his brothers into the hands of the people" (p. 204). With this pamphlet, the Cardinal had exploded a myth which members of the nobility had tacitly agreed to believe in.

[68] M. J. Benardete, *Hispanic Culture and the Character of the Sephardic Jews,* New York, 1953, pp. 43-45.

145

logue to his *Biblia* ascribes to the Jews "quatro preheminencias": "en linaje, en riqueza, en bondades, en sciencia."[69] Lineage significantly is put in first place. So too, according to Castro, the poet and aphorist, Sem Tob, believed Jews to be "fidalgos de natura."[70] Mosén Diego de Valera who was at once a *converso* intellectual and an exemplary fifteenth-century knight errant (wandering around Europe, challenging local champions to single combat, and enlisting in the crusades of foreign kings), in his translation of Honoré Bonet's compendium of chivalric doctrine, the *Arbre de batailles*, adds a section of coats-of-arms of famous past heroes. Along with King Arthur, Hector, and others we also find those of Joshua, King David, and Judas Maccabeus.[71] At least as far as roles and self-definitions for the benefit of others were concerned, such Jews and *conversos* were (as we surmised) no less Spanish and men of their time than those who opposed them. They may have been alienated, but in their language and the roles they played, they were not alien.

This particular "fusion" of values had become so commonplace by the seventeenth century that the prestige of *hidalguía* itself was increasingly controversial. Castro and others point out numerous passages in the theater of Lope and his successors in which peasants encounter *hidalgos* and allude more or less openly to their tainted ancestry—merely because they were *hidalgos*.[72] It is difficult for modern audiences to grasp such slurs. They have forgotten the fifteenth- and sixteenth-century social history which now pre-

---

[69] *Realidad*, edn. I, p. 466; *Structure*, p. 489.

[70] *Ibid.*, p. 532.

[71] See El Márqués de Laurencín, "Mosén Diego de Valera y el *Arbol de batallas*," BRAH, LXXVI (1920), 294-308.

[72] It was natural, as Madariaga points out (*Vida del muy magnífico señor Cristobal Colón*, Buenos Aires, 1940, p. 183), for men confronted by a hostile and suspicious society to try to find effective and convincing defenses in their own tradition that would be understandable to their antagonists. Ideal for this purpose was the Jewish sense of undefiled lineage easily translatable into chivalresque and feudal terms. Jewish pride in genealogy (so irritating, as we have seen, to humble and obscurely born peasant neighbors) was thus identifiable with the arrogance of the noble families with which they intermarried. Salomón ben Verga has a Spanish King remark ruefully: "Everybody knows that no people on earth can prove the purity of their origin and lineage as well as these unhappy Jews." Castro, Caro Baroja (I, 401 ff.), and Lea (I, 152) all comment on this aspect of the encounter between the two castes.

occupies us; they have forgotten, to be specific, that every *converso* family that could afford it, in one way or another (by bribery, by purchase, by marriage, or by sheer self-assertion) had attained *hidalgo* status. Nor were the two classifications (in spite of the Francos' sad fate) as mutually exclusive as they might theoretically seem. The vocation of *mayordomo*, for instance, with its steward-ship of castles and distant properties often involved the sword and command of armed forces as well as the pen and accounts. Diego de Rojas from the Puebla de Montalbán (a contemporary of uncer-tain relationship to the Bachelor) presents a typical case. Begin-ning as household administrator for the Lords of Montalbán, he afterwards became a captain under "el Gran Capitán," Gonzalo de Córdoba, and *"alcaide"* or seneschal of a fortress. The several wit-nesses who recall his career (in a *probanza* to be examined later) seem to regard it as a perfectly natural transition.

Adoption of Christian class characteristics did not exempt the caste of *conversos* from continued involvement in Spain's endemic social antagonisms. As we shall see in future chapters, the fusion of *converso* with *hidalgo* led on the part of the *villanos* to a cor-responding fusion of anti-Semitism with rebellion against exploita-tion. It was natural in what Américo Castro aptly terms a "conflic-tive age" that the scorned and underprivileged peasants should respond to their neighbors' pretensions by asserting for themselves a new and revolutionary kind of nobility: *limpieza,* a lack of defile-ment of the bloodline which they believed to be guaranteed pre-cisely by the humility of their origins.[73] It was this consciousness of being unpolluted children of the earth that the inhabitants of Fuenteovejuna pitted against their Commander's doubtful quarter-ings and that was at the root of the uniquely Spanish notion of peasant honor.[74] Nevertheless, what was admired and admirable

[73] *De la edad conflictiva*, p. 36.

[74] Domínguez Ortiz cites a protesting 17th-century document: "In Spain there are two kinds of nobility: one which is major and is called '*hidalguía*' and one which is minor and which we call cleanliness of blood, the posses-sors of which we call Old Christians. And, although it is more honorable to possess the first (*hidalguía*), it is more insulting to lack the second, because in Spain we value a commoner with pure blood more than an *hidalgo* who is not of pure blood" (p. 196). Villalobos was more amused than bitter when a certain "acemilero mancebo que tenía" became alarmed and disdainfully refused when his master teased him by offering him his daughter's hand ("Los problemas," BAE, vol. 36, p. 425).

in the theater was malignant in social practice.[75] The mania of *limpieza* not only caused an infinite amount of personal suffering, but also, when it went to the extremes of which we saw a sample in the Palavesín *expediente*, it brought about a built-in and historically debilitating falsification of interpersonal relations. It has even, as we have seen, marred much contemporary literary and historical scholarship.

These long term reactions against *converso hidalguía* described by Castro, Sicroff, and others again surpass our present concerns. What matters directly to us is something much less easily determinable: its degree of authenticity as a way of comprehending one's place in the world. To what extent and in what manner did Fernando de Rojas view himself as an *hidalgo*? Since in his case we know far more about his grandchildren than we do about him, let us begin by considering the spectacular parallel furnished by the Madrid branch of the Montalbanes—into which his daughter Catalina married. The founder of the Madrid family was a first cousin of Alvaro's, another grandson of the original Garcí Alvarez, named Alonso de Montalbán. During the reconquest of Granada, he served with such distinction that he was given command of a Galician contingent. In the words of one of the *probanza* witnesses, "the present witness took part in the wars of the reconquest of the Kingdom of Granada and saw how Alonso de Montalbán was a captain of the soldiers from Galicia, and afterwards they gave him the post of Royal Master of Lodgings" (*Aposentador real*).[76] Thus

---

[75] Other examples may be found in Domínguez Ortiz, p. 199; Castro, *De la edad conflictiva*, pp. 205 ff.; and Caro Baroja, II, 278. At the end of Act II of Lope's "Niño inocente de la Guardia," admirably studied by Edward Glaser (*BHS*, XXXII, 1955), the equation *converso = hidalgo* is particularly explicit.

[76] Alonso de Montalbán; Riva, II, 420. In the *Cuentas* of Gonzalo de Baeza, ed. A. de la Torre and E. A. de la Torre, Madrid, 1956, II, 318, Alonso de Montalbán is mentioned as having received 5,000 maravedís in 1496. In 1503 he was paid for lodging certain members of the Royal household in his home (p. 578). Another curious reflection of a family quarrel is furnished by the *Registro general del Sello* in Simancas for 1487 (ed. M. A. de Mendoza Lassalle, Valladolid, 1950-59): "A las justicias de Madrid a petición de Elvira Hurtado, mujer de Alonso de Montalbán, aposentador real, que desea no permitan a su madre vender bienes de la ligítima a cambio de mantenerla y vestirla" (262). Other Montalbánes mentioned are two Toledan cloth merchants, Juan and Alonso, who frequently sold their wares to the Royal family (see pp. 471 and 545). The former is probably not the same as the

a successful career of military service ended with Alonso de Montalbán's joining that group of able *conversos*—the Royal Secretary, Gabriel de Santangel; the Queen's confessor, Fray Hernando de Talavera; the legal theorist and lawmaker, Doctor Alonso Díaz de Montalvo; and many others[77]—who administered the court and kingdom of the Catholic Monarchs. It was during his life in the field, and in the new world of the court, that Alonso de Montalbán took on the appearance, the manners, the appurtenances, and eventually the reality of *hidalguía*.

By 1548, some twenty-seven years after his death, Alonso de Montalbán had become a respected and honorable forebearer proudly recollected by his grandchildren and great-grandchildren in their *"probanza de hidalguía."* His sumptuous house in the parish of San Ginés with its stone coat-of-arms ("three leaves and a *fleur-de-lys* and a bar crossed by two mouths of dragons") over the door was their ancestral mansion. There he had "treated himself" as an *hidalgo* and, like his son and his grandson in following years, had enjoyed proudly the privileges and exemptions to which he was entitled.[78] Nor did any of the friendly and probably well paid witnesses to these facts find it necessary to remember the catastrophic picnic in 1525 when the family name was tarnished. Like the numerous Montalbanes who had been burnt after death or shamefully reconciled in the Puebla, that event, if not forgotten, was irrelevant to the formal certification of status now being

---

Juan de Montalbán, "husband of Juana Díaz and father of Juana and Francisca de Montalbán," who dwelt in the parish of San Ginés in 1544 (Serrano y Sanz, p. 256).

[77] See, among many other studies, *Investigaciones*, p. 54 and Amador de los Ríos, pp. 671-84.

[78] In his brief and pro forma statement attacking the petition the "fiscal" bases himself on the same point: "I say that the aforesaid Alonso de Montalbán the grandson and his father and grandfather were and are of the lineage and caste of '*pecheros*,' and, if on occasion they avoided paying taxes, it was because their grandfather was a servant of the Catholic Monarchs and they allowed them to do so." The phrases "tratarse como hidalgo" or "representarse como hidalgo" occur not only here but in the *probanzas* of the Francos, the other Rojas of the Puebla, and the Cepedas. In the last, a witness states: "Viben como buenos muy limpiamente e tienen e an tenido cavallos muy buenos e sus personas muy atabiadas, e se tratan como hidalgos e aun como cavalleros" (N. Alonso Cortés, "Pleitos de los Cepedas," *BRAE*, xxv, 1946, p. 91). The irony of such testimony is almost audible.

149

sought.[79] And in Madrid there was no vindictive counterpart of don Antonio de Rojas intent on interfering. Three generations of royal favor and administrative responsibility (the post of *aposentador* was still held by a member of the family),[80] three generations of inherited wealth, and three generations of scrupulous conformity were now to be recognized officially. That was all there was to it.

Despite parish gossips, the Montalbanes were what they seemed —or wanted to seem. They travelled to the new world with a retinue of servants;[81] they established their own private chapel within the church of San Ginés (the "Capilla del Lagarto" which still exists today with its stuffed alligator brought back from America)[82] where their weddings, burials, and baptisms were celebrated lavishly. It is impossible—since they left no trial records or masterpieces of dialogue behind them—to fathom their minds or hidden feelings, but on the level of being called by Sartre, "l'être pour

---

[79] Otis Green, in his "Fernando de Rojas, *converso* and *hidalgo*," *HR*, xv (1947), 384-387, is concerned to establish Rojas as a reputable *hidalgo* no different from any other (thereby, one supposes, saving him for the "Western Tradition") that he goes to the other extreme and overlooks the delicate rites of legal transition that had to be so carefully prepared. The two categories could be and in many cases were brought together, but to present them as unproblematically identical indicates a grave lapse both in investigation and meditation. The failure of the Francos is a case in point. Green's further conclusion that, because Rojas was an *hidalgo*, "We may safely assume . . . that he did not know 'cosa alguna de judaísmo o del rito de él'" (p. 385) represents a scholarly carelessness (given information easily available about life in the Puebla de Montalbán) that is surprising in an individual so intransigent with others.

[80] The last traceable *aposentador* was probably Melchior de Montalbán, the eldest son of Pero de Montalbán's second marriage (to Alvaro's daughter, Constança Núñez). One of the *probanza* witnesses states, "que no conoze a otros dos hermanos deste que litiga [the grandson, Alonso, mentioned in n. 78] que biden casados en la dicha villa de Madrid, y el uno es aposentador de su Alteza. . . ."

[81] *Catálogo de pasajeros*, ii, 4563: "Alonso de Montalván, hijo de Pedro de Montalván y de Isabel de Monzón, vecino de Madrid, a la provincia de Cartagena. Lleva consigo dos criados naturales de Madrid y Villafranca. Dimosle licencia que pasasen por quanto parece por los libros desta casa *que otras vezes han pasado*. —7 Marzo [1538]." Italics mine.

[82] See n. 38. In spite of several serious fires, this chapel still exists. I am grateful to don Fernando del Valle Lersundi for pointing it out to me. The importance of the Montalbanes is also manifest in the instructions for a lavish funeral given in detail in the 1528 will of Pero de Montalbán (Serrano y Sanz, p. 298).

150

autrui," they were *hidalgos*. In this sense their *probanza* should be understood less as an elaborately arranged social deception than as a certification of social truth.

We may now return to Fernando de Rojas whose conversion into an honorable ancestor was also (although more timidly, as we have seen) attempted by his grandchildren. Biographically speaking, it would be erroneous to limit his range of reactions to the capacity for ironical withdrawal and veiled counterattack that is revealed in the pages of *La Celestina*. There was for one thing the strong vocational dedication to his "principal estudio," and along with it— as the result of a life-long successful performance of the role of small town *hidalgo*—a concern with status. The picture of Rojas' life that emerges from the inventory of his household made at the time of his death supports this supposition with concrete details. Indeed, in a number of ways the possessions of the Bachiller resemble those of that most illustrious of all *hidalgos*, Alonso Quijano "el bueno." The two "lanzones viejos," the pikes, the crossbows for hunting, and the copies of *Amadís, Esplandián, Primaleón*, along with some five other romances of chivalry will all seem familiar to readers of Spanish literature.

In addition, we may note that Rojas' eldest son, the Licentiate Francisco, had no doubts about his rights and privileges as an *hidalgo*. When in his old age he was threatened with imprisonment for unpaid debts, he replied: "Because I am an *hidalgo*, because I and my forebearers are known to be such, and because I have held noble judicial and legal office, I cannot be arrested for civil indebtedness."[83] The claim is convincing not merely because it was upheld by the *corregidor* of Talavera (probably a friend or a friend of friends) but because it would hardly have been made if those bringing suit had had a good chance of disputing it. And, if the son felt at once confident and proud of his *hidalguía*, these were feelings which he must at least in part have inherited from his father. Like their cousins, the Montalbanes, and like the Francos (if they had been successful), the Rojas were *hidalgos*—in that they lived as such. In this sense their two *probanzas* testify as much to a social reality as to a social fiction.

The frozen society in which Rojas lived was acutely aware of rank, that is to say, of each individual as a fixed social image to be

[83] VLA, 34-9.

treated in a predetermined way. Precedence and protocol were matters of unquestioned importance.[84] And Rojas, precisely because of his creative concern with the psychic mutations beneath the roles of servant or mistress, did not fail to share in this awareness. That he esteemed his *hidalguía* as a fount of personal worth may well be doubted by readers of *La Celestina*, but, that he insisted in his daily intercourse with the world that he be treated in accordance with the rules, may be taken for granted. In the "*probanza de hidalguía*" three witnesses give similar explanations for his leaving the Puebla and moving to Talavera. In the words of one of them:

> The present witness has heard tell that the town council of the Puebla de Montalbán and the collectors of the head tax and Royal assessments [from which *hidalgos* were exempted] insisted that the aforesaid Bachelor Fernando de Rojas contribute because of the property he owned in the town, and the aforesaid Bachelor Fernando de Rojas because he was an *hidalgo* always refused to pay the Royal head tax or to allow his property to be sequestered as a penalty. In the same way the present witness knows and saw himself that, on account of the bad treatment which the lord of the aforesaid town who was called don Alonso[85] meted out to the *hidalgos,* some of them moved away. One called Hortiz [*un fulano Hortiz*][86] went to Toledo and one called Sahabedra went to the town of Torrijos and the aforesaid Bachelor Fernando de Rojas went to Talavera."[87]

As we shall see, Rojas' reasons for moving were probably more complex than is explained in this apparently agreed upon and schematic account. At the same time, upon reading it, we are in-

---

[84] A typical reflection of this situation is the self-exile of Lazarillo's third master, the Squire. The pages of Lea are filled with example after example of complex, picayune, and bitterly contested rivalries for status. The conflictive caste encounters noted above were later on converted to competition between those representing different varieties of authority (civil, Inquisitional, noble, ecclesiastic, Royal, etc.). A situation in which no status was settled and the masses could identify with the cry "Del rey abajo ninguno" paradoxically could only result in an infinity of unresolvable confrontations.

[85] For further details on don Alonso Téllez Girón, First Lord of Montalbán, see Chap. V.

[86] See Chap. V, n. 94.   [87] VL, I, p. 392.

evitably reminded of Lazarillo's third master, the Squire, who left his native town to go to Toledo because a local gentleman persisted in greeting him in a fashion offensive to his rank.

✒ The "Selves" of Authors

The three kinds of *converso* reaction to social circumstance that have here been proposed—angry rejection, ironical withdrawal, and partial acceptance—are, thus, not mutually exclusive. The state of mind of a Rojas or of anyone else living within the *converso* situation was surely a mixture of all three, a mixture the proportions of which differed not only from individual to individual but also from day to day and year to year within a given individual. Even in that complex structure of verbal irony called *La Celestina* there are, as we have seen, moments of thinly veiled anger and others of affirmation. Witches, too, are human beings and deserve something better than Inquisitional "justice," while Pármeno and Sempronio caught *in flagranti* are dealt with in exemplary fashion. "A biography is considered complete," Virginia Woolf remarks, "if it accounts for six or seven selves, whereas a person may have as many as a thousand."[88] Which should serve as a warning not to try to compensate for our biographical ignorance and impotence with abstract efforts at characterization. We are fated never to know or be able to account for a single one of all the selves that bore the name of Fernando de Rojas, but we may at least surmise that they were many and fluid, combining in ever changing proportions ironical evanescence with inner vocational solidity beneath an outer identification with the role of *hidalgo*.

Recognition of the immense modesty of these biographical speculations serves at least one good purpose. It leads to a further recognition and more exact definition of our subject. We are not interested in the life of Fernando de Rojas just because a man so named wrote most of *La Celestina*. As we announced at the beginning, nobody's curiosity about him is going to be satisfied, and no incidents or characters are going to be explained anecdotally. But, by considering Rojas in his family as a member of a caste, we may at least gain some comprehension of the larger relationship

[88] *Orlando*, London, 1928, pp. 189-190, quoted by Leon Edel, *Literary Biography*, New York, 1959.

153

between the *converso* situation and the prehistory of fiction, a relationship that was incarnated in his life. The *conversos* contributed many things to Spain: administration, intellectual achievement, great poetry, religious reform, and all the rest. But what they contributed to the world was nothing less than the possibility of the major literary genre of modern times: the novel. Cervantes and the men who provided him with his tradition—Mateo Alemán, Alonso Núñez de Reinoso (Spain's first reviver of the Byzantine novel),[89] Jorge de Montemayor (creator of the first pastoral novel in Castilian), the anonymous author of the *Lazarillo de Tormes,* Fernando de Rojas, the "sentimental novelist" Diego de San Pedro, and, earliest of all, Alonso Martínez de Toledo, who in his *Corbacho* first brought speech into Castilian prose—were *all,* although certain scholars fight rear guard battles in individual cases, *conversos.*[90] And the way of their creation, the cohesive shape of the tradition to which they contributed, reflects the unprecedented situation which they shared.

Racial characteristics and whatever remnants of Jewish culture and attitudes that may be reflected in some of their works are completely beside the point. What matters is the existence of such individuals at once inside and outside the social circumstance. It was this that provided the ironical distance and the identification with and knowledge of society that were equally necessary for the task of mirroring the world in fiction. Insight joined to perspective were the components of novelistic vision then as now, and it was with this vision that Rojas and some of his fellows were blessed—as well as cursed. Quevedo forced to the margin of his world is driven to

[89] See Chap. I, n. 26.

[90] Our degree of certainty about the hidden origins of these writers naturally varies. In the disputed case of Diego de San Pedro, Caro Baroja (1, 284) accepts (both because of the name and of the "humorismo agrio" and "ironía templada" of *La cárcel de amor*) his *converso* provenance. For a more detailed discussion of these subterranean aspects of the book, see Francisco Márquez, "*Cárcel de amor,* novela política," *RO,* IV (1966), 185-200. Dorothy Vivian in her study of the *Passión trobada (Anuario de estudios medievales,* I, Barcelona, 1964) sums up other arguments in this connection. Other names which might enrich the list would include many of those continuing or influenced by *La Celestina*—for example, Francisco Delicado (see Chap. VII, n. 18). Marcel Bataillon has recently dedicated himself to studying the presence of "Les Nouveaux Chrétiens dans l'essor du roman picaresque" (*Neophilologus,* 48 [1964], 283-298), finding in the genre a persistent thematic mocking of caste pretensions.

satire;[91] Lope at its vital center invented the celebrative *comedia*; but Cervantes as a novelist had to be in both places at once. Or as Alberto Moravia has recently phrased it, simultaneously "dentro e fuori del suo mondo."[92]

It would be pointless to try to argue that the novel could not exist or even that its birth in England and France would have been delayed without the caste of Spain's converted Jews. But, nevertheless, since literary history is concerned less with suppositions than with verifiable traditions, the Spain of Fernando de Rojas should be taken into account by students of prose fiction. Although not formally a novelist, his characteristic withdrawal and ironical exploration of all that he had intimately known and experienced was at once novelistic and unprecedented in the rest of Europe in 1499. Ultimately we shall have to try to distinguish between Rojas' personal gifts as a creator and his social situation (shared by countless contemporaries), but for the time being it is fruit of the latter—what might be called pedantically the sociology of the birth of the novel—which is of importance. In the chapter to follow we shall meditate on the same problem not in personal or collective terms but historically.

[91] This should not be taken to imply that I would include Quevedo too among the ever increasing roster of embittered *conversos*. Quite to the contrary, his particular sort of marginality and his anything but anonymous satire would seem to make him a companion in verbal arms with the statues of Laín Calvo and Nuño Rasura.

[92] *Corriere della Sera*, 29 Sept. 1963. In after centuries our greatest novelists —Faulkner, Joyce, Dickens, Twain—have found other varieties of insideness and outsideness, those of a novelistic society, but they inevitably repeat Cervantes' double stance.

CHAPTER IV

The Times of Fernando de Rojas

"¡ . . . cuánta desaventura le sigue y a
seguido en estos nuestros tiempos, y
las bueltas que este amargo reyno ha
avido y dado en tan breve espacio, y
los muchos ricos tornados pobres,
y las crueles guerras, y la amarga
muerte que de continuo llovizna!"

—Juan Alvarez Gato

❧ The *Anusim*

Jean-Paul Sartre describes the first critical moment in the life of a Jew growing up in a gentile society as the discovery of his own uniqueness, of his specialness in the eyes of others. "Sometimes," he says, "the discovery is made through the smiles of the people among whom one lives; sometimes it is brought about by gossip or insults. The later the discovery is made, the more violent is its impact. Suddenly each one perceives that everybody else knows something about him of which he himself was ignorant."[1] We have no way of determining when and how Rojas discovered he was a *converso* (a far more fearful discovery in his Spain than Jewishness in Sartre's France), but we can be sure that he made it. And we know too that once made (perhaps only at the moment of his father's arrest)[2] it generated an attempt at understanding. A period of questioning followed this as it does all discoveries: not the hopeless, unanswerable, ultimate questions Rojas and Pleberio were to ask later on, but rather the kind of questions which call for a story. The new being—himself as a *converso*—which he had just discovered could not be comprehended without a biography, without a "life and times." Which is to say, Fernando de Rojas, like all his fellows, necessarily sought for a preliminary narrative understanding of his own being as belonging to a historical circumstance. As Ortega remarks, we can only grasp the meaning of life through narration, through telling it first as a story and then as history.

Who it was who first undertook to answer Rojas' questions we shall never learn. But we can at least try to approximate the grown-up historical version which he put together for himself on the basis of the different answers he was progressively given. I do not propose here to retell in detail the fascinating history of the Spanish *conversos*, a history available to the English reader from several points of view.[3] Castro's chapters on the Jews and *conversos* in

[1] *Réflexions*, pp. 91-92.

[2] According to Lea and other standard authorities, if the family practiced Jewish rites, it was usual for a young *converso* to be informed of the secret only after reaching the age of discretion.

[3] In addition to Lea and translations of Castro and Llorente, see Cecil Roth,

IV. THE TIMES OF FERNANDO DE ROJAS

The Structure of Spanish History are particularly to be recommended for their profound and renovating insights. What I cannot avoid, however, is a brief recapitulation of the things that Rojas learned from his queries. To begin with, we should stress that the story was one of horror and violence, decade after decade of continual aggression, of relatives killed, of houses burned, of property stolen, of narrow escapes, of hopeless flight, of hatred in depth, and of unceasing danger. One was what one was because one was forced violently so to be. Of all the words for *converso,* perhaps the most appropriate was the Hebrew, *"Anusim,"* meaning "the forced."

The first major outbreak had occurred in 1391, almost exactly a century before the young Fernando de Rojas began to try to understand his own biography. Previously—as Castro, Menéndez Pidal,[4] and Amador de los Ríos have shown with striking examples—the three "castes" of medieval Spain had lived together with a harmony remarkable in European social history. Although violence was woven deeply into the texture of medieval life, Christian, Moor, and Jew had managed to achieve a kind of functional and even institutional co-existence. During the 1300's, however, increasing social unrest (of the kind that was spreading all through Europe), the loss of the frontier as a mission and as a safety valve for aggressive instincts, anarchical rupture of the stable forms of social existence (Rojas returns again and again in *La Celestina* to the theme of the disruption of human relationships), the daily spectacle of Jewish power and riches derived from their ever more necessary administrative functions, and many other desiccating factors created a tinder dry society. In 1391 the spark was ignited by the fanatical preaching of a few Franciscans, and within a few months almost every Spanish town was a scene of inflamed souls and violated flesh.

Flight to the countryside with its population of frightened *moriscos* and enraged revolutionary peasants (who thought of themselves as crusading warriors) was impossible. Noble and royal protection was haphazard and ineffective. Indeed there seemed to

---

A History of the Marranos, New York-Philadelphia, 1959; Abraham Neuman, *The Jews in Spain,* Philadelphia, 1948; and Yitzhak Baer, *A History of the Jews in Christian Spain,* Philadelphia, 1961, 1966.
[4] Particularly in *La España del Cid.*

be no place to turn except to the baptismal font. And great masses
of Jews did so choose safety—many of them reassured by the fervent oratorical welcome to the faith of Saint Vincent Ferrer, who
took advantage of the violence to become one of the most successful missionaries of all time. If in doing so they incurred the scorn
of their brethren outside Spain, they had at least preserved a situation of power, wealth, and social importance without parallel in
any other country. Settled in the cities and towns across the land,
the new *conversos* continued the business of their forefathers—arts
and crafts, tax collecting, money management, medicine—and, as
we saw, added many new ones. They intermarried with noble
families; they conducted diplomacy; they revived commerce and
industry; they entered the church with conspicuous success; they
wrote poems and argued ignorantly or well about theology; they
studied law; they engaged in civil administration; and, almost without intending so to do, they formed a kind of political party which
made its weight felt in the confused struggles for predominance
which characterized fifteenth-century Spanish history. The downfall of the one great political figure of the period, John II's royal
favorite, Don Alvaro de Luna, was apparently due in part to his
policy of favoring the Jews over the *conversos*. It was a time of
gathering power, a time which produced, as is noted by Amador
de los Ríos, "great characters" in the Marlovian sense, a time when
a "caste" could hope to turn itself into a ruling class.

But it was not a long time. The initial welcome was soon worn
out. In 1449 the *conversos* of Toledo experienced the kind of mob
violence that their Jewish grandparents had been subjected to at
the end of the preceding century. Numerous houses were burned
down, and efforts at armed resistance were decisively defeated by
the enraged mob. Worst of all, King John II and don Alvaro de
Luna were unable to help, and, after the rioting was over, the
Mayor, Pedro Sarmiento, promulgated a *sentencia estatuto* (statute
of exclusion). Some thirteen city councillors, notaries, and judges
were thereupon ousted for no other reason than the impurity of
their blood. It was the first of a large number of such statutes,
statutes which, however ineffective and ductile in the hands of professional fixers like the Licentiate Fernando, were ultimately to influence Spanish history and society in fundamental ways. Many
conversos recognized the danger inherent in the original statute

161

and attacked it both in practice (by obtaining papal intervention) and in theory (in a legal treatise by the outstanding jurist, Alonso Díaz de Montalvo, and a theological discussion by Alonso de Cartagena).[5]

All was in vain. During Rojas' lifetime more and more associations (colleges, guilds, orders, and others) adopted such rules, with the result that by the time of his death a *converso* political party was inconceivable. Although discrimination was resisted (a *converso* general of the Jesuits called the statutes a "national error")[6] and not given full royal support until 1548, its existence kept *conversos* from the acknowledgement of origins that joint action would have implied. An era of deceit, hypocrisy, and genealogical falsification had set in which was to last for centuries and which, as we have seen, still affects certain sectors of Hispanic scholarship today.[7] Indeed, it could be maintained that these statutes (particularly in the extreme seventeenth-century form represented by the Palavesín *expediente*) and the dishonesty they compelled on the part of candidates and witnesses were as responsible as the Inquisition for the petrifaction of Spanish society. That is to say, for Spain's slow death as a body politic. They can be thought of as complementing and later even replacing the Holy Office as a major instrument of social pressure. Once doctrinal deviation had been reduced to a minimum, acute consciousness of racial background performed on a day to day basis the same function as the climactic humiliation of the *autos de fe*. But this was later on. What Rojas was told about was the germination of the myth of Old Christian "cleanliness of blood" and *converso* impurity some thirty years before he was born.

To return to our synopsis, this first taste of violence and discrimination did not frighten the *conversos* of Toledo. In 1467 they took the offensive themselves with an attack on the cathedral, but, al-

---

[5] A detailed account of all this is given in exemplary fashion in Sicroff.

[6] Diego Lainez' frequently cited, "humor o error nacional," echoes Saint Ignatius' comment that attack on and exclusion of the *conversos* could be attributed to "el humor español." See E. Rey, "San Ignacio y el problema de los cristianos nuevos," *Razón y Fe*, 153 (1956), 173-204.

[7] In addition to Sánchez Albornoz and Eugenio Asensio cited in Chap. I, see the curious efforts to protect the reputation of Saint Teresa's ancestors as discussed by Homero Serís, "Nueva genealogía de Santa Teresa," *NRFH*, x (1956), 365-384.

though inside the city they could at times achieve superiority of numbers, they were soon defeated by masses of Old Christian peasants who poured in from the countryside. The resulting persecution was frightful: 1,600 dwellings burned, a general massacre of stragglers, and slow starvation for many of the rebels who, abandoning the town, wandered over the inhospitable countryside until they died. In 1473 the same scenes were repeated on an even greater scale in Córdoba (where one of Cervantes' ancestors was the first victim), and, after that, massacres and mob violence spread over Spain like a fever. Jaen, Valladolid, Segovia, and many smaller towns erupted in the same way. It was a time of great fear, a time of nerve-racking uncertainty, a time when every *converso* scrutinized his Old Christian neighbors for those slight changes of attitude or manners which might foretell a coming storm. In the Puebla de Montalbán where there was, as we shall see, a preponderance of *conversos*, the immediate danger was not as great, but the inhabitants were necessarily affected by the bloody events in Toledo only five leagues away. In the 1450's on another such occasion many of them took refuge with their cattle and goods in the nearby castle of Montalbán. For this protection they were forced to pay "one calf or lamb out of 20 born and, from each hundred sheep or goats, one milk giving and another dry."[8]

As was natural, after being commented on and told about over the years, the brutal events of 1449 and 1467 became institutionalized as a central part of the historical lore of the *conversos* of Toledo. Each person knew himself as a member of the group insofar as he or his forebears had participated in common suffering—and were likely to participate again. That is to say, although families and individuals had separate experiences and atrocities to tell about, they were not told in isolation. Rather they were thought of as belonging to the group story, a story which gave to each of

---

[8] ". . . cuando la Condesa de Montalbán, doña Juana Pimentel, muger de don Alvaro de Luna, residía en esta villa por señora della, se levantó cierta guerra en Toledo sobre la tenencia del alcazar y había grandes disensiones por esta tierra, y que al dicho castillo y fortaleza de Montalbán se iban a recoger muchas personas desta villa y tierra y llevaban sus haciendas para las poner en salvo allí, y por intercesión de se las guardar la dicha Condesa impuso cierta impusición sobre los ganados de villa y tierra que de veinte crías que naciesen le diesen una y de cient ovejas y vacas una parida y otra vacía . . ." (*Relaciones*, II, 260).

the years of atrocity an institutional name by which it might be known. Rojas heard about the 1449 rioting and robberies as "lo de Pedro Sarmiento," while the second and more definitive pogrom was referred to as "lo de la Madelena."[9] In order to sense directly the way these years reverberated through *converso* consciousness, we may read a passage from the trial after death of one Fernán González Husillo (probably the father of the Hernán Husillo who had advised Alvaro de Montalbán not to testify against his family).[10] His children are defending him from the usual charge of apostasy and they aver "that [on the occasion of the robbery of Pedro Sarmiento and 'lo de la Madalena'] the aforesaid Fernán González, because he was a Catholic and faithful Christian went to his front door and stood there, and, although he lived where the fire was greatest and the danger most pressing [next door to the *converso* leader, Fernando de la Torre],[11] none of the *hidalgos* or Old Christians robbed him or took any part of his goods. . . ." Here the feeling of participation in a common story is the more clear precisely because the individual concerned escaped the common dénouement. Ignorance of the particular anecdotes and reminiscences in terms of which this tale of violence was told to Fernando de Rojas is not the least of our misfortunes.[12]

It was not surprising under these circumstances of mass hatred and imminent violence that certain prominent *conversos* (among them the jurist Montalvo) would have asked for an inquisition.[13] Confident of their own scrupulous conformity to orthodox standards of behavior, they hoped that a weeding out of those actually

[9] Serrano y Sanz, p. 290. In the trial of Fernando González Husillo already cited (Chap. II, n. 9), the two events are referred to as "el robo de Pedro Sarmiento . . . e el de la Madalena." The second name, according to Caro Baroja (i, 124), derives from the fact that it was the "barrio de la Magdalena" that was sacked.

[10] Serrano y Sanz, p. 265. In the trial record just noted, it emerges that the accused died in 1469 leaving a large number of heirs—among them a Fernán Husillo—who protected their father's reputation and their own legacies against the Inquisition.

[11] Since Fernando de la Torre was well known as the hanged leader of the *converso* insurrection which brought on the reprisals, Husillo's escape was all the more remarkable.

[12] The kind of atrocity stories that were told and retold among *conversos* and Jews are represented in the *Chebet Jehudah*. See, for example, the narration of the exile (pp. 209 ff.) or of the 1506 massacre in Lisbon (p. 215).

[13] Sicroff, p. 66.

164

guilty of Judaic practices would allow them to pursue their careers unmenaced by the society around them. Others, of course, saw more deeply into their true situation and realized that the new institution would try to destroy them as individuals, as families, and as a caste. Hence the revolts—sternly suppressed—against the Inquisition by the *conversos* of Seville and Saragossa in 1481 and 1485 respectively. Even in Toledo where the *converso* cause had been twice decisively defeated there was one more attempt at self-defense.[14]

If some *conversos* still believed four years after the events of Seville that the Inquisition might ultimately be of benefit to them by exonerating them and freeing them from fear, they soon discovered that they were in the clutches of an antagonist as merciless and violent as any mob and in addition far more efficient. Instead of confining its aggression to a few days of continuing terror, the Inquisition's bureaucratic menace was longer than life itself, enfolding the dead as well as the living and reaching out to punish generations not yet born.[15] And, instead of merely grabbing or destroying tangible property, it knew how to gain legal possession of intangibles: debts, deeds, inheritances, mortgages. Finally, instead of just taking the life of its victims, it also specialized, as we have seen, in destroying their honor. The increase in efficiency, however, did not necessarily imply efficient separation of the innocent from the guilty. Like the mobs it replaced, the Holy Office, at least in its early decades, was frequently indiscriminate in its aggression.

We must also realize that the narrative was not all in the past

---

[14] Lea, I, 168.

[15] I refer, of course, to the stringent prohibitions in dress and occupation inflicted on the descendants of Inquisitional victims. The classic text describing these prohibitions is the Edict of Faith reproduced by Lea (II, 588). Sebastián de Orozco describes almost poetically the function of the displayed *sambenito* (the penitential garb worn by all the condemned, including such diverse individuals as Candide and Alvaro de Montalbán) in maintaining family dishonor: "The *sambenitos* of everyone who had been burned were hung in the cloister of the Holy Church of Toledo on beams near the garden, but in the course of time with its winds, waters, and suns, they rotted and were torn, and the names inscribed thereon could not be read, and, as a result, our Lords the Inquisitors commanded that they be renovated and hung up in the parish churches which each . . . had attended" (F. Fita, "La Inquisición toledana," *BRAH*, XI, 1887, p. 302). Those interested in the author of *La Celestina* would give a great deal to know whether one of them bore the name of his father.

tense. New paragraphs and chapters were added every year and indeed every month. An annalist of the Toledo Inquisition recounts the events of the beginning of the year 1501 (the year Rojas was busy amplifying *La Celestina*) in the following way:

Auto of Carnival Monday, 22 February 1501
On the 22nd of February, 1501, the day of Saint Peter of Cátedra, an *auto* of the Holy Inquisition was held in which they brought out for burning 38 men from the towns of Herrera and Alcocer. They had all been reconciled and had been deceived by a false prophetess only fifteen years old who claimed she had spoken with the messiah. He was coming, had taken her to heaven, and even had shown her the souls of those who had been burned by the Inquisition rewarded for their martyrdom with places of honor and golden thrones.

Auto of Shrove Tuesday, 23 February 1501
Then on the following day, the 23rd day of the aforesaid month and year, they brought out for burning 77 women from the aforesaid villages . . . and they say that some of them died in the Christian faith recognizing their error, and these were smothered before being burned. At this time news came to the city that in Córdoba they had burned some 90 persons. . . .

Auto of Holy Tuesday, 30 March 1501
On the 30th of the month of March of the aforesaid year an *auto* of the Holy Inquisition was made in which they brought out for burning six men and three women. They were natives of this city, and they had been reconciled, and it was found that they had gone back to "Judaizing" [*tornaron a judaizar*]. And they were all burned as having relapsed.[16]

The atmosphere of fear and horror suggested by these schematic annals is confirmed in the journals of travelers to Rojas' Spain. For example, in 1494 the Bavarian Hieronymus Münzer describes a madhouse in Valencia in which a crazed *converso* in a tiny cage was to be heard praying in Hebrew.[17] He remarks in passing that the madman's father had been burned as a result of his insane indiscretion. An infinite number of such scenes and stories constitute the grim texture of what we have called the Spain of Fernando de Rojas.

[16] *Ibid.*, pp. 307-308.　　　　[17] See Chap. III, n. 11.

It is also worth noting that, according to Caro Baroja's calculations, there was a marked acceleration of Inquisitional activity during the years immediately following the appearance of the *Comedia*. Basing himself on Vignau's *Catálogo* of the fragmentary archives of the Holy Office in Toledo, he concludes: "One observes that the Inquisition of Toledo was most violent and unbridled in its persecution of *judaizantes* as such at the beginning, concretely in the decade 1480 to 1490 (the climax being in 1485). The number of trials decreases somewhat between 1490 and 1499 only to increase again in 1500 and in the first years of the 16th century."[18]

The tale of horror that was told to Rojas will surely make more sense to a reader of the 1970's than it would have to his grandparents. If previously the Inquisition seemed to have been invented by Edgar Allan Poe, today we are better prepared to understand it from within. The zeal of certain *conversos* in preaching and helping to establish the Inquisition is particularly comprehensible in our time. As Castro brings out, the half-revolutionary, half-anti-Semitic violence of the masses, their "embestida anti-judaica" (blind bull-like charge), was now joined to the "theological fury" of certain neophytes whose only inner solace, whose only means of purging themselves of guilt, lay in attacking and destroying their fellows. The names of Fray Alfonso de Espina, Fray Jerónimo de Santa Fe (previously Rabbi Josué Lurquí), Fray Diego de Deza (Columbus's protector), and even Torquemada, himself, were all famous (or infamous) in this sense. Their administrative aptitudes as well as their fervent self-identification with their new faith made them well qualified to found and to organize such a tribunal.[19]

The elaborately ordered *autos de fe* in which *converso* Inquisitors and their victims, elevated upon scaffold or dais, were surrounded by the immense crowd of eager Old Christian spectators was a physical representation of the hateful alliance. The mob was now adequately administered, and a fundamental discovery about

---

[18] Vol. I, p. 352. These conclusions are not confirmed by the more complete archives in Cuenca (see S. Cirac Estopiñán, *Registros de los documentos del Santo Oficio de Cuenca y Sigüenza*, Cuenca-Barcelona, 1965), which indicate 1492 and 1496 as years of peak activity. Few Toledan records remain from the early 1500's.

[19] Castro convincingly—although not without partisan rebuttal—attributes Inquisitorial fanaticism to the Hebrew heritage of these early Inquisitors. The fiercely maintained orthodoxy of the medieval ghetto, he maintains, was now extended to all Spain (*Realidad*, edn. I, pp. 496-518; *Structure*, pp. 521-544).

the government of modern states had been made.[20] The result of this joining of forces, however, was not limited to *autos de fe* and burnings at the stake. The Inquisition was a continuing institution unique in its combination of cunning and sheer hatred, calculated greed and self-righteous piety, secrecy of procedure and public display of punishment. In their omnipotence, their mystery, and their power, the Inquisitors seemed God-like to some of their victims;[21] in their passion and ruthlessness, others compared them to animals ("wolves, lions, dragons . . . who hated to the point of madness").[22] Nor was there any evasion of Inquisitional power aside from flight—and that was frequently unsuccessful.[23] Appeals to the Pope only resulted in paying bribes for restraining orders that were never enforced;[24] appeals to the King and Queen never penetrated the blind piety of the one and the political calculation of the other.[25]

Man was, thus, submitted to an organized and institutional inhumanity of a sort only too familiar to the twentieth century. But in a land traditionally devoted to measurement of the world in human terms, in a land whose heroes were a Cid in the past and an Hernán Cortés in the present, such submission seemed to many strange, unheard-of, and without precedent. The reactions re-

[20] See Márquez' introduction of Fray Hernando de Talavera's *Católica impugnación*, p. 27, n. 26, for a cogent discussion of the Inquisition as an instrument of government.

[21] Among the imprudent outbursts attributed by a *"mosca"* to the physician Bachelor Francisco de San Martín, referred to previously (Chap. II, n. 89), was that his Inquisitors (who had jailed a butcher for not delivering meat to a "familiar") acted as if they were "second gods."

[22] The amount and variety of animal imagery used by Montes (as in this sample) is noteworthy. The key image seems to be Biblical in derivation: Christians are sheep whose shepherds have been changed into savage beasts who devour their own flock.

[23] Lea discusses both successful escapes from Inquisitorial power, mostly in the 1480's and 90's (I, 183-184) and the later efficient organization set up to prevent them (II, 513).

[24] Llorente (II, 99) discusses the resulting bitter complaints of prominent *conversos*, including those of Juan de Lucena, the Royal Councillor (cited previously, Chap. III, n. 59).

[25] A. C. Floriano Cumbreño's fascinating factual account of the hopeless efforts of the city fathers of Teruel (*conversos* to a man) to persuade King Ferdinand to relieve them of a particularly remorseless Inquisitor (intent, as his later behavior confirmed, on multiple burnings and confiscations) throws harsh light on royal greed and implacability. See Chap. VIII, n. 137.

corded by Father Mariana stress precisely this: the Inquisition behaved in a way "completely contrary to that which was the custom of other tribunals"; the fact that children should be penalized for the sins of their fathers was "specially surprising"; the death sentence for minor deviations in ritual behavior "seemed to be a new thing"; the loss of freedom of speech constituted a "servidumbre gravíssima y a par de muerte."[26] As Francisco Márquez observes, "The Inquisition was not one more event in political or religious history; from the very beginning, it belonged to that special category of happenings which on certain occasions oblige each man to consider anew the deepest foundations of his existence and his attitudes."[27] Which is to say, those who experienced and lived under it belonged to a different historical generation from those who had not. When Leonor de Lucena, the daughter of the printer used the expression "vivir muriendo" in a letter to her sister, she only intended to communicate the hopelessness of her immediate situation. But, in the ready-made phrase, used in very different contexts by Saint Teresa and others, there is also expressed a generational sense of life as anguish.[28]

To conclude, we may roughly divide the history of the caste into three periods. In the times of violence before the establishment of the Inquisition the *conversos*, too, were violent. Such rebellious and anarchical individuals as a Fernando de la Torre in Toledo fought back against the statutes and restrictions and resisted or collaborated (on those occasions when it could be manipulated to *converso* advantage) with popular unrest. As we shall see, the last and disguised eruption of the latter possibility was the rebellion of the "Comunidades."[29] Secondly, there were the tormented, imprudent, and maladjusted fellows of Alvaro de Montalbán who with Erasmistic fervor, ironical self-display, or hopeless skepticism attempted to live their own lives under the pressure of an institution and a social situation not yet fully comprehended. Finally, there were the dissemblers, the late sixteenth- and seventeenth-century clients of the Licentiate Fernando who dedicated themselves full

---

[26] See Chap. II, n. 85.   [27] *Investigaciones*, p. 95.

[28] The letter was written after flight to Lisbon where her son had died shortly after arrival. After asking urgently for news of relatives and friends, she describes her exile as follows: ". . . de acá, señora, no sé que diga, sino que yo siempre bibo muriendo . . ." (Serrano y Sanz, p. 287).

[29] See Chap. VIII, section 4.

169

time to camouflage and assimilation. Naturally this division is to a certain extent arbitrary, a single life often partaking of all three (each "period" roughly corresponding to one of the three varieties of personal reaction set forth previously) at different times and in changing combinations. In any case, Fernando de Rojas, seen from a historical point of view, had heard about the earlier period but belonged himself to an intermediate generation somewhere in between the second and the third. Still aware of his own existence as radically different (*La Celestina*, among other things, is a manifesto of discrepancy), he was also capable of an irreproachable conformity that lasted over forty years. Hence, perhaps, the unique combination in the prologue material of anonymity and display, of self-withdrawal and self-revelation. Unlike his father and father-in-law, he had evidently learned from the story he had been told.

The Fall of Fortune

In preceding chapters we have observed the effects of exposure to the Inquisition and to the social atmosphere which accompanied it, first, in the biography of an individual and, second, among *conversos* as a group. In the following chapter we shall discuss the disruption caused in the life of a small community, the Puebla de Montalbán, where Alvaro de Montalbán and his son-in-law were brought up. Our present concern, however (now that our brief narrative is finished), is with a historical generation: the first generation of *conversos* to grow up under Inquisitional pressure. What were the feelings of its members, their thoughts, their characteristic ways of understanding and expressing what was happening to them?

Perhaps the most apparent reaction was the special intensity and new meaning given the age-old topic of fortune and its fall. Fernando de Rojas belonged to a falling caste, a caste which during his lifetime lost all ability to act in its own interest and was beginning to realize that its children would have to go into hiding forever.[30]

---

[30] *Converso* community efforts to mitigate Inquisitional procedure by offering the Crown substantial sums (a traditional recourse of the medieval Jews, as we have seen, Chap. III, n. 28) practically ceased after the Comunidades (see Lea, I, 217-223). Partly perhaps this was due to their futility (see Peter Martyr's *Epistolario* edited by J. López de Toro as volumes IX through XII of the *nueva serie* of *Documentos inéditos para la historia de*

This was, of course, a gradual process (like Sempronio's "casa que se acuesta"); yet as it went on from day to day and year to year the individual falls of friends and neighbors were painfully noticeable. Many did not have very far to drop—such as Rojas' humble protégé and agent, Alonso de Arévalo, who in 1517 was forbidden to exercise his profession as watchman in Talavera because of a chance remark offensive to the Holy Office.[31] More conspicuous were falls from a higher altitude: the falls of noblemen (those persecuted in Córdoba by Lucero), high churchmen (Fray Hernando de Talavera), leaders of professions (Doctor Alonso Cota), and in general of all those who, like Pleberio, had been successful in their life-long pursuit of wealth and honor.

Sudden changes were the rule of the day—and not always caused directly by the Inquisition. In 1496, for example, the president and all the "*oidores*" of the Royal Court of Chancery were summarily dismissed as being "cristianos nuevos y poco limpios de manos" (*conversos* whose lack of cleanliness extended to their sticky fingers).[32] As Rojas and his fellows year after year observed such immediate "casos de fortuna," as they looked at each other and wondered who would be next, their world seemed increasingly hazardous, more and more strewn with pitfalls. It was a tightrope world of vertical danger in which a life of precaution could be destroyed by one moment of carelessness. The *conversos* who in the fifteenth century had in many cases been fortune's darlings[33] now felt themselves singled out as her special victims.[34]

España, Madrid, 1955-57, XI, 322; hereafter referred to as *Epistolario*) and partly also to the dissimulation forced on individual *conversos* by the statutes, as mentioned above.

[31] Inquisición de Toledo, p. 257; and VLA 28 B.

[32] Vicente de la Fuente, *Historia de las universidades*, Madrid, 1885, II, 41.

[33] I refer less to such established families as the de la Caballerías, the Coroneles, the Santa Marías, and the Dávilas than to cases of spectacular ascension such as that of Alonso de Montalbán or the tailor Juan de Baena, who, as mentioned previously, changed his name to Juan de Pineda and was given by his noble protector, don Juan Pacheco, the rank of Commander in the Order of Santiago. His subsequent fall at the hands of the Inquisition (Inquisición de Toledo, p. 218) may be considered an exemplary turn of the wheel in the hands of its new masters. Caro Baroja, unaware of Pineda's origins (although mentioned in the trial record and discussed by Baer, II, 347 ff.), considers him a noble influenced by his Jewish servitors (I, 509).

[34] Prior to the Inquisition, *converso* sensitivity to fortune was prepared for by the pogroms and turbulence mentioned above. Thus, an Alvarez Gato

171

In order to understand this renovation of an age-old vertigo, we must realize that the Inquisition operated in the way fortune had been traditionally thought to behave—which is to say, its malevolence was attracted by wealth and high honor. As a *converso* who had fled is reported to have remarked: "que el que tenía fazienda feziese cuenta que tenía el fuego consigo" (whoever owned an estate should realize that fire might own him).[35] Or in the words of Raimundo Montes, one of the few who managed to escape successfully from an Inquisitional prison, "What greater avarice than this confiscation of property! What practice could be more pernicious, more absurd, more alien to the profession of Christianity?"[36] These frequent charges were only admitted once—in the case of the infamous Lucero who was eventually tried (but not punished) for his extortions and use of perjured testimony. Lucero aside, however, the practice of trying and burning the dead in order to deprive the living of their patrimony is sufficient indication of motive. The austere Torquemada, according to Lea and Llorente, was not free of such temptations. His frustrated efforts to condemn the bones of Diagarias (Diego Arias de Avila, mentioned previously as Henry IV's *converso* treasurer) can only be attributed to the desire to gain possession of his riches.[37] During his lifetime Diagarias had been careful about his religious obligations.

Frequent royal denials are hardly convincing in the face of the facts. Even Isabel sounds unnecessarily self-righteous—at once rhetorical and evasive—when she deals with the charge: "I have

---

laments "las *bueltas* que este amargo reyno ha avido y dado en tan breve espacio, y los muchos ricos tornados pobres y las crueles guerras y la amarga muerte que de continuo llovizna" (cited in *Investigaciones*, p. 391).

[35] Fritz Baer, *Die Juden im christlichen Spanien*, 2 vols., Berlin, 1929, 1936, II, 473. This compilation served the author (Fritz was changed to Yitzhak upon emigration to Israel) as a source book for the *History* previously cited. The frequency of such charges and the sensitivity of the Crown and the Inquisition to them is apparent in a 1519 letter of instructions from Charles V to his envoy in Rome. In order to keep Leo X from modifying Inquisitional methods, the envoy was instructed to argue that reform would give credence to false *converso* accusations of avarice: ". . . tal renovación . . . dar[ía] a entender que es verdad lo que falsamente algunos conversos han querido dezir e afirmar que los ynquisidores condemnavan a muchos sin culpa por tomarles sus bienes y haziendas . . ." (F. Fita, "Los judaizantes en el reinado de Carlos I," *BRAH*, XXXI, 1898, p. 334).

[36] *Artes*, p. 19.   [37] Llorente, II, 120-123, and Lea, III, 82.

caused great calamities," she writes the Pope, "and depopulated lands, provinces, and kingdoms, but I have acted thus from love of Christ and His Holy Mother. There are liars and calumniators who say I have done so from the love of money, for I have never myself touched a maravedí from the confiscated goods of the dead. On the contrary I have employed the money in educating and giving marriage portions to the children of the condemned."[38] Yet in spite of this disavowal, a typical trial was initiated by greed and terminated in the gratification of the masses at the fall of the mighty in a public *auto de fe*. As we have seen, religious fervor and class resentment went hand in hand. In the Inquisitors the goddess Fortune had found willing and efficient human agents for her labor on earth.

A second factor to be considered is the peculiar importance of the notion of fortune during the century preceding the Inquisition. As Huizinga has shown, the semi-pagan play of noble ambitions, the sudden soaring and diving of feudal politics, the gambling on all or nothing which replaced acceptance of medieval order, all turned men's attention to fortune with augmented fear and enthusiasm. In Castile don Alvaro de Luna, described by Juan de Mena as riding on fortune's back and "taming her with harsh reins," ultimately fell off and became a figure as exemplary as any in Boccaccio's standard collection, the *De casibus*. As late as the composition of *La conquista de la Nueva Castilla* (1537?) the success of Pizarro is explained as the result of his superb handling of fortune both as an enemy and as an ally.[39]

In the peninsula, however, the Catholic Monarchs brought the reign of noble anarchy to an end and sent titled warriors either off to crusade on the frontiers of Granada or back to their estates where they busied themselves with their neighbors and tenants— with no more mutations of fortune than those resulting from their lawsuits. A typical example is don Alonso Téllez Girón, the Lord of the Puebla de Montalbán and the third son of the most notorious of the turbulent grandees of the fifteenth century, don Juan Pacheco, Marquis of Villena and Master of Santiago. After the siege of Granada, don Alonso spent land-poor decades (he died in

---

[38] Cited by R. Merton, *Cardinal Ximenez and the Making of Spain*, London, 1934, p. xlvi.

[39] Edited by F. Rand Morton, Mexico, 1963, pp. xvii-xxi.

1526) quarreling with his neighbors about boundaries, squeezing taxes out of the inhabitants of the Puebla, and collecting tolls from shepherds in their annual migrations. The change is most nobly represented (as Pedro Salinas shows)[40] in Jorge Manrique's *Coplas on the Death of his Father*, one of the two or three finest poems in Spanish. Time, fortune, and death erase the transient glories of don Alvaro de Luna and his fellows, but the poet's father, don Rodrigo Manrique, defeats fortune in terms of the religious destiny that was to give glory to his country for almost two centuries more.

When the *ci-devant* goddess turned her attention away from her previous devotees and victims, she found a new class ready for her care. It was the class of those who administered the estates of the nobles, of those who bought and sold and gave credit: the *conversos* who had been subjected to the Inquisition in the same years that their masters went off to renew the struggle against the Moors. This is the profound sense of the remark of Villalobos to the effect that "the children of fortune are the great lords of the land, and the favorites of fortune are those who govern their estates and accompany the aforesaid children."[41] The reference to *converso* majordomos and tutors is clear, but the word "favorite" may not fully express the contrast that Villalobos intends. "Children" are loved by their mother, fortune, without change or mutation, but her favorites are elevated to the heights or cast aside at her whim.

Thus, too, the philosopher Luis Vives writes in 1525 (from his safe haven as a professor at Oxford): "Fortune continues the same and faithful to her being, acting against my father, against all my family, and even against myself, since in my opinion what it does to them it does to me, for I love all of them no less than I love myself."[42] The use of the term fortune as a euphemism for the Inquisition is clear. According to Américo Castro, Vives' father was burned in the following year, and his mother's remains were disinterred and similarly disposed of. As for his three sisters, they were left "orphaned, unmarried, and poor." It was unnecessary to

---

[40] In *Jorge Manrique, Tradición y originalidad*, Buenos Aires, 1948, which contains an admirable essay on and résumé of medieval views on fortune.

[41] *Algunas obras*, p. 212: ". . . es de saber que los hijos de la fortuna son los grandes señores y los príncipes del mundo, porque estos son los heredados de sus bienes. Y los privados de la fortuna son los que gobiernan sus estados y andan siempre al lado de los dichos sus hijos. . . ."

[42] *Realidad*, edn. I, p. 551, n. 44. The translation is mine.

add "dishonored." As Castro sums it up, "The Jew and his adversary, the convert, were something more than the usual run of people: they carried in their souls the agony of their feeling that they were being dashed from the summits of fortune into the terror of massacres, burnings at the stake, torture, *sambenitos,* and harassment by a crazed society, which continually pried into the Jew's actions and conscience, always subject to exposure through torture."[43]

More interesting for our purposes than post-Inquisitional discourses and poems on fortune (for example, Diego de San Pedro's commonplace *Desprecio de la fortuna*)[44] is *converso* fascination with Petrarch, particularly with the *De remediis utriusque fortunae,* the reading of which was one of Rojas' most decisive experiences. A. D. Deyermond in his recent *The Petrarchan Sources of "La Celestina"*[45] has a well-documented first chapter summing up what is known about the presence of Petrarch's Latin works in Spain. They were indeed influential, but he remarks with surprise that the *De remediis* (a fundamental treatise on antidotes to fortune), although known in Italian or Latin to such aristocratic writers as the Marquises of Santillana and Villena, and to scholars such as Alfonso de Madrigal "el Tostado" and the Arcipreste de Talavera, was not translated or printed before 1510. There were, however, at least six more editions before 1534.[46] Which is to say,

---

[43] *Ibid.,* pp. 543-544. It is surprising that Bataillon, in view of his insistence on interpreting *La Celestina* as a work in its time for its time, does not stress the theme of fortune and its peculiar treatment by Rojas.

[44] Mrs. Dorothy Severin has called my attention to the unusually concrete description of the rich man (*converso?*) persecuted by Fortune in the *Desprecio*: "Ella [la pobreza] dormirá / sin dar buelcos en la cama / no teme lo que verná / ni llora que perderá / la hazienda *ni la fama*" (*Obras,* Clásicos castellanos, Madrid, 1950, p. 241).

[45] Oxford, 1961.

[46] Indications of Spanish interest in Petrarch overlooked by Deyermond are the following: (1) that Fray Hernando de Talavera's *Invectiva contra un médico rudo y parlero* was presented as a preliminary essay for an apparently never achieved translation of the *De remediis* (see J. Domínguez Bordona, "Algunas precisiones sobre Fray Hernando de Talavera," *BRAH,* CLIV, 1959, p. 228); (2) that *De vita solitaria* was cited in the *Retablo de la vida de Cristo*; (3) that the *De remediis* (bound together with *De vita solitaria,* Boethius, and Valerius Maximus) was one of the 30 manuscripts mentioned in the will of Alvar García de Santa María (see Cantera Burgos, p. 198); (4) that the *Flores philosophiae,* and apparently the *De remediis* as well, were in the library of the Colegio viejo de San Bartolomé in Salamanca (see F. Ruiz de

only when fortune widened her field of operations from a few dozen frenzied nobles to a caste that was by definition more or less intellectual did the *De remediis* find a sizeable public. A treatise which awakened so much enthusiasm in Fernando de Rojas also appealed to those who, like him, lived under the shadow of a malevolent fortune and were in need of appropriate remedies.

Why was this so? It is a question which I have endeavored to answer elsewhere in literary terms,[47] but for our present purposes a historical approach is more suitable. As we have seen, before the reign of the Catholic Monarchs, fortune, although often the target of moral castigation (for example, Santillana's *Bias against Fortune*), was not always thought of in wholly negative terms. Fortune was Machiavellian and two-faced, at once a chastiser of the greedy and unwary and a provider of opportunities for the brave and the skillful. Don Alvaro de Luna played the game of fortune, and, if ultimately he was the loser, he at least had known the chances he was taking. He and his fellows had "staked their lives"[48] on success, and they would hardly have been interested in the interior, neo-Stoic protection against fortune's siege offered by Petrarch. Such men may have thought of themselves as characters worthy of the *De casibus*, but they wanted no pamphlets explaining how to reform themselves from within or how to mend their bad habits.[49]

The *conversos*, on the other hand, were in a far more anguished situation: they were the passive recipients of fortune's mutations, subject from day to day and minute to minute to her incalculable aggressions. They had not chosen the game of fortune. Nor did

---

Vergara, *Historia del Colegio Viejo de San Bartolomé*, Madrid, 1766, II, 331); (5) that the Marqués de Santillana possessed a *Prospera ed adversa fortuna* (surely the *De remediis*) which probably did, in spite of Deyermond's assertion to the contrary, exercise minor influence in his writings on fortune (see *Obras*, ed. Amador de los Ríos, Madrid 1852, p. 629).

[47] See chap. VI of *The Art*.

[48] The typical phrase "poner la vida al tablero" was used by such master players of the game of fortune as don Rodrigo Manrique and Celestina. That is, although existing in a Petrarchist world of hopeless subjection, Celestina guides her life willfully in an older tradition. The encounter of these two visions of fortune in the pages of the book is thematically central.

[49] Fray Martín de Córdoba did address a treatise entitled, *Compendio de Fortuna*, to don Alvaro, but there is no reason to believe that his interest was awakened or his behavior influenced thereby.

176

their responsible careers lead them to envision a goddess whom they might challenge.[50] Instead they found themselves in a state of exposure, exposure to the Inquisition, to the society which supported it and spied on them, and ultimately to the careless world of nature into which, shelterless and penniless, they might be thrust at any moment. One of the saddest parts of the story of his kind that was told to the young Fernando de Rojas was of the expulsion of whole families from Toledo in 1449 and 1467, families which had wandered till they died through an inimical countryside. And the fate of the children of those incarcerated or executed rambling over the land and waiting for Queen Isabel to provide them with education and dowries furnished daily epilogues of the most heart-rending variety. For such as these Petrarch's neo-Stoic interpretation of fortune and his recipes for mental self-discipline made special sense.

We may also observe that while the traditional purveyors of consolation—Seneca, Job, and Boethius—were also widely read, they lacked one thing which Petrarch provided: a portrait of man exposed to the world in all its aggressive immediacy. Boethius was intent on setting the soul free for its flight to Heaven and on accounting for the apparently arbitrary acts of providence. Failing to meditate on the immediate surroundings of the individual, his muse was inspirational and theoretical. As for the Book of Job, the tragic relation of man to God draws the writer's attention away from daily existence. Evil, as an inexplicable intrusion on prosperity, is posed as a metaphysical problem, not described as an immediate experience. We are not really told how Job's boils hurt. Seneca, too, though admired by Petrarch and at least as widely read, lacked this quality. Most of the time he seems to speak from a classical stage upon which pain is extreme and patience, heroic, but both somewhat rhetorical, unreal, foreign to domestic worries and humiliations.[51] Unlike these predecessors, Petrarch thought in terms of specific situations, in terms of the joys and sorrows that

---

[50] I except, of course, certain *conversos* belonging to generations prior to the Inquisition and the major pogroms. Such men as Diagarias, Ximeno Gordo, Mossén Diego de Valera, and (I strongly suspect), Pedro de Baeza, don Juan Pacheco's *mayordomo* and slayer of Jorge Manrique, do not differ in their attitude towards fortune from the grasping nobles with whom they played her game.

[51] For *converso* interest in Seneca, see *Investigaciones*, pp. 187 ff.

arise from being in the world as it is.[52] The passage on noises that fascinated the author of Act I of *La Celestina* is perhaps the best example of the circumstantial density of the *De remediis*:

> Who hath not endured the nightlie conflicts of birdes? Also the crying of owles and scritches, and the bootlesse watching of dogges all night barking against the Moone, and cattes making their meetings vpon the tyles & toppes of houses, and the quiet silence disturbed with horrible clamour, and whatsoeuer else maketh anie grieuous noyse in the darke? Wherevnto may be added, the croaking of frogges and toades in the night, and the lamenting and threatening of the swallowes in the morning: so that a man would think that Itys and Tereus himselfe were present. For as touching the quietnes of birdes by day, the squeeking grasshoppers, the arrogant crowes, and braying asses doe disturbe it, and the unwritten cackling of hennes without surceasing, who sell their small egges for a great price. But aboue al things is either the crying of swyne, or the common clamour and laughter of fooles, than which foolish thing, there is nothing more foolish, as saieth Catullus: and the singing and merimentes of drunkardes . . . and the iangling and scoulding of olde wiues: and sometime the battailes, sometime the lamentation of children: and of weddings, either their vnquiet feastes, or their daunsing: and the merrie mournings of wiues, who by craft do seeme to lament the death of their husbands: and the unfeigned howlings of parents at the decease of their children. . . .[53]

If Seneca or Job were more meaningful to those submitted to torture or condemned to burning at the stake, Petrarch spoke to a far larger group, to those who were forced to live out their lives in a situation of alienation. The individual consciousness forced back on itself, unsure of its beliefs, pursued by the suspicion of countless watchers and spies, resentful, fearful, above all sensitive, adopted the *De remediis* as its breviary. Petrarch's Stoic "remedies" were advanced less confidently than those of his predecessors (defensive psychic armor against a wailing cat or the malicious gossip of a

---

[52] *The Art*, pp. 166 ff.

[53] From Thomas Twyne's translation, *Phisicke against Fortune, as well prosperous, as aduerse, conteyned in two Bookes*, London, 1579, fols. 157-158.

neighbor is in a way more difficult to forge than against an executioner), but his identification of adverse fortune with continuous aggression from without was in profound accord with one aspect of *converso* experience. Local humiliation, helpless subjection to uncontrolled hazard, unending exposure constituted the daily foundation of fortune's major catastrophes and mutations. It was this sense of life that Fernando de Rojas and his kind found reflected and defined in the *De remediis*.

Villalobos in his *Canción con su glosa* (evidently drawing on the *De remediis*) expresses the *converso* feeling of subjection to fortune on every level as follows:

Anyone choosing to think about it can *see within himself* all the servitude and yokes which man has to bear in this world. Because from the moment we are born we are *captive and subject* to the necessities of the world into which we are born, to wit: hunger, thirst, extreme cold and heat, sickness and pain, . . . *to tyrants and cruel judges*,[54] and to the passions of the flesh and its concupiscence. Finally, whom do we not serve? We serve the land which was created to serve us by plowing it so it will give us whereof to eat. We serve the domestic animals who were given to us as slaves. Because, who doesn't have to tend to his horse? Who doesn't have to get him food? Who doesn't scrub him and scratch him and clean him? And sometimes this is carried so far that, if it weren't for the brains of the one, we would much prefer to be the horse than the master. We even serve oxen and other cattle. And we are also *subject* to the dangers and disturbances and corruptions of earth, water, and air: earthquakes, storms at sea, and thunder and lightning. And we are *subject to the wars and tumults and dissensions of the human species*. To conclude, to what are we not subject? For even flies and vermin offend us, and we can do nothing against them, not to mention fleas and grasshoppers and garden pests. . . .[55]

[54] The topic of judicial rapacity was well suited for application to Inquisitional behavior. See my "The Sequel to *El villano del Danubio*," RHM, XXXI (1965), 175-185.

[55] *Algunas obras*, pp. 205-206. In his *Tratado de la gran risa* (*Curiosidades*, p. 454), there is mention of the "simulation of laughter and joy with which certain men deceive others" (p. 454). For Villalobos even laughter can be a weapon in his world of "contienda y batalla."

179

To sum up, as fortune extended her sway, as a whole class grew used to existing in a vertical circumstance in which to fall was a routine event rather than a biographical climax, there was a metamorphosis in her fundamental nature. The horror story that was told to Rojas' generation about itself and, what was even more decisive, the experience of living in the world of the story, of coping with its minor manifestations on a day to day basis, made it receptive to the world outlook of the *De remediis*. Petrarch the philosopher and Petrarch the lyric poet come together in concern with the solitary consciousness exposed to the slings and arrows of outrageous objectivity. In one phase, Petrarch attempts to explain and cure the condition; in the other, he expresses it poetically, but it is the central theme of much of his writing. It was primarily the former phase that interested Rojas and Villalobos and all the other purchasers of the seven editions of the *De remediis* which came out between 1510 and 1534. Here was a book which explained to them in clear prose what Ortega y Gasset might have called the "theme of their time."

These readers, like the writer although evidently in a different way, felt themselves to be exposed and solitary consciousnesses: the prey of inner concupiscence, social antagonism, and ultimately of Heavenly unconcern. And the last was worst of all. Jacques Maritain—referring primarily to the France described by Huizinga, all distraught with Death and Fortune—speaks of "existentialist distress" at the end of the fifteenth century.[56] A breakdown of the medieval order, he generalizes, prepared the way for the sixteenth-century revival of Stoicism (in which Petrarch played an important role)[57] and ultimately for scientific investigation. In Spain, the same crisis, at first a pale reflection of what was going on all over Europe,[58] became acute in terms of a special social and human agony. Those who lived in a world presided over by the Inquisition understood as few have been able to do until our own time the import of alienation. That is to say, they understood that, when one speaks of a hostile and alien world, the two adjectives are not really contradictory.

[56] *Creative Intuition in Art and Poetry*, New York, 1955 (Meridian Edition), p. 21.

[57] L. Zanta, *La Renaissance du Stoicisme au XVIᵉ siécle*, Paris, 1914, p. 12.

[58] Only one Castilian *Dance of Death* has come down to us and there is no extant version in Spain of the much translated dialogue of the *Trois morts*.

". . . as if in contest or battle"

The remark of Villalobos (writing at the time of the rebellion of the Comunidades) that "we are subject to wars and tumults and dissensions," reminds us of that section of the *De remediis* which Rojas translated in the prologue as a gloss to Heraclitus' "all things come to pass through the compulsion of strife."[59] The introduction to the second part of the *De remediis*, "Remedies against Adverse Fortune," is a breathless compilation of anecdotes depicting the natural world as a battleground. Animals, insects, birds, fish, and even the four elements (as we saw in the passage from Villalobos), all are engaged in constant warfare. But worst of all is the world of men. The "human species" (a pessimistic rather than scientific description which neo-Stoics used in order to subtract dignity from man)[60] has a conscious perversity lacking in all the other species, and its history is a meaningless catalogue of cruelties, violations, arbitrary changes, and general degradation. We have just read the Breughel-like description of interpersonal relations in Petrarch's prologue, a description emphasizing such bellicose interchange as the "conflicts of birdes" troubling men with their "horrible clamour," "the iangling and scoulding of olde wiues," as well as the camouflaged "merrie mournings" of insincere widows. It is a fitting introduction to a book which is dedicated to a presentation of human life as a *"pannier de crabbes."*[61]

[59] If Rojas had known Heraclitus directly, he would surely have found congenial such fragments as 24: "Time is a child moving counters in a game; the royal power is a child's," 25: "War is both father and king of all; some he has shown forth as gods and others as men; some he has made slaves and others free," and 26: "It should be understood that war is the common condition, that strife is justice, and that all things come to pass through the compulsion of strife" (P. Wheelwright, *Heraclitus*, New York, 1964, p. 29). Above all, he would have agreed with the statement attributed to Heraclitus to the effect that "war and Zeus are the same thing" (p. 35). For the deep and fruitful influence of Heraclitus on Petrarch, see M. Françon, "Petrarch, Disciple of Heraclitus," *Speculum*, XI (1936), 265-271.

[60] *La Celestina*, I, pp. 101-102. In contrast to animals, Stoics traditionally maintained that the "human species" was at a disadvantage because of the curse of consciousness.

[61] We may contrast this vision to that of the earlier *converso*, Alonso de Cartagena, who two generations before had translated a central phrase from the Book of Job in chivalresque terms: "Caballería es la vida del ome sobre la tierra" (Santillana, *Obras*, p. 494). Similarly Mosén Diego de Valera translates Honoré de Bonet's *Arbre de batailles*, giving a chivalresque context

The *De remediis* appealed to Rojas (as a member of his caste and generation) because of the frequency of such vivid passages in all its parts. Although the Spain of his time had been united in terms of a renewed destiny, although its national history was given epic and religious significance by the Catholic Monarchs and their successors, many of the *conversos* who lived through the riots of the 1470's and the first years of the Inquisition had a very different sense of the present and past. Like Petrarch they had experienced history as a complex and senseless warfare of individuals and groups, a warfare in which they were helplessly involved. The major battle was, of course, that waged by the Old Christians against the *conversos,* all of them Jews in disguise according to Fray Alfonso de Espina. Or as a scurrilous poem of the time phrased it: "You, the 'marrano,' and he, the Jew—are birds of a feather."[62] But such a definition of the warfare and antagonism suffered by the *conversos* is misleading. The racial solidarity of the two groups was exceedingly fragile. As Castro puts it, "Among the converts, some, under the protection of their new faith, attacked the Jews, whether they were converts or not, impelled, as we have seen, by their fear and their ambition. The Jews, for their part, denounced the converts by way of reprisal, and Spain was choking in an atmosphere of espionage and counter-espionage."[63]

It is true that at times and in protected places harmony and even deep affection characterized the relations between the two groups. As we have seen, the Puebla de Montalbán in the 1470's and early 80's was a striking example of such friendly co-existence. It was a lost idyll which Rojas was told about along with later anecdotes of horror and violence, anecdotes which must have seemed all the

---

to his answers to such philosophical questions as, "si es posyble que este mundo esté en sosyego e paz" (cited Chap. III, n. 71). Such writers, happily for them, did not share the generational desperation of a Villalobos, a Rojas, an Alvarez Gato ("todo es peligro o batalla quanto ay sobre la tierra," *Investigaciones,* p. 280), or a Torres Naharro. Constance Rose in the dissertation cited previously (Chap. I, n. 26) gives a number of examples from the group around Núñez de Reinoso. Some of them coincide with Rojas in citing (again at second hand) Heraclitus.

[62] *Cancionero de obras de burlas provocantes a risa,* Valencia, 1519, facsimile ed. A. Pérez y Gómez, Valencia, 1952, sin fo. "De un galán a Juan Poeta."

[63] *Realidad,* edn. I; p. 517; *Structure,* p. 542. Father Fidel Fita gives documentary details in "La Inquisición toledano" (cit., above, n. 15). He cites Pulgar as accusing Jewish denouncers of delighting in false testimony.

more atrocious by comparison. But such exceptions were rare or half forgotten; in general it can be said that jealousy, hatred, and fanaticism prevailed. We shall have occasion to refer again to a *converso* called Juan de Sevilla who fraternized with Jews in the Puebla when to do so was still possible and who later on was denounced to the Inquisition by a series of Jewish witnesses. It was a typical case.[64]

But even a two-fronted battle plan would be a gross oversimplification. As Domínguez Ortiz in his sociological and historical study of the *conversos* of Castile demonstrates at length, the New Christians were violently and viciously divided among themselves. He refers not merely to their persecution by the fanatical Catholic neophytes in their own ranks, the Inquisitors and would-be Inquisitors of whom we spoke previously. In addition to these, *conversos* belonging to families converted in the 1390's and whose Christianity had become habitual resented being bracketed with later converts whose Judaism, evident in appearance and habits, rendered the whole caste suspicious. These, they felt, were the authentically *New* Christians, and they denounced them and discriminated against them in various ways. The latter, in their turn, envious of the social and financial entrenchment of the older *converso* families, fought back in any way they could.[65] For example, as we remember, the well established *mayordomo* of the Lord of the Puebla refused to marry Alvaro de Montalbán's niece, because he considered the family to be *ajudiada*, whereupon her parents initiated a retaliatory campaign of slander against him.

It is a sociological commonplace that minority groups tend to develop internal patterns of discrimination resembling those imposed on them—just as they assimilate the terms and values of the society which oppresses them. Everett Stonequist in *The Marginal Man* presents a number of case histories of American Jews which illustrate the point strikingly. It was, thus, only to be expected that

---

[64] Chap. V, n. 70. Also see F. Fita, "La Inquisición de Torquemada," *BRAH*, xxi, 1893, p. 407. The special quarrelsomeness of Spanish Jews is a recurrent theme of the *Chebet Jehudah*. *Converso* reprisals were, of course, equally violent. Madariaga explains the reaction against those following the law of their fathers convincingly: "The persistence of the Jews who were 'different' when they [the *conversos*] had sacrificed their faith precisely to eliminate that 'difference' had to produce in them a deep irritation and profound resentment" (*Vida*, p. 176).

[65] Domínguez Ortiz, p. 31.

under the violent pressure from the Christian world, *converso* solidarity should develop fissures and cleavages in a number of directions. There was indeed such an exacerbation of the social dimension of the individual that not just deviations and personal idiosyncrasies but all signs of rank or caste tended to involve their bearer in unwelcome conflict.

Related to this (and perhaps more characteristic of Spain because of the unique role, at once marginal and central, of the *conversos* than of social behavior in general) was the impingement (already touched upon) of anti-Semitic feeling into other areas of class strife. The traditional rivalry between town and country was embittered by the belief of the peasants that their urban oppressors were all of Jewish origin. We have already mentioned the decisive eruption of country-dwellers into Toledo during the 1467 *converso* uprising, and Domínguez Ortiz presents a number of other conclusive examples. In at least two localities (Nájera and Almagro), he points out, the word for town dwellers, *"ruanos"* (those who walk in the streets), came to be synonymous with *converso*.[66] In general it can be said that rage against the *conversos* was in many ways a disguised form of revolutionary feeling, and that the resentment of the lower class against their economic exploiters tended to express itself in religious terms.[67] This was a fact half-recognized at the time. The *conversos* with good reason were wont to call their enemies *villanos*, and the Old Christians, often with equally good reason, returned the compliment by calling all nobles and *hidalgos* Jews.[68] It was, as Castro has brilliantly demonstrated, out of this partially disguised (and for that very reason all the more aggravated) class war that many of the fatal peculiarities of Spanish social life, the myth of *limpieza* and the exaggerations of "honor," were to arise. For our purposes, however, it is enough to try to

[66] *Ibid.*, p. 144. This had been commented on previously by Castro.

[67] In addition to Domínguez Ortiz (p. 51, p. 180, and elsewhere), the matter is discussed by Francisco Márquez in his Introduction to Fray Hernando de Talavera's *Católica impugnación*, Barcelona, 1961, with his usual reliability. Castro was again the initiator of the new insight with his depiction of the "Siglo de Oro" less as a willed continuation of the Middle Ages (this traditional view is only superficially enlightening) than as a kind of frozen social revolution. *De la edad conflictiva* contains the most recent development of these views.

[68] In addition to Castro's *De la edad conflictiva*, see Domínguez Ortiz, pp. 198-199.

imagine the life of a man irretrievably and perilously involved in an insane history which he had no way of controlling. This may not be too difficult after all, for although Rojas' history and ours are totally different, his way of being involved was not unlike our own.

As we have seen and shall see again (in our discussion of daily life in the Puebla de Montalbán), all these sectors of conflict extended from the level of history deep into that which four centuries later Unamuno was to call "intra-history."[69] Indeed, aside from major riots and *autos de fe,* the war around Rojas was primarily intra-historical, and its most ferocious contestants were envious neighbors, resentful servants, crazed and ignorant *beatas,*[70] as well as members of the immediate family who with their ingrown hatreds were often the most bellicose of all. The continuity of history into intra-history is a major theme of *La Celestina* and first appears in the Prologue in a series of synonyms for conflict: "What shall we say of men . . . ? Who can explain their wars, enmities, envies, sudden wraths, and changes of mind, and discontents?" Once meaning and importance are subtracted from history, war and minor discontents, decisive battles and family squabbles, come together. They are expressions of a single phenomenon. This sense of alienation from history is basic to *converso* interest in the *De remediis.* When Petrarch reduced fortune from a goddess supervising the life histories of famous men to the level of daily occurrence —a child fallen from a window, thieving servants, a nagging wife— his *converso* readers in Spain understood him from within their own lives.[71]

---

[69] By this was meant the daily texture of human relations and activities, the changeless customs and repetitions, which underlie those superficial events, battles, royal marriages, and the rest, traditionally deemed more worthy of the historian's attention. There, according to the Generation of '98, is to be found the permanence of nations.

[70] See, for example, the lengthy dossier containing the malicious and obviously paranoic accusations made over a number of years (1557-1559) by the Talaveran *beata* Catalina González against her neighbor the Licentiate Alonso de Montenegro (cited Chap. II, n. 58). It is appalling to observe the scrupulous attention paid by the Inquisitors to her insane ravings—although it must also be said that eventually and reluctantly they decided not to follow up her charges. As we shall see in Chap. VIII, the Licentiate and his wife seem to have enjoyed the game of stringing her along.

[71] One may apply to the *converso* experience of Petrarch the same observation Bernhard Groethuysen applies to Petrarch's own understanding of the Stoicism of the ancients. Stoic concepts of life, he says, "acquire a new im-

All of *La Celestina* with its texture of argumentation, squabbling, and agonizing inner debate can be considered a kind of giant *exemplum* of the Petrarchist sense of life. But perhaps where the author's *converso* alienation most explicitly merges with the intimate misery of conflictive daily existence is in the speech of Sempronio's on the war of time with value discussed previously. The battles with Turks and Moors, the aggression of thieves against Pedro's possessions, and the inner discord which led to Cristóbal's drunkenness and Inés' suicide, all taken as manifestations of the same reasonless *contienda* to which man is exposed, form a generational manifesto. It is a passage which could only have been written by a man who was an exile at home, axiologically "de su tierra absente." And it spoke directly to the hearts and minds of those who shared that situation.[72]

Awareness of life as warfare, warfare ranging from major clashes of nations and cultures through the minor skirmishes and aggressions which make up the texture of human existence, to the historyless ferocity of the animal world, was, thus, at once a theme of *La Celestina* and a fundamental part of the experience of being a *converso*. Hence, the dissimulation and camouflage to which Rojas' characters have continual recourse is a reflection of the dissimulation and camouflage which he and Alvaro de Montalbán and their friends and relations found necessary for their survival. Madariaga sees the *conversos* as an army in retreat, divided against itself and with very low morale; their ranks are shot through with "profound

---

portance and significance because they are felt by a new kind of man and appear in a new reference to life" (*Philosophische Antropologie*, Munich and Berlin, 1931, p. 105). With similar perceptivity to history (unfortunately missing in Menéndez Pelayo who saw in the *De remediis* only pedantry) Cassirer analyzes the "excitement and liveliness of these dialogues" for men of the time (see *The Individual and the Cosmos*, p. 37).

[72] We must distinguish ironical distance and apparent unconcern first of all from the attitude of writers caught up in the enthusiasm of the epic moment: Juan del Encina, el Cartujano, and the Italian Peter Martyr ("this is the happy ending of Spain's calamities"). But it is even more important to remind ourselves of the other option considered in the previous chapter: nihilistic and aggressive hatred particularly of everything official. Domínguez Ortiz cites a Venetian ambassador who describes certain *conversos* as "having a particular and immeasurable hatred of the King, the crown, the government, justice and everything indiscriminately." As descendants of those persecuted by the Inquisition, they were condemned to "perpetual infamy and live therefore in the greatest desperation and anger" (p. 180).

resentment and deep irritation."[73] Nevertheless they survive, because "pretending and dissimulation become a second nature to them."

Yet we must never forget that it is also an army which along with cowards (as we pointed out, the theme of cowardice in *La Celestina* is noteworthy in its penetration) was also capable of producing heroes. The very subjection of the individual *converso* to fortune as well as the sense of being "a victim of social disdain" led to the kind of vocational heroism we have seen. From an Old Christian point of view, this was interpreted as "ambition" and "restlessness," a terminology of prejudice not unfamiliar in our own time. But this is misleading. Although the will to win often merely involved getting to the top in a given profession, it also could express itself in the exaltation of martyrdom,[74] religious reform, and feats of conquest.[75] Cowardice and heroism, dissimulation and exaltation, necessarily accompanied each other in the world of "contienda y batalla" in which the *conversos* were *criados* (brought up). It is not surprising they are *all* to be found in the make-up and behavior of the inhabitants of *La Celestina*.

The literary expression of this world is not limited to Fernando de Rojas and his predecessor. We find it again in the *Lazarillo de Tormes* and even more explicitly in the *Guzmán de Alfarache* and the picaresque novels of the seventeenth century. Lazarillo begins his story, we remember, by telling us of his father's death in the battle of las Gelves (Djerba), but, as in Sempronio's discourse, he immediately brushes past the plane of history and begins to chronicle the battles and skirmishes, the offense and defense, of daily living at the lowest levels. At once anti-hero and hero, Lazarillo makes

---

[73] *Vida*, p. 176.

[74] See Chap. III, n. 45. Montes recounts moving examples of self-conscious martyrdom in the *autos de fe*, and, indeed, as in the case of the Blessed Juan de Avila, the mere attribution of martyrdom to Inquisitional victims was sufficient motive for denunciation. See Lea, II, 588, and the moving statements of Fray Francisco Ortiz reproduced by Angela Selke in *El Santo Oficio*, p. 143 and elsewhere.

[75] Although such *conversos* as Saint Teresa or Alonso de Ercilla may in a sense have been opposed to "official history" (the Saint sees the hypocrisy of her order's self-presentation, while the poet-conquistador in one of his last cantos depicts Spaniards as corrupting a natural Indian Golden Age), nevertheless, unlike Rojas, they did believe that history could and should be profoundly meaningful.

187

war on his masters with calculation and courage in a world which demands both for survival. As for the *Guzmán*, passages such as the following echo both Petrarch and Rojas with high fidelity:

> Everything is turned upside down; everything goes too fast and is all mixed up. No man truly communes with another; we all live in ambush, lying in wait for each other the way cats do to rats or the spider which, upon catching a snake unawares, hangs from a strand and seizing it by the neck, tightens it hard, not letting go of it until the snake dies of the poison.[76]

"I know nothing about what lies beyond"

The expression of this "conflictive" sense of life in the *Guzmán de Alfarache*, published exactly a century after *La Celestina*,

---

[76] *Guzmán de Alfarache*, Part I, Book II, Chap. IV (translation mine). There has been much discussion of the *pícaro* as literary and social type, discussion usually involving lists of necessary or common characteristics. But, as Castro maintains, such typification is meaninglessly abstract without complementary comprehension of the *pícaro* as living in a picaresque world. Novels—and this includes even these proto-novels—are not stories of heroism or anti-heroism but rather an interplay of experience between person and circumstance. Hence, the classification of the *Lazarillo*, the *Guzmán*, and their successors as "picaresque" implies the existence of the protagonists (or as Castro phrases it, "how it felt to exist within the happening") in a recognizably identical literary world: a world of hostility, brutality, and small-scale bellicosity. That is to say, the picaresque novel presented life adapted to a world—and this in itself is profoundly ironical—as it appeared to *conversos* in the tradition of Fernando de Rojas. Even authors who were not *conversos* (Vicente Espinel) or who attacked *conversos* (Quevedo), as Bataillon has recently stressed ("Les Nouveaux Chrétiens"), imitated not only the type but the satire of honor and lineage as irrelevant to such existence. Unremitting daily warfare and evacuation of values coincide in an environment as hard and alien as the stone column with which the blind beggar is induced to collide. This does not mean, of course, that I think Rojas, the author of the *Lazarillo*, or Mateo Alemán were themselves in any sense *pícaros*. Rather, these novels, like *La Celestina* although in a different way, may be thought of as simplified literary projections—narrative parables—of the Heraclitean and Petrarchan world view which had taken root in the post-Inquisitional generation of marginal lives and which subsequently "sprouted branches and leaves" of words. A reading of the continuations both of the *Lazarillo* and the *Guzmán* (I rely on Bataillon for the latter part of the assertion) demonstrates that the *converso* tenor of the picaresque narrative metaphor was clearly understood at the time. Reading these novels in terms of *Til Eulenspiegel*, the *Decameron*, Rabelais, or Saul Bellow is an anachronism.

shows far greater clarification and codification. Attitudes that are implicit or under the surface of Rojas' work become explicit in that of Mateo Alemán. This is particularly true of the sense of a loss of relationship between supernature and the devalued and incessantly bellicose world in which we live. As Carlos Blanco has pointed out, the beginning of Guzmán's autobiography is a reenactment of man's fall and expulsion from paradise.[77] After that, the two planes, the mundane and the celestial, are held apart and contrasted the one against the other all along the narrative course. The basic biographical pattern of the Middle Ages had been the saint's life, a life in which the human and divine are intertwined by definition. In the life of this archetypal *pícaro*, however, the two are rigidly separated and referred to in alternating segments. Petrarch would have dissented bitterly from such a conclusion, but it is nevertheless true that to present the world as he and Rojas and Mateo Alemán present it implies a withdrawal of God from human affairs. This might (as in the *Lazarillo*) or might not (as in the *Guzmán*) reflect doubt or even tacit denial of His existence. What matters to us is the sense of separation. The fascination the *De remediis* had for Fernando de Rojas and for others like him may, thus, be related not only to their experience of life as daily warfare but also to a concomitant loss of religious immediacy.[78] Having abandoned one faith and not yet gained another, they were themselves abandoned, the first community of men since the Romans to face a universe of withdrawn hope and alien dimensions. In Rojas' particular case, the feelings of Alvaro de Montalbán are revealing but not decisive. They need not be. As we shall see, a straightforward reading of *La Celestina*, particularly of the climactic speeches made before and after Melibea's suicide, can lead to no other conclusion. Al-

[77] "Cervantes y la picaresca," *NRFH*, XI (1957), 316-328.

[78] For more general discussion of *converso* incredulity and its Jewish background, see, in addition to Castro, Caro Baroja (I, 229 ff. and 445; II, 193, 220, 229, 383), and Baer. Benardete discusses the difficulties in reintegration to the "Law of Moses" experienced by *conversos* after emigration (p. 41). According to J. Nehama whom he cites, the Ashkenasis were generally suspicious of the Sephardim, holding them to be lukewarm in faith and rationalistic. I.S. Revah, in his studies of Spinoza and João de Barros, indicates lively polemics among exiled Spanish Jews and reconverted *conversos* concerning the immortality of the soul and punishment after death (*Spinoza et le Dr. Juan de Prado*, Paris, 1959, and others).

though God remains in the language of the speakers, He is withdrawn from their world of contention and battle.

Again—as Lucien Febvre warns us—we must make an effort to comprehend this withdrawal in terms other than our own.[79] If today we speak of the "death of God" or of Martin Buber's less definitive "eclipse of God" with a certain complacency, it is because scientific discoveries have acted as a buffer between ourselves and ultimate mystery. But in Rojas' time the removal of divine sense from all the ritual activity of daily life, prayers, food preparation, dress, greetings, and all the rest, left a vacancy and rootlessness far more alarming than most of us have experienced. It was not just a question of disbelief or doubt but of being caught between "laws," without foreordained meaning and direction in the paths of existence.

The story of the 1492 baptism of Abraham Senior (a principal advisor of the Catholic Monarchs and, in fact, the agent in arranging their marriage) is revealing. The ceremony was to be an important one; the King and Queen, themselves, were to be the godparents; but on the appointed day it was learned that the future *converso* had gone to the synagogue to pray. The royal sponsors were deeply chagrined, fearing that he might have changed his mind and that this important conquest for Catholicism (according to Lea, they had put a great deal of pressure on him in order not to lose his services)[80] might be lost. Abraham Senior explained, however, "that until his baptism he might not abandon his obligations as a Jew, because he did not wish to live for a single hour outside the law" (*sin ley*).[81] Religion was far more rooted into the habits and the basic rhythms of existence than it is for most of us; and conversion, as Alvaro de Montalbán discovered, demanded an effort far greater than mere intellectual acceptance.

Not many *conversos* had the strength of will of Abraham Senior or his full comprehension of his own situation. Instead they tended to waver between the two laws, keeping portions of each, and ending by losing the comfort that unthinking conformity to either might have given them.[82] There is confirmation of this in the anti-

---

[79] *Le Problème de l'incroyance au XVIe siècle*, Paris, 1942, pp. 496 ff.
[80] I, 138.　　　　　　　　　　　　　　　[81] Sicroff, p. 147.
[82] See Márquez' Introduction to the *Católica impugnación*, and for a series of graphic examples of mixture of laws, as well as Lea's reproduced list of Inquisitional cases in the year 1486 in Zaragoza (I, 601).

Semitic literature of the time. Predictably most of those who attacked the *conversos* concentrated their fire on secret practices and conspiracies: obscene rituals and defilement of objects of Christian worship, plans to overthrow the government and poison the neighbors, and other such misbehavior. But in the midst of these atrocious clichés, we are surprised to find moments of authentic insight into the *converso* situation. The best example occurs, perhaps, in a polemic between the chronicler of the Catholic Monarchs, Hernando del Pulgar, and an anonymous antagonist. Hernando del Pulgar, himself a *converso*, was well aware of the deviations of his fellows, and in his *Chronicle* he defends the establishment of the Inquisition in Toledo: ". . . among the Christians who were of Jewish lineage . . . some were found . . . who in their great ignorance endangered their souls *by not keeping either law*."[83] On the occasion of the polemic, however, he came to the defense of the New Christians, maintaining that at the worst they were "good Jews" in a world of very "bad Christians." The anonymous answer, unusual for its moderate tone, goes to the heart of the problem: admitting that there are bad Christians and that, "although some of them defile the walls of our Holy Church with their evil lives, even so the edifice of its law remains entire. But if one takes out the cornerstone of the edifice which is faith, tell me, what then remains? And this is what is done by those you call 'good Jews' but who are really liars in both laws."[84] The danger presented by the *conversos*—in spite of all the frenzied accusations that were current—was not to morality but to belief. The nature of their experience had made them skeptical.

A frequently cited anti-*converso* pamphlet which stresses this particular danger is the anonymous *Libro del Alborayque* (1488). The word "*alborayque*" refers to the monstrous animal which carried Mohammed on his back from Jerusulem to Mecca and which,

[83] F. Fita, "La Inquisición en Ciudad Real," *BRAH*, xvi-xvii (1890), 510.
[84] See F. Cantera Burgos, "Fernando del Pulgar y los conversos," *Sefarad*, iv (1944), 318. Such accusations were frequent in the anti-Semitic literature of the time. The notorious Bachelor Marquillos de Mazarambros (instigator of the first discriminatory statute) calls *conversos* "the hated, tainted, detested, fourth class and estate of baptized Jews and of those proceeding from their tainted lineage, adulterers, children of incredulity and infidelity" (E. B. Ruano, "El memorial contra los conversos," *Sefarad*, xvii [1957], 321). The Cura de los Palacios is just as violent: ". . . they were neither Jews nor Christians . . . but rather heretics without any law" (quoted by Domínguez Ortiz, p. 19).

like the *conversos*, belonged to no known species. All *conversos*, according to the polemicist, may be divided into two groups: the *mesumad* whose change of faith was voluntary and sincere and the *hanuzaym* (*anusim*), the "forced." These latter are "circumcised like Moors, guard the Sabbath like Jews, and are Christians only in name. Really they are not Moors, Jews, or Christians, and, although they may wish to be Jews, they do not keep the precepts of the Talmud or observe Jewish ceremonies. Still less do they observe the law of the Christians. That is why they have all been called in vituperation, *alborayques*." The result—it is asserted—is a special receptivity to heresy. The *anusim* tend to credit "as many heresies as the ancient philosophers, some of whom said that there was nothing but being born and dying, or as their grandparents, the Jews. . . ."[85] The author of the *Libro del Alborayque* was strongly partisan (it is easy to guess he was a member of the group he calls the *mesumad*), but he seems as much concerned with analyzing a real situation as with venting his passion. Our glimpse into the marginal and skeptical minds of Alvaro de Montalbán and his fellows provide his *Libro* with moving confirmation.

In a case not yet referred to, Inquisitional testimony allows us to overhear a *converso*, Micer Pedro de la Caballería (previously don Bonafós), one of the most powerful men in Aragón, express his own situation as such an *alborayque*. The testimony is probably false (it was given by a hostile Jew long after his death), but it is not for that reason less interesting. In conversation with a Jewish friend, Micer Pedro was heard to say, "Who keeps me from fasting on Yom Kippur if I wish to or from celebrating your holidays and all the rest? Who prevents me? But when I was a Jew I dared not walk as far as this on Saturday[86] and now I am free to do whatever I like." The Jewish friend, somewhat scandalized, replied, "Ha, Sir, don't you know that the law imposes this and that upon you, and

---

[85] From the summary and excerpts of F. Fita, "La inquisición de Torquemada," pp. 379-82. Heretical sects among the Jews are listed as "marbonios, saduceos, oseos (Essenes?), fariseos, meristeos, ymerobatistes." The use of hybrid images (such as "alborayque") to depict individual *conversos* as belonging to no fixed species was a commonplace of 15th-century satirical poetry. For one example see E. Grey, "An Ingenious Portrayal of a Split Personality," *Romance Notes*, IX (1968), 1-4.

[86] In his *History*, Baer interprets this to mean that he would not have been able to go "beyond the prescribed limits of a Sabbath day's walk" (II, 227).

that you, being a Christian, are not acting right in so doing!" Micer Pedro's answer is almost Marlovian: "Now I am free to do whatever I wish, for the old days are well past."[87] He can speak with such revealing frankness precisely because he glories in his liberation from ritual. If at the end of the century, many of the *anusim* felt lost, exposed, and exceptional in their fervent world, Micer Pedro de la Caballería (who was assassinated in 1465) had no regret for lost certitudes. And, as he spoke, so might have spoken the pagan courtiers and favorites of Henry IV of Castile who were attacked by the partisans of Prince Alfonso in a 1464 propaganda blast: "It is well known that there are individuals at your court, in your palace, and indeed close to your very person who are nonbelievers, enemies of our Holy Catholic Faith and others who, although nominally Christians, are suspicious in their faith and who believe and say and affirm that there is no other world and that we are born and die like animals, a heresy which destroys our Christian faith, and they are continually blaspheming and denying Our Lord and Our Lady, the Virgin Mary, and the Saints. And it is to these that your Majesty has given high honors and estates and dignities. . . ."[88]

[87] My translation from the document as reproduced in *Die Jüden* (II, 464) was made prior to the publication of the *History*. In the latter, Baer devotes considerable attention to the family, one excellent source being the long drawn out trial of Alfonso de la Caballería, Vice Chancellor of Aragón who was finally acquitted in 1501. From it emerges a fascinating portrait of a man of brilliant legal attainments, keen mind, and skeptical views, "a typical Renaissance personality." A number of witnesses testify to having heard him repeat a proverb, "En este mundo no hay más que nacer y morir; no hay otro paraíso" (pp. 372-379), even more explicit than "En este mundo no me veas mal pasar. . . ."

[88] Alfonso de Palencia, *Crónica de Enrique IV* (cited by Castro, *Realidad*, edn. II, p. 238). This description of the Royal Court is confirmed by the scribe Gabriel Tetzel, who accompanied Leon von Rozmital of Blatna on a journey through Spain in 1465. He portrays the temporary capital of Olmedo as full of "pagans" who were irreverent during Mass and who lived a life of "impurity and sodomy." The lack of fanaticism during this reign is surprising to the same observer. When he passes through Mérida, for example, he comments on the co-existence of six different sects, the names of which are not given in the Spanish translation (*Viajes de extranjeros por España*, cited Chap. III, n. 11): "heiden, juden, confessen, pauletten, grechen, und de la centura" (*Des böhmischen Herrn Leo's von Rozmital, Ritter-, Hof- und Pilger-reise durch die Abenlande*, ed. J. A. Schmeller, Stuttgart, 1844, p. 185). From the context we may conclude that the "heiden" were "moriscos," while

❧ "Razón y sinrazón"

The *Libro del Alborayque*, when it speaks of the heresies of the "philosophers," suggests a tradition reaching far behind the arrogant paganism of some members of the preceding generation. As Lea, Caro Baroja, and Baer demonstrate, there had long been an Averroistic movement in Saducean Jewish circles which was favorable to skepticism and rational judgment.[89] Baer, in particular, in his recent *History of the Jews in Christian Spain* provides much new information concerning the ideas lying behind *La Celestina* and the ordeal of Alvaro de Montalbán. Citing a number of violent attacks by orthodox rabbis on fifteenth-century holders of Averroistic views, he observes that rational disillusionment with inherited beliefs and with the rigidities of ritual seems to have been widespread among those who were well off. Even worse, the danger represented by Averroism to the continuity of the Jewish community was rendered especially grave by the existence of the *conversos* and by the tempting and profitable possibility of joining their number. Although Christianity was "even more . . . inconsistent with the religion of reason than Judaism," lack of fervent belief in the latter made baptism seem a less significant step. Why not, in other words, submit to one more rite demanded by society, since all of them would have seemed unreasonable to Aristotle and his Moorish prophet? "To be born and to die; all the rest is a snare and a delusion," Baer concludes, summed up the "whole faith" of "philosophical intellectuals, Averroists, and nihilists," whether they appeared as bankers and physicians "in their modest Jewish garb" or as "*conversos* in the magnificent array of courtiers or knights."[90] I would not be inclined to assert that the lives of either Fernando de Rojas or his father-in-law (in view of what we know of the more or less humble Judaizing of their families) can be explained in terms of such a well defined and ultimately unproblematical philos-

---

"juden" and "confessen" offer no problem. My colleagues Morton Bloomfield and George Williams tentatively identify the others as Albigensian refugees, Greek Orthodox, and spiritualist Franciscans.

[89] It is interesting to note that Fray Alonso de Espina in an enumeration of Jewish sects in the *Fortalitium fidei* identifies the Saducees with denial of immortality: "alii vocantur saducei qui non credunt almas post mortem manere" (cited by Caro Baroja, I, 489).

[90] Baer, II, 270-277.

ophy. Neither great books nor unwary self-betrayals are made directly from ideas; living experience must be the incubator. But, on the other hand, there can be no doubt but that their anguished view of the world as deserted by providence and only justified by the transitory "*gozo*" of a blazing love affair or of a cool glass of wine delivered by a single page was not entirely the product of immediate circumstances. There was evidently an appropriate fifteenth-century intellectual tradition to which their questing minds could direct themselves.

Direct evidence to this effect is offered by a book in Rojas' library, *La visión delectable* (an allegorized and semi-Christianized version of the *Guide for the Perplexed*) which, purporting to be a reasonable man's answer to materialism and agnosticism, thereby effectively reveals their existence. Among others, the author, Alfonso de la Torre, proposes to correct such errant opinions as the following: "There is no difference between the death of a rat caught by a cat when going out to drink and that of a prophet bitten by a serpent on his way to preach"; "God has removed His protection from the earth He created"; or "Once a man dies, that is the end of him."[91] I do not intend to suggest, nor do I think Baer would argue, that such Spanish Jews and some of their *converso* descendants were eighteenth-century paladins of reason crusading against faith or even that Alvaro de Montalbán was necessarily more rational than his Inquisitors. What does seem to be the case, however, is that interest in philosophy and reasonable discussion of its problems led, long before the epoch of the *conversos*, to a view of the universe as distinct from man, alien to him, inexplicable perhaps, but free from ghosts and auguries.

Castro's brilliant discussion of the fourteenth-century Jewish poet, Sem Tob of Carrión, centers on this point: "This refined rationalist, this rebel against boredom, rejects the commonplaces of those who denounce the world: 'There is no evil in it save ourselves, neither monsters nor anything else. . . . It becomes neither appeased nor enraged, it neither loves nor hates, it is not crafty, nor does it answer questions or cry out . . . for the world is always

---

[91] *Curiosidades bibliográficas*, BAE, vol. 36 (Madrid, 1871), pp. 358, 373-374. Atheism is specifically refuted with the following argument: "Just as a blind man might think that blindness afflicts everyone's eyes, fools ordinarily think that, since they can't see anything incorporeal, neither God nor angels exist . . ." (p. 350).

one and constant'" (i.e. the world has a constant being).[92] Words such as "atheism" or "agnosticism" seem somehow out of place, but when individuals to whom remnants of this intellectual tradition were available had an unfamiliar faith forced on them, doubt and concealed (or aggressive) questioning of providence were only to be expected. Their existence in *La Celestina* should certainly not surprise critics interested in interpreting it in terms of its time.[93]

A not unnatural corollary of the rational approach was interest in and understanding of space and time as dimensions. On the lowest level this may be related to the traditionally Jewish capacity for monetary abstraction: calculation of interest, management of estates, surveying, division of real estate and inheritances. But, aside from this traditional and practical knowledge of how to measure space and time and how to calculate human desires in terms of monetary value, the *conversos* naturally shared in the spatial preoccupation of their contemporaries. That is to say, they saw space in a way it had not been seen previously. Long before *La Celestina,* Sem Tob (in a passage discussed by Castro) had described his careless objective world as the "lueñe tierra" (the long land).[94] Just as Calisto in the soliloquy of Act XIV proceeds from a realization that external dimensions will not change according to his desires ("there is an equal course for all, a single space for life and death") to a vision of the heavens ("the high celestial firmament"), so too Sem Tob had associated the dimensionality of the world with its lack of interest in human affairs. And in the century of Columbus and Uccello, the century when background in painting began to replace foreground, spatial awareness was far more acute.

It will not be necessary here to discuss Jewish excellence in astronomy (Abraham Zacut had left Salamanca in 1492 just prior to Rojas' arrival) and navigation or the later acceptance of Copernicus by *converso* professors. What concerns us primarily is consciousness of space as alien to human concerns, a consciousness that was characteristic of the period as a whole and that could not

[92] *Realidad,* edn. I, p. 528; *Structure,* p. 554.

[93] In his Celestinesque *Diálogo,* Villalobos portrays himself being teased by his noble interlocutor about his skepticism and doubts concerning the Trinity. Elsewhere he remarks that Pliny in "nostro aevo" would be jailed by "moderna charitas" for his views on the mortality of the soul (*Algunas obras,* p. 200).

[94] *Realidad,* edn. I, p. 547; *Structure,* p. 573.

fail to be shared with special acuteness by *converso* intellectuals.[95] One of the false opinions referred to in the *Visión delectable* is "that beyond the sky there is an infinite body, that is to say *all empty*."[96] When Juan de Lucena in his *De vita felici* presents the well-eroded topic of transitory fame, he renovates it in precisely these terms: by substituting space for the temporal commonplace. Why strive for fame, he asks, if "the earth according to mathematicians is no more than a tiny point in the middle of the universe surrounded by the abyss of the rotating Heavens"?[97]

Our comprehension of the world around Fernando de Rojas would be dangerously oversimplified, were we to imagine the *conversos* as an inner circle of rationalists, intellectuals, and technicians, persecuted by an insane and fanatical society. The truth is that fanaticism and passion (characteristic of a period alert for signs of the coming of the Anti-Christ)[98] were rife all through the ranks of the *conversos*—and not just among those who tried to be more Christian than their Old Christian neighbors. The Inquisition trials are full of blasphemies often involving a hatred of the newly imposed ritual so intense that they became (like the black mass) a kind of worship in reverse. Crucifixes and other objects of Christian worship were defiled and beaten; hosts were stolen, tortured, and used as ingredients in magic concoctions; ritual crucifixions were talked about if not actually performed. The mother-in-law of Fernando de Montalbán (a probable relative from the Puebla) was typically accused not only of having washed the baptismal water off her child's head but also of having thrown a crucifix into a cesspool.[99] Of course, many of these accusations are malicious lies while others are gross exaggerations. But nevertheless, after reading a number of trial transcripts, I would conclude that such be-

---

[95] See my "The Fall of Fortune: from Allegory to Fiction," *Filología Romanza*, xxv (1957), 340 ff. for further discussion of *La Celestina*'s spatial presentation in its relationship to art and art history.

[96] p. 345.

[97] pp. 139-140. For a definitive discussion of this new sense of space in terms of Renaissance philosophy, see Cassirer's *The Individual*, pp. 176 ff.

[98] The coming of the Anti-Christ had been effectively preached by Saint Vincent Ferrer, and fear of his advent remained latent through the century. See J. Wadsworth, *Lyons*, Cambridge, Mass., 1962, pp. 27-31. In 1497 a "biography-chronicle" of the Anti-Christ appeared in Spanish (presumably related to those cited by Wadsworth). See Chap. VI, n. 120.

[99] Baer, *Die Juden*, ii, 448.

havior (understandable under the circumstances) was not infrequent.

Thus, in a way both antithetical and complementary to the tired disbelief of Alvaro de Montalbán, other more superstitious *conversos* were willing to do anything which might give relief to their feelings or believe anything which promised redress. We have already mentioned one example: the Messianic wave which swept over Castile and Andalusia as a result of the preachings of a fifteen-year-old false prophetess. Another kind of consolation was found by the *conversos* who swelled the ranks of the *"alumbrados,"* a sect of *illuminati* to be discussed briefly in Chapter VI. Witches and magicians, some of them admittedly charlatans and others (like Celestina) more or less convinced of their own powers, made large profits. A contemporary of Rojas who began practicing in 1501 was the physician Eugenio Torralba, famous for a familiar spirit named Zequiel who characteristically transported him through space (as in the original legend of Dr. Faust), brought him news from all the world capitals, but was unable to protect him from the Holy Office.[100] It was the one power that even Celestina was afraid of.

Not all of this irrationalism deserves condescension—Voltairian or otherwise. Much has been written about *converso* contributions to the renascent spirituality and mysticism of the sixteenth century. Although it was a phenomenon for which Rojas probably had little sympathy, he surely had read and admired the eloquent Spanish translations of the Old Testament which circulated among *conversos* as well as the poetry of their clandestine prayers. Some of the latter are preserved in Inquisition records and are written with a passionate intensity moving even to the non-believer. In words of desperation and hope, the tortured human spirit, like that of Kafka's ape (in the *Report to the Learned Society*), found new meaning in its highest faculties. A typical lament *de profundia* expresses directly the anguish of the time:

> I return to Thee, with tears and sighs and great repentance like a son to his father asking for pardon and mercy . . . praying that Thou wilt lift me out of the mud and the great tribulation into which I have fallen. . . . O Adonai, Adonai, Adonai! Take pity on me . . . Thou who art light of lights, flame of char-

[100] See Llorente, III, 228ff.

ity, law for the good, merit of crowned heads, king over kings, peace with sufferance, patience of love, will fulfilled, the way and the life, sun before dawning, star of light, heaven of delight, angel of good company, paradise of rest. . . .[101]

However much Rojas might have admired the style of these prayers or sympathized with his fellows crying out, like Pleberio, from the depths of "hac lachrymarum valle," he could not share their exaltation. Harried by brute force, carefully administered hatred, and outrageous fortune, he apparently felt, as did those Jewish heretics attacked by Maimonides, that God had "abandoned the world." As we shall see, the sense of hopelessness is so strong at the end of *La Celestina* that a translator into French felt compelled to add a new character whose role it was to console the stricken father with a set of commonplaces which Rojas had refused to intone: those which explain why God permits evil to exist and how grateful we should be that He does.

What was left after the departure of divine significance from life? The answer has already been given: an acute and special form of that "existentialist distress" which Maritain sees characterizing the end of the fifteenth century. One felt oneself adrift, exposed to naked and careless space, subjected to days and years and decades of meaningless history. Petrarch's *De remediis* with its vision of the world as incessant conflict, a place of rancor and change in which to confer value on anything was an act of folly (albeit an unavoidable one), found in the Spanish *conversos* some of its best prepared readers. Georg Lukacs describes the novel as founded on a sense of "Obdachlosigkeit," which is to say rooflessness or shelterlessness. It was understandably in such times as these and for such readers

---

[101] F. Fita, "La Inquisición en Guadalupe," *BRAH*, xxii (1893), 325-326. The above fragment was taken from a much longer prayer of which one initial sentence suggests a reason for *converso* predilection for Erasmus: ". . . syn ymagen esculpida nin pintada, e sin ningund abogado que me fie delante de ty, ca non es menester, señor . . ." (p. 323). On other occasions orally transmitted versions of the Psalms were employed ritually. Versions of the 114th, a sheer celebration of divine power as surpassing all bounds of nature and reason, were not uncommon and are to be found both in Spanish and American archives: "Los montes baylaron como ciervos; los cerros como fijos de las ovejas. ¿Qué as la mar? ¿Porqué fuyes? Et el Jordán ¿porqué torrnas atrás? . . ." see F. Fita, "Fragmentos de un ritual hispano-hebreo del siglo XV," *BRAH*, xxxvi (1900), 87. Also in B. Lewin, *Mártires y conquistadores judíos en la América Hispana*, Buenos Aires, 1954, p. 16.

that the oldest representatives of the genre should have been written.

But not even a Taine would pretend that times can weep or put pen to paper. The true significance of the story assembled by Fernando de Rojas lies not in things he heard about or even in events he may have witnessed but in the nature and quality of his reaction. Here is the Rojas who has not disappeared, the Rojas who lives in us. When the old story died and was reborn in a new story called *La Celestina*, his unique experience of his times, not what he knew but the way he felt, became immortal. Such self-evident generalizations apply to any major author; the special thing about Rojas and his fellow proto-novelists is the acute self-consciousness of their investigation of history and their correspondingly acute creative concern with the nature of the individual consciousness in its relation to others and to the world. All the atrocities of these terrible years are, of course, not less atrocious because of *La Celestina*, the *Lazarillo*, or ultimately the *Quijote*. And yet the newly intense, ultimately non-Medieval self-consciousness expressed in these masterpieces and generated by a need to comprehend incomprehensible times has been a blessing to mankind ever since.

The adjective, "self-conscious" in English is usually associated with social awkwardness, shyness, lack of the "naturalness" that Stendhal used to try to imitate. Overconcerned with the impression he may be making upon others, the self-conscious person watches himself behaving, hears himself talking, and criticizes himself as if he were somebody else. Insofar as we may have participated in such feelings, we are in a better position to understand the situation of the young Fernando de Rojas trying to explain the new being imposed on him by society. How did this stranger come to be me? Who is he? What does being him entail? These were the questions which the first oral biography (not autobiography) of the future author of *La Celestina* was designed to answer. For such as he the entity we now call "contemporary history" was a form of self-consciousness.

It will be objected that self-consciousness of the sort familiar to us is commonly thought of as a stage of adolescence through which we pass on the road to maturity, a stage terminated when we come to terms with ourselves and with the others among whom we must live. The objection is valid. The profound and important difference between the self-consciousness of sixteenth-century *conversos* and that which we ourselves may have experienced is that theirs never came to an end. The more they heard about the story of their kind, the more strange and alien they seemed to themselves. Like men watching their mirror images, they practiced facial expressions and observed their own movements with wonder.[102] To live such times as these was to be hopelessly aware of awareness. Or, seen more positively, to grow older without growing up and so being able to combine accumulated wisdom with an undiminished capacity for intense experience. In a profound and unorthodox sense, I would maintain that not only the novels just mentioned but also the poetry of Fray Luis de León, the autobiography of Saint Teresa, and even the plays of Juan del Encina originate in a permanent identity crisis.

This should not be taken to mean that I propose any sort of fixed characterization for *converso* writers and their writing. Quite to the contrary, from the vantage point of self-consciousness the number of paths is limitless and freedom to choose among them, guaranteed. What they share is not themes or fixed traits or style or genre but a sense of self as different and inexplicable. Inexplicable, among other things, because always changing. Over and over again in these writers we discern a special perceptiveness for time: the moment passed, the moment passing, the moment to pass sensed not with Baroque display but as an intimate inner mutability. As one observes curiously all the feelings, reactions, and fleeting ideas that constitute on-going awareness, one perceives therein a new region of time. Which is precisely why Rojas was far more concerned with his lovers' "process of delight" than with their fixed characterization—and why Fray Luis circumscribed his feelings in a

---

[102] Stonequist points out: "The hypersensitiveness of the marginal man has been repeatedly noticed by sociologists. This trait is related to the exaggerated self-consciousness developed by continually looking at himself through the eyes of others." He goes on to cite, among many other examples, William Du Bois' presentation of Negro existence as characterized by "double consciousness." Stonequist's explanation of the term is interesting for our purposes: "In the case of the marginal man, it is as if he were placed simultaneously between two looking-glasses, each presenting a sharply different image of himself." Hence the marginal situation with its "fluctuating and contradictory opinions, its tendency towards 'self-rejection,' and all the rest" (*The Marginal Man*, pp. 145-150).

frame of temporal adverbs: "cuando," "ya," "mientras," "luego," "aún." It would be overbold to assert, according to the formula of Ortega, that the theme of Rojas' times was time. Rather, we must try to imagine from within how the new kind of consciousness he shared absorbed the frenzied time of history and the inexorable time of clocks and transmuted them. Thus it was that *La Celestina* and Luis Vives' *Treatise on the Soul*—the one creatively and the other meditatively—ask and answer the same questions. Instead of the "Quid est anima?" of the theologians, these unprecedented sensibilities wondered "how the soul works and what are its operations . . . as manifested to our intelligence little by little and in bits and pieces?"[103] Beneath what Juan Marichal has called Antonio de Guevara's "previously composed image" of authority, piety, and wisdom,[104] the latter was, he confesses, "variable in appetites, profound in the heart, mutable in thoughts, and indeterminable in goals."[105]

Many other examples could be added, and yet, as I said, it would be mistaken to claim that the creation of human and inhuman time by historical times was a *converso* characteristic. As authors, a Rojas or a Vives or a Fray Luis were not *conversos*; they were awarenesses subjected to the *converso* situation. Only by thinking in such terms can we hope to understand how *La Celestina*'s remorseless irony expresses a mind at a distance, conscious of itself in time because all else is alien, even its name and the reflection of its corporal envelope in the mirror. *Converso* biographies taken as a group are biographies of captivity and liberation. From without each individual was imprisoned, "forced" to accept the identity of his caste, but from within his mind in the course of time could discover means of consolation, seek out avenues of escape, or realize, like Fabrice del Dongo in the Tour Farnese, that awareness of captivity is the highest form of freedom. At which point a *Celestina* becomes possible and its author stops being a *converso*.

[103] I have slightly rearranged the quotation. Vives' Latin reads as follows: "Anima quid sit, nihil interest nostra scire: qualis autem et quae eius opera, permultum . . . quae paulatim se per partes ad intelligentium totius proferant" (*De anima et vita*, Basel, 1538, facsimile ed. M. Sancipriano, Turin, 1959, p. 39).

[104] *La voluntad de estilo*, Barcelona, 1957, p. 96.

[105] From the *Relox de principes*, as cited by A. Castro, *"El villano del Danubio" y otros fragmentos*, Princeton, 1945, p. xi.

Some of Rojas' fellows tried to extinguish their ardent consciousnesses—to stop time—in irrationalism or fanaticism. That is, they tried to either destroy or become their image as Christians. Others, like the printer Juan de Lucena, dissipated the heat in "grandes yrronías" and "humor chocarrero." Still others enclosed their minds in psychic hearths and warmed themselves for decades on carefully tended feelings of resentment and hatred. And finally there were an exceptional few possessing the serenity necessary for exploration of new inner and temporal worlds discovered in captivity. It should be noted that in all these different reactions what we have called self-consciousness was the stimulus, an initial fate imposed on life by history. To be a *converso* was to be condemned to a fire as fierce as any kindled by the Inquisition (or by Nero as Calisto prefers to phrase it), but in occasional well aerated souls it could at times provide a great deal more illumination. Castro makes the same distinction between the two aspects or moments of *converso* biographies when he says that "Inquisitional persecution would not have sufficed to motivate the splendid literary flowering. . . ." An inborn capacity "to express in valuable terms the phenomena of consciousness" was also necessary.[106]

The notion of self-consciousness is not quite the same thing as introspection. The latter was inevitably a part of the process, for, as Castro says, "External circumstances incited the Spanish *converso* to return to the most profound roots of his own existence." But by going inwards, individual *conversos*—Rojas is the supreme example—often found a place from which to look outwards. To be forcibly tagged by society and to feel oneself an axiological orphan, cast out by God and History, turned the individual in upon himself but at the same time provided him with matchless perspective for seeing things as they are. The shy adolescent measures himself in the world's eye; the introspective adult retreats into the world of his own mind; but Fernando de Rojas, alone in his room with his chin in his hand watching himself pursue truth from all sides like a hunter (his thoughts are "pointers" which sniff the wind and his judgment is a soaring falcon), learned how to measure the world against itself. And, at the same time, like Celestina, he knew how to project his questing mind imaginatively into the selves of others less emancipated than he was, how to dictate to himself their ef-

[106] *Realidad*, edn. I, p. 545.

203

forts to communicate and express—each from within the separate time of his life.

In saying this we go far beyond the story we have just retold. Rojas' unique, creative utilization of the *converso* situation is ultimately not susceptible to any sort of sociological or psychological or historical or existential explanation. The biography of such a man, like the biography of a Shakespeare or a Picasso, is a journey to the edge of mystery. And once there, the most that we can attempt is to clear the view in order to look across in silent reverence. Yet, admitting these rigorous limitations, our reading of *La Celestina* has much to gain from two realizations: first, that its author was a human being (not a "non-crystallized personality" or a mouthpiece for the commonplace morality of the time); and, second, that he was a human being, not determined by his race, milieu, and moment, but rather made conscious by them.

CHAPTER V

❧ La Puebla de Montalbán

"E fue nascido en la puebla de Montalvan"

—(El bachiller Fernando de Rojas)

". . . si saue o a oydo dezir que el dicho pretendiente y sus ascendentes sean descendientes de los Francos desta ciudad y de los Rojas que salieron della para la villa de la Puebla de Montalbán y Talavera de la Reina . . ."

—(El doctor don Carlos Venero y Leiva)

❧ "And he was born in the Puebla de Montalbán"

Whether or not Fernando de Rojas was born of Garcí González Ponce de Rojas and Catalina de Rojas in the Puebla de Montalbán or of the "condemned" Hernando de Rojas in Toledo is a question (actually two intertwined questions)[1] which will probably never be answered definitively.[2] Although I myself am inclined to accept the second set of alternatives, I would not for that reason wish to de-emphasize the importance of the Puebla to the biography of the author. That Rojas returned to the town after studying in Salamanca, that he owned property there, that close relatives were among its inhabitants, and that he visited them from time to time during the Talavera years, are all facts supported by documents.[3] Thus, even supposing that the acrostic is a deliberate deception and that he spent a tormented early childhood in Toledo, we must still assume two separate periods of residence in his "clara nación" and "patria chica." First, as a boy sheltered by surviving relatives (the household of Garcí González?) after the disruption of the family in 1488, and, second, as a young lawyer beginning his professional career. A *probanza* witness states specifically: "he was a resident of the town for a certain time until he went to Talavera."[4] The most significant fact of all, however, is that by self-

[1] Although the double deception seems more probable to me (in view of the several indications of Toledan origin for the Rojas in the Palavesín *expediente*), there is no documented reason for denying an earlier departure of the family—say, as a consequence of "lo de la Magdalena" (1467). If this were the case, the acrostic would be truthful.

[2] Hope for documentary clarification seems slight. Systematic parish records of vital statistics ("libros parroquiales") were first introduced by Cisneros in the early 1500's (see V. de la Fuente, *Historia de las universidades*, II, 39). In any case, the earliest parish records available in the Puebla begin in the 1520's.

[3] In VLA 5 Rojas is still referred to in 1512 as a "vecino de la Puebla," when he purchased a "censo perpetuo" on a dwelling there from his wife's aunt, Elvira Gómez (see n. 129 below). This was probably during an intermediate period of movement back and forth between the two towns. The *probanzas* refer to repeated visits to supervise such property as the "huerta de Mollegas" and the "majuelo de la Cumbre." Contact with members of the family (presumably including that of his brother Juan, a local *regidor* or alderman) is also mentioned. See VL I, pp. 388 and 389.

[4] VL I, p. 391.

definition, Rojas was, or wanted to be, a native of the Puebla, and it is he who must be given the last word.

At this point the problem of determining four dates is unavoidable. They are: the year of Rojas' birth, that of his departure for Salamanca, that of his return to the Puebla, and that of his establishment in Talavera. Since, except for the last, no documentary evidence is available, we must calculate on the basis of three things we know (or at least which seem likely) about the years spent in Salamanca. The first is that the *Comedia* was written—or rather "finished"—after 1496, the year of publication of the Basel edition of Petrarch used therein as a reference book for commonplaces.[5] At that time Rojas, according to his own statements, was a student. The second is that he had received the degree of Bachiller by 1500, the date of the first edition to bear the acrostic verses. Finally, there is the strong indication in the *Prólogo* that the additions and interpolations which were first printed in 1502[6] were written while still at Salamanca. I refer particularly to the statement that it was "la alegre juventud e mancebía" (happy youth) which discussed the work and urged that it be lengthened and to the statement that the task was accomplished during moments filched from the writer's "principal estudio." A work begun in the University and provisionally concluded there, a work conceived of by a self-styled "filósofo" for an academic audience—it is only reasonable to assume—was also brought to final perfection in the same environment. Which is to propose that the watershed of Rojas' life, the divide between author and lawyer was his final leave taking from Salamanca.

Now, if we combine these three strong probabilities (the third is arguable, but, as we pointed out earlier, we must accept the first two if we are to talk about Rojas at all) with what we know about

[5] See F. Castro Guisasola, *Observaciones sobre las fuentes de "La Celestina,"* Madrid, 1924, p. 48 (to whom all credit) and Deyermond, *The Petrarchan Sources*, chap. II.

[6] Bibliographers (most recently J. Homer Herriott in his *Towards a Critical Edition*, pp. 5-6) have proposed a lost first edition of the *Tragicomedia* dating from 1500. Although the hypothesis is not to be dismissed (the reasons for it need no explanation here), continued printings of the *Comedia* in 1500 and 1501 make it risky from a biographical point of view. Were we to accept the work of continuation and interpolation as taking place in 1499 or at the beginning of 1500, the first three dates of our chronology would have to be set back one or two years.

the course of study for future civil lawyers, approximate dates will suggest themselves. Since the Bachelor of Law degree normally required six years of preparation and since the Licentiate filled four more,[7] we may provisionally assume that Rojas arrived in Salamanca in 1493 or 1494 (that is, some six years before the display of the degree in the acrostics) and that he stayed on until 1501 or 1502 (that is, after finishing up the *Tragicomedia*). The reasoning behind these assumptions is simple. Had Rojas started much earlier or remained much longer, he would in all likelihood have had time to have qualified for the higher degree. Or at least he would have been close enough to it to have made it worthwhile to finish in spite of all hardships. Having read *La Celestina,* we cannot question Rojas' intelligence and ability, and, having read the acrostic verses and the epitaph (both stressing the title *bachiller*), we can hardly question his professional motivation. Indeed it would appear that only a grave financial or family crisis could have been responsible for bringing his studies to a halt. Had he been able, he would surely have completed the requirements for the degree of Licentiate[8] as his eldest son, Francisco, and two of his grandchildren were to do.[9]

Acceptance of the year 1494 for arrival in Salamanca will in its turn allow us to estimate the most important date of all, that of Rojas' birth. The usual age of first-year students was between fourteen (Fray Luis de León, Juan de Segovia, and Juan del Encina are examples of such customary precociousness) and sixteen, although there were more individual deviations in either direction than is usual today. Twelve-year-old students and some even younger were often admitted to the preparatory courses in Latin and grammar—so that perhaps Vicente Espinel did not exaggerate too much when he remembered leaving Ronda for Salamanca still wearing

[7] See the documents reproduced by C. M. Ajo y G. Sainz de Zúñiga, *Historia de las universidades hispánicas,* Madrid, 1957, I, 618 and II, 222 (hereafter referred to as Ajo). Thus, too, V. de la Fuente (*Historia,* II, 39) estimates that the average fifteenth-century licentiate was 25 upon graduation.

[8] Such speculation must take into account the well-known high costs of taking the advanced degree. As in the time of Ruiz de Alarcón (whose remarks are quoted by J. García Mercadal, *Estudiantes, sopistas, y pícaros,* Madrid, 1934, p. 151), fees, customarily generous tips and the elaborately prescribed banquets, might have represented an insoluble problem for a candidate whose family was in financial straits.

[9] See Chap. VI, n. 3.

diapers. However, in Rojas' case, most readers of *La Celestina* will be inclined to accept a later age. We may guess then—knowing full well it is a guess—that Rojas was perhaps eighteen when he set out on the long journey from the Puebla to Salamanca for the first time. Which in turn fixes the date of his birth as 1476, the year of don Rodrigo Manrique's death. This would make him twenty or twenty-one when he acquired the Basle edition of Petrarch and twenty-one or twenty-two (1497 or 1498) when he sat down during his spring vacation to continue the *Comedia*. Menéndez Pelayo indulges in another guess when he remarks that Rojas may have attributed his own age to Calisto; that is, when Celestina tells Melibea (who had not asked), "Podrá ser, señora, de veynte e tres años."[10] This is not unlikely. It would merely imply that Rojas was even more conspicuously senile among his classmates than we have assumed, that he was further along towards the higher degree than we have guessed, or that his studies had been interrupted for some reason.

Fortunately the date of the move to Talavera is less speculative. In the 1517 trial of a local resident, Diego de Oropesa, Rojas, as a rather noncommittal witness for the defense, testified that he had known the accused "for the last ten years."[11] The date of 1507 is further confirmed by two Talaveran witnesses in the *probanza* arranged for in 1571 by his grandchildren in order to qualify for emigration to the Indies. Both of them, one eighty and the other eighty-six, remember first knowing the Bachelor "more than sixty years earlier."[12] And if they were coached by the Licentiate Fernando, it only confirms the probability of our supposition. To sum up, the four half-guesses and half-estimates put together appear as follows: birth, 1476; attendance at Salamanca, 1494-1502; and professional establishment in Talavera, 1507. In meditating on their interrelated likelihood, we may further observe that birth in 1475 or 1476 would make Rojas a reasonable fifteen years older than his wife[13] and sixty-five at his death in 1541.

[10] *Orígenes*, p. 26. See P. Ariès, *Centuries of Childhood*, New York, 1962, part II, chaps. I and IV, for age variations among medieval students.

[11] Serrano y Sanz, p. 252.

[12] VLA, 32. The 1512 document referred to in note 3 above indicates that establishment in Talavera was, as might be expected, a gradual process involving trips back and forth and not a sudden and definitive exile.

[13] "*Hijos deste confesante* . . . Leonor Alvarez, muger del Bachiller Rojas

Before concluding these chronological speculations, it is necessary to discuss a perturbing new fact which came to my attention after the above paragraphs were written. In the list of *Judaizantes del arzobispado de Toledo habilitados por la Inquisición en 1495 y 1497* recently published by Francisco Cantera Burgos and P. León Tello (see Chap. I, n. 52) we find the following entry for the Puebla de Montalbán: "Leonor Alvarez, muger de Ferrando de Rojas, e sus hijos menores 500 maravedís." This means, as we saw previously in the case of Alvaro de Montalbán (Chap. II), that she was assessed the indicated sum in exchange for the annulment of clothing and perhaps other restrictions imposed after her reconciliation. It also seems to mean that Rojas was already married and had children at the time of writing *La Celestina*—a supposition which will be much to the taste of those who find it improbable that a relatively young student should have been its author.

Yet, in spite of the coincidence of the names of husband and wife, a number of other facts eliminate the need to re-estimate the dates just presented. First, there is the direct and unequivocal statement of Alvaro de Montalbán that Rojas' wife was about thirty-five years old in 1525 and hence only seven at the time the list was compiled. He could, of course, have been confused, but likelihood of such a substantial error is small. Second, Rojas himself tells us that he was a student when he found and completed the original fragment, a task for which, as we just saw, the earliest possible date is 1496. And students with wives and children (even supposing the family remained behind in the Puebla) were exceptional both for economic reasons (as Guzmán de Alfarache quickly learned) and because of the semi-monastic nature of a university which forbade its students even to visit married couples. Finally and most conclusively, the birth dates of Rojas' children indicate that he was married in 1507 or some time afterwards rather than a decade before. Although two daughters may have preceded him (Catalina de Rojas provided the first recorded grandchild in

---

que compuso a Melibea, veçino de Talavera; avrá XXXV años" (Serrano y Sanz, p. 263). The remote possibility suggested by some that this could be interpreted as referring to the date of composition of *La Celestina* is eliminated by the preceding entry: "Johan del Castillo, escudero, veçino de Montalbán, moço; dixo que avría treynta años." The date of the document is, of course, 1525.

1530), the eldest son (later to become the Licentiate Francisco) was born in Talavera after 1511. A number of witnesses in the 1571 *probanza* just referred to so agree, and on this point there was no reason for prevarication. One of them, a man sixty years old, states specifically that Francisco was born in the house in Talavera and that he had known him since the age of two. As for the three remaining brothers and sisters, in the division of property made just after Rojas' death in 1541, they state specifically that they are between eighteen and twenty-five years old. That is to say, the bulk of the family was born between 1513 and 1523 more or less. In available documents there is no indication at all of births before 1507, let alone before 1497.

It is, of course, remotely possible that the couple might have lost an earlier family through disease or the plague, but these dates so naturally grouped together corroborate clearly the statements of both Rojas and his father-in-law. All three facts converge to rule out identification of the person referred to in the Cantera entry with the author of *La Celestina*. Who, then, it will inevitably be asked, was this mysterious Ferrando de Rojas whose wife, Leonor Alvarez, lived in the Puebla. Perhaps we shall never know, but my guess is that it was his father, the Fernando de Rojas who was condemned in 1488. As for the coincidental names of mother and wife, we need not be too surprised. Leonor and Alvarez were such a frequent combination at the time that there were no less than three of them in Alvaro de Montalbán's immediate family and eighteen on the list of those reconciled in Toledo. In any case, my conjecture is that at the time of her husband's trial she was reconciled and sanctioned, that she moved to the Puebla (perhaps to the house of a brother-in-law, Garçí Gonçález), and that she afterwards applied for exemption along with the rest of the family. And our Fernando de Rojas would have been one of her "hijos menores," meaning "menores de 25 años," to use the phrase of his children when they state their ages.

The importance of giving a date for Rojas' birth goes beyond the convenience of being able to put it after his name (with the usual question mark) in histories of literature and the—to my mind meaningless—question of whether so young an author could have written so mature a masterpiece. As we have pointed out, even though 1476 may be wide of the mark by several years, the date does establish him as a member of the first generation of *conversos* to grow up under Inquisitional pressure. Furthermore, it confers upon him a sense of historical reality which—in his self-chosen anonymity—he badly needs. Just by the magic of writing down a number, we are able, according to the present fashion, to include Fernando de Rojas in the European generation of Erasmus (1469), Luther (1483), More (1478), Michelangelo (1475), Raphael (1483), Ariosto (1474), Bandello (1480), Castiglioni (1478), Guicciardini (1483), Cranach (1472), Patinir (1475), Magellan (1480), Copernicus (1473), and Doctor Faust who, like Rojas, died in 1541. Such a list as this, it goes without saying, is an unforgivable abstraction. To suggest generational unity or spiritual resemblance (spiritual in the sense of *Zeitgeist*) for these diverse figures and nationalities would be frivolous. On the other hand, the identity which emerges from a moment of history lived, and lived through with others, is a not insignificant part of one's personal identity. Rojas becomes less of a "semi-anonymous" subject of scholarly dispute merely by inclusion in the generation which has traditionally been given credit for inaugurating two major abstractions in which most historians still believe: the Renaissance and the Reformation.

꧁ Mollejas el ortelano

In the darkness of Act XII of *La Celestina* Pármeno and Sempronio converse in hushed voices while they wait for the outcome of Calisto's first rendezvous with Melibea. In spite of their arms and in spite of their master's belief that they are "esforzados," they are ridiculously frightened and ready to flee at the first sign of danger. As they talk, they work on each other's fears. Was the assignation part of a carefully laid trap? Are Pleberio's bellicose servants "who would rather fight than eat" waiting to ambush them? Has Celestina lied? Standing there nervously, shifting from foot to foot, their arms and armor girded not for battle but for flight, the miserable pair have only one consolation: their newly-cemented friendship permits them to reveal their fears to each other without shame. Sempronio is speaking:

Oh Pármeno, my friend! How pleasant and profitable is the conformity of true companions! Even if Celestina had nothing

213

else to offer us, in bringing us together she has been of great service.

PÁRMENO.—No one can deny a truth that is self-evident. It is manifest that if things were otherwise, we would out of shame, each afraid the other would accuse him odiously of cowardice, stay waiting for death alongside our master. . . .

However, in spite of their vaunted shamelessness, they are shamed, so deeply ashamed that, when Celestina later accuses them of cowardice, the insult is unbearable and becomes the immediate cause of her murder.[14] We get an initial hint of this complexity of feeling, when the abject pair walk back towards Pleberio's house after a false alarm has sent them scurrying away. In their conversation they excuse themselves by exaggerating their present danger and by bragging feebly of past affronts and tight spots faced with greater coolness:

PÁRMENO.—Never in my life can I remember being so afraid nor in a situation so threatening, although I've served in people's houses for a long time and in places where the going was rough. Why, during the nine years I worked for the Friars of Guadalupe, the other fellows and I would get into fist fights all the time, but never did I fear death as I did just now.

SEMPRONIO.—And didn't I serve the priest of the Church of San Miguel *and the innkeeper of the plaza and Mollejas*[15] *the gardener? And I also had my troubles with the boys who threw rocks at the birds roosting in a big elm tree he had, because they were damaging the vegetables.*

Here is an interchange characteristic of coexistence inside *La Celestina.* As the late María Rosa Lida de Malkiel has stressed, its

---

[14] For the motivational structure of Act XII, see chap. IV of *The Art.*

[15] Cejador, following the 1514 edition, gives "Mollejar," but "Mollejas," closer to the transcription of the *probanza*, appears in the *Libro de Calisto y Melibea* (Seville, 1518-1520). Secondly, as we shall see, Mollejas, although uncommon, is a real *apellido* (the only non-Latinized one in the text, significantly enough). Finally, as we shall also see (n. 20), Mollejas was the form which Feliciano de Silva took from *La Celestina.* The italics of the passage refers, of course, to the fact that it is an interpolation inserted in the earlier text of the *Comedia.* As such, inclusion of the name Mollejas provides a fresh although minor argument against those who still doubt Rojas' authorship of the *Tragicomedia.*

inhabitants are unique among those who appear in other works of the time because of the pervasive presence of the past in their lives.[16] In the most intense and immediate situations, fragments of past experience come to the surface and participate in each speaker's stream of self-revelation.

Where do these elusive and suggestively employed memories come from? Rojas' art, as we have observed at length, is mysterious in its ability to create the illusion that the characters themselves, as autonomous beings, have dredged them up out of their own minds. Celestina's past is supremely hers; in its peculiar exploits and satisfactions, it could only be hers; and her constant reference to it in argument or reminiscence is central to her existential density. Here resides what Unamuno would term her "reality." But in this case, at least one (and perhaps more) of the servants' nervous boyhood recollections resembles a tooth with twin roots. In addition to its source in Sempronio's past, it also extends out of *La Celestina* and into another biography, that of the author, Fernando de Rojas. The boyhood adventure in the market garden of Mollejas is—by historical accident—the unique window opening from the work out into the forgotten life from which it sprang.

As I pointed out in *The Art of La Celestina*,[17] witnesses testifying in the *probanza de hidalguía* identify the garden of Mollegas, Mollejas, or Moblejas (the paleographical problems of the transcription are grave)[18] as a part of the Rojas estate in the Puebla. The double coincidence of the names, "huerta de Mollegas" and

[16] "By an extraordinary innovation the characters not only vary within the work, each one changing according to his own law—that is living—but also give the reader the feeling that they have already lived and changed. The characters have a history behind them" (*Two Spanish Masterpieces*, Urbana, Ill., 1961, p. 87). The only change I would propose would be, as we shall see, the substitution of "revolutionary" for "extraordinary." In her brilliant *Memory in "La Celestina"* (London, 1970), Professor Dorothy Severin has studied in detail various aspects of this "innovation."

[17] p. 218.

[18] VL I, pp. 388 and 393. Valle Lersundi published his transcription of a copy made for the family archives by the Licentiate Fernando in the late 16th century. I have also had access to the original in the Archivo de la Real Chancillería in Valladolid as transcribed for me by no less an authority than don Agustín Millares Carlo (Appendix III). In his opinion the "letra procesal" of the latter document is so hasty and careless as to render firm judgment on the correct form difficult. "Huertas" still exist along the Tajo but none still possesses such a designation—according to the inhabitants of advanced age whom I questioned.

215

"Mollejas el ortelano," thus, indicates the external source of Sempronio's anecdote. It would seem that Rojas in 1501 or thereabouts, at the moment of enlarging the sixteen-act *Comedia* and looking for an effective way to amplify Sempronio's relatively short answer to Pármeno's adolescent boasting, suddenly came across a boyhood memory of his own. He recalled being sent—perhaps by Garcí González—to guard the family garden plot; he felt again his childish fear in the face of greater numbers and his pride in having stood his ground; the birds, the flying stones, the damaged "*ortaliza*," all returned to his mind and then were transplanted into that of his character. At which point the garden itself was converted into a picaresque master.

Surely other memories and vignettes in *La Celestina* were "created" in a similar manner (it is thus that fictional experience is made), but this is the only one in which chance, in the form of coached witnesses and the preservation of a document, has revealed to us.[19] But aside from our historical good fortune, it is not

[19] Two other students and lovers of *La Celestina* have noticed independently the coincidence of the "huerta de Mollegas" to "Mollejas el ortelano." Marcel Bataillon admits the probable identity but interprets it as due to the popularity of the work: "Etant donné qu'il s'agit de documents tardifs (1588) posterieurs de 86 ans à la révision de la *Célestine*, il est très possible que ce détail de notre *Tragicomédie* ait servi à baptiser après coup une *huerta* appartenant à la famille de Rojas. La gloire de l'œuvre était suffisante pour cela, comme pour créer la tradition de la 'casa de Celestina' à Salamanque" (p. 143). Two objections suggest themselves. The first is simply that, although the documents were written 86 years after *La Celestina*, what is written in them (the answers to questions given by old men, one 84 years old and the other 71) goes much further back into local history. The second is that the house of Celestina and the garden of Melibea, quickly discovered in Salamanca and pointed out then and now to tourists by local readers, involve—as was to be expected—principal characters and places, known to all and vivid to all. Here, on the other hand, we are concerned with a name—not a character—mentioned only once and in passing. Why, in other words, should a transient shadow from the past of Sempronio have been specially remembered and conserved by readers in the Puebla? Those interested in conferring local reality on the fiction would have been far more likely to call the property "la huerta de Sempronio." Furthermore, for whatever it may be worth, while visiting the Puebla in the company of Valle Lersundi, he pointed out to me the following entry in the parish register: "Sabado en diez y seis del mes de marzo, año de mil e quinientos e sesenta años se baptizó Juan, hijo de Juan de Mollejas y de su muger, Ana Sánchez . . ." (fo. 203). Could these be descendants of an earlier gardener or owner? Certainly they were not so named in order to celebrate Sempronio's first master. Don Fernando, himself, goes to the other extreme. In a 1958 newspaper article in the *Diario Vasco* (5 August), he incurs in

216

without significance that in this particular moment of recollection
—however minor it may appear—the lives of author and character
should coincide. Boyhood presents to all boys in all ages (to Fernando de Rojas, to Sempronio, and to the reader and writer of this
page) a central experience: the experience of vulnerability when
grown-up protection is gone and one must search for his own courage. A man's first fight remains as vivid in his memory as his first
love. So it was here. Rojas' clear recollection of his anguished
moments in the family garden is used to contribute to Act XII's
complexly orchestrated theme of cowardice and bravery (the fears
of the servants ranged against the individual recklessnesses of
Calisto and Celestina) by referring to the homely and childish be-
ginnings of the two antithetical reactions to danger. That in so doing Rojas paused to smile ironically at an earlier self, is a gift we
had no right to expect. For a moment we have been privileged to
peek at his boyhood in the Puebla de Montalbán.[20]

---

what Bataillon terms (impersonally since he had not seen the article) a
"naïve recherche des 'modèles vivants'." His intent in publishing the *probanza*
some 33 years earlier, Valle Lersundi informed me, had been precisely to
call attention to the biographical importance of Mollejas el ortelano. If that
is accepted, he feels, other incidents in the dialogue between the two servants
can also be interpreted as reflecting Rojas' early life. For example, when
Sempronio says, "¿E yo no serví al cura de San Miguel?" the reference is to
"la iglesia de San Miguel." So too there is a fifteenth-century "*mesón*" in the
plaza and enormous "*álamos*" in the "*huertas*" along the Tajo. The whole
passage may then be interpreted as a nest of personal reminiscences with the
priest and the "frayles de Guadalupe" being references to Rojas' primary and
secondary schooling. Personally, I believe there is a strong possibility that Valle
Lersundi may be right. This is, of course, a matter better suited for supposition than for assertion, but, in any case, the descendant of the Bachelor is to
be admired for his lack of fear of naïveté.

[20] It is curious to note that the same Mollejas who slipped so unobtrusively
from biographical into created experience was later to traverse the frontiers
of Rojas' work and to reappear in Feliciano de Silva's *Segunda Celestina*.
Along with other minor details (such as Melibea's ships) and fringe characters (such as Crito), Mollejas was not ignored in the continuing author's
extraordinarily close reading of *La Celestina*. He is mentioned on two occasions as the grandfather of Pandulfo, the principal servant of the enamored
Felides. The passage commented on by Bataillon is interesting in that it
associated him to a burlesque genealogy comparable to those of Torres
Naharro and Juan del Encina. Pandulfo remarks at the beginning of the
"vigésima-séptima cena": "Pues voto a la Casa Santa, que mi agüelo Mollejas,
que no debía nade a D. Brasco, su agüelo, sino por la renta, que aunque
era hortelano, él era muy buen hidalgo." In addition to being, according to

✑ La Villa de la Puebla de Montalbán

Aside from being—like every town in the world—a juvenile battlefield, what kind of a place was the Puebla de Montalbán? And what was it like to grow up there? In order to ask and to answer fairly, we must begin by revising our usual notions of childhood as a moment of intense and self-evidently meaningful experience. That is, we must use as pattern of comprehension not *Tom Sawyer* or *Le Grand Meaulnes* (books which would surely have disconcerted Rojas) but the *Lazarillo de Tormes*. By this I do not mean to say that the author of *La Celestina* was a *pícaro* or even that the *Lazarillo* and its fictional progeny portray child life as it really was. The point is rather that the contrast between children in nineteenth- and twentieth-century fiction and those appearing in that of the sixteenth is our best means of grasping the sense of the incident in the garden of Mollejas just dredged up through five centuries of oblivion. In the world of the miniature men[21] who were the children of our ancestors, the circumstances of life (landscape, relations with parents, houses and furnishings, and all the other elements of our nostalgia) tended to be institutional—which

---

Bataillon, a "plaisanterie raciste de Feliciano de Silva, hidalgo fort mêlé, comme Rojas, aux nouveaux chrétiens d'origine juive," it is also an indication (we shall examine others in a later chapter) of *La Celestina*'s acceptance among and relevance for *conversos*. That is to say, Mollejas has become involved in a form of literary counter-attack against rustic and rude Old Christians who despise *manchas* and who cover their ignorance of their own lineages with presumption. For further discussion, see my "Retratos de conversos en la *Comedia Jacinta* de Torres Naharro," *NRFH*, XVIII (1964), 20-21. I further suspect that the occupation of "*hortelano*" suggested to Feliciano de Silva that Mollejas was a "*morisco*." *Conversos* often sneered at the rival caste's pretensions to "limpieza de sangre" by pointing out that "*labradores*" (those of El Toboso are examples) either did not know or tried to cover up the Moorish element in their ancestry. The very name Mollejas, which sounds ridiculously rural in Spanish, may have had some such connotation.

[21] Erasmus' surprised observation (in his *De pueris instituendis*) that children learn in a fashion quite different from adults and that teaching methods, which up to that time had not taken those capacities into account, needed to be modified is itself a significant indication that 15th-century childhood was quite different from that which we remember. Children have not changed, of course, but rather the concept of childhood provided by grown-up culture and lived by children. For a complete discussion with abundant examples, see Ariès' *Centuries of Childhood*, part I, chaps. II and V.

is to say, accepted and ignored unless suddenly emphasized by violence. Garden and gardener are remembered because of flying stones and not as a *vert paradis*.[22] Realizing, then, how radically Jean-Jacques Rousseau and his successors have changed our sense of our own lives, let us try to reconstruct the Puebla de Montalbán as an institution rather than as an experience. If we avoid as self-consciously as possible anachronistic notions of childhood, and even of biography, we may attempt to fill out the empty clause of the acrostic, "e fue nascido en la Puebla de Montalvan," with whatever information we can find. What kind of an institution in which to start life was it?—that is the more adequate question.

Physically, the Puebla has changed very little since Rojas' time. The church of San Miguel where Garcí González Ponce de Rojas was buried under "a large brown stone" has disappeared leaving only a tower (not yet erected in the fifteenth century) behind it. The palace of the Lords of Montalbán (now the Dukes of Osuna) which dominates the plaza had not yet been constructed in its present ostentation. But otherwise only electric wiring, a certain amount of cement paving, and recent buildings on the outskirts would seem unfamiliar to Rojas. The handsome plaza with its fifteenth-century inn (where Sempronio may have gotten his first hard knocks) is probably the same as it was when Rojas lived there. From the central square there extend irregular streets of white-washed houses over the hills above the Tajo until the last dwellings and barnyards give way to wheat fields, vineyards, and olive

---

[22] When certain humanists did attempt to portray their own childhood, the results sound more like a topical recital of childish activities than an experience lived through. Let us listen to Nebrija's "Salutatio ad Patriam suam multis ante annis non visam, et, memorata infantia sua . . .": "Here I used to hang from the neck of my father, and I was a gentle weight for him and a pleasant burden on my mother's lap. Here I used to crawl on the ground; in this small threshing floor I would creep around held up by my tender hands; it was here that I took my first steps, and, shaking my rattle, I would say sweet things to my mother in my garbled language. These walls saw me play with other children of my age and win or lose at a game of marbles [*nueces*]. It was here too that I played at war mounted on a long stick which served as a horse, but my favorite game was playing with a top" (F. G. Olmedo, *Nebrija*, Madrid, 1942, p. 221). As against this evidently artificial memory of infancy, Villalobos' mockery of his own cowardice already cited ("When I was a child I was the worst *judihuelo* in my village") sounds more authentic. And it was probably closer to what Fernando de Rojas remembered about the Puebla.

groves. The "Calle Real" no longer is the main road to Toledo, almost a day's journey away, but it is still the most important street. On the flatlands below, on either side of the road leading to the bridge (antique now, but still a replacement of the wooden affair crossed by Rojas) and to the Castle of Montalbán over the hills, irrigated *huertas* are plotted out in squares and oblongs. There are even a few huge and leafy *álamos*[23] of the sort which shaded "la güerta de Mollejas"—probably only one generation removed from the tree defended by both Fernando de Rojas and Sempronio. And over all, the wide reach of the sky from the low hills behind the town to their distant counterparts on the other side of the shallow valley is identical to its timeless self. As Lucio Marineo, called the "Sicilian," wrote in 1539 in a humanistic guide book to Spain, "The province of Toledo exceeds all the other regions of Spain in its nobility, in the fertility of its land, and in the *disposición* of its sky."[24]

There are, however, other less immediately perceptible things which might impress an imaginary visitor from the Puebla's fifteenth century with the immensity of time gone by. The region as a whole is much dryer and more deforested than in the time of Rojas. So much so that Philip II's partially successful project for making the Tajo navigable all the way from Lisbon to Toledo would be inconceivable today.[25] It is a physical change which may not have caused, but which at least has appropriately accompanied, the drying up of history in the Puebla and its neighboring centers of population, Torrijos, Maqueda, Casarrubios, and even Toledo. Along with persecution and anguish, along with intensities of faith and skepticism, along with skilled handicrafts, weaving, forging, and their pervasive noises ("puta vieja, puta vieja") and repeated motions ("todo oficio de instrumento"), there has been a corresponding and enormous loss of pace and rhythm. And it is this slowing down of human time that Rojas would surely find most strange and disturbing. Unlike Azorín, who hears the clocks of Argamasilla de Alba strike with "marvellous deliberation," the author of *La Celestina*, a work overflowing with experienced time

[23] Still called *álamos*, they seem to be a variety of elm, and not poplars.
[24] *De las cosas memorables de España*, Alcalá de Henares, 1539, fol. XII.
[25] See A. Martín Gamero, *Historia de la Ciudad de Toledo*, Toledo, 1862, pp. 981-982.

and within which clocks cannot possibly satisfy impatience, was not prepared for that peculiar, melancholy sloth which Ganivet was to call "*abulia*" and to diagnose as a national disease. It is unnecessary here to elaborate on the familiar contrast between the Spain of 1498 and that of 1898: the loss of will (Azorín's "*voluntad*"), of traditional skills, of creative impetus, and the rest. What matters now is to record our awareness that the intense, strife-ridden, ingrown, yet vitally burgeoning town in which Rojas grew up was utterly unlike the desiccated, decelerated, and drained mirror image of itself which can be visited today.

Mention of Azorín reminds us of one of his most frequent and effectively used sources, the so-called *Relaciones hechas a Felipe II*, a town-by-town census and national inventory already cited for its report on the grammar school in Torrijos.[26] Compiled in 1560 and 1566, approximately a century after the royal grant of the Puebla to don Juan Pacheco, its report on the town serves as a revealing introduction and description. Although during the decades after *La Celestina*'s first publication rigidity and withering were already beginning to show, Juan Martínez and the Bachelor Ramírez de Orejón (each of whom wrote out answers to sixty royal questions)[27] lived within the same historical structure as their grandparents. In this sense—in spite of their awareness of the community's nascent petrifaction—they are still Rojas' contemporaries. Indeed, as they informed his Majesty's representative, a part of their information about the past of the Puebla had been obtained from an aged priest, one Francisco Esteban "que hobiera ahora más de ciento y diez años." Born in 1456, this curator of local traditions was surely acquainted with the Bachelor and shared with him a common fund of historical lore.[28]

"The town of the Puebla de Montalbán," we are told in the *Relaciones*, "is five leagues from the city of Toledo . . . and it con-

---

[26] Chap. III, n. 47.

[27] The version (that of 1560 being in the Academy of History) here cited was written in the presence of "the apostolic notary, Garcí Díaz de Rojas, a resident of the town," *Relaciones*, III, 254-274.

[28] A priest named Francisco Esteban testified in the 1555 *probanza* of Diego de Rojas (to be examined at the end of the present chapter). There he states that he is 73 years old "poco más o menos" and so born in 1484. The coincidence of name and occupation would indicate that, despite the discrepancy of dates, he is the person referred to in the *Relaciones*.

tains 700 houses[29] with 800 heads of families. It is an old town, dating, as far as is known, from the time of the Knights Templar[30] who populated it and owned it. It was first situated and settled on the bank of the river Tajo opposite to where it is today, and it was called Villa Hermosa. Afterwards the town was moved across the river and was called Villa Harta . . . and (later) Villa de Ronda." In the primitive period of local history, we conclude, the Puebla was a shifting settlement of imported frontiersmen, an entity uncertain of its name and even of its location. But then, probably early in the fourteenth century, a definitive move was made which was to prove of enormous importance to the future history of Spanish literature: "The dwellers in the land of Montalbán, still searching for a healthier place to live because they were sick down by the river, settled in a town of Jews [*población de Judíos*], and they stayed there, and after that the town was called the Puebla de Montalbán, because the land where it is is the land of Montalbán."[31]

If the pioneering and tolerant origins of the town seem to represent in miniature those of Spain as a whole, there are equally typical elements in its subsequent history. Doña María Coronel and, after her, Peter the Cruel were the first persons of importance to pay any attention to the newly flourishing community. The latter installed his mistress, doña María de Padilla, there "in palaces surrounded by a large and excellent garden,"[32] palaces which in 1508

[29] A description of the houses in the town of El Viso (also in the province of Toledo) is contained in the *Relaciones*: "The houses are supported by buttresses . . . and they are white inside with plaster and possess garrets; the most common to be seen are made of earth with tile roofs and wood from the mountains . . ." (III, 773).

[30] The Templars existed in Spain from the time of their foundation in 1128. Among their possessions were castles and fortified towns, the chief of which was Monzón. The order was dissolved in 1312 by Pope Clement V. The Puebla, thus, probably had existed for some three centuries prior to Rojas' birth.

[31] A similar version is given by the Bachelor Ramírez de Orejón: "Andando a buscar los vecinos de la tierra de Montalbán donde vivir más sanos, porque vivían enfermos junto al río, hallaron una población de judíos en el lugar donde está aora fundada la dicha villa, y se vinieron con su juredicción al dicho lugar donde está fundada, y ansí lo oyó decir a sus padres y algunos ancianos desta villa" (p. 263).

[32] In his *Crónica*, Pero López de Ayala relates how Peter the Cruel at the time of his reluctant departure for his wedding in Valladolid "left doña

(a year after Rojas' departure?) were converted into a nunnery. Under Peter, the Puebla enjoyed a substantial amount of political liberty: "In former times it was a *behetría*, as the oldest inhabitants relate, and every *vecino* [head of a family] had the right to speak and vote in the town council, and the council meetings were open to all." King Peter, who was more "cruel" to nobles than to villagers, "confirmed these privileges and ordered that the aforesaid town should elect two men of good standing as mayors, and there would be no superior over them save only the King himself, and they could cut wood in the oak grove of Montalbán and in the common forests at their pleasure." Although the equalitarian sentiment and its wording sound like a Golden Age *comedia*, the history of the Puebla did not have a happy ending. In the troubled and anarchical times that followed, two men of good standing did not offer much protection, and the dwellers in the Puebla were forced to elect a series of powerful "lords to defend them." This was supposed to be a lifetime arrangement, but the last of them was no less a personage than one of the arrogant Infantes de Aragón, whose ambition and transient glory are referred to in the *Coplas* of Jorge Manrique.

The Infante—the informants relate with barely suppressed bitterness—was delighted with the town, "because it was such a good place, and he kept it, and, when he became king in Aragón, he gave it to the Queen doña Leonor, wife to the King don John" (Juan II of Castile). Its next master was King John's well-known favorite, don Alvaro de Luna, and, after his execution, it was bestowed as a royal gift on the Master of Santiago, don Juan Pacheco who in his turn converted it into a hereditary fief for "one of his sons called don Alonso Téllez, the great grandfather of the Count who now owns it." This first Lord of Montalbán held the title until 1527 (outliving his son and heir), so that it was he whose bad treatment, as we have seen, is supposed to have caused Fernando de Rojas and some of his fellow *hidalgos* to leave. The gift of what had once been a "town of Jews" to a nobleman of remotely Jewish origin (it

---

María de Padilla in the castle of Montalbán, a castle which is strong and well constructed" and how he then returned to her immediately after his celebrated flight from his bride" (ed. A. Llaguno Amirola, Madrid, 1779, p. 86).

was well known at the time that don Juan Pacheco, the overbearing antagonist and favorite of Henry the Impotent, was descended from a medieval *converso* called Ruy Capón)[33] is without doubt a coincidence. But it may prepare us to understand some of the things we shall see later on: the Lord's failure to be at all concerned at the fraternization of his *converso* subjects with the remaining Jews, the penetration of the Inquisition into his very household with the arrest and trial of his *mayordomo*, and the marriage of a great-grandson to a Rojas who was descended from a family tutor ("*ayo*") and who seems to have been distantly related to the Bachelor. Although heartily disliked for many reasons, the Lord don Alonso was at least not inclined to disturb the last years of the small world of happy coexistence remembered pathetically by Alvaro de Montalbán.

Other answers have to do with the physical environment and natural resources of town and countryside: "The land called Montalbán is cold in winter, but in the summer it is not too hot. It is a temperate land partly forested with hills (where it is difficult to walk), and it is healthy." Of the surrounding forest we are told elsewhere: "There is an abundance of firewood; the trees are of live oak and *madroño*, and there are patches of rosemary; but in the last fifteen years many forests have been cut down in order to plant wheat, and the game that there is—rabbit, hare, partridge, deer, wild boar, and roebuck—has diminished greatly." The Spain, or at least the New Castile, of Fernando de Rojas' youth was still wooded, still a land where cleared settlements were surrounded by expanses of wilderness, and not the denuded man-plagued *campo* we ride through today. Aside from hunting, there were other attractions to the forest. We wonder if Rojas remembered as well as did the writer of the *Relaciones* that in its depths, free for all to gather, "there are wild cherry trees which bear dark little cherries which are good to eat and wild apples too."

---

[33] In the vengeful *Tizón de la nobleza* (cited in Chap. III, n. 67) there is a whole chapter devoted to the descendants of "Ruy Capón, judío convertido, almojarife de la reina doña Urraca." In the main line of descent he not only includes don Juan Pacheco but also "la casa de la Puebla de Montalbán, que heredó su hijo tercero" (p. 65). This third son was don Alonso Téllez Girón, and he was, as we shall see, to exercise an important influence on the biography of his most famous vassal.

Human collaboration with nature centered and still centers on the river Tajo coming down from Toledo on its way to Talavera, Portugal, and the sea. Along the banks a quarter of a league from town, "there are three *güertas*, one belonging to the Count and two to private owners. The fruits picked therein are apricots, cherries, both small and large and tart and sweet, pears, apples, and all kinds of plums; and the vegetables and ground fruit [the '*ortaliza*' of Mollejas] are melons, cucumbers, garlic, onions, beans, turnips, eggplant, radishes, and lettuce; and the fish that are in the aforesaid river are barbels, eels, mendoles, and others. . . ." In addition to fish, the river furnished water power, there being three mills including the large one belonging to the Count. Other mills usable only in winter and smaller garden plots are along the two tributary streams, the Torcón and the Cedeña. On the hills there is much pasture land and many grainfields "where bread is harvested" and "the grains are wheat, barley, rye, chickpeas, and bitter vetch." "Salt and fish from the sea" are the only things lacking. But to make up for these, "there is the clearest and best honey and the best asparagus in all Spain and red, white, and claret wines which are very good and healthy, although this is not a village famous for its wines; and there are kids and milk and goat cheese and sheep cheese and better melons than any place else, for ours are exported to the Court and to Toledo." The rural cornucopia here has emptied itself in a burst of paratactic celebration.

Outside the town there are two centers around which local history and legend have accumulated. One is the "ancient and noteworthy" hermitage of Our Lady of Melque, "formerly called Mecca," built of stones so curiously joined that no mortar is needed. It used to be gilded from top to bottom,

> but in the old days, thinking it was covered with gold leaf, they set fire to it, and now it is all streaked with smoke. Some say it was built by the Templars,[34] for it is in the shape of a cross, and there are half moons carved in the stone. But it may

---

[34] This is apparently a fact. According to Luis Moreno Nieto, "Este mismo rey Alfonso VII a finales del primer tercio del siglo XII hizo donación del territorio de los Templarios, que hicieron de Melque uno de los doce conventos que poseían en España . . ." (*La provincia de Toledo*, Toledo, 1960, p. 499).

have been built to replace an earlier Roman structure, for all around there are ruins of ancient buildings where a rock with an inscription in Latin was found. Nearby are olive groves too far from the Puebla to have been planted by its inhabitants and old stone dams three yards thick which hold no water in their pools. . . . And up above on the hill there are ancient brambles and a fountain carved out of the living rock with running water, and they say that, nearby, treasures have been found.

From the Hermitage of Melque a paved stone road leads to the Castle of Montalbán about a league away. Long ago the castle used to be the haven of two sisters "who would sally out armed and on horseback and attack and rob anyone who passed by, and they did so much evil and damage that no one dared go near, until two men, a father and his son, came, and the father had a lance in his hand, and he threw it at one of them and drove it through her breast, and she cried out, 'Oh Sister, they have killed me.' For which deed the pair were appointed by the King to be the first 'alcaldes de la hermandad vieja de Toledo.' "[35] More factual and more recent was the story of the young King, John II, and his favorite, don Alvaro de Luna. Feigning a hunting excursion on a November morning in 1420, the two of them drew away from their escort and escaped from Talavera—the boy king having been held a semi-prisoner by one of the same arrogant Infantes de Aragón referred to earlier. After a desperate ride, King and favorite took refuge in the Castle of Montalbán up the river and endured a siege of some months. Although the garrison almost starved, each day two partridges were sent in for the King, as was recounted by local peasants who rallied to their King and eventually helped drive off the besiegers.[36] Later (after having served as a haven for the Puebla *conversos*), the castle was successfully taken by the troops of Henry IV. He was, as we have seen, determined to dispossess don Alvaro's widow and to bestow it, along with the Puebla, on his own favorite, don Juan Pacheco. Grateful for the help offered by the vil-

[35] The "hermandad vieja" refers to irregular regional defense forces established long before the Catholic Monarchs founded the "Santa" or "Nueva Hermandad."

[36] A detailed narrative of the siege is contained in Fernán Pérez de Guzmán's *Crónica de don Juan II*, chaps. 29-45.

lagers (who had had no idea what they were getting into), the King granted them a free market to be held on Thursdays.[37]

In contrast to these reigns of strife, the accession of Ferdinand and Isabella brought tranquillity to the land of Montalbán. The castle was gradually abandoned, and, by 1560, its arms and munitions were obsolete, its garrison reduced, and its fortifications in a state of disrepair. The land that used to be set aside for the support of the *alcaide* had been rented out for many years. Nevertheless, both informants insist, this rural peace was deceptive. The arbitrary actions and the avarice of the Lords (later the Counts) of Montalbán made things worse than they had been before. Don Alonso and his grandson not only had driven away local *hidalgos* but also, and worst of all, they had cut down the forest lands that used to be the common property of the town and sold them as wheat fields to private individuals. The result, as we have seen, was that the town could no longer export firewood and charcoal, and the wild game had disappeared, and "our honey, the whitest and best in all Spain, is no longer abundant." Typical of these noble masters was their failure to repair the old wooden bridge over the Tajo in spite of the excessive tolls they demanded for its use. When migrant sheep have been crossing it for three days (at a rate of three florins per thousand), "pieces begin to fall out, and many animals and even people are endangered. Because it is in such poor condition, many people have perished and perish even now."

The despotism of the Téllez Girones, we further learn, was political as well as economic and gravely affected the traditional freedoms of the town. When the *alcaldes*, *regidores* (aldermen), *alcaldes de la hermandad*, and the *alguaciles* (constables) are voted for "on the day of the Nativity of Our Lady," they do not choose from among those who have the most votes as they are traditionally obliged to do but rather pick those who will be subservient. The second Lord even dared to jail an *alcalde* who refused to obey him. Of all the feudal masters of the town, this family—the complaint directly to the King here becomes emphatic —has done the most damage.

Lest from these reports of Romantic ruins and reflections on political and economic decadence we should derive the impression

[37] This meant simply that the Lord was not allowed to collect duties on produce brought into market.

that the *Relaciones* were really written in the nineteenth century, the candid report on local relics and miracles serves to remind us that their origin was far more remote. Aside from such muzzled and tormented individuals as Alvaro de Montalbán, most of the dwellers of the Puebla still lived in the medieval cosmos in which Heaven and earth were not separated but intimately interlocked or superimposed. It was still a time when (as Paul Ludwig Landsberg has emphasized nostalgically) if sufferings in Purgatory could be shortened by prayer, it was also expected that frequent miracles might alleviate many of the evils of life on earth.[38] The concepts of the natural and the supernatural and of their corresponding varieties of causation, as distinguished today even by fervent believers, were not habitual mental patterns among those inhabitants of the Puebla who went willingly to church. It was a world, in short, in which priests (and others unordained) could easily aspire to acceptance as shamans.

We should not be surprised, therefore, at the great importance given by the two informants to certain local holy days—particularly that of Saint Michael on May 8, a day which had been promised to him by the ancestors of present believers if he would rid their vineyards of worms. Hence, too, the stress laid on the town's supply of relics as well as the interest of Philip II (who tabulated his own Escorial collection at some 7,422)[39] in using the *Relaciones* to take a national inventory of Spain's holdings in this regard. The relics owned by the Puebla, primarily "the heads of two of the 11,000 virgins," had unfortunately performed no known miracles.[40] But the image of Our Lady of Peace, an image which had been re-

---

[38] "La edad media y nosotros," *RO*, ix (1925), 327.

[39] Fray José de Sigüenza, *Historia primitiva y exacta del monasterio del Escorial*, ed. M. Sánchez y Pinillos, Madrid, 1881, p. 202. Sigüenza himself does not cite the figure but rather describes the King's wild excitement at the arrival of a large shipment rescued from Protestant Germany followed by his subsequent arrangements for tabulation. The final figure is given in a 1754 index conveniently broken down into categories—"insignes," "casi-insignes," "menores," etc.—each affixed to the "relicarios."

[40] The Puebla's poverty as far as relics were concerned may be contrasted with the riches claimed by such a backward and credulous town as Coria. There the local reporter proudly mentioned possession of the "jawbone of St. John the Baptist with teeth," "most of the head of the same," "a giant canine tooth of Saint Christopher six fingers long and thick as a thumb," along with some 15 others including wood from the Cross and dirt from Golgotha.

vered ever since the eleventh century when it was displayed as a sign of welcome to the advancing troops of Alfonso VI (presumably by the neutral inhabitants of the "town of Jews") had several to its credit. She was not only used against the depredations of grasshoppers and caterpillars but even against the plague itself. The story is told by the priest Ramírez de Orejón in this way:

> In time of war and of drought she is carried out in a formal procession. . . . There are witnesses that during the pestilence, which was in the year seven (1507), the inhabitants left their sick relatives (who told them to go, saying they felt better), and with their feet bare they took her in procession all the way to the Hermitage of Melque. And it rained for three days, and the plague was mitigated, and a new kind of grass grew up, and they cured themselves with its roots, and they ate them because hunger was everywhere and there was no bread, and, when they were cured, the grass was never seen again.[41]

The interpenetration of the natural and the supernatural was also manifest in black magic. Understandably omitted by Philip II's pious informants (while surely of great interest to the young Fernando de Rojas) was the Puebla's share in the prevalence of Spanish witches. There is only one extant record of proceedings against a witch known to the future author of *La Celestina*, but later trials from the region indicate that clandestine recourse to sorcery for influencing events and human behavior was as common there as elsewhere. Unfortunately the specific case we do possess, that of Alvaro de Montalbán's prisonmate, Inés Alonso, reveals activity that is clearly more intermittent and amateur than professional. Known by her nickname of "la Manjirona" in the outlying village of El Carpio, she confessed under torture to having been called to break a spell (that she herself had cast by use of a leaden figure) and to having at least twice invoked Satan, Barrabas, and Beelzebub for trivial reasons. On one occasion it was to bring home the straying husband of a daughter's friend.[42]

---

[41] Nuestra Señora de la Paz as a miraculous intermediary was later replaced for pragmatic reasons by El santísimo Cristo de la Caridad, who in 1598 was believed to have saved the inhabitants from an epidemic of bubonic plague. See Moreno Nieto, *La provincia de Toledo*, p. 504.

[42] Caro Baroja concludes: ". . . era una vieja curandera más o menos injerta en hechicera y que—como otras veces ha ocurrido—su clientela se

Probably of far greater interest than this ninety-year-old dabbler in magic and folk remedies (whose wretched appearance may have helped turn her neighborhood clientele against her) was another long term resident of the Inquisition's prison in Toledo, one Mayor de Monçón usually referred to as "la física de la Puebla de Montalbán."[43] "La física" (the lady physician) was apparently her local nickname and, like "la Manjirona," quite enough to identify her to anyone in town or even in the region. Although her dossier has disappeared and along with it the record of her offenses, we know from the reports of the prison spies who contributed evidence against Abraham García that she was arrested in 1514. And she was still there (indicating that the case had not yet been decided) in 1518 according to another transcript. We also gather from the same fragmentary reports of goings on among the prisoners that she was a knowledgeable professional as well as a woman of character. On one occasion, like Celestina herself, when she discourses to Pármeno on the erotic imperative, she was overheard citing the "authority of Aristotle,"[44] and, on another, she cried through the bars to a fellow prisoner, "Bernaldino Díaz,[45] how are you?" When the answer came back that he was badly off, a prisoner, and all alone, "she told him to pluck up his courage and not to moan, for she too was a prisoner and a woman and alone."[46] She was to need

---

volvió en contra" *Vidas mágicas*, ii, 15. Thanks to Américo Castro, who located the reference in the Academy files, I learn that "*gironas*" are defined in the *Biblia* of Arragel as "omnes de mal bevir e ladrones" (Madrid, 1921, i, 23).

[43] Her name is given in records of the trial of the Licentiate Diego Alonso (Inquisición de Toledo, p. 161): ". . . el alcaide . . . sacó a este testigo . . . para barrer el patio de la cárcel, y que estando barriendo . . . llamó a este testigo el licenciado Diego Alonso . . . y le puso dos cartas en la mano . . . la una a Mayor de Monzón, física, presa en la dicha cárcel, vecina de la Puebla de Montalbán. . . ." The letters contained news and advice about the prisoners' individual situations.

[44] Concerning prison conversations, a cooperative inmate reports "que oyó hablar a un hombre y una mujer no entendiendo bien lo que decían, pero que la mujer mentó una autoridad de Aristotelis, pareciéndole ser esta mujer la física de la Puebla, cosa que resultó ser cierta . . ." (Abraham García, Inquisición de Toledo, p. 184).

[45] If this Bernaldino Díaz (who was arrested at the same time as "la física") from Talavera is the same as the defiant and bellicose priest whose case is presented by Lea (see below, Chap. VIII), the latter's dates must be in error. Lea has him escaping to Rome in 1512.

[46] "Bernaldino Díaz . . . declara que una mujer llamada 'la física' vecina

all the courage she could muster, for, according to a later document, she was burned at the stake sometime before 1529.[47]

It would be misleading, not only because of the sparseness of the evidence, but also on general principles to propose "la física" or anyone else as a living model for Rojas' greatest human creation. But, at the same time, if we are to understand the Puebla as an institution for growing up, we must also realize that women such as these, institutional in their occupations and their very nicknames, were a part of his life—present in his life. The final truth, perhaps, is that between Celestina and these sorceresses of flesh and blood "influence" was exercised in both directions. It is moving to overhear (in the 1547 trial of Juana Núñez Dientes, discussed at length by Caro Baroja) a witch who lived in Toledo during Rojas' lifetime invoking Satan with these words: "Conjúrote con todos los siete conjuros de Celestina. . . ."[48]

Returning to the *Relaciones* and their closing description of the town, we are told that its population, now 800 *vecinos*, has doubled during the last fifty years. Since this period takes us back more or less to the time of Rojas' departure, the total during his childhood (according to the standard multiplication of each *vecino* or head of family by five) would have amounted to something less than 2,000 inhabitants.[49] How did they make a living? In 1560 (perhaps for the 1490's the figures should be halved) there were three *escribanos*, seventeen priests (as against one today), and eleven *hidalgos*, of which three were exempted from paying the Royal *alcabala*.[50] The rest of the inhabitants, witches aside, are poor and

---

de la Puebla de Montalván le llamó a voces diciéndole: 'Bernaldino Díaz, ¿qué tal estais?' respondiéndole este testigo que mal puesto, que estaba preso y solo, y que la tal física le dijo que se esforzara, que no tuviese pena, que también ella estaba presa y era mujer y sola" (Abraham García).

[47] In that year her son, Diego de Adrada, also from the Puebla was denounced for violating the restrictions on dress imposed on children of those condemned (Inquisición de Toledo, p. 139).

[48] *Vidas mágicas*, II, 43.

[49] Juan Martínez mentions 600 "casas de morada" adding "podrá aver ochocientos vecinos y que la dicha villa no a sido tan poblada como al presente porque en sus días se abrán augmentado quatro cientos vecinos." By 1535 according to various entries in the *Catálogo de pasajeros a Indias*, the Puebla had begun to export population to the New World. The population in 1958, as given by Moreno Nieto, was 7,642.

[50] This is a small proportion, since in the province of Toledo, according

"work with their hands at farming or at carding, spinning, and weaving the wool cloth that is made in the town."[51] All live in well-built houses of adobe or brick. But water is scarce; either one has to dig very deep wells or go all the way to the Tajo. There are two free "hospitals" and two churches, San Miguel (where Garcí Gonçález reposed), adorned with the moons of don Alvaro de Luna, and Nuestra Señora de la Paz, in which the miraculous image is kept. There are also two monasteries, one of Franciscans with some thirteen begging friars and the other a convent for forty nuns founded by don Alonso Téllez.

Lastly, comes the usual list of famous men who are native to the Puebla. Three are famous warriors: one Bolonia "now a Captain General on the marches of Hungary" and "Captain Peñas and Captain Bartolomé López, well-known persons in Italy and other theaters of war." Another is "don Pedro Pacheco, a son of don Alonso Téllez . . . who became Viceroy of Naples and a Cardinal in Rome and . . . even sat on the Papal throne and was adored as Pope, but, for the lack of a few votes, he lost the honor. However, he was always a favorite of the Popes, and, in spite of all his power, he never accomplished any good for our town, nor did he leave here any memory."[52] Resentment against the local establishment is still audible. Of much lesser importance was one of the last names mentioned, "the Bachelor Rojas who wrote Celestina."[53]

---

to a 1541 census, there was one *hidalgo* for every 12 *vecinos pecheros* (*Documentos inéditos para la historia de España*, ed. M. Salvá and P. Sainz de Baranda, Madrid, 1848, XIII, 529).

[51] In 1573, according to Moreno Nieto, there existed "cuatrocientos telares, numerosas curtidurías, varios molinos aceiteros de los llamados de viga, bodegas, alfares, etc. De la importancia que alcanzaron los gremios en aquella coyuntura nos hablan los nombres de algunas de sus calles, tales como Tenerías, Bataneros, Canastas, Labradores, Bodegones, etc." (p. 499).

[52] A biography of this don Pedro Pacheco born in the Puebla a few years after Rojas (1488) is given in F. Fernández de Bethencourt, *Historia genealógica y heráldica de la monarquía española, casa real y grandes de España*, Madrid, 1897-1920, II, 428 (hereafter referred to as Bethencourt).

[53] Rojas is mentioned only in passing by Ramírez de Orejón and not at all by Juan Martínez. An illustrious native of the Puebla, born a little too late for mention (1514?) was Dr. Francisco Hernández, the so-called "proto-médico de las Indias" and author of the monumental *Historia natural de Nueva España*. Hernández married a girl from his home town, Juana Díaz de Pan y Agua (see *Obras completas*, México, 1960, I, 119). In the Serrano

◈ "A town of Jews"

The most suggestive remark in the *Relaciones* is not the pass-ing reference to *La Celestina* but the information that the nucleus of the Puebla was a "población de judíos" to which a disorganized and errant Christian settlement later appended itself. For in its light the reply of Alonso Ruyz, the parish priest of San Ginés in Madrid, when asked about "the reputation of the aforesaid Alvaro de Montalbán and who were his parents," takes on added signifi-cance: "He said that he had heard that the accused and his parents are from the aforesaid Puebla and that in all the aforesaid Puebla there is hardly a person who has not been 'reconciled.' "[54] It would seem, then, that, in accord with its history, the Puebla de Montal-bán was one of those towns, like Almagro, Carrión, Lucena, Llerena, Montilla, Monzón, and Madrid itself, where a substantial proportion of the inhabitants were of Jewish origin.[55]

We must allow, of course, for exaggeration on the part of Alonso Ruyz. Were we to take his statement literally, there would have been no one left in town to torment those who had been reconciled "to the brink of suicide" during the subsequent years of extreme civil tension. Curiously enough, according to Lea, the paradoxical situation of an entire community of "reconciled" inhabitants with no one in a position to put anyone else to shame did actually obtain in Cifuentes. The Inquisitors there had filled the Church with so many *sambenitos* that, rather than singling certain families out for dishonor, the effect was to keep everybody from attending mass. Every name in town was represented, and the parish priest was

---

trial there are mentioned a "Diego Paniagua y su mujer" as servants in the noble household, who may have been her parents.

[54] Serrano y Sanz, p. 272.

[55] See Domínguez Ortiz, p. 141; Amador de los Ríos, p. 158, and *Investi-gaciones*, p. 52. For Montilla, see R. Porras Barrenechea, *El Inca Garcilaso en Montilla*, Lima, 1955. For Almagro, see Sicroff, p. 211. Regarding the Puebla itself, Bernhard Friedburg in his *History of Hebrew Typography* (in He-brew), Antwerp, 1934 remarks: "About the year 1485 typography had already made great strides forward in the lands of Spain. The forcibly converted Jew, Juan de Lucena, established two printing shops, one in his native Toledo and the other in the town of Montalbán which is near it and which was also an ancient town and full of Jewish inhabitants from former years" (p. 71; translated for me by Ernest Grey).

forced to petition the Inquisitors for the removal of the shameful garments.[56] Unfortunately for those who suffered, things did not reach this extreme in the Puebla, but, if Alvaro de Montalbán's *sambenito* was displayed after his death in one of the two churches, we can be sure it was accompanied by many others. Friends, neighbors, and relatives (many of them conspicuously *ajudiados*) rubbed long empty sleeves whenever a draught passed through their clustered emblems of dishonor. Admitting exaggeration, Alonso Ruyz still offers useful testimony about the human make-up of the town. To a considerable extent, the ancient "población de judíos" was now a "población de conversos."[57]

Nevertheless, the true significance of this characterization of the Puebla is not demographic. The very element of exaggeration in the priest's testimony points to the fact that he is less interested in population groups and percentages than in what, as a man of his time, he considered to be the tainted *opinión* or reputation of the community. The implication is that Alvaro de Montalbán, origins and actions aside, was a native of a dishonored town and that that dishonor affects all born there. Such an attitude is difficult to grasp today—when most of us think guilt by association to be an aberration—but it was accepted as true by all parties in sixteenth- and seventeenth-century Spain. Arguing in this forgotten context, a frequent and—to us—paradoxical point made by *converso* opponents of the Inquisition was that public *autos de fe* and exhibition of *sambenitos* had the effect of dishonoring Spain among Christian nations. A France or an England, they claimed, had known how to absorb their converted Jews and punish their backsliding far more surreptitiously.[58]

For Alonso Ruyz and for the Inquisitors who asked him to testi-

---

[56] III, 168. Llorente also refers to the incident.

[57] Documents concerning Jewish life in the Puebla are few and far between. Aside from that revealing the comparatively small size of the *aljama* in 1485 (see n. 75), the only one I have seen was provided by Ernest Grey from the *Response* of Isaac ben Sheshet (1326-1408), Constantinople, 1547, concerning a quarrel between Jews over rented land (1510). Professor Grey believes the reference given by Joshua Bloch ("Early Hebrew Printing in Spain and Portugal," *Bulletin of the New York Public Library*, 1938, p. 375) to Responsum 560 of the same author's *Sheelot Teshubot* (Riva di Trento, 1559) to be in error.

[58] See Sicroff, p. 130 and elsewhere.

fy, however, it was not all Spain which was dishonored but only certain tainted enclaves and communities. Before Spain could be truly honorable, it was first necessary that these be exposed and cleansed. Such men were incapable of thinking on a national scale; neighbors and neighboring towns were all that mattered. Today a Camilo José Cela can describe with perverse fascination the reputations which still characterize villages in the isolated region known as "la Alcarria." But there was nothing rural or backwards about such notions in the Spain of Fernando de Rojas. Even a Madrid priest who counted the Montalbán family among his principal and most affluent parishioners knew and was not hesitant in saying what it meant to be born in the Puebla de Montalbán.

The relationship between the ancient history and the contemporary reputation of Rojas' self-announced birthplace will help us to comprehend one of the major ambiguities of the prologue material. As we remember, when Rojas' friend Alonso de Proaza in his closing verses solves the mystery of the initial acrostic, he promises that it will reveal not only the *nombre* of the author but also "su tierra y su clara nación." And when we follow Proaza's directions, we find that the first two—*nombre* and *tierra*—are clearly spelled out: "ELBACHJLERFERNANDODEROIAS" and "PUEVLADEMONTALVAN." But what about the *"clara nación"*? At first glance, we are likely to consider it a more or less rhetorical repetition of *tierra*: "native land and distinguished birthplace." Although in contemporary Spanish this meaning has been lost ("*nación*" now meaning "nation"), there can be found a number of cases of such usage.[59] What is hard to comprehend, though, in this unproblematical interpretation is the adjective "*clara*" applied to such a humble and dishonored place of origin. Are Rojas and Proaza playing with us ironically, or do they overlook the gap between Proaza's elevated description and Rojas' actual revelation? The second alternative seems to me no more likely than to propose that Cervantes was unaware of the comic bite of "Don Quijote *de la Mancha*" as a title.

Our suspicion that a stylistic joke has been played on us will be confirmed if we take into account another and complementary

[59] For example, in Hurtado de Mendoza's *Guerras de Granada*, BAE, vol. 69: ". . . la aldea que llaman Alfacar en mi niñez vi abierta y tenida por lugar religioso donde los ancianos de aquella nación . . ." (p. 2).

meaning of *"nación."* In addition to *"place* of birth" it also signifies *"line* of birth" or lineage.[60] As Castro observes, *"nación"* has a special connotation of caste reference that does not accompany "nation" either in French or English.[61] In the *Vocabulario* of Diego de Guadix, for example, the two words are put together as synonyms, "casta o nación." That Proaza intended to refer to the Puebla not only as a locality or *tierra* of origin but also as a source of lineage is also indicated by the preceding adjective, *"clara"* ("clear" in the double sense of undefiled and famous) used to celebrate ancestry in such formulae as "claro linaje" or "claros varones."[62] Which is to say specifically: Fernando de Rojas' *tierra* is the Puebla de Montalbán while his *"clara nación"* is the Jewish caste which (as Alonso Ruyz testifies) was identified with it. In the acrostic Rojas, with the rhetorical help of Proaza, hints at the same family background his grandson less than a century later tried so hard to conceal. If the Licentiate Fernando had composed the hidden message, he probably would have concluded with "e fue nascido en Asturias."

Examination of this aspect of Rojas' prefatory strategy is of biographical value in that it indicates his attitude towards his own origins. Marcel Bataillon does not go astray when he remarks that the originality of the preliminary octaves does not derive from their artifice but from their length.[63] Other such acrostics limit themselves to the revelation of a single hidden identity. But Rojas, taking far greater poetic pains, composes a line for each of the

---

[60] Thanks to Rafael Lapesa I was able to consult the file on "nación" in the Royal Academy. In a note to the *Quijote* (III, 209) Rodríguez Marín equates "de nación" with "de nacimiento." In the *Baladro del Sabio Merlín* (NBAE, vol. I, pp. 120-121) we find the same thing: ". . . e de su nascencia e de los nuevos linajes de nación." There are a number of other examples.

[61] In *Realidad*, edn. II, he explains: "El modelo para la estructuración colectiva no fué ni el visigodo, ni el francés, ni el inglés, en los cuales la dimensión política predominaba sobre la religiosa. La base de la nación fué la circunstancia de haber nacido la persona dentro de la casta religiosa a la que pertenecía cada uno de los tres grupos de creyentes. Por eso se dice aún en español 'ser ciego de nación'; es decir de nacimiento. . . . La nación iba determinado por la creencia, mientras en Francia *nation* refería a la tierra en donde se había nacido" (p. 246).

[62] This was, of course, the Latin meaning of *"clarus."* It should be noted that if Proaza applies the adjective to Rojas' "nación," at least by implication he includes himself within the same lineage, which—given his particular vocation—is not surprising.

[63] p. 205.

nineteen letters of the name of the humble—and, in Old Christian circles, despised—town where he claimed to have been born. Why? I would answer: because he believed that his claim to a "dígna fama" and a "claro nombre" could not be separated from his birth-place and from the caste which it represented. For the Old Christian priest, Alonso Ruyz, to be a native of the Puebla was suspicious per se, a stain on any man's reputation. But what Proaza and Rojas are up to in their calculated and ironical game of hide-and-seek is precisely the reversal of that evaluation. For them, the Puebla and the *conversos* who inhabited it together constitute a *"nación"* which, far from dishonored, is "clear" by definition. It is an assertion which, by the way, does not in any way conflict with the probability that Rojas was at the same time concerned to hide an acutely painful and socially humiliating family tragedy. Rather, at one stroke and with a subtlety to be expected of the author of *La Celestina*, the announcement "e fue nascido en la Puebla de Montalbán," is simultaneously an act of shamed concealment and of proud display.

As we have already seen, there were many precedents for such an expression of pride. One of the typical reactions—which can be overheard in the argument of Abraham García with his jailer[64] or read on the indignant pages of Villalobos and Fernán Díaz de Toledo—of *conversos* to their marginality was to defend Hebrew lineage in medieval Christian terms. Some *conversos*, even before the coming of the Inquisition, tried to pretend to be what they were not, but others preferred to launch a proud, although ultimately hopeless, counter-offensive. It is for our purposes particularly interesting to find an echo of these feelings in the time of *La Celestina* and in its immediate tradition—that is to say, in a contemporary imitation which was quite obviously the work of a fellow *converso*. A speaker in the anonymous *Thebayda* (1504)[65] contrasts the authentic nobility of Hebrew descent to the borrowed and artificial nobility of recently purchased titles in these words: ". . . ask the Israelites if there were no nobles among them, and more than just noble: illustrious and super-illustrious. . . . [In view

[64] Chap. III, n. 50.
[65] See M. R. Lida de Malkiel, "Para la fecha de la *Comedia Thebayda*," *RP*, xvii (1952), 45, for the anonymous author's sympathetic view of the *converso* situation.

of this] do you think it necessary for me to mention nobility acquired the day before yesterday?"[66] It is better, in other words, to be proud of the lineage of Abraham and Isaac than to hide behind such epic names as Diagarias or such spurious titles as Count of Puñonrostro.[67] So also Rojas and Proaza seem to feel: it is better to praise the "clara nación" of the Puebla than to live in shame. That this is said evasively and ambiguously rather than with the resentful assertiveness of other *conversos* can be explained both in terms of personality and strategies of self-presentation. But it is said nonetheless and, I would maintain, in a way clear to the kind of readers Rojas hoped to find.[68]

In view of the repeated assertion in the Palavesín *expediente* that the Rojas family "left Toledo for the Puebla," there is a related aspect of the "reputation" of the town which must be examined. In the years before the Inquisition the Puebla was commonly thought of as a place of refuge for all those half-converted individuals (particularly those harassed in Toledo) who were reluctant to lose contact with their Jewish past. Along with Alvaro de Montalbán's nostalgic memories of a time when Jew and *converso* lived as one, the use of the Puebla by Juan de Lucena for experiments with printing in Hebraic and for the eventual establishment of a press and bindery seems significant in this connection. As is brought out in the trial of his daughter, Lucena owned houses both in Toledo and in the Puebla but in the latter he felt more free to exercise his new vocation. There, too, on Saturdays his daughters would invite "women friends and relations . . . and behind closed doors they would rest and enjoy themselves all dressed up and primped for the occasion."[69] Another example, for which we may thank Baer, is that of Juan de Sevilla, accused by a Jewish informer in Toledo of going to the Puebla in order to celebrate Passover. While there, "he called himself don Ysaque, and he consorted with Jews, and he walked with them, and he ate in their houses during the whole of

---

[66] Edited by Marqués de la Fuensanta del Valle, Madrid, 1894, pp. 488-490.

[67] For information on the conversion and transformation of the Arias, see Caro Baroja, I, 121-122.

[68] Even Serrano y Sanz centuries later sensed something hidden behind the emphatic assertion: "Que Fernando de Rojas *fue nascido* en la Puebla de Montalbán, según él dice en los famosos versos acrósticos, es cosa indubitable; ¿a qué fin iba a inventar una patria tan humilde . . .?" (p. 250).

[69] Serrano y Sanz, p. 285.

Passover, and he went to the synagogue."[70] Similarly in the 1487 confession of one Beatriz González, she admits that while in the Puebla "she gave alms to Jews and money to buy oil and wax for the synagogue and to pay for prayers."[71]

The same contrast between the repressive atmosphere of Toledo and the freer air of the Puebla may be deduced from the marital difficulties of Leonor Jarada—one of the women friends of Juan de Lucena's daughters and possibly one of the very ones observed celebrating the Sabbath with them in their house. As her husband later explained to the Inquisitors, fear that Toledan neighbors might remark on her backsliding caused him to send her back to her mother in the Puebla. There the family, he says, "publicly performed Jewish ceremonies," and his wife made a gift of money to a Jewish maker of wine skins.[72] From these substantial fragments of fact not much imagination is needed to reconstruct the singular atmosphere of the former town of Jews which Fernando de Rojas was proud to acknowledge as his own.

The common factor of these separate incidents, as well as of the early portions of Alvaro de Montalbán's autobiography, is the fraternal coexistence of nominal Christians with remaining Jews. It was precisely this "participation, conversation, or communication" which Ferdinand and Isabella emphasized in order to justify the 1492 Edict of Expulsion. According to this much cited document, the Jews

> try in every possible manner and way to subvert the believers in our Holy Catholic Faith, and they seduce them from it and into their own noxious belief and opinion, instructing them in its practices and ceremonies, calling meetings where they read to them and teach them how to keep their law, trying to convince them to have themselves and their children circumcised, giving them books so that they may read their prayers, declaring days of fasting . . . notifying them of Passovers . . . giving

---

[70] *Die Juden*, 1/2, p. 446.   [71] Inquisición de Toledo, p. 189.

[72] Not only did they keep the Sabbath and work on Sundays but also they observed traditional days of fasting, "a remenbrança de la reyna Ester porque libró los judíos de la maliçia de Hammar [*sic*]; e su desayuno destas donzellas diz que hera con lechugas e sal e vinagre, en vasijas nuevas." Their prayers were recited from a "citurí de oraciones de judíos en romance . . . bueltas a la pared" (Serrano y Sanz, pp. 285-289). Jarada was a typical *converso* name. (See Domínguez Ortiz, p. 152.)

them unleavened bread . . . persuading them that they should obey as well as they can the law of Moses, and making them understand that it is the only law and the only truth. . . .[73]

Although the expulsion was the inevitable corollary of the Inquisition, and although Ferdinand and Isabella may have correctly described the long-run inevitabilities of coexistence, at least for the Puebla their generalizations are misleading. Juan de Lucena and his family and the pathetic individual alternatively named Juan de Sevilla and don Ysaque hardly seem to be either in danger of seduction or in need of indoctrination.[74] My conclusion would be just the opposite: it was the *conversos* who helped and influenced the Jews. The *aljama* of the Puebla was small and, if it resembled others in neighboring towns, at a social disadvantage.[75] The community of *conversos*, on the other hand, had been rewarded politically and economically—a principal reason for baptism in the first place having been the threatened loss of wealth and position. And from this position of dominance, for reasons of conscience or nostalgia they did what they could to help the humble artisans—basketweavers, potters, shoemakers, saddlers, and the rest—who remained faithful to the older law.[76]

To conclude, if in the larger cities the material disparity between the parts of the sundered caste would eventually lead (under Inquisitional provocation) to Jewish denunciation of *converso* neighbors,[77] in the Puebla the relationship seems to have been one of

[73] Amador de los Ríos, p. 1006.

[74] For a similar conclusion on the part of Caro Baroja, see I, 387.

[75] See F. Fita, "Documentos anteriores al siglo XVI, sacados de los archivos de Talavera," *BRAH*, II (1882), 309 ff. He describes the depressed economic and social conditions of the Talavera *aljama* after the mass desertion of wealthy members to Christianity. There is no reason to believe that the same situation did not exist in the Puebla. Serrano y Sanz concludes that by 1474 there remained no more than 15 Jewish households (p. 249). Which would confirm Lea's discussion of the general decline of Castilian *aljamas* during the 15th century (I, 125). Baer offers a specific basis for calculation: in 1485 the *aljama* of the Puebla was asked to contribute "60 castellanos" in a special levy assessed for the war against Granada. We may compare this to the 227 assessed from the Talaveran Jewish community and the 225 from Santolalla (a town on the scale of the Puebla). Toledo's share (as a result of pogroms) was minimal (*Die Juden*, 1/2, p. 370).

[76] See the article by Fidel Fita just cited.

[77] See F. Fita, "La inquisición toledana," *BRAH*, XI (1887), 289 ff. for the problems that resulted.

brotherhood, protection, and sought-for identity—with the *conversos* taking the leading role. Teresa de Lucena and her friends are charged with frequently giving "alms to the Jews and oil to the synagogue"[78] as well as "fasting whenever a Jew or Jewess was sick or had just given birth." Similarly Leonor Jarada, we remember, angered and frightened her husband by her charity to a Jew. There were exceptions, of course, one of them being a Jewish intellectual and physician, Abulafia, who was still a resident in the Puebla in 1490.[79] He had books to lend and was known to have discussed religious matters with Christians old and new, but it is hard to think of him convincing or seducing more effectively than a Juan de Lucena. And there were surely other *conversos* who tried to cut all ties with the past. However, in general, the evidence seems to indicate that, during the years prior to Rojas' birth and in such small towns as the Puebla, the difference between *converso* and Jew was often far more economic and social than religious.

"Enmities, envies, sudden rages, changes of mind, and discontents"

Prior to the coming of the Inquisition, the inhabitants of the Puebla could remember only one public execution—for a case of incestuous rape. But, as we saw both in the life story of Alvaro de Montalbán and in our discussion of the pessimistic sense of history prevalent among *conversos*, the year 1485 disrupted the harmony of the rural haven. Not only was the physical safety it had offered gone, not only were the "reconciled" Christians tormented to the "brink of suicide," but also the mere presence of the new institution led to a profound disarticulation of community life. Part of this was due to amateur people watchers such as the "odious" Puebla priest, Juan Alonso, a "man of evil entrails" who was delighted at the op-

[78] This was also one of the accusations against Fernán González Husillo (mentioned previously in connection with advice given to Alvaro de Montalbán prior to reconciliation). Admitting the charge, his children defended him by pointing out his parallel charity to "churches, monasteries, nuns, *beatas,* and needy Old Christians of any sort." He was acquitted.

[79] Before their quarrel (which we shall mention later on), Abulafia lent a translation of the Bible ("brivia en romançe") to Pedro Serrano. The Abulafias were a distinguished family of moralists, mystics, cabalists, and courtiers during the Middle Ages (see the index to Baer's *History*). The name is Arabic and means physician, literally "father of health."

portunity to "wreak revenge on his 'relatives' for it is thus that he mockingly calls the *converso*," and who remarked in public of a colleague, "I'll see to it that that old man is the first to burn."[80] But even more disrupting was the fear that any disagreement with a neighbor could result in denunciation. The minor incidents and quarrels of daily existence were thus magnified and remembered, and all human relationships within families and without became problematical. Every encounter with another was potentially fatal.

The Inquisitors were, of course, aware of the danger of receiving false information and took precautions. A second witness was usually required to substantiate individual accusations, and, although confrontation with accusers (a privilege fervently requested of the Crown by potential victims)[81] was forbidden, the defendant was permitted to list his known enemies and those with whom he had quarrelled. If he could identify the persons who had brought about his arrest, it was a point in his favor. Finally, severe penalties were provided (but seldom applied for fear of stopping the flow of information), if malicious denunciation could be proved. These were fragile safeguards at best, and, whatever their effectiveness in individual cases, they could not stem the fast rising historical tide of passion and conflict. The result was that community living during Rojas' childhood was strained every day to the limits of human tolerance.

The most effective way to comprehend the special tensions of small towns during the first years of the Inquisition is through direct testimony. "Voices . . . which come to us out of the . . . misfortunes of the age," quaver with suppressed hysteria in lists of the sort just mentioned: those compiled from the memories of desperate prisoners in order to identify possible accusers. Let us, therefore, listen

---

[80] So described in the Serrano trial. Such threats were not infrequent during the early years of Inquisitional presence. We remember, for example, León de Castro's remark to the same effect about Fray Luis de León during a faculty meeting (Bell, *Luis de León*, p. 115). Angela Selke de Sánchez provides an even more horrifying example in her "Un ateo español," previously cited (Chap. 2, n. 44). The enemies of the accused, she points out, took advantage of his being a *confeso* to exercise their rancor. One of them, an *escribano*, used to go around saying "that the Doctor was a Jew and that he and all his family would be burned." He had even trained his little boy to cry out in public: "They're going to burn the Doctor and his mother." And according to a witness, "When the boy would say that, everybody would laugh" (p. 8).

[81] Lea, II, 574 ff.

to an unusually lengthy and detailed example presented in 1490 by the Puebla *converso* whose case has already been referred to several times, that of Pedro Serrano, the mayordomo of the Lord don Alonso.[82] Serrano was charged (among other crimes) with "praying face to the wall, bowing and nodding like a Jew," with reading a Jewish Bible "falsely translated into Castilian," with conspiring with his brother, the Lord's Chaplain, to avoid "reconciliation," and with assuring those who were tormented by their neighbors that they would be "blessed" in the life to come[83] as compared to those who were "enjoying their plight." The truth was that these charges resulted from a series of malicious misinterpretations. In the trial record Serrano appears as a good hearted, although naïve and self-righteous, converted Christian given to arguing about theology with the Jews, displaying devotion, and defending the Inquisition. But the charges were grave, and, in spite of much favorable testimony (his noble master appeared as a character witness), without the establishment of bias, he knew he would be convicted.

A man in a mortal predicament, Pedro Serrano set out to try to remember every single one of the incidents and arguments which might conceivably have brought about his denunciation. The written result was a diary of daily warfare in the Puebla de Montalbán which, if efficient for Pedro Serrano (it did identify his accusers), is invaluable to us. Here is a window into a variety of "intrahistoria" antithetical to that of *Niebla* or of *Paz en la guerra*. That is to say, not misty but sharply outlined memories of war within peace. What is called in the Prologue all the "enmities, envies, sudden rages, changes of mind, and discontents" which compose the day-to-day biography of Everyman are here recounted in specific local detail. Furthermore, these were events which Rojas as a boy was in a position to witness or at least to hear about soon after. From such encounters, hideously dangerous however petty in origin, sprang the continuing tension of his youthful experience.

We must as usual try to understand what these voices from the

---

[82] Don Alonso was named for his paternal grandfather, "señor que fué de Belmonte" (Bethencourt, *Historia genealógica*, II, 425), and it is possible that this connection was responsible for his importation of the Serrano brothers from that town as chaplain and mayordomo. As we shall see, there was a certain amount of friction and suspicion between this out of town *converso* and local members of the caste.

[83] See Chap. III, n. 45.

past have to say on their own terms. Specifically, we must keep reminding ourselves that the atmosphere of physical violence that was described by Pedro Serrano did not seem as abnormal or strange to him as it may to anyone likely to read these pages. Although our century may be the most atrocious in history, our attitudes towards stabbing people or even striking them have changed significantly. John U. Nef, writing in 1956, may sound complacent when he comments on the change, but his usual perceptiveness to history works for him nonetheless:

> What we miss in all these "humanists" of the Renaissance is any sense that the deliberate infliction of bodily suffering beyond the field of battle is so grievous an abuse of power that it lies beyond the bounds of accepted conduct. What we miss in Montaigne, writing as he was in the shadow of the French religious wars, is the idea that the human conscience ought never to resign itself to the commission of "atrocities," the idea that unrestrained violence lies beyond the bounds which a decent community, even of independent states and of differing religious practices, can ever accept. The word atrocity, as a term for condemning the cruel and heinous conduct of a people, hardly seems to have existed in English before the late eighteenth century.[84]

We must, in other words, grasp clearly that it was not because violence characterized so many of them that Pedro Serrano picked out these incidents as potentially dangerous. To him the violence was as routine and tangential as it is in the *Quijote*. What was new and "specially surprising" (to use again the phrase of Father Mariana) was the facility offered by the Inquisition for offended persons to settle scores with their offenders.

With some editing, this notebook for a documentary novel of village life in fifteenth-century Spain may be reproduced in English as follows:[85]

[84] *The Cultural Foundations of Industrial Civilization*, Oxford, 1958, p. 77.
[85] The original text is highly colloquial and confused, shifting frequently between the first person of the accused's reminiscences and the third person of the lawyer. In translating, I have used only the first person and have supplied missing connectives. A number of insignificant items have been omitted. The writer uses the form don Alfonso instead of the Alonso found in most other documents.

A black friar called Fray Diego Sarmiento is my enemy, because, when I asked him to preach [presumably to the noble household] last year, one of the pages who did not know him said that he had heard from Nicolás de Arenas that he made love to the women who confessed to him. I asked him about it and made an investigation, and the aforesaid friar got angry and threatened me. My witness is the priest, Juan Rodríguez.

Fernando de la Coleta hates me and is my enemy, because, when he refused to sell me a barbel for the palace one day during Lent, I took it from him and also cancelled his prebend on account of his ingratitude. He complained about this and threatened me. My witnesses are Lope Majón and don Alfonso to whom he complained.

Pedro de Sylva, a neighbor of the Puebla, is my enemy. He hates me bitterly, because I once warned him to read the Scriptures instead of [historical] chronicles. He answered me with great fury, telling me to leave him in peace and that I was not his priest. He also said that it was forbidden to read the Bible [in translation], and that, if I didn't want to read chronicles and vanities and only an evangel without error, I had better read the Koran. My witness is the priest, Juan Rodríguez.

Diaguito, the son of Pedro Terciado, hates me and is my enemy, because he "dishonored" (slandered) a master [of a military order] named Quincoces who complained to me and I had him whipped. My witness is the aforesaid Pedro de Quincoces who lives in this city [of Toledo].

Martín Navarro, the cook for don Alfonso, is my enemy, because one day at table he called everybody present rascals and good for nothings. Quesada told him to shut up, because he wasn't man enough to sit at the table with the rest of us, and I took out my dagger and attacked him. Afterwards he formed a band with Juan de Murcia and others in order to do me all the harm they could. He is an evil man who lives sinfully. He keeps a whore, has little conscience, and less honor. He says he would give up a member of his body if it would result in my perdition. My witnesses are Diego de Cordoba, Alcubillete, and Saravia, the page of don Alfonso, and Pedro Palacios.

A Jew of the Puebla called Mosen Seneor is my enemy, because once I was lodged at his house and, while I was in bed,

245

he and his son, hoping to gain favor with Fernando Gómez who hates me, came to kill me with swords. Don Alfonso ordered the sword broken, and, on account of that, the enmity began. My witness is don Alfonso.

Abulafia,[86] the physician, hates me and is my enemy; after quarreling with me because I said that I disapproved of the Jews' praying for rain one day and the Christians the next and that that was why no rain had fallen, he came to me in great fury and asked me if I meant what I said. He said he would complain to his Grace [don Alonso], because Kings and grandees had always sponsored such prayers. He told me I couldn't deny belonging to his lineage, and, while we were arguing in the kitchen, he picked up a stick and said he would beat me. Thus, the hatred began and the insults, for he called me another fat-tailed one [otro rabigordillo]. I'll never speak to him again except when I have to. . . . My witness is Jaco Abeales.

Beltrán, a fellow from la Montaña, is my enemy, because my lady ordered me and Maldonado to arrest him and bring him to the Puebla on account of his rascally deeds. And before that, one night when I went to bed, I found him lurking in the dark and, imagining him to be a thief, drew my sword, cried out, and threatened him. My witness is Maldonado.

Juan de Murcia and Francisco de Murcia, his brother, hate me and are my enemies because (Juan) is cuckold, and don Alfonso commanded him to pardon his wife and promised to give him a present, but afterward he complained about it and said he'd been deceived. [He is also angry] because I beat one of his servants. My witnesses are don Alfonso and Villegas, the butler.

Leonor, the wife of Matute, who was the mistress of the Comendador and bore him a child, is my enemy. A woman of

---

[86] When Serrano y Sanz mentions Abulafia as living in the Puebla in 1487 and as being "distinguished for his fanaticism" (p. 249), it is probable that his source is this trial. Solomon ben Verga speaks of traditional Jewish prayers for rain as follows: "As for rainfall, our Talmud speaks of many just men who were able to induce it. Thus, the Christians requested of the Jewish inhabitants of Toledo to make rain fall, and they were able to do so by prayer" (p. 240).

bad repute and evil conscience, she hates me because I was waiting for Matute one day in the inn of Alonso Varica with the intention of killing him. He had kicked a brother of mine who used to live with don Alfonso. My witness is Alonso Varica.

Sancho Ortiz Calderón has been my enemy ever since the Comendador, Diego Sedeño, ordered me to make up some *coplas* accusing him of loving an old woman called Marihoz who worked for him as a maid, and the aforesaid Comendador had the *coplas* made in order to anger him. This is known by don Alfonso and Fernando de Valladolid.

Andrés de Ocaña hates me and is my enemy. He is an accuser and stirrer up of trouble [*malsyn e alborotador*], and don Alfonso arrested him and was going to have him whipped through the streets but desisted at the pleading of doña Marina de Guevara.[87] He is an evil man who starts trouble. My witnesses are don Alfonso and others.

Pedro de Polanco of Peñafiel is my enemy, because he was persuaded to testify against me by Andrés de Ocaña and Fernando Ruiz. [They told him to say] that when I prayed I turned my face to the wall like a Jew. They urged him on saying, "You poor fellow, you'll lose your soul, go on and tell them what you are supposed to" [*Ve di eso que entiendes*]. And since he's a drunkard and a fool, he did what they told him and afterwards said he was sorry and that he had said all this to his confessor, Fernand García, the priest. He is an inconsequential person, easily swayed [*hombre liviano*], who was induced and urged to give false testimony. My witnesses are

---

[87] The Guevaras intermarried with the Téllez Girones and are described in the *Relaciones* (see also VLA 4) as large landholders in the Puebla region. The doña Marina referred to here was the wife of don Alonso, a descendant on her mother's side of the Rojas of Poza (Bethencourt, II, 428) later punished for "Protestantism" in the 1559 *auto* in Valladolid. Although I have tried hard, I have not been able to find indication of any relationship between the family of the Bachelor and these ennobled *conversos* of the same name—except, of course, for the former's tenuous and doubtful ties with the Téllez Girones to be examined later. At the time of the 1559 *auto*, don Alonso Téllez Girón II, as a member of the family, intervened in favor of another doña Marina de Guevara who had been imprisoned (Llorente, IV, 224).

Diego de Corral and Antón Cachiperro and Catalina de Toledo, the housekeeper of Alonso Davila.[88]

Diego Paniagua and his wife,[89] administrator for my lady María, hate me and are my enemies, because I struck a son of theirs one night, and Don Alfonso heard about it and scolded the aforesaid administrator very harshly, and Bitoria, the pastrycook, is also my enemy, because he wounded a page called Castellanicos. . . . My witnesses are Garnica and Villegas.

Comendador Alonso de Fuentesalida is my enemy. Although he is of good lineage, he is envious and has no fear of God. He schemed with Fray Andrés to replace me as majordomo, and he snooped around to see if I was a *converso* in order to cause me trouble. Later the aforesaid Comendador, hoping to possess himself of the estate of my wife, caused false testimony to be raised against me with the help of a Moor called Maestre Abdullah the potter. My witnesses are Juan Rodríguez, the Clergyman, and Pedro Baruero.

Pero González Oropesa and his wife hate me and are my enemies. Fray Andrés who used to lodge with them came to me with the proposal that I marry their daughter, and I answered him saying that [I would have nothing to do] with people who were still so Jewish in aspect and habits [*ajudiadas*]. On account of this, they conceived a great hatred for me, and they sent a crazy woman out to say dishonorable things about me. My witness is Fray Miguel de la Puente.[90]

Alonso Alvarez, the brother of Pedro González' wife,[91] is my enemy. [I heard about it] when Diego de la Fuente,[92] a servant of don Alfonso, came to me with threats from Gonzalo, the son of Fernando Gómez, and told me to watch out for him. My witness is Diego de la Fuente.

Fernand Gómez Quemado is my enemy. He hates me because, when I came to serve don Alfonso, I replaced him in his functions. And also because I said to him once that the bones

[88] The reference is undoubtedly to Alonso de Avila "el viejo," still living in the Puebla in 1500 (VLA 4) and brother-in-law of Alvaro de Montalbán.
[89] See n. 53.   [90] See Chap. II, n. 32.
[91] Alonso Alvarez de Montalbán, born after 1460 and dead in 1525, was a brother of Alvaro de Montalbán. He married a Francisca Rodríguez.
[92] Probably the Diego de la Fuente identified in Chap. III, n. 35.

248

of my father were safer than those of his. [Another reason is that] I found out about some letters that he falsified [*cartas que falseó*] for the wife of don Alfonso de Aguilar. My witness is don Alfonso.

Alfonso de Arenas, a neighbor of the Puebla, is my enemy, because once, when we were in Escalona, the tutor of Don Alfonso sent us out on watch together, and I said I didn't want to go on watch with kids [*rapaces*]. Then, because I had laughed at him, he called me a drunkard. When I sought him out with arms, he hid from me, and we've been enemies ever since. My witness is Briones, a neighbor of Mesegan.

Juan Nieto, a neighbor of the Puebla, is my enemy. He was sent to collect some money in Valladolid, and he didn't dare come back because of the snow, and I made up a satirical song [*coplas de escarnio*] about it. After that we exchanged harsh words, and, for these reasons, his mother-in-law, one of those who were reconciled, felt herself to be mortally insulted by me. Both of them have hated me unceasingly ever since. My witnesses are Alfonso and Fernando de Valladolid.

Colaneche, a *baldosa* player, who lived with don Alfonso, my master, is my enemy. One day he took my hat from the hall, and, when I went to look for it, I couldn't find it, and, when he left it for me, my brother found out that he had taken it. So we quarrelled, and the other day he waited for me with a sword and a stick near a corner. When I saw him, I went up to him, but he didn't wait for me. We are now enemies. My witnesses are don Alfonso and Fernando de Valladolid.

Diego Sedeño is my enemy, because, through jealousy of a kept woman, he wounded Mena with a sword on a Palm Sunday. . . . Just afterwards I met a page who had picked up Mena's sword, and I took it and attacked the aforesaid Comendador Diego Sedeño, and I asked him if he thought it was praiseworthy to steal from his Lordship and kill his servants. And they made him prisoner and took him to [the Castle of] Montalbán, and after he was released he went to Torrijos and threatened me from there. My witnesses are don Alfonso and Pedro Sánchez the priest of Burujo.

Lira, a servant of don Alfonso, is my enemy, because we

have had many quarrels both in Medina del Campo and in the Puebla. He said he'd have me beaten and make me kiss his mule. He sent Villegas the butler to tell me that, and, that if he were not made majordomo within three months, he would consign his soul to the devil. Well, within two and a half he was put in jail. We have even exchanged blows on numerous occasions and he has always spoken badly of me and threatened me with beatings [*veinte palos*] out of jealousy. My witnesses are don Alfonso and Villegas the butler.

Alonso de Cota, don Alfonso's mule driver, is my enemy, because he pretended to be sick week after week in order to avoid working, and I had to find somebody else to drive the mules. Finally I had to dismiss him. He lived with the aforesaid Clergyman Juan Alonso [the one who denounced and threatened the local *conversos*]. My witness is Andrés, the mule driver of don Alfonso. [In the margin: "He did not confirm this."]

Maldonado, the servant of don Alfonso, is my enemy, because I affronted him when he was talking through a *reja* with a lady-in-waiting who later went to court. After that our friendship was pretended. Neither of us dared show our enmity because of fear of don Alfonso. My witness is Villegas who first saw him talking to the woman and called me over to witness it. [In the margin: "This is insufficient."]

García Martín, a shoemaker and neighbor of the Puebla, is my enemy, because in my capacity as majordomo I denied him the custom of the household. He found out [that I was responsible], and we quarreled, and he said to me that he thanked God that none of his relatives were Jews or reconciled *conversos*. He even complained to the Mayor, and, because it was a matter which had nothing to do with the law, his hatred was all the more bitter. My witness is Pedro Rodríguez Baruero.

Pimienta, a Jewish shoemaker, is my enemy. I ordered some slippers for doña Francisca from him, and she didn't like them and threw them in a big jar full of dirty water that was nearby and splashed his beard and face. He considered himself dishonored and mortally offended. My witness is Nicolás de Arenas, the Mayor. . . .

250

Juan Herrero of the Puebla is my enemy, because he used to do the horseshoeing for don Alfonso; but he didn't know how to do his job, and he used to take the mules to the Jewish smiths . . . , and I reproved him every month . . . and quarrelled with him, and he has been hateful and indignant ever since. . . .

"The aforesaid Bachelor had departed from the aforesaid village"

The appalling view through this documentary window deepens our comprehension not only of Alvaro de Montalbán's preference for Madrid and Valencia but also of the Bachelor's decision to move to Talavera. In addition to the irritability and the petty obsession with personal honor resulting from the close quarters of village existence, the intrigues of the local palace, the rivalries of Christians, Jews, and *conversos* in their different degrees of assimilation, and the competitiveness of artisans made each day bristle with strife. And if we add to this the shadows of mortal suspicion cast by the Inquisition, the strain on interpersonal relations will be understood to have been intolerable. It was necessary to abandon hope that the Puebla would in some way become again a communal refuge and to seek out, family by family, whatever semi-anonymity might be available in new and larger towns. As we saw in the case of Alvaro, and as is quite evident from Pedro Serrano's list, camouflage was out of the question in such a place. In the Puebla everyone knew everyone else's "life and miracles," as they say in Spanish; nor did they forget them as scatterbrained Alisa forgot Celestina's when they no longer lived in the same part of town.[93]

These considerations are meant to supplement rather than to deny the explanation for Rojas' decision to leave the Puebla offered by the witnesses of the "probanza de hidalguía." External evidence tends to confirm their memory that it was the "malos tratamyentos"

---

[93] Rojas' background was probably even better known in the Puebla than we have seen it to be in Toledo long afterwards. It is significant that in preparing the Indias *probanza* (VLA 32) Rojas' grandchildren were careful not to ask Puebla witnesses to testify to the *limpieza* of their paternal grandfather. Only the Avilas were referred to in the questionnaire, while witnesses for the Bachelor were all selected in Talavera.

251

of don Alonso Téllez combined with his efforts to "empadronar" (to include on the list of tax payers) Rojas and other local *hidalgos* which were directly responsible. This is fortunate, since those familiar with the procedures of military intelligence would surely give a "C" rating to information derived from such obviously fabricated "proofs." And particularly so, when three successive individuals remember the same incident in much the same way. On the other hand, as in the case of the two witnesses who mentioned the "huerta de Mollejas," it does not seem that the Licentiate Fernando's prior coaching necessarily meant incitation to perjury. Apparently his technique was to remind the ancient inhabitants of things they ought to remember. Thus, two other *hidalgos* who left town for the same reason and at the same time as Rojas are mentioned by name, and one of them, "un Fulano Ortiz que fue a Toledo," is probably the "bachiller Francisco Ortiz" whose name crops up in the Serrano trial.[94]

Further corroboration is supplied by information available about don Alonso's credit rating, a rating so unenviable that frantic efforts on his part to milk every possible source of revenue were to be expected. We have already noticed the resentment felt by the inhabitants of the Puebla as a result of the exactions of don Alonso's great-grandson, and in Rojas' time the land poverty of the family seems to have been even more extreme. In his will don Alonso lists a number of creditors, among them, Alonso de Montalbán, the "aposentador real," from whom he had borrowed small sums in cash.[95] But most telling of all is a special legacy to a daughter still unmarried, "because I have not found anyone suitable to her rank and because of the great need in which I have always been."[96] Which is to say, he could not provide a suitable dowry.

[94] "Es su enemigo un mochacho que era rapaz del bachiller Ortiz, por la enemiga que tenía y tiene el dicho Lira porque posaba en su casa [the "rapaz" in Lira's house?] e [Lira] le avisó e truxo para que testificase falso testimonio. [El rapaz] es un loquillo e liviano y de mal tyento, por tal lo echó el dicho bachiller de sy, y andava diciendo muchas liviandades y paresce ser sobornado e ynducido y con liviandad aver dicho lo que no sabía ni oyó: que rezaba el dicho Pedro Serrano. Testigo el dicho bachiller Francisco Ortiz." In addition to identifying Ortiz, the above will illustrate the difficulties of Serrano's text.

[95] Salazar y Castro, doc. 20,561: "Iten, mando que se paguen a Alonso de Montalbán doce ducados que me prestó en dinero."

[96] *Ibid.*: "Yo no la he podido casar, ansí por no aver hallado persona que

252

A principal reason for don Alonso's threadbare condition was his tendency to get involved in lawsuits. Not only were the usual disputes with neighbors about boundaries and areas of jurisdiction,[97] but also he was involved during his entire tenency in a very expensive legal encounter with the Duque del Infantado who, as an heir of don Alvaro de Luna, claimed nothing less than the lordship for himself. A provisional compromise settlement arranged by Pedro de Baeza (don Alonso's father's *mayordomo*) in 1506 entailed a series of substantial cash payments by don Alonso.[98] But lawsuits are hard to kill. Renewed litigation from 1520 to 1526 (when final settlement was reached)[99] indicates that Baeza may have overestimated his young master's ability to pay. In any case, in 1506, just about the time that Rojas appeared in Talavera, don Alonso must have been forced to bear down heavily on his tenants and vassals, and as a result he was probably most annoyed at those who claimed tax exemptions. It should be added that Ferdinand and

---

la convenga segund su nobleza y merecimiento como por las grandes necesidades en que siempre me he hallado."

[97] Particularly with his neighbor, don Carlos de Guevara (see n. 87) about the possession of a property known as "Gramosilla." *Registro general del sello*, III, 2308 and 3618 (1484) and with the city of Toledo, *ibid.*, III, 2005 and 3051.

[98] Documents referring to the Téllez Girón family in the Puebla are to be found in the Salazar y Castro archives in *legajo* D-14. That specifically referring to the preliminary settlement in 1506 is numbered 20,565 in the *Catálogo*. Pedro de Baeza, the trusted representative of don Juan Pacheco, describes his long negotiations with "el doctor de Talavera" (representing the Count of Alba who derived his claim from the widow of don Alvaro de Luna) regarding the Lordship of the Puebla in his fascinating "Carta que Pedro de Baeça escrivió a el marqués de Villena sobre que le pidió vn memorial de lo que por él avía fecho" (*Memorial histórico español*, vol. v, Madrid, 1853, pp. 485 ff.). Among Baeza's claims to merit as a faithful servant is his defense of the Téllez Girones' castle of Garçí Muñoz during which he killed Jorge Manrique: ". . . peleé con don Xorxe Manrrique, e le desbaraté e tomé la cabalgada que llevaba de la Motilla . . . e a la postre la noche que Vuestra Señoría sabe que peleé con don Jorxe como vuestro capitán, él salió herido de una herida de que murió . . ." (pp. 503-504). In 1503 Pedro de Baeza whose services were inherited by don Alonso was a witness to the marriage agreement of the latter's son with doña Leonor Chacón, daughter of Gonzalo Chacón, "Adelantado de Murcia, Señor de Cartagena, Contador Mayor, Mayordomo Mayor de la Reina" (Salazar y Castro, doc. 20,568).

[99] Bethencourt, II, 427.

Isabella, aware of don Alonso's difficulties and of the responsibility of their open-handed royal ancestors in creating them, took the unusual step of allowing him during his lifetime to retain the royal *alcabalas*,[100] precisely the taxes which *hidalgos* traditionally did not have to pay. Hence, the departures in 1506 or 1507 of "Fulano Ortiz" for Toledo, of "Fulano de Sahabedra" for Torrijos, and probably of Fernando de Rojas for Talavera.[101]

After his early glory at the taking of Granada, don Alonso's years of harassed coping with money problems (and perhaps, too, his years of heading the strife-ridden household that is remembered by Pedro Serrano) turned him into an embittered and crusty old gentleman. Francisco de Villalobos, writing in 1520, describes him as "loaded with rosaries, grown old and wasted with fastings and abstinence, battered, in poor health, and long bearded." Even worse, in spite of his piety, his bad luck is notorious. At the very moment when his grain is ripe, "a hail storm from the devil or a thick fog from the world" will blight it. "Such are the secret judgments of God!"—the physician concludes perversely.[102] *Converso* skepticism about divine justice aside, such audible gloating indicates that the disagreeable old fanatic was not much liked by those who knew him.

Along with the tenor of life in the Puebla and the irascible reactions of its Lord to his difficulties, a number of other factors may have influenced Fernando de Rojas' decision to abandon "su tierra, su clara nación." Precisely during the years 1506-07 (those which marked Rojas' departure and don Alonso's new financial obligations) there was the famine and the outbreak of the plague that were vividly remembered in the *Relaciones*. Both, of course, ex-

---

[100] As narrated in the *Relaciones*, III, 261: "Y ansimesmo tiene las alcavalas tercias de la villa y de la tierra, las quales se dice aver hecho merced della el rey don Hernando y la reyna doña Isabel a don Alonso Téllez, sucesor del dicho maestre don Juan Pacheco, por los días y vida del dicho don Alonso Téllez; lo qual es mucha suma de maravedís, que lo desta villa valdrá un cuento o más de maravedís."

[101] I use the word "probably," because it is at least conceivable that the Licentiate Fernando might have reminded his witnesses of a familiar event in municipal history and then suggested to them that his grandfather's departure was connected with it.

[102] *Algunas obras*, p. 46. He also describes him as a busybody "podreciendo su sangre con los negocios ajenos, perdiendo todos los días el sueño y el comer por mil cosas en que no le va nada."

tended far beyond municipal boundaries. Rodrigo de Reinosa describes the year 1506 in the title of a broadside as "the year of hunger,"[103] while the accompanying epidemic was virulent as far away as Lisbon. There, we are told, popular rumor blamed it on *converso* emigrées from Spain, and, as had happened before, the result was a ferocious massacre.[104] It is not hard to imagine the alarm of the *conversos* of the Puebla when faced with natural and human catastrophes of such proportions. Would they be infected? Would supplies last? Would a similar rumor excite the resentful Old Christian peasants who surrounded them as if they were a human island? In addition to these worries, we may also meditate upon the skeptical distaste with which those *conversos*, who, like Alvaro de Montalbán, "knew nothing of what lies beyond," regarded the religious fervor of their fellow townsmen during this period. As we remember, the stricken inhabitants resorted to elaborate parades, vows, and pilgrimages. And, even worse, when conditions were eventually mitigated, they, like Lazarillo's starving master when a *real* comes his way, were pathetically eager to attribute the change to divine intervention. It is curious to think of the author of *La Celestina* living in such an atmosphere.

The particular moment in Rojas' biography may also have played its part. Here was a young man who had already written nothing less than *La Celestina,* a young lawyer, who, as we shall see in the following chapter, had returned home after years of free intellectual fellowship with others of his age and kind—that is to say, with his University *socios,* "happy in their young manhood." And now, with immeasurably increased awareness, he was submitted not merely to the petty yet dangerous dissension described by Pedro Serrano but also to the enforced diet of mental pablum which even an Alvaro de Montalbán, far less educated than his son-in-law, found impossible to swallow. Back in the 1480's when Serrano, as a *converso,* "would meet a Jew in the plaza or whenever we happened to sit down together and the Jew would cite an authority of those which the Church admits and would argue about it, then we would go to his house and he would 'sing' his Bible, and we always

---

[103] "Otras coplas suyas a una moça q̃ en el año de la hãbre de mill y quiniẽtos y seys a la q̃l req̃ria damores." Quoted by J.M. Hill, "An Additional Note for the Bibliography of Rodrigo de Reinosa," *HR,* XVII (1949), 244.

[104] See the *Chebet Jehudah,* p. 8 and Caro Baroja, I, 201.

255

found it to be the way I maintained it was. Thus did I, before the coming of the Inquisition and afterwards, uphold our Holy Catholic Faith against the Jews." But the departure of the latter and the tightened pressure of the former had, by the time of Rojas' return, brought all such discussion to an end. Pedro Serrano's is a case in point. After torture and much hardship, he was absolved of heresy and apostasy but condemned to fifty lashes for daring to argue about theology "syn letras e syn ciencia."[105]

It is doubtful whether a Fernando de Rojas would have been much interested in the naïve opinions of Pedro Serrano and others like him, but, at the same time, his punishment represents—in contrast to the intellectual liberty still possible in Salamanca—the closing in of a fog of conventionality over small town life. As Solomon ben Verga informs us, daily conversation in the Spain he remembered from exile dwelt obsessively on major and minor discrepancies of the three coexisting "laws."[106] But now such speculation and arguments had perforce to leave the public square and retire to universities, monasteries, and to the reserved communication of such groups as the *alumbrados*. In a curious volume of theological polemic against Jewish beliefs entitled *Las epístolas de Rabí Samuel embiadas a Rabí Ysaac doctor y maestro de la synagoga* published (along with the *Libro del Anticristo* mentioned earlier) in 1496, the "Prólogo" carries the following significant warning: "I now wish to warn all laymen who are not masters of theology who

---

[105] Prior to the sentence and after being imprisoned for years, he was subjected to repeated torture. From the recorded deliberations, we learn that the Inquisitors absolved him of the major charges with their usual reluctance.

[106] The *Chebet Jehudah* is constructed on the basis of such argument, the thread of unity among its dispersed reminiscences being a continuing dialogue between Christians and Jews. As a member of the "generation of '92," ben Verga is concerned to analyze critically the behavior of his own people in their daily relations and conversations with Christian neighbors as contributing to the disaster. We are, as a result, led to see the oral confrontation of members of different "laws" as one of the most intense aspects of small town existence in Spain before the coming of the Inquisition. Sports being non-existent and politics being secret, questions of faith had the conversational field to themselves. The *Cancionero de Baena* (admirably analyzed from this point of view by C. W. Fraker in his *Studies on the Cancionero de Baena*, Chapel Hill, N.C., 1966) contains a number of poems which express the same amateur theological disputation. Read today, they seem to belong to a Spain so alien to the one with which we are familiar as to be virtually from another country.

256

may read this work for that reason not to presume to argue with any Jews and above all not publicly, since it is forbidden for laymen to dispute matters of faith publicly. . . . Because, if the opponent should answer with some sophistry and the layman should be at a loss for an answer, scandal might be engendered in the hearts of those listening. . . ."[107] To return to the Puebla must have seemed to the young graduate a return to a silence that was without the one advantage silence has to offer: privacy.

Finally, we must not forget the actual prosecutions and convictions that were falling hither and yon among friends and neighbors —as one victim under pressure involved another. These were not the more or less unknown victims Rojas might have seen in Salamancan *autos de fe* but people he knew intimately whom he liked or disliked, admired or despised. Unfortunately, due to the fragmentary nature of the archives, no records of Puebla cases from these years (1502-1507) survive. But that they existed cannot be doubted, and only one hitting close enough might have been sufficient to impel the change of residence. Admittedly these additional motives for Rojas' leaving the Puebla are speculative; there may have been any number of others such as those having to do with his marriage or with opportunities for advancement offered by friends and relatives in Talavera. However, at worst such speculations are no more illegitimate than those dedicated to identifying the purposefully nameless town where Celestina lived, and they do have the advantage of helping us to comprehend the Puebla as a home to which (unlike Stratford-on-Avon) it was extremely difficult to go again.

✒ "As many or more than there are Rojas"

A typical example of the unreliability of *probanza* testimony is the following statement made by a single witness: ". . . as such *hidalgos* [Rojas and his family] were familiar with the Counts of Montalbán, and the latter considered them to be their protégés

---

[107] Zaragoza, 1496, fo. LXVII. I have also seen a reference to a 1497 edition. In a book filled with echoes and repetitions of centuries of religious argument (from the Christian point of view), this initial warning reveals the author's half awareness that his whole endeavor is somehow pointless and obsolete. In the 1537 trial of Juan López de Illescas (see Chap. II, n. 44) we learn that a great part of his difficulties resulted from a barber shop argument about Erasmus.

and relatives by direct descent. . . ."[108] The repeated testimony and corroborative facts just examined have led us to believe in the estrangement of noble lord and *hidalgo* vassal, and now we are informed of a vague but intimate relationship between the two. Luckily (for the tentative conclusions here proposed) the contradiction is explained by another *probanza* initiated in 1555 by one Diego de Rojas of the Puebla.[109] In this document it is revealed that the aspiring *hidalgo*'s grandfather had served don Alonso as *ayo* (tutor) to his children and that his descendants held similar family posts. And we learn elsewhere that a daughter, once the claim to *hidalguía* had been granted, did marry one of the Téllez Girones. What evidently happened, then, is that the sixty-three-year-old witness had heard village gossip about the social success story of these particular Rojas, and, in his confusion or his desire to help the cause of the Licentiate Fernando, he attributed it to the family of the Bachelor. We need not be surprised that this kind of mix-up should occur. Anyone who has examined the incredibly complex sixteenth-century genealogies of the Rojas in the Toledo region will understand that, even in such a lineage-conscious age, it was often impossible to keep things straight. A proverbial way of expressing multiplicity repeated by Juan de Lucena in *De vita felici* was "son más de los de Rojas": the Rojas in Spain were like grains of sand on the shore.

Nevertheless, we must try as well as we can to deal with these genetic ramifications. The existence in the Puebla of two families of Rojas, each of which in due time attempted a change in status, suggests the possibility—and even the likelihood—that they were interrelated in some way. Let us see, then, if there is anything more to be learned about the Bachelor's blood ties. If our information about his father's identity is contradictory, about the mother claimed in the *probanza,* Catalina de Rojas, we know nothing at all. In the same *Libro de memorias* in which the Licentiate Fernando claims family origin in the "puebla de Tineo," he began a sentence about her and then (unfortunately for us) thought better of it and inked it over thoroughly. According to Valle Lersundi the blotted words only say "deuda de la casa de . . ." Concerning the Bachelor's brother Juan de Rojas, the *probanza* offers more information. He

---

[108] See Appendix III.   [109] Riva, III, 238.

is mentioned several times, the most suggestive being the following: "the present witness says that he never knew any relatives who were *pecheros*; rather they were all *hidalgos*. He was specially known to be a relative of a Martín de Roxas, resident of the village of Carriches, and a Juan de Rojas, resident and former *regidor* of the Puebla."[110] Beyond this, it seems reasonable to assume that Juan was married and left descendants in the Puebla. In the Palevesín *expediente* a number of Puebla witnesses state that the grandchildren of the "Hernando de Rojas who composed Celestina . . . had relatives in this town with whom they communicated. . . ."[111] The assertion is confirmed by a 1548 entry in the parish register recording the baptism of a Fernando de Rojas, son of Miguel, whose godfather was the Bachelor's eldest son, the Licentiate Francisco.

The casual mention of "Martín de Roxas, vecino del lugar de Carriches," thanks to information provided by Valle Lersundi, turns out to be more helpful than we had any right to expect. Alfonso López' *Nobiliario genealógico de los reyes y títulos de España* (Madrid, 1622) in the section dedicated to the descendants of Iñigo López de Ayala identifies Martín de Rojas as follows: "The aforesaid Martín Vásquez de Roxas and doña Leonor de Ayala, his wife, had the following children: Francisco de Roxas called 'the hoarse,' Martín de Ayala, Knight of the Order of Santiago, Rodrigo Dávalos, Knight of the Order of Calatrava and afterwards of Santiago, Governor of Alexandria in the state of Milan, doña Ynés de Ayala, lady-in-waiting to Queen Germana, second wife to King Ferdinand the Catholic. . . . Francisco de Roxas called 'the hoarse,' married doña Francisca de Acuña, and they had, among other children, *Martín de Roxas, a resident and heir to property in Carriches*" (p. 115).

From this information and from other sources a fragmentary genealogy of the family may be prepared, a genealogy which reveals two relationships of particular interest to us. The first is that Martín Vásquez de Roxas, his son, and his grandson, Martín (the supposed relative of the Bachelor) were all directly descended from Diego Romero, the treasurer of Henry IV, and his wife, Aldonza Núñez, known as "la romera," who was condemned and

---

[110] VL I, p. 389. Elsewhere he is called "hermano del dicho bachiller" and "tío del dicho licenciado Hernando."

[111] Gilman-Gonzálvez, p. 15.

burned after death.[112] Honors and orders and royal service aside, this family was as much a prey of gossip as the Rojas who left Toledo for the Puebla. The second is that Martín Vásquez de Rojas was (according to the sworn testimony of another grandson) a cousin of the Rojas who served the Counts of Montalbán.[113] Thus, if the witness who stated that the Bachelor was "specially known to be a relative of Martín de Roxas" was telling the truth, we have at one blow connected his family to a well-known line of slightly "stained" aristocrats and—at a considerable distance—to the servants and relatives of the Lords of Montalbán.

Although there may be legitimate doubt about the reliability of the testimony linking the two families (this witness, too, seems anxious to help the Licentiate Fernando), the possibility of relationship remains. In any case—whether related or not—it is still pertinent to examine briefly the family history of these protégés of three generations of Téllez Girones. Their careers will add one more perspective—as Ortega would say—to the Puebla "circumstance" of the author of *La Celestina*. From their 1555 *probanza*, we learn that the other family of Rojas was originally from Illescas, where they lived in "principal houses," rode on horseback with a retinue of servants, and, in general, "treated themselves as knights and *hidalgos*." The grandfather of the petitioner, Diego de Rojas, appeared in the Puebla as "a handsome and well disposed young man," married there in about 1495, and, as we said, was given the post of *ayo* for don Alonso's young children. Some four years later, after a quarrel with his difficult master, he left to become the *alcaide* of a fortress belonging to the most famous military man of the time, Gonzalo Fernández de Córdoba, known as the "Gran Capitán."

After Diego's premature death, his wife returned to her home in the Puebla where their son, Gonzalo de Rojas, was in his turn received into the Téllez Girón household, first as a *camarero* and afterwards, like his father, as an *ayo* for the children of the second

---

[112] Serrano y Sanz, p. 250 and Esténaga, p. 83.

[113] The witness, Rodrigo de Rojas, was a priest born in Illescas in 1505. He states that "su padre . . . se llamaba Francisco de Rojas" and that he was a "primo en terzero grado" of "Diego de Rojas, abuelo del que litiga." Later on, when we learn that his grandfather's name was Martín, we realize that he was among the "other children" of Francisco de Rojas "the hoarse" and a brother of the landowner of Carriches.

Lord. His son, Diego (who initiated the *probanza*) was even more favored: having begun his career as a page, in the early 1550's he married a lady in all likelihood related to his master's family, doña Juana Téllez de Toledo.[114] In 1555 he received considerable help from his new relatives in establishing his *hidalguía*. In the *probanza* the description of the second don Alonso's uncle dressed in the full regalia of a Commander of Calatrava and refusing, for the sake of good form, to be sworn without the permission of the Master of the Order is quite dramatic.[115] However, the black robes of the lawyer in charge of the proceedings turned out to have the upper hand. After being threatened with a fine, the Commander agreed to testify—naturally in favor of Diego de Rojas. Then, another generation later, Diego's aristocratically named daughter, doña Beatriz de Rojas y Toledo, climbed the final step in the social ladder when she married a legitimate son of the Téllez Girones, don Alonso de Cárdenas.[116] The latter through his family, as we

[114] From the Téllez in her name and from other circumstances, it would seem that she was an illegitimate daughter of a member of the Puebla's ruling family. Aside from the fact that she is always referred to as "doña" in documents (the 1555 baptism of their son Gonzalo and the 1608 "Prueba de Santiago" of their grandson don Juan Girón de Rojas, AHN 3414), the substantial help afforded the bridegroom in obtaining his *hidalguía* by the Téllez Girones is in itself suspicious. Finally there is the *probanza* testimony of the same priest, Francisco Estéban, whom we saw mentioned as a source of information in the *Relaciones*: He said he knew Diego de Rojas "desde hocho años a esta parte, poco más o menos, porque lo a bysto estar con su padre, que se llama Gonzalo de Roxas, e con su madre, bybiendo e morando en la dicha villa de la Puebla, e después lo a conoscido casado desde dos o tres años a esta parte, poco más o menos . . . e teniendo byenes y haçienda . . . *que le dieron con su muger en casamiento*." The same statement is also made twice by Diego Ruiz, "pechero llano."

[115] "E luego el dicho don Alonso Téllez dixo que él hera comendador suxeto al mayoral de su encomienda, e no podrá jurar syn lyçençia de su prelado e patrón de su encomienda, e que trayéndolo, que estaba presto de luego jurar e declarar. E yo el dicho rreçebtor le notifiqué que luego a la ora, syn embargo de su rrespuesta, sopena de mill castellanos de horo para la camara e fisco de su magestad, luego jurase e declarase. El qual dixo que por temor de la pena que estaba presto de luego jurar, e del yo el dicho rreçetor tomé e rrescibi juramento en forma debyda e de derecho, poniendo sus manos sobre una cruz que tenía de su encomienda e horden de caballeria que en sus pechos tenía e jurando por ella e por el abyto de su encomienda en lo demás como se contiene de suso, e a la confusyon del, dixo e rrespondió 'sy juro' e 'amén.' "

[116] "Don Alonso de Cárdenas . . . ya era muerto en 1608 y había cassado con doña Beatriz de Rojas y Toledo, hija de Diego de Rojas, Alcalde del estado de

remember, was related to our old friend, don Antonio de Rojas, the nemesis of the Francos. As might have been expected in a genealogy traced sideways, we have come full circle: to the democratic discovery that everyone may be kin to everyone else.

The social success story we have just retold is typical of the period[117] and should serve to make us wary of oversimplified explanations of Calisto's failure to propose to Melibea. To my mind there is little doubt that these Rojas—like those descended from the "condenado por judayzante"—were *conversos* who "had the aforesaid race in all parts" (to use the phrase of the period) and that the Téllez Girones knew it. I assert this not because of their distant relationship to the descendants of Diego Romero and Aldonza Núñez, but rather on the ground of their vocations. As we have seen, the career of administrative and intellectual service in noble households is highly indicative. Then, too, as in the case of the Francos, there is muted irony in portions of the *probanza* testimony, particularly in the description of the Illescas house and the pretentiousness of its owners who "treat themselves" and "present themselves" nobly. Finally, the grandfather's choice of the Puebla as a place to marry and settle down and of don Alonso as a master is suspicious in the light of what we have learned of both. The attractions of the town for errant *conversos* need no further comment, and, as for its Lord, we know the caste of his *mayordomo* and chaplain. Don Alonso's father, don Juan Pacheco, had on occasion fought the political power of the nascent *converso* "party," but he was nonetheless served by an able team of *conversos*, particularly Pedro de Baeza and the Cordoban tailor, Juan de Baena,[118] whom he raised to the rank of Commander of Santiago. It is not surprising, then, that his son should look for similar assistance in

---

los hijosdalgo de la Villa de Montalbán, y de doña Juana Téllez de Toledo, su mujer, naturales y vecinos de la Puebla. De esta unión: nació Don Juan Girón que fué Caballero de la Orden de Santiago . . ." (Bethencourt, II, 439 and Salazar y Castro, doc. 20,571). The *probanza* required for entrance into the order is listed in the AHN catalogue for 1608 and gives identical information.

[117] Another such case alluded to in the *Libro verde de Aragón* (cited Chap. II, n. 38) is that of the tailor of the Count of Belchite who was promoted to "procurador general de toda su tierra, y el mismo Conde le armó caballero." But, unlike the Rojas, fortune's fall was rapid: "Ambos marido y mujer fueron presos por la Inquisición y salieron penitenciados" (p. 267).

[118] See n. 98 and Chap. IV, n. 33.

his legal struggles and in his daily effort to live in a manner be-
fitting his station.[119]

Admitting the discrepancy in rank and blood between these
Rojas and the Téllez Girones, we still need not be surprised that
their long association ended in intermarriage. As Marcel Bataillon
points out, such matches, more or less disguised, were not infrequent in the time of *La Celestina* and afterwards.[120] It is hard today, in the light both of our experience of race prejudice and of our
knowledge of the later myth of *limpieza*, to understand the attitude
towards Jews and *conversos* of late medieval and Renaissance
nobles. When in his long correspondence with the Admiral of
Castile, Francisco de Villalobos half-affectionately and half-mock-
ingly taunts him about his fraction of Jewish blood,[121] we naturally
fear dangerous reactions of rage and shame. But not at all. The
Admiral jibes back in his turn, and their genuine friendship is
undisturbed. Part of the explanation, I think, is that pride was so
built into these grandees that their being ashamed of themselves
about anything is almost inconceivable. Then, too, the notion of
Hebraic nobility, as discussed previously, is more than a mere defensive reaction against Christian values. When Villalobos reminds
the Admiral that "we are descended from great and anointed
kings and from strong captains,"[122] he demonstrates positive belief
in the honor of their shared origins. There is always a certain
amount of "*humor chocarrero*" in such remarks (on one occasion
Villalobos refers slightingly to the presumably Old Christian
origins of don Antonio Manrique by calling him a *villanazo*, or
clodhopper, from Ocón),[123] but there is also genuine pride.

Lastly, from the historical and sociological points of view, we

[119] Diego de San Pedro, as is well known, was a mayordomo for another
member of the family, don Pedro Téllez Girón, Maestre de Calatrava, and for
his son, don Pedro Girón. See *Obras*, ed. S. Gili Gaya, Madrid, 1950, p. xxxiii.

[120] p. 175. See also Caro Baroja, I, 248-258.

[121] One of many examples may be found in *Algunas obras*, p. 91.

[122] "Y pues que somos nacidos / de grandes reyes ungidos /y de fuertes
capitanes, / no nos den tantos afanes / que turben nuestros sentidos" (*Algunas
obras*, p. 90). In the prologue of the Franciscan Fray Martín de Lilio to Fray
Pedro de la Vega's *Flos Sanctorum* (Alcalá de Henares, 1521), we hear
a similar echo of the same pride: "Acordemenos que fueron salvos nuestros
padres (como se lee en los Machabeos) quando los perseguía Pharaon, que
es el demonio, en el mar bermejo."

[123] *Algunas obras*, p. 133.

should not forget that the *converso* middle class and the aristocracy were subjected together to intense pressure from the newly-united and self-conscious masses. Social unrest and religious fanaticism had for over a century exploded in sporadic outbreaks of violence, and during the 1470's and the 1480's Ferdinand and Isabella channelled them into an effective and continuing political force. To unite the Kingdom around themselves, they sought through such pressure to counterbalance noble power and *converso* wealth. Later, of course, noble families had to pay at least lip service to the doctrine of *limpieza*—circumventing it, if necessary, with fraudulent proofs.[124] But in the time of which we speak, this had not yet affected matrimonial behavior. Instead, a Lord such as don Alonso and his administrators were natural allies, allies who were friends,[125] who spoke the same language, and who, when dowries and the search for status impelled them, were willing to cement the alliance by inter-marriage. Such was the more or less typical—however curious to us—household which presided over life in the Puebla de Montalbán and to which Fernando de Rojas, his father, and his brother may have been distantly related.

The degree of the relationship (if it existed) and the feelings of the Bachelor and his children (whether of warmth or dislike and envy) towards these social climbers who shared their name are beyond our ken. But it is certain that they knew each other in view of the continued contact with the Puebla of the Rojas who had moved to Talavera. In the will there is unfortunately no mention of the "huerta de Mollejas" or of any other local holdings, but the Bachelor seems to have kept his share of the family property there

---

[124] The gross hypocrisy of this practice as well as the self-satisfied and self-righteous images of self and lineage which accompanied it is the specific target of the *Tizón de la nobleza*. The irate author was less interested in maliciously revealing individual *manchas* than in showing up the wholesale self-falsification of his society.

[125] This is a valid generalization that is, nevertheless, a foreshortening when applied to individual cases. The ambiguity of the interpersonal relations of these full blooded *converso* physicians and mayordomos and their more or less tainted noble masters may better be understood by listening to Villalobos' partially Celestinesque *Dialogue* with a "grande de este reino de Castilla" (*Curiosidades*, BAE, vol. 36, p. 442). Familiarity, contempt, fear, affection, adulation, and impertinence all make themselves heard as Villalobos records for posterity his grotesquely Rabelaisian treatment of the Count of Benavente.

264

at least until after the Licentiate Francisco's marriage (probably between 1536 and 1540).[126] In addition to the testimony in the Palavesín *expediente* regarding relatives with whom the Rojas continued "to communicate," several *probanza* witnesses remember knowing the Bachelor not when he was a resident of the Puebla (some 77 years before) but on his many return visits "to look after the property he owned in the aforesaid town."[127] This included "a house he left there,"[128] probably the one in which he had been brought up. Furthermore, Rojas not only held on to his Puebla estate but also added to it. In the Valle Lersundi Archives there is a lengthy contract for his purchase in 1512 of a mortgage held by Elvira Gómez, a sister of Alvaro de Montalbán.[129] Such facts are insignificant in themselves, but, insofar as they offer some indication of Fernando de Rojas' long-lasting and deep concern for his *tierra,* they are worth our attention.[130] The composer of a verse in "arte mayor" for every letter of "y fue nacido en la Puebla de Montalvan" was a man who had learned much of what he knew about people (and he knew as much as any Spaniard has ever known)

---

[126] The problem of the lack of reference to Puebla property in the inventory offers no easy solution. In the "probanza de hidalguía" local witnesses testify repeatedly that both father and son owned real estate in town (VL I, pp. 389-90). It is possible that Rojas' heirs in order not to excite official cupidity preferred not to list out of town property in a document publicly available in Talavera.

[127] VL I, p. 389.   [128] VL I, p. 393.

[129] See above n. 3. The mortgage was on a house next door to that of Diego de Ladrada, probably, because of name and date, the husband of "la Física" (see n. 47). In addition to being Alvaro's sister, Elvira Gómez was also the grandmother of Catalina Alvarez de Avila who married the Licentiate Francisco. In document 1 of the Valle Lersundi Archives we find her in 1496 and 1498 mortgaging "certain houses which they had in the aforesaid town." A widow by 1500 and apparently in need of cash, she afterwards sold agricultural property to her brother Alvaro (VLA 4). The deal with the Bachelor in 1512 indicates continuing financial difficulties.

[130] As we know, the Licentiate Francisco, like his father, married a girl from the Puebla, and it is probable that, if the ceremony took place there (as would naturally be the case), the Bachelor and his family all went home for the occasion. Alfonsina de Avila, a Puebla witness in the "probanza de Indias" (VLA 32) who was "parienta de la dicha doña Catalina no sabe en qué grado y ansimismo . . . del dicho Licenciado Francisco de Rojas poca cosa," states only: ". . . este testigo estubo presente a sus desposorios quando se belaron." In any case, a second witness remembers the couple living in the Puebla (presumably in the family house) for a time after the marriage, "e despues se fueron a bibir a la villa de Talavera."

while living there. No wonder he is remembered as often return-ing.[131] The roots were deep; and although—like Stendhal's Grénoble—the past into which they burrowed may have been viewed more with irony than with affection, they were still roots, and Rojas never sought to cut them.

[131] Francisco Hernández, too, the self-styled Aristotle of the Indies and the only other famous intellectual to acknowledge the Puebla as his home, also held property there until the end of his life. He seems to have returned home a number of times after coming back from Mexico (*Obras*, 1, 288).

CHAPTER VI

Salamanca

"Yo vi en Salamanca la obra presente"
—Fernando de Rojas

✑ Students and Faculty

A discussion of Fernando de Rojas' years at Salamanca takes the form of an inverted pyramid. All that we shall have to say about the structure of University society, about the historical moment, and about faculty, courses, and classmates ultimately rests on one specific statement. Speaking as the continuing author in the acrostic verses, Rojas tells us that it was in Salamanca that he found or "first saw" the anonymous first act. It is reasonable to conclude therefrom that the degree of *Bachiller* of which he was so proud was awarded by the University of Salamanca. And, if that is indeed so, it behooves us now to meditate upon attendance there during the last years of the fifteenth century as a central experience of his life.

But is it so? We must begin by admitting that, however reasonable such a conclusion may seem, it is not susceptible to documentary proof. Only in the course of the following century did the University begin to employ its own *escribanos* and to record its graduates and their degrees. Before that time academic records were kept only by the individual professors and by the town notaries who prepared the illuminated parchment "letters of *bachilleramiento*" which cost the candidate 10 maravedís.[1] Since both these possible sources of information have been dispersed or destroyed, no direct evidence of the Bachelor's University career has been, or is likely to be, uncovered.

Fortunately, a number of buttresses support the otherwise precarious conclusion. In the first place, there is the prefatory letter's much discussed claim that *La Celestina* was completed during a

[1] As prescribed in the 1538 Statutes contained in E. Esperabé Arteaga's *Historia pragmática e interna de la Universidad de Salamanca* (Salamanca, 1914, I, 195). Ricardo Espinosa Maeso in "El maestro Fernán Pérez de Oliva in Salamanca" (*BRAE*, XIII, 1926, p. 434) mentions the University's belated assumption of record keeping functions. This failure was general in medieval universities and corresponded, according to Istvan Hajnal (*L'Enseignement de l'écriture aux universités médiévales*, Budapest, 1959, p. 30), to the capacity for memory of those living within a primarily oral culture. Individual graduations ceremonially conducted ("cérémonies spectaculaires et compliquées") served to reinforce the "recordatio" of fellow students who could be called on to testify in case the degree was disputed.

fortnight's vacation from Rojas' "principal study" of jurisprudence. In the same context the writer speaks to his unknown friend about absent *socios* (presumably the fellow students who were later to listen to his dialogue and discuss it heatedly) and about writing while away from home. Whether or not these remarks be considered a strategic attempt to minimize Rojas' own labors, they do lead us to conclude that at least some portions of *La Celestina* were written in Salamanca during the Easter recess of 1497 or 1498.[2] Probably the latter for reasons we shall soon see. In the second place, we must not overlook the air of recently acquired learning, of bouyant erudition, which pervades Rojas' composition (as well as that of his predecessor)—an air which fits in well with its adoption as a representative University work by the student body.

As has often been noted, local tradition quickly accepted Rojas' characters and places as its own, and from the sixteenth century until today student guides have pointed out to visitors such landmarks as Melibea's garden and tower and Celestina's decrepit house. When Rojas' grandson Fernando was studying in Salamanca (in itself an indication that he was following the footsteps of his family),[3] it is even recorded that he was nicknamed "Celestina." As

[2] The 1538 Statutes describe the University vacations as follows: "los quarenta días de vacaciones y los ocho de la fiesta de la Natiuidad y los quinze de la Resureción" (Esperabé Arteaga, I, 198). It is curious that a work concerned in its last act with the finality of death should have been written at precisely this time of year.

[3] In his "Libro de memorias" (VLA 25), the Licentiate Fernando describes his education as follows:

I was taught to read and write [las primeras letras] in the town of Llerena while my father was there in that province of León as resident judge in 1546 and afterwards in Talavera under 'el maestro Barreda.' I began grammar with the Bachelor Martínez on the day of San Lucas in 1549 and I finished with the Bachelor Ballesta. I went to Salamanca around the day of San Lucas in 1557 (that is, at the age of 16) where I studied law for five years. I took my first orders [Hízome de corona] the following year from don Fray Bartolomé de Carrança y Miranda, the Archbishop of Toledo. I graduated as a Bachelor of Law at the University of Salamanca on the 11th of May 1562. The famous Doctor Emanuel de Acosta conferred the degree on me. I graduated as a Licentiate at the University of Toledo on the 12th of May 1565.

It was while studying for this last examination that he lodged in Toledo with his cousins the Francos (see Chap. I, n. 50). Elsewhere (Gilman-Gonzálvez, p. 14) we learn that the Licentiate Fernando and his brother

a fellow student testified in after years, "the present witness was a companion in Salamanca in the *pupilaje* of the Licentiate Velasco (who resided in the street called Doctor de la Parra) of Fernando de Rojas, a native of the town of Talavera. Like his fellow pupils, this witness always called him 'Celestina' because he was a grandson of the Bachelor Rojas who wrote it and because his face was somewhat effeminate."[4] Finally there are the facts stressed by Menéndez y Pelayo that, of the two law faculties of Rojas' Spain, Salamanca was by far the most outstanding as well as the closest to the Puebla.[5]

Juan, who later practiced as a Licentiate in Madrid (VL I, p.; 387), went to the University together where they lived in the "pupilaje de Velasco."

Ricardo Espinosa Maeso has been kind enough to send me a copy of their respective *matrículas* in the University archives. Those of Juan in the "Facultad de Canones" read as follows: (1) "juebes vispera de san nicolas a cinco de diz[e] de 1560 años juan de rrojas natural de talabera diocesis toledo" (*Libro de Matrículas*, 1560-61, fo. 21, Archivo de la Universidad de Salamanca, no. 277); (2) "lunes a diez y siete de nobi[e] 1561 juan de Rojas natural de Talavera de la Reyna diocesis de Toledo" (*ibid.*, 1561-62, fo. 21, no. 278); (3) "martes a xvii de noviembre 1562 juan de rrojas natural de talabera de la rreyna diocesis de toledo" (*ibid.*, 1562-63, fo. 26, no. 279); (4) "sabado 13 de nobiembre 1563 juan de Rojas natural de talavera diocesis de toledo" (*ibid.*, 1563-64, fo. 21, no. 280); and (5) "sabado xviii de nobiembre 1564 juan de Rojas natural de taluera [*sic*] de la Reina diocesis de toledo" (*ibid.*, 1564-65, fo. 24, no. 281). Professor Espinosa has only found two *matrículas* in "Leyes" for the Licentiate Fernando: (1) "xxix de noviembre 1562 hernando de rrojas natural de talavera de la rreyna" (*ibid.*, 1561-62, fo. 37, no. 278); and (2) "viernes a xiiii de noviembre 1562 hernando de rrojas natural de talavera de la rreyna diocesis de toledo" (*ibid.*, 1562-63, fo. 42, no. 279). The same scholar also informs me that in the *Libro de Pruebas de Cursos*, 1562-65, now missing from the archives, both brothers were referred to. According to Espinosa's notes, the Licentiate Fernando was inscribed as a "bachiller legista" on May 11, 1562, while Juan's academic record was entered on May 5, 1565. The folios were respectively 14 and 185. The dates for Juan are confirmed by the AHN archives of *Universidades* (Libro 1254, fo. 237). There we find that "Juan de Roxas natural de Talavera de la Reyna" in 1571 "pidio licencia para se graduar de licenciado en canones" offering as his credentials a "título de bachiller en canones de la Universidad de Salamanca firmado por Bartolomé Sánchez" and dated 1565. Evidently the two brothers pursued different careers at the same time.

[4] Gilman-Gonzálvez, p. 14.

[5] "No había más que dos Estudios de Leyes en todo el territorio de la corona de Castilla, y el de Valladolid estaba más lejos de Talavera o de la Puebla que el de Salamanca y tenía menos nombradía que él" (*Orígenes*, p. 241).

We have already proposed the years 1494 to 1502 as the probable dates of Rojas' sojourn in Salamanca. Assuming that this is approximately correct, we may now attempt to place the young Rojas in his university circumstance, that is to say, in a particular moment of Salamancan history. It would be anachronistic and artificial to try to classify the author of *La Celestina* as a member of a definable school or literary generation. The historical generation suggested previously is sufficiently controversial. But we may at least surround him with the names of those fellow students and faculty members whom we know to have been at Salamanca at the turn of the century. Among the former were the professional jester and physician Francisco de Villalobos (of whom we have already spoken), Luis de Lucena (of whom we shall speak later), and Cervantes' grandfather, the turbulent Juan de Cervantes, who received his bachelor's degree in 1499 and began his career by joining Lucero's infamous team of inquisitors. Others worth mentioning are the humanist disciples of Nebrija, Francisco de Quirós and the bachiller Villoslada, the musicians, Diego de Fermoselle and Lucas Fernández (b. 1474),[6] and two future professors of law, Fernando Rodríguez de San Isidro and Tomás de San Pedro.[7] The student rectors between 1494 and 1496 were Pedro Manuel del Madrigal and Rodrigo Manrique, a younger relative of the author of *Las Coplas*. But in the long run the best known figure of all Rojas' fellow students was to be Hernán Cortés (b. 1485) who began his studies for the degree of Bachelor in 1499.[8]

The faculty members active during these years—aside from the imported humanist, Lucio Marineo, el Sículo (the "Sicilian") and

[6] Rojas probably did not coincide with Juan del Encina, who left Salamanca in 1492 and did not return until some 10 years later. Lucas Fernández, however, was born in Salamanca in about 1474, entered the University in 1490 or thereabouts, and seems to have lived in the city all his life.

[7] Esperabé Arteaga, vol. II, provides a catalogue of faculty biographies, including the above. Caro Lynn in her biography of Lucio Marineo, *A College Professor of the Renaissance* (Chicago, 1937), mentions some of these in chap. V, "The Circle at Salamanca," a sketch of university life during the years of Rojas' sojourn.

[8] It is unlikely that Cortés was long enough in residence to qualify for a degree, but his command of Latin and knowledge of legal procedures testify to some years of university study. In addition to these names, J. E. Gillet accepts Menéndez Pelayo's surmise that Torres Naharro began his studies in Salamanca in 1500 (*Propalladia*, IV, Philadelphia, 1961, p. 402).

a few others—are hardly remembered today. Arriving after the 1492 exile of Abraham Zacut, the Jewish astrologer and cosmographer, and during the absence of Nebrija (1486-1503), Rojas had been a Bachelor for 20 years when the great tradition of sixteenth-century learning began with such appointments as that of Francisco de Vitoria (1526) and Fernán Núñez, the so-called "comendador griego" (1524). Nevertheless, we may single out three names known to Rojas for special comment. First among them is the physician Fernando Alvarez de la Reina, frequently called to court, as were many of his colleagues in medicine and law. Then there was the curious professor of mathematics and astrology Rodrigo de Basurto (or Basuarto) who, in spite of his Jewish origins, was elected in 1495 to the one residence college existing at the time, the Colegio Viejo de San Bartolomé, and who is supposed to have predicted Prince John's sudden death during a 1496 visit to Salamanca.[9]

Finally, we must mention Rojas' older admirer, corrector, and collaborator (in the strategy of self-revelation), Alonso de Proaza (b. 1445?), who seems to have held a teaching position in the preparatory program (the "Escuelas menores") during these years. That he was a man and a mentor loved and respected not only by the student author of *La Celestina* but by all who knew him is attested to by a eulogy from the pen of the anthologist of a definitive *cancionero*, Hernando del Castillo: "You . . . in whom all wisdom shines, you to whom famous men, those lesser known, and those obscure, all come asking for help and always receive in full measure what they need . . ."[10] In view of his greater age, Proaza's unstinting admiration for *La Celestina* confirms both these qualities, that is, both his wisdom and his generosity. Not only did he edit the text but, in his closing verses, this professional humanist and poet

[9] In addition to Esperabé Arteaga's catalogue, see Gillet, *Propalladia*, III, 630, and Ruiz de Vergara, *Historia*, I, 229-30, for information on Basurto.

[10] *Cancionero de Castillo*, Madrid, 1882, I, 622. For Proaza's age and education, see D. W. McPheeters' *El humanista español Alonso de Proaza*, Valencia, 1961, pp. 22-24. McPheeters attaches little importance to Hernando del Castillo's flattering description (p. 114) and even seems to doubt personal collaboration between Rojas and his admiring "corrector" (p. 201). However, the collusion between the two in the simultaneous preparation and revelation of the acrostic would seem clearly to indicate prior confidence and friendship.

in Latin unhesitatingly and with sharp critical insight elevates his young friend to the summit of Parnassus: "The comic hand of Naevius or of Plautus, those prudent men, did not draw so well . . . in Roman meter." As for the Greeks, "Cratinus, Menander, and ancient Magnes . . . hardly knew as well how to paint in the first style of Athens as this poet in his Castilian." In Proaza's view, Rojas, a veritable Amadís of "poets," had won his battle against the ancients with one stroke of his pen.

Of the others about all we can say is that their names—Andrés de Carmona, Antón de Salamanca, Pedro de Gomiel, Pedro de Burgos, Martín de Avila, Juan de la Villa, etc.—indicate that they, like many of their famous successors, were of *converso* origin. As we have noted elsewhere, the identification of personal name with a place was generally accepted as a sign of Hebraic lineage. There was undoubtedly a certain amount of anti-Semitism in Salamanca. It is very evident, for example, in the gossipy annals of Pedro de Torres,[11] and in 1498 a fractious *converso* was scandalously and forcibly ejected from the Colegio Viejo de San Bartolomé (an institution whose early Statute of "Limpieza" was still laxly observed, as is indicated by the election of Basurto).[12] Nor, as we have seen, were many known *conversos* exempt from this sentiment. The violently anti-Semitic former Jew, Fray Alonso de Espina, had been rector a generation before, and the professor of theology and head of the Colegio Viejo, Fray Diego de Deza, who had defended Columbus and who was made Bishop of Zamora in 1496 (Sempronio's "aquel es ya obispo" in the discourse on time in Act III?), went on to become one of the most vindictive of all Inquisitors in spite of (or because of) his own lineage. Nevertheless, I

---

[11] Extracts from his *Cronicón* are given in de la Fuente's *Historia*, pp. 58-71. Among other things, Torres accuses "esta malvada gente judiega" of having ruined Castilian handwriting with their "garabatos," a grave charge indeed, as anyone who has had to learn to read the *letra procesal* of the period knows to his sorrow.

[12] The incident is described by Ruiz de Vergara (I, 234) and alluded to briefly in Caro Baroja, II, 271. Other known *converso* members were Alfonso de la Torre and Juan Arias Dávila. Apparently this unnamed scholar irritated his fellows by his extreme haughtiness. When, after the invocation of the Statute, he refused to leave, they appealed to Isabella. In spite of the fact that he was a "persona favorecida de parientes poderosos y nobles," her reaction was to order him to be thrown out the window if he chose not to leave by the door.

think it is safe to say that the Salamanca which Rojas attended was, among other things, a haven for harassed *converso* intellectuals.[13] A large percentage of the students and surely a majority of the faculty must have shared uneasily or comfortably awareness of a common origin.

ε2 Literary Portraiture

When the adolescent Rojas arrived in Salamanca to begin his studies—just about ten years after Columbus' mixed reception there—he felt lonely and strange. There are certain human situations which are not susceptible to history—although, as we shall see, the loneliness and strangeness of newcomers to Salamanca far exceeded anything to which freshmen today are exposed. Furthermore, we may assume from contemporary accounts, he was acutely uncomfortable. Salamanca was well known for its hard winters, its damp quarters, and its frigid lecture halls. A future Archbishop of Valencia describes his arrival at the University as follows:

> It was decided that we should arrive in Salamanca in the month of November, 1528, but since the building of our college was of restricted size and the residents from León were constantly quarreling with those from Uclés, we were poorly received and lodged. I kept to my room to try to study at night, because during the daytime I listened to lectures on Saint Thomas, my principal teacher for the year being the late lamented Fray Francisco de Vitoria . . . Because of the rig-

[13] Aside from the specific years of Rojas' attendance, known *converso* professors at the end of the 15th and the beginning of the 16th centuries included the physicians Fernando Alvarez de la Reina (who spent most of the time at court) and Alonso de la Parra (whose name is still remembered today in ballads narrating the illness and death of Prince Juan), the philosopher and theologian Francisco de Vitoria, as well as several members of the Coronel family. Pablo Coronel who held a chair in the Scriptures is discussed by Amador de los Ríos in his *Estudios sobre los judíos de España* (Madrid, 1848), along with Alfonso de Zamora, the University's first professor of Hebrew, and another physician, Alfonso de Alcalá. As far as Fray Alonso de Espina is concerned, his Jewish background (mentioned by Lea, I, 120) has recently been denied by I. S. Revah, who seems to be irritated beyond measure by Castro's proposition that the peculiarities of the Spanish Inquisition show signs of Jewish tradition. As for Deza, see Márquez, *Investigaciones*, p. 148. Ricardo Espinosa Maeso was the first to relate his bishopric to Sempronio's remark ("Dos notas para *La Celestina, BRAE*, XIII, 1926, pp. 182-184).

orous winter and extreme cold we spent uncomfortable days. My room was on a lower floor and at times my feet were completely numb without any feeling at all. I did not get sick ..., but we could not stay there, and they decided to send us to Alcalá.[14]

Rojas' stoic armor may have provided him with more protection than was available to the plaintive student of Father Vitoria. Or perhaps (as the "son" of the owner of a prime piece of irrigated land) he had more suitable lodgings. Nevertheless, there were surely times when he concurred in the imprecations of Juan del Encina's Rodrigacho: "Water and snow—and savage infectious winds—I curse that whore the weather!" Actually, this passage, from the *Egloga de las grandes lluvias*, refers to a fall and winter famous for their inclemency, those of 1498, the year when *La Celestina* was most probably written. Encina's rustic speakers undoubtedly exaggerate for comic effect, but the drowned cattle, fallen houses, endangered lives, hunger, and general lamentation may well have entered the complex of personal experience lying behind the work. Ricardo Espinosa Maeso supposes that Sempronio's inclusion of "la puente es llevada" (the bridge has been swept away) in his list of transitory current events refers to a historically recorded result of the flooding of the Tormes in that year —and he may well be right.[15] The medieval winter in general and that of Salamanca in particular—although not always as spectacular as that of Rojas' fourth academic year—was a period of extreme discomfort and fear.

To return to the fall of 1494, aside from feelings of loneliness and exposure, what happened to Rojas on his first day? It is a question which any reader of Spanish literature can answer for himself. Generations of students subject to the experience of arrival converted it into a tradition which in turn eventually became a topical scene for the picaresque novel. Whether or not the rites of initia-

---

[14] M. Serrano y Sanz, *Autobiografías y memorias* (NBAE, Madrid, 1905), p. 215: "Discurso de la vida del ... señor don Martín de Ayala." Temperature becomes a part of the picaresque tradition in Descanso XII of the *Marcos de Obregón* when Espinel inserts personal reminiscences of his own suffering at the University. The anecdote of the mule bone mistaken for kindling because it was undoubtedly true stands at the crossroads of life and literature.

[15] "Dos notas," cited above, n. 13.

tion to which Rojas had to submit were as brutal and soggy as those portrayed by don Pablos "el Buscón" (who describes himself covered with the expectoration of the "antiguos" or upperclass-men), it is still true that entry into the new world of the university was in a sense entry into a world of fiction. In contrast to universities of our own time and country (so poor in traditions that administrators sometimes try to create them), Salamanca was strongly traditional, aware of itself as a separate, unique entity removed from the ordinary world from which its members came. That is to say, for centuries Salamanca told itself a story, and the first duty of the newcomer was to get inside the story and live in it as a character. Hence the importance of initiation.

The picaresque portrait of Salamanca is so well known that lengthy description is unnecessary. We should remark, however, on the fact that student life brought out an aspect of the picaresque tradition quite different from the bleak and remorseless daily warfare of Lazarillo's childhood in the same town. Insofar as the students thought of themselves as *pícaros*, it was with a gaiety and youthful verve which reminds us more of Cervantes than of the *Lazarillo*. Rojas, in his *Prologue*, speaks of his fellows as "la alegre juventud y mancebía" (the happy fraternity of the young). And in Alarcón's *La verdad sospechosa* (unjustly famous as the source for *Le menteur*), the description is expanded:

> In Salamanca, Sir
> All are young with good humor to spend;
> Each one to his own pleasure,
> Turns vice into gaiety,
> Pranks into fame,
> Folly into grandeur;
> Youth, in conclusion, does its work well.

Here was a world of roving juvenile bands intent on novelty and excitement, a world "penetrated," as doña Emilia Pardo Bazán phrases it, "with the anarchism that palpitates in picaresque literature," a world whose inhabitants "were drunken with liberty, mischief, and idleness."[16] The negation of generally esteemed values

[16] Cited by J. García Mercadal, *Estudiantes, sopistas, y pícaros*, p. 39, from a speech which, as far as I can determine, is not reproduced in its entirety in her *Obras completas*.

277

which is fundamental to the picaresque vision is achieved, in other words, not through individual desperation and discrepancy but in terms of sheer vitality, vitality unconcerned with anything beyond its own explosion. Salamanca was a chain reaction which, according to the rules, physical as well as sociological, for such reactions, depended on a high concentration of youth.

The truth to life of the picaresque portrait of Salamanca is not lessened by the fact that it was a fiction, a self-conscious literary interpretation, as is brought out by its coexistence with a pastoral portrait. Less well-known and flamboyant than the Salamanca of Marcos de Obregón, Guzmán de Alfarache, and don Pablos, the pastoral tradition was just as inherent and extends at least as far back as the description of the ideal university town in the *Siete Partidas* (1252) of Alfonso the Wise: "The town where the university is to be established should be of healthy air and inviting promenades, so that the masters who expound their disciplines and the scholars who study them may be healthy and may enjoy themselves and take their pleasure when in the afternoon they go out tired from their efforts."[17]

The same ideal takes on humanistic elaboration and a coloring of Renaissance perfectionism in Cristóbal de Villalón's description of Salamanca in the summer: "When summer comes and reading and study are made difficult by the heat, the scholars and teachers devote themselves to virtuous pastimes. In each other's company in order to recreate and aerate the spirit, they have kept the custom of walking out to nearby villages or to the delightful gardens which surround the city, and there, the better to enjoy themselves, they invent games and honest diversions."[18] The rural—Virgilian and Horatian—Salamanca of Fray Luis de León is surely the best and most definitive expression of the tradition. But it is preceded by these and other examples.[19] Just as valid as picaresque reporting of student strife and mischief, was this proposition of the university as a place of pastoral communion and authentic dialogue. Whether Fernando de Rojas walked in the country or experienced such com-

---

[17] Partida 2, título xxxi, ley 2. Cited by García Mercadel, p. 56.

[18] From *El escolástico*. Cited by Serrano y Sanz in his introduction to the *Ingeniosa comparación entre lo antiguo y lo presente*, Madrid, 1897, p. 81.

[19] Caro Lynn, for example, cites and translates the following lines from Lucio Marineo: "so we went through green gardens, and down by the shadowy river. / As we walked, sped the hours in wise conversation" (p. 66).

munion cannot be known, although in the prologue he indicates that he found a few listeners who understood him perfectly ("those who knew how to add up the total for their own profit"). But like students on one of our own pastoral campuses, or Melville when he jotted down impressions of Oxford ("Garden girdled by river. Meadows beyond. Oxen and sheep. Pastoral and collegiate life blended"), Rojas was surely aware of the literary dream that was built into this special world.

A curious feature of these portraits of Salamanca is their failure to be mutually exclusive. Not only do they coexist, but on occasion they intertwine. In addition to purely picaresque reminiscence— thievery of capes and books, solicitation of votes, mock ceremonies and all the rest—Guzmán de Alfarache remembers his student days as a time of pastoral perfection and communion:

> Where doth a man enjoy more liberty, than in the Universitie? And who lives so merry and quiet a life, as your schollers? What entertainments of all sorts whatsoever, have not your Students amongst them? There is not one thing you can name that they want. If they will be civill and retyred, they may fit themselves with companie that shall jump just with them: If loose and dissolute, they shall meet with as mad waggs as themselves. There every birde shall finde some of his owne feather, such as shall equally sute with them in their disposition. The studious shall have those that will conferre with them about their studies, that will keepe their set hours, write out Lectures, compare their Notes, and punctually perform all those laudable exercises, that appertaine to a good student: and if they are disposed to walke abroad, they are like unto your Biskayners, those women that live in the mountaynous Countries; who wheresoever they goe, carry their distaffe along with them, that a man may truly say of them, That they plow spinning. Wheresoever you light upon a Student, though he be out of his Colledge, and walkt abroad, with a purpose onely to recreate himselfe by the Rivers side, in those sweet and pleasant fields, yet even then doth his wit and his memory also goe a-walking, calling to minde what he hath read, arguing and reasoning upon this, or that other point, and conferring with himselfe on those things, which he

279

hath studied, being never less alone, than when he is thus alone. For men that employ their time well, though alone, cannot be truly be said to be alone. If once in a yeare, he will take his liberty, and ride into the Country, slacking for a while the stringe of his bowe, fetching some vagaries abroad to make merry with his friends; what sports or what pastimes can be equall'd with theirs?[20]

If the pastoral and the picaresque come together in an intuition of freedom, a "Fay ce que vouldras" in grove or city, they diverge when it comes to enjoying it. As against the student "shepherd" free from disturbance to his meditations, the student *pícaro* enjoys the freedom of action that is inherent in warfare, mischievous daily warfare against his fellows and against the long-suffering inhabitants of the town. At this point, however, a third literary self-portrait joins the other two, that of the student cavalier. As soon as the *pícaro* attacks with sword instead of with hands or mouth, he abandons gaiety and dialectic for honor and enters the Salamanca "de capa y espada." The major text here is the second lie of Alarcón's *La verdad sospechosa*, a lie which paints university life as one long gallant intrigue in the best tradition of the Spanish *comedia*. The portrait was in general so flattering (although not without some truth) that the only person who seems fully to have accepted it was Espronceda some three centuries later when he wrote his Romantic *El estudiante de Salamanca*. Rojas certainly did not. The night scene of Act XII with its comic depiction of the armed cowardice of Pármeno and Sempronio was surely understood by his first student listeners as a take-off on this pretense.

The extreme susceptibility of Salamanca to literary portraiture (Don García, the student whose whole life is a fiction, is an appropriate human representative) is illustrated strikingly by the effects of *La Celestina* on the town. As we pointed out, soon after

---

[20] Book III, chap. 4 (*The Rogue*, tr. James Mabbe, London, 1924, IV, 207-208). That this coexistence had its counterpart in life is attested to in a document cited by Julio González in his *El maestro Juan de Segovia y su biblioteca*, Madrid, 1944: Even the canons of the Cathedral of Salamanca walked about "armas portando ad taxillos et alios illicitos ludos ludendo, *ad tabernas, ortos, vineas, prata, blada* at alia loca vetita et inhonesta intrando . . ." (pp. 30-31, italics mine).

280

its publication visitors to the city were shown "the house of our mother, Celestina" and the "celebrated but not elaborate tower of Melibea."[21] The best imitation of the work, Sancho de Muñón's *Lisandro and Roselia*, replaces Rojas' profoundly anonymous urban setting (it is misleading to think of it as a city) for one decorated with university local color.[22] And, in such later prose works as Avellaneda's apocryphal *Quijote* and *La tía fingida*, Celestinesque and university references come together as a matter of course. That is to say, traditionally but without imitation. In the first, Barbara "la mondonguera," a sordid, grotesquely vile descendant of Rojas' go-between, purveys to student viciousness in the most debased fashion,[23] while in the second there is a gaiety and careless humor far removed from the original. Thus, *La Celestina* as a unique, demonstrably inimitable, masterpiece, all by itself created a new version of Salamanca. In after years to go to Salamanca was to go not only to a pastoral resting place, not only to a scene of picaresque deceits or to a realm of gallantry and adventure, but to the very town where Melibea and Celestina lived and died so intensely.

Why is this so? Why did the university and the town adapt themselves so readily to literary self-presentation? It is a question which directs our attention towards certain general features of all university society, features which were peculiarly accentuated in Salamanca. Like other universities of its time (and in ours, although to a lesser extent), Salamanca was an "independent state" (the words are Modesto Lafuente's), conscious of itself as distinct from the town and the nation which surrounded it. Its students came from

---

[21] *Orígenes*, p. 279.

[22] Typically, Sancho de Muñón's Celestina scolds one of her protégées: "Damn you! Why don't you follow the example of our neighbor la Calventa, who always demands something before she gives anything away? If they have no money, they leave things in pawn. Where were you looking yesterday when we visited her? Didn't you see the shelf she had full of the Decrees, Baldos, Scotos, Avicenas, and other books?" (*Lisandro y Roselia*, ed. J. López Barbadillo, Madrid, 1918, p. 29). The books mentioned are, of course, the principal texts of the three major faculties, law, theology, and medicine. There are many other examples. J. E. Gillet sees indirectly something of the same ambiance in Rojas' work, going so far as to explain Sempronio's erudition and his ambiguous relationship with Calisto as reflecting the behavior of the servant-scholars locally known as "capigorrones" (*Propalladia*, IV, 182).

[23] Since Barbara operated in Alcalá, it is curious to note that the younger university quickly assimilated the literary traditions of the older.

the outer world, and eventually almost all of them were sent back
to it. But while they were citizens of "the republic called the University,"[24] the social conditions of their existence were profoundly
alien to anything that could be found outside. To go to Salamanca
was to go on a journey to a foreign country, a country which, in
spite of its smallness (Lucio Marineo, the Sicilian, calculates the
student population in Rojas' time at seven thousand),[25] was resolutely determined to maintain its prestige and independence. The
history of Salamanca seen from the outside was the usual one of
town and gown dissension and of negotiations with the Crown
(when, for example, it interfered or demanded the services of the
university's medical and legal experts) and the Papacy. But we are
here less concerned with foreign relations than with understanding
from within the laws, customs, folklore, and peculiar national consciousness of the new country to which Rojas emigrated and within
which *La Celestina* was written. It was precisely because attendance in Salamanca involved profound readjustment of social behavior, because the University was a self-consciously autonomous
state of naturalized citizens, that it delighted in literary portraiture
of itself. The picaresque and pastoral images of Salamanca, in other
words, provided patterns of self-understanding. They were the appropriate legends—the one, a legend of freedom told by the students, and the other, a legend of perfectibility told by the faculty
—of a society at once wholly literate and wholly artificial.

The Republic Called the University

The full extent of the social change experienced by Rojas
when he left the Puebla de Montalbán and went to Salamanca is
brought out by the simple fact that the first was a world run by old
men who gave orders while the second was a democracy of youth
in which the great majority of the professors and even the rector
were elected to their posts.[26] It is true that the faculty deplored this

[24] Cited from the 1538 Statutes by Gustave Reynier in his *La Vie universitaire dans l'ancien Espagne*, Paris, 1902, p. 30. According to de la Fuente,
effective independence of civil power dated back to the 1421 *constituciones*
of Pope Martin V. Through Papal authority at a time when royal power
was almost non-existent, "la Universidad se erigió ya en estado independiente"
(I, 274).

[25] Caro Lynn, p. 60.

[26] Not all university posts were elective. Characteristic of Salamanca was

from time to time. In 1554, according to de la Fuente, a report was presented to the faculty on the poor quality of grammar study at Salamanca as compared to Alcalá. The specified cause of this situation was envy and greed arising from the practice of student voting. The conclusion is sharp: "As long as students elect their teachers, the latter will be forced to conceal the laziness and self-indulgence of the former."[27] In 1503, when the Greek scholar, Arias Barbosa, was defeated in an election for a chair in grammar, his friend Lucio Marineo wrote him a letter reproaching him for a candidacy which "entrusted his dignity and honor to the votes of light-minded boys, knowing very well how easily they are suborned by cakes or sweets or even a few chestnuts."[28] But in spite of such objections and of occasional poor appointments, at its best the system worked as well as any in use today.[29] For one thing there was proportional allocation of the voting power according to years of residence.[30] For another, as Gustave Reynier pointed out, "the young students in Salamanca, as in all the great schools of the Middle Ages, almost always were influenced, in spite of intrigues and cabals, by their older and more serious comrades. There were many who had passed their thirtieth year and had received the licentiate or even the doctorate and were themselves future candidates for the same chairs. These were at once capable of judging the candidates and concerned that true merit should be rewarded."[31]

It is, however, less our purpose to judge the system than to try to comprehend its meaning for those belonging to it. In addition to accumulating knowledge and skills presumably for later use in the outside world, the young student, as a result of his right to vote, had a sense of participation in the academic profession which is comparatively unknown today. Furthermore, the way the voting

its curious dual administration. As well as the rector there was a *maestrescuela* appointed by the Church. The structure of councils and committees was also interlocking and complex, according to the standard histories cited.

[27] *Historia*, ii, 240. See also Bell, *Luis de León*, p. 81.

[28] Caro Lynn, p. 100.

[29] The decadence and latter-day corruption of the system of electing professors in the 17th and 18th centuries was closely related to the decadence of the *colegios* and the corruption of their admission policies. See Reynier, Part II, chap. 3.

[30] See Bell's description, *Luis de León*, pp. 79ff.

[31] p. 78.

was conducted tended to reinforce this feeling of participation. Election days were tense with excitement, and victory celebrations were often explosively jubilant. The annals of the university are replete with election campaigns conducted with bribes, conspiracies, violence, intense canvassing, and torchlight processions. Academic politics were surely no more enlightened and altruistic then than they are today, but, conducted in this fashion, they resulted in a new relationship of the individual to his immediate society. One became a citizen in the academic state or—to use Rojas' own term, a *socio* or partner in the academic enterprise. At a time of hotly-contested *oposiciones* even new students on their way to enroll would be welcomed outside of town by partisans from their own province. For the sake of their single votes, such newcomers not only escaped the rites of initiation but were treated royally in the bargain.[32] Rojas, to sum up, had entered into a world in which everyone voted and dressed more or less alike,[33] and in which the distinction between kinds of Christians was not important enough to prevent anyone from rising to academic heights. If Rojas' first discovery was that he did not belong to his world, his second, upon arriving in Salamanca, was that he did. Hence, at least in part, the extreme importance he gave to his degree and to his "principal study."

The feeling of participation, of belonging to a corporate whole, is as much a denial as it is a confirmation of the pastoral view of Salamanca. Participation was more than anything else participation in a continuing struggle. Although the University presented a common front against the outside world, its history resembled that of the Puebla de Montalbán in its tendency to intramural "conflict and battle." Bitter, prolonged, and often picayune quarrels among the faculty and students fully confirmed Huizinga's description of medieval universities as "in general tumultuous and agitated. The forms of scientific intercourse themselves entailed an element of irritability: never ending disputations, frequent elections, and rowdyism of the students. To those were added old and new quar-

---

[32] Reynier, p. 77.

[33] Reynier, p. 30. University regulations for uniformity are replete with penalties for various infractions, usually those of the richer students or *generosos* who sought to display their wealth by means of fur collars, slashed sleeves, or silk material. See Esperabé Arteaga, I, 204-205.

rels of all sorts of orders, schools, and groups. The different colleges contended among themselves, the secular clergy were at variance with the regular."[34]

As we have said, Rojas was a student during the absence of the celebrated Spanish grammarian, Nebrija (1488-1503), but the latter's long and bitter quarrel with Lucio Marineo, the Sicilian, over prestige and over their competing introductory Latin textbooks was typical.[35] Fray Luis de León, whose celebrated moments of tranquillity were infrequent, describes his academic life in a way which reminds us both of the Prologue to *La Celestina* and of its source, Petrarch's *De remediis*: "We all lived as if engaged in warfare because of pretensions and competitions, and, for the same reasons, we all had enemies."[36] The involvement of disciples, of religious orders, and of regional solidarities in these rivalries was inevitable. The result was that the student body not only voted but took full part in the strife of their elders, arguing incessantly about the opposing doctrines of the party leaders. The university was dedicated to the principle of dialectical learning, and, indeed, the most academic features of *La Celestina* are both the arguments it occasioned ("the dissonant and variant judgments" of the Pro-

[34] *Erasmus and the Age of Reformation*, New York, 1957, p. 20. Elsewhere Huizinga comments on the resemblance of scholarly disputations to chivalric tournaments: "The medieval university was in the full sense of the word an arena. . . . In it one played a serious and often dangerous game. The activities of the university, like those of knighthood, had the character either of a consecration and an initiation or of a contrast, a challenge, and a conflict" ("The Task of Cultural History," *Men and Ideas*, New York, 1957, p. 17). In this sense the very study of Latin could, according to Father Ong, be compared to the puberty rite calculated to separate the individual from his past and qualify him—by proof of courage as well as learning—in the "close-knit jealously guarded internal organization of the university." Thus boys who earlier had been afraid of those who threw stones at the birds were prepared for the specialized intellectual battles of their new manhood. "Latin Language Study as a Renaissance Puberty Rite," *Studies in Philology*, LVI (1959), 103-124.

[35] Caro Lynn, pp. 96-99. When Marineo complained to Peter Martyr about Nebrija's arrogance, the latter advised him that in university life one has to accustom oneself not only to "arguments but also to insults and affronts." He who contemplates revenge only succeeds in "tormenting and torturing himself" (*Epistolaria*, IX, 46-47). The introduction of new textbooks was particularly controversial both because of the profits to be made and because of the shock waves which we shall see altering university life as a result of the printing press.

[36] Bell, *Luis de León*, p. 77.

logue) and the continuing argument and debate which run all through it. To go to Salamanca from the Puebla was to leave a country where argument had been stilled (we remember the lashes meted out to Pedro Serrano for arguing about theology with his Jewish neighbors) and to arrive in another where it was both loud and required.

The warfare of Salamanca—as readers of its literary portraits know—was not limited to words. The students, except in lectures and classes, carried swords and concealed daggers and very frequently wore armor under their robes. In an age of arms,[37] the place was an armed camp where it was customary even for those who had taken orders to go abroad prepared for attack and defense. In such circumstances, when tempers rose or when candidates of rival factions were competing for a single chair, the streets frequently were the scene of mass conflict. Private duels, nightly skirmishes with the town watch, even armed assault and robbery were as common as might be expected in such a society. It is difficult for us to imagine our gangs of delinquent juveniles engaged in sustained intellectual endeavor, but in their youth, their factionalism, their bellicosity, and their passionate concern for honor, the Salamancan student body bears marked resemblances to these contemporary counter-societies. So far have we risen—or fallen.

Rojas' student years were particularly turbulent, so much so that in 1504 royal attention was attracted to the "scandals, damages, and inconveniences" caused by "the many arms which the students have in their houses and carry about the city."[38] King Ferdinand's proposed remedy was a new statute limiting each student to one sword.[39] Salamanca provided for its continually changing population a liberated society, a society liberated from the resentful stasis of small town existence. But its daily warfare, waged with tongue and sword, was far more intense and exciting—or, if the student

---

[37] Juan de Mal Lara (cited by García Mercadal, p. 167) saw university armed violence as an unseemly exaggeration of that inherent in Spain where "men are born armed and kill each other without reason for very trivial causes." The reminiscences of Pedro Serrano are a case in point.

[38] In a letter dated April 22, 1497, Prince Juan orders the civil authorities of Salamanca to help the *maestrescuela* discipline ("punir y castigar") the rebellious students (Ajo, I, 634).

[39] *Ibid.*, I, 353. Royal displeasure at the failure to enforce this order was expressed in a series of follow-up letters dispatched during the next two years.

was sensitive or cowardly, more frightening. Here was a world fully suited to the figurative language of the acrostic verses: the "shield" of silence and the "wounding" or "cutting" of reproaches and objections.[40]

The Salamanca of alarums and excursions, of ebullient youth expressing its vitality in horseplay and swordplay, that has just been sketched seems to confirm the picaresque and "cape and sword" portraiture. However, we must not be misled. Like all good portraits, the Salamanca of the *Guzmán* and of the *Tía fingida* has a strong element of caricature. For, complementary to turbulence and disorder, there was a continuing and persistent effort to organize and to impose order on all phases of student and faculty existence. The university regulations of 1538 were as severe as the irrepressible spirits of those regulated made necessary. Expulsion was apparently rare, but fines were levied and incarceration in the university prison imposed even for minor infractions. Two days was the standard sentence for rudely turning one's back on a professor. Furthermore, legislation was invented for areas of daily life and personal deportment into which even the most militant of present-day administrators might hesitate to enter. Along with the usual prohibition of gambling, wenching, and fighting, details of dress, diet, and even speech (the most frequently violated rule was that Latin be spoken at all times)[41] were prescribed positively. The rule-makers were particularly stringent about the hour by hour and week by week use of time. The parietal hour for the younger students was seven o'clock, and during the day, which began with a morning bed check, there were set times for lectures, class repetitions, private study periods, as well as "hours destined for recreation"—to use Rojas' own phrase. The living shape of a horse is expressed in the contours of its harness. So too the time-free, anarchical aliveness of student existence is expressed in the barriers and restrictions of these sixteenth-century regulations.

Here again is a fundamental contrast between university society

[40] From the acrostic verses: ". . . a mí estan cortando / Reproches, reuistas e tachas."

[41] In Rojas' time the rule was universally violated. See Olmedo's *Nebrija*, chap. XIII. Caro Lynn cites Arias Barbosa writing in 1503: "Hardly two or three [instructors of grammar] are to be found who speak Latin, rather more who speak Spanish, and many more a barbarous tongue" (p. 101). By the last he presumably refers to regional dialects.

and that of the Puebla de Montalbán. Back at home the ordering of life had been traditional; patterns of behavior and interpersonal relations had been slowly drawn in time by economic and biological necessities acting through the culture of the community. There was disorder, as we have seen, profound and critical disorder, but it was posterior to the medieval rhythms and certainties which it disturbed or destroyed. It was a disorder which by its very existence implied an underlying and violated order of individual and communal life. At Salamanca, the opposite was the case. In that temporary society of youth, ebullience and verve constituted a non-order or orderlessness upon which order had to be more or less successfully superimposed. Thus, when the degree of licentiate was granted, the 1538 statutes attempt to limit the celebrative parade put on by the recipient and his friends to "six trumpets and three pairs of drums." "Chirimías" (a reed instrument) were prohibited altogether. Each examiner (apparently the purpose of all this was to protect the poorer candidates and to prevent the favoring of wealth) could *only* be given "two 'castellanos' and a torch and a box of 'diacitrón' and a pound of sweets and three pairs of chickens." Even the banquet which the candidate was expected to offer had a strictly prescribed menu.[42] Those who drew up these artificial customs were apparently attempting to hold in check much greater extravagances. Conscious of the lack of order and harmful effects of exuberant lavishness, the academic legislators attempted by a combination of acceptance and restraint to superimpose at least a semblance of permissible regularity.

The important feature of all this is that the students themselves, as a result of their participation in the academic enterprise, shared in the arrangement of their own lives. That is to say, to study at Salamanca—an institution far more democratic than military—was to become aware of order and disorder as a problem with which one was personally concerned. If at home the students had been trained to accept more or less unconsciously the order of long established custom, at Salamanca the encounter of the new student with the regularities and rules—some time-worn and others recent —laid down by his fellows was a conscious one. And because it

[42] Esperabé Arteaga, I, 170. The menu consisted of "one partridge or chicken or two turtle doves and a bowl of pudding and a fruit before and another after the wine and bread. . . ."

was conscious, rebellion against or adjustment to an imposed order of daily existence was a profound personal experience. For six years or more each student, by the mere fact of being so, was intensely aware of a problematical relationship of self to society.

In *La Celestina* this awareness appears not only in Rojas' introductory concern for the reactions of his comrades and his public but also, and more profoundly, in such passages as Calisto's reflection on the public execution of his servants. It is a monologue that goes far beneath the topical "¿Qué dirán?" and which was unprecedented in its time. Boccaccio in the plague description of the *Decameron* shows us the painful breakdown of medieval order (a breakdown seen as an erosion of loyalties by Rojas)[43] as a frame for the self-conscious reordering of life (ten stories, ten days, prescribed topics, strict yet graceful decorum) by his youthful story tellers. In the Boccaccian villa (as in More's Utopia of restored medieval order) there is an academic and artificial arrangement of existence comparable to the society into which Rojas was naturalized after leaving the Puebla de Montalbán. We need not be surprised that in the dialogue of the one and the stories of the other we contemplate amorous and vital spontaneity in conflict with social order.

A related change experienced by Rojas and his fellow students was the national and international character of their new surroundings. All of them had come from communities which were essentially local in their points of view and preoccupations. The sense of self as a Spaniard had gained in intensity during the reign of the Catholic Monarchs, but, even so, the outlook of both small town and city dwellers was to a large extent provincial. And as one's vision withdrew to the town boundaries and then to the separate parishes and neighborhoods (the *barrios* so esteemed by Areusa), things loomed larger and events seemed more important. This was a world without newspapers in which news that was not local was exotic, and in which men were drawn in upon themselves and their immediate neighbors. At Salamanca, on the other hand, students

---

[43] This is not to say that comments on disruption of the prescribed ordering of life were not prevalent throughout all the Middle Ages (see, for example, quatrains 126 and 127 of the *Libro de buen amor*), but rather that in Rojas' time, for reasons already examined, they were far more anguished. Torres Naharro (Jacinto's complaint), Alvarez Gato, Villalobos, Núñez de Reinoso, and many others, as we have seen here join Rojas in doleful chorus.

from all parts of Spain and even from abroad mingled and fraternized. They spoke (or were supposed to speak) an international
language, and they wore more or less the same clothes: mantles,
robes, and square hats. In other words, in addition to the intellectual ferment of this particular moment in Salamancan history, the
very fact of attendance was in itself an expansion of horizons.

We must not, of course, overemphasize the homogeneity of the
student body. The importance of money in maintaining features of
the class structure of the outside world was as inevitable then as it
is today.[44] The clothing restrictions referred to previously, although intended to diminish class separation, reflect its existence.
And there were other customs, such as the allotment of the best
lecture seats to rich students (hopefully referred to as "generosos")
and the special dress of the student servants (the "capigorrones"
or cape and cap wearers), which were frankly based on discrimination. Hereditary social distinction and lineage, on the other
hand, lost some of their importance in this world of the intellect.
Nor was this entirely due to the new hierarchy of values. Cervantes
in the *Colloquy of the Dogs* remarks on rich "merchants" (I suspect
strongly that the implied meaning is *conversos*) who live modestly
at home but who take pride in providing a luxury and ostentation
for their sons at the university comparable to that of the scions of
aristocracy.

Regional differences were also noticeable and recognized politically in the election of the student council by "naciones."[45] The
provincial characteristics described in *La tía fingida*[46] and the
rallying cries—"Viva la espiga" for the Castilians, "Viva la aceituna"
for the Andalusians, and others—are frequently cited bits of university lore. The individual necessarily brought his past with him
not just in his memory but in his accent, dietary preferences, and
manners. And to a greater or lesser extent he conserved it. Salamanca, like certain universities in our own time and country, took
pride in being a gentleman factory, a "*nutrix equitum,*" as well as
a school.[47] But, at best, training in manners was a superimposition.
In many cases, the sudden revelation of new intellectual horizons

---

[44] Reynier, part I, chap. 3 and Bell, *Luis de León*, pp. 66-67.
[45] *Luis de León*, p. 63.
[46] Edited by A. Bonilla y San Martín, Madrid, 1911, pp. 63-67.
[47] *De Laudibus hispaniae*, Burgos, ca. 1496, fo. XVIII.

290

and alien points of view actually reinforced attachment to the past. When one of Rojas' contemporaries, the student author of a poem designed precisely to teach decorous behavior, identifies himself as "Gratia Dei, a Galician son of the University,"[48] we can sense his complementary loyalties. Who knows if the words, "Bachelor . . . born in the Puebla of Montalbán" did not in part express similar feelings?

In spite of such partition and inner segmentation in the student body, the changes demanded upon arrival were profound. The 7,000 kinds of past that were guarded in the bosoms of Rojas and his fellows, if not eliminated, were necessarily submitted to unfamiliar standards. Which is to say, the locality which each student carried within himself was reinterpreted *sub specie universitatis*. When Rojas went back to the Puebla on his vacations (as he must have done on some occasions) or after taking his degree, he saw it through new eyes. The painful moments in the Huerta de Mollejas, for example, were not just far away and reduced in importance; they were also a comic demonstration of the applicability of Heraclitean and Petrarchist doctrine: *Omnia secundum litem fiunt.* *La Celestina* is, as we shall see, one long example of what might be called the university approach to local reality. It is a more profoundly Salamancan work than the later *Lisandro y Roselia*, precisely because it does not refer to student life (aside from a few teasing allusions) but rather chooses to present its world of physical and verbal "contienda y batalla" in ostensibly classical terms.

A related aspect of the book appreciated by its student listeners is its recurrent satire of parochial concerns and limitations. I refer to such things as Areusa's eulogy of back-fence gossip, Sempronio's sardonic catalogue of local news items, or Celestina's intimacy with Alisa when they lived near each other, an intimacy forgotten when the latter moved away. But even these barbed allusions avoid genuine specificity; they are samples of reality, "a typical selection," according to María Rosa Lida de Malkiel, which purposefully avoids even a resemblance to local color.[49] In this sense, Rojas'

---

[48] *La crianza y Virtuosa doctrina dedicada a la Illustre y muy esclarecida Doña Isabel primera Infante de Castilla en la Universidad de Salamanca por un gallego, hijo del dicho Studio renombre Gracia Dei*, ca. 1490, ed. A. Paz y Melia, Madrid, 1892, p. 381. Identified by the editor with Pedro Gracia Dei who published a *Blasón general* in 1489.

[49] *Two Spanish Masterpieces*, p. 77. In *La originalidad* she makes the same

comic vision may be contrasted to that of his Salamancan contemporary, Lúcas Fernández, whose dialogue reproduced the language, grotesque genealogies, and limited points of view of the peasants who came into town on market days.[50] In an eclogue such as *Mingo, Pascuala y el escudero* the university audience easily recognized the comic rusticity of the surrounding countryside. *La Celestina*'s *barrios*, on the other hand, are, like its city and its language, nowhere and everywhere. As Mrs. Malkiel puts it, the work aspires "to an artistic representation which is concrete but not particular."[51] Or as Rojas might have rephrased it in the jargon of his studies, his art of comedy was to treat "particulars" as if they were "universals."

A final contrast between the two worlds in which Rojas lived has to do with a key aspect of any culture: the purpose and style of its ceremonies. Guicciardini, a generally unsympathetic visitor, describes the Spain of Rojas' time as obsessively ceremonial: "In appearance and in external show Spaniards are very religious, but not in reality. They are prodigal in ceremonies and they perform them with much reverence."[52] But even for such a country and such a century (the last of Huizinga's ceremony-crazed medieval autumn), Salamanca seems to have been spectacular. As we shall emphasize later on, university life and work were predominantly oral, a situation which by its very nature requires ceremonial ordering. Marshall McLuhan points out that even twentieth-century universities—in spite of libraries, laboratories, and printed catalogues—still depend on "regular oral communication"[53] and accordingly on a reverence for ceremonial cycles, ritual observance, and traditional status that is not entirely vestigial. We operate in the time of speech, and insofar as repeated ceremonies,

---

point more emphatically: "los autores de *La Celestina* han sacrificado todos los elementos particulares que hubiesen ligado su representación a tal o cual localidad. Así lo subraya el contraste con Juan del Encina . . ." (p. 166).

[50] Although the *Farsas y églogas* were published in 1514, Cañete believes that Fernández' earliest work goes as far back as 1500. If they were represented orally while Rojas was still in Salamanca, their failure to influence the added five acts is noteworthy. As we remember, Sosia, the *villano*, may be foolish, but his language is not comically rustic. He is also in his very simplicity the only uncorrupted inhabitant of the work.

[51] *La originalidad*, p. 167.   [52] *Viajes por España*, p. 201.
[53] "Culture without Literacy," *Explorations*, 1 (1953), 120.

always accompanied by the proper words, are ways of recognizing and celebrating the meaning of our mutual time, we need them still. If we project this familiar situation back into Spain and into the fifteenth century, we may begin to grasp the incredible display of ceremony which was the daily experience of Rojas and his fellows.

Understood as a way of formulating human time, the most important ceremonies in Salamanca were those accompanying changes of status. We have already alluded to the elaborate processions and banquets attendant upon the graduation of a licentiate or doctorate; but even Rojas' humble bachelor's degree was awarded to him individually and according to a prescribed ritual. Having attended lectures for the required number of years and hours according to the testimony of the *bedel* (an official who was at once master of ceremonies, registrar, campus policeman, and crier of the college bulletin), the candidate bachelor asked the rector to set a date. This was announced publicly by the *bedel*, and, when the time came, the student presented himself in one of the lecture halls accompanied by the doctor who sponsored him. The doctor first occupied the *cathedra*, and the aspirant stood up and requested the degree: "Accedens prope cathedram gradum postulet." The sponsor would then step down, place the bachelor's bonnet on the head of the candidate, and allow him to occupy the seat of honor. There, after the customary beginning, "Explicaturus agrediar" (to which the *bedel* replied "Satis"), the new bachelor would discourse briefly in Latin on a point related to his studies. The cost of the concluding reception was limited to five Aragonese florins.[54]

In addition to ceremonies accompanying advancement in status (Rojas witnessed in 1496 the elaborate celebration of the doctorate granted to Palacios Rubios, one of the two legal mentors of the age), there were numerous regular and special celebrations. Among them, typically, were readings and "representations" in Latin, debates, pilgrimages, bullfights[55] and chases, and lavish wel-

[54] de la Fuente, I, 279-280.
[55] The bullfights involving knights on horseback were typical and attracted the attention of visitors from abroad. One may speculate that the characteristic taurine imagery both in Act I and in those by Rojas ("Aquella cara, señor, que suelen los bravos toros mostrar contra los que lanzan las agudas frechas en el coso . . .") was derived from such spectacles.

293

coming displays for visiting princes and distinguished foreign professors. These added to the religious festivals, observed by students and townsfolk alike, gave a special, ceremonial quality to almost every day in the academic year.

The remarkable thing is that from a circumstance so drenched in ceremony, there should have emerged a book uniquely concerned with states of awareness beneath the surface of traditionally prescribed behavior. In this sense, *La Celestina* may be thought of as a kind of anti-ceremonial manifesto. I refer here, not only to its well-known failure to provide for two essential sacraments, marriage and final confession and absolution, but also to a number of lesser expressions of the same antipathy. Celestina uses ceremonies ("missas del gallo," "procesiones de noche") to communicate with women otherwise inaccessible, and, when she tells the beads of her rosary, she is really doing her accounting. Sempronio sees no difference between the investiture of a bishop or the welcoming of a king and the drunkenness of a neighbor. Even the central ceremony of the mass is interrupted by Celestina's corrupt presence in Rojas' caustic parody of an inoffensive ballad, *La misa de amor*.[56] Only Elicia in her brief mourning for Celestina—the irony of this is at its most biting—behaves with ceremonial propriety.

As we have suggested, Rojas' antipathy to the ceremonies of his time was derived from a human situation more anguished and more deeply-rooted than that of attendance at Salamanca. But if we limit ourselves to university terms, we may consider this aspect of *La Celestina* as an example of student mockery and irreverent burlesque. In general it can be said that, although Salamanca equalled or even surpassed other parts of Spain in ceremonial density, the attitude of its academic citizens towards ceremony was unique. We have already seen something of the seriousness which the Spaniards of Rojas' Spain accorded to ritual and festival. In the fourteenth-century *Libro de buen amor*, a poem referring again and again to ceremonies of all sorts and in a sense organized ceremonially,[57] there had been a joyous sense of participation and com-

---

[56] *"La Celestina" como contienda*, pp. 96-98.

[57] After the courtship and marriage of doña Endrina, the major episodes include a pilgrimage, the mock epic battle of don Carnal and doña Cuaresma, an Easter parade converted poetically into a Triumph of Love, and the play funeral of Trotaconventos. Continuing delight in the ritualistic and cere-

mon celebration (almost like a Dickensian Christmas) that was missing in Inquisitional times. The fanatical intensity of the *autos de fe*, the conversion of the Mass into an occasion for displaying fervor and for trapping unwary heretics, the parades of relics and images during which whole populations cried in anguish for a miracle, all testify to the self-conscious gravity which had replaced the lightheartedness of earlier centuries.

Furthermore, the gloomy Inquisitors were specially concerned with irregularity or suspicious happiness where ceremony was concerned. Among trials for sacrilege (listed in the catalogue of the Toledo Inquisition), there are a number of convictions of groups of peasants (apparently Old Christians) for ceremonial parody and burlesque. In 1538, for example, 16 inhabitants of Valdegrudas, Taracena, Iriepal, and Guadalajara were accused and tried because "these criminals [*reos*], gathered together in reaping time, parodied certain ceremonies of Palm Sunday and took part in a burlesque funeral."[58] Their defense was that "it was not a thing they had done to offend God but only in order to enjoy themselves," but, for all that, they were condemned to a humiliating penitence. It was a world in which mockery, unless skillfully managed, was sacrilegious, a world in which Alvaro de Montalbán and others like him avoided as many ceremonies as they dared.

Within the frontiers of "the republic called the University," however, ceremonies were performed with gaiety and careless enthusiasm. To a certain extent this can be explained in terms of the sheer quantity of ritual behavior that was expected of students and professors. Huizinga's analysis of the way the ceremonial excess of late medieval court life was relieved by parody and burlesque would seem applicable. But if, in the society of chivalry, ceremony like armor only gradually became topheavy and artificial, in academic society it had an inherent artificiality. Witty reversal of serious patterns is an ageless tradition among scholars whether

---

monial ordering of existence is manifest in every part of Juan Ruiz' creation and constitutes the major difference between its "festiveness" and that of later centuries—to be specific, the tradition running from the Arcipreste de Talavera through Quevedo. The joy derived from the yearly cycle of activities depicted on the tent of don Amor is typical. In his treatment of ceremony Juan Ruiz seems comparable to Chaucer.

[58] *Inquisición de Toledo,* p. 308.

grown up or juvenile and would seem to be a corollary of the self-conscious nature of scholarship both as an endeavor and as a variety of existence. Thus, at Salamanca an integral part of the long and complex ceremony accompanying the doctorate was the *vejamen*, a derogatory speech about the candidate which, on occasion, descended to gross insults hugely enjoyed. So, too, student writing—from the Goliardic poems to Luis de Lucena's half-burlesque *Repetición de amores* (*The Lesson of Love*), written and read aloud at Salamanca just before Rojas sat down to continue the *Comedia*—has never hesitated to treat impertinently the language and literary forms of the curriculum.[59] Rojas, in other words, left a society in which ceremony was remorselessly grave and entered one in which festivity and joyous make-believe accompanied its moments of greatest pomp. It must have been a shock to the young Rojas when he first witnessed the "fiesta del Obispillo" in which the students dressed as priests parodied religious ritual.[60] The Puebla de Montalbán had never been like this.

We have in the preceding pages applied a fair number of adjectives to the academic world within which and for which *La Celestina* was written. We have characterized it, among other things, as youthful, autonomous, self-conscious, artificial, non-local, exciting, dynamic, bellicose, argumentative, festive, highly ceremonial, and relatively classless. These are adjectives which to a greater or lesser extent are applicable not just to Salamanca at the

[59] J. Ornstein in his recent edition (Berkeley, 1954) seems to imply that the *Repetición* was seriously intended to be read for an academic degree (p. 2). This seems highly unlikely not just because of the Castilian but also because Lucena himself presents it as an implicitly frivolous imitation: "el orden de mi repetición no difiere del que en las scientíficas letras se usa." Furthermore there are recorded other examples of such university burlesque at the time. See L. Thorndike, "Public Recitals in the Universities of the Fifteenth Century," *Speculum*, iii (1928), 104-105.

[60] García Mercadal (*Estudiantes*, pp. 136 ff.) gives an account of the custom. Beginning prior to the year 1400, it became sacrosanct, and, in spite of later restrictions and disapproval on the part of 16th- and 17th-century authorities, it continued into the 18th and even the 19th century. The Salamancan Inquisitor, Fray Diego de Deza, forbade its performance inside the Cathedral, and in the rules of the Colegio Viejo de San Bartolomé which he headed for a time there is a rather plaintive paragraph (reproduced by Ruiz de Vergara) deploring it. The "fiesta del Obispillo," the writer remarks, is disrespectful and causes feelings to be hurt "for many days afterwards." Nevertheless, the University being what it was, not even the Inquisition and the Counter-reformation could achieve its complete suppression.

end of the fifteenth century but to all universities in every century. They apply to university society as such, and we can validate them —although to a far lesser degree than at Salamanca—from our own experience. Adjectivally speaking, Salamanca was an extreme and superlative example of university society.

Nevertheless, granting that creation in such a highly-charged milieu is a significant fact about *La Celestina*, we should avoid naïvely positivistic derivation of the one from the other. We might well describe the work with the same words—youthful, autonomous, self-conscious, and the rest—but they would not signify at all the same qualities when applied to the newly-created literary reality. *La Celestina* is *not* a university work like the *Repetición de amores*; it is—to intone once again our litany—a unique masterpiece written by a great writer. And if this is so, it is less interesting to think of Salamanca as a determining milieu than to try to intuit (however arbitrary this may appear) the experience of going there. Which is to say among other things: since experience is cumulative by definition, we must try to imagine Salamanca not only as an institution but also as a change from the Puebla de Montalbán and from the *converso* situation in the outside world.

Adjectives aside, then, the important thing is to re-create with historical imagination Rojas' sense of belonging, of sudden and even giddy liberation from social pressure, of meaningful relationship with others, of growing intellectual power, and, above all, of freedom to experiment creatively with received forms. It would be wrong to equate *La Celestina* with the humanistic comedy and think of it only as a half-jesting student imitation of Terence. Yet this traditional academic genre (as María Rosa Lida de Malkiel brings out) and the disrespectful tradition of university writing in general were essential to the one important thing Salamanca had to teach Fernando de Rojas: not the laws of the land but freedom to see and express and make sense of the sound and fury that had been put inside him. The traditional attribution of the *Lazarillo* to a student at Salamanca, whether true or not, testifies to popular awareness of the at once subversive and festive atmosphere of the university. Readers sensed in both works, it would seem, the fundamental irreverence of minds initiated into a new society and looking back at the old one they had left behind. Father Ong observes in general about this aspect of the possibility of *La Celestina*: "The

297

break with the past thus reached a kind of maximum in the Renaissance, and the sense of the Latin school as a special marginal environment reached its greatest intensity."[61]

"The fair of letters"

Our imaginative reconstruction of Rojas' experience in Salamanca is still dangerously incomplete. We must now add "moment" to "milieu" ("race" having been well taken care of) and turn our attention to the university and the town as they were in the years when *La Celestina* was conceived and written and read aloud to its argumentative audience. To begin with, we may point out the obvious fact that the history of Salamanca is a part of the history of Spain. Contrasts between what went on inside and what went on outside can no longer be neatly drawn, for, although there were some special features to academic annals, the history of the university, the town, the nation, and the Christian world was ultimately of a piece. The university may have defined itself as a separate sociological entity, but it could not help being joined organically to its time. At its best it made history, as when its theologians went to Trent and its lawyers inspired the legal reforms of the Catholic Monarchs. At its worst, it submitted to history as when in 1492 Abraham Zacut was forced into exile or when in the early 1490's some 60,000 of its books (on magic and Judaism) were burned.[62]

But whether at its best or at its worst, at least this much may be affirmed: in the fifteenth and sixteenth centuries the town and university were a focal point for historical happening and value creation in much the same sense that Madrid was in the nineteenth century. To go from the Puebla de Montalbán to Salamanca was comparable to the emigration of the members of the Generation of '98 from the provinces to the capital. It was a journey from intra-history into history. Or, to use terms that are even more anachronistic, from the Middle Ages into the Renaissance. In the Puebla, as we have seen, men's minds were already turning back regretfully towards the past; at Salamanca they gazed—sometimes desperately, sometimes hopefully—into the future.

---

[61] *Op. cit.* (n. 34 above), p. 113. Attributions of the *Lazarillo* both to Hurtado de Mendoza and Fray Juan de Ortega have this assumption in common.

[62] Lea, III, 480.

When Rojas arrived in Salamanca in 1494 or thereabouts, he could hardly have been aware of these generalizations. The town was for the most part still old-fashioned in its architecture. The new Cathedral had not yet been built and most of the houses, dating from the time of municipal factions, were fortified with towers, crenelated walls, and embrasures for archers.[63] A few dwellings displayed the more confident and monumental qualities of the style called "Isabelino," but the great period of construction was to begin a generation or so later.[64]

Nor were the preoccupations of the inhabitants as optimistic and forward looking as the above homage to Burckhardt might indicate. Salamanca, traditionally tolerant, had in past centuries been singularly free from the mass violence which had brought so many enforced conversions elsewhere. Its *aljama* or Jewish colony was large and prosperous, and the Edict of Expulsion was consequently a severe blow.[65] The Inquisition, still possessed with its initial ferocity, was another cause of general apprehension. Rojas probably was not one of the 50,000 spectators—among them Lucio Marineo, the Sicilian—who in July 1494 during the long vacation crowded the square to witness public burnings.[66] But there were undoubtedly other such spectacles.[67] The university itself had not

---

[63] According to Emilio Salcedo many of these urban castles were torn down during the reign of the Catholic Monarchs in order to suppress the warring *bandos* (Spanish Montagues and Capulets) fortified therein. *Bandos* were characteristic of city life not only in Salamanca but also in Toledo, Valladolid, and almost every other Spanish town before pacification at the end of the 15th century. See "Notas sobre *La Celestina*," *Boletín informativo del Seminario de Derecho Político*, 1962, p. 109.

[64] Angel de Apraiz, *La casa y la vida en la antigua Salamanca*, Salamanca, 1917.

[65] Although San Vicente Ferrer had preached in Salamanca in 1411, he was not conspicuously helped by local persecution. The *repartimiento* or assessment assigned to the Jewish community was comparatively large, and it appears to have enjoyed a special *fuero* and atmosphere of tolerance until the very end. See F. Cantera Burgos, *Abraham Zacut*, Madrid, 1935.

[66] *De hispaniae laudibus*, fo. xix, where it is pointed out that in that year (the year of Rojas' arrival?) many heretics were burned: "Quo anno haeretici Salamanticae incendium passi sunt." See also Caro Lynn, p. 81.

[67] Facts on Inquisitional activities in Salamanca during Rojas' years of residence seem unavailable, but since the period was one of intense persecution all over the peninsula (as we have seen, Caro Baroja notices in 1500 a substantial recrudescence of trials almost equalling the atrocious situation of the 80's), there is no reason to assume that Salamanca was exempt.

yet been deeply affected by the new institution, at that time in a phase of social persecution rather than of ideological repression. But its many *converso* professors and students could not help but share the anguish of the well-to-do townsfolk.

In this connection we should add that Salamanca's philological and theological learning (Nominalism had just been introduced by Fray Alonso de Córdoba who had studied and taught at the Sorbonne)[68] had not in general advanced to a point of obvious danger. The recantation of questionable doctrines by Pedro de Osma, a professor of theology, was still being talked about 14 years later,[69] but major confrontations of the Inquisition with prominent members of the faculty—Fray Luis de León, Juan de Vergara, Francisco Sánchez "El Brocense"—were not to occur for decades. The conflict between the new and the old in the realm of thought was not yet openly engaged.

Another reason why Rojas, on first arriving, might not have sensed the winds of historical change that had begun to blow through the University was that the branch in which he was professionally enrolled was the most traditional and the most honored. Salamanca in earlier centuries had been above all a law school. The budget stipulated by Alfonso the Wise in 1254 provided twice as much money for five professors of law than for all the rest of the faculty (some six teachers of grammar, logic, and science).[70] It was a preeminence which was still strong under the Catholic Monarchs. Distinguished professors of law, such as Doctor Palacios Rubios or the *converso* Alonso Díaz de Montalvo, continued to be accorded all the honors and privileges of grandees, and their best students found it easy to enter the highest echelons of the new bureaucracy. In 1496 Palacios Rubios began his opening address as a professor in Valladolid with these words: "Among the other institutions of the human arts, through which men are daily elevated to high levels and to the greatest honors, Canon and Civil Law are known to occupy the first and most eminent position. For besides the clarity of thought which they give, those men who are most versed

---

[68] Fray Francisco Méndez, in his *Tipografía española*, Madrid, 1861, cites Fray Alonso de Orozco's praise of Fray Alonso de Córdoba: "Our Spain is much in debt to this doctor because he brought Nominalism [*la vía que dicen de los nominales*] and spent many years lecturing on the liberal arts in Salamanca" (p. 43).

[69] Caro Lynn, p. 89.   [70] *Ibid.,* p. 6.

in them are guided more easily toward the administration of private and public affairs, and sometimes we even see them admitted to the presence and council of the King."[71] To study civil law at Salamanca was thus to share in the time-honored prestige of a central branch of learning and at the same time to prepare a distinguished personal future.

Under these circumstances and with such incentives, the individual law student or *civilista* probably did not object greatly to the audition, explication, repetition, and memorization of the four Justinian codices—the Codex or Code, the Digest or Pandects, the Institutes, and Novels or Novellae—which was his academic fate.[72] During his childhood he had got accustomed to learning in this approved medieval fashion, and he probably would not have agreed with Luis Fernández de Retama's presentation of fifteenth-century legal studies:

The state of legal studies in Salamanca corresponded to the decadence of the century. There were twenty-five principal chairs in the university of which six were devoted to Canon Law and four to Civil Law. These last were preferred because of the future careers which they offered, opening the path to honors and magistracies. Theological and philosophical studies which were to flourish in the sixteenth century were still in a disadvantageous situation, waiting for the renovating influence of Francisco de Vitoria and the stimulus afforded by the rival theological faculty founded a short time later by Cisneros. But

[71] Eloy Bullón y Fernández, *El doctor Palacios Rubios y sus obras*, Madrid, 1927, p. 357. As is well known, the Catholic Monarchs were distinguished for their high esteem for *juristas* and for the legal profession as a source of judicial and administrative reform. Thus, don Diego Hurtado de Mendoza affirms:

Pusieron los Reyes el gobierno de la justicia y cosas públicas en manos de letrados, gente media entre grandes y pequeños, sin ofensa de los unos ni de los otros, cuya profesión eran letras legales, comedimiento, secreto, verdad, vida llana sin corrupción de costumbres; no visitar, no recibir dones, no profesar estrechura de amistades; no vestir ni gastar suntuosamente; blandura y humanidad en el trato; juntarse a horas señaladas para oir causas o para determinarlas, y tratar del bien público. (*Guerra de Granada*, p. 70.)

We may compare this attitude of respect and admiration (shared by Rojas, as we have seen) with the satire and mockery of a Rabelais.

[72] The *Siete Partidas* and other texts in Castilian were studied but far less thoroughly.

301

even the law studies in which Salamanca specialized suffered —as in the rest of Europe—from grave weaknesses. In the first place, deficient education in philosophy prevented the emergence of legal theoreticians of importance and favored the mass production of pettifoggers and unscrupulous legal logic choppers. In the second place the excessive predominance of Canon law and Roman law with the accompanying disregard of the national legislative tradition limited the student to a region of abstractions useless for ordinary practice and daily application. If we add to this the barbarity of legal language, the refined scholastic subtleties and the ample medley of commentary, based not on original sources but on other commentaries equally indigestible, we understand how right Luis Vives' later criticism of the system was.[73]

A favorite disciple of the Sicilian, Alfonso Segura, answers these charges for us (as well as for Rojas, proud as he was of his "Principal study") when in 1510 he writes a friend about his first impressions as a law student:

I know you are wondering what I think of civil law, and I will give you my impressions briefly. There is in the civil law a holy justice which, if jurists did not invert it, would not, as is com-

[73] *Cisneros y su siglo*, Madrid, 1929, I, 43-44. This would indicate that legal studies in Rojas' Salamanca continued the medieval tradition of Bartolus and his school of "post-glossators" who—according to Myron Gilmore—"were much more interested in the elaboration and application of a system of rules than they were in the achievement of any historical understanding of the growth of law or even of the existence of different periods in the history of institutions." Gilmore goes on to cite Petrarch's expressions of regret at having wasted his time in law school and Lorenzo Valla's violent (and violently answered) attack on Bartolus as anti-historical and barbarous (*Humanists and Jurists*, Cambridge, Mass., 1964, pp. 30-31). What we shall see to be the striking absence of humanistic texts in Rojas' personal library may therefore be understood in part as a result of his intellectual commitment to his "*bartulos*" (as law books were collectively termed) and not merely of a lack of continuing interest in Latinity. On the other hand, since the only evidence of open dissension between humanists and jurists at Salamanca is Nebrija's scorn of the Latin of all his colleagues and since Rojas (as we shall see) seems to have been a competent Latinist, it would seem likely that, even though his "*principal estudio*" was "medieval," he did share the new sense of importance and of excitement which characterized academic activities at the time. One way of describing *La Celestina* would be as expressing a kind of negative (not anti-) humanism.

monly thought, bring us all to destruction but would lift us to higher things. It has a reverence-compelling dignity, and a care for the dealing with minute affairs that amazes me when I contemplate its scope. It contains a pregnant dignity of speech; for I call laws pregnant[74] when they include within themselves so many and such varying purposes. Civil law is in all parts so outstanding that I feel the genius of the lawmakers is not less to be admired than the body of laws is to be praised and respected.[75]

Later on Segura complains that because of the "grind of successive hours of study" he is "rusty, musty, tarnished, and washed out," but another friend consoles him with two arguments of interest to readers of *La Celestina*. He reminds Segura, first, of his "frequent release from studies, days given to vacation and rest" when (like Fernando de Rojas) he can take "a brief holiday from the jurists' task" and turn to humane studies and, second, of the high quality of the Latin with which he works.[76] In addition to prestige and material rewards, the study of the law, as Stendhal was to remark centuries later, had certain inherent advantages for anyone interested in words and their meanings.

Although Rojas, in his concern with a discipline deeply rooted into the academic past, might not at first have been aware of the

---

[74] The Latin for this sentence reads: "Et postremo praegnans quaedam dignitas orationis: praegnantes enim appello leges quod intra se tam multa et varia contineant" (Lucio Marineo, *Epistolarum familiarium*, Valladolid, 1514, epistle ix). It may well have been this professional application of the word that Segura's fellow law student had in mind when he wrote in his prologue, "toda palabra del hombre sciente está preñada." That is to say, like the words of a legal generalization which can be applied to different cases, so Heraclitus' *sentencia* expresses a natural law which *personas discretas* can observe operating in all spheres and in innumerable ways. In general, in the rhetorical usage of the time pregnant words were important or "loaded" words with the possibility of double or multiple significance. Fray Francisco Ortiz explains, for example, that a statement of his misinterpreted by the prosecutor was really a "palabra preñada," which should be understood in quite a different way (Selke, *El Santo Oficio*, p. 196). Going one step further, we might even propose that the "pregnancy" which, according to Rojas, characterized "omnia secundum litem fiunt" is a way of expressing the applicability of the citation to the innumerable kinds of daily warfare (including that of language) which are the texture of *La Celestina*. Rojas would thus be stating the irony of his "theme."

[75] Caro Lynn, p. 214.   [76] *Ibid.*, pp. 264-265.

special historical effervescence which distinguished the Salamanca of the end of the fifteenth century from that of even a generation earlier, it could not have taken him long to sense that change was in the air. He probably perceived it first in the new stress placed on the study of the Latin language and in special significance accorded to its cultivation. Within the university the instigator was, of course, Antonio de Nebrija, the one-man "debelador de la barbarie" (extirpator of barbarity) whose basic credo was that linguistic reform is the foundation on which all other reforms must ultimately rest. Language—he points out at length in the Prologue to his *Introductiones latinae*—"is the first principal of, and gate leading into, all the sciences, and any error therein, although it may seem inconsequential, afterwards leads to a labyrinth of confusion."

The semanticists and logicians of our own time (as well as Ezra Pound and his Chinese sages) have once again made current the proposition that in order to act correctly, one must judge correctly and, in order to judge correctly one must choose and arrange words correctly. But we should not overstress the resemblance. Nebrija was no linguistic theorist or semantic reformer. He was a Humanist, and he found in Latin a ready-made language not just sacred but so humanly apt that, if used correctly by a guiding élite, it could create a perfect society based on reason and full mutual comprehension. It could even, by improving medical science, heal the body of its ills. Aside from its cultural or historical value, Latin was conceived of as a means of remaking national institutions and ultimately of saving the city of man. To go to Salamanca was to go to a place where Utopia was getting under way. Hence, both the zeal with which Nebrija (like nineteenth-century Spaniards in Germany) spent his youth studying in Italy and the daring of his successful capture of the university "as a fortress" from which he could dominate Spain and "all my Spaniards."

Nebrija had left Salamanca some eight years before Rojas' arrival there (1486), and he was not to return until 1503. But, although he was greatly missed,[77] his influence, exercised through his *Introductiones latinae* and his disciples (among others, Rojas' fellow student authors, Alonso de la Cámera and the Bachelor

[77] So concludes Pedro Urbano González de la Calle on the basis of Nicolás Antonio's remarks (*Elio Antonio de Lebrija*, Bogotá, 1945, p. 25).

304

Cerezo)[78] was enormous. The tempting comparison of Nebrija with such later academic reformers of future national history as Sanz del Río and Ortega, is in a sense, misleading. It would be quite wrong to think of him as the leader of a band of dissident intellectuals engaged in a battle to wake up the nation or influence its youth. Instead, as has often been pointed out, Nebrija and his work were in a real sense an incarnation of a major aim of royal policy: that of making the newly-united kingdom not only the military and political but the intellectual leader of Europe. In the times of Sanz del Río and Ortega, history was divided by generations; in those of Nebrija, it was divided by reigns. Or as Juan de Lucena (not the printer in Hebraic but the royal chronicler) puts it simply: "When the King used to gamble, we were all gamblers; but now that the Queen studies, behold us all turned into students."[79] As far as Salamanca was concerned, this involved not only sponsorship and patronage for Nebrija and others, but also continuing royal protection, frequent visits, and hopeful projects of reform. If Rojas entered in 1494 as we have assumed, it should be noted that this was only two years after the Catholic Monarchs had characteristically suppressed abuses of the University immunities (*fueros*), at the same time issuing orders against laxness in granting degrees and corruption in faculty elections. Rojas' Salamanca was in a period of renewed academic purpose and rigor.[80]

Symbolic recognition of the University's future national importance had been given in 1480, just after the pacification of the realm was completed. In combining a state visit both to Santiago and to Salamanca, Ferdinand and Isabella stressed geographically that arms and letters were equally important to them. The royal tour of inspection was appropriately commemorated by an inscription in Greek placed on the university façade: "The Monarchs for the University and the University for the Monarchs."

Salamanca had had to fend for itself during the lean and anarchic reigns preceding that of Ferdinand and Isabella and could do little more than try to preserve its own tradition. But now under these two and after its "conquest" by Nebrija, it found itself

---

[78] Olmedo, *Nebrija*, chap. xiv.
[79] "Epístola exhortatoria a las letras" in *Opúsculos literarios*, p. 216.
[80] de la Fuente, ii, 28-37.

at the very center of history. The humanist Juan Ginés de Sepúlveda, as cited by Prescott, sums up the change in this way: "While it was a most rare occurrence to meet with a person of illustrious birth before the present reign who had even studied Latin in his youth, there were now to be seen numbers every day who sought to shed the luster of letters over the martial glory inherited from their ancestors."[81] These young men were presumably the future makers of national history, but the capable latinity of those born more obscurely—such as Fernando de Rojas[82]—could lead to results even of greater importance. Renascent insistence on accurate and elegant use of a literary language brought with it—in Salamanca as elsewhere in Europe—awareness of the creative possibilities of the spoken language. The improvement of Latin was a prerequisite for the outburst of student literature which, as we shall see, occurred at the end of the century. Rojas and Mena are not only separated by reigns but also by the kind of Latin letters the new monarchy did so much to foment.

In order to experience in a more direct way the heady atmosphere of Salamanca in this period, we have only to read Peter Martyr's account of two celebrated visits. The first was of a famed Italian humanist—the narrator himself—and the second, of the Crown Prince of the realm. In his *Epistolary*, we are told how in 1488 the newly-arrived humanist announced his presence by posting on the doors of the cathedral and the lecture halls a twelve-line Latin epigram praising the university. This attention caused the institution "to pour its affection over him." His special lecture of Juvenal was then announced by town criers, the *bedel*, and his assistants:

> The day was Thursday and on that account free from public lectures. So great a crowd had assembled before our arrival that we were not able to enter the hall. Many of the doctors armed themselves with spears and clubs to help the bedel clear the way. With shouting, threatening, and thrusting, a path was opened. I was lifted on the shoulders of the men and so pendant was carried to the desk. Your kinsman, Gómez de Toledo, in all his regalia, and Alfonso de Acebedo, son of the

[81] *Ferdinand and Isabella*, New York, 1837, I, 485.
[82] So one concludes from the scant list of only four minor errors detected by Deyermond in Rojas' translations of borrowings from Petrarch, p. 92.

Archbishop of Alcalá, and many less conspicuous persons were carried out half suffocated. Sandals innumerable and berets not a few were lost. The bedel lost his crimson mantle which had fallen off; he consulted the doctors whether he might not hold me responsible for the loss, and was laughed at. But to return to myself, when the day was mine, I inquired from the lectern what they wished. "The second satire of Juvenal," called out Marineo the Sicilian who professes poetry here. . . . I had begun before the second hour, as I said; and until the third hour I was listened to with the closest attention, without any confusion or moving about. At the third hour, when I was inwardly accusing myself of prolixity, two youths, following their custom, shuffled their feet upon the floor. They were frowned down by their elders. Would I continue, they begged. I finished the point I had begun, and asking their pardon descended. I was carried home like a victor from Olympia.[83]

The second visit illustrates the special importance which both town and university accorded to their relations with royalty. It has the added interest for us of having taken place in 1497—that is to say, it was an occasion which Rojas himself very probably witnessed. Salamanca was one of the cities granted as a marriage portion to Prince Juan, and the inhabitants were determined to make a good impression on their new master:

On the 28th of September the Prince entered Salamanca; and the applause of trumpets and drums with which he was received seemed to rend the air with jubilation. Oh what melodies, what a diversity of song, what nuptial hymns were prepared by the clergy! . . . The formation of lightly armed

[83] Caro Lynn, pp. 95-96. Lynn also cites Lucio Flamminio's account of a lecture on Pliny to another such group. The tone of personal complacency and scholarly braggadocio in both descriptions is typical of these knights-errant of the mind. But, at the same time, the excitement was real. As Gilmore points out—commenting on a similar letter describing a 1511 University of Paris lecture on Ausonius: "If there should be matter for surprise that a discourse of such length on a third-rate ancient author could create such a sensation, we must remember that the popular appeal of humanist scholarship lay less in its content than in its method. Here was a new way of looking at literature, at history, and at the world. It seemed to convey to its practitioners a heightened sense of vividness and reality" (*The World of Humanism*, New York, 1962, pp. 183-184).

knights in the surrounding fields were worthy of contemplation. It was admirable as well as beautiful to see the harnesses
and the adornment of the riders. You would have thought that
all the wealth of Spain had kept a rendezvous in this place.
The choruses of boys and girls on the platforms constructed
in the plazas and in the windows of the houses imitated celestial harmonies and refreshed the spirits of all who passed by.
Every doorway was adorned with green branches, and the
walls of the houses were covered with tapestries admirably
woven by Flemish artisans. . . . These solemnities in honor of
the Prince were arranged with the greatest care and lavishness, because this city is the literary fountain of all Spain, and
it hoped that the future king—himself a lover and cultivator
of letters—would grant it favor and protection beyond all
other cities.[84]

At this point the letter, like the visit it describes, takes an unexpected turn. What began as a celebration of rank and youth and
love ended, in Juan del Encina's words, as "a terrible case of mutable fortune," when a few days later the young Prince died of a
fever. But if the pathetic contrast held the attention of these writers, what interests us is the historical self-awareness of the city as
revealed in their accounts. The Encina poem goes so far as to include an apostrophe to the city which laments its dishonor and predicts future "mala ventura."[85] As the seat of the university,
Salamanca thought of itself as a source of intellectual renovation
deservingly cherished by royal authority but now in danger of losing favor. To conclude, the buoyant enthusiasm which greeted
Peter Martyr's own visit and lecture involved something more than
love of learning. Salamanca aspired to be and was—Nebrija saw
this clearly—the intellectual capital of Spain at a climactic moment
of national history.

[84] *Epistolario*, IX, 344-345.
[85] *Cancionero* (facs. edn.), Madrid, 1928, fos. A and Aiii. For the "romancero" tradition, see Castro's *Santa Teresa y otros ensayos*, Madrid, 1929, and
Paul Bénichou, *Creación poética en el Romancero tradicional*, Madrid, 1968.
In *Realidad*, edn. II, Castro compares the continuing legend of Prince Juan's
death to that of the guilt of King Roderick, the "last of the Goths"—in the
sense that both provide personal and human explanations for a decadence
otherwise inexplicable (p. 243). If the Prince had lived, the Hapsburgs
would not have taken over, and then. . . .

Profiles are by definition one-sided and foreshortened. And the profile of Salamanca at the turn of the century that has just been displayed is even more distorted than most. A treatment in depth would reveal that Nebrija, for all his importance, was only one of a number of distinguished classical scholars—some of them foreign, such as the Sicilians Lucio Marineo and Lucio Flamminio, or the Portuguese Arias Barbosa—who also contributed to the intellectual excitement of the time. Nor did the newly-intensified study of Latin result only from the two motives suggested here: the generous desire for national regeneration (Nebrija) and the more selfish need to prepare oneself for a given vocation (Palacios Rubios). At least a few students believed in the humanistic ideal of mundane salvation through absorption of the classics—the expectation of finding in them a portal to the eternal and incorruptible life of the mind. The correspondence of the Sicilian and of Peter Martyr with their younger Spanish disciples and friends reveals the extent to which the topic, "Per aspera ad astra," was fleshed with life.[86] I would surmise that Rojas in his devotion to the

---

[86] The letters of Lucio Marineo and his students are full of topical references to such salvation. Another typical example occurs in a 1494 letter of Peter Martyr to a disciple (the heir to the Duchy of Alba) whose studies have been interrupted by his father: ". . . if you see that your father delays your return to the Court, beg him to let you go, making him know that those things one obtains from books of learned men are better and more precious than those things which come to us from the abundant patrimony of our ancestors. Tell him that the former are eternal, sweet, celestial, and incorruptible: the latter earthly and corruptible" (*Epistolario*, IX, 283). Again in *De hispaniae laudibus* we find Salamanca described as a place of shelter for those "Spaniards who apply themselves to the study of letters, not out of self-interest, but for knowledge and who follow the journey which they began, flying to greater heights each day, until they reach the sky" (fo. XXIX). These tendencies were accelerated among succeeding generations of students. Prescott cites both Erasmus and Sepúlveda to the effect that 16th-century Salamanca attained an enviable cultivation of humanistic studies and that it was considered a "model" European university. The interesting thing about all this for us is Rojas' apparent apartness from the new faith. He, like his characters, is destined for the Earth in Spanish and not for the Heavens in Latin. The surprise and excitement that greeted Peter Martyr indicates that in Rojas' time—in spite of Nebrija—humanistic philology was still very much of an intellectual novelty. It had not yet affected in any intimate way the vocations or the traditional disciplines of the mass of students. Specifically, Rojas used Terence according to the way he had been understood by preceding medieval generations: as a moralistic point of departure for creating dialogue and not as a text to be restored. For which we may be thankful in view of the restric-

law, his self-proclaimed apartness, and his sardonic assessment of generally accepted ideals never fully shared this one (his library, as we shall see, hardly indicates assiduous reading of the classics), but he could not help but be aware of what was going on among his fellows. In his own ironical way, he was as concerned as any discoverer of Juvenal with the new world of the mind.

Finally, although Latin language and literature were predominant in the Salamanca of those years, a more rounded portrait would reveal nascent interest in Greek and Hebrew as well as in the language of mathematics. Salamanca, however, does not concern us in and of itself; what matters is that we see in sharp outline the profile of that particular Salamanca which was the circumstance of *La Celestina*. For Rojas and his fellows it was a "fair of letters"[87] in which the traditional dignity of legal studies, although undiminished, was supplemented by a new fervor for words and sentences, conceived of as beautiful and important in themselves.[88]

❧ "The author speaks"

A favorite way of dismissing the deep literary mystery of *La Celestina* has been to label it a work of transition. The impropriety of the term—insofar as it implies a mixture of Renaissance and medieval elements—is patent. Aside from the fact that history is

---

tive influence of the classics on the vernacular writing (for example, the efforts at classical drama) of later generations of students. Rojas, historically speaking, attended Salamanca at exactly the right time, a time of burgeoning intellectual and linguistic excitement in which the ancient order was crumbling but no new formulae had been generally accepted as correct by students and faculty.

[87] Lucio Marineo repeats the commonplaces of local self-consciousness in his *De las cosas memorables de España*, Alcalá, 1539. Here he calls Salamanca "the most brilliant city, mother of the liberal arts and all virtues. . . ." It is the center of legal studies, and from it all parts of Spain "piden leyes y derechos para bien vivir." It also provides professional men for the court. All in all, it is the capital of Spanish intellectual life: "Al estudio desta ciudad vienen como a feria de letras y todas virtudes no solamente de muchas ciudades y lugares de España mas tanbién estrangeros de otras naciones" (fos. ii-iii).

[88] In addition to Nebrija, Arias Barbosa (the Portuguese professor of Greek) sought to reform university studies on the basis of linguistic purity, concision, simplicity, and rigorous definition. See *A Carta do helenista Aires Barbosa sobre a reforma dos estudos*, ed. A. do Amaral, Coimbra, 1935, p. 14.

310

transitional by definition, any attempt to sort the contents of the work into separately labelled piles is a murderous denial of organic unity. But there is one sense in which *La Celestina* may be properly described as representing a transitional period. When Rojas tells us in the preliminary *Letter to a Friend* that the style of Act I is so "elegant" that nothing like it has ever been *"seen* or *heard* in our Castilian language," the two participles reflect composition at a time when the advent of the printing press was transforming the intellectual world—a phrase in Rojas' Spain which was almost synonymous with Salamanca. If previously the university had been a predominantly oral institution, it was now more and more pre-occupied with reading. Students two generations before Rojas had spent most of their time listening and repeating, and recourse to the text, although as matchless an argument then as it is now, was achieved with difficulty. Caro Lynn remarks of this: "At the opening of the fifteenth century there was such a lack of books in Castile that those found in the cloisters were rented out by the year, like houses, under bond; and at such a price that the rental was an appreciable source of income to the churches. Many known works could not be got by trouble or money, and books of law and theology were farmed out at public auction to the one contributing most highly to the church."[89] But by the 1490's when the first generation of master printers in Spain had finished its task, text books were beginning to be available in quantity.

It would be mistaken, of course, to think of the change as revolutionary in nature. Even today—in spite of the publicity given to machines as effective replacements for both books and teachers—words spoken by men seem to be in little danger of academic banishment. We need not be surprised, therefore, that the Salamanca of Rojas' time was still primarily an oral university and that it was only beginning to explore the possibilities of visual learning. Resistance to the innovation is implied in one of the 1538 rules which requires that students take their books to class in order that they may—in a phrase characteristic of this period of transition—"oyr por libros."[90]

Another indication of continuing dependence on spoken language is the special emphasis placed on oral behavior and misbe-

[89] pp. 18-19.
[90] 1538 Statutes, Esperabé Arteaga, 1, 149.

311

havior. Castilian is prohibited time and again by the rule makers; blasphemy is treated as a specially serious offense; recommendations for courteous argumentation are spelled out in detail; and, during class and lecture hours, "there is to be an *alguazil* who shall silence the noise of those who impede lessons, such as the pages of the students who play outside."[91] Finally, the importance of oral repetition is stressed as a means both of learning and presenting knowledge. Formal *repetitiones* and dissertations (much of today's academic vocabulary stems from oral centuries) were required of the faculty and advanced students at stated times, and Saturday was set aside for drill and oral review of each week's work. The reason given for this arrangement is indicative: "because the greatest help to professional competence is the discussion and oral exercise of the students."[92]

In a university governed by such rules as these, the daily experience of the individual student was primarily aural. Instead of looking at a bulletin board, he heard the *bedel* cry out announcements of important events: lectures, debates, or even dramatic performances in Latin. In addition to classroom study of Terence, performance or at least dramatic reading of the dialogue of classical and humanistic works seems to have been a regular custom. Although there are no specific records of such events in Rojas' time, the 1501 publication in Salamanca of Alberti's *Philodoxus* would indicate that the 1538 regulation to the effect that certain Sundays be set apart for the representation of a "Comedia de Plauto o Terencio o Tragicomedia" was based on earlier tradition.[93] During

---

[91] *Ibid.*, p. 197. Interruption of those engaged in "oyendo y leyendo" had been legislated against as early as 1426 (Ajo, I, 350).

[92] *Ibid.*, p. 200. The term *"repetición"* was used loosely and could mean anything from a mere oral drill to "an eloquent and thoroughgoing discussion of a chosen theme." In the latter sense it corresponded to our doctoral or magisterial dissertations and was "eminently fitted to serve as a sample house from the writer's repertory, for by its very nature . . . its purpose is to make a wide display of learning" (Caro Lynn, "The *Repetitio*," *Speculum*, 1931, pp. 126-129). With such training it is hardly surprising that Rojas should have been proud of his "gran copia de sentencias entretexidas." But what training cannot account for is that he should have known so well how to "entretexerlas" into spoken life. For a general discussion of kinds of "repetitions" see Hajnal, pp. 138-141.

[93] For the date: *La originalidad*, p. 37. For the regulations: García Mercadal, p. 144. For assignment of Terence: Ajo, II, 237. For general background: E. J. Webber, "The Literary Reputation of Terence and Plautus in Medieval and

meal times—as is usual in monasteries still today—edifying books were read aloud. And after the routine of morning lectures and afternoon drills, the student might well join his friends in song or listen to a private recitation of a classmate's literary experiment.

All examinations were, of course, oral, the most feared of all being the one which qualified the aspiring beginner as a Latinist and permitted him to pass from the "Minor Schools" to work in his chosen field. During this ordeal the frightened and self-conscious student could hear not only the aggressive and even brutal sound of the questions but also his own voice timidly answering as if from a distance. Fray Luis de León's enemy, León de Castro, was particularly feared for his oral violence on these occasions and was in some cases known to have passed from words to deeds, chasing the terrified and mute candidates away with his stick.[94] There was, all in all, little silence and a limited time for reading, writing, or meditation in the daily routine of the student at Salamanca. It was not surprising, then, that Rojas should have transcribed the voices of his characters during a vacation—when he could listen to them without interruption. As Luis Vives remarked in his bitter criticism of the advanced education of his time, *De causis corruptarum artium*, "as novitiates they are trained never to be silent, but always to maintain whatever comes into their mouths, lest they should seem to have yielded. Nothing seems to them more base than to fall silent or to pause for thought."[95]

The resistance of speech to substitution by the printed page was not entirely a matter of deeply-rooted tradition or even of enchantment with sonorousness. The oral concept of learning was defended by two unquestioned and invincible champions: Catholic faith and the classics. Speech and learning through speech were not

---

Prerenaissance Spain," *HR*, xxiv (1956), 191-206. Father Olmedo notes that Ovid and Terence were standard texts for grammar classes, p. 163.

[94] See Francisco Sánchez, el Brocense's criticism of the oral ordeals imposed by León de Castro in de la Fuente, ii, 251.

[95] Cited by Caro Lynn, p. 36. The oral character of medieval and renaissance university life and its influence on prose style has more recently been discussed by Father W. J. Ong in his "Oral Residue in Tudor Prose Style," *PMLA*, lxxx (1965), 145-154. Hajnal, who describes these forgotten educational techniques at length, concludes: "Chaque passage est commenté avec chaque personne, à haute voix, aux cours d'exercices prolongés; chacune des matières de la science pour ainsi dire personnifiée accompagne l'étudiant dans la vie" (*L'Enseignement de l'écriture aux universités médiévales*, p. 29).

only habitual; they were ordained. Thus, the climax of the three-and-one-half-hour ceremony prescribed for the doctorate was a reading of St. John's "In principio erat Verbum." García Mercadal describes the moment picturesquely: "When the candidate was approaching the end, the senior *bedel* struck the platform a blow with his staff, and everybody, *maestrescuela*, rector, assembled doctors, and public, fell to their knees. They kept this posture with head bent low while the candidate, also kneeling, pronounced his final words as if he were himself a new-born Christ: 'Et verbum caro factum est, et habitavit in nobis.' "[96]

Just as important as this sense of the continuity of the divine "Verbum" and the academic word[97] was humanistic reverence for Ciceronian rhetoric. Newly understood in Rojas' time, the various treatises of Cicero were studied diligently both as a textbook in persuasion and as a path to improvement of the self. Cicero's notion that the perfected orator was also a perfected human being may not have been shared by the more cynical among his student readers; but it contributed nevertheless to a new assertion of the prestige of the spoken word. When Nebrija, for example, wanted to praise Terence as a literary artist, he described him as a master of speech: "Terentius est summus orator et omnium hominum gestus sciat effingere."[98] It was to such praise as this that Rojas aspired. He may have been skeptical about the moral benefits of rhetoric—Celestina is Spain's finest orator—but he was clearly fascinated by the potentialities of speech for the creation of new human beings.

This point may need some clarification. As Charles Homer Haskins and others observe, medieval rhetoric consisted primarily of recipes for composition.[99] It served as a key to the mysteries of

[96] *Estudiantes*, pp. 156-157. John 1:14 is read at Christmas mass.

[97] Reverence for speech as a divine faculty of the intellect is, of course, built into the Western tradition—and, as far as I know, into all traditions. Limiting ourselves to books read by Rojas, in the *Visión deleitable*, "la lunbre intelectual" constitutes the "speech" of God, while the basic distinction between an *"idiota"* and a quasi-sacred *"sciente"* is knowledge of rhetoric (pp. 343, 347, and 392). To speak was to be human, and so to be capable of salvation. Four generations later we find Guevara identifying deaf mutes with soulless beasts (*Relox de príncipes*, Seville, 1543, fo. cvi).

[98] Cited by Webber, p. 201.

[99] *The Renaissance of the Twelfth Century*, New York, 1957, p. 138. See also M. B. Kennedy, *The Oration in Shakespeare*, Chapel Hill, N.C., 1942,

written language, in Latin or the vernacular, as opposed to the art-
lessness of the oral tradition. But first in Italy with the early development of humanism, and later in France, Spain, and England,
there came a gradual realization that rhetoric as understood by
the ancients had, in Aristotle's words, to do with the "effects produced by speeches and dialogues." It was precisely at this time of
refreshed comprehension of oratorical antiquity that *La Celestina*
was created. The elements of fifteenth-century *retoricismo* which
Spitzer and Samonà[100] find so prominent in it are undeniable, but,
as the latter points out, they are mutated by the fact of individual
pronunciation. It would be hard to maintain that Rojas' view of life
was humanistic, but he is undeniably Ciceronian both in his mastery of and his respect for spoken language. To sense the magnitude of the innovation it is only necessary to compare Rojas' prose
style to that of Juan de Mena or of the Marqués de Villena in his
Tratado de la consolación.[101] *La Celestina* is, in short, the product
of a relatively brief but immensely significant moment in the history of literature. The quasi-magical creative power of oral language (which we shall discuss in a moment) had not yet been seriously weakened by the printing press, and, at the same time, it was
accorded new dignity and respect as the true object of rhetoric.

Discussion of the new possibilities of literary importance
(Proaza, as we remember, declares Rojas to be superior to Terence) acquired by oral language through renascent interest in and
understanding of Latin thus adds a new level of significance to the
notion of transition. Transition would be an oversimplified and misleading label were we to limit it to undecided and indecisive war-

---

and more specifically D. L. Clark, *Rhetoric and Poetry in the Renaissance,*
pp. 44 ff. and 62 ff.

[100] "A New Book on the Art of *La Celestina*," *HR*, xxv (1957), 1-25,
and *Aspetti del retoricismo nella "Celestina,"* Rome, 1953.

[101] *RH*, xli (1917), 110. Clearly the unknown author of Act I initiated the
movement from written to oral rhetoric, but it was Rojas' achievement to
have comprehended creatively the stylistic innovations of his model and to
have improved upon them substantially. If here and elsewhere I seem to
give too much credit to the continuing author, it may be attributed to my
admiration for the extraordinary organic growth of the whole when confided
to his horticultural care. For discussion of a specific example (the oral portrait
of Celestina's arcane warehouse) of this evolutionary step forward, see
"Rodrigo de Reinosa and *La Celestina*," *RF*, lxxiii (1961), 255-284, by M. J.
Ruggerio and myself.

fare between spoken and written words, between reading and listening. The somewhat more subtle truth just observed is that the oral tradition itself was in a state of change. Rojas, Proaza, and their *socios* were admittedly fascinated by printing, but—because of their lack of historical perspective and their reverence for the classics—they had not yet foreseen the future schism between language on paper and language carried by the human voice. They had not realized that Gutenberg's invention—as Marshall McLuhan asserts—was already beginning to create a new world of written words which could be scanned at a far greater rate of speed[102] than ear and tongue could ever hope to rival.

We are now able to assess the gains and losses that ensued. What was eventually lost in intonation, personality, and immediacy of relationship between author and public was to be compensated for not only in efficiency and quantity but in a new ability to communicate experience in depth, to grasp in the Cervantine novel the complexity and simultaneity of living.[103] But this had not yet happened.

[102] *The Gutenberg Galaxy* (Toronto, 1962) which suggested much of the present discussion is particularly convincing in its treatment of the so-called "transitional" period to which *La Celestina* belonged. Within Rojas' lifetime reading had turned from a scholarly ritual into a habit—as the romances of chivalry in his personal library demonstrate. The gradual emergence of a public of habitual and silent readers—readers who, like their paladin, Alonso Quijano, could consume up to a book a day—was, as McLuhan stresses, at least as important as ideological change for the transmutation of medieval literature during the first half of the 16th century.

[103] In so stating, I differ with McLuhan who prefers to explore the linear, rational, and abstract conceptualization of "typographic man." Such a limited view leads away from a comprehension of the new possibilities of exploring human life from multiple perspectives as a growth of temporal experience. Which is to say essentially that Alonso Quijano–Don Quijote is as much a "typographic man" as Peter Ramus. This should not be taken to mean, however, that, like Ulrich Leo ("Die literarische Gattung de *Celestina*," *RF*, LXXV, 1963), I consider *La Celestina* to be a primitive or embryonic psychological novel. Many of today's habitual readers when confronted by its dialogue find themselves disconcerted, generically uncertain, and intimately uneasy. Here is a work which presents its "characters" changing in time and constantly varying according to their momentary situations—the kind of characters we are used to meeting in novels. And yet at the same time it completely lacks analysis on the part of the omniscient author, revelatory indirect dialogue, and experienced relationship with a systematically constructed narrative world. The inhabitants of *La Celestina* react to each other in depth (on several internal levels) and at length (from memory of previous experience) but solely in spoken words. Hence, the puzzlement and foreshortening generic definitions both of Ulrich Leo and of Mrs. Malkiel, who goes to the opposite

Reading was still thought of as reading aloud to oneself or to some-body else. The Sicilian's *De hispaniae laudibus* was written in seven books, each intended for an evening session; the humanistic epistles that he and Peter Martyr delighted in sending and collect-ing are written in a style that has evidently been listened to appre-ciatively; even the Latin grammar of that first academic exploiter of the market for textbooks, Nebrija, was rhymed in order that it might be read aloud and learned by heart.[104] The printing press, in other words, had not yet created a public of silent readers; it had merely multiplied the number of texts available for reading aloud.

It is in precisely this sense that the Salamanca of Fernando de Rojas may be thought of as transitional. There was a flourishing commerce in printed books along the new "Calle de los Libreros"; a new university library had been finished in the 1480's; reading for personal pleasure and freer circulation of texts within the minia-ture student public began to supplement academic repetition. But at the same time, none of those affected by such potentially revolu-tionary changes had modified their habitual sense of language. They wrote to be heard not read, and they read as if they were de-claiming, moving their lips and making abortive gestures as they went along. To compare them with school children would be

---

extreme and tries abstractly to understand what goes on in terms of a non-existent theater. The truth is, I think, that Rojas' creative meditation on what Luis Vives was to term a few years later the "how" of conscious life *does* lead to the *Quijote*, but, at the same time, his vision (or perhaps his "audi-tion") of what is significant about his characters is always in terms of his oral medium. As a result he tends above all to probe those intense regions of sentimental awareness—explosive anger, violent love sickness, fierce joy, demoniac glee, stark fear, heartrending grief—which are susceptible to direct spoken expression. To hear these passions (not in themselves dissimilar from those expressed in the *Romancero*) not only intensely present but growing and receding in time constitutes the unique—however enigmatic today—greatness of the work. The 19th-century novelist, on the other hand, must be understood as trying to penetrate into the subsoil of interiority, into shades of feeling and motivation, which the life being observed could never explain or bring to full consciousness.

[104] Caro Lynn (pp. 97 ff.) suggests that Marineo's rival grammar was less successful, although more conveniently and rationally organized than Nebrija's, because unrhymed and presumably more designed for silent study. Apparently the students of Rojas' generation were not yet ready for the "typographical" step forward.

grossly unfair, for they knew how to read with sonorous grace and with an awareness of verbal implication which have been forgotten today and which only men highly trained in an oral university could have achieved. But they did have one thing in common with first and second graders: their whole sense of language was still profoundly a sense of speech.

At such a time and in such a place it was the most natural thing in the world that Rojas should have "found" the fragmentary first act in circulation among his fellows, that he should have read it aloud to himself over and over again: "As many times as I read it, so much the more necessity was there to read it again, and it pleased me so much the more, and, in the process, *I heard new sayings!*" ("*. . . nuevas sentencias sentía*"). Rojas did not *learn, see,* or even *find* old maxims which had previously passed unnoticed. Rather he *hears* new ones. "*Sentir,*" as readers of *comedias* know (and as defined in the *Diccionario de autoridades*), is generally used in an auditory sense,[105] while "*sentencias*" (according to the same dictionary) are "grave and succinct sayings which enclose doctrine or morality." Which is to say that Rojas discovered ever deeper significance beneath the spoken signs as he pronounced them and listened to them over and over again. In essence he is describing the process of acquiring oral wisdom.[106]

Nor is it surprising that Rojas' oral intimacy with the speakers of Act I, his virtual identification with them in speech, should have led him to continue their lives. Comprehension of the way Rojas read leads to comprehension of the way he wrote. Istvan Hajnal has stressed the extent to which all writing and particularly the process of learning to write was in medieval universities a profoundly oral affair. Every stage of the student writer's apprenticeship was accompanied by the exercise of careful pronunciation (*pronuntiatio*). One spoke and listened as one wrote—with the result that words were never divorced from sound and calculated intonation. As Hajnal concludes, "In the Middle Ages writing was auxiliary, the

---

[105] "Particularmente se toma por oir o percibir con el sentido del oído."

[106] Father Ong (in the article cited in n. 95) comments brilliantly on the relation of the use of commonplaces (including those culled from printed collections) to the "orally oriented mind" (p. 152). See also McLuhan, pp. 102 ff., beginning: "When it is understood how entirely oral these thesis defenses were, it is easier to see why the students would need to have memories furnished with a large repertory of aphorisms and sententiae."

materialized expression of the extremely sensitive and disciplined technique of verbal culture; and, as such, writing found its place in all areas of oral work. It did not eliminate oral work; it did not efface it; on the contrary, it contributed to its reinforcement."[107]

In such an environment (Hajnal stresses that oral training was given in universities as well as grammar schools) Rojas continued to hear the speakers of Act I as he transcribed his own acts. As we surmised in the Introduction, he can be thought of as dictating to himself[108] as he proceeded from one speech to another. A man of prodigious—to us inconceivable—oral sensibility, Rojas heard voices as true and real as any heard by Joan of Arc. His, however, did not come from above but from the hell of human consciousness, and in the simultaneous act of reading and writing they made themselves audible through his own mouth. *La Celestina* demonstrates how oral penmanship in the right hand of a genius could become oral creation.

Just as *La Celestina* was written, so its author expected it to be read: out loud to an in-group. The notion of numberless future generations of silent scanners was alien to authors of the time. They were concerned rather with groups of "ten persons who would come together to listen" to their words. In a way antithetical to, say, a novel by Stendhal, *La Celestina* is aimed point blank, the

---

[107] p. 153. Hajnal is cited extensively by McLuhan, pp. 94-99. His work, as we have seen, is of great interest to anyone concerned with the university background of given literary works—providing as it does abundant details about the kind of oral training undergone by the students. Among other things, Hajnal stresses the peculiar concern of 15th-century academics (p. 17) with "the art of writing as proof of a solid oral formation" (p. 127) and with the use of reading aloud as a major means of editing and improving upon the obscure manuscripts of earlier copyists: "On croirait que c'est la parole prononcée à haute voix et avec précision que provoque ce progrès" (p. 41). Perhaps Proaza in his instructions to the reader was also revealing an aspect of his technique as an editor.

[108] Hajnal discusses (pp. 117-134 and elsewhere) in detail lecture hall and classroom dictation as a teaching method (and also as a way of reproducing old and new texts). The practice, called at the time either simply *"legere"* or *"pronuntiare ad pennam,"* helps us understand Rojas' approach to writing (as suggested in Chapter I) as a kind of private dictation of the speakers' voices to himself. Or, putting it in another way, once invented and known orally, these voices begin to dictate the rest of the things they have to say to their author. This unfamiliar and obviously paradoxical notion may indeed (as suggested earlier) deepen rather than solve the mystery of how *La Celestina* was possible, but I do think it helps put it in its proper context.

way spoken language must be aimed. But there was danger, too, in such a flat trajectory. Rojas had been stricken and indeed overwhelmed by the direct oral impact of Act I, but other readers might well react differently, and to avoid "detractors and poisonous tongues," secrecy—or at best carefully calculated strategies of self-revelation—might be necessary.

About twenty years after the writing of the Prologue, Antonio de Guevara included in the "argument" to his European best seller, *The Diall of Princes*, a description which illustrates in caricature Rojas' report of the violent "battle or contention" which his dialogue stimulated among its listeners. Guevara describes a scene in which three or four persons discuss a work of literature at the table after a meal: ". . . taking the book in his hand, one says it is prolix; another says it is nonsense; another that it is difficult, another that everything it says is fictitious; another that it is without a moral; another that it is skillfully written; another that it is malicious; the result being that in the best of circumstances the doctrine of the book is left open to suspicion and the author does not escape without a stain [*mácula*]. Of course, those who speak so should be pardoned because they are at table and they speak not really about books but according to the meal they have just eaten. . . ."[109] Flesh and blood being what they are, such an audience, as compared to an anonymous public, might well be so obstreperous as to make necessary authorial anonymity.

To think of *La Celestina* as transitional in this limited sense is, I believe, much more revealing than to think of it as mixing medieval and Renaissance characteristics. Some of the most puzzling of the "paradoxes" for which the work is famed are illuminated—if not explained—by comprehension of the oral tradition underlying its printed façade. For example, in the early editions the lack of marginal directions, of underlinings, of punctuation in the modern sense, and even of indentation can only be understood in terms of the oral power still possessed by the word, its ability to suggest pronunciation and intonation without external help.[110] Hernán

---

[109] Translated by myself (North's version being taken from the French) from the prologue material to the edition previously cited.

[110] A key example at the very beginning is the following: "*Cal.*—¡Sempronio, Sempronio, Sempronio! ¿Dónde está este maldito? *Semp.*—Aquí soy, señor, curando destos cauallos. *Cal.*—Pues ¿cómo sales de la sala? *Semp.*— Abatióse el girifalte e vínele a endereçar en el alcándara. *Cal.*—¡Assí

Pérez de Oliva remarks in the introduction to his translation of *Amphitryon* (printed in this tradition in 1525 and, aside from the *Propalladia*, the only work in dialogue owned by Rojas): "In comedies the style of speech is as diverse as the emotions of men. Sometimes it's lukewarm; sometimes boiling; some speeches are hateful and others tender; gravity can alternate with humor; narration, meditation, and familiar interchange succeed each other. . . ."[111] But without specific instructions from the author as well as detailed typographical help, the modern reader will be left at a loss about how to sort out such a variety of intonations.

We sense in these comments of Pérez de Oliva the implied uncertainty of Alonso de Proaza's famous lesson in elocution: "If you wish to move your auditors / to great attention while reading / [the book of] Calisto / you will have to know how to speak mumbling / at times with joy, hope, and passion / or at other times angrily with great excitement. / Learn to feign as you read a thou-

---

los diablos te ganen! . . ." Only by hearing the tone of Sempronio's two rapidly conceived but lame excuses for idling in the *sala* during his master's absence (as well as the tone of the latter's incredulous irritation) can we ascertain what is actually going on. Tone-deaf translators such as Simpson (Berkeley, 1955) and Hartnoll (London, 1959) entirely misinterpret the interchange because of oral incomprehension. The former has Calisto ask Sempronio, "Why did you *leave* the room?" And the second, concerned with tying up loose ends of the plot, believes Sempronio's story since the falcon must have "flown home" to its perch. Singleton (Madison, Wis., 1958) and others translate correctly, but fail to help the silent reader to visualize what Sempronio has been up to. The best solution I have seen is that found by E. Hartmann and F. R. Fries (Bremen, 1959), who have Calisto ask Sempronio, "Why, then, did you *run* out of the room?" Here action cleverly supplies what has been lost in intonation. Perhaps somewhat too explicit is the interpretation of Barth who pictures Sempronio lolling on a "triclinium" in his master's absence.

111 "El estilo de dezir en comedia es tan diuerso como son los mouimientos de los hombres. A vezes va tibio, y a vezes con heruor; unas con odio, y otras con amor; graue algunas vezes, otras vezes gracioso; unas vezes como historia, otras como razonamiento, y otras vezes es habla familiar" (cited by W. Atkinson, "Hernán Pérez de Oliva," *RH*, LXXI, 1927, p. 400). Pérez de Oliva who arrived in Salamanca in 1508 at the age of 14 was (like his fellow translator of the *Amphitryon*, Villalobos) clearly influenced by the style of *La Celestina* —as the above remarks on oral decorum indicate in themselves. Like Nebrija ("Terentius est summus orator"), Pérez de Oliva was well aware of the similitude of *comedia* dialogue and oratory: "Las comedias antes escritas fueron fuentes de la eloquencia de Marco Tulio, que muncho amó su muy familiar Terencio."

321

sand ways and manners, / to ask and answer through the mouth of each speaker / crying and laughing at the proper time and season."[112] It is as if Rojas (using Proaza as his spokesman) and Pérez de Oliva were confident of the oral capability of their written dialogue until the moment came for relinquishing it to new and unknown readers. Then and only then do they begin to wonder whether instruction may not be useful. Proaza's advice is in this sense indispensable for the modern reader who has lost what a student imitator of *La Celestina* called his "auditory appetite"[113] and for whom printed words no longer possess the seemingly magic power of being able to speak for themselves.

A second paradox, which may be observed more clearly from this point of view, has been best described by María Rosa Lida de Malkiel: "No matter how much the eating, sleeping, nightfall or daybreak, which serve to mark off segments of the action, create the illusion that everything unfolds before the eyes of the reader, the action projected in the *Celestina* is not the uninterrupted flow of reality, but rather a typical selection from it, which at no point coincides with the continuous sequence of life."[114] She refers, of

[112] McPheeters interprets these lines in anachronistically Platonic terms. The Greek rhapsode as described in the *Ion*, he says, was inspired by the Homeric poetry he recited to relive emotionally the lives and speeches of the heroes. And so too in *La Celestina*. Aside from the fact that Plato was little more than a name in the intellectual world around Rojas (the evidence presented for Proaza's neo-Platonism is sketchy), such a comparison overlooks a number of obvious differences. Rojas' work is an unheroic or even anti-heroic prose dialogue printed for reading aloud, not a wholly oral epic poem half known by heart by most of the auditors. The medieval disciplines of effective oral comprehension and expression (Hajnal's "*pronuntiatio*") rather than epic "inspiration" are what are at stake here (*El humanista español*, p. 34).

[113] Alfonso de Villegas Selvago, *La Selvagia*, Madrid, 1873, p. iv. The reference to *La Celestina* reads as follows: ". . . dando gusto al *apetito auditivo* con el estilo de sus razones." Writing in 1554, Villegas goes on to attribute Act I to Cota but does not for that reason stint his praise of Rojas: "Sabemos de Cota que pudo empeçar / Obrando su ciencia la gran Celestina. / Labrose por Rojas su fin con muy fina / Ambrosia que nunca se puede estimar." The image of "fina ambrosia" for style indicates that his gustatory joy in the word is more than a matter of broadly sensual, Rabelaisian pleasure. Although this too is present (primarily in Act I with the "puta vieja" passage, the excoriation of women, etc.), the oral tradition of the universities paid "close attention to precise nuance of word use" (McLuhan, p. 156) and derived refined pleasure therefrom. *La Celestina*, for a reader such as Selvago, was an exquisite marvel of oral precision at every level of expressive decorum.

[114] *Two Spanish Masterpieces*, pp. 76-77.

course, not only to the much discussed sequences of time (one that of actual speech and the other that perceived or experienced by the speakers) but also to remarks such as the following addressed by Sempronio to Calisto in Act II: "As soon as you find yourself alone, you rave like a madman, sighing, moaning, singing out of tune, retreating into darkness and solitude, and in general looking for new ways to torment yourself mentally."[115] Calisto has only been alone at most for some three or four minutes at the beginning of Act I, but the spoken word has the power to create *ex nihilo* a habitual dedication to amorous despair.

In order to comprehend the possibility of such creation we must begin by revising our expectations. As readers accustomed to the post-Renaissance genres of the novel or the drama, we tend to view individual works as fictional worlds, as imaginary regions each with its own interdependent space and time which contain, as it were, the things signified by the words. The author and the reader are in fact in tacit generic agreement that this shall be so. With the result that, just as in our daily experience, the word is a sign for something which we believe (or pretend to believe) has prior existence. But in *La Celestina* the opposite situation holds: words create their realities in the very act of being pronounced, and the author never needs to worry about fitting them into a completed and congruent whole. For Rojas language had not lost what Leo Spitzer, referring to the *romancero*, called its vocative force,[116] that is to say, its power imaginatively to *invoke* new and wholly unexpected realities. Predefined space and time are not only not in control; they themselves come into being when the speakers need them and invent them in their speech. Melibea creates "many many days of love" by mentioning them in spite of the fact that the dialogue up to that point (Act X) only provides for two, and so on.[117] Such power does not seem strange in fully oral and unsophisticated

---

[115] "Que en viéndote solo, dizes desuaríos de hombre sin seso. . . ."

[116] "Los romances españoles," *Asomante* I (1945), 13.

[117] For more examples see my "El tiempo y el género literario en *La Celestina*," *RFH*, VII (1945), 147-159. If I had read it at that time, Lewis Mumford's discussion of medieval space and time as forming "two relatively independent systems" would have been most helpful. See *Technics and Civilization*, New York, 1934, pp. 18-22. I might then have understood that it was the transitional printed condition of *La Celestina* and not generic mixture that made its dimensional anomalies seem so mysterious.

medieval literature—a ballad or a fairy tale—but on the printed novel or drama-like pages of *La Celestina* it seems uncanny.

⟨⟨ "Read histories, study philosophers, look at poets"

A similar transition is apparent in *La Celestina*'s relation to the immediate literary history of its time. As we pointed out, students at Salamanca had not yet foreseen or experienced the profound metamorphoses of language and culture which the printing press was to bring about, but they were fully aware of the intellectual excitement it stimulated. Printed books, McLuhan observes, were "the first uniform, repeatable, and mass produced items in the world" and their advent on the market resulted in literary shock waves. The classics either in imported anthologies such as Albrecht von Eyb's *Margarita poética* (a textbook still in Rojas' library at the time of his death) or in annotated editions (Terence with ever more elaborate glosses was frequently reprinted)[118] were suddenly available to all who could read them. And aside from the standard Latin texts of law, literature, and theology (usually imported), numerous locally printed translations began to appear in the newly-established bookstores and in the hands of friends. History, fiction, moral treatises with handy indices of commonplaces circulated widely in Salamanca and in the other Spanish cities where foreign masters and native apprentices had set up shop. Seneca in various compilations and editions was a great success along with Petrarch understood as a modern disciple of the Stoics. As for Boccaccio, the *De casibus*, the *Decameron*, and the *Fiammetta* first appeared in 1495, 1496, and 1497, respectively. Another work imported from Italy with notable success was Aeneas Silvio's *Historia de duobus amantibus* (1496). There were even indications of interest in the *converso* market. Aside from the clandestine Hebraic press of Juan de Lucena, Josephus (translated by the "humble chronicler" Alonso de Palencia) appeared in 1492 and served as a justification for caste pride.[119] The same purchasers

---

[118] E. R. Robbins, *Dramatic Characterization in Printed Commentaries on Terence*, Urbana, Ill., 1951.

[119] According to J. Puyol y Alonso (*Los cronistas de Enrique IV*, Madrid, 1921), Alonso de Palencia was both a *converso* himself and an apologist for the caste. Because of *converso* fondness for this chronicle of their ancestors' glory, Lope has the Jews who crucify "el Santo Niño de la Guardia" speak of

may have recognized the strong influence of Maimonides' *Guide for the Perplexed* behind the semi-Christianized allegory of *La visión deleitable* (prepared for the press in 1480 by the *converso* Alfonso de la Torre).[120]

Nor were the best writings of the Spanish fifteenth century neglected in this first tentative exploitation of the non-professional market. Juan de Mena's allegorical *Laberinto de la fortuna* (Salamanca in the 1480's), Fernán Pérez de Guzmán's *Coplas* (otherwise known as *Las setecientas*) (1492) and later his *Mar de historias*, the Arcipreste de Talavera's *Corbacho* (1495),[121] the Marquis of Santillana's *Proverbios* (1490) as well as chronicles (Valera's *Crónica de España* was the most popular), *cancioneros*, and works of piety were all gathered from the past and distributed in quantity.[122]

But what do these scattered facts signify? We must remember that we are speaking of a period just prior to Garcí Rodríguez de

---

"nuestro Josefo." The facts that Columbus cites Josephus in his "Carta a los Reyes" and that his "escribano mayor," Diego Méndez, possessed a copy in his library, are considered by Madariaga as possible indications of *converso* background (*Vida del magnífico señor, Cristóbal Colón*, Buenos Aires, 1940, p. 539). As we shall see, Rojas possessed his own copy.

[120] Gillet surmises that Rojas was thinking of Maimonides when Calisto prays: "Tu que guías a los perdidos . . ." (*Propalladia*, VI, 345). For those opposed to *conversos* the printers provided such works as the forgotten *Libro del anticristo y Juicio final, sermón de San Vicente, y las epístolas de Rabbi Samuel a Rabbi Isaac*, Zaragoza, 1496, variously attributed to Alonso Buenhombre de España and Martín Martínez Dampiés. Aside from the despair and the doubts about the validity of their faith expressed by the Rabbis in their apocryphal letters (letters clearly intended to make Christian readers feel smug), in the second part the Anti-Christ is described as a circumcised false Messiah leading the Jews to eventual defeat at the hands of the Christians they have persecuted. A third section is entitled "el libro del judicio postrimero."

[121] The 1495 edition is listed as "muy dudosa" by Simón Díaz, but the unquestionable influence of the work on *La Celestina* speaks for its existence. The first extant edition was printed in 1498, a date which would hardly have given Rojas time to assimilate the creation of his predecessor. Access to the work in manuscript is, of course, another possibility, but, since so many of the traceable sources emerge from books made available by the press, I would tend to doubt it.

[122] Scholars seem to agree on the tendency of early printers to make newly available long known medieval material. See J. B. Wadsworth's *Lyons* cited previously, as well as L. Febvre and H.-J. Martin, *L'apparition du livre*, Paris, 1950.

Montalvo's revision of a mediocre medieval romance called *Amadís de Gaula*. The appearance of this world's first best seller in 1506 has commonly been considered a major step towards the formation of an entity still unforeseen by Rojas and his oral-aural circle of "colleagues": a national reading public. However, we should not overstress the novel and its date as a sharply defined watershed. That the process was gradual and that a community of isolated silent readers was not born overnight, is attested to by the familiar scene from the *Don Quixote* in which an innkeeper describes the reading aloud of a romance of chivalry to harvest hands gathered in his inn on a summer's day. Similarly one might say that the national success of the *Amadís* was prepared for by the turbulent reception among scattered local groups (one imagines them at the beginning to be composed primarily of university graduates and their families) of books published in preceding decades.

Admitting, then, the importance of Montalvo's achievement in creating a fictional prose which could be read silently by the lonely Don Quixotes of this world (as against the spoken dialogue of *La Celestina* and the *Corbacho*),[123] we should still take care not to overlook the sudden upheaval in the relationship of literature and society experienced by Rojas and his generation. Reading for these people, while still primarily oral, had rapidly become a fascinating activity and an absorbing topic of conversation. Rojas' intense reaction to Act I, as well as the book-inspired dissensions he and Guevara describe, seem typical of the first years of printing activity. As a disciple of Nebrija observed wryly, "he who publishes a new work has to listen to many opinions."[124]

---

[123] The distinction proposed is not rigid. Just as it is possible and profitable to read these texts silently (in spite of the meaningful intonations which go unheard), so too the Innkeeper in the *Quijote* only knows the Romances of Chivalry from hearing them read aloud. But the essential *printed* difference between the *Amadís* and the *Corbacho* or even the *Cárcel de Amor*, I would maintain, is its tentative efforts at visual description of exotic and ever changing people and scenes. The result was that a silent reader could picture immediately in his imagination the castles and grottoes witnessed by the hero. This in turn tended to increase his sense of identification with him. Accelerated reading rather than slow savoring of words and speeches, McLuhan suggests, was the necessary precondition of the novel.

[124] The Bachelor Cerezo reminds us of Rojas when he comments (in his colloquial letter on the reception of his 1485 grammar) on "críticos caninos que necesitan carne en que cebarse" (reproduced in Olmedo, *Nebrija*, pp. 172-174). However, his counterattack is far more aggressive than anything

From all of which we may intuit an important conclusion: for the genesis of *La Celestina,* the sudden discovery of oneself as a reader is at least as important as the sudden discovery of oneself as a *converso.* Rojas became, in other words, a writer in the same fashion that Cervantes, Shakespeare, and their heirs became writers: as a result of reading. We need not strain our capacity for historical imagination in order to recapture the excitement which reigned among the students and faculty of Salamanca when they discovered what it meant to read, not consecrated texts in manuscript, but books which they were far more free to enjoy and judge on their own merits. Aside from individual fields of specialization, they found themselves sharing, disputing, and possibly adding to a common intellectual and imaginative life. These avid young men —ready like Cervantes to pick up scraps of printed paper from the street—may be compared to fish suddenly transferred from a quiet pool to a running stream. Although still immersed in the oral world of their ancestors, they found a sudden new exhilaration to living in it.

La Celestina, as a new book sent to the press for printing, was not a unique sort or even the first of its kind. Once a market for past books hitherto unavailable had been created, the next step— the fabrication and circulation of new books—was easily taken. Editors and revisers had now to make room for authors. Aside from Rojas himself, the *converso* majordomo, Diego de San Pedro, was the most successful and noteworthy of these. After publishing the manuscript of his *Tractado de amores* (probably finished years before) in 1491, he seems to have written his better remembered *Cárcel de Amor* (first edition, Seville in the annus mirabilis of 1492) with a view to publication.[125] Aside from the merits of the

---

to be found in the prudent prologue material of *La Celestina*: "A vosotros que uncís las zorras y ordeñais los cabrones, a vosotros que lleváis a los niños por precipicios y derrumbaderos . . . a vosotros, digo, es a los que había que azotar. ¿Qué estudiantes habéis formado? ¿En qué laberinto se ha metido vuestra zafia Minerva?" As a sample of the intellectual activity of the time, Cerezo's Castilian rhetoric is striking.

125 A number of facts are relevant to this hypothesis. As is well known, San Pedro's first "sentimental novel," the *Tractado de amores,* was written in 1483 and published belatedly in 1491. It was an immediate success, and a year later the *Cárcel*—intended for the same avid public—appeared on the market. That it was written after the *Tractado* is attested to by San Pedro

work as a "sentimental novel," its appearance in that year as the first novel written for the press is an event at least as significant to the sociology of Spanish literature as that of the *Amadís*. The intellectual climate of Salamanca since the time of the Bachelor Alfonso de la Torre had been particularly favorable to this new activity. Students and faculty were trained for oral composition (the preparation of *repetitiones*, dissertations, rebuttals, and the rest) and, given their failure to distinguish between spoken and written language, it was only natural that they should find themselves qualified to provide the printing presses with new writing. Which is to say that, in a sense, Salamanca—precisely because of its oral tradition and its primary emphasis on grammar and rhetoric—centered its whole curriculum on the teaching of creative writing.

Latin was, of course, the language of rhetoric and oratorical training. In addition to the "Sicilian" Lucio Marineo's topical but curious volume of oral adulation, *De hispaniae laudibus* (1495), publication of academic repetitions and other treatises by the faculty and advanced students was not uncommon.[126] Nevertheless (and in spite of their newly-learned and newly-esteemed latinity) the inhabitants of Salamanca were not reluctant to exploit the much greater market for books in Castilian. The list of Spanish titles published during the few years of Rojas' residence is impressive. Francisco de Villalobos summed up his freshly-learned medical wisdom in his *Sumario de Medicina* (1498), written (presumably for oral repetition) in verse like his model, Avicenna. Luis de

---

himself, and that it was written long afterwards is suggested by Gili Gaya's discussion of its stylistic simplification (Introduction to the *Obras*, Madrid, 1950). Francisco Márquez provides additional evidence of years of experience separating the creation of the two works in his "*Cárcel de amor*, novela política," *RO*, IV (1966), 185-200. San Pedro's early enthusiasm for the Catholic Monarchs evident in the *Tractado*, Márquez demonstrates, was replaced by horror of royal despotism. There are even—as in *La Celestina*—half-concealed thrusts at the Inquisition and its special *justicia* (see Chap. III, n. 45). Once we admit a substantial passage of time between the two periods of composition, the supposition that the stimulus for undertaking the *Cárcel* was the popularity of the first edition of the *Tractado* seems reasonable. The symbiosis of novel and printing press had begun.

[126] Aside from Villalobos' *Sumario* and Cerezo's *Gramática*, Fernando de Roa published his *Repetitiones* in 1502. For other publishing disciples of Nebrija, see Olmedo, *Nebrija*, chap. XIV.

Lucena, the son of the Juan de Lucena who had written *Libro de la vida beata* (1483) followed his father's footsteps by publishing his *Repetición de amores e arte de axedrez* (1497) while "estudiando en el preclarissimo studio de la muy noble ciudad de Salamanca."[127] As for poetry, in addition to the presumptuously didactic *Crianza y virtuosa doctrina* (cited in note 48) dedicated to doña Isabel by a "son of the University," Juan del Encina, a recent graduate, published his *Cancionero* in Salamanca in 1496.[128]

To proceed from this résumé of University publication to Rojas' own creative behavior as a student would lead directly to the problem of sources. The first question we should have to ask would be exactly what books the avid young reader had consumed and later incorporated into his writing. Fortunately, this aspect of Rojas' biography has been adequately investigated (by Menéndez Pelayo, Castro Guisasola, and María Rosa Lida de Malkiel, among others) and needs no further discussion here. We may be startled, however, to realize how many of the known sources stem from the books in Latin and Spanish stocked by the booksellers who competed for the academic trade on the Rua Nueva (later Calle de los Libreros) during the 1490's.[129] It has long been known that

---

[127] The *Repetición de Amores* was probably written at about the same time as *La Celestina*, since, in spite of certain similarities in subject and technique, there are no unmistakable signs of influence in either direction. As far as the similarities are concerned, in the *Repetición*, as in both parts of *La Celestina*, general statements are immediately followed by supporting examples (the oral form of the academic footnote); routine changes are rung on the topics of amorous blasphemy and love as a disease; and there is a scolding *alcahueta* whose dialogue is reproduced with a typical grossness much enjoyed by the listeners. All of which constitutes unnecessary testimony to the genius of the authors of *La Celestina*. One unanswerable question remains: why had not Lucena read Act I? Its absence in his text may indicate that, when Rojas "found" it, it was still relatively uncirculated.

[128] Another student author of the time (unlisted above because his work was not published until the 19th century) was the Bachelor Palma whose *La divina retribución* (Madrid, 1879) reflected the epic exaltation of contemporary history in a fashion diametrically opposed to *La Celestina*. It consists of a virtual hymn of patriotic celebration after the victory of the Catholic Monarchs in the battle of Toro, 1476. He may later have changed his attitude as Márquez shows Diego de San Pedro to have done (see n. 125).

[129] That many Italians, presumably prepared by humanistic studies, entered this flourishing new commerce, we learn from Manuel García Blanco's "La casa de Nebrija" in *Seis estudios Salmantinos*, Salamanca, 1961. Apparently Nebrija himself set up a bookstore in one of the *casas* of his residence and kept it in operation even during his absence in Alcalá. The same close intellec-

Rojas' conveniently indexed edition of Petrarch was a literary *nouveauté*[130] and that Terence to a much greater extent than the humanistic comedies[131] was a student best-seller. The textbook anthology of ancient and modern Latin letters of Albrecht von Eyb mentioned previously is another possibility (although doubtful, as we shall see). As for Spanish, translations of the *Fiammetta* and the *Historia de duobus amantibus,* as well as the works of such native authors as Rodrigo de Cota,[132] Diego de San Pedro, Jorge Manrique, Martínez de Toledo, Rodrigo de Reinosa, and Juan del

---

tual ties between booksellers, readers, editors (such as Proaza), and printers are apparent in the little that is known about Fadrique Alemán de Basilea, the printer of the first extant edition of *La Celestina.* Karl Wehmer sums up his activities as follows: "The German printer, Friedric Biel, who was active in Basel during the early 70's in partnership with Michael Wennsler, moved to Burgos in 1485 where he called himself Fadrique Alemán de Basilea. In the intervening period he may have been in the South of France, at that time a favorite place to work for printers from Basel. His press, the first in Burgos, lasted until the second decade of the sixteenth century, after which it continued to produce under Juan de Junta and his successors until the beginning of the seventeenth. Biel published distinguished works of literature and scholarly learning. He was in close relation with leading men in the humanistic movement in Spain who entrusted him with the editing of their writings. It was considered the characteristic specialty of his press that Biel from the end of the fifteenth century used Roman type" (*Deutsche Buchdruck im Jahrhundert Gutenbergs,* Leipzig, 1940, Tafel 96).

[130] Castro Guisasola's discovery of the use of this index was, as we have seen (Chap. V, n. 5) and as is well known, essential to the dating of Rojas' composition.

[131] As mentioned previously, only the *Philodoxus* is known to have been published in Salamanca during Rojas' sojourn. However, there may well have been others available to him, either imported (like Petrarch) or printed in Spain and since lost. That he knew of the existence of the genre is certain since fragments of a number of such plays are included in the Latin school anthology entitled *Margarita poética* which was in his library. For its possible influence on *La Celestina,* see Chap. VIII, n. 67. In the same tradition was the curious "dramatization" of a current event (the attempt on King Ferdinand's life) by Carlo and Marcelino Verardi: the *Fernandus seruatus,* Rome, 1493. According to Menéndez Pelayo, the hybrid generic designation of the 21-act *Celestina* as a *tragicomedia* may have been derived therefrom (*Orígenes,* p. 291).

[132] In addition to Castro Guisasola, see M. J. Ruggerio, *The Evolution of the Go-Between in Spanish Literature through the Sixteenth Century,* Berkeley and Los Angeles, 1966 (for the tradition within which both Cota and Rojas displayed their originality) and Elisa Aragone's introduction to her edition of the *Diálogo,* Florence, 1961, pp. 48-54 (for a more complete survey of specific borrowings).

Encina, are all present.[133] *La Celestina* is not only a timeless masterpiece; it is also—or was also—integrated into the literary and intellectual life of its age, a book written in a society and a decade in which reading was no longer a ritual and not yet a habit.

These considerations will also help us understand Rojas' peculiar way of incorporating what he had read into what he was writing. *La Celestina*'s shameless mosaic of borrowings from sources presumably known to his readers, as well as the author's confidence that the oral expressiveness of his style could rejuvenate and refreshen them, are both phenomena of transition. The *Don Quixote*, as a prodigious masterpiece of written words, was self-conscious about its borrowings and about its own printed condition. But *La Celestina*, composed entirely of speech, is natural in its irresponsible quotation. That is to say, it could borrow from another orally composed text as freely and unproblematically as one ballad does from another—or as one lecturer from another. The difference, of course, between Rojas' practice and that of a folk poet is that the former, as we have seen and shall see again, was well aware of how to exploit the irony which the incrustation of stolen commonplaces into specific dialogue situations allowed. Aside from this—as Menéndez Pidal was the first to point out[134]—the oral prosist and the oral poet work in the same way. Or, to look at the same thing from another point of view: if today it is customary to stress the disparity between erudition and life, Rojas' Salamanca recognized no such impassable gulf. The result (as Mrs. Malkiel observes)[135] is the singular vulnerability of *La Celestina* to anachronistic criticism and misinterpretation. Even Menéndez Pelayo thought Rojas' use of Petrarch to be "pedantic" and the closing orations, "affected." The first task of a teacher of *La Celestina* is precisely this: to provide comprehension of an age of transition in which borrowed learning was a component of spoken life.

Don Ramón, of course, was concerned to stress the oral nature of Rojas' creation in order to solve in his own fashion the classical problem of *La Celestina*'s unity. And he was right. Only by think-

---

[133] Only the last two need annotation. For Reinosa see n. 101, and, for Juan del Encina, see C. Real de la Riva, "Notas a *La Celestina*," *Strenae* (Homage to Manuel García Blanco), Salamanca, 1962, pp. 387-391.

[134] "La lengua en tiempo de los reyes católicos," *Cuadernos Hispanoamericanos* (Madrid), no. 40, 1950.

[135] *La originalidad*, pp. 130 ff.

ing in terms of the *romancero* and the epic, can we begin to understand how separate authors could collaborate so intimately. In this sense it might be said that Act I was at once the most important and the most completely assimilated source of *La Celestina*. But, in addition to the peculiar ability of the oral artist to graft himself into another's creation, we must also accept as a fact (or at least as a strong probability) that Act I was as much a university product as those that follow. Salamanca was where Rojas "found" it, and Salamanca was where one learned to cite Aristotle and the other authorities admired by its speakers. Both authors were nurtured in the same academic hothouse and roughly in the same decade, since internal evidence (despite the supposed archaism of certain words and expressions) indicates that the original fragment was written after 1490.[136] It was this community of training and inter-

[136] The first edition of the *Crónica troyana* containing a pen portrait of Helen of Troy that is the direct source for Calisto's description of Melibea appeared in 1490. I do not deny the obvious fact (insisted on by Mrs. Malkiel, *La originalidad*, p. 449, and Otis Green, "On Rojas' Description of Melibea," *HR*, XIV, 1946) that the *Celestina* passage is ordered according to a conventional medieval pattern and that it is made up of conventional rhetorical comparisons. However, a number of specific verbal coincidences indicate beyond reasonable doubt that the author of Act I had this particular lady in mind. In both cases their "cabellos" resemble "madexas de oro"; they are of great "longura" and are divided by a part or "pequeña cerda" (an apparently unfamiliar usage of the word which suggests Sempronio's comic "essos tales no serán cerdas de asno" and which is corrected in Pero Núñez Delgado's Seville, 1509 revision to "carrera"). Then come the eyebrows which for both Melibea and Helen are "delgadas"; the noses, "no grande ni pequeña" in one case and "mediana," in the other; the "little" mouths; the teeth which are "menudos"; the lips which are "colorados"; the fingers which are "luengos"; the breasts which are "pequeñas"; and the complexions each as snowlike as the other. Admittedly many of these adjectives are topical (the first two are not), and, again admittedly, the imitator abbreviates the original and makes changes ("labrios grosezuelos" instead of "delgados" and "uñas coloradas" instead of "de marfil") according to his personal taste. But the overall coincidence of words and sequence is nonetheless decisive. The attribution is further supported by Calisto's closing remark: "Aquella proporción que ver no pude, no sin duda por el bulto de fuera juzgo incomparable ser mejor, que la que París juzgó entre las tres Deesas." Here his reference seems to be to an earlier chapter of the same *Crónica* in which Paris "respondió que no podia dar verdadero juyzio de aquel fecho si ellas todas tres no se presentassen desnudas ante él para que las viese y con la vista esaminase por todas las faciones de sus cuerpos." The origin of the description is evidently Guido delle Colonne's *Historia Destructionis Troiae* (ed. N. E. Griffin, Cambridge, Mass., 1936, pp. 71-72), of which the earliest extant manuscript translation in Castilian (*La Crónica*

ests that brought the two minds close enough together to enable a continuous flow of dialogue to cross from one to another.

A final factor, not susceptible to proof but, to me, virtually certain, would be the further community of caste. It is possible and

---

troyana, ed. F. P. Norris, Chapel Hill, 1970) dates from the end of the fourteenth century. That the author of Act I used the printed version is apparent from a number of small but conclusive details. Only there is the part referred to as a *cerda;* only there is the *longura* of the hair mentioned; and only there are the eyebrows *delgadas.*

Menéndez Pelayo was aware of the resemblance of the two descriptions but since he had seen only the word-for-word plagiarism which concludes the 1501 Valladolid *Tristán de Leonís,* he found it difficult to account for chronologically: "No dudo que también la tuvo presente el autor de la *Celestina"* (*Orígenes,* p. 333). Apparently the writer of this version of the *Tristram* romance (quite unlike the ironical and skeptical author of Act I) saw in the passage a bravura amplification of medieval rhetorical description which would provide him with a closing flourish and a physical justification of the tragic love affair.

I have not been able to examine the original Burgos, 1490 edition of the *Crónica troyana* and have had to rely on a microfilm of the Pamplona, 1500 reimpression in the British Museum. Pero Núñez Delgado's edited version is in the Ticknor collection.

It should further be noted that Rojas recognized the source of the description—as is indicated in Act VI when he has Calisto remark: "Si oy fuera viva Elena . . ." He also understood the ironical intent of the comparison. Although Mrs. Malkiel sees in *La Celestina's* classical references merely a "repositorio didáctico" (*La originalidad,* p. 337), the vision of Melibea as Helen, of Calisto as "en esfuerço Etor," and of the assault on her virtue as the siege of Troy ("Más fuerte estaba Troya") function as a way of exposing by contrast the tawdry, sordid, and ineffectual aspects of the love affair. As in the case of Galdós' Orbajosa, classical models recurrent in the dialogue are betrayed by human existence.

A second indication of the proximity in date of Act I emerges from Menéndez Pidal's observation that Rojas' mistaken reading of Erosístrato in the Act I manuscript as "Eras y Crato," later corrected to "Hipócrates y Galeno," resulted from his ignorance of an anecdote in Valerius Maximus' *Dictorum factorumque memorabilium exempla,* first translated in 1495 (*Antología de prosistas,* Buenos Aires, 1951, pp. 58-59). This, however, is less decisive since the author of Act I could have read it in one of the many Latin editions printed in the 70's and 80's. His Latin was certainly up to the task, since his translations of Seneca seem to be his own. As far as I can see, they do not proceed from available printed versions of Pérez de Guzmán and Alonso de Cartagena.

To return to Rojas, it is possible that he remembered his youthful puzzlement and recognized his error when he read the Erosístrato anecdote either in his copy of *Los Triumphos de Apiano,* Valencia, 1522, or in his translation of Petrarch's *I trionfi,* Logroño, 1512, where it is referred to in that of Love.

even probable that Rojas knew the identity of his predecessor,[137] but, in any case, the feigned and significantly tardy speculation that he might be either "Cota or Mena with their great knowledge" indicates awareness of similar origins. These assumptions (that the author of Act I was another *converso* educated in Salamanca) are the best rebuttal I can offer to those who interpret the dual authorship as a demonstration of Rojas' "unreality." Both men, precisely because of the social and intellectual circumstances they shared, led lives that were highly conscious and painfully real. On the other hand, neither this nor any other attempt at comprehending the mystery of their collaboration (which is to say of their shared irony) should lead to diminished admiration of its marvel.

To sum up, the Salamanca of Fernando de Rojas was not only an intellectual haven, not only a milieu of intense historical innovation; it also represented what, in more than one way, was the highest cultural level ever reached by an oral society. The printing press had not yet diluted or blurred the edges of language. Nor had it yet created a public capable of limiting literary creation by habitual expectations: this is a novel; this is a drama. But it had, in the two decades of its effective existence in Spain, multiplied many times the possibilities of literary experience. Even more it had given that very important kind of experience an intensity, a sense of novelty, and a sudden self-consciousness which it had hardly possessed before. Here was a world in which neither reader nor writer had explored the limits and exigencies of creation in words.

---

[137] I so suppose primarily because of the proximity of the dates established above. But there is another minor anomaly in Act I which indicates that Rojas had some awareness of his predecessor's plans for completion, an awareness which perhaps indicates his possession of other unrevealed information. That Erosístrato is the correct reading for Rojas' Eras y Crato is a certainty in view of the reference to Seleucus (the royal father who relinquished his bride to an older son by another marriage in order to cure him of lovesickness) which follows. And if that is so, the phrase "plebérico corazón" must refer to Pleberio—which is surprising since his name is not mentioned in Act I. Rojas himself neither could have understood the reference and then gone on to use the name nor could he have inserted it after naming Melibea's father. Both these alternatives depend on knowledge of the Erosístrato anecdote— knowledge which he did not have. Therefore, the unknown first author must have intended to use the name from the beginning. And Rojas must have learned of that intention from some source outside the text, possibly by word of mouth, possibly by a summary of the plan of the work such as the "Argumento de toda la obra."

334

For example, it was not yet known that speech must be decorous, time, consequential, and actions, motivated in conventional ways. But it was also a world in which both parties were deeply excited by the newly perceived possibilities of writing, possibilities which it seemed were open to anyone who had been trained in the arts of speech.

A comparison with the America of Hernán Cortés may be helpful—however farfetched. Cruelty and greed aside, it can be fairly maintained that the conquests of Mexico, Peru, Chile and the rest represented the highest expression of the chivalric way of life. Which is essentially to propose that they were only possible for people unaware of the limitations of heroism. The first years after the discovery of America and the discovery of the printing press were unique moments in military and literary history. They had in common a quality of adventure, of limitless new possibilities for inherited ways. For an unknown student at Salamanca to dare to write and to succeed in creating *La Celestina* and for his classmate to dare to attack and to succeed in conquering Tenochtitlán, are exploits of comparable incredibility.

❧ "Listen to Aristotle"

We have already alluded to the revolutionary change in point of view which accompanied Rojas' university experience. To go from the *Puebla* de Montalbán to the *Universidad* de Salamanca, we said, was to leave a world of particulars for a world of universals, the only world in which it was possible to create *La Celestina*. In saying this, we referred less to the academic "fountains of philosophy" and the erudite references which are woven into the argumentative texture of the work than to its consistent treatment of individuals, localities, events, and momentary estimations from the kind of distance that is implied in the expression, "higher learning." The opportunity to compile a sardonic commonplace book was less important than ascension to a philosophical view of life—than becoming, like the author of Act I, a "great philosopher." Thus, the style of *La Celestina*—meaning by style not just rhetoric but what Ortega called a "posture towards life"—is profoundly Salamancan. A Rodrigo de Cota or an Antón de Montoro, "the clothes-dealer," tried to use the fifteenth-century tradition of court poetry in order

335

to give objective form to their experiences as *conversos* and as men. But the distance, the perspective into themselves and into life provided by this shallow tradition, was insufficient. With the partial exception of the *Diálogo entre el amor y un viejo,* neither poet ever did more than to convert his outbursts into brilliant occasional pieces. *La Celestina,* on the other hand, thanks to its author's years at Salamanca, contemplates a wider and more complex landscape of life from a higher elevation: from the altitude of "philosophical" meditation. It is in this ambitious sense that Rojas referred to his predecessor as a "great philosopher" and not as a great writer or great author. And, he surely aspired, despite his professions of modesty, to no less an honor for himself.

Scholarly elevation, of course, is not in itself a virtue or a prerequisite for literary value. The infinitely inferior *Repetición de amores* was written by one of Rojas' classmates for the same listeners and treats comparable subject matter in a comparable style. Nevertheless, as in the case of the University's oral sense of language, training in meditation, if not a cause, was at least a condition of *La Celestina*'s peculiar greatness. Discussion of Fernando de Rojas' years at Salamanca would be incomplete, accordingly, without some understanding of the philosophical views there available. What kind of a great philosopher might he have hoped to be?

To begin with, although Stoicism (particularly Seneca as studied, translated and preached by "el Tostado," Fernán Perez de Guzmán, and Alonso de Cartagena) was increasingly renascent, Aristotle was still "the philosopher" in Salamanca.[138] But far from confronting each other in rivalry, coexistence of the two was easy. Moral philosophy, after all, was directed to the will of an individ-

---

[138] In chap. xviii of *La visión deleitable,* Understanding, guided by Truth and Reason, enters the house of Nature. There she is seen sitting on her throne with a panoply of courtiers, natural philosophers all, at her feet. And in the very center is "el filósofo," Aristotle. Nor was he to lose this pre-eminence. In the course of the 16th century as his works became known more directly and closely, he made incursions into the realm of moral philosophy with the teaching of the *Nicomachean Ethics.* Hence, Quevedo's 1638 complaint that Stoicism had all but disappeared "no solo en el vulgo siempre rudo, pero aun entre los que encanezen en las universidades." See Arnold Rothe, *Quevedo und Seneca,* Cologne, 1965, pp. 22-23. For a recent general appreciation of Aristotle's importance in the times of Rojas, see Michael Levey, *Early Renaissance,* Middlesex, 1967.

ual reader or listener, while natural—meaning Aristotelian—philosophy dealt in reason. One has to choose or be persuaded to take his Stoic medicine, but how to think in syllogisms and how to understand nature as a complex chain of cause and effect has to be learned. We may imagine then individual students reading Seneca and Petrarch and excitedly discussing the brand-new incunabula which contained their doctrine, while in class Aristotle continued to be the central text, the very substance of their apprenticeship in reason and disputation. As a University, Salamanca was necessarily founded on Aristotelian methods of recognizing and using truth, and at the same time, it provided an intellectual climate which favored independent moral reflection.

The complementary character of the two "schools" is nowhere more evident than in *La Celestina*.[139] Individual characters speak of their problems and situations in terms of Seneca and Petrarch: one must arm oneself against Fortune; one must keep one's passions under control; and all the rest. And, at the same time, as is evident in *Argument of the Whole* (a summary of the action appearing at the beginning), all are caught in a remorseless chain of cause and effect, a chain which, in spite of their good resolutions, they are unable to evade or control. The initial cause is love: "Haven't you read the philosopher," Sempronio remarks in Act I, "where he says, Just as matter desires form, so woman desires man."[140] And once the natural course of events is set into motion nothing—neither social decorum nor individual armor—can stop it.

[139] The fact, observed by Castro Guisasola, that frequent citations of Aristotle in Act I are replaced in Rojas' acts by Petrarch as the most audible authority should not be understood as denying this conclusion. In both parts, as I try to show above, natural and moral philosophy are complementary. Seneca is the spokesman for the latter in Act I.

[140] Also in Act I Celestina impresses Pármeno with a—to us—amusingly pompous Aristotelian argument: love ("el soberano deleyte") is natural and biologically necessary for the preservation of the species ("la humana especie"). The argument loses its picaresque charm, however, when at the end we come to understand the fatal consequences of this natural law. As *La Celestina* proceeds toward its inexorable conclusion, our initial enjoyment of the mock Aristotelianism of Celestina (and Sempronio above) seems hideously superficial. Both of them doomed by the inevitable sequence of amorous cause and effect, the truth they announce is more grim than they or the reader realize at the time. There is in these initial flirtings with Aristotle an irony not only of event but of tone appropriate to an authentic *tragicomedia*.

337

Although overt references to Aristotle are more frequent in Act I than in those following, Rojas allows his characters on other key occasions to glimpse the implacable ordering of their lives. One occurs in Act II when Pármeno (just taken over by Rojas and not yet fully drawn into the destructive course of events) sums up for his master all that has taken place up to that point: "Losing your falcon was the cause of your entering Melibea's garden to ask for it, which entrance caused you to see her and speak to her. From speech love was engendered, and love in its turn gave birth to grief. And grief will cause you to lose your body and soul and fortune."[141] Or again, after the action is all over, Pleberio is granted a more profound moment of insight. He "laments . . . the disastrous cause of Melibea's death" and comes to the terrible realization that he, his daughter, her lover, and even Celestina and the servants are victims of the order of nature.[142] They have fallen like leaves. But only when free from the toils of the plot, do the speakers so sense their doom. At other times they confide in an illusion of free choice or in Stoic maxims which they seem incapable of relating adequately to the truth of their ailing lives.

It goes without saying that Fernando de Rojas' creative knowledge of human behavior was deeper and more subtle than anything he could have learned at the University of Salamanca—or, for that matter, than anything to be found in the writings of Aristotle and all his commentators. Nevertheless the intentional shape of *La Celestina* was Aristotelian, for only in these terms could its author explain to himself its structure as a consequential machine of happening progressing from initial cause to ultimate effect.[143] As for

[141] For further discussion of how "Rojas se complace en ajustar causas y consecuencias recorriendo sin cesar su bien urdida tela, y mentalmente, en el recuerdo o la imaginación, repasa el encadenamiento perfecto de los hechos," see *La originalidad*, p. 235.

[142] As Pleberio discovers—with the listener or reader alongside—in *La Celestina* the concept of natural order so consoling to other "philosophers" is fearfully ironic. From the individual point of view it represents the most abominable disorder. Moral philosophy has run headlong into natural philosophy and both are undone—as we shall see in the chapter to follow.

[143] See Groethuysen's *Philosophische Antropologie* (cited previously, Chap. IV, n. 71), p. 40:

I can explain why every detail exists and what it means in relation to the whole; I can conceive of the whole and interpret everything within it as a significant integrating element. Everything is susceptible to explanation if we

the reader, it is his responsibility—and Pleberio will remind him of it, if in the course of his reading he should become carried away —to be aware of the fatal relationship of the parts to the whole. The overall irony of *La Celestina* would perhaps have pleased Aristotle as much or more than that of Sophocles. It is based not just on foreknowledge of what is fated but also on an incredibly detailed understanding (hidden from the speakers) of how each tiny step towards destruction is inevitable. From the vantage point of reason, we overhear a world of unreason and are led to comprehend its most intimate workings. In this sense, *La Celestina* is a profoundly rational work. Reason is as much or more a condition of its being as it is of any French seventeenth-century drama—although Corneille's or Molière's notions of the faculty might not coincide with Rojas'. The Spanish work does not necessarily recommend reasonableness (Pleberio seems to be the most reasonable member of the cast) nor does it base its catastrophe on the admirably heroic unreason of its characters. Rather it peeks with dispassionate intelligence and sardonic irony inside the irrationality of human lives, and it records in the greatest possible detail the inexorable logic of their doom. And in Spain at the end of the fifteenth century the only place offering such a vantage point was the University of Salamanca.

---

start with the whole, the total concept, the contemplation of the larger form. Everything then becomes embraceable. Each thing belongs to another and all to the whole.

This criterion is systematically applied by Aristotle everywhere. Whether it is a work of man or a product of nature . . . , the individual can be understood only if seen in terms of the whole. . . .

Aristotle is concerned with the philosophical elaboration of human experience but always in terms of the whole sphere of human experience and with a continuing aspiration not to leave anything out, not to misplace anything.

The careful student of *La Celestina* will remember therein a similar preoccupation with and view of the whole in relation to the parts. As Rojas says, the best reader is the one who knows how to "coligir la suma": that is, how to integrate "las particularidades" not into a story ("los huesos que no tienen virtud, que es la historia toda junta") but into a meaningful structure. Rojas clearly did not aspire to *be* the new Aristotle of his Spain (in the fashion of his fellow townsman, caste member, and student, the physician and natural scientist Francisco Hernández—see Chap. V, n. 53), but, while presiding over his cast of voices, we should think of him listening as he believed Aristotle might have listened.

Portrayal of Salamanca as a citadel of reason in a country and an age more characteristically devoted to passion, fanaticism, and heroism brings together two central threads of our hidden biography. In our discussion of the times of Rojas we commented first on the horror story told to each new *converso* in the course of growing up, and then we passed on to significant kinds of reaction to the fearfully discovered historical situation. Perhaps the most typical of these reactions (precisely because of its deep roots in the past) was reliance on reason for a practical understanding of the human condition. The natural result was that commented on at the beginning of this chapter: *conversos* from all over Spain flocked to Salamanca and later to Alcalá. There they could obtain the degrees that would enable them to get ahead in the world; there, as we have seen, they could find surcease from the suspicious eyes of their home towns; and there, above all, they found their own traditionally rational approach to problems respected and cultivated professionally. We have already mentioned the student authors Francisco de Villalobos, whose *Sumario de Medicina* (1498) is a somewhat brash effort to propagate medical common sense in a superstitious profession,[144] Luis de Lucena with his commonplace denunciation of feminine irrationality, and Alfonso de la Torre, whose curious allegorization of Maimonides' *La visión deleitable,* gave contemporary academic relevance to the older rational tradition.[145] We should now add that of Rodrigo Basurto whose *De*

---

[144] In a letter to his father written in the same year, Villalobos, defending Avicenna, expresses himself about contemporary practice of medicine with a rational skepticism that reminds us of a more recent century. In closing—curiously enough—he makes the first known reference to a folkloric figure later made famous by another physician: ". . . todas estas son, en mi sentir, falsas invenciones acreditadas por los que corren detrás de los charlatanes como los carneros de Panurgo . . ." (*Algunas obras*, p. 120). As a man of reason, Villalobos—like his *socio*, Fernando de Rojas—was also acutely aware of the ambiguities and mutations of human life beneath the deceitful definition called character. Typically, he writes to his Flemish friend, Jufré: ". . . así que vos . . . soys compuesto de diversas maneras . . ." (p. 9). And again in an earlier letter: "Vos soys amigo de buenos y amigo de ruynes, diligente y floxarrón, muy cuerdo y muy loco . . ." (p. 1).

[145] Typical of the book is its dismissal of the Goths as "bestial," its attack on prejudice and "passión" as blinding to reason, and its dislike of those realms of human life known as history and custom. The author is particularly concerned with all forms of irrational change (just as is Rojas in the Prologue), the most obvious being changes in styles of dress (p. 391). Against such as

natura loci et temporis (Salamanca, 1494) contains a brilliant explication of the Aristotelian theory of time and motion that is directly applicable (as Dorothy Severin has shown)[146] to their presentation in *La Celestina*. These names, however, are merely a few of the most prominent of the long list of *converso* bachelors, licentiates, and doctors who passed through Salamanca as an indispensable step in their new-fashioned careers in administration or who stayed on to become distinguished members of the faculty. In spite of all its turmoil and bellicosity, the opportunities offered by Salamanca must to some of these men have seemed an earthly approximation of de la Torre's "Paradise of Reason": "Here it was never night and everything was clear day and the sun shone seven times more bright than usual, without obstacle or impediment of clouds . . . and it was admirable that there should be so much clarity without excessive heat. . . ."[147]

At this juncture a brief return to the sociological point of view may be useful. Thorsten Veblen, wondering why "the Jewish people have contributed much more than an even share to the intellectual life of modern Europe," comes to the foregone conclusion that racial factors have little to do with the matter. Instead, as we saw Robert Ezra Park suggesting, it is the Jewish penchant for creative marginality that seems to be responsible:

> The intellectually gifted Jew is in a peculiarly fortunate position in respect of this requisite immunity from the inhibitions of intellectual quietism. But he can come in for such immunity only at the cost of losing his secure place in the scheme of conventions into which he has been born, and at the cost, also, of finding no similarly secure place in that scheme of gentile conventions into which he is thrown. For him as for other men in the like case, the skepticism that goes to make him an effectual factor in the increase and diffusion of knowledge among men involves a loss of that peace of mind that is the

---

these right reason is the only bulwark: ". . . bien me place ser desnudo de toda fantástica opinión, et no me moverá más la verdad dicha por boca de cristiano que del judío o moro o gentil, si verdades sean todas, ni negaré menos la falsía dicha por la boca de uno que por la boca de otro" (p. 352).

[146] *Memory in "La Celestina"* (London, 1970).

[147] p. 352.

birthright of the safe and sane quietist. He becomes a disturber of the intellectual peace, but only at the cost of becoming an intellectual wayfaring man, a wanderer in the intellectual no-man's-land, seeking another place to rest, farther along the road, somewhere over the horizon. They are neither a complaisant nor contented lot, these aliens of the uneasy feet; but that, after all, is not the point in question.[148]

Veblen goes on to indicate that this intellectual eminence—exactly as in the case of our *converso* graduates in Roman law and Christian theology (medicine being an obvious exception)—was exercised in gentile fields and disciplines. Lacking the conventional and traditional preconceptions of his gentile rivals ("the inertia of habit"), the "gifted young Jew still flexible in his mental habits" can more easily excel. Or, as we have just concluded, it was the *converso* situation which enabled those whose existence it defined to derive so much from Salamanca.[149]

The gradual replacement of the Marlovian *conversos* (the Caballerías, the Arias Dávilas, the Toledan rebel Fernando de la Torre, the Comendador Juan de Baena, or Amador de los Ríos' favorite "great character," the Saragossan, Ximeno Gordo)[150] who had dominated the fifteenth century, by this ever increasing class of university trained intellectuals is a phenomenon not less true because it has never been attended to by historians.[151] As we have

---

[148] *Essays on our Changing Order*, New York, 1934, p. 227.

[149] Castro would, of course, rightly insist that Spain with its eminent Jewish tradition, its division into *castas*, and its Old Christian suspicion of all forms of intellectual labor represented a special and aggravated case of such pre-eminence. As far as *converso* excellence in legal studies is concerned, Baer goes so far as to suggest that jurisprudence "came easily" to *conversos* as a result of their "training in Talmudic dialectics" (*History*, ii, 273). It is a possibility which perhaps better applies to the tradition behind Rojas than to his own pre-University education.

[150] Speaking of the political power of Aragonese *conversos* just prior to the Inquisition, Amador de los Ríos remarks: "Y esta preponderancia, que así se refería a las regiones superiores de la gobernación y de la nobleza como a las más llanas y populares del municipio y de la gente menuda, daba ocasión y aliento al desarrollo de grandes caracteres . . ." (p. 670). In a sense, the following generation, that of Rojas, was also composed of great characters—but deprived of recognition and forced to substitute a carefully studied role and a compensating vocation.

[151] Domínguez Ortiz and Caro Baroja are primarily sociological in orienta-

seen, adventurers, royal favorites, and municipal rebels had to make way for professional men, men of reason and ordered careers better suited to the new century and the new nation. But, as we have also seen, neither university degrees nor a more pacific group image erased the suspicion and resentment of their Old Christian neighbors. The access of these new *conversos* to invisible and rationalized sources of financial and legal power was perhaps even more intolerable to minds conditioned by the frontier than had been the presumption, arrogance, and turbulence of their fathers and grandfathers. Thus, the stony brains of Laín Calvo and Nuño Rasura typically attribute the social, commercial, and official success of the busy *conversos* not to cultivation of reason (of which they have no notion) but to hereditary and dishonest *agudeza* or sharpness.[152]

Another reaction not necessarily infected with anti-Semitism was to deride what could not be understood. The know-it-all wordy Bachelor of the sort represented by Don Quixote's rival, Sansón Carrasco, became a minor comic type, and reference to Salamancan pompousness and hair splitting was a frequent source of laughter. But ridicule, even at its most biting, was less significant and dangerous than hatred. In general it can be said that the status proud *conversos* who graduated in ever greater numbers, took posts on the front line of one of the most bitter of the intra-mural struggles of the Spanish Renaissance: the struggle between the intelligentsia (I hasten to admit the anachronism) and the resentful society it served.

Indications of a peculiarly bellicose commitment to enlightenment are frequent in the writings of educated *conversos* and are more interesting for our purposes than Old Christian antagonism. If the *converso* intellectual lived in a world which tended to regard him resentfully, suspiciously, or mockingly, his disdain for his ignorant neighbors provided a measure of retaliation. In a 1521 letter, referring to certain participants in the "Comunidades" rebellion against Charles V, Villalobos asks, "How can barbarians and wage earners who have never had the use of reason be made to

---

tion while Castro, Márquez, and Sicroff have observed the matter historically either from wider or narrower perspectives than mine.

[152] For the commonplace of Jewish *agudeza*, see Chap. III, n. 17.

listen to it?"[153] And in his famous letter attacking the anti-*converso* prejudice of the Franciscans, he remarks that many members of the order don't know enough Latin to say Mass, "and some of them are so stupid and rude that they can hardly understand Spanish." In general they are "passionate, unworthy, moronic, brutes of low extraction," the offspring of "ignorant peasants" who bite enviously at any *converso* who rises in the hierarchy of the Church because of his studies and abilities. In the same way Juan de Lucena in his *De vita felici* mourns for "men of genius and excellent doctrine" who are ignored and forgotten while the King sends as his ambassadors veritable "trotters who if they can't speak, bray in Spanish."[154] In his *Hortatory Epistle on Letters* written in the 1490's, Lucena anticipates one of the major complaints of the Erasmists and other sixteenth-century reformers. Those who pray in Latin without understanding it are "two footed donkeys." "They neither pray nor bray in their own language; they neither understand themselves nor, in my opinion, does God understand them, for God only understands the speech of the heart."[155]

In view of such feelings as these, we need not be surprised that one of the most frequent counter-charges made by Inquisition victims against their accusers (the trial of Fray Luis de León is full of such references) is failure, through stupidity and ignorance, to understand the meaning of what they report. The *converso* felt himself surrounded by a world that was not only malicious but also, as they said, so barbarous and thick-headed that it was almost impossible to deal with. María Cazalla, in the trial already referred to,[156] reacts spontaneously after hearing one of the accusations read

---

[153] "El Almirante . . . haze cartas más elegantes que Séneca y Tulio, las quales leydas en púlpito . . . la gente baxa e menuda . . . entienden los primores y sutilezas dellas como las ouejas y las uacas entendían los altos versos que les cantaba la sibila. No sé como se podrán someter a razón los jornaleros y báruaros que nunca tuuieron uso de razón humana" (*Algunas obras*, p. 53). For the letter on the Franciscans, see pp. 165-179.

[154] *Opúsculos literarios*, p. 160. Much of the dialogue of the nascent theater (particularly that of Torres Naharro) furnishes striking testimony of scorn for the speech of Old Christian peasants.

[155] *Ibid.*, p. 213.

[156] Melgares Marín, *Procedimientos*, I, 117. A note of exasperated impatience with "ignorantes de mala vida" is everywhere present in her lengthy defense. Her description of the adverse witnesses taken as a group is typical: ". . . son solos o singulares, varios e inconstantes, confusos . . . contrarios en si mismos . . . deponen de oídas y vanas creencias, y no dan razón de sus dichos deponen

to her and cries out, "only a person of torpid and dull understanding could have said such a thing." And Raimundo González de Montes, whose *Artes de la Inquisizión* is loaded with such disdain[157] concludes with this apostrophe: "Oh one thousand times detestable barbarousness! Since you cannot restore what you have destroyed, how can you repay the world for the clear lights [of reason] you have extinguished?"[158] If the nineteenth century saw the Inquisition historically as a force of reaction, Montes sees it rather as a kind of army of unreason at war with intelligence.

Merely to have taken a degree at Salamanca did not in itself enlist one in the ranks of reason. To be given a commission by the defending forces one had to choose the right side. *Converso* polemicists were specially scornful of Old Christian graduates who opposed their interests. Fernán Díaz de Toledo attacks the Bachelor Marcos García de Moyos (the "Marquillos de Mazarambros" who had instigated the first "sentencia estatuto" in Toledo) in these words: "He is of villainous descent from the village of Mazarambros" and he would be well advised to go back there and return to the customary occupations of his lineage: "digging and plowing and grafting grape shoots."[159] There is a bitterness and

---

con odio; juzgan . . . por congeturas y pareceres" (p. 112). Similar feelings of frustration at the stupidity of witnesses and accusations appear from time to time in the replies of Fray Francisco Ortiz. One witness is referred to as a "neciarronazo" and "simplonazo" (Selke, *El Santo Oficio*, p. 193) and the words of another are described as "habladas por infinitivo, que es lengua de negros" (p. 269). See also Caro Baroja, I, 447.

[157] Two random examples will be sufficient. On one occasion he describes the monks of San Isidoro as sleeping "el sueño profundo de la ignorancia en medio de aquella inveterada superstición" (p. 267). On another, he remembers with pleasure Dr. Constantino de la Fé saying to his Inquisitors: "que eran más a propósito para andar de arrieros con tres o cuatro burros, i que esto les estaría mejor que arrogarse la censura de una fe que tan torpemente ignoraban . . ." (p. 279).

[158] p. 330.

[159] *Contra algunos zizañadores*, p. 201. Elsewhere Marquillos is referred to as being of "baja sangre pastoril." Here is a combination of intellectual scorn and class antagonism so widespread as fully to confirm Castro's views of "la edad conflictiva." From the point of view of "naturales de Toledo" Mazarambros was a particularly despicable *nación*, a hamlet of "jornaleros de açadón" where—according to the *Relaciones*—no *hidalgos* or *caballeros* deigned to live and "los dos escrivanos mueren de hambre." Another expression of the view that Old Christians were unsuitable for education is Montes' description of Cardinal Siliceo as a "doltish bishop who without virtue or

hopelessness in these champions of reason which is missing in the *philosophes* of the Enlightenment. We can sense in the violence of their remarks that the battle is going badly and will ultimately be lost. The so-called pessimism of *La Celestina* is, in the last analysis, the antithesis of eighteenth-century optimism: it is the pessimism of reason's last long battle of attrition.[160]

However, we must avoid oversimplification. If, as I believe, a sense of self as a doomed paladin of reason is indeed expressed in *La Celestina,* it is in disguise. As we shall see in the following chapter, it was unthinkable that Rojas should present in his dialogue the complex and tense relations of *conversos* to Old Christians. In the absence of the novel as we know it today, the only genre that could express such problems was the person-to-person poetry of the *cancioneros.* Fiction—and in this Bataillon is correct—was not social but moral, with the result that Rojas expressed his social anguish and his pessimism in terms of a traditionally moral struggle: the struggle of reason not with external unreason but with the inner passion of love. In this sense, *La Celestina* may be thought of as a kind of last major offensive undertaken by the negative in the tired debate on women and love in which Spanish intellectuals had been engaged for some sixty years.[161] It is difficult today to estimate the degree of serious preoccupation of those who took part in the anti-feminist polemic of fifteenth-century Spain. When Sempronio remarks to Calisto in Act I, "Consider the pea brains which women carry underneath their high thin toques," we may surmise that

---

education rose from plow and clods . . ." (p. 310). See also Caro Baroja, II, 278.

[160] Emblematic of reason's defeat in Spain were the weird scenes of exorcism at Charles II's deathbed in 1699. Two hundred years after *La Celestina*'s ironical presentation of its protagonist's magic, the most arrant superstition had effectively taken possession of national life. Witchdoctors had replaced such men as Villalobos. Thus, it can be said that a Feijóo not only relied on the rationalism of neighboring nations but also revived the defeated campaigning of a host of forgotten *conversos.*

[161] In spite of infinite antecedents in classical and Christian traditions, this particular polemic got under way in prose with the completion of the *Corbacho* in 1438 and in verse with the appearance of Pere Torrellas' celebrated *Coplas de maldezir* in the *Cancionero de Estúñiga* 20 years later. Torrellas' Aristotelian verses, "Muger es un animal / que se dize imperfecto . . ." are repeated as a commonplace by Sempronio: "Que sometes la dignidad del hombre a la imperfección de la flaca muger."

author, reader, and listeners enjoyed the lightheartedness of the reference to the Aristotelian doctrine (a doctrine central to the whole debate) of feminine irrationality.

To a great extent the quarrel had become a topical routine of standardized arguments and ready-made lists of virtuous and vicious women which could be either repeated pompously or—if one was a disrespectful scholar—paraphrased frivolously. Here was a variety of unreason which by its very nature provoked humor, which could be safely used in half-mocking disputations and repetitions. On the other hand, beneath this level we shall observe in *La Celestina* a deep and authentic concern with the erotic impetus not only because it is a "mysterious and terrible deity which poisons and corrupts human life" (Menéndez Pelayo's own moral commitments echo through these words)[162] but also because it is capable of reducing any man to the level of a mindless animal. Love—"enemigo de toda razón"—has a force which experience shows to be invariably greater than the strength of reason's armor. Beneath the level of argumentative commonplaces by the fact and fashion of our creation, we are the cannon fodder of a hopeless war.

The irresistibility of love and the futility of trying to combat its fatal urgency were notions which appeared in such diverse places as the "matière de Bretagne," poems, allegories, sentimental novels, and learned treatises. Fear and reverence for Venus, a goddess as implacable as Fortune or Death, pervaded the whole of the western world. And in that small part of it called Salamanca, where Rojas, perhaps, first learned about and experienced her power, she occupied a large part of everyone's attention. The assembled scholars, precisely because of their professional dedication to reason, spent much time bewailing and discussing the imperious ways of love. More than forty years before Alonso de Madrigal, "el Tostado," a professor still famous in Cervantes' time for his solemn prolixity, composed his *De como al ome es necesario amar*, a treatise recommending resignation, which was much argued about and which seems to have been a source for Act I.[163] Villalobos in his *Sumario*, on the other hand, seemed to take seriously the Ovidian presentation of love as a disease susceptible to therapy.[164] His

---

[162] *Orígenes*, p. 381.   [163] Castro Guisasola, p. 176.
[164] This tradition should be kept separate from that used by Celestina in

medical description of its symptoms sounds almost as if Calisto, himself, had gone to him for treatment. Understanding, Villalobos claims, is deceived by the false testimony of "corrupt imagination" with the result that judgment, strength, wisdom, prudence, and reason itself are all lost. There is a burning fire ("ardentíssimo fuego") in the heart continually fed and brought to white heat by desire. After that, "You will see the patient abandon his daily affairs, his eating, drinking, and sleeping, for grief, sighs, and a thousand follies. He desires solitude, dotes on his own miserable tears, and no one helps him or can help him. . . ."[165] In spite of the fact that the description is topical, we are again tempted to suspect that Villalobos was a member of *La Celestina*'s Salamancan circle of auditors.

A third attitude toward love which Rojas might very well have encountered in Salamanca involved neither hopeless resignation nor clinical prescription but ecstatic surrender. In Act I Pármeno answers Celestina's enticing description of amorous pleasure by comparing her to "those who, basing themselves on opinion instead of logic, founded sects coated with sweet poison in order to capture the will of the weak and who blinded reason by throwing delicious dust into its eyes." The possibility that Pármeno is referring to the so-called *"alumbrados"* (a movement of *converso* illuminati later persecuted by the Inquisition and noted for the special fervor of their fusion of sensuality and spirituality)[166] is supported by the fact that some of their earliest activities may be traced to Salamanca at the beginning of the sixteenth century. In the trial of the priest, the Bachelor Antonio de Medrano,[167] meetings and prose-

---

Act X. For an excellent discussion of the latter (primarily a poetic conceit) see Márquez, *Investigaciones*, pp. 223-224.

[165] *Algunas obras*, pp. 322-323.

[166] More balanced views of the *"alumbrado"* movement as a whole are given by Angela Selke (see the bibliography cited at the end of her *Santo Oficio*) and Bataillon in *Erasmo y España*, chap. IV. By no means in all cases does "abandonment of self to God" result in "moral laxity." Yet in the popular mind, *"alumbramiento"* was indeed equivalent to sexual transgression. One of the earliest references to the movement ("unprintable" according to Menéndez Pelayo) is that of Villalobos in his *Sumario de medecina* (written, as we remember, in Salamanca, in 1498, probably the same year as *La Celestina*): "Los aluminados padescen dolencia / de ser putos . . ." (*Algunas obras*, p. 400).

[167] M. Serrano y Sanz, "Francisca Hernández y el Bachiller Antonio de Medrano," *BRAH*, XLII, 1903.

lytization in Salamanca as far back as 1516 are referred to, and it is quite probable, in view of the hidden continuity of such cults, that his group had predecessors in the city.[168]

The trial of Medrano is particularly suggestive to students of *La Celestina* in that his blasphemous identification of human and divine love is as serious as Calisto's. There would be no point in denying that the conventional rhetoric of the *cancioneros*—the courtly lovers who with a thousand and one conceits "say that their mistresses are their god"—is a source for the initial thesis.[169] Yet at the same time as we read on from act to act we encounter a tacit cult of love that goes beneath verbal extravagance and that may well reflect certain aspects of *alumbramiento*. The priestress or headmistress of the Salamancan coterie was an extraordinary woman called Francisca Hernández, so beautiful and so spiritually and sensually intense, that Medrano and his friends had no hesitation in admitting that "they adored God in her" and that "no saint in heaven could compare with her." She was "holier than Saint Catherine," and she could miraculously "bring flowers to a dry meadow" by walking across it. All this was accompanied by confessions of such unblushing erotic behavior that we are reminded of Sempronio's remark that Calisto wished to "make abominable use" of the very person "he confessed to be God." Items of Francisca Hernández' dress were revered as relics, including a girdle which Medrano actually wore during Mass.[170] Melibea's *cordón* worshipped by Calisto not "because it had touched many relics" but because it had "the power and the virtue of encircling" Melibea's body finds here an historical counterpart. And Melibea, herself, when she speaks of her lover's *visitación*, reminds us of another suspected *alumbrada* reported to have said that "in carnal inter-

[168] Another indication that Salamanca was an early center of *alumbrismo* was the presence there in 1519 of Sor María de Santo Domingo, the much discussed "beata de Piedrahita" who was accustomed to kiss her male adherents "con la mayor sencillez del mundo, sin recatarse" (*Erasmo*, I, 207). It is also suggested that Sor María and Francisca Hernández may have both been active there in that year (*ibid.*, p. 81).

[169] Márquez gives the essential bibliography for this much discussed series of rhetorical substitutions (*Investigaciones*, p. 235).

[170] In the trial of Fray Francisco Ortiz, it is indicated that she had a whole supply of *cintas* and other personal objects which she distributed freely among her admirers—although she claims she did not herself believe in their miraculous powers (Selke, p. 302).

course with her husband she was in closer union with God than during the highest prayer in the world."[171] With such goings on in its midst, no wonder that the defenders of the citadel of reason were preoccupied with love.

A not unrelated sector of unreason or anti-reason at once embraced and wrestled with by Salamancan scholars was magic.[172] Menéndez Pelayo thinks that the legend of the Cave of Salamanca—a kind of continuing underground seminar in the occult limited to seven students—was posterior to the sixteenth century.[173] He may well be right, but the lack of clear distinction between the natural and supernatural sciences made it inevitable that theoreticians and practitioners of magic (traditionally Jews, Moors, or *conversos*) should have gathered in Salamanca. At a time when astrology and astronomy had not yet parted company (after Abraham Zacut's enforced departure, the holder of this prestigious chair was the *converso* Diego de Torres) and when medical theory was still laden with superstition, it would have been difficult to exclude them. Rojas and the author of Act I may well have believed that Celestina's arcane lore was false ("E todo era burla y mentira"), but they were not for that reason less fascinated with her elaborate pretenses.

Many others among these scholarly contemporaries of Doctor Faustus, who were less determinedly skeptical than a Sem Tob, a Rojas, or a Villalobos, were disposed to accept the possibility of magic and to experiment with it. That is to say, to investigate "la razón de la sinrazón." As we remember, of the some 60,000 volumes burned in Salamanca in the early 1490's many had to do with the occult.[174] Even among those who were concerned to reprove

[171] Melgares Marín, *Procedimientos*, I, II.

[172] Closely related, in the sense that love—as in the legend of Tristram and Isolde and ostensibly in *La Celestina*—could be induced by magic. According to Menéndez Pelayo, one of the contemporary explanations of the strange behavior and symptoms of the *alumbrados* was that they were under a magic spell (*Heterodoxos*, II, 189).

[173] *Heterodoxos*, I, 696. Traditionally the Cave was related to the activities of the Marqués de Villena "a partir de 1332" (García Mercadal, p. 181).

[174] The figure is given in a 1623 letter of the Inquisitor Andrés Pacheco "sobre la aprobación de los libros" (C. Pérez Pastor, *Bibliografía madrileña*, Madrid, 1891-1907, III, 442-443). According to Pacheco, these books dealing with "artes vanas y sciencias ilicitas, supersticiones de mágica, y encantamientos" were confiscated from "judíos y los nuevamente convertidos dellos y otras personas."

and condemn occult practices we find a measure of credulity about their effectiveness. Pedro Ciruelo (who departed from Salamanca in 1495 just after Rojas' arrival) provides a relevant example with his *Reprouación de supersticiones* (1497)[175] as does Father Vitoria in his *De arte mágica* which appeared later.[176] According to Cas-

[175] The earliest extant edition is Alcalá, 1530, but there is positive evidence indicating that the *princeps* was Salamanca, 1497. I refer to the listing in the *Inventario de la librería del Sr. D. Lorenzo Ramírez de Prado* (ed. J. de Entrambasaguas, Madrid, 1943): "Maestro Ciruelo contra las hechicerías, Salamanca, 1497" (p. 73). Actually, Ramírez de Prado possessed three editions, one of which, without indication of date, was bound together with *La Celestina.* Justo García Morales in his edition of the Alcalá text (Madrid, 1952) questions the earlier date, but offers no convincing reasons aside from those used to question Rojas' own authorship. That is to say, the fact that at the time Ciruelo had just finished his studies in Salamanca and could not have been much over 20 or 25 years of age. This, of course, leads me to the opposite conclusion: Ciruelo was one more student author of the sort with which we have here been concerned. Salamanca was precisely the place in Rojas' Spain where intellectual excitement and the new possibilities for publication came together. In any case, the coincidence of Celestina's concern with "agüeros" on her first visit to Melibea and Ciruelo's discussion of them is itself an indication of a 1497 edition. Rojas seems to have looked up (or to have just come across) the reproof of those who believe in omens and to have found in it a fitting conclusion for Celestina's alternately valiant and timid monologue: "Todos los agüeros se adereçan favorablemente o yo no sé nada desta arte. Quatro hombres, que he topado, a los tres llaman Juanes e los dos son cornudos. La primera palabra que oy por la calle, fue de achaque de amores. Nunca he tropeçado como otras vezes. Ni perro me ha ladrado ni aue negra he visto, tordo ni cuervo ni otras noturnas" (Act IV). Of these, four are catalogued by Ciruelo: the sight of birds ("el cuervo o la graja o el milano"); the tripping ("cuando el cuerpo del hombre se hace algun movimiento puro natural y se hace a deshora sin pensar el hombre en ello; ansi como toser, estornudar, tropeçar . . ."); the dog, an urban transformation of Ciruelo's wild animals ("lobo o raposa o conejo"); the overheard word ("dichos o hechos que otros lo hacen a otro proposito y los adevinos lo aplican a otro"). This naturally may be purely coincidental, but it is at least an interesting coincidence and one which corresponds to the way we know Rojas to have selected material from Petrarch and Reinosa. I have found no other concrete examples of utilization of Ciruelo, aside from the usual magic circles, inscribed papers (Celestina's "papel escrito con sangre de murcielago") and invocation of the devil—who is described by Ciruelo as a kind of a highly rational super-scientist. For further discussion, see A. V. Ebersole Jr., "Pedro Ciruelo y su *Reprobación de hechicerías, NRFH*, xvi (1962), 430-437. It should also be noted that the name indicates that he was a *converso.* Three daughters (one with children of her own) of a Bachelor Ciruelo are listed in *Judaizantes.*

[176] *Obras*, Madrid, 1960, pp. 1123-1291. Like the Neo-Platonists, Vitoria admits the existence of secret and "admirable natural forces" and, like Calderón, the devil's power to "transform marvellously the matter and nature

sirer, the very nature of Renaissance science with its inability to separate "the 'necessary' from the 'accidental'" led reasoners like della Porta and Campanella towards serious consideration of magic.[177]

What concerns us now, however, is the fact that the whole question of magic, both its licitness and its possibility, continued to be debated as intensely (and much more seriously) in the fifteenth and sixteenth centuries, as was that of women and love.[178] In this sense, *La Celestina*'s ambiguous, yet at the bottom clearly rationalistic, presentation of the subject corresponds to its presentation of amorous excess. In both cases, the intention is to utilize creatively a palpitating contemporary concern. I do not mean by this, of course, that Rojas intended to take sides (as we shall see, *La Celestina* has no sustained thesis or theses), but rather that from the point of view of reason, he observed and recorded sardonically the tragicomedy of its normal absence from human *razones*. But, had he been asked directly his views on magic, I think he would have answered in much the same way as the *gracioso* in Alarcón's *La cueva de Salamanca*: "Señores / Contra estudiante gorrón, / Salmantino socarrón, / non praestant incantatores."

We may conclude by observing that these debates on women, love, and magic exemplify the polarity inherent in human awareness, the tendency of the human mind to perceive, and hence to think, in terms of opposites. Dedicated professionally to the use and cultivation of reason, the University and its inhabitants were nonetheless almost obsessively concerned with the irrational. This was so, not merely because they were annoyed by contradiction, but because reason knows itself and its own usefulness in the process of coping with the irrational or non-rational. The vocation of reason is to rationalize, to bring grammar to language, laws to nature, and regulations to student conduct. Or to say the same thing in another way, a healthy man, happily unaware of his health, seldom broods about illness. But a self-consciously rational man

---

of bodies" (p. 1242). Yet all along one senses the same preoccupied skepticism that we find in Ciruelo: "Many times the desired result is not obtained in spite of exact fulfillment of all the rites and ceremonies" (p. 1274).

[177] *The Individual and the Cosmos*, p. 152.

[178] See *Heterodoxos*, I, 699, and for the wider European range of the debate, Wadsworth, *Lyons*, p. 80.

can hardly avoid being concerned with stupidity and ignorance (which he hopes to reform) with passion (which he hopes to control) and with humbug (which he hopes to disprove). So it was that our Salamancan rationalists spent as much of their time thinking about the lurking danger of love, the false pretenses of magic, and the disappointing intellectual attainments both of women and of their uneducated neighbors, as they did in contemplating geometry, reading the classics, or calculating the movement of the stars.

In these terms, *La Celestina* may be thought of as a kind of ultimate example of the polarity of reason and unreason. Within its borders one of the most rational minds ever produced by the human race listens to and broods upon not the bright sunlight of "La Visión Deleitable" but the dark night of irrational, animal-like, logically doomed human existence. And it came to understand far more about how people think and behave and, above all, interact than its own rational tradition was equipped to explain. *La Celestina* surpasses the university milieu in which it was born, but, in its fundamental exploitation of the confrontation of reason with realms beyond itself, it was profoundly academic.

CHAPTER VII

☙ Fernando de Rojas as Author

¡Gran filósofo era!
                    —Fernando de Rojas

The Intention of *La Celestina*

If Fernando de Rojas was less the author of his own life than men of his genius and station are likely to be today, if in his semi-anonymity and conventional legal career he accepted fully the requirements, the impositions, and the routine of the world into which he was born, during the weeks when *La Celestina* was being written he was one of the most extraordinary creators of imaginary life ever to exist. By which I mean, not only that he is a peer of Shakespeare, but also that it is impossible to overestimate the unconventionality of his art. The late María Rosa Lida de Malkiel's exhaustive and passionate *La originalidad artística de "La Celestina"* will be durably important for its widening of the chasm between the sources and the new classic. Evident now to all of us, this chasm appears as a deep fissure running through literature in Castilian and dividing the human geography of Juan de Mena, Jorge Manrique, and Diego de San Pedro from that of the *Lazarillo*, Cervantes, and Gracián. In other regions of this literature continuity and tradition present unbroken beauty to the reader's eye, but he who would deal with Fernando de Rojas and *La Celestina* is confronted with discontinuity, the unprecedented greatness of a sudden and unexpected leap into a new world. Thus it is that his would-be biographer (as Marcel Bataillon insists) must concern himself with Rojas' comprehension of his own achievement. He must ask not what *La Celestina* is (a question for critics), but how Rojas felt about what he was doing during the short period when his life was giving birth to lives of a sort which had never lived before in literature. How did Rojas view his own unconventionality? Was he aware of it at all? In what terms might he have understood it if he had been? These are the demanding and elusive questions which I must now try to answer.

Everything that has so far been said about Fernando de Rojas—the few facts, the many conjectures, the collected background—has really been aimed at this one problem. Rojas' life is meaningful to us only insofar as the lives of *La Celestina* emerged from it during vacation hours spent in writing and musing "chin in hand and elbow on table." What was he thinking about as he sat there in his room in this topical pose? If, as was affirmed in the Introduction, our purpose is to try to understand how *La Celestina* was possible, how Rojas understood it as possible becomes more than a matter of antiquarian curiosity. What is called today the "intention of the artist" is for us a crucial question.

These are fighting words. On the one hand, the New Critics warn us against the Intentional Fallacy and advise us, if we love literature at all, to abandon the problem as distracting and improper. On the other, many old-fashioned historians of literature not merely defend the propriety of reconstructing past intentions but go on to assert its necessity. Only by examining what the writer meant to say can a given work be understood properly. Only a thorough knowledge of the poetics and the rhetoric of the period can save us from anachronistic impressionism. To my mind, both sides oversimplify. Just as Rojas' reaction to the narrative of his times was ultimately personal, so too his encounter with received literary doctrines (another way of saying ready-made intentions) was personal. Indeed, it was a key sector in his private war with the history he found waiting for him. Understood in this fashion, we can speak of Rojas' intention without debasing whatever is timeless in *La Celestina* (as the New Critics would claim) and also without reducing it to the least common denominator of fifteenth-century literary theory (as certain more conservative scholars have demanded). Like its peers, *La Celestina* is made of life as well as ideas.

The implications of what we have said are as follows: first a potential author receives from his tradition a doctrinal notion of what literature should be and mean; then, as an actual author, he puts it into practice; and, in the process of doing so, he learns how to express what he feels, what he wants to say, and how to transfer his life into the lives of others. Every significant work must, in other words, redefine the received poetics with which it began. In the particular case of *La Celestina*, this redefinition is not only revolutionary (as we have just insisted) but also complicated by the problematical, separate existence of Act I. There, too, the unknown first author began with an original intention, an intention which was modified as he listened to and transcribed the dialogue of his speakers. The comic debate on women engaged in by Sempronio and his master and Pármeno's Rabelaisian inventories of

358

Celestina's warehouse and interpersonal relations (the "puta vieja" passage) are quite different from the intense dialogic encounter of Celestina and Pármeno at the end. The act of creation has begun to transform the intention which first set it into motion.

It would probably be wrong to claim that the anonymous writer was aware of having surpassed the declaration of his probable title: "There follows the Comedy of Calisto and Melibea composed in order to reprove mad lovers who, conquered by their disordered desire, call their ladies divine and say they are a god for them, and also to warn against the deceptions of go-betweens and bad and flattering servants." But if his intention had not had time to mature, he must have been at least partially aware that his attention had turned from predefined virtue and vice to an exploration of how human minds operate in changing situations. We may even go on to surmise that it was this innovation that fascinated Rojas and incited him to embark upon the continuation. In any case, taking *La Celestina* as a whole, it is to my mind undeniable that the original intention to reprove and improve was replaced by a much less optimistic moral.

Here, it seems to me, is the fundamental error of Marcel Bataillon in his recent book on Rojas' intention, *"La Celestine" selon Fernando de Rojas*. Bolstered by the title cited above, by other selected prefatory remarks, by the closing "Habla el autor" (probably as suggested elsewhere an ironical form of disappearance),[1] and by the commonplace literary doctrine of Rojas' time, Bataillon equates the ultimate with the initial intention of *La Celestina*. It would be difficult to deny that the work is morally concerned with

---

[1] In my opinion the very word *autor*, as applied by Rojas to himself, has ironical overtones. A typically serious and non-ironical *autor* of the time was Juan de Padilla, "el Cartujano," who uses the word to describe himself as a kind of final link in a chain of *auctoritas* stretching back into the classical and ecclesiastical past. He is a respectable *persona* whose speech gathers the moral wisdom of the ages. As such an *autor*, Padilla locates himself here and there on the margin of his *Retablo de la vida de Cristo* (Sevilla, 1513) to indicate his responsibility for explanatory and didactic comments on the events described. Thus, when Rojas at the end of *La Celestina* uses the same formula "Habla el autor," he tips his listener off that in this role he will provide briefly the standard piety, the mention of Christ, and the moral admonishment that are conspicuously missing in Pleberio's lament. The title of the closing verses might also be translated as "The Preacher Speaks" or the "The Moral Philosopher Speaks" rather than "Author" in our sense of the word as artist or creator.

the human condition, that, in the last analysis, it *is* "un *exemplum* de grand envergure."[2] But to conclude therefrom that Rojas only intended to repeat or renovate Christian moral castigation as inherited from preceding centuries is to ignore the import of Pleberio's valedictory address. It amounts to nothing less than preferring appended material of uncertain sincerity to the text itself.

Bataillon, anticipating this charge, answers that there is no need to identify Rojas' intentions with the statement of a single character, a character who is moreover distraught and "inconscient" after the catastrophe which has befallen him. There is some justice to the argument; indeed we might even imagine Rojas using it himself had he been charged with impiety, inappropriate pessimism, or (like his father-in-law) failure to be concerned with "what lies beyond." But what Bataillon cannot explain away is the extreme emphasis accorded to the closing "planctus" in both versions of *La Celestina*. It occupies a final act all to itself; it serves as a concluding monologue after all the participants in the dialogue have died or disappeared; it emerges from the soul of the one character who has not been undermined ironically during the course of the work;[3] and above all it sums up and attempts to make sense—or nonsense —of all that has taken place. In view of these self-evident facts— and although later readings of the work need not coincide and have not coincided with that of Rojas—it requires a suspicious amount of critical dexterity to avoid attributing to the young author the words of the aged character. As Menéndez Pelayo affirmed explicitly (and as almost all other readers before or since have assumed tacitly) Pleberio in Act XXI is the spokesman for Rojas' final intention, the intention as redefined in the course of writing *La Celestina*.[4]

---

[2] p. 255.

[3] Bataillon states: Si Rojas se décide a mettre en plus vivre lumière les parents de Melibée, c'est pour faire d'eux, plus nettement, des personnages ridicules, aussi comiques, dans leur genre, que le Calisto du premier auteur" (p. 186). But he himself is forced to admit that he can make a far better case against Alisa than against Pleberio.

[4] This does not necessarily reduce Pleberio to a mere puppet. As T.S. Eliot points out, "There may be [heard] from time to time . . . the voices of the author and the character in unison, saying something appropriate to the character, but something the author could say for himself also, though the words may not have quite the same meaning for both. That may be a very different thing from the ventriloquism which makes the character only a

To challenge a master-scholar as impartial and as courteous as Marcel Bataillon is neither easy nor pleasant. Anyone who concerns himself with Rojas' view of his own work may therefore be grateful to María Rosa Lida de Malkiel for her detailed and expert refutation of the thesis of *"La Celestine" selon Fernando de Rojas*. Her central argument is historical in nature. Basing herself on the moral condemnations of Vives, Guevara, Venegas, Fray Luis de Alarcón, Fray Juan de Pineda, Lope, Cervantes, Gracián, and a number of others, she concludes that, if Bataillon were right, *La Celestina* would present the rare case of a didactic work the fundamental intention of which was so disguised that it eluded the majority of readers in its own and following centuries—all of which implies a total didactic failure."[5] Aside from Gaspar von Barth (a pedantic seventeenth-century German on whose interpretation Bataillon bases much of his thesis)[6] and a few imitators and editors (in whose interest it was to affirm moral profit)[7] the initial intention as re-stated here and there in the prologue material was understood to be purely conventional. Almost everybody read *La Celestina,*

---

mouthpiece for the author's ideas or sentiments" ("The Three Voices of Poetry," *On Poetry and Poets,* p. 100).

[5] *La originalidad,* p. 296. The point may be reinforced by listening to the tone of a typical denunciation, that of the Augustinian *converso,* Fray Luis de Alarcón: "¿Qué otra cosa hace el que da a leer en estos tales tratados o libros sino estar soplando y encendiendo tizones que tiene a si apegados, conque sea de cada día encendida y abrasada con la cobdicia carnal en este mundo, y después con mayor fuego en el infierno? Del número de estos libros son en latín: Ovidio y Terencio en algunas obras y otros tales. En romance: un *Amadís* o *Celestina* y otros semejantes. . . . Los que estas cosas han escrito o escriben no son sino hombres ya muy perdidos o pestíferos, hombres que han perdido el temor de Dios." *Camino del cielo y la maldad y ceguedad del mundo,* Barcelona, 1959, pp. 88-89.

[6] That certain French critic-moralists of the 15th century attempted to explicate the *Decameron* in didactic terms (see Wadsworth, *Lyons,* p. 163) is interesting but no more revelatory of Boccaccio's intention than Barth is of Rojas'.

[7] *La originalidad,* p. 297. Francisco Delicado, the author of *La lozana andaluza* (a Celestinesque work which even a Barth could hardly have justified) prefaces his 1531 Venice edition of *La Celestina* with remarks which I take to be a parody of such self-interested justification: "Y porque en latín ni en lengua italiana no tiene ni puede tener aquel impresso sentido que le dió su sapientíssimo autor; y también *por gozar* su encubierta doctrina encerada [*sic*] debaxo de su grande y maravilloso ingenio . . . lo acabé este año de 1531." In *La originalidad* there is noted a similar parody by Velázquez de Velasco, p. 308.

and almost nobody thought of it as uplifting. Readers of the time knew—as we know—that all authors had to pretend to be moral, but they also knew, as a contemporary moral poet phrased it, "that the troubadour ought not to imitate the tinker who, while trying to mend one small hole in a pan, opens twenty all around it."[8]

One might add to the direct testimony collected by Mrs. Malkiel Francisco de Villalobos' mockery of just such commonplace moral self-justification in a 1515 letter concerning his translation of *Amphitryon*: "Jupiter's lasciviousness is my feathered fly for fishing gallants like trout, in order that they may be deposited in the holy doctrine of virtuous love."[9] Another source of evidence which she does not fully exploit is the evident contrast between *La Celestina* and those later "*Celestinas*" (none of which Rojas thought worth purchasing) which took seriously the didactic pretense of the original title. Instead of supporting Bataillon's notion of a moral intention by showing how the work was understood by all contemporary readers, certain continuations by their changes, lapses, and tasteless emphases show how it was misunderstood by a few of them. Avellaneda's didactic *Don Quijote* does not prove Cervantes' identical intention but rather illustrates the uniqueness of the masterpiece. For example, while in *La Celestina* no single character represents virtue and points out infractions against it,[10] in *La Thebayda* (1504), a work as boring as it is lascivious, Menedemo holds to a forlorn and inflexible posture of Christian virtue. Another contrast just as obvious is provided by the more readable *Lisandro y Roselia* (1542) which (like a number of others) spells out the moral in continuing commentary. The "argumento" to Act IV scene 4 is indicative: ". . . Lisandro not tolerating the good advice of his loyal servant dismisses him. . . . This Act is very learned and full of doctrine."[11]

In general the continuations and imitations may be divided into

---

[8] Padilla, *Retablo*: "por ende no haga ningún trobador—assí como haze cualquier calderero—que por remediar un pequeño agujero—abre los veynte por alrededor." Seville, 1518, "Tabla primera, Cántico xvii." The pagination of this edition is irregular.

[9] "Con las liviandades de Jupiter como con plumas de gallo, he pescado aquí galanes como truchas, para metellos en la sancta doctrina del amor virtuoso" (*Algunas obras*, p. 159).

[10] *La originalidad*, p. 308.

[11] Sancho de Muñón, *Lisandro y Roselia*, ed. J. López Barbadillo, p. 155.

those which exaggerate eroticism and crude humor (*La Thebayda, La Seraphina, La loçana andaluza*) and those which attempt to compensate morally for their subject matter—either by concluding the love affair with marriage (*La Eufrosina, La segunda Celestina, La Selvagia*) or by underlining the relation between transgression and punishment (*La penitencia de amor* or *La tercera Celestina* in which the *alcahueta* falls to her death). Both varieties are, as might be expected, replete with the direct preaching which we are grateful not to find in the original. Finally, there is a noticeable difference of attitude towards the prevailing religion. Even in *La Thebayda* and the *Comedia Ypolita* (both of which were highly shocking to Menéndez Pelayo) repeated references to Christ and Christian precepts stand in marked contrast to Rojas' sardonic treatment of the routine and superstitious faith of his characters, characters who never once utter the name of the saviour. This failure to name Christ (also conspicuous in the *Lazarillo*) carries through into the closing verses where one of the two clear references to Him in the whole of the text ("amemos aquel . . .": Let us love the one who . . .) is a circumlocution.[12] It would seem that Rojas shared the hateful reluctance of certain of his fellow *conversos* to name directly an imposed and spurious messiah. Perhaps he too used such evasions (recorded in numerous Inquisitional transcripts) as "Otohays" (meaning "that fellow"), "aquel enforcadillo" (that strung-up wretch), or "barbillas" (Mr. Beard) whenever in appropriate company it was necessary to speak of Christ. In any case, in contrast to those imitations which chose to reinterpret their model in terms of conventional morality, *La Celestina*'s virtual a-Christianity is startling.[13]

The above considerations should not be understood as a denial that for Rojas *La Celestina* was both initially and ultimately a moral work—that is, a work concerned with the moral posture of man in the world. In his mind it was neither immoral, as many of his contemporaries proclaimed, nor amoral and so comparable to

---

[12] I am not counting, of course, the expletive *jesú*, which is used only by the women in moments of excitement. Apparently Rojas heard it as expressing a special feminine irrationality—a reaction which further supports my thesis. The other mention of Christ is again that of the "author" praying piously for the soul of his predecessor in the acrostic verses.

[13] See the cogent discussion in *La originalidad* of the characters' self-interested religiosity (p. 365).

the creations of certain of ours. What must be emphasized, however, is the point already made: that its creation was not controlled by the original didactic intention (the mirroring of amorous blasphemy and wicked wiles). Rather, *La Celestina* evolved toward an original and far more profound moral view during the course of its speech. Bataillon is, thus, not wrong, in spite of his oversimplified concept of intention. Had he proceeded differently he might well have come to some such conclusion as that of Henri Fluchère on Elizabethan tragedy: ". . . a school of morality to a degree which even propaganda plays have never achieved. *For it contains no thesis* and its appeal to ethical ends is quite instinctive. . . . There is, indeed, no play of Shakespeare or of his contemporaries which does not contain to some degree, under the discreet veil of allusions, wealth of metaphor or incisive epigrammatic maxims, essential revelations about the meaning of life, the moral significance of an attitude or a gesture, so that the shock to the audience's sensibility is prolonged in its mind on the ethical plane."[14] Should we accept such a notion of *La Celestina*'s moral vision, however, we should then have to claim—perhaps overboldly—that Rojas went one step beyond Shakespeare. In Pleberio's desperate soliloquy when dialogue was finished, the Spaniard attempted a feat the Englishman was wise enough to eschew. He made explicit what he believed to be his "essential revelations about the meaning of life." Which is to say in simpler words, Pleberio provides us (or hopes to provide us) with a specific program of tragic "morality."

But, before we can reexamine directly the conclusion of *La Celestina*, we must comment on another view of Rojas' intention which has had wide circulation in recent years. Three critics have propounded independently the idea that the work portrays the impossible love affair of an Old Christian of good family and a wealthy *conversa*—that it is nothing less than a racial Romeo and Juliet.[15] The notion is tempting in view of both Rojas' background

[14] *Shakespeare and the Elizabethans*, tr. Guy Hamilton, New York, 1956, p. 91.

[15] E. Orozco, "*La Celestina*, Hipótesis para un interpretación," *Insula* (Madrid), xii, 1957, no. 124; F. Garrido Pallardó, *Los problemas de Calisto y Melibea*, Figueras, 1957; and S. Serrano Poncela, "El secreto de Melibea," *Cuadernos Americanos*, 3, 1958, later published under the same title as a book, Madrid, 1959.

and the relationship suggested earlier between that background and the possibility of irony.[16] By which I mean Rojas' tacit communication with readers who were also "conversos" and who shared his corrosive vision of society and the universe. Would not such as these find in *La Celestina* meanings that are hidden from us today?

That this communication was real and not a product of erudite fantasy is attested to by *La Celestina*'s immediate literary influence. Both the earliest imitation, *La Thebayda*, and the earliest continuation, the so-called "comedia que ordenó Sanabria," contain significant references to the situation of the caste.[17] Later on the preoccupations of *conversos* who had emigrated to Italy appear in such neo-Celestinesque works as *La lozana andaluza* and Torres Naharro's *Comedia Jacinta*.[18] Even Feliciano de Silva's much more commonplace *Segunda Celestina* is not without hints of this sort,[19] although nowhere near as many as those to be found in the dialogue fragments of Villalobos or in *La Eufrosina*.[20] Considering that out of Rojas' contemporary public these were the few readers whose reactions we are in a position to intuit, such references seem particularly significant. But perhaps the most surprising reader of all was the Jewish physician and Oriental philologist Joseph ben

[16] Chap. II, n. 88 and Chap. I, n. 22.

[17] In the one act which is extant (the so-called *Auto de Traso*, first interpolated in a 1526 edition of *La Celestina*—see Chap. II, n. 40) Centurio admits that he is afraid to cross the market place because he might fall in the hands of those who would condemn him to "purgar en la prisión" his "pecados viejos." He goes on to remark on the greed of "los alguaciles de hogaño" willing to go without sleep for five nights in a row in order to confiscate a poor man's cape. Such as these "en lugar de ayudar al que poco puede, no le dejan cera en la oreja, saben bien trasquilar a cruces" (*La Celestina*, ed. J. Bergua, Madrid, n.d., p. 251). Reference to the Inquisition though not provable, seems highly likely to me.

[18] For the *Comedia Jacinta*, see Chap. I, n. 26. For Delicado, see Castro, *Realidad*, edn. 1, p. 545, n. 37 (*Structure*, p. 571, n. 35) and Caro Baroja, 1, 244.

[19] One example is the mock peasant genealogy mentioned previously, Chap. V, n. 20. Another is the fact that Feliciano de Silva (who was married to a fullfledged *conversa* and who, as a member of the Silva family, undoubtedly had a strain of tainted blood himself—see Chap. III, n. 24) dedicated the continuation to the well-known ex-*converso* in exile, João Míguez. See Caro Baroja, 1, 223.

[20] Not only in the "Diálogo" with a "grande deste reino" (see Chap. II, n. 78) but also in that preceding it.

Samuel Zarfati, who before 1527 translated *La Celestina* into Hebrew.[21]

Yet, in spite of Rojas' success among his fellow *conversos* and of his artful rapport with them, the proposition that *La Celestina* contains a secret message about racial prejudice and matrimonial discrimination seems dubious. None of the reader-authors just mentioned alludes to it; in fact, there is no evidence at all that before the second half of the twentieth century anybody over-interpreted Calisto's failure to propose in this fashion. Although an author's intentions may be secretive (we shall see an example before this chapter is completed), a wholly secret intention is critical nonsense. Hints and allusions recognizable at least to the readers he hopes to reach must be present. It may also be noted in this connection that, while Rojas (through Celestina in Act VII) does communicate his judgment of Inquisitional procedures, there are no detectable references to *conversos* as such in the entire book.[22] Melibea is specifically described by Calisto in Act XII as possessing "limpieza de sangre e fechos," and, since in this matter it is his judgment that counts, there is no point in taking issue with him. The real ironical dig here may be at the meaningless purity of her *sangre*, given what we know about the impurity of her *fechos*.[23]

[21] See U. Cassuto, "The First Hebrew Comedy," *Jewish Studies in Memory of George A. Kohut*, New York, 1935, pp. 121-128.

[22] An exception might be the phrase from Act I, "¡O qué comedor de huevos asados!" if we accept Peter Goldman's very reasonable interpretation of the phrase. "A New Interpretation of *comedor de huevos asados*," *RF*, LXXVII (1965), 363-367.

[23] Such a slur at those proud of their clean lineage repeats in a veiled way the gross implications of Sempronio's "Lo de tu abuela con el ximio," as interpreted by Menéndez Pelayo, *Orígenes*, p. 277. Otis Green's dismissal of the phrase as a commonplace (on the basis of a display of erudition) fails to be convincing. Even the most evident commonplaces are given dialogue force and human immediacy in the speech of *La Celestina*. If Calisto fails to react violently in the manner Green expects, a more appropriate explanation would be his moral weakness made ironically evident by the unknown author. One can imagine Rojas appreciating the slur at the caste of his oppressors but preferring a more subtle way of getting at the same point. See "Lo de tu abuela con el ximio," *HR*, XXIV (1956), 1-12. Earlier in Act IX similar irony accompanies Sempronio's snobbish approval of the love affair; "Calisto es cauallero, Melibea fijadalgo; assí los nacidos por linaje escogido búscanse unos a otros." If there were any possibility of a stain on either, surely the banquet gossip would have alluded to it.

Finally as Bataillon has shown with conclusive erudition,[24] this interpretation bears little relation to the social situation at the end of the fifteenth century. Later on when the mania of *limpieza* was at its height, knowledge of a suitor's Jewish antecedents might make things difficult for him (as in Lope's *El galán de la membrilla*), but during Rojas' lifetime mixed marriages, although perhaps less frequent than during the reign of Henry IV, were still possible. Thus, while Bataillon and others are content to remain with the initial intention, these searchers for concealed prejudice go far beyond Rojas' and Pleberio's last words. They invade regions of pseudo-historical supposition that lie outside the text, the very regions in which Lady Macbeth's children were born and grew up.

In hac lachrymarum valle

In what crucible did Rojas initial understanding of *La Celestina*—his first intention—become transformed? This is a question leading beyond our present concerns and one to which those interested in his art would find diverse answers. That is, they would find them provided they were willing to ask the question in the first place. For my part, as I have already suggested (and as I have tried to demonstrate elsewhere at more length),[25] I would rest my case with irony. The constant bifurcation of static moral prescriptions from human mutability (which, as we have seen, was a *converso* "theme of the time") allowed ironic vision, distance, detachment, implacable unconcern. Or to say the same thing in another way, imported into a continuity of self-betraying dialogue, moral commonplaces can be seen around and through. The result is that "the initial exemplary intention has been absorbed into an artistic organism of a more complex and less comforting significance. Rojas was not a rebel but an ironist, an ironist outside the realm of accepted values and explanations, who watched his characters and their society from a distance and allowed them to be-

[24] Bataillon, pp. 175-176. See also Caro Baroja, II, 249-250 and *La originalidad*, pp. 475-476.

[25] *The Art*, pp. 174-175. Spitzer, apparently without being aware of so doing, confirms this in his hostile "A New Book on the Art of *La Celestina*," *HR*, XXV (1957), 1-25. The support of his authority in this matter should help to convince those who might otherwise be convinced by naïve and anti-ironical interpretations.

tray their own rationalizations and corruptions."[26] As Northrop Frye phrases it, "the ironist fables without moralizing, and has no object but his subject."[27]

Up to now we have been concerned with providing social and biographical contexts for this irony, an irony so caustic and sardonic as to make the young author of *La Celestina* seem humanly monstrous when compared to that older and more gentle ironist who after him was to write *Don Quixote*. But now that we have done our best to comprehend how such a relentless view of "lo humano" (Cervantes' way of saying "human things" in his criticism of *La Celestina*) was possible, it is our next task to observe the monster observing his own monstrosity. He has finished listening to and writing his dialogue, and, in the figure of Pleberio turning to his fellow citizens, he turns to tell us what he intended, what he thinks *La Celestina* portends.

The classic discussion of Pleberio's soliloquy is that of Menéndez Pelayo. In it, he situates Rojas as a kind of precursor of Denis de Rougemont[28] as a castigator of those who find sinister and romantic comfort in the worship of *Liebestod*. If the work had finished with the suicide of Melibea in Act XX, Menéndez Pelayo observes, "one might believe that the poet had wished to give a halo of glory to the two unfortunate lovers, concluding with what today would have

---

[26] For convenience I am citing my own "Rebirth of a Classic, *Celestina*," *Varieties of Literary Experience*, ed. S. Burnshaw, New York, 1962, p. 298.

[27] *Anatomy of Criticism*, Princeton, 1957, p. 41. Frye goes on to remark, "Irony is naturally a sophisticated mode, and the chief difference between sophisticated and naïve irony is that the naïve ironist calls attention to the fact he is being ironic, whereas sophisticated irony merely states and lets the reader add the ironic tone himself." Herein lies the difference between the irony of a Rojas and the "grandes yrronías" of his fellow-townsman, Juan de Lucena—as well as those of Villalobos, Antón de Montoro, and Francesillo de Zúñiga. Later failures—such as that of Barth—to comprehend the messages within the message may be attributed to the same sophistication. Elsewhere in commenting on the opposition of irony to myth, Frye remarks that "the ironic tone is central to modern literature" because of its accompanying "thematic detachment" (*Myth and Symbol*, ed. B. Slote, Lincoln, Neb., 1963, p. 11)—thereby confirming our comprehension of a *Celestina* relevant to us precisely because of the stance described in the letter. That is to say, the stance of a man preoccupied with his "patria" and the lives of his "conterráneos" at a distance. For a comparable discussion of Rojas' apartness from the society he knew so intimately, see Mrs. Malkiel's *Two Spanish Masterpieces*, p. 14. In *La originalidad* this emerges less clearly.

[28] I refer, of course, to the thesis of *L'Amour et l'Occident*, Paris, 1939.

been called the apotheosis of free love."[29] It would have been comparable in its intention to the story of Tristram and Isolde. But Pleberio's words cast a very different light on the action. Through his eyes we see love for what it is, "a mysterious and terrible goddess whose evil influence poisons and corrupts human life" and brings sudden and terrible death to her servitors, Celestina, Melibea, Calisto, Sempronio, and Pármeno. But, admitting this grim moral, Menéndez Pelayo hastens to say, *La Celestina* is nevertheless lamentably unorthodox. It may not be "scandalous" or "libidinous" and it may "fulfill, at least externally, the law of expiation," but at the bottom what we find in the work is "epicurean pessimism lightly veiled, a transcendental and bitter irony."[30]

Although Menéndez Pelayo's literary judgment is as usual intuitively keen, he does not, in my opinion, either go far enough or take all the necessary intermediate steps. By the latter objection I mean that he fails to point out that Pleberio's lament, like both the Letter and the Prologue, is to a large extent Stoic (and not "Epicurean") in its sources and tenor. Written at about the same time as the Letter (that is to say at the conclusion of the dialogue of the sixteen-act Comedia version), it is derived less from medieval *plancti* (Juan Ruiz, Juan de Mena, Diego de San Pedro) than from certain of the cases debated in Petrarch's *De remediis utriusque fortunae*: *De tranquillo statu, De infantis filli caso misero,* and *De amisso filio.* Pleberio, in a way different from (yet comparable to) Calisto and Melibea, has in Stoic terms "disarmed" himself through love. He has made his situation as secure as he can; he has planted trees; built towers and ships; accumulated wealth without really caring for it; he has even accepted his age and approaching death, sagely planning (only a month too late) for the marriage of his daughter. But he is vulnerable through the one thing he loves beyond reason: Melibea. His pathetic observation, "Now I shall lose along with you, my unfortunate daughter, the terrors and fears which haunted me every day; your death is the only thing that could free me from worry," is a clear echo of Petrarch's "Ratio" in *De amisso filio,* an echo which was to be heard again at the end both of *Riders to the Sea* and *Bodas de sangre.*[31]

---

[29] *Orígenes*, p. 379.   [30] *Ibid.*, p. 385.

[31] *The Art*, p. 177. This has since been accepted and elaborated upon by Bataillon in his review-article of *La originalidad* (see below, n. 46).

Or again, his conclusion, "I complain of the world, because it created me. If I had not been given life, I should not have engendered Melibea. If she were not born, I would not have loved her, and, without loving, this disconsolate and pitiful agony would cease," is the reasoning of an orthodox Stoic. Pleberio's failure to bewail the manner of his daughter's death and the automatic damnation it entailed has often been explained in terms of Rojas' insincere conversion. This is, to say the least, very probable. But, looked at from another point of view, her suicide can also be seen as the classic "solution" of Stoicism. Recognizing *her* "disconsolate and pitiful agony" in his own, Pleberio is in a position to be understanding.[32]

In view of Pleberio's repeated emphasis on the agony of consciousness (as he remarks, Alisa is relieved by fainting, one of Petrarch's most painless remedies), we cannot help but conclude that, when Rojas looked back over his work, he saw it from a neo-Stoic Petrarchist standpoint. The initial didactic moral, the warning by *exemplum* against blasphemy and the deceit of servants, had been converted into a Stoic contemplation of the human condition. Rojas' intention is still exemplary and moral, but the example functions in a way hardly predictable in Act I and its title. There we were led to expect that the lovers would be punished for their misbehavior, imprudence, and hyperbole. Witnessing the punishment would teach us a lesson. But at the end the principal sufferer is guiltless Pleberio, "punished" for loving his daughter too much and so leaving a weak spot in his Stoic defenses against the world.

---

[32] Villalobos gives a neo-Stoic diagnosis of suicidal states of mind which it is interesting to relate to that of Melibea: "Y que sean mayores los trabajos del pensamiento que los del cuerpo manifiestamente se paresce en esto. Que ninguno por cavar y remar, ni por otros afanes por grandes que sean, se desesperan; y muchos hombres y mujeres por una congoja o triste pensamiento se dan crueles muertes, unos *despeñándose*, otros dándose de estocadas, otros ahorcándose, otros en agua, otros en fuego. Porque es tan grande la pasión del alma que qualquier muerte tienen en muy poco por acabar la tormenta que padescen" (*Algunas obras*, p. 208). As far as Pleberio's silence about damnation is concerned, we may compare it to Suplicio's explicit warning to Placido when the latter is on the verge of suicide: "¿Tu quieres perder el alma con el cuerpo?" (Juan del Encina, *Teatro completo*, ed. M. Cañete, Madrid, 1893, p. 324). We may also note that Encina (p. 353) and Villalobos use the same word for self-destruction, "desesperarse," a term later used by Cervantes to let us know the nature of Grisóstomo's death. Inquisition records frequently employ it. See, for example, Chap. II, n. 29.

Hence, in the Letter, Rojas tells us that *La Celestina* will provide its reader with "defensive armor . . . not manufactured in the great armories of Milan but by the clear genius of learned Castilians . . ." (4-5). This familiar Stoic image (used also in the *De remediis*)[33] indicates that as Rojas looked back on what he had done he saw it less as a guide to behavior than as a guide to evaluation.

Only in such terms do the final catastrophes make sense. Calisto's death, an accident resulting from his passionate behavior, is a weapon which penetrates the chink in Melibea's armor as does Melibea's in that of her father. Rojas has expressed his revised moral intention with precision. Neither father nor daughter are ethically guilty or socially to be reproached. Pleberio does not appear to conceive of Melibea's surrender as a sin and, unlike Calisto, he does not worry about his besmirched honor. As has often been pointed out, he is in these respects antithetical to the typical fathers of Golden Age theater. The only error of father and daughter—and in this they share equal blame—is to have overlooked fundamental Stoic precepts on evaluation. And in retrospect we can see that in this they were accompanied by Celestina and the servants—basely and avariciously in love with the gold chain. Only those who in one way or another are cynical or relatively unattached come off unscathed.

This unorthodox moral (from the point of view of conventional social and religious beliefs) is by no means an isolated appendage of *La Celestina*. Instead, as we indicated previously, the explicit lesson, as ironical as it is pathetic, is the necessary end product of Rojas' peculiar art of dialogue. The forthright Stoicism of the conclusion cannot be divorced from Rojas' use—evident, as I have tried to show elsewhere, from the beginning of Act II[34]—of Petrarchist commonplaces to communicate an ironical understanding of speaker, speech, and thought. This relationship between irony and Petrarch is, in fact, the only aspect of *La Celestina* about which recent critics seem to agree.[35]

Specifically, if I may be allowed for a moment to retrace steps

[33] In the "Epistolaris praefatio." See *The Art*, p. 225.
[34] *The Art*, p. 171.
[35] In addition to Spitzer, Bataillon, pp. 103-104, and *La originalidad*, p. 253. An exception is A. D. Deyermond who continues to read *La Celestina* as a grab-bag of *exempla* no different from any other (*The Petrarchan Sources*, p. 111).

taken years ago, Rojas causes his speakers to cite Petrarch in order that they may betray the gap between exemplary commonplaces ("Control yourself"; "Don't be proud of your lineage"; "Only communication and friendship make experience worthwhile"; etc.) and the particular purposes and situations to which they are attached. The onflowing of consciousness is always juxtaposed ironically to the static recipes the individual pretends to live by. Petrarch's neo-Stoic Latin treatises are major sources of *La Celestina* for precisely this reason. Their copious inventory of *sententiae* on firm self-control provides intellectual counterpoint to the uncontrollably vital processes of loving, hating, desiring, attacking, and defending in which the speakers are engaged. They offer a fixed standpoint for Rojas' ironical observation of human life—which is to say, Stoically conscious life—in ceaseless operation. That the resulting view of the way consciousness works should have been caustic is not surprising in view of the biography here proposed. *La Celestina* is a work in which the Stoic moral, although never denied, is always betrayed by living and which ends by inflicting the most suffering on the character who is least responsible. Insofar as it fulfills the author's intention, this "exemplum de grande envergure" is ironically inverted, vengefully turned upside down.

Menéndez Pelayo would probably have replied to this interpretation by pointing to the fact that Pleberio does not spend all or even the greater part of his soliloquy bewailing his own state of mind. He also attempts to fix the blame, to try to understand how the sudden, incredible catastrophe happened. Suspending introspection, he lashes out in a bitter apostrophe to Fortune, the World, and Love (listed in the order of their ascending importance) whom he accuses of responsibility for all the deaths. To the Stoic analysis is added what at first glance appears to be a return to the great personified commonplaces of medieval tradition. Far from denying the validity and importance of these central accusations, I would maintain that it was precisely in his interpretation of them that Menéndez Pelayo did not go far enough. Let us listen again to Pleberio in his role, not now as a Stoic failure, but as a prosecuting attorney for mankind:

O changeable Fortune, minister of worldly goods, *why didn't you exercise your cruel wrath, your waves of mutability, on*

372

whatever is properly subject to you? Why didn't you destroy my patrimony? Why didn't you burn down my house? You would have left me that flowering plant over whom you should have no power. You should have given me a sad youth and a happy old age; *you should not have perverted order. . . .*

Oh World, World! Many people have said many things about you . . . but I can speak from experience as a person ruined in the commerce of your deceitful fair, as a person who has up to now been silent about your falsity in order that my hatred should not excite your wrath and bring about the untimely withering of the flower you have plucked today. But now I am without fear, since I have nothing to lose. . . . In my younger *days I used to think that you and your events were ruled by some kind of order,* but now that I have seen the pros and cons of your blessings, you seem to me to be a labyrinth of errors, a thorny plain, a dark forest, a stony field, a meadow of serpents, a garden of flowers but without fruit, a fountain of sorrows, a river of tears, a sea of misery, work without profit, sweet poison, false happiness, true grief. Oh false World, you fish for us with bait of pleasure, and just when it tastes the best you set the hook!

Oh Love, Love. I never thought you had the strength or power to kill your subjects. Wounded by you in my youth, I passed through your flames. Why did you then let me go, if you were going to punish me for my escape in my old age? When I was forty and was content with my conjugal spouse, when I possessed the fruit that you cut off to me today, I thought I was free of your snares. *I didn't think that you visited the sins of the fathers upon the children.* I don't know whether you wound with steel or burn with fire. You leave the clothing unharmed and hurt the heart. You make the ugly act of love seem beautiful. *Who gave you so much power? Who gave you such an unsuitable name?* If you were Love, you would love those who serve you. If they could live happily they would not kill themselves as my beloved daughter has just done. What has become of your servants and ministers? The false go-between Celestina died at the hands of the most faithful assistants in her envenomed profession that she ever found. They were beheaded. Calisto died of a fall. My unhappy daughter chose the same death. You cause it all. They give you a sweet name, but your deeds are bitter. Nor are your rewards equally shared. The law which is not equal for all is unjust. Your reputation is happy; your acquaintance, sad. *Blessed are those who never knew you or whom you ignored. Others,* betrayed by some error of the senses, *have called you a god. But observe that God kills those whom He created; you kill those* who follow you. Oh enemy of reason; you give the greatest gifts to those who serve you the least, until you finally lure them into your *grievous dance.* Enemy of your friends; friend of your enemies, *why do you behave without order or pattern?* ... The fuel for your fire is the souls and lives of human creatures, so many that I wouldn't know where to begin were I to take a roll call. *Not only Christians but also gentiles and Jews* are paid for their faithful service in the same way.

After rereading these three accusatory passages, one is struck by the coincidence in all of them of a sense of the chaotic impersonality of the universe. The external frame of allegorical personification —and hence of implied order—contains within it an explicit denial of order, a denial which as in the plague description of the *Decameron* could be utterly devastating to the medieval mind and one to which *conversos,* as we have seen, were particularly prone. Fortune for Pleberio (as Rojas' spokesman) accordingly perverts order and does not exercise her wrath on whatever should be properly subject to her. He used to think the World and its events "were ruled by some kind of order," but now he knows better. Love is unjust, arbitrary, cruel and so belies its harmonious and gentle name. It behaves "without order or pattern." This view of the universe— whether it reflects Rojas' conclusions or merely Pleberio's frenzy— is unorthodox in every sense. It is not Stoic, for Stoicism's first principle is that it is the individual who is out of order, not nature. Nor is it Christian (although some of the epithets for the World sound Christian), since it ignores the existence and even the possibility of a hidden providence.

We should not, therefore, be surprised that in a seventeenth-century French translation there is introduced a new character, "Ariston, frère d'Alise," whose task it is to console Pleberio and to lead him from metaphysical pessimism to Christian resignation.

374

Pleberio's answer indicates that his faith in ultimate order has been restored: "You have given me back my life. You have dispersed the deep shadow into which I was cast by my recent grief."[36] Rojas and his spokesman, however, are willing to admit no such consolation. For them there is no law to which they may cling nor is there any faith (*"ley"*)—Christian, Jewish, or gentile—in the arms of which rest is to be found. Adherents of all three are equally subject to arbitrary aggression.

If the universe is for Pleberio permanently out of joint, unconcerned, chaotic, senselessly hostile, its very disorder suggests, paradoxically, a familiar literary pattern: that of the Dances of Death so popular in the century preceding *La Celestina*. In these dances, portrayed profusely in poetry and the graphic arts, Death chooses his successive partners without regard for age or hierarchical importance. Pope, peasant, king, knight, maid, beggar, child, and the rest are made to speak their last words, cavort, and die according to the grim whimsy of the dancing master. So that when Pleberio mentions the "grievous dance" of the "enemy of reason" and Rojas in the closing verses advises his readers to "flee the dance" of Calisto and Melibea, they both suggest that Love acts in the same arbitrary fashion as Death in its most popular portrait. By an assimilation of commonplaces not at all uncharacteristic of the time,[37] Rojas looks back on *La Celestina* as a Dance of Love, a

---

[36] Paris, 1577, cited by Deyermond, p. 110. The provider of consolation was a familiar figure in desperate *plancti*, a custom which makes his absence in Act XXI all the more noteworthy. In the *Fernandus servatus* (1493) the role was taken by no less a personage than Cardinal Pedro González de Mendoza to whom the "play" was dedicated. In the imitative lament at the end of Sancho de Muñón's *Tercera Celestina* (cit. Chap. II, n. 56), the speaker effectively consoles himself with a moral soliloquy and concludes: ". . . determino irme a servir a Dios en un yermo, donde esté apartado de tu furia [referring to "Amor"] y de los placeres y halagos y deleites de la vida, para conseguir la suma bienaventuranza *ad quam Deus optimus nos vehat*" (p. 182). The contrast with the end of the original could not be more striking. Both Muñón and Jacques de Lavardin, the translator into French, sense that from the moral point of view something essential is missing in the *Tragicomedia*. As Deyermond points out (although he seems to have no conception of the significance of the change), in this respect Rojas diverged significantly from the larger pattern of the *De remediis* with its constant provision of some sort of consolation.

[37] A common example (also offered by *La Celestina*) is the assimilation of topics having to do with divine and human love. M. J. Ruggerio in his *Evolution of the Go-Between in Spanish Literature* (Berkeley, 1966), bases his

dance as fatal, frightful, and carelessly ordered as its predecessor
—and with the added perversity of deceitful promise. It should be
noted, of course, that the auditors and viewers of the Dances of
Death, usually members of the oppressed lower classes, seem to
have found mass consolation and grim amusement in contemplating the common fate of all mankind,[38] while Pleberio (and, by ex-
tension, Rojas) is alone in passionate and intellectual horror. Fortune, the World, and Love are all outrageous. The terms, like the
pace of the two dances, are not identical. But it is important for our
purposes to see how Rojas, just as he did with the neo-Stoicism of
the *De remediis,* avails himself of a familiar pattern in order to
understand his otherwise incomprehensible innovation. The *Dance
of Death* which expressed Jacques Maritain's "existential distress"
of the fifteenth century[39] all over Europe is here used to translate
the far more radical and ultimately desperate alienation of the solitary Spanish *converso.*

Rojas does not and cannot stop here in his efforts to express his
resentful and vengeful intention. As the mind presiding over the
work and concerned with its Aristotelian coherence (a coherence
antithetical to meaningful human order), it is his duty to assign a
final cause for the conditions he describes. It is all very well to
blame Love, but human nature with its inherent erotic urge cannot
ultimately be blamed. "Who gave you so much power?" Pleberio
asks Love directly and leaves the listener to draw his own conclusions. The latter, if he has listened carefully to the tightly knit,
premonition-loaded dialogue now approaching its end, will remember that the question was answered specifically not far from the
beginning. Early in Act I Sempronio had exclaimed the correct
reply: "Oh sovereign God, how deep are your mysteries! You gave
as much force to love as is necessary for the undoing [*turbación*]

---

approximation of Venus to "alcahueta" on the same sort of substitution.
Bataillon notes the assimilation of the two dances in the closing verses but
explains it as a further indication of moral punishment rather than as a
representation of disorder (p. 218).

[38] See, of course, the appropriate chapter of Huizinga's *Waning of the
Middle Ages* as well as H. Rosenfeld's more recent *Der mittelalterliche
Totentanz,* Munster-Köln, 1954.

[39] *Creative Intuition in Art and Poetry,* New York, 1955 (Meridian Edition), p. 21.

of the lover!"[40] Here is the secretive intention of which we spoke previously. Once the reader realizes that Rojas without saying so openly intends Love to be understood as a euphemism for God ("Others . . . have called you a god"), additional phrases of the soliloquy take on unexpected significance: the Old Testament visiting "of the sins of the fathers upon the children," the bitter observation that God "kills those whom He created," and the potentially blasphemous paraphrase of the Beatitudes, "Blessed are they who never knew you or whom you ignored." But the definitive betrayal of the half-hidden intention occurs at the very end when Pleberio remarks "I complain of the World because *it* created me" ("Del mundo me quexo porque en si me crió"). The implication of a Godless natural universe is about as explicit here as at the time it could be. Or at best, assuming that behind the masks of Fortune, the World, and Love there lurks some sort of overseer, he is capricious and heartless, comparable to those gods in *King Lear* who are like wanton boys to flies.

What is the fate of man born into such a situation? It is precisely the answer to this question that Pleberio's unseen audience has just listened to in the previous twenty acts of *La Celestina*. Man is engaged in a feverishly logical Dance of Life composed of two fundamental movements. On the one hand (as explained in the Prologue and copied directly from Petrarch), there is continuing, relentless conflict—a conflict of words, fists, swords, minds, and talons among all who live: masters, servants, classes, children, fathers, cities, nations, and the opposed faculties of the soul. "All things are nurtured in contention and battle," and, as Castro has emphasized, even chaos is "litigioso."[41] On the other hand, there is an equally relentless erotic urge (to which even Cota's "Viejo" was forced to succumb) reducing us all to animal fury. Sempronio continues the apostrophe to God cited above with a vivid descrip-

---

[40] Celestina gives the same answer to Pármeno: "el soberano deleite, que por el Hacedor de las cosas fue puesto."

[41] ". . . lo propio de esta literatura finicuatrocentista es el relieve y la inquietud del 'animus tacendi,' expresivo del 'caos litigioso' en y desde la cual el autor escribe. En una adición introducida en la edición de 1514, Rojas cambió la expresión 'eterno caos' de Petrarca en 'litigioso' caos" (*"La Celestina" como contienda*, p. 70). The change was probably made in 1502 and not in 1514. I am not convinced that Rojas personally intervened in later editions.

tion of the love-driven, lemming-like human race: "Each lover seems to think he is falling behind the others. They all pass by; they all break through; pricked and spurred with banderillas, all unchecked they jump over barriers and fences." Aside from the specific intimation of the manner of Calisto's future death, we may remark on the disordered dynamism of both movements of Rojas' Bosch-like Dance of Life. In earlier years society had told him a horror story compounded of a thousand and one atrocious anecdotes about the persecution of his kind. And now in *La Celestina*, he, in his turn, as the author of the *Lazarillo* was to do a few decades later, has told society a horror story. He has told it the story of a world of vertiginous cause and effect without Providence or asylum before or after death, a world in which death was a blessing because of the insane, helpless dynamism of being alive.

If on one level Rojas regards life with the ironic eye of a Stoic moralist—that is to say, as a series of errors and faulty evaluations —on another, and this is the very heart of his intention, he tells us that "remedies" for life are hopeless. Those who live in his bleak neo-Aristotelian universe are all in one way or another, whether like Calisto or like Pleberio, inexorably doomed. On the first level Rojas is comic; on the second, tragic; so that the whole is appropriately the world's first tragicomedy.

To sum up, when Rojas looked back over the strange thing he had created and then attempted to explain his intention, he availed himself of familiar patterns of comprehension: Stoic moral precepts, the Dance of Death, and personification allegory. In each case, however, the pattern was infiltrated with unfamiliar implications. Rojas surely would not have shared our view of the revolutionary nature of his originality. His sense of living at a historical dead-end would by itself have been sufficient to blind him (even granting that such a prediction was possible) to the future development of modern genres, genres enabled by and first made visible in *La Celestina*. Nevertheless, in his redefinition of received "poetics," in his abandonment of conventional didacticism, he demonstrates his awareness of having fulfilled Ezra Pound's injunction to "make it new." Rojas knew, as well as we know, that, although *La Celestina* had set out to do one thing, it had ended doing something else. Indeed it was precisely his acute consciousness of possibly dangerous originality which led him to employ the various protective strategies of the prologue material. However many insights they offer into Rojas' sense of himself as an "author" or "philosopher," taking the Letter and the Prologue literally is as naïve as taking the Prologue of *Don Quixote* literally. It is Pleberio during his climax of consciousness who best reveals what Rojas had in mind—and not the appended camouflage.

৫৫ "Cortaron mi compañía"

At this point we must be careful not to claim too much for what we have done. Assertion that Rojas was an artist conscious of his subversive intention need not commit us to unquestioning acceptance of Pleberio's *explication de texte*. Critics of the Intentional Fallacy have served as well in their insistence that the meaning of a work should not be limited to an authoritative interpretation almost surely irrelevant to later generations of readers. Even such self-conscious and ironical authors as Stendhal and Fernando de Rojas are not in a position to judge how new they have made it or the full implications of the newness. This warning is strikingly justified by *La Celestina*'s oft-noted change of title. If Rojas centered his attention on the lovers and his intention on Pleberio, readers soon saw that a deeper originality lay in the self-revelation in dialogue of the avid and corrupt vitality of the heroic go-between. It is necessary to search for and define the author's intention, I would maintain, but it is equally necessary to remember that any literary creation of lasting importance presents a vision of life which cannot be accounted for by his personal interpretation.

Although reiteration of this critical litany may seem impertinent, if we are to discuss relations between author and work which transcend the level of intention, we must be fully aware that we are entering dangerous and forbidden territory. To this prohibition, curiously, both the literary historian and the proponent of a-historical criticism would agree. The former would say that an understanding of the intention is as much as we can or ought to expect from our efforts, while the latter, disdaining such knowledge as fallacious, would prefer to retrace the patterns of an isolated artistic universe. Neither would be willing to try to relate understanding derived from criticism to the life of the author. There is a good deal to be said for their reluctance, but the biographer of Fernando de

Rojas cannot afford not to take chances. His most meaningful document is *La Celestina*, and he must use it in every way he can.

In my own case, I have chosen as a guide for the perilous journey my late teacher and friend, Augusto Centeno. His notion of the "intent" of the artist (as distinct from the "intention") indicates a possible passage from critical interpretation to biographical understanding. Centeno defines the "intent" as a "sense of life deep and intense" which informs the world of art and which springs from realms of personal experience far wider and deeper than can be expressed by direct self-interpretation.[42] From this it follows that, if we move with due caution and support our conclusions with carefully assembled exemplification, we can come to know Rojas through *La Celestina* in a way he could not, for all his intense consciousness, know himself.

Perhaps the most visible and attractive point of departure would be the art of characterization. On the pages of *La Celestina* we can overhear Rojas listening to and observing other people. How does he judge them?—we might ask ourselves. What is his attitude towards them? Yet, since answers to these questions (unless supported by a critical structure too elaborate for presentation here) would seem arbitrary, I have chosen a less obvious and more modest path. It was remarked previously that great works redefine the received poetics of their time. We may add now that they also redefine language, particularly a few key words intimately related to their theme—or, as Centeno would put it, to their "intent." Close observation of Rojas' use of certain words, it may be hoped, will take us from the style to the "man himself." In any case, granting the risk of the whole enterprise, an investigation of language is less likely to mislead a biographer who was trained as a philologist. As a point of departure for a journey into Rojas' mind, this one has the advantage of pertaining to my area of supposed competence.

It is pointless to wonder which of all the words uttered by the speakers of *La Celestina* have been most significantly redefined, because Rojas, himself, must necessarily underline them for us. We may begin again, therefore, with the most underlined portion of the work, Pleberio's lament, and try to read it from this point of view. Previously we concentrated on those sentences which betrayed Rojas' half-concealed interpretation of the previous twenty

[42] *The Intent of the Artist*, Princeton, 1941, p. 22.

380

acts. Now, instead of reading what Pleberio says as a statement of the concluding intention, let us listen to it as a speech, a speech uttered by a man attempting to communicate his private desperation. The difficulties inherent in this effort lead him to repeat over and over again a single word. It is the word *solo*, and it sums up Pleberio's personal plight, a particular paternal solitude which cannot be shared by Rojas. As we remember, when Melibea is poised for her fatal leap, although fearless of death and damnation, she does have one moment of hesitation. She has stopped to think—she states explicitly—because she regrets leaving her father "in a state of great solitude." And only after justifying herself with a series of *exempla* (perhaps to be found under the heading, "Cruelty within Families," in her girlhood commonplace book) and asking God to be her witness that her freedom is a captive to love, does she destroy herself. That Melibea's foreboding is justified is amply proved by Pleberio when at long last he reacts to her speech and her deed.[43] He begins by remarking to Alisa: "Look at the one that you bore and I engendered lying there broken . . . look in order that I may not have to weep *alone* for the painful loss we have both suffered."

Even in this first appearance redefinition can be detected. It is not mere physical companionship which Pleberio desires but rather another consciousness which can accompany his in its pain. This Alisa denies him by fainting (or, for all we know, dying of shock) and he reproves her: "Get up from where you lie over her body, and, if you have life left in you, *spend it with me* in sad mourning and sighing and grief . . . or, if you have deserted this painful life, *why did you leave me to take the brunt of it all?*" Alisa failing, he turns to the townspeople and neighbors "who have come to witness [his] pain": "Oh friends and noble sirs, *help me to feel* my grief!" Pleberio's mind is cut off from all other minds—assuming, of course, that only in reason is communication possible—by the very force of his feeling. A few lines later on he asks why death has de-

---

[43] We must accept Pleberio's failure to interrupt Melibea's long speech— however psychologically improbable it may seem—not only as resulting from her warning ("No la interrumpas con lloro ni palabras; si no, quedarás más quejoso en no saber porqué me mato . . .") inserted by Rojas as a lame explanation but also as an indication that we are approaching the frontiers of the dialogue world. As we near the end, closely knit interchange naturally gives way to oratory.

parted from its natural order to leave him "all alone." And he concludes his denunciation of the World by observing that, although that entity might try to justify itself by its mistreatment of all men and its resulting provision of each one with "companion in grief," this has not been so in his case: "Pues desconsolado viejo, ¡qué solo estoy!"[44] Other examples are: his imagined picture of the "solitary" room of Melibea; the question, "Who will accompany my unaccompanied dwelling?"; and the final rhetorical address to the broken body at his feet, "¿Porqué me dexaste *triste e solo* in hac lachrymarum valle?" Thus, in the lament as a whole there are two complementary varieties of solitude. There is a special awareness of the unbridgeable gap between consciousnesses as well as a natural feeling of personal abandonment. In the world of *La Celestina* incessant dialogue is balanced against—and in a deeper sense made possible by—the radical loneliness of the mind unto itself. Pleberio is the ultimate Stoic "subject," alone in a world which he perceives to be at once a "frightful desert," anticipating Góngora's never achieved *Soledad del yermo*, and a "choral game for men," a futile and pointless game of dialogue.

The special implications in *La Celestina* of the word *solo* (and of the state of solitude it represents) are also apparent in Act XX when father and daughter confront each other for the last time. Melibea's plan depends on being left alone, and, after having sent her father to arrange for comforting music, she subtly converts her own preoccupation with solitude into an excuse for ridding herself of Lucrecia: "Lucrecia, this is a very high place. *I am already sorry for having left my father's company.* Go down and tell him to come to the foot of the tower. . . ." This order having been obeyed, she exclaims with pathetic exultance, "*They have all left me now*; the manner of my death has been well arranged. . . ." The single figure

---

[44] In the section of the lament which follows, Pleberio, like Melibea a few moments before, looks for appropriate classical *exempla* but with even less confidence. For all their prestige, past heroes of Solitude cannot accompany him: "Yo fuí lastimado sin hauer ygual *compañero* de semejante dolor, aunque más en mi fatigada memoria rebueluo presentes e passados . . . ¿Qué compañía me ternán en mi dolor aquel Pericles . . . ?" Mrs. Malkiel sympathetically and perceptively stresses the real human anguish which informs these commonplaces: "La máscara docente que recita la moraleja . . . es al mismo tiempo un personaje, un concreto caso humano, y su lamento atestado de aforismos y ejemplos generalizadores, acaba en una desgarradora pena individual" (*La originalidad*, p. 473).

of Melibea perched high on her tower is, thus, a visual representation, an emblem of solitude. When Pleberio then comes and looks up, his first words are: "Oh daughter Melibea, what are you doing up there alone?" At which point the emblem comes to life and begins to speak. During all the years of Melibea's life Pleberio had been deceived by domesticity—the dialogue of daily coexistence—into believing that he was accompanied. And only now across vertical space and a unsubstantial bridge of words does he realize the distance between her mind and his. Only now, only when his daughter finally does tell him all that she had kept hidden, does he understand the radical nature of his loneliness.

As usual in *La Celestina*, the physical situation and the human situation have merged. The tower and Melibea's confession together express Rojas' acute realization that to be conscious is to be isolated—cut apart by space and cut off by time (Salinas' "fragile wall of winds, heavens, and years") even from those who are closest to us. Lyric solitude of the sort studied by Karl Vossler is also present (particularly at the beginning of the second garden scene), but what Pleberio has learned and is about to express in his *planctus* has little relation to languor or melancholy. His is an irremediable loneliness, built into the human condition.

Unlike their mentor Petrarch, the inhabitants of *La Celestina* cannot derive from their separate solitudes the consolations of Vaucluse. Instead they all strive frenziedly for company of one sort or another, the very intensity of their dialogue demonstrating the inefficacy of Stoic remedies or lyric sublimation. Only in the garden and only for a few hours during a few evenings does acute awareness of time and space (the external forms of individual isolation) give way to pastoral immersion in nature. The rest of the time—like Rojas himself, we may well imagine—the lives from which the voices of *La Celestina* emerge not only pursue each other "in contention and battle" but also regard each other as coveted booty. Even the apparently self-sufficient Celestina refers again and again nostalgically to her past companionship with Claudina. She remembers the nine girls who lived with her during the height of her lost prosperity as a source of "rest and consolation." Nor should we overlook the affectionately querulous domesticity of the homecoming dialogues with Elicia and the transient but nonetheless genuine grief the latter feels after the murder. Despite the vicious irony of

383

Rojas' treatment of these aspects of Celestina's life and death, on their own terms they are genuine. Although she is an invincible and unrelenting word warrior, the verbal hero of her book, only a complementary need of company can explain her celebrated redefinition of "*deleyte*." Carnal intercourse, she tells Pármeno in Act I, is better performed by donkeys out in the field than by human beings, but only the latter can talk with companions about it and become fully conscious through dialogue. "What delight can there be without company," without being able "to recount and communicate the details of love?"

A far more intimate and intense relationship between otherwise lonely consciousnesses is that referred to by the lovers as their "*gozo*." Celestina's *deleyte*, redefined as the camaraderie of dialogue, amounts only to the remembered pleasures of shared life with Claudina or of Areusa with her neighbors. But *gozo* provides, however briefly, not for a superficial conjunction of souls, but for the highest and most intimate form of company. The dictionaries give two familiar definitions for *gozar* and *gozo*. On the one hand, it means "carnal knowledge" and is used by Tirso's don Juan in his refrain, "Esta noche he de gozalla." On the other, it merely signifies "to be pleased or happy," "a movement of the spirit taking pleasure in the possession of desired objects."[45] Both of these meanings are occasionally appropriate in *La Celestina*, particularly during the early acts. When Celestina advises Areusa in Act VII, "E pues tu no puedes de ti propia gozar, goze quien puede," the first is clear; but, when she says, "¡O, si quisiesses, Pármeno, qué vida gozaríamos!" (Act I) the second is used as a matter of course. But eventually in the course of creation (after Act X according to Bataillon), the notion of *gozo* repeated and emphasized by Calisto and Melibea merges these two meanings in a way that is highly significant. *Gozo* becomes nothing less than love's antidote for the awful solitude which Pleberio sees as man's fate. "¿Cómo no gozé más del gozo?" is the apparently immoral reaction of Melibea to Calisto's death. But really what she is asking is not the sensual question, grotesque under the circumstances, "Why didn't I make more physical love?" A more adequate paraphrasing might be: "In

[45] The first is given in the *Diccionario de autoridades*, and the second is to be found in all standard dictionaries.

384

my present solitude, how much I regret not having partaken more of the intense company which only love can provide!"

It is of course true, as Marcel Bataillon points out in a recent revision of his moral interpretation,[46] that, on the level of intention which permits us to read *La Celestina* as a neo-Stoic "comedy," pursuit of *gozo* types the lovers as living representatives of Petrarch's "Gaudium," always candidly optimistic and always disappointed. "Gaudium" along with "Spes" fill the pages of the *De remediis* with their vain efforts to win a continuing argument with "Ratio." Thus, the moral lesson that Petrarch's readers learn from the ever-repeated intellectual defeat of "Gozo" (as this speaker was rendered properly in the translations) is represented by Rojas as the sudden death of those who choose to live only on its terms. Which is to say, those who choose to live without reason. *Gozo* in the world of *La Celestina* is temporally limited and by definition can only exist for a few brief hours and weeks. And every time we hear Calisto and Melibea exclaim at its marvel we also shudder at the fate we know is in store for them. It is perhaps the most pathetic and the most remorseless of the many varieties of dramatic irony with which Rojas engages our continuing attention. When all is over, as Bataillon says, "The desperation of Pleberio explodes in the proverbial formula, 'Nuestro gozo en el pozo,' " which according to modern taste may seem dissonant within the tragic decorum but which by that very fact attracts attention to the ephemeral *gozo* with its vanished illusions."[47]

[46] "La originalidad artística de *La Celestina*," NRFH, xviii (1963-64), 264-290. Since this chapter was written in 1963 (a preliminary version with the same title appearing in *RF*, lxxvi, 1964, 255-290) we apparently coincided in focusing on this key sentiment and word. Although Bataillon with great insight and perceptiveness here affirms the neo-Stoic and ironical significance of the tragic ending, he does not seem to see clearly the extent to which such an interpretation modifies his earlier defense of the title, the "Argumento de toda la obra," the Letter, and the closing verses as explanations of the full meaning. A medieval and ascetic morality play is hardly the same thing as a Stoic and ultimately a-religious presentation of self-destruction. That is, that retribution is mundane, with fortune transmuted into space (as in the *De remediis*—see my "Fall of Fortune," cited Chap. IV, n. 95) and not divine. Our would-be "gran filósofo" is sardonic rather than pious.

[47] Bataillon, *op. cit.*, p. 47. Apparently Rojas or one of the "correctors" shared this "modern taste," since the exclamation was deleted in some later editions.

And yet, I think, Rojas' treatment of *gozo* need not be irrevocably tied to Stoic error and defeat. At a more profound level—that of "intent" rather than "intention"—it becomes independent of its own termination. It becomes the one, the only possible, human experience which affords justification for life in the desolate *mundo* excoriated by Pleberio. It may lead to doom, but without it, there would be nothing. We would face an even worse fate than sudden disappearance: to be forced to live only in terms of the fierce, feral, and even more transient urges that control most of the other members of the cast. For as Bataillon himself points out, *gozo* represents something far more consoling than sensual alleviation: "In reality it is the happiness which the mere sight, the mere evocation, of her lover [brings to Melibea] and which she feels her garden shares upon his arrival (p. 287). Which is to say in other words: *gozo*, even though its timelessness is illusory, transcends rational and moral transgression and is therefore not properly punishable. Instead of feeling self-righteous satisfaction, at the lovers' "fall of fortune," we feel that deep sense of loss which is the sign of authentic tragedy.

In order to defend and clarify this judgment, let us see in the text exactly how this second "palabra preñada" (as Bataillon terms it) has been redefined. Let us listen for a moment to Calisto remembering his first seduction of Melibea. At the end of a long monologue mostly devoted to bemoaning the loss of honor which his servants' public execution may cause, he finally turns for solace to memory and imagination:

But you, sweet imagination, you who can provide all things, come to my assistance. Bring to my fancy the angelical presence of that shining image. Bring back to my ears the soft sound of her words, those half-hearted attempts to repulse me, when she would say, "Please, sir, don't touch me; don't be discourteous," uttered with rubicund lips. Or when from time to time she would repeat, "Don't be the cause of my perdition," each word separated from the other by amorous embraces. How she would hold to me and then let go, flee and then return to bestow her sugared kisses! But above all, bring back the words with which she took leave of me. How sadly they emerged from her mouth! How many signs accompanied

386

them! How many tears—each one a pearl—dropped from her clear and shining eyes and she all unaware! (XIV)

What is striking here is the lack of erotic meditation and masculine complacency about the conquest. Sensual recall—sight, hearing, touch, and even taste (the sugared kisses)—points instead to Melibea's otherness as a person, to her intense companionship at the frontiers of eyes and fingers. The corporal signs of her awareness—which is to say her *gozo*—are treasured as an essential element of his *gozo*. The act of possession matters less to Calisto than the acute conscious joy of mutual possession. Thus, the reiterated insistence on those acts and gestures which betray Melibea's feelings. As against superficial *deleyte* and deceptive domesticity, *gozo* emerges from the depths of its participants and testifies to its own truth.[48] So it was that Fabrice del Dongo experienced the "happiest moment of his life" when he saw Clélia Conti betray her love for him in one embarrassed gesture.

Redefined in this way, the word *gozo*, instead of signifying merely a Stoic illusion, can also be understood as representing what might be called the triumph of consciousness. When Melibea in Act XVI explains to her maid, Lucrecia, why she rejects her parents' marriage plans, she significantly equates her passion for Calisto with parental love: "If my father and mother want to enjoy [gozar de] me, they will have to allow me to enjoy him." And then she goes on to say: "The only sorrow I have now is the time I lost without enjoying him, without knowing him since I learned to know myself." The literal rendering in English is obscure. What Melibea is actually regretting is that between her first attainment of consciousness of self ("desde que me sé conoscer"), and her meeting with Calisto she had not exploited that state to the full. She had not found the intense company that her meetings with Calisto

---

[48] This is the deepest meaning of the repeated (in Act VII cynically by Celestina and in Act XVI proudly by Melibea) commonplace: "el amor no admite sino el solo amor por paga." Bataillon sees this merely as "vice, comme dans un roman picaresque" (p. 103), but I am more impressed with Mrs. Malkiel's perception of the difference between "breve deleyte" and the heartbreaking question cited above, "¿Cómo no gozé más del gozo?" which she attributes to Melibea's "noble franqueza" (p. 431). In the *Visión deleitable* there is an explanation of "gozo" which helps us comprehend Rojas' redefinition: "delectación o gozo . . . lo alcanzamos y nos holgamos en él" (p. 384).

now provide. Thus too her statement that the satisfaction her company gives her parents is comparable to—although hardly as intense as—that received from love. Love is relief from solitude, a merger of minds as well as of bodies. The result is that the theme of the rhetorical blasphemy of Calisto underlined in Act I is at the end taken over by Melibea in an unexpected way: "My lord, I am the one who enjoys, the one who gains, and you, my lord, grant me an incomparable favor with your visitation" (XIX). The word *visitación*, with its mystical implications underlines the extent to which love is felt to provide ecstatic relief from the mind's imprisoned loneliness. *Gozo* in its fusion of divine *gloria*, human *deleyte,* and animal *placer* acts as a thematic counterpoint to the pessimism of Pleberio. It is for that reason, at once deeply ironic and deeply pathetic (rather than moral), that these words of Melibea should conclude the "process of love" and that a moment later Calisto should stumble into ultimate solitude and ultimate unconsciousness.

Although it is clear that the *gozo* of the lovers is founded on uninhibited physical desire and consummation, they are both aware that their pleasure is the foundation of a more exalted edifice. We have already seen this in the case of Melibea, and, by the end— once he has fully absorbed the experience of love—it is also true for hotblooded Calisto. In Act XIX we find him perched on the fatal wall listening to the singing of his beloved and her maid and enjoying in full measure the melodic testimony of his presence in their minds. Once again in accord with Rojas' repeated practice (the initial example occurs in Act II),[49] the larger meaning of the dialogue encompasses not just those who speak but also the silent eavesdropper whose reactions become apparent later on. Calisto, however, cannot remain passive for long and suddenly precipitates himself into the scene. He explains and deplores this action with the following significant words: "Oh well accompanied melody! *Oh joyful moment!* [gozoso rato] Oh my heart! Why could you not resist a little more time without interrupting your *gozo*. . . ?"

The "noble conversation" which is shortly to come and which leads to the physical climax of *gozo* is, thus, subordinate to the encounter of consciousness.[50] Mutual awareness—awareness that the

---

[49] *The Art*, pp. 67-68.

[50] As Calisto indicates when he refuses food and drink, *gozo* prevails not

loved one too is aware—is the essence of the new definition. It is this that the lovers have learned to savor during their month of amorous experience. If on the wall Calisto is able to spend a rapturous interval listening to the "suave canto," during the original and naturally agitated seduction such patience had been out of the question. As Calisto said, "There dwells in my person such a turbulence of pleasure, that it hinders my feeling of all the *gozo* that I now possess" (XIV). Without this triumph of consciousness the act of love is reduced to a "brief delight," rapidly accomplished and soon regretted as both Calisto and Melibea quickly discover.[51] But, once discovered, the lovers feel immune to time, "ever ready," as Melibea puts it in a 1502 interpolation, "because of the *gozo which remains in me*" (XIV).

This perhaps overlengthy and unnecessarily detailed discussion of Rojas' presentation of *gozo* cannot be justified in terms of its originality. As centuries of readers (Lope is surely the greatest example) have seen for themselves, *La Celestina*'s treatment of love and lovers is profoundly and meaningfully ambivalent: on the one hand, traditional reprobation (love is fearsome, and lovers are either ridiculous or hypocritical) and, on the other, sympathetic compenetration. However, although I may have belabored the point, it does serve to remind us of something essential. It demonstrates with great clarity that Rojas *cannot only* be understood (as the evidence at our disposition has led us to understand him) as an alienated and ironical *converso* revenging himself artistically against the society in which he lived or as a university student observing life at a Stoic and Aristotelian distance. In addition to what

---

only at love's climax (as it does for don Juan) but also all throughout the scene: "¿cómo mandas que se me passe ningun momento que no goze?"

[51] Both use the same commonplace to express their remorse for their lost honor (Melibea's lack of virginity and Calisto's publicly executed servants) after the first seduction in Act XIV. Another term with which *gozo* may be contrasted is *solaz* as used by Elicia in Act IX: "Madre, a la puerta llaman. ¡El solaz es derramado!" Here she seems to refer to orgiastic lack of consciousness, withdrawal into intoxication and animality. *Gozo*, on the other hand, is above all attained and maintained through vision. Just as love archetypically comes from the eyes and enters through the eyes, so sight and consciousness of seeing remain central to the truly amorous relationship. See, among other examples, "Goza de lo que yo gozo, que es ver y llegar a tu persona" (XIV), and "en verlo me gozo" (XVI).

Centeno calls "separation" from his subject, that is to say, in addition to his almost vicious use of erotic compulsion to expose the animality lying beneath social pretense, Rojas was also deeply and necessarily a part of the thing he made. He was a man who, in terms of a personal experience we shall never be able to narrate, understood love from within as a salvation for the human condition—as an ecstatic if temporary release from loneliness. The theme of solitude and company culminating in the contrast between the enclosed garden and the exposed tower, in other words, may be identified as one layer of the seemingly bottomless "intent" of *La Celestina*. As such, it represents Rojas' "deep and intense" but not necessarily fully conscious "sense of life." As well as being a self-righteous moralist and an ironical philosopher, he was also in the fullest sense an artist, an artist supremely gifted for making new experience out of old.

✑ The Rhetoric of Unease

Let us now return to our point of departure, to the mystery of the relationship between the life of Rojas and the lives to which he gave voice. We have guessed that the love of Calisto and Melibea—insofar as it involved not only the uncontrollable, irrational passion of fifteenth-century doctrine but also experienced *gozo*—reflected an experience of the author. But granting that direct reflection of one life by another can and does exist, such reflection is only one small phase of a complex process of vital metamorphosis and human sea-change. T. S. Eliot, in an essay on Ben Jonson, remarks on "transfusion" of the self into other roles: "The creation of a work of art, we will say the creation of a character in a drama, consists in a transfusion of the personality or, in a deeper sense, the life of the author into the character."[52] And Manuel Azaña, maintaining that the roots of Cervantes' "marvellous inventiveness" are autobiographical, goes even further. He explains the transferral as arising from "dream and delirium in which one sees oneself as another."[53] In the case of *La Celestina*, in which the solemnly intoned commonplace performs the ironical function of Castro's

[52] *Essays on Elizabethan Drama*, New York, 1956, p. 79.

[53] "Cervantes y la invención del *Quijote*," *Obras completas*, ed. J. Marichal, México, 1966, 1, 1106.

390

"palabra escrita" in *Don Quijote*,[54] we should perhaps replace the visual with an auditory supposition. Did not Rojas, as we suggested in our discussion of oral creation, hear voices? Did they not, to use a phrase Eliot borrowed from Dickens, "force themselves upon his ears"?[55] And is it because of the pervasion of our minds with print that neither we nor whatever saints or heros we still possess can hear them any more?

All of this, however, amounts to nothing more than restating the mystery. And although a genuine mystery is by definition without solution, this one entices those of us who do not share Eliot's reluctance to "penetrate this maze" to greater speculative effort. The only critic-theologian I have found who has dared to think systematically about the creation of others out of the self is Kenneth Burke, and it may be provoking (however controversial) to try out his conclusions on Rojas. Burke proposes essentially that the relationship between author and character is comparable to that of the feelings of a dancer with the patterns of his dance. That is to say, what the character does or says or feels, although wholly different from anything the author might do or say or feel, provides relief for the "burdens" of the latter's existence. The creator dances himself out in words, words spoken by others. On one occasion Burke discusses the rhetoric of physical disease (the characteristic literary metamorphoses of various illnesses),[56] and, redefining his terms slightly, *La Celestina* may be taken to exemplify the rhetoric of social disease. Or, changing the prefix, we might more appropriately say social unease, the uneasiness of being a *converso* in fifteenth-century Spain.

Rojas—Burke might maintain—did not need to write directly about *converso* problems or "feelings" as did others of his caste, because he created characters who, faced with very different situations could use and use up his own resentment, fear, deceit, and cynicism. The function of the work for the author (and Burke insists that this is unlikely to apply to the reader) is one of self-purgation, in extreme cases of self-obliteration. A Montoro or a Villalobos were never relieved of such unease throughout a life of

[54] "La palabra escrita y el *Quijote*," *Hacia Cervantes*, Madrid, 1967, pp. 359-420.

[55] *On Poetry and Poets*, p. 92.

[56] *The Philosophy of Literary Form*, New York, 1957, p. 16.

autobiographical expression—perhaps because they hopelessly and repetitively talked about their feelings. Rojas, on the other hand, having obliterated himself in a major masterpiece, never needed to write again. He had found others to bear his burdens "symbolically," just as did a few decades later the anonymous author of another single book, the *Lazarillo de Tormes.* In this sense it may be significant that *La Celestina,* like the *Sorrows of Werther* (the best known example of this kind of rhetoric) ends in a suicide.[57] Melibea's self-destruction may thus be interpreted as at once expressing and obviating Rojas' own need of self-destruction. It soothed his intense and painful consciousness—a consciousness sharpened by the loneliness inherent in the particular employment of his "vacation"—and allowed him to live out the rest of his days professionally and domestically. In the language of the time to kill oneself was to "desesperarse" (see note 32), and it might be said, following Burke's interpretation, that it was nothing less than Rojas' "desperation" that Melibea took with her in her mortal leap.[58]

[57] Burke's discussion of this point deserves meditation on the part of those preoccupied by the relation of *La Celestina* to its author: "In fact, even though every action and person in the plot led downwards, we should find an assertion of identity in the constructive act of the poem itself. I should want to treat even suicide in real life as but the act of rebirth reduced to its simplest and most restricted form (its least complex idiom of expression). However one may feel about that point, the act of will in poetic organization justifies our claim that a *symbolic* suicide (on the page) is an assertion, the *building* of a role and not merely the abandonment of oneself to the disintegration of all roles" (*ibid.*, p. 34).

[58] Since the first publication of this chapter in 1963, a number of articles have taken one side or the other on the matter of the relevance to the whole (to my mind unquestionable) of Act XXI. Otis Green corrects rightly my interpretation of "Del mundo me quexo porque en si me crió," pointing out with pertinent examples that "mundo" signifies the created world in which we live, "la tierra," rather than a creating universe. But I fail to see that this lessens to an appreciable extent the underlying desperation of Pleberio's view of existence or that it cancels the implication that, if there is anyone responsible for mundane disorder and all powerful love, that someone should be blamed ("Did the 'World' Create Pleberio," *RF*, LXXVII, 1965, 108-110). Green's view of Pleberio as a "foolish and wordly man" whose words are not to be identified with Rojas has met the sensible opposition of Charles Fraker ("The Importance of Pleberio's Soliloquy," *RF*, LXXVIII, 1966, pp. 515-529) and Frank Casa ("Pleberio's Lament for Melibea," *Zeitschrift für Romanische Philologie*, LXXXIV, 1968, pp. 20-29). Bruce Wardropper, although primarily concerned, as his title indicates, with the tradition behind such speeches, also seems to see it as a purposeful summation. See his "Pleberio's Lament for Melibea and the Medieval Elegiac Tradition," *MLN*, LXXIX (1964), 140-152.

And yet, and yet . . . once again I draw back appalled from statements which the very writing of such a book as this has led me to make. To think of *La Celestina* only—or even primarily—as a ritual of personal salvation is a denial of its deeper relevance to men in Rojas' time and to men in our own. To interpret the work biographically in the several ways proposed by an Eliot, an Azaña, or a Burke may be both fascinating and (in a chapter entitled "Fernando de Rojas as Author") indispensable. But it is also a grievous act of critical foreshortening. Whatever may have been accomplished by my years of effort to retrieve the man of flesh and blood who wrote *La Celestina* from his semi-anonymity must ultimately be assayed in the light of C. G. Jung's vision of the artist not as a person "who seeks his own ends, but one who allows art to realize its purposes through him."[59] To be a great artist is not only to be a special and superior individual; it is also to be an agent of mankind, the human means of "an impersonal creative process." Hence, the impropriety and the danger—and who better qualified to warn us than Jung?—of setting up a short circuit from "psychology" to "rhetoric." Speaking personally, I would not use either of these terms (at least in their usual limited sense) to describe what has been attempted here, but at the same time I cannot fail to recognize the profound validity of the stricture. To proceed from life to dialogue and back again in a continuing process has been indispensable for my purpose, but my reader ought not to think—or think that I think—that *La Celestina*'s greatness can be either explained or estimated thereby.

Probably none of these critics would agree with the kind of interpretation suggested here.

[59] "Psychology and Literature," in *The Spirit in Man, Art, and Literature*, Collected Works, vol. 15, New York, 1966, p. 101.

CHAPTER VIII

&c Talavera de la Reina

"...hizo asiento en Talavera: aquí
vivió y murió y está enterrado."
—Cosme Gómez Tejada de los Reyes

Why Talavera?

When Fernando de Rojas left Salamanca and, for reasons unknown, abandoned his studies for the degree of Licentiate, he returned to the Puebla de Montalbán. But he only remained for a few years, probably from 1502 or 1503 to 1506 or 1507. The social and intellectual asphyxiation of village life (particularly intolerable after existence as a student), the financial exactions of the Lord don Alonso, and disruption resulting from the plague have all been suggested as reasons for dissatisfaction and departure. But now let us speculate from a vocational point of view. What did Talavera de la Reina have to offer a young lawyer that was missing in his "clara nación"? Opportunities for professional exercise of Rojas' brand new legal knowledge were necessarily limited in the rural and semi-feudal society he had left behind eight years earlier. In the Puebla, as we saw in the *Relaciones*, more often than not don Alonso Téllez' will was all the law there was. A person in Rojas' position either had to serve in his household, an uncomfortable and strife-ridden occupation at best, or else resign himself to a static and perhaps needy life as a country *hidalgo*. To supervise the cultivation of the "huerta de Mollejas" and the "majuelo de la cumbre" and to follow a weekly routine not dissimilar to that ascribed to Alonso Quijano by Cervantes was surely less than the Bachelor had been trained for. Whether Rojas refused the choice preferring to try himself out elsewhere as an independent lawyer, or simply found that there was no choice—that no patronage was available and that recognition as an *hidalgo* had been denied him by Lord and community—is uncertain. The only thing we can be reasonably certain of is that, once the move was made, the pattern of his life was set until death came thirty-four years later.

But why Talavera as a place to settle down in? Since it is the next sizeable community down the valley of the Tajo and, like the Puebla, under Toledan jurisdiction, Rojas could hardly have hoped to conceal (as his grandchildren attempted to do in Valladolid) his origins. But other probabilities may be conjectured. To begin with, living in Talavera only seven leagues away from his original home would not impose a rupture with the past. As we have seen, Rojas continued to visit his property and relatives in the Puebla long after his departure. It is, of course, true that he might have gone to Toledo, as did a fellow *hidalgo* similarly persecuted by don Alonso. But Toledo, particularly in 1507, could not have been attractive to a *converso* starting out in professional life and perhaps more interested in living unobserved than in rapid success. Not only was it tense from the severe social strains of the century that had just ended, but also, as the headquarters of the Inquisition, the resentments, suspicions, and intrigues of its inhabitants were never abated. As we have seen in the case of the Francos, frequent *autos de fe* and the gossip they occasioned gave an Inquisitional quality to life in Toledo that was only comparable to that of Seville. As Hernando del Pulgar, Royal Chronicler and *converso*, expresses it: "What can I say of the noble city of Toledo, the seat of Emperors, where the inhabitants of high and low degree live lives that are sad and forsaken by fortune?"[1]

In Talavera, however, *converso* elements of the population were far less intimidated. As we shall see, as late as 1517 they still dared to use their control over the municipal government to hamper the investigations of the Holy Office. Which is to say, Talaveran *conversos*, in spite of the tendency of their kind to develop internal patterns of discrimination when under pressure, had something of a mutual protection society at their disposal. Finally, there were relatives living in Talavera on whom Rojas may have counted for help in overcoming initial difficulties. Leonor Alvarez' aunt, Beatriz, had moved there with her husband, Francisco de Torrijos, and it is reasonable to assume that the two families, the Rojas and the Montalbanes, had other useful connections in the neighboring town. And there may have been any number of other relevant factors—perhaps Talaveran classmates in Salamanca—involved in the final choice.

Rojas' advantageous marriage to Leonor Alvarez probably coincided in time with his establishment in Talavera. In 1507 she was of eligible age—17 to be exact—and the fact that their first grandchild was born in 1530 tends rather to confirm than to deny the supposition. However, it is also likely that he journeyed to Talavera ahead of time to make practical arrangements for his new life and only afterwards undertook the slow ride up the valley of the Tajo

[1] Quoted in E. B. Ruano, *Toledo en el siglo XV*, Madrid, 1961, p. 158.

for the purposes of getting married and bringing home his bride and his sizeable dowry of 80,000 maravedís.[2] It was a route that he had travelled before and was to travel many times again, the last being perhaps on the occasion of the marriage of his eldest son, the Licentiate Francisco, to one of his Puebla cousins.[3] Events during these years which may be dated with more precision are: the purchase of a mortgage on Puebla property in 1512;[4] testimony in behalf of Diego Oropesa in 1517; the ordeals of Alvaro de Montalbán and his nephew (?), Bartolomé Gallego, in 1525; negotiations to obviate confiscation by the Inquisition of half of his dowry in 1527; legal dealings with the municipal government in 1527 and 1535; election as mayor for five weeks in 1538; and, finally, death sometime between the third and eighth of April, 1541.

[2] This sum, mentioned in the will as reverting to Leonor Alvarez before the division of the estate ("yo recibí con ella en dote y casamyento de sus padre y madre ochenta myll maravedis, ansy en dineros como heredades y bienes muebles . . . mando ante todas cosas sea pagada la dicha mi muger . . ."), amounted, as we shall see, to about one fifth of Rojas' estate at the time of his death and to at least twice what I estimate to be his peak annual income. Provision of a dowry of this size (when three daughters had to be considered) indicates the financial well being of Alvaro—and at the same time helps explain the continuing interest in his orthodoxy on the part of the Holy Office.

[3] The Licentiate Francisco married Catalina Alvarez de Avila from the Puebla, probably in the late 1530's. Their first child, the Licentiate Fernando, was born on November 5, 1541, some eight months after his grandfather's death (VLA 25). As we saw (Chap. V, n. 130), the testimony of a Puebla relative in the 1571 "probanza de Indias" (VLA 32), who attended the "desposorios" indicates return there for the ceremony. Rojas did, however, have the opportunity of dandling on his knees at least one grandchild, Ysabel Hurtada, born in 1530 (Serrano y Sanz, p. 298).

[4] VLA 5. See Chap. V, notes 3 and 129. The extremely thorough and indeed —to modern eyes—picayune text of the agreement generally follows the style of the model provided by *Las notas del relator* by Fernando Díaz de Toledo (1st ed., Burgos, 1490) which was in Rojas' possession. Two minor bits of specific information appear. The first is that in 1512 Rojas was still considered to be a "vecino de la Puebla": "I authorize and I recognize that I do sell to— and under oath do now and forever renounce the heritage in favor of—you, the honorable Bachelor Fernando de Rojas, neighbor of the Puebla de Montalbán, who are here present." The second is that Rojas is presented as kind to his relatives—or at least to Leonor's Aunt Elvira from whom the purchase was made: "I of my own free and agreeable will do hereby make a contribution, donation, and transfer of all future increments without conditions or contradictions . . . because of the many honors and good deeds which I owe to the aforesaid Bachelor. . . ." In evaluating this we must take into account both its somewhat formulaic sound and the probability that Rojas wrote it himself.

From these events and dates, we can only conclude, along with Menéndez Pelayo, that Rojas after marriage centered his life on his home and vineyard, on his legal practice and modest investments (mostly mortgages on rural properly), all in Talavera. The ratio of resignation to contentedness or of prudence to modesty during these thirty-four years we shall never ascertain. However, since the person who submitted himself to such an apparently unexceptional existence was none other than the author of *La Celestina*, we may at least try to find out all we can about it. Let us not think of the Talaveran years merely as a long and monotonous biographical postscript to a brief moment of literary glory. They were perhaps not exciting, but they do concern us. They are years of the life Rojas invented for himself—or was allowed to invent for himself—after he had finished inventing the lives of *La Celestina* for the world.

"La ynsigne villa de Talavera"

In medieval and Golden Age Spain men were defined by their places of birth to an extent that is difficult for us to comprehend. What Siegfried Giedeon terms the "communal ethos of the Gothic"[5] acquired for Spaniards an almost mythological permanency. To begin with, local pride occupied a large section of each individual's emotional spectrum, although of a kind not entirely identical with that which we ourselves have been brought up to feel. Less attention was paid to the customs, costumes, folklore, and regional dishes which fascinated the Romantics than to fame: the fame of monuments, origins, virgins, relics, heroes alive and dead, fertile land, water, and even bad weather. The Romantic cherished sentimentally the most insignificant details of life—particularly rural life—in his *patria chica*, while his ancestors asserted passionately the notability of the town (the surrounding country was secondary) that was his birthplace. Yet beneath the contrast, there is one significant likeness. In both the sentiment of the folklorist and the assertive pride of the Golden Age booster, locality serves as a shield against time. It is a way of associating oneself with the atemporal: that which either surpasses time (fame) or is impervious to its changes (custom). In the former case, one was given a perma-

---

[5] *Space, Time, and Architecture*, p. 55.

nent *ser* or identity as a Talaveran which armed the vulnerable consciousness against the ceaseless erosion of the world of *estar* or day-by-day existence in which one lived. The men of Rojas' era and afterwards were as deeply preoccupied with mutability ("that change of styles in clothing, that tearing down and replacing of buildings, and all the other different movements and variations to which our weak humanity gives rise") as the men in that of Sir Walter Scott were preoccupied with history. And in both cases locality was exalted as an antidote.

Intimately allied to this reassuring identification with something more permanent than naked personal existence was the sense of belonging genetically to a distinguished stem of mankind. Racism in a national sense is the worst temptation of the Romantic, and in the Spain of Rojas the *casta* represented another sort of biological timelessness more susceptible to identification with a particular locality. A person's *casta*, we remember, could be either famous or infamous, honored or dishonored (hence the practice of stigmatizing the descendants of victims of the Inquisition) and in this sense was not conceptually different from a locality. Furthermore, depending on the context, the word could refer to genetic units of all size from the race as a whole (the three *castas* of Jews, Moors, and Christians) to the individual family. The result was, as we have seen, that birthplace and birth were not conceived of as distinct and that the individual felt himself to belong almost carnally to the province, town, and even the neighborhood of which he was a "natural."

This confluence of municipal pride and clan identity—still a striking peculiarity of the Spanish-speaking world[6]—was a familiar theme of classical literature in Castilian. It appears in *La Celestina* when Rojas and Proaza exploit ironically the double valence of *nación* in their preliminary game of hide and seek. And in *Fuenteovejuna* Lope uses the same simultaneous geographical and biological connotations of the word *pueblo* in order to celebrate the human dignity of the villagers. The cry "¡Valiente pueblo!" expresses the sudden joining of Old Christian peasants and village

---

[6] For a contemporary anthropological discussion, see J. Pitt Rivers, *The People of the Sierra*, New York, 1954. However, one only needs to have talked to a few Spaniards or Spanish-Americans in order to realize the obsessively geographical quality of their sense of identity.

into a single and invincible organism. No matter how worthless or unsuccessful an individual might be (and Fuenteovejuna was not without examples), he was intuitively sure that he derived physical and spiritual virtues from those of his birthplace. The wandering and nationless bands of actors who carried Golden Age drama to the farthest corners of Spain and America were so aware of this myth of locality that they customarily prefaced their offerings with *loas* (poems of local praise) designed to flatter and appease their unruly audiences. These topical *loas*, repeated incessantly in one performance after another, are stale today, but at the time they functioned as effectively as folklore and local color for our more immediate forebearers.[7]

I do not insist here on the peculiar value of locality in Rojas' Spain because he—skeptical as he was of all passionately asserted values and beliefs—necessarily revered it. As we have seen, *La Celestina* is merciless with the honor of its significantly nameless city and with the local fervor of some of its inhabitants, notably Areusa. It might even be proposed that, having picked time as the winner in its war with value, Rojas cheered it on. Thus, when Rojas referred to his own *nación* in the acrostic verses, we surmised that he did so with a certain amount of defiant irony, sardonically reversing normal patterns of local and racial pride.

Nevertheless, if Rojas did not share these evaluations, he still had to cope with them—and so must we. Admitting that in the solitude of his consciousness he may have rejected the protective identity of person and place (or that he only subscribed to it in sarcastic terms), it is important to us now to understand what he was up against in Talavera. When *La Celestina* was written at the university, it was easy to express therein a point of view tangential to local assertiveness and to locality as a personal commitment. But now faced with the prospect of leaving the Puebla for good, Rojas' adjustment to community beliefs of this sort must have been both indispensable and difficult. Not only was it hard to move at all in such a world, but also Talavera, like other medium sized towns (2,000 heads of family were reported to Philip II in 1576)[8] seems

---

[7] In the negative world of the *pícaro*, as is well known, the topic of locality is parodied sardonically with the mention of such places as the *potro* of Córdoba and the *arenales* of Seville.

[8] *Relaciones*, II, 200. Of these some 200 were *hidalgos*. Ramón Carande gives the figure of 6,035 for the total population in 1530. This may be compared to

to have been particularly self-conscious and hard to penetrate. Extreme urban vanity is apparent both in the *Relaciones geográficas* and in that more abundant source of information, Cosme Gómez Tejada de los Reyes' *Historia de Talavera*,[9] from which I am about to quote at length. Whatever Rojas' hidden feelings may have been, Talavera, the way it thought about itself, and the magnitude of Rojas' success in being chosen as its mayor,[10] all need prefatory explanation before they can be understood by what I imagine to be the municipally alienated minds of some of my readers.

Cosme Gómez begins his *Historia* by informing us that the ancient name for Talavera was Elbora and that it is "one of the oldest towns in all Spain." In order to reassure the inhabitants that they did indeed belong to a diamantine, time-impervious community, it was customary for local historians to stress antiquity. Etymological "proof" of continuous existence from ancient times was a minimum requirement for the kind of monumentality demanded both by Cosme Gómez and his readers. As Galdós knew, doña Perfecta could not have *been* doña Perfecta without the derivation of Orbajosa from Urbs Augusta. Only an immutable identity for the town could provide immutable identities for those who participated in its being. Thus, at the end of the first chapter the proud author attributes the foundation of the town to the Greeks and discusses its continued existence under the Romans and—inexplicably enough—the Hebrews.[11]

Toledo's 31,930, Burgos' 8,600, and Madrid's 4,060 (*Carlos V y sus banqueros*, Madrid, 1965, I, 60).

[9] BNM 2039. See E. Alarcos García (*Homenaje*, Valladolid, 1965, pp. 616-634) for a presentation of Cosme Gómez' attack on "culteranismo" in his curious allegorical novel, *El león prodigioso* (Madrid, 1636). His interest in *La Celestina* accordingly was due not just to its local provenance but also (like Quevedo's interest in the poetry of Fray Luis) to its provision of an old-fashioned example of forceful style: "He fulfilled the obligations of that kind of writing, in such a way that modern writers of books of entertainment and others may understand that the art and elegance of expression does not consist of affected 'culturas,' the words of which resound in the air and flatter the ear but do not wound the soul because they lack solid ammunition" (*Orígenes*, p. 244).

[10] The importance of the mayoralty is emphasized by Cosme Gómez at length as well as by the reporters of the *Relaciones*. The former stresses Rojas' appointment as a major honor accorded to this "abogado docto": "y aún hizo algunos años oficio de Alcalde mayor" (*Orígenes*, p. 244).

[11] In the *Relaciones*, there are frequent proud references to stones with

In spite of the doubtfulness of this information, it is worthy of note that Cosme Gómez disdains popular myth making and rejects the belief that no less a figure than Hercules founded the town. Ascertainable antiquity is worth far more than "vulgares rumores"— as is further evident in the careful discussion of the municipal etymology in Chapter III. There the age of the town is ingeniously and probably correctly extended back to Iberian times: "I suspect the 'tala' is the same as town in the ancient language of Spain; thus names such as Talabán, Talarrubia, and Talamanca. . . ." The result of this speculation is another etymology, tala ebura: Talavera, meaning "town of the plain."[12] With such a pedigree the inhabitants did not really need to depend on Hercules or the legendary King Briga (who, according to the *Relaciones*, founded the town exactly 1,917 years before Christ) as guarantors of municipal fame. Unlike the humble Puebla de Montalbán which lacked an etymology, a history prior to the reconquest, and even a coat of arms, Talavera in its own opinion was an impressively antique and famous place to live.

Cosme Gómez was not a writer to be contented with mere assertion of municipal immutability. He prefers, and this is the fascinating thing about his *Historia* as compared with ordinary *loas* and town eulogies, to portray Talavera's timelessness within time, contrasted to time, engaging in uncertain war with time. In Chapter I immediately after proclaiming the ancient origins of the town, he begins to speak of the weather (a word that in Spanish as in other romance languages is significantly homonymous with time) and portrays his birthplace not elevated monumentally but submerged under a sea of changeable air:

Talavera occupies a pleasant valley floor that is about a league wide and runs from East to West. In both directions the valley opens out into spacious fields. Talavera lies in the fifth climate at 40 degrees North Latitude and lacks a few minutes of nine degrees Longitude. Geminis is dominant, and Mercury, the

---

Roman inscriptions, taken and reused from Roman buildings. Several are cited textually.

[12] Cosme Gómez apparently took this etymology from Mariana's *Historia* (book IV, chap. 13). Contemporary scholars agree on "ebura," but Menéndez Pidal relates "tala" to an identical Mediterranean root meaning "tierra pedregosa" (*Toponimia prerrománica hispana*, Madrid, 1952, p. 120, n. 30).

Lord of that sign, influences the town. The temper of the climate inclines towards humidity and heat, and because of this and because of the pernicious south winds that blow in summer and autumn, the place is not thought to be healthy. But the malice of these winds is corrected by the westerly winds which are frequent and pleasant, and at times the north wind comes and brings the freshness of the mountains of Segovia and of the inaccessible highest part of the Sierra de Gredos which is almost above the second region of the air.

Along with wind, there is water, the river Tajo—at once a symbol of time and of changlessness—flowing down from Toledo and the Puebla de Montalbán past the very walls of Talavera: "It is the most celebrated river in all Spain, famous for its golden sands, for its 'thin' and healthful water, and for the fertility and beauty of the land it irrigates. . . . Its wide banks enclose various channels which make agreeable little islands verdant with grass and poplars. . . ." Under the weather and by the river Talavera is not only a monument but a subject—"subjected" Stoically to influences and forces beyond its control.

The encounter of municipal timelessness with time is nowhere more apparent than in Cosme Gómez' rhapsodic description of the town fortifications. Although they now have almost entirely disappeared, when Rojas moved to Talavera in 1507 the town was girded by walls that were impressive (Father Mariana describes them as of "fearful aspect")[13] even in those days.[14] Three tiers of walls, some seventeen round towers standing out from them, other square towers each with a barbican, formed a grandiose structure which seemed to have been "specially exempted from the law and jurisdiction *de los tiempos.*" Here reference is made to the sort of time that is divided into seconds and centuries. But Cosme Gómez

[13] In the preface to *De rege et regis institutione*, quoted in P. F. de Paula Garzón, S.J., *El padre Juan de Mariana*, Madrid, 1889, p. 29.

[14] According to the *Relaciones*, the walls were 15 feet thick and 50 feet high, with protruding towers 60 feet high. Their existence represented a major improvement both in prestige and safety over life in the Puebla. As S. Sobriqués observes, "El río y la muralla son siempre elementos indispensables en una ciudad medieval. Una población por pequeña que fuese, si no la defendían un muro y un foso era tenida por cosa de poca monta que se tomaba a broma" (*Historia económica y social*, ii, 399). Here is one more excellent reason for suspecting Proaza and Rojas of irony in their treatment of the latter's "birthplace."

characteristically does not forget the other edge of the word: "The towers," he tells us, "have held fast and shown no weakness in their fierce combats with weather [*tiempo*] and water even when ferociously attacked during the rainy months of winter. . . ."

In spite of the confidence here displayed, the fact (also remarked on by Andrea Navagero)[15] that many of the stones used to construct the walls had been taken from "ruined edifices and sepulchres which occupied the fields" and that they were "cut by other hands for other buildings" with inscriptions in other languages is interpreted mournfully. In view of this past, the first signs of decay in walls and towers (the work of the elements, of time, and of the inhabitants who remove stones for new buildings, "a daring worthy of Castile") are ominous. Talavera, Cosme Gómez half admits and half denies, because of its very monumentality is fated to become a ruin. There was even a supernatural prediction of this fate on a stone inscribed in Arabic which, according to local belief, lay half way up the wall and read as follows: "When Tajo reaches so high, woe to Talavera!"[16] But we are "not yet" in ruins, he concludes ambiguously, and the fabric which surrounds us is a structure so grandiose that it "could never be built twice nor destroyed once."

Within the enclosure of the walls, the same assertions of monumentality and uneasy intimations of mutability coincide. The Alcázar, once one of the finest in the Kingdom with its halls, rooms, ceilings of inlaid wood, and courtyard is an uninhabitable ruin. Although the Archbishop of Toledo "has the obligation of maintaining its ancient splendor, the peace of the realm occasions disdain for castles, and, in order to save a moderate sum of money, it has been abandoned to the inconstancy of time." In the same way, the countless tournaments, bull fights, fiestas, displays of fireworks, horse races, and masked processions which had traditionally filled the town's twenty plazas during the long medieval autumn are at once praised and mourned by Cosme Gómez. These celebrations of urban fame were beginning to seem more and more expensive, and a special *regidor* had to be appointed to see to it that "their ancient

---

[15] *Viajes por España*, p. 261.

[16] "Cuando Tajo llega aquí, Talabera guay de tí!" Something of the same temporal uneasiness is to be heard in Sebastián de Orozco's complaint that *sambenitos* hung up in churches as permanent monuments of shame become ragged and lose their identifying names "in the course of time with its winds, waters, and suns." See Chap. IV, n. 15.

glory did not decay," a functionary who "in our constrained times is very necessary."

Inside the individual lives of the citizens of Talavera—a realm far beneath the horizon of the historian—a comparable duality obtained. On the one hand, each inhabitant constructed by force of will a social monument out of his own existence. He was honorable, poised (*sosegado*), capable of maintaining indefinitely rigid postures of gravity and reverence, a hero in potentiality. Yet all the while he senses life slipping away inside himself, undermining the prescribed corporal mask. It is hard to imagine—Castro tells us— "the intensity with which the Spaniard felt the process of self-creation and self-disintegration within his life."[17] This disintegration however, should not be understood merely in terms of old age, weakness, and disease (the corporal decadence which tormented Guillén de Castro's Diego Laínez)—conditions which, taken by themselves, were susceptible to the remedies of religious consolation and biological rebirth.[18] The really treacherous antagonists of these walking statues (Castro calls them "retablos de su propio existir")[19] was a sense of falsehood and vital inauthenticity. Each had his hidden secret—perhaps a carefully concealed stain in lineage, perhaps awareness of a moral incapacity that could never be confessed as in the case of Cardenio, or perhaps a nagging sense of inner vacancy of the sort that tormented Alonso Quijano. Intimacy and honor, lonely self-knowledge and rigidly maintained *opinión, estar,* and *ser,* thus, reproduced among the participating human organisms the dilemma of the colony as a whole.

The aspect of Talavera that is most easily—and most unconvincingly—portrayed as a monument to itself is the countryside: the fertile river valley and mountains of the municipal jurisdiction. Cosme Gómez spends pages on a neo-Virgilian description of pastoral parks, olive groves, sweet springs, laden vineyards, cunningly irrigated gardens, straining udders, overflowing beehives, bending branches of fruit trees, fragrant butter from mountain pastures, and even of fresh fish from the Tajo packed in snow for export to Toledo and Madrid. This rural cornucopia is true, which is to say

[17] *Realidad,* edn. II, p. 134.
[18] That is, not only in terms of the life to come in which we shall all be thirty years old according to Berceo, but also, as in the case of Rodrigo Díaz, in terms of the regeneration of the caste with the birth of new heroes.
[19] *Realidad,* ed. II, p. 244.

not falsified or even exaggerated. These products were produced, and they made Talavera when Rojas moved there, as it still is to-day, the center of a region of agricultural abundance outstanding in Castile. But, by portraying nature only in terms of plenitude and harvest, Cosme Gómez excises from it its crucial temporality. He converts it into its own culmination, a vegetable and animal monument which transcends the change and growth which brought it into being. Precisely for this reason, such topical word paintings of nature seem alien to experience, hopelessly citified.

Fernando de Rojas, who owned a vineyard outside of Talavera and who made his own wine with loads of grapes brought in on muleback (loads which were exempted from the municipal duties called "el portazguillo" because of his status as an *hidalgo*)[20] surely had a different vision of rural abundance. Having spent much of his life in the country (from the early days when he guarded the Huerta de Mollejas from local idlers to his later journeys of inspection of mortgaged properties around Talavera), he knew the treachery of seasons and the often catastrophic results of crop failure. As a result, he could hardly have subscribed to Cosme Gómez' Virgilian optimism. As the organic—both zoological and horticultural—imagery of *La Celestina* demonstrates poetically, Rojas was deeply aware that nature's bounty was weather- and time-fraught, as essentially temporal as consciousness itself.

The great herds of nomadic sheep which twice a year filled the stone bridge over the Tajo on the other side of the wall from Rojas' home also served as a reminder that the cyclical time of nature was alien to the monumentality of the city. Moving slowly from the mountains of León in the summer to Extremadura for the winter, the sheep were an herbivorous tide—a tide channelled by the few available bridges over the rivers flowing into the Atlantic, the Tajo and the Duero. As we remember, even the rickety wooden bridge at the Puebla, an alternate route expensive in its tolls and its accidental falls, received some of the spill over. Nor was the passage by Talavera as idyllically pastoral as Cosme Gómez might have described it. Exactly as if it were a real sea-tide, the annual ebb and flow attracted predators: the sheep thieves called *golfines* (literally "wolf-men") who gathered twice a year in the forested

[20] See Appendix III. The institution is referred to confusedly in the *Relaciones*.

ranges below town (the "Jaras") to prey on the passing flocks. Against them, Talavera used to send out mounted posses of archers from the municipal *Hermandad* (a militia which had been organized for protection during the anarchy of preceding reigns), and at times pitched battles were fought and substantial casualties suffered by both sides.[21]

There were, thus, two natures around Talavera: the inner belt of fields and gardens where insects and birds were a constant danger and a more savage outlying realm of mountain and forest. There shepherds wandered fearfully; wild animals (bears, wolves, and wild boars are mentioned by another historian)[22] and wilder men were hunted; pagan deities were still worshipped;[23] and there were even said to be giantesses and prodigious serpents lying in wait for lonely travellers.[24] In neither of these zones of nature did time behave as it did within the city walls. Instead of draining away in measured intervals, here and there held back by fragile dikes of fame, it flowed like the sheep, came to its flood, and then receded only to return again.

To conclude, both in its profound and rhythmic temporality and in the ceaseless "war and contention"—men against sheep, worms against crops, and the rest—nature around Talavera was far better described in the Prologue to *La Celestina* than in the *Historia* of Cosme Gómez. Whatever else may be said about the elusive figure of Fernando de Rojas, he did not share the city man's failure to grasp the country man's perception of time, a failure which lay at

---

[21] F. Jiménez de Gregorio in his detailed and fascinating study of Belvis, a hamlet in the jurisdiction of Talavera remarks on this: "The members of the Hermandad patrolled the *Jaras* tirelessly in pursuit of the *golfines*. . . . These latter armed with bows and arrows lived in a semi-savage state in a scented forest of shiny brambles, large cork trees, and live oaks. In mountain clearings many *golfines* were tied to the oaks and were executed by archery" ("El pasado económico-social de Belvis," *Estudios de historia social de España*, Madrid, 1952, p. 637).

[22] Fray Andrés de Torrejón, "Historia de Talavera por un monge de San Jerónimo," 1595, BNM 1498.

[23] *Ibid*. "De la villa de Mejorada que está una legua desta villa detrás de los cerros de la parte del norte traían en memoria de la diosa Palas, cuyo templo estava en aquel pueblo, una pala de madera muy adornada y compuesta de joyas y los demás trajes de una mujer galana lo cual duró hasta poco menos deste tiempo, y a pocos años que murieron unos viejos que la vieron traer, y, considerando los perlados era gentilicia superstición, mandaron que cesase."

[24] Jiménez de Gregorio, p. 635.

the roots of their antagonism. In earlier chapters we spoke of the rivalry between those who lived in the streets (*ruanos*) and those who lived in fields (a rivalry as bitter in Rojas' Talavera as anywhere else) in economic and social terms. The town was resented because of its financial power, its mysterious manipulation of money and credit in order to enmesh the land in a web of mortgages.[25] In Spain, too, the resentment was all the more bitter because of the unfair suspicion that all town dwellers were *conversos*. But beneath resentment and suspicion there was scorn—scorn on both sides—arising precisely from the way time was perceived and understood. As we shall see in a moment, it was from such facile scorn as this that Rojas' mind was blessedly exempted.

The rural occupations of the peasant populace—plowing, clod breaking, grafting, each in its season—were, as we have seen, despised as basely manual labor by those who attacked Cardinal Silíceo, Marquillos de Mazarambros, and the prejudiced Franciscan friars. It was a feeling that was returned with interest. Countrymen knew intuitively that city dwellers, on a level deeper than rapacity or questionable faith, had an inauthentic sense of time. As they looked at calendars or listened to the striking of the hours (Lewis Mumford sees hourly measurement of time as the fatal disease of medieval order),[26] they dreamed and prated to timelessness, of the monumental eternity of the city, of their tombs, or, if they could afford them, their private chapels. Money made temporally—indeed made from time conceived of abstractly—was supposed to render them timeless. This was not only contradictory and unconsciously hypocritical; it was also on both its terms untrue to temporal reality. Neither clocks nor monuments were relevant

---

[25] See Carande, I, 75. Jiménez de Gregorio offers precise details concerning the economic aspect of rural resentment against Talavera and concerning vain peasant efforts to escape town domination.

[26] When bells stopped ringing for prayers and began to strike the hours, human life underwent an intimate revolution: "The idea of time, or rather, temporality, resumed its hold over men's minds. All over Europe, beginning in the thirteenth century, the townsmen erected campaniles and belfries to record the passing hour. Immersed in traffic or handicraft, proud of his city or his guild, the citizen began to forget his awful fate in eternity; instead he noted the succession of minutes and planned to make what he could of them" (*The Golden Day*, New York, 1957, p. 3). These ideas are further developed in *Technics and Civilization*, pp. 12-18.

to natural time, the time of seasons and weather, the only time that really counted.

A priest in Rojas' parish church of San Miguel and a prominent member of a prominent family of Talaveran intellectuals, Gabriel Alonso de Herrera, presented these two antithetical perceptions of time in contemporary terms. In the prologue to a book that was to be reprinted almost as many times as *La Celestina,* the *Libro de agricultura* (1513),[27] he compares the life of a merchant with that of a cultivator of the fields. Beginning with Pliny's commonplace (used later by Cervantes and Lazarillo de Tormes) to the effect that "there is no book so bad that it does not contain something worth saving," he justifies his as neither heretical nor fictional.[28] Instead, it may persuade the reader to follow a way of life which will be "without offense to God": "For if we speak of merchants, what other vocation or trade is there in which danger grows more lushly for the soul? Their bodies are bent over with toils and fears. They never feel safe on land or sea because of their trials, perjuries,

[27] *Libro de agricultura que es de la labrança y criança y de muchas otras particularidades y provechos del campo,* "copilado por Gabriel Alonso de Herrera, Dirigido al muy illustre y Reverendíssimo señor don fray Francisco Ximénes Arçobisbo de Toledo y Cardenal de España su señor." I have had access to a Córdoba 1563 version "nuevamente corregido y añadido por el mesmo." The first recorded edition is Alcalá de Henares, 1513. Bonilla (in his "Un antiaristotélico del Renacimiento, Hernando Alonso de Herrera," *RH,* L, 1920, p. 73) lists 28 other editions (omitting the one used here and probably others) in Spanish, Italian, and Latin. He also provides biographical data which, although we shall deal with the family as a whole later on, may be mentioned here. Probably born after 1460, Herrera received the degree of Bachelor at Salamanca (possibly in medicine since he discourses at length on the medicinal properties of agricultural products) and later travelled and studied extensively in France and Italy. At some point he joined the entourage of Fray Hernando de Talavera in Granada where he studied Moorish agricultural techniques and planted an experimental orchard and garden. That he wrote the treatise in his native town is indicated in the text by sentences beginning "Aquí en Talavera . . ." and the like. Bonilla concludes from other comments that, in addition to his interest in science, he was an ecclesiastic, and, indeed, in 1515 a person of his name is listed as "Beneficiado en San Miguel." Since Rojas lived precisely in this parish, it is certain that he not only knew Herrera but saw him frequently.

[28] Books such as his, he states, will keep their readers out of trouble: "Esto entiendo yo conque no sean libros de doctrinas heréticas ni tampoco de fábulas ni mentiras que despiertan y abivan a pecar que los avían de quemar con sus autores" (fo. iii). One wonders how such an opinion may have struck the author of *La Celestina.*

411

deceits, and falsehoods. They spend most of their time away from home, and they always desire repose and tranquillity." In contrast to this wretchedness, agriculture offers "quietude, security, and innocence, . . . a safe and saintly life, foreign to sin, . . . healthy, . . . and without rancors and enmities." Thus, the Bachelor Herrera invites his fellow townsmen to abandon their perilous dedication to the abstract measurement of time and money and to rediscover the natural and divine order that exists on the other side of the walls: "¡O vida del campo ordenada por Diós!"[29]

How has God ordered natural life? The answer is the substance of Herrera's treatise and particularly of the last section, a detailed theoretical and practical amplification of the medieval topic *Laus omnium mensium*.[30] Here in rational rather than traditional terms, he instructs the apprentice farmer in his seasonal and monthly activities. The time to sow and the time to reap, the signs for good and bad weather, the menace of erosion—all these represent an ageless time alien to that measured by clockwork or percentages of return. In a world lashed to the wheel of fortune and impelled by measureless ambition, Herrera in his curiously technical "alabanza de aldea" proposes return to the existence of the "patriarchs and prophets" and the founding fathers of Rome.

Because of the well-advertised hazards involved in proceeding directly from biography to creation, I would not try to relate Rojas' life first in the rural Puebla and afterwards in urban Salamanca to the presence of these two antithetical varieties of time in *La*

[29] Herrera is ambiguous in his attitude towards the Old Christian peasants who actually were engaged in the work of agriculture. He begins by lamenting that "los labradores a quien pertenesce saber esto no saben leer" and so cannot learn from his work. And later he exclaims with even more benevolence: "¡O quánto devemos y somos obligados a los labradores de cuyo trabajo nos sustentamos! Y ellos son dignos y merecedores de mas favores y libertades que muchos que heredan hidalguías" (fo. iiii). On the other hand, it is clear that his book is clearly intended for a public of gentlemen farmers and *mayordomos*. For example, when he discusses the time for planting and harvesting, he advises the owner or a trusted representative to be on hand to avoid thefts and to defeat the countless stratagems employed by hired hands in their ceaseless war with their masters. Elsewhere, mourning the agricultural decline of Castille, he places the blame squarely on the laziness, carelessness, and ignorance of its farmers.

[30] This section of the book is accompanied by emblematic woodcuts clearly in the medieval tradition.

412

Celestina.[31] However, certain passages in the work can be used to illustrate the author's awareness of their duality. The conflict within human lives of measured, urban, rational time with natural tempos and biological drives that begins in Act I and extends all the way through expresses a basic predicament of man in society. The very haste and impatience of the lovers (illustrated with striking animal imagery)[32] are concomitant with the community's artificial damming up of natural channels. But against these frenzied individuals, Rojas' opposes the figure of Sosia, the groom, "born and brought up in a village and better suited for breaking clods with a plough" than for amorous posturing. He alone—and how sympathetically Rojas portrays him as compared to the rustics of a Lucas Fernández or a Torres Naharro!—is really at home in time, contentedly integrated to its flow. Thus, he describes himself "driving his horses to water on moonlit nights, taking his pleasure in singing *cantares* to lighten the burden of work and to put aside bad temper" (XVII). Unlike his master, Sosia lives in profoundly rhythmic tune with his own life.

And it is Sosia, appropriately enough, who brings the opposition of urban and rural time to the surface of the dialogue. "Tristán," he says, as the two accompany Calisto on his return from Melibea's garden, "it now behooves us to go silently, for there arise at this hour rich men, those who are greedy for worldly goods, the devout who frequent temples, monasteries, and churches, lovers such as our master, those who go out to work in the fields, and shepherds who now bring their sheep to yonder pastures for milking . . ." (XIV). This mixture of motives and rhythms constitutes a marvel-

---

[31] In Talavera Rojas may be thought of as living at once an urban and a rural existence. While practicing as a town lawyer, he also was engaged in agricultural activities ("la viña que es al pago de Terunbre"), activities which the family continued and expanded after his death. In 1578 the Licentiate Francisco (we learn from the Valle Lersundi archives) made a special provision in his will for his son Garci Ponce (whom we encountered previously as a solicitor in Valladolid married to doña Maria de Salazar) because of his help in this connection (doc. 20). Nor was this duality of concern exceptional. As Lewis Mumford points out, it was common for burghers all over Europe to have their own orchards and vineyards in the suburbs while towns themselves were "persistently rural" in character (*The City in History*, New York, 1961, pp. 288-289).

[32] As studied in detail and with remarkable insight by George Shipley in "Functions of Imagery in *La Celestina*," Harvard diss., 1968.

413

lous range of temporal experience: from the clock-harassed rich men and lovers, through those obedient to the canonical ritual of matins, to the diurnal acceptance of ploughmen and shepherds. City and country have come together in a passage which communicates poetically the sense of the writer's future existence just behind the city wall in Talavera. Although the treatment of time in *La Celestina* is far more complex, in the figure of Sosia literary expression can at least be said to coincide with a biographical experience that was lifelong. Once again we have observed human existence from the high soaring of Rojas' untrammelled *juyzio*.

Reentering the gates of Talavera accompanied now by Max Weber instead of Cosme Gómez, we observe that its strong sense of identity and self-importance corresponded to a municipal autonomy which, though much reduced by the Catholic Monarchs, was still considerable. Talavera was in effect "economically a seat of trade and commerce, politically a fortress and a garrison, administratively a court district, and socially an oath-bound confederation."[33] As such, it was aware of itself as a functioning individual entity with a distinct "pattern of human life, . . . a total system of life forces brought into some kind of equilibrium."[34] According to municipal archives, it was Talavera as such that was responsible for raising and dispatching troops, and in them there is still preserved a 1522 letter from Charles V thanking the town, as if it were a human vassal for its good behavior during the rebellion of the Comunidades. The Emperor gratefully promises his royal favor in the future.[35] Like a military regiment, the community is recognized as a unique entity.

Existence as a *polis* or at least as a partially independent city state depended, as Weber suggests, primarily on effective local participation in the government, and in Rojas' century this seems to have been very much the case. Talavera was a fief of the Arch-

---

[33] *The City*, tr. D. Martindale and G. Neuwirth, New York, 1958, p. 111. The last item in Weber's minimum list of requirements would seem to correspond to the annually elected *jurados*, sworn to preserve municipal traditions and to observe critically the functioning of the government. In a sense, we may think of such selected but ordinary citizens as swearing fealty to the town as an entity.

[34] Quoted from Martindale's prefatory summary, p. 38.

[35] L. Jiménez de la Llave, "Archivo municipal de Talavera de la Reina," *BRAH*, XXIV (1894), 188.

bishop of Toledo with his representatives (usually of local origin) holding ultimate administrative power. In practice, however, this power was exercised in terms of a complex web of local customs, ranks, offices, privileges, and institutions jealously maintained by the citizens in the medieval tradition.[36] The outstanding privilege and honor of the town (discussed both by Cosme Gómez and in the *Relaciones*) was local appointment of the mayor in periods between the death of one Archbishop and the investiture of his successor. Unlike Toledo, Talavera had not undergone sustained periods of internal disorder, factionalism, massacres, or uprisings, and the fabric of its existence as a community was far more intact.[37] Guilds, parishes, traditional festivals, religious brotherhoods[38] all continued to define existence within the walls and to create stable patterns of interpersonal relations. It was precisely this that made possible the substantial degree of autonomy that Talavera continued to enjoy even during the reign of Philip II. It also, as we shall see, seems to have helped limit to some extent the disruptive activities of the Inquisition, an institution more at home either in the strife-ridden cities of Toledo, Córdoba, and Seville or in villages more easily prey to ingrown caste resentments.

The population of Talavera contained a high percentage of *con-*

---

[36] Cosme Gómez explains in detail how the twelve permanent posts of *rexidores* are sold to rich citizens "for not less than 5,000 ducats"; how the *jurados* are appointed (first by electing three from the estate of *hidalgos* and three from that of *hombres buenos* and afterwards by selection, the Archbishop choosing four from those nominated); how the *procurador general* is picked by the town council from among the three who obtain the highest number of parish votes; etc.

[37] Amador de los Ríos, p. 483.

[38] In discussing the twelve local *cofradías* (which paraded at funerals and religious ceremonies) Cosme Gómez pays particular attention to that of the thirty *hidalgos* which began when "in ancient times the *caballeros* of Talavera grew proud of their nobility and power and made themselves intolerable to the *hidalgos*, and these latter, finding themselves oppressed, formed a confederation to defend themselves from knightly excesses." He also remarks that in the first years of the 16th century one of the *cofradías* demanded proof of cleanliness of blood, but that afterwards "on the advice of holy and wise men the requirement was dropped." Torrejón, on the other hand, discusses a "cofradía de nuestra señora" as imposing a statute of discrimination and goes on to defend it. " 'La gente maculada,' " he says, "tend to be restless and ambitious, although not all of them in general have that fault, and it would be unsuitable for those who crucified our Lord to serve His sovereign mother. Moreover it is necessary to respect the demands of 'la honrra humana.' "

415

versos. In addition to those who, according to Amador de los Ríos, had flocked to the baptismal font in the panic year of 1391,[39] there was a substantial colony of unconverted Jews throughout the fifteenth century. In 1450, for example, a 9,000-ducat assessment imposed on the town was apportioned as follows: 3,000 from the Christians (both Old and New), 2,500 from the Jews, 500 from the Moriscos, and 3,000 from the outlying territories and dependent villages.[40] Many of these hitherto resolute Jews, willing to face manual labor[41] and discrimination of all kinds in order to remain true to their faith, must nevertheless have weakened in 1492. The result was that, when Rojas moved within the walls of Talavera, he found not only some 200 other *hidalgos* and *caballeros* but also a medium-sized community in which perhaps a majority of the inhabitants shared his racial origins. All of which leads to a tentative conclusion: in Talavera (and presumably in other communities like it) the assimilation of *conversos* to Christian habits and social behavior had been more successfully achieved than in the Puebla or in Toledo. Here was a town ideal for the kind of existence we imagine Rojas proposing for himself. On the one hand, it was a structured community, proud of its coat of arms, customs, monuments, guilds, noble families, and famous citizens, and, on the other, it had accepted, integrated, and made good use of the New Christians who were willing to contribute to its way of life.

❧ "First of all, the principal houses of his home"

For all its elusive recession into time, the life of Fernando de Rojas has left us two major souvenirs: the quality of its consciousness as revealed enigmatically in *La Celestina* and the contents of its dwelling place as listed specifically in the will and in the two inventories taken after death.[42] Anything else that we dare say about

---

[39] Amador de los Ríos, p. 483.

[40] F. Fita, "Documentos inéditos, anteriores al siglo XVI, sacados de los archivos de Talavera de la Reina," *BRAH*, 11 (1882), 317. For further discussion of this *reparto* together with general comments on the Jewish community of Talavera, see Baer, 1, 202.

[41] The *padrón* of some 168 named contributors lists a great many basket weavers, smiths, harness makers, and shoemakers along with the more expectable *físicos*, *tenderos*, and *sastres* (*ibid.*, p. 332).

[42] The first, of course, was that published along with the "Testamento" by

it is based either on speculative reconstruction or on chance shards of information which more often than not seem to tease and mislead more than they illuminate. Only the text and the post-mortem documents can fully and satisfactorily be known. It is therefore particularly ironic that these two records should appear so alien and unrelated to each other that they almost seem to refer to different human beings. Is the Rojas, at once enthusiastic and meditative, who describes himself sitting chin in hand musing excitedly on a fragmentary masterpiece and who boasted confidently about his "principal study" identical with the one who carefully organized his own funeral, weighed gold on tiny scales, supervised wine-making, and held "certain books" belonging to his colleague, the Bachelor Cáceres, as security for a loan of twelve ducats? One answer, of course, is that he is not. The student in 1498 and the dying man in 1541 are separated not merely by years but by the day-by-day choices made during each of them and the experience thereby determined. Four decades and the innumerable leagues covered during their span are sufficient to turn any man—even the most biographically humdrum—into somebody else.

On the other hand, there is an organic continuity to any life—even the most biographically unstable. When we read the inventory of Rojas' books, the old ones he brought back from Salamanca as well as those accumulated in Talavera, or when we discover among his possessions "a chessboard with all its pieces," we sense that this may be the same person after all. We sense that his mind has gone on living inside itself, talking uninterruptedly to itself, over the years. It is precisely these meager indications of a continuing intellectual life that point to the authentic difference between meeting Rojas in *La Celestina* and searching for him in his testamentary documents. The first is a construct of consciousness—organic, complex, ambiguous—and the second is a souvenir—a casual, straightforward, and factual description of the tangible domestic camouflage worn by consciousness.

The risks involved in such a simplified dichotomy are apparent. Rojas, like all men, necessarily became to some degree identified

---

Valle Lersundi (VL II), and the second was made after the death of Leonor Alvarez in 1546 (VLA 27A).

with the domestic and municipal roles which society offered him after graduation. As we surmised both in connection with his *hidalguía* and his law practice, he *was* the person known to his neighbors. For, as James Baldwin warns us, roles, although constructed to "help us survive," are dangerous by definition: "The world tends to trap you and immobilize you in the role you play; and it is not always easy—in fact it is always extremely hard—to maintain a kind of watchful mocking distance between oneself as one appears to be and oneself as one actually is."[43] On the other hand, who could be better equipped to cope with this danger than an artist who premised his art on ironical distinction between internal and external forms of existence. Which really amounts to saying that Rojas, as a *converso* and above all as author of *La Celestina*, is an unlikely subject for naturalistic description. His domestic milieu was surely less a determinant than itself determined by desire for survival and by the resultant cautious and self-conscious approach to daily living. From which we may further conclude that the chasm between the Rojas who, in the words of Kenneth Burke, "danced out" his dilemma and resentment in 1498 and 1501 and the Rojas who sat back and counted his possessions in 1541 is more an appearance than a reality. Like the neighbors in Talavera, we suspect that something secret lies behind the display of conventional living, but we cannot be sure what it may be.

With these reservations in mind, let us now examine Rojas' domesticity as revealed in the Valle Lersundi archives. Since we have been given the raw material for the kind of portrait which might better have been drawn by Azorín—which is to say, a portrait of an existence which has learned to accept triviality and console itself with each day's less than climactic portion of experience—we should not refrain from exploiting it. Can we be sure after all whether the immobile, bittersweet, and gentle Rojas whom Azorín might have described was not one of his innumerable selves? Let us imagine him, then, waking up one morning early in 1540. His wife is at his side; his head rests on a new French pillow embroidered in black silk; and he looks up at the "painted canopy" which covers the "matrimonial bed." Painted in what style and representing what?—Azorín would have asked, and we share the

---

[43] *Nobody Knows My Name*, New York, 1962, pp. 218-219.

curiosity. It is cold, and the two dress quickly, Rojas putting on his "slashed doublet," his hose (made by "Diego López, calçetero" to whom he owed "two reales"), and perhaps even his ankle-length brown serge cape. Leonor Alvarez, now 50 or 51, wears a silver ring worth ten maravedís and, if there is any reason for celebration, a dress with "three velvet ribbons" and a "necklace with ten chalcedon beads and two of jasper." She looks at herself before leaving the room in one of her two mirrors. The image is blurred if she picks the metal mirror, distorted if it is the glass one.

As husband and wife dress, they think of the activities of the day that is beginning: meals must be prepared, accounts calculated, colleagues, clients, and friends visited, and the adolescents still living home instructed and helped. Perhaps they have just learned of the pregnancy of Catalina Alvarez de Avila, their cousin and daughter-in-law, and speak of the future of the first born of their first born. When they leave the room, they push aside the heavy green curtain, embroidered with a woolen eagle, which covers the door and keeps out draughts.

Breakfast is eaten in the kitchen under the enormous chimney where the fire of vine prunings and mountain kindling crackles. There are three braziers in the house, but it will take time to kindle or revive their heat. At this hour it is more agreeable to sit at a big wooden table in the kitchen and watch the fire blaze under the iron tripod with its hanging cauldron. There are two maidservants, Francisca del Alamo and Juana de Torres (who lived out with her husband), and during the modest breakfast they are not excluded from the family circle. As Lewis Mumford points out, cohabitation of masters and servants (even to the extent of sleeping in the same room) was normal at the time.[44] Some years later both women were to be remembered in the will of daughter Juana,[45] probably about 13 or 14 years old when she appears at breakfast on this particular morning. The other children still living at home were the future *escribano*, Alvaro, about 19, and Juan de Montemayor (who

[44] *The City in History*, p. 286.

[45] A Francisco del Alamo (perhaps a relative of Francisca) testified in favorable terms in the Indias *probanza* in 1571. At that time he was about 60 years of age. Alonso Martín, the husband of Juana de Torres, was sent to Toledo when the Bachelor's estate was settled to collect the 44 ducats which, as we shall see, he had lent interest free to his sister-in-law, Ysabel Núñez.

departed for Nombre de Dios in Panama after his father's death and never returned) aged somewhere between his brother and sister.

In spite of the Dickensian cosiness and intimacy suggested by these remarks, were we to listen to the conversation around the fire, we would probably be surprised at its formality. Rojas was undoubtedly addressed as "Señor padre," and when he referred to his wife, he probably found most suitable the words spoken by Pleberio in Act XVI: "Señora muger." A 1555 letter written by Rojas' daughter Catalina to her elder brother, the Licentiate Francisco, begins: "Sir, the letter I received from your grace [*vuesa merced*] brought grace with it, for I had wished for it for a long time, and I was delighted to learn that your grace and my lady, Catalina Alvarez, and the rest of the household are in good health. May God continue to grant it to your graces and guard you [*los*] for many years and allow me to visit you as is my wish."[46] Family greetings on the morning of which we speak may have been less stilted than this epistolary sample of sixteenth-century interpersonal relations, but they were probably just as respectful. One might even propose that from Rojas' point of view, Calisto's domestic establishment as described in Act I was not so much immoral as unseemly. The intimacy of relationship among servants and master was closely related to their wrangling and their lack of human respect and liking one for another.[47]

The kitchen was on the ground floor and opened on to a courtyard with a well in the center. From the description given in the

---

[46] VLA 28B.

[47] We ourselves seem closer to the informal interpersonal relations of the Cid and his vassals than to those of either Pleberio and Alisa or Calisto and his servants. The point is that the comic effect of Rojas' portrayal of the unwholesome intimacy and mutability of what went on in the latter's house depended for 16th-century readers on its contrast to their own standards of behavior. In the times of the frontier, reactions had been spontaneous and immediate; but now society had taken over and the individual attempted to conceal his own passions, vices, and tides of inner change beneath a conventional mask. Decorum, status, rank, and their recognition by others (as readers of 17th-century history are well aware) seemed all important. For such readers, *La Celestina*, the picaresque novels, and above all the *Quijote* furnished a release which could be either shocking or wholesome (or both)—and which was always accompanied by laughter. As we remember, Cervantes remarks that socially oppressed pages and varlets sick and tired of the anteroom and of the stuffed shirts they served were his most enthusiastic admirers.

420

will, it would appear that the back of the courtyard was the city wall and that around it extended the three wings or *casas* of the dwelling. There is no way of calculating the exact size of the place, but the modest quantity of furniture listed in the inventory indicates that it was anything but palatial—not at all comparable to the dwellings of Pleberio or Calisto with their stables, towers, servants' quarters, and the rest. Buildings and land, together, were valued at 80,000 maravedís in the division of property made after Rojas' death, a substantial but not enormous sum. That Leonor Alvarez' dowry was exactly the same amount may indicate that this was the original purchase price. Which is to say, when Rojas went to Talavera, Alvaro de Montalbán provided him with enough capital to allow his daughter to live in the modest but comfortable style to which she was accustomed.

The furniture in the wing used for living was equally unimpressive. Two rugs and seven floor pillows upholstered in green rug material gave a note of Moorish comfort not unusual at the time. There was also an "old divan," but the rest of the furniture consisted of hinged tables, benches, beds, and a few of those peculiarly uncomfortable backless Spanish chairs.[48] There were, of course, no closets. Both clothes and Leonor Alvarez' good supply of table and bed linen were stored in locked chests of which some ten are listed. Smaller chests and coffers were reserved for special purposes such as the storage of wax, candles, and sewing materials. There was also a strongbox for money and for other valuables including the gold jewelry, silver spoons, and silver salt shaker which were apparently held as security for loans. In the inventory there is no indication of plates or glassware, all apparently so inexpensive as not to be worth the trouble of listing. Talavera's Morisco artisans were famous for their pottery, and during Rojas' lifetime were beginning to introduce the likenesses of fantastic animals and birds into their traditional blue and white geometric designs. These, we surmise, were used both at table and for wall decoration. All in all, however livable, it was an establishment unlikely to excite the envy of its

---

[48] A description of a similar house is given by S. Sobriqués in his previously cited section of Vicens Vives' *Historia*. He remarks that such accessories as "tapices, alfombras, almohadones, y arquillas" were more important than furniture in the sense we think of it today (p. 398). Two of the chairs are mentioned specifically in the inventory as possessing the luxury of backs.

neighbors or the greed of the Inquisition. It was, in fact, almost self-consciously modest, far removed from the "insulting luxury" for which many of Rojas' fellows (including his relatives, the Francos) paid dearly.

Rojas' home was more than an address—on the street of Gaspar Duque in the Parish of Saint Michael—and more than an elaborate form of social camouflage with walls behind which to hide and furniture on which to sit, lie, or rest the elbow while doing so. Like all homes, it was also a place for using and organizing time, which is to say, for carrying on activities necessary for the maintenance of life. This is still the case today, at least as far as meals, relaxation, and sleep are concerned, but in the sixteenth century the home was an almost autonomous unit of production both for its own needs (baking, weaving, etc.) and for those of the community (as a workshop, pharmacy, or whatever). Rojas' house, accordingly, was also his law office. There he kept his professional library of some 45 tomes, a work table, his account books (the outstanding debits and credits are listed in the inventory), two scrivener's tables (I assume for clerks) with scissors and knives for preparing quill pens, a scale for weighing gold, and the strongbox.

If it was to his office or perhaps to the stable to see to the saddling of his mule for the road[49] that Rojas went after breakfast, Leonor Alvarez had more numerous alternatives. Aside from fill-in occupations such as spinning, knitting, or embroidering on her two frames, her supervisory functions were constantly changing: baking, washing, cleaning, cooking, and the rest, according to long established daily and hourly routine. The symbol of her authority was (as still today in provincial Spain) the great bunch of keys carried at her waist. For example, on the day set aside (perhaps once a month) for making candles she opened the chest containing the wax, locked it again, and saw to it afterwards that the newly-made candles were secure in their own receptacle. Constant inspection and watchfulness becomes a second nature in such an existence— just as carelessness characterized that of Calisto's housekeeperless domicile. The cleanliness of the various rooms, the state of the family clothes (so expensive at the time that Celestina preferred

---

[49] No domestic animals are mentioned in the *inventario*, but there is a "freno viejo y unas cabeçadas de mula, viejas" (p. 380).

a "saya" to a gift of money), the supplies on hand, all had to be kept under constant review.[50] If we add to this the necessity of visible and audible religious devotion—praying, reading aloud from the *Flos sanctorum* or the other pious books in the family library, and telling the beads on her "ebony rosary" in a part of the house where the servants might take note—we come to the conclusion that Leonor Alvarez did not find time hanging heavy on her hands. The idleness and folly of Melibea's mother, Alisa, seem out of the question in the household described by the inventory.

A large portion of Leonor Alvarez' time was spent on food preparation, not excluding the staples of bread and wine. Baking was done at home with flour made from wheat stored in the house and taken to one of the mills on the Tajo (the remains of one at the other side of the old bridge may still be seen) for grinding. As for wine, once a year everything else was put aside when loads of grapes were brought in from the vineyard into the court and piled high in baskets and panniers before being pressed. Daily preparation of food began with shopping for the fresh fruits and vegetables of the season, fish, and more infrequently meat at the town market —although many of these items must also have appeared in the house as gifts from Rojas' rural clients or as rent in kind. As we remember from Act IX, this was the case in Calisto's establishment. On special occasions, Leonor Alvarez may have looked in the market place for such local delicacies as partridge, trout from the high streams of the Sierra de Gredos, or capons. And when she got out her cookbook, the *Libro de cozina* of Ruperto de Nola (1525), she may have gone further and taken a hand in the kitchen herself. We may imagine her, for example, following the recipe for "manjar blanco," a dish of chicken, rice flour, and milk, sprinkled with sugar and "considered to be one of the three most principal delicacies in the world."[51]

---

[50] The two inventories in themselves provide evidence of careful supervision of what was owned and owed.

[51] *Libro de cozina*, reprinted, Madrid, 1929. Most of Nola's dishes were highly spiced and relied on a combination of sweet and sour ingredients for a determined assault on the palate. Among the more interesting recipes are several of Moorish origin prescribing olive oil (for example, "calabazas a la morisca") and roasted cat ("gato asado como se quiere comer") alternately basted and flayed with green branches.

On most days, however, either Francisca del Alamo or Juana de Torres could be trusted with the pots, skillets, roasters, and cauldron mentioned in the inventory. Maidservants knew then—as they still know from the same oral tradition—how to prepare excellent stews and well cooked fish, fowl, and egg dishes. Pork, ham, and the mildly spiced sausage called "chorizo" were served frequently (judging by reports on other *converso* households) and eaten with as much ostentation as suppressed resentment.[52] As Castro explains, the ham and eggs regularly reappearing on Alonso Quijano's table were termed in the sarcastic slang of the time "duelos y quebrantos" (afflictions and miseries).[53] On the other hand, olive oil was the basic fat, as it had been for Rojas' ancestors and as it was becoming (its replacement of lard was the one great triumph of Mohammedan and Jewish dietary laws) in most Spanish households. Another satisfaction was the long anticipated seasonal appearance of *primicias* or first fruits and vegetables (Talavera was specially proud of its asparagus), a pleasure lost to an age of artificial preservation and long distance marketing. All in all, and aside from the imposition of pork, there seems to be little reason for commiserating with the culinary fate of Talavera's sixteenth-century burghers.

Were we to enter Rojas' house, as don Quijote and Sancho entered that of don Diego de Miranda, the Knight of the Green Overcoat, we would undoubtedly share their admiration for the enormous *tinajas* (earthenware containers like those in which Ali Baba hid) in the courtyard. In both families (the Mirandas and the Rojas) these were the outward indications of bourgeois security; in them were stored the wheat, oil, and wine that in those uncertain times would enable the members to survive an interruption in supplies. No one knew better than the creator of Pleberio the hazards of overconfidence in such material security, but that awareness does not in any way imply willingness to dispense with it. Like his father-in-law, Rojas apparently felt that a glass of wine, a serving of chicken, and a warm coat were not to be despised. He and his wife took good care, therefore, that their 34 *tinajas* of vari-

---

[52] "I con esto verás criar en sus casas gruesos lechones y marranos; y sáuete que cada gruñido que dan les es una gruessa lanzada, como si el Cid los hiriesse" (*Diálogo entre Laín Calvo y Nuño Rasura*, pp. 178-179).

[53] *Cervantes y los casticismos*, p. 15.

ous sizes (the largest held 60 *arrovas*, or about 240 gallons) were properly cleaned with a special brush, filled to the brim, and tightly capped with the right *tapadores*.

Thus if Rojas' residence provided, as I have surmised, social camouflage (conventional refuge for the errant consciousness of its inhabitants), it was at the same time a place of physical sanctuary. It was a place where—as Sancho knew when he saw don Diego's *tinajas*—there would be always something to eat and drink. Even in an age of bomb shelters, piped-in utilities, vulnerable freezers, and match-box construction, the words "house" and "home" still carry connotations of safety, independence, and comfort. And in Rojas' Spain the difference between inside and outside, between being provided for and abandoned to chance, between shelter and exposure was so great as to be almost palpable. Hence, the emotion of Sancho and even of don Quijote when they are taken in from the road, and hence, too, Celestina, when she goes out of doors, echoes the classical cry of "Goodbye, walls!" with personal fervor. The 34 *tinajas* were a tangible part of this sense of domestic reassurance. They were nothing less than Rojas' biographical answer to the picaresque and shelterless ("*obdachlos*," in the German of Lukacs) existence of the multitudes who in his Spain were forced out of doors or who, according to their individual *fortunas y adversidades*, moved continually from house to house. The life of a Cervantes is a case in point.

Domestic time could not, of course, be entirely devoted to business, to manifest piety, and to the semi-ritual labors required for provision of life's three necessities. As Rojas phrases it in his Prologue, there were "other hours destined for recreation." Or, in the words of his most illustrious reader and admirer, "one is not always in church; not always are the chapels filled with the devout; nor always are we occupied with business matters, however important they may be; there are also hours for recreation during which the afflicted spirit may find repose." If Cervantes here sounds somewhat apologetic, we must remember that we are speaking of an age which doted on rigidly prescribed domestic schedules. Fray Hernando de Talavera, for example, sets forth the ideal interval for rest in a Christian household: "Having risen from the table, and having said prayers before and after eating, you may then devote your time—perhaps half an hour—to recreation: perhaps honest and profitable talk with a few good people, honest music, or good reading (which would be the best, although not for the digestion). You may then, if you wish, repose and sleep for another half hour."[54]

Even though we need not imagine so inflexible a routine or so brief a refreshment for Rojas and his family, they and their contemporaries were people who worshipped orderliness in life, people, who—like Sir Thomas More—when finding it shattered, dreamed and strove for its restoration. The concept of *"ley"* discussed previously as the interpenetration of religious belief into daily activities meant exactly this: a ritual ordering of behavior. And Rojas, having so clearly determined on outward conformance to his borrowed "law" (whether in his soul he believed in its dogmas and promises is another matter), surely was meticulous in his day-to-day and hour-to-hour Christian living. Antonio de Guevara typically relates the careful ordering of daily activities both to "maintaining honor" (a maintenance necessary both to personal safety and family prestige) and to classical precepts: "Today there is no generous gentleman or delicate lady who would not rather suffer a stone thrown against his forehead than a prick into his honor. . . . For as Diogenes pointed out, the whole doctrine of harmony of the ancients was designed to teach citizens of the republic how they should speak, conduct business, eat, sleep, bargain, dress, work, and rest, how each one should reform his household and bring his personal life into order. . . . Men who wish to live quietly and in peace [*assosegados*] in this life must adopt a recognized status and manner of living."[55] And so we may imagine Rojas to have lived. In his house, orderliness as well as cleanliness (he undoubtedly inherited from the tradition of his ancestors a concern for personal hygiene) was next to godliness.[56]

---

[54] *De como se ha de ordenar el tiempo*, NBAE, vol. 16, p. 102. Even more of a *locus classicus* was furnished by Guevara in his significantly titled *Relox*. See particularly Book II, Chap. 13 for Marcus Aurelius' stringent and detailed ordering of daily activity. Such prescriptions, of course, abounded in previous centuries but, if the *Siete partidas* is typical, not in so self-conscious and emphatic a fashion.

[55] From the "Prólogo general" of the *Relox*.

[56] As is well known, the public bathhouses frequented by all castes during the late Middle Ages disappeared during the reign of the Catholic Monarchs, but we may assume that Rojas remembered the traditional cleanliness of his

There is a clear anticipation of Rojas' future manner of daily existence not only in the Letter and Prologue but also in the ambiguous morality of *La Celestina*. Perhaps the most immoral and exciting effect of love is its temporal anarchy. Love alternately chafes at the hours and forgets them, failing foolishly to distinguish between night and day. Ecstasy and misery, both well-known temporal reagents, have replaced the regular march forward of domestic life. The lover, morally speaking, is a lost man (*un perdido*) not only because of his blasphemy and his concupiscence but also because he lives a rudderless, disordered existence. Having no temporal skeleton, no sure schedule, for his life, he is prey both to forgetfulness and to sudden accesses of ineffective awareness. For which he is clearly to be reproved rather than pitied. But Rojas— even though he may have essayed the sublime and transitory rewards of such passionate liberation—was no Calisto. In his life as well as in his work, we judge him to have been a preeminently time-conscious man. Domesticity for him, as still for many of us, was comforting not just because of the bulging bellies of the *tinajas* but also because of its tranquil repetition of customary activities.[57]

How did Rojas and his family fill their "hours destined for recreation"? In earlier years there had been hunting, excursions into the wild lands to the north and south, or even up into the foothills of the Sierra, in search of small game and birds. The Bachelor would come back of an evening in a manner reminiscent of Lope's description of Peribáñez: ". . . with his crossbow slung sideways and hanging from the saddlebow a brace of partridges or rabbits."

---

family during childhood and perhaps even tried privately to maintain it. See *Realidad*, edn. I, p. 117; *Structure*, pp. 107-108.

[57] In the course of the treatise just cited, Fray Hernando paints a vivid and almost Celestinesque picture of domestic and vocational disorder: "Never, as the holy Job tells us, do we remain constant, not even those of us who separate ourselves from the movement of the times. First we are sick, then we are healthy; sometimes strong, sometimes tired; sometimes overheated, sometimes with colds. When we are not devout and pious, our faith becomes lukewarm. When the hour of sleep comes, we stay awake. When we are supposed to be wakeful, we doze. Domestic arguments break up the interval set aside for prayer. During business hours and when it is time to take care of our clients, people visit us, some of them so close to us or so important that it is necessary to receive them and talk to them. Who then dares to lay down rules and to establish order for a humanity so subject to diversity?" (p. 102).

427

Two such weapons (one still in commission) are listed in the inventory, indicating that he was often accompanied by a son, relative, or friend. Then, too, there was social intercourse. One Diego Hernández, a *probanza* witness, remembers frequent visitors at the house: ". . . *hidalgo* relatives who were neighbors of Talavera and other people from out of town who came to the house of the Bachelor Rojas. . . ."[58] Since the speaker was an Old Christian, had known the author of *La Celestina* "for some 15 years before his death," and had even been present at the Licentiate Francisco's wedding (probably in 1538 or 1539), there is reason to believe him. For those who were known and trusted it was a hospitable home. Another possibility was chess played with members of the family or friends. Even alone, Rojas could amuse himself with the end game problems Sempronio had recommended to Calisto as a distraction from amorous torment. If, like most chess players, he took the game seriously, by 1541 he had progressed beyond the simple problems and elementary doctrine contained in his copy of his classmate Luis de Lucena's *Arte de Axedrez*, published together with the *Repetición de amores* in 1497.

As for intellectual conversation, we need not suppose that a man of Rojas' intellectual capacities was as alone in sixteenth-century Talavera as he might be today. Cosme Gómez points out proudly: "Innumerable are the youths who leave their parents for the universities" and who, after completing successful careers in church, army, or public administration, retire to their native town. There is something touching and deeply Spanish in the phrasing of his conclusion: "Buena es Talavera para nacer en ella y no suele ser mala para morir en la vegez."[59] Rojas, as a result, was not entirely divorced from the company of his *socios*, those who had attended Salamanca at the turn of the century and now resided in Talavera as well as those who came and went (in later years the fellow students of Francisco) and brought news of academic changes and scandals. From which we may conclude that in Talavera Rojas did not suffer the sort of intellectual exile ascribed by a friend to Guevara's antagonist, the Bachelor Pedro de Rua, because of his residence in Soria: "How many times have I lamented that a person

---

[58] See Appendix III.

[59] "Talavera is a good place to be born, and it is usually not bad for dying in old age."

as learned and worthy of all praise as yourself should live among uncultured Uracos, Pelendones, and Arevacos! . . . Is there any compelling reason why, while you cultivate the clear light of Athens, you should suffer Scythian barbarity?"[60] Talavera naturally had its share of Uracos, Pelendones, and Arevacos (names of primitive Iberian tribes used here to refer slightingly to the peasant population), but, unlike Soria as seen by Rua's friend, they did not dominate municipal existence or determine the town's image of itself. Noteworthy among the intellectuals stemming from Rojas' adopted town were the three Herrera brothers, one of whom, Gabriel Alonso de Herrera, we mentioned previously as the author of the *Libro de agricultura*. Born about a generation before the Bachelor's arrival, he and his brothers apparently were close relations of Fray Hernando de Talavera.[61] As a priest with a benefice from Rojas' parish church of San Miguel, Gabriel Alonso remained at home, but the other two, Diego Hernández and Hernán Alonso, followed academic careers which took them to the two major universities. The former professed music at Salamanca as a "maestro del órgano,"[62] while the latter, a disciple of Nebrija, held a chair of grammar and rhetoric in Alcalá. Known primarily for his pre-Erasmistic dialogue, *Disputa en ocho levadas contra Aristótil y sus secuaces* (written in Salamanca in 1517), Hernán Alonso, would have been interested in meeting Rojas whenever he re-

[60] F. Zamora Lucas y V. Hijes Cuevas, *El bachiller Pedro de Rua humanista y crítico*, Madrid, 1957, p. 107. The reason for these reproaches was that Rua had refused a post at Alcalá that had been arranged for him by the writer, Alvar Gómez de Castro. The latter goes on to say with typical humanistic playfulness that Rua must have been drinking "human blood" and have made a pact with the "Pelendones y Numantinos." Otherwise, he would surely not stay in Soria. In spite of their classical prestige, the Numantinos seem as barbarous to the writer as they appear in Cervantes' play, and from their stock, it is implied, present day peasants have sprung. We have once again witnessed a skirmish in the verbal war between castes, levels of culture, and birthplaces.

[61] I so conclude in view of their common municipal origin and the fact that, while in Granada studying Moorish techniques of agriculture, Gabriel Alonso was a *comensal* of Fray Hernando. It is well known that the latter, not believing nepotism to be a sin, maintained a number of relatives (including a nephew and sister whose given name was also Herrera) in his official household (*Investigaciones*, pp. 132-133).

[62] Bonilla seems overscrupulous in questioning this statement of Alvar Gómez de Toledo in view of its partial documentary confirmation (p. 72).

turned home.[63] The lively dialogue of this work is even more determinedly popular than that of *La Celestina* and contains at least one direct reminiscence of Act I.[64] Hernán Alonso, according to a contemporary, was "a person of reckless wit and facile speech,"[65] and, if it pleases us, it should not be hard to imagine the two men engaged in brilliant conversation. Rojas' "hours destined for recreation" could hardly have been more fittingly employed.

"All the books in romance that I own"

At Salamanca—we have said—Fernando de Rojas discovered himself in his new role as a liberated student engaged in the university's ritual transition from childish apprenticeship to adult professional status. But even more important from our point of view was his discovery of himself as a reader, as a full-fledged member of a highly excited student reading public. As such, we saw him entitled to absorb, judge, and discuss such varied books as the *Fiammetta*, the *Cárcel de amor*, Juan del Encina's *Cancionero*, the *Philodoxus*, or the *Visión deleitable*. And eventually out of the highly fertilized soil of this intense experience as a reader there grew a new book, *La Celestina*, with its "flourishing branches and leaves."

However, the "abundant fruit" of this achievement did not and could not mark the end of Rojas' self-cultivation. What Unamuno once called "the terrible vice of reading which carries with it the punishment of continual death" is, like all vices, extremely difficult to give up. Furthermore, even admitting that each new volume as it proceeds towards its end provides a foretaste of the reader's own end, reading also offers abundant solace—particularly for the kind of life Rojas was living in Talavera. In the *Relox de príncipes* we find an answer to Unamuno that might have been written by Rojas

---

[63] If he was born in 1460 as Bonilla surmises, he probably was not in Salamanca during Rojas' stay. He had left after his student years and returned to profess sometime between 1513 and 1517. As for his "erasmismo," only in his attacks on "medieval corruption of the liberal arts" and particularly of Aristotelian doctrine, does he seem to be a half-jesting precursor of things to come. See *Erasmo*, I, 17-18.

[64] "*Maestre Pedro.*— . . . Mas bien me acuerdo aver leído que de ombruno y cavalluno han salido y biuido los centauros. . . . *Diego de Herrera.*— ¿Cómo? ¿Y philósopho tan grande como vos days fé en hablillas?" (Bonilla, p. 120).

[65] "hominem ingenio promptum et extemporali facundia praestantem." Alvar Gómez de Toledo quoted by Bonilla, p. 67.

himself: "If we consider the sudden fears of the flesh, the dangers of the world, the temptations of the devil, the traps laid by our enemies, the importunities of our friends, [we may well wonder] how the heart can withstand so many and such continual tribulations if not by reading and consoling itself with books."[66]

Discussion of Rojas' library on Guevara's terms—as a refuge or portal for the escape of the spirit—may help to mitigate our disappointed surprise at its contents. For, although Rojas, like Montaigne and Sem Tob, may have thought of his books as his best friends (they are first among the specific bequests of his will), we might well have expected a richer accumulation during the four decades which separated departure from Salamanca and departure from the world. Aside from his "principal estudio," Rojas—judged on the basis of the inventory—clearly did not keep up with the explosive intellectual life of his time. There is, for example, nothing to indicate that he continued the exploration of Latin letters that had begun with his study of Cicero and Terence and his absorption of the *De remediis*. In an epoch when the whole classical canon was becoming available, Rojas possessed only those few texts which he had brought back from the university: his "Petrarca en latín," his "oraciones de Tulio," and that monument to the futility of medieval teaching of rhetoric, Albrecht von Eyb's *Margarita poetica* (15 editions between 1472 and 1503). This last did provide him with awareness of the existence of numerous authors and titles (among others, Plutarch, Lactantius, Apuleius, eighteen plays of Plautus, and three humanistic comedies), but its carefully indexed excerpts of "elegantiae et auctoritates" are no more than pulverized fragments run together in such a way as to communicate no idea at all of the literary organisms from which they came. In the case of the dramatic works, not only plot and characterization but the very form of the dialogue disappears. The *Margarita poetica* is nothing more than a compendium of rhetoric followed by an enormous commonplace book which, as far as I can determine, Rojas never bothered to use.[67] Quite as telling in this connection is

---

[66] *Relox*, "Prólogo general."

[67] This statement is based on three long days spent checking for commonplaces from *La Celestina* both in the text and in the copious index. My search was hardly exhaustive, but a complete lack of positive results led to the above conclusion. The adjective "complete" also includes Mrs. Malkiel's mistaken assertion that Rojas' source for Melibea's soliloquy in Act X was Eyb's ex-

the purchase of the *Golden Ass*,[68] the *Metamorphoses*,[69] Boethius,

cerpt from the soliloquy of Philogenia waiting for her lover. See her review of J. M. Casas Hom's edition of the *Polidorus* (*NRFH*, x, 1956, p. 423). As usual without any indication of dialogue, Eyb reproduces three of Philogenia's more exemplary sentences, none of which correspond to anything said by Melibea. It is possible that Rojas had access to the *Philogenia* itself, since this speech (in which the victimized heroine wishes she had not been so adamant and fears that her lover may have turned to somebody else) does resemble in its contents that of Melibea. Also, as mentioned in *La originalidad* (p. 492), the worried parents (one of whom is named Calisto) awake in a fashion similar to that of Pleberio and Alisa in Act XII. What seems to be missing are the specific verbal echoes which usually accompany Rojas' borrowings. I was unable to locate in the *Margarita* a second minor resemblance mentioned by Mrs. Malkiel: the possible source of Pleberio's "En quién caben las quatro principales cosas que en los casamientos se demandan . . ." (Act XVI). However, Pérez de Guzmán's *Coplas* 141 and 142 also speak of the four qualities: honesty, beauty, lineage, and wealth (see below, n. 114).

For interpretation of the *Margarita* as a medieval adaptation of humanistic learning, see J. H. Hiller, *Albrecht von Eyb, Medieval Moralist*, Washington, D.C., 1939. Eyb's resolutely moral interpretation of Plautus not only in the *Margarita* but also in his translations (as discussed by Hiller) may help explain Rojas' failure to make use of the former. The contrast between the moralistic tenor of parts of the prologue material and what actually goes on inside *La Celestina* may be due not only to routine repetition or the desire to camouflage the author's intention but also to purposeful parody of just such stale distortion of what texts actually say. This was certainly true of Villalobos' statement of his intention in translating the *Amphitryon* (see Chap. VII, n. 9).

[68] Since the *Golden Ass* only appears in the 1546 inventory, it may be a copy of the Medina del Campo, 1543 edition acquired after Rojas' death by Leonor Alvarez. But had he read it before writing *La Celestina*? Castro Guisasola and Mrs. Malkiel (*La originalidad*, p. 338, n. 43) reject Menéndez Pelayo's proposition of Apuleius as a source on the grounds that Pármeno's "diacitrón" remark at the end of Act VIII could just as well have been taken from Petrarch. On the other hand, the following seems reminiscent of Melibea's post-mortem speech to Calisto: ". . . la hermana [psyche] incitada de imbidia mortal, compuesta una mentira para engañar a su marido, diziendo que auía sabido de cómo su padre estaba a la muerte, metiose en un nao y fue nauegando hasta que llegó a aquel risco, en el qual subida, dixo: 'O Cupido recíbeme que soy pertenescente para ser tu muger; tu viento cierço recibe a tu señora.' Con estas palabras dio un salto grande del risco abaxo . . ." (Alcalá de Henares, 1584, fo. 84). In other parts of the work we find repeated falls, insistence on height, and an attempted suicide from a tower. There is even an implicit equation of the fall of fortune with a tumble through space: Alcino "que no pudo huir la sentencia de la cruel fortuna" is pushed out of a high window by an evil "vejezuela" (fo. 60). Palau lists Seville, 1513 as the first published translation, but there is no reason that Rojas could not have read the original or a lost edition in Spanish while in Salamanca.

[69] There was apparently no translation prior to *La Celestina*, but Rojas (whether he read it in Latin or in Spanish afterwards) might have been in-

and Seneca's *Epistolae*,[70] all in Castilian. Like many others before and after his time, the author of *La Celestina* seems to have allowed his knowledge of literary Latin to go to seed.

Two curious Latin treatises among the law books help confirm this judgment—if only because they seem to have been acquired during the Salamanca years. The first *De secretis mulierum et virorum* (attributed to Albertus Magnus),[71] is manifestly medieval in provenance while the second, the *Fasciculum temporum*, represents a typographical innovation which would delight Marshall McLuhan. The *De secretis* is a mixture of astrology, superstition, and traditional scientific doctrine about the mysteries of human procreation. Divided between alternate portions of *textus* and *commentum* it deals with such matters as "mal de la madre"which is said to occur when the "matrix de propio loco tollitur." But aside from this, I have seen nothing which bears on *La Celestina*. As for the *Fasciculum*, it represents an extraordinary effort to coordinate graphically all available knowledge of the past. In the world before Gutenberg, history was comprehended in long parallel narrative

---

terested, among other things, in Daedalus' lament for Icarus as well as in the following Heraclitean interpretation of the process of metamorphosis (cited from the Antwerp, 1551 edition): "Los elementos nunca están en una figura; siempre se mudan y renuevan; ninguna cosa perece; antes de nuevo torna a renovar y paresce que nascen otra vez. Ninguna cosa puede luengamente durar en un ser" (fo. 228).

[70] Zaragoza, 1496, with three extant editions prior to 1541. Translated from an Italian translation by Fernán Pérez de Guzmán, it is more demonstrably a source for the *Coplas de vicios y virtudes* (later gathered with other pieces in *Las setecientas* also on our list) than for Rojas. The author of Act I, as far as I can determine by detailed textual comparisons, used the original Latin rather than either this or Alonso de Cartagena's *Cinco libros de Séneca*, Seville, 1491. In Rojas' acts there are a number of suggestive but not conclusive similarities. Of particular interest are letters discussing speech with its gestures, intonations, and facial expressions. Some untrustworthy speakers, Seneca remarks, "inclinan y abaxan el rostro a tierra" just as does Pármeno in Act II (Epistola 11 with additional discussion in 15, 40, and 41). Celestina's cure of Melibea in Act X may perhaps be read in the light of "El decir que se hace por melecinar al corazón . . . deve entrar dentro a la fondura" (41). In general, the Stoic substratum of *La Celestina* is explicit in the letters on fortune, love, old age, and others.

[71] It is impossible to determine which edition Rojas owned. Haebler lists none, but in the rest of Europe there were at least five between 1475 and 1490. Unfortunately for students of Celestina's laboratory, the custom of printing the *De secretis* in conjunction with such other treatises as *De virtutibus herbarum* was initiated in the 17th century.

433

sequences, oral in conception and then (as in the Old Testament) written down for permanency. However, a German Carthusian named Werner Rolevinck (1425-1502) had the genius to see that, if on the printed page these separate lines could be coordinated chronologically, the coordinator would produce a best seller.[72] And so it was that this *Fasciculum* with its series of double-paged charts of emperors, kings, prophets, and popes accompanied by inserted boxes of essential information became one of the most reprinted of all incunabula. By comparing the three or four lines which divide the page horizontally, the reader could, for example, ascertain without laborious checking through individual chronicles what personage from the Bible was contemporary with a given period in classical history. It was the first visual aid for students, a sign of the new times.

Perhaps even more disappointing than the absence of the classics is that of Erasmus' works either in the original or in translation. There was, it would seem, no place among Rojas' books or interests for the *Enchiridion*, the *Colloquia*, or the others that were widely circulated in Spanish. Two comments suggest themselves. In the first place, *La Celestina* itself—assuming it can be taken as an indication of its author's mind in later decades—is anything but Erasmistic or pre-Erasmistic in its presentation of human life. Its traditional criticism of the clergy is the surface manifestation not of a desire to reform but of a deeper skepticism about the human condition. And its irony, like that of the *Lazarillo*, probes depths of despair and disbelief beyond the reach of the playfully intellectual satire of the *Moriae encomium*.[73] Rojas and Erasmus attended their respective universities in roughly the same years; they were both marginal to society and its accepted beliefs; and they were both ironists. But there the resemblance ends. My reading of *La*

---

[72] There were some 30 editions printed during the author's lifetime, including one in Spain (Valencia, 1480) listed by Haebler.

[73] See my "Death of Lazarillo de Tormes," *PMLA*, LXXXI (1966), 149-166. There I am more in accord with Bataillon's thesis that the whole tenor of the work, including the anticlericalism, is alien to Erasmism (*El sentido de "Lazarillo de Tormes,"* Paris, 1954) than with that of Francisco Márquez (*Espiritualidad y literatura en el siglo XVI*, Madrid, 1968). To give one specific and—to me—decisive example, when Lazarillo describes his unvoiced and ferocious exclamation, "¡San Juan y ciégale!" as a "secreta oración," the author refers ironically to one of the movement's central propositions for devotional reform.

Celestina leads me to believe that unlike many of his fellow *conversos*, Rojas never accepted his imposed religion with enough sincerity to preoccupy himself with its purification. The external formalities of Catholicism may indeed have suited him more than they annoyed him—as we shall see when we examine his religious literature—precisely because they were external. That is to say, because they could provide him with camouflage.

In the second place, in spite of the absence of Erasmus' best known works, there was at least one translation (and perhaps two)[74] of the lesser pieces. I refer to the *Querela pacis*, which, as the first to appear in Castilian (1520), was used to fill out an overslim edition of a past author at that time more familiar to the reading public, Aeneas Silvio. The book appears in the inventory only as *Tratado de miseria de cortesanos*, and its first part is indeed a curiously specific and unrhetorical source for Guevara.[75] Then

---

[74] In the 1546 inventory there is a "libro de la mala lengua" which has been tentatively identified by myself and M. J. Ruggerio (following a suggestion of Valle Lersundi) as Rodrigo de Reinosa's "pliego suelto," "Aquí comiençan unas coplas de las comadres no tocando en las buenas salvo de las malas y de sus lenguas y hablas malas . . ." (see Chap. VI, n. 101). Since Reinosa's *Coplas* served a source for Rojas as well as for the author of Act I, the identification seemed reasonable to us. However a second possibility is perhaps more likely: *La lengua de Erasmo nuevamente romançada* of which there were several editions in the 1530's. Since the title of part one is "Libro primero de los malos oficios y daños de la mala lengua," it seems probable that the taker of the inventory opened to this page to check the title. Or perhaps Rojas himself so inscribed the binding. If Rojas did possess this anonymous translation, he surely found much therein of interest to him. The initial praise of reason, the comparison of the wise man's word to a burgeoning seed, the attack on slanderers and perjurors who use words as deadly weapons to bring about imprisonment, confiscation of goods, or social dishonor, all sound familiar. A detailed comparison of the Spanish to the Latin original (now being undertaken by Professor Dorothy Severin) will probably reveal substantial accommodation of Erasmus' thought to the *converso* situation. Aside from this aspect, Rojas surely found congenial the satirical descriptions of the "senseless" monologues of lovers and of the pointless viciousness of "rameras" who with their evil tongues cause "quistiones y muertes."

[75] Aeneas Silvio's view of court life as perpetual warfare presided over by a king who delights in fattening up his favorites for future slaughter and despoliation is far more grim than Guevara's. Instead of false good manners, court banqueters are described as drooling through decaying teeth and picking fleas out of their beards. The constant travel, dirt, and intrigue that make the courtier's life unendurable, rather than topical, seem to be direct reflections of the writer's experience. Also included in the book is a short allegory by the same author entitled "Sueño de la Fortuna" in which the commonplace

comes Erasmus, introduced to his new readers (the opening title, as often was the case, served much the same function as today's book jacket) as follows: "Y otro tractado de como se quexa la Paz. Compuesto por Erasmo, varón doctíssimo."[76] But the exception may not really be an exception. By its singular proximity to the theme of "Omnia secundum litem fiunt," this particular treatise seems to confirm my conjecture that Rojas was not particularly interested in Erasmus for his own sake. Peace—in an anthropomorphic fashion comparable to Folly—begins her long monologue of complaint (*querela*) by observing the insanity and insensiblity of human-kind. Among certain animals there is charity and peace (we are reminded of one of Celestina's speeches in Act IV), but men are subject to a "vast ocean of war" which rushes over them: "If familiarity had not blunted the sense of evil, who could be prevailed upon to believe that those wretched beings are possessed of rational souls, intellects, and feelings, [since they] contend with all the rage of furies in everlasting feuds and litigations ending in murders, robbery, blood, butchery, desolation . . . ?" It almost sounds as if Erasmus had read *La Celestina*.

What follows by way of specific examples continues to echo what we have heard on Rojas' pages and what we have surmised were his feelings about the human condition, his own and that of all men. Among Christians—Peace asserts—"the voice of strife [resounds] more loudly than was ever heard by nations that knew not Christ." And, if this is true, "Will the nation to whom we intend the favour of conversion to Christianity by fire and sword believe that we ourselves are Christians when they see what is too evident to be denied, that no people on earth quarrel and fight more than we . . . ?" Therefore (Erasmus refers to the general religious repression of the time, although we may easily surmise Rojas' personal interpretation): "Let the Christians vote what the heathens sometimes voted, an entire amnesty of all past errors and misfortunes." Furthermore, aside from actual warfare and bloodshed (conducted by kings who are often no more than "crowned miscreants" who kill for money), there are infinite less virulent but

images of the goddess (two faces, one "manso" and the other "sañudo," etc.) are vividly presented.

[76] Translated by the Arcediano of Seville, Diego López de León. English citations are taken from *The Complaint of Peace*, London, 1802.

still incapacitating forms of strife. "I behold a city," Peace observes, "enclosed with walls. Hope springs in my bosom that men, Christian men, must live in concord here, if anywhere, surrounded as they are by the same ramparts, governed by the same laws. . . . But, ill-fated as I am, here also I find all happiness . . . vitiated by dissension. . . ." "Scholar wages war with scholar,"[77] and even in domestic life the "Goddess of discord has insinuated herself." Finally, clearly echoing Petrarchist Stoicism, "One and the same man is at war with himself. Reason wages war with passions; one passion with another passion.[78] Duty calls one way, and inclination another. Lust, anger, avarice, ambition, are all up in arms, each pursuing its own purposes, and warmly engaged in battle." Whether by chance or by design, the one work of Erasmus that Rojas did possess must have appealed to him with as much urgency as the *De remediis*. Had he been able to read the *Querela pacis*, Pleberio would have found passage after passage suitable for his final lament. Let us listen to one more exclamation: "What is more brittle than the life of man? Supposing it unbroken by casualties, how short its natural duration! Yet how liable to disease; how exposed to momentary accidents!"

Positive conclusions based on missing titles are extremely precarious. The possibility of carelessness of those charged with taking the inventory (as suggested by the ten additional items listed in 1546) is only one of several reasons for not equating it with the whole of Rojas' reading experience. *La Celestina* testifies to the fact that its author had read and absorbed a number of books (the *Fiammetta*, Encina's *Cancionero*, and the *Corbacho* are the most obvious), copies of which were no longer in his possession in 1541. Among the members of the excited reading public in Salamanca books were passed around, read aloud, owned for a while, and ex-

[77] In connection with our previous discussion of life in Salamanca the passage deserves further citation: "In the same kind of profession, the scotist contends with the thomist, the nominalist with the realist, the platonic with the peripatetic; insomuch as they agree not in the minutest points, and often are at daggers drawing *de lana caprina*, till the warmth of the disputation advances from arguments and from arguments to abusive language and from abusive language to fisty-cuffs; and if they do not proceed to use real swords and spears, they stab one another with pens dipt in the venom of malice; they tear one another with biting libels, and dart the deadly arrows of their tongues against their opponent's reputation" (p. 22).

[78] See *The Art*, p. 167.

changed with an ease made possible by their sudden new availability. Nor, as we have seen, did the move to Talavera imply intellectual isolation. As was already mentioned, when dictating his will Rojas remembered specifically that his colleague, the Bachelor Cáceres (accused years before of having expressed unorthodox views on tithing)[79] had left him certain books as security for a loan of twelve ducats. The congenial social and racial background of many of the local readers is also manifest in that of the ill-fated town bookseller, Luis García, who, as we remember, was known to his intimate clientele as Abraham. Here are facts from which we can only conclude that Rojas all during his life had access to many more books than he owned and that, as far as the classics and Erasmus are concerned, lack of interest is not proven. On the other hand, if hardly an exhaustive record of Rojas' intellectual life, the inventory *is* an indication of it, and, on the face of it, a disappointing one. The books Rojas chose to purchase and preserve—the *Querela pacis* and the law books aside—reflect less an open and exploratory mind than one content to remain with its undergraduate illustration. There is, in spite of the several travel books, not a single one dealing with (or even mentioning) the exciting new discoveries in the West.

It is only when we view Rojas' books, not as belonging to a possible Montaigne but to an Alonso Quijano of flesh and blood, that we begin to realize the extent of our debt to the Licentiate Fernando and to Valle Lersundi. If we consider this provincial sixteenth-century library (to repeat what we proposed at the beginning) as a source of "refuge" from Guevara's daily round of "tribulations," we become aware that we have been given a unique document, a document which suggests less what the author of *La Celestina* learned from books than how he lived them and lived with them in his house. The inventory is our single advantage over biographers of such comparably great and elusive figures as a Shakespeare or a Marlowe. Without it, for example, I for one would never have imagined Rojas sharing the enthusiasm of Juan de Valdés, Cervantes' Canon, and Saint Teresa (among many other

[79] During the trial of Diego de Oropesa (already mentioned several times and in which, as we shall see, Rojas was called to testify) a Bachiller Bernaldino de Cáceres was accused of having stated that tithing was a matter of custom and not a divine law.

438

unlikely addicts) for the romances of chivalry. But such would seem to be the case. Among the some sixty non-professional books, no fewer than ten romances are listed: *Amadís de Gaula* and one of its sequels, *Las sergas de Esplandián, Clarián de Landanis, Palmerín de Oliva* and its two sequels,[80] the *Historia de Henrrique fi de Oliva,* the *Guarino Mesquino,* and one of the several versions of the story of Tristram and Isolde.[81]

How to explain this apparent fondness for a genre so alien in its themes and vision from *La Celestina*? Perhaps, as we suggested in the preceding chapter, there was more of Calisto in his author than he would have preferred to admit. Perhaps these were books purchased for reading aloud to the family and retainers, a custom the Innkeeper of the *Quijote* was later to describe. But the truth of the matter is that neither of these extra-literary explanations is necessarily valid. Precisely because the sense of life expressed by Montalvo and his successors was so unlike Rojas' own, such books offered evasion. Instead of the concentric and concentrated world of *La Celestina*'s strife-ridden city, here (as Cervantes' Canon knew intellectually and his insane interlocutor knew vitally) space and time are open and endless. Adventure replaces domesticity; heroism, haggling; and imagination's elastic horizons, walls and streets. Through "a more transparent sky . . . a sun with newer clarity . . . exiles melancholy and . . . betters the human condition." Which is to say in terminology already overexploited, for the reader of the romances of chivalry the daily perils of *fortuna* have given way to the surrogate pleasures of *ventura*. As Esplandián explains after drifting for ten days to an unknown shore, "I am not from this land but from far away, and *la ventura* brought me here."[82] And so too Rojas could drift away from whatever Celestinesque qualities of life he found to amuse, circumscribe, or horrify him in Talavera.

[80] Listed in the editorial notes to the inventory as *Libro segundo de Palmerín: que trata de los altos hechos de armas de Primaleón su hijo: y de su hermano Polendos* (Salamanca, 1516, Seville, 1524, Toledo, 1528. Venice, 1534) and *La crónica del muy valiente y esforçado Platir, hijo del invencible Empãdor [sic] Primaleón,* Valladolid, 1533.

[81] The "Don Tristán" listed in 1546 could have been *Libro del esforçado cauallero don Tristán de Leonís,* (Valladolid, 1501, and Seville, 1528 and 1533); *Crónica de don Tristán de Leonís en español* (Seville, 1520); or *Corónica nuebamente enmendada y añadida del buen cauallero don Tristán de Leonís* (Seville, 1534).

[82] BAE, vol. XL, p. 407.

In the space of a paragraph his spirit could rest in what Ortega called a "world lacking communication with [his] authentic one,"[83] a world in which *ventura* reigned.

To be fair, however, we should point out that two of the books listed, the *Hystoria* of the crusading "Enrique, fi de Oliva, rey de Iherusalem, emperador de Constantinopla" and the curious chivalric travelogue called *Guarino mesquino*,[84] take us into instructive geography rather than into imaginary realms. But even so, these two, like the others, provided welcome relief from the constraint of urban and domestic roles. They could, by surpassing the limitations of locality, "give life and even get rid of gray hair"—to repeat the defense of the oft-mentioned Innkeeper.

As we have just suggested, the generic frontiers of the romances of chivalry are not sharply drawn. In one direction they blend into history and legend and in the other into the travel narratives that in those years were becoming ever more popular. Of these latter Rojas owned four: Santesteban's *Libro del Ynfante don Pedro de Portugal*, as well as translations of Mandeville, of Ludovico Varthema's *Itinerarium* of a journey to Egypt and points East, and of Bernhard von Breydenbach's *Peregrinationes* to the Holy Land.[85] Accuracy of observation and narration was hardly a factor in the choice of these books. Santesteban's insane geography and weird customs (in part corresponding, as Francis Rogers shows,

---

[83] *Obras completas*, Madrid, 1947, III, 410.

[84] *Crónica del noble cauallero Guarino Mezquino*, Seville, 1527. The title goes on to promise "hazañas y aventuras," but the appended "argumento" indicates mixed intentions: ". . . en el qual se muestran los nombres de las provincias quasi de todo el mundo y de la diversidad de los hombres y de sus diversas costumbres y de muchos y diversos animales." As a result, the book is even more invertebrate than standard romances. However, it comes to a moral climax when the author, Andrea de Barberino (a 14th-century Italian), consigns his hero to the Purgatory of Saint Patrick (he enters alive through a cave) for having dallied with "la muy sabia Sybila." Virgilian and Dantesque influences are both manifest and curiously primitive.

[85] Breydenbach, who made his journey in 1484-85, saw the possibilities offered by the press and almost immediately went to work on his *Peregrinationes in Terram Sanctam* published two years later. The Spanish translation, *Viaje de la tierra sancta*, appeared in Zaragoza in 1498. Varthema seems to have profited by his example, publishing his *Novum itinerarium* in 1510, again two years after returning home. The Spanish version entitled *Ytinerario del venerable varon micer Luis patricio romano: en el qual cuenta mucha parte de la ethiopia, Egypto: y entrambas Arabias: Siria y la Yndia* appeared in Seville 1520 with a second edition in 1523.

to the hidden purpose of suggesting clerical reform along the lines of Prester John's Christian Utopia)[86] would have been as incredible to a man of Rojas' skepticism as Mandeville's tall stories. Varthema, too, although basing his narrative on an actual journey, frequently gets carried away by the fact that he longs "for novelty as a thirsty man longs for fresh water." He has seen the unicorn and, what is even more unlikely, resisted as successfully as Byron's Don Juan the seductive charms of an Oriental queen. Only Breydenbach reports on his travels factually and with detailed wonder at scenes, customs, and encounters.

How may we comprehend interest in such far-fetched tales on the part of a reader as skeptical as Rojas? To begin with, as we just observed, these fifteenth- and sixteenth-century "itineraries" and "peregrinations" provided a sense of liberation that was hardly distinguishable from that to be found in the romances. Our serious bachelor, too, like other customers of Luis "Abraham" García within the walls of Talavera, must have thirsted for novelty as much as Varthema himself. But it is also suggestive that these books (like the two last mentioned romances and the translations of Josephus and Jacobus Fontanus' *De bello Rhodio*)[87] were concerned with the Orient. Like many Europeans of his time, Rojas dreamed, not of the newly found and inexplicable West, but of the East which offered, in addition to geography, ageless civilization and half-forgotten history. Here were lands to which a man "withdrawn in his chamber, chin in hand and elbow on table" might allow his spirit to wander. But not just for wandering's sake or for fascinated contemplation of the marvellous! Somewhere to the East was a garden—of which Melibea's was a transitory and deceitful simulacrum —where the mystery of being human might be resolved and alienation surpassed. In Rojas' case, however, an even more poignant and specific loss may be surmised. In the East was the land promised to and taken away from his *linaje*.

Rojas' collection of chronicles composes a category of reading as extensive as the romances. In addition to the two just cited, he

---

[86] For a definitive discussion of the book and its background see Chap. VII of Francis M. Roger's *The Travels of the Infante Dom Pedro of Portugal*, Cambridge, Mass., 1961.

[87] *La muy lamentable y cruenta batalla de Rodas*, Seville, 1526, translated by the same Cristóbal de Arcos, "bachiller y clérigo," who was responsible for the Spanish of the *Ytinerario*.

owned six books relating to the past of Spain, translations of Sallust[88] and Appian of Alexandria,[89] as well as a narrative of the exploits of Joan of Arc.[90] Of the books of national "history," at least two, a "libro del Cid"[91] and the legendary *Crónica del rey don Rodrigo* (Seville, 1499 and 1511) probably did not seem to Rojas to be generically distinguishable from his romances of chivalry. If so, it was a failure to discriminate similar to that of another *hidalgo* reader well known to all of us. Somewhat less novelesque was the *converso* Mosén Diego de Valera's sketchy but widely read *Crónica de España*[92] listed as "la valeriana." Printed in 1482, it was the first history in Spanish to be prepared with the press in mind. Finally and of more interest, there were a treatise by Lucio Marineo,[93] Pero López de Ayala's *Chrónica del rey don Pedro*[94]

[88] *Cathalinario e Jurgurthino de Salustio*, Valladolid, 1519 or Logroño, 1529, included only in the 1546 inventory. The translator was Francisco Vidal de Noya.

[89] *Los triumphos de Apiano*, Valencia, 1522, described in the British Museum Catalogue as "containing the books on the Lybian, Syrian, Parthian, and Mithridatic Wars translated by Juan de Molina."

[90] The editors of the *RFE* cite three possible chronicles.

[91] Identified in the *RFE* as the *Crónica del Cid Ruy Díaz* (reprinted six times between 1498 and 1541) which contained a mixture of historical fact and epic invention. However it might also have been the *Crónica del famoso cavallero Cid Ruy Díaz Campeador*, Burgos, 1512, embodying an even greater proportion of fantastic material from later "refundiciones." See F. J. Norton, *Printing in Spain 1501-1520*, Cambridge, Eng., 1966, for a discussion of its special preparation by royal command for the monastery of San Pedro de Cardeña (pp. 59-60).

[92] In spite of the title, more than a third of the text is a résumé of world history and geography reflecting the medieval concept of the past as divided into universal ages. Valera's eulogy of the printing press as a means of bringing all these ages into one new Golden Age indicates the transitional nature of the work. For further discussion, see Juan de Mata Carriazo's introduction to the *Memorial de diversas hazañas*, Madrid, 1941.

[93] Listed only as "el siculo" in the 1546 inventory, the volume might have been the *Crónica daragón* (Valencia, 1524), *De la vida y heroicos hechos . . . de los católicos reyes* (Valladolid, 1533), or—more probably—*De las cosas memorables de España* (Alcalá, 1539). The last is curious for its treatment of Jewish and *converso* matters. The discussion of the disorders during the reign of Henry IV is accompanied by a childishly smutty description of Jewish customs ("pasan el sábado limpiándose el culo con los dedos"). But when Marineo comes to the problem of *converso* backsliding, he goes beyond the official line ("la conversación que tenían con los judíos") towards a dawning realization of their human situation: ". . . es cosa dificil dexar las cosas acostumbradas" (fo. CLXIII). Most remarkable of all is his invention of ancient

442

with reference to local events in Torrijos, Talavera, and the Puebla de Montalbán,[95] and Fernan Pérez de Guzmán's *Mar de historias* (printed in 1512).

The last is best known today for its collection of fascinating and vivid pen portraits of the great Spaniards of the period prior to Rojas' birth. But, aside from this section, called by the author *Generaciones y semblanzas*, there were other stories which might have appealed to the author of *La Celestina*. Although Pérez de Guzmán dedicated himself primarily to moralistic meditation on individual lives (some of them *conversos* and Jews)[96] selected from both classical and Biblical traditions, he also demonstrated a continuing preoccupation with reason and unreason in history.[97] While Rojas surely derived a pleasure from some of his chronicles comparable to that offered by the romances of chivalry, we may nevertheless imagine him finding another sort of satisfaction in Pérez de Guzmán's characteristic assessment of the Grail narrative: "However delightful and sweet [it may be] to read because of the

---

Roman etymologies and lineages for such well known *converso* names as Merlo, Coronel, Deza, Coscón, and Cota. In this passage it is impossible to ascertain if the humanist is betraying his naïveté, expressing irony, or attempting to be helpful.

[94] The *RFE* editors propose only the *Chrónica del rey D. Pedro*, Seville, 1495, but it might just as well have been the *Crónica del rey D. Pedro aumentada con las Crónicas de Enrique II y de don Juan I*, Toledo, 1526.

[95] Talavera, Torrijos, and the Puebla were important as points of strength and rest half way between Old Castille and the newly conquered cities of Andalusia, the two main centers of power and population. From these smaller towns (free from the urban pressures and dangers of Toledo) 14th-century kings could react to events in either direction. Specific references here include the murder of Alfonso XI's mistress, doña Leonor de Guzmán, in the Alcázar of Talavera, the wounding of don Pedro at a tourney in Torrijos, the gift of the castle of Montalbán to his daughter, and his romantic flight back to the Puebla where doña María de Padilla was waiting for him after his arranged marriage.

[96] Among others, all highly praised, are Philo, Josephus ("noble varón de la generación de los judíos"), and Pero Alfonso.

[97] Using the same techniques of portraiture that were to make famous the section known as *Generaciones y semblanzas*, Pérez de Guzmán makes a continuing effort to endow remote history and biography with the vividness of present experience. In this sense the *Mar de historias* may be considered a precursor of the *Marco Aurelio*, the portrait of Charlemagne being a particularly good example. Also Guevaresque are apocryphal letters of moral purport attributed to various historical figures.

strange things that are related in it, it should be taken with a grain of salt."[98]

The *Mar de historias*, as another generic hybrid, lies somewhere between history and catalogues of human *exempla*. The latter, widely circulated in the Middle Ages, were represented in Rojas' library by translations of Boccaccio's *De casibus* and *De claris mulieribus*. Such works provide less a sense of the past than an appreciation of the enormous range of possibilities for being human. In a way comparable to Juan de Mena's visionary *Laberinto,* in these compendia human figures are held up in an eternal present for our inspection as if they were exhibits in a moral museum. The reader gaped at them, learned from them, educated his friends by their good and bad examples (Sempronio reminds Calisto that books are full of the *caídas* of those who esteemed women), and might even go on to find in them commonplaces useful for his own experiments in creative writing. In this connection, as I have observed elsewhere,[99] it is worth meditating on the fact that Rojas, who had surely thumbed through the *De casibus* (*Cayda de príncipes,* Seville, 1495) before continuing *La Celestina,* did not so employ it. Boccaccio's vision of fortune as a moral entity for the punishment of individual cases of pride and excess was alien to Rojas' more intimate sense of fortune as resulting from exposure built into the human condition. The falls which occur on Rojas' pages are caused by nothing more—or less—than gravity. To have employed Boccaccio extensively would have blunted the double-edged irony of Sempronio's warning, a warning as true in his own case as in Calisto's and, at the same time, inappropriate in its absolute morality.

We may imagine a similar lack, not of interest (Rojas was certainly curious about extreme human behavior), but of thematic utility for the *De claris mulieribus* (*Mujeres ilustres,* 1494). One feature about it, shared by the *Crónica troyana* (which Rojas owned and which, as we saw, was a source for the description of Melibea),[100] is its awkward attempt to reduce classical mythology to purely human and historical terms, the most flagrant example being the presentation of Venus as a famous whore mistress. Nor is this the only resemblance between the two works. Like Boccac-

[98] Quoted in *RH*, 1913, p. 600.   [99] *The Art*, Chaps. V and VI.
[100] See Chap. VI, n. 136.

cio, the authors of the *Crónica* convert the narrative of the Trojan war into a sequence of *casos de Troya* generically not dissimilar to the works now under consideration. Hector is the virtuous hero, and the *exemplum* of treachery and cowardice is Achilles, who stabs him in the back.

Fortunately for his personal illustration, Rojas later purchased Juan de Mena's *Yliada en romance* composed in part—as we are told in the "prohemio"—to correct the "sinister" distortions of Guido delle Colonne and to return Homer (known to him through a Latin verse résumé) to his place of honor.[101] The story line is as a result strengthened, authenticated, and unified, even though Mena, like his predecessor, conceives of the *Iliad* as a book "of clear deeds of past men which will encourage and strengthen the will" of his readers. The effort to persuade as well as to inform is further manifest in the style with its forced rhetorical eloquence and (like certain passages in *La Celestina*) its hidden lines of the verse form called "arte mayor." In these versions of the story of Troy we have approached again the blurred medieval frontiers between history, poetry, and moral exemplification.

More rigidly selective than these but belonging to the same ambiguous category, is the *Chrónica llamada el Triunpho de los nueve mas preciados varones de la Fama* (translated from the French in a Lisbon, 1530 edition). Among the nine are three Jewish heroes,[102] Joshua, David, and Judas Maccabeus, whose exploits are told not in schematic *exempla* but at some length. Whatever Rojas' reaction to this exaltation of the past of his kind may have been, he could

---

[101] Although almost certainly not a source (the first known printing being Valladolid, 1519), Crisis' lament for Crisida (Cressida) must have impressed Rojas with its similarities to that of Pleberio. The capricious and disordered behavior of a deity (in this case, Apollo), the wish for death, the complaint that the daughter has been unjustly punished for the father's sins, all are present. There are even some inexplicable verbal similarities: "¿Estos son, Phebo, los galardones que tu me das en la postremería de la mi desierta vejez?" *Yliada en romance*, ed. M. de Riquer, Barcelona, 1949, p. 53.

[102] The anonymous *Triomphe des neuf preux*, Abbéville, 1487, stemmed from an earlier manuscript tradition. The other six include three pagans, Alexander, Hector, and Caesar, and three Christians, Arthur, Charlemagne, and Godfrey of Bouillon. The Spanish version was reedited in 1581 by López de Hoyos who described it as an "ejemplar obra para afficionar a la cavallería a honestos exercicios y obras históricas." Presumably he would have recommended it to the hero created by his most renowned student as reading more suitable than the romances of chivalry.

445

not have helped but attend to one particular passage in the story of Judas Maccabeus. In it Antiochus IV offers a certain Mattathias wealth and high position if he will renounce Judaism. The latter answers that he and his sons and brothers "will only obey the law of our fathers" and, after killing the King's messenger (a renegade Jew), takes his faithful band out into the desert to fight.[103]

Against these annals of intransigence, we find in Guevara's monumental and far more cunningly arranged accumulation of *exempla, El relox de príncipes*, reiterated pleading for tolerance. The portrait of the ferocious Roman judge, Licaónico (quite evidently an inquisitor)[104] and the speeches of the Villain of the Danube and the aged ambassador "del reyno de Judea" form the core of the book—precisely because in these episodes the traditional genre becomes relevant to contemporary history. In restyling medieval *exempla* for the press with pseudo-humanism and sonorous rhetoric, Guevara, for all his appearance of insincerity, could not avoid the pressing human and intellectual problems of his new public. How gratefully Rojas and some of his fellows must have listened to the nominally Jewish but really *converso* Ambassador: "In return for all the advice Judea has received from Rome (Christianity and its culture) let Rome be advised by Judea . . . to appoint judges who will conserve its dominion, not with rigor and bloodshed, but with clemency and the uniting of hearts [*juntando corazones*]."[105]

The remaining profane books in the library can be dealt with

---

[103] The incident stems from Josephus' *Antiquities*, Book XII, Chap. 6. I am citing from the Alcalá, 1585 edition, p. 31.

[104] See my "The Sequel to the *Villano del Danubio*," RHM, XXXI (1965), 175-185. Although I do not there so note, the name is apparently a derivation from that of the bloodthirsty Lykaon, king of Arcadia, converted by Ovid into a wolf. However, if Guevara was aware of the derivatives of the root *Lyko* signifying light (e.g. Apollo Lykios), he might well have intended a second level of reference to Lucero.

[105] Admittedly the parallelism between Roman and Inquisitional "justice" is awkward to maintain, but such remarks as the following clearly demonstrate Guevara's intention: "en el pueblo romano no tienen crédito los que sanan con olio sino los que curan con fuego" (fo. CXLVII). Or again: "De una cosa estoy muy espantado . . . en que siendo de derecho la justicia de los dioses y *siendo ellos los ofendidos* se quieren llamar piadosos y nosotros teniendo la justicia emprestada y no siendo ofendidos, nos gloriamos de ser crueles" (fo. CXLV). Italics mine.

more briefly. Either they are quite well known (Aesop,[106] the *Decameron*, the *Cárcel de amor*, the *Golden Ass*, Boethius, Seneca's *Epistles*, Castiglione's *Courtier*, and Ovid's *Metamorphoses*, all in Spanish prose), or they have been discussed previously in detail (the *Visión deleitable* and the *Repetición de amores*). However, two points may be made about the list as a whole. In the first place, these books represent a worthwhile selection of what was on the market at the time. Rojas, if neither a Latinist or an Erasmist, was not content merely to escape through literature. Along with addiction to the romances of chivalry he did not disdain what used to be called "the best of the good reading." Secondly, we again observe a lack of sharp generic frontiers. The fiction of Diego de San Pedro and Apuleius blend imperceptibly into the philosophical allegories of Boethius and Alfonso de la Torre. That is to say, the prevalence of fable and allegorical frames makes impossible our customary division of fiction from non-fiction. Only at the extremities of the spectrum can a Boccaccio, for example, be clearly set apart from a Seneca. And even in these cases the occasional moral pretense of the one and the rhetorical artificiality of the other must be taken into account. From which we may conclude once more that attribution of a conventional moral intention to Rojas' own efforts at creating good literature, if not untrue, is somewhat pointless. What must be determined in each case is the direction and significance of the author's moral purpose and the manner and degree of its artistic transmutation. To judge by external or generic criteria will tell us little about works written in this tradition.

A somewhat more valid case may perhaps be made for separate formal classification of the surprisingly few works in dialogue and verse present in the library. Of the former, it is at first glance disconcerting to notice the absence of the continuations of *La*

---

[106] Typical editions included a proto-picaresque biography of the fabulist as a slave "de muchos amos" which was probably derived from medieval tradition. Curiously from our point of view, Aesop on one occasion warns a treacherous adopted son that he is "subjeto a las caídas humanales" and at the end, when the latter's misdeeds come to light, "desesperando de una alta torre se ochó." *La vida y fabulas del clarissimo y sabio fabulador Ysopo*, Antwerp, 15–, p. 30. The inventory listing, "fabulas de Ysopo," may indicate that Rojas owned the edition so entitled, Salamanca, 1491.

Celestina. How could Rojas—we wonder—have been so uninterested in his own influence and literary fortune? But if we meditate for a moment on our own reading of his imitators, we may well imagine that their dialogue and development of action were painful to him. This is in a sense confirmed by the two partial exceptions, Hernán Pérez de Oliva's translation of the *Amphitryon* and Torres Naharro's *Propalladia.* The former, as we saw, theorizes on the oral presentation of speeches in a fashion similar to Proaza and in practice endows them with a colloquial fluidity reminiscent of *La Celestina.*[107] Used for revelation of Plautus in living language, Pérez de Oliva's dialogue is far removed from the intolerable and interminable caricature of the *Thebayda* and most of the other continuations. In a quite different way, Torres Naharro also put Rojas' stylistic achievement to new artistic purposes. Instead of resuscitating a classical masterpiece, he fused what he had learned from *La Celestina* to the nascent theatrical tradition of Juan del Encina and emerged with the first full-length plays in Spanish.[108]

Although Rojas with justified satisfaction may have recognized in these works a personal contribution to literary history, his single copy of the tragicomedia[109] seems to indicate relative unconcern with himself as a man of letters. Unlike Ercilla who, as we remarked previously, cherished several elaborately bound volumes

---

[107] See Chap. VI, n. iii.

[108] For consideration of references to *conversos* and their problems, in Torres Naharro, see my "Retratos de conversos en la *Comedia Jacinta,*" NRFH, xvii (1963-64). It is worth noting that, unlike Rojas, Torres Naharro alludes in immediately decipherable fashion to various aspects of the *converso* situation. Thus, insofar as it demonstrates the possibility of what *La Celestina* avoids, the *Comedia Jacinta* may be used as an argument against the thesis that Melibea and her family were of Jewish extraction. That is to say, if Rojas transformed his "desesperación" into other terms, Torres Naharro—perhaps less profoundly anguished than his predecessor—was able to use dramatic dialogue to give comprehensible form to his own experience.

[109] Because Rojas' copy was listed in the inventory as "el libro de Calisto," Bataillon identifies it as the *Libro de Calisto y Melibea y de la puta vieja Celestina,* the sole remaining copy of which is identified by F. J. Norton as printed by Cromberger in Seville between 1518 and 1520 (*Printing in Spain 1501-1520,* p. 151). Apparently, however, it is a reprint of a lost 1502 edition with the same title—which may have been that retained by the Bachelor. This text has been edited by M. Criado del Val and G.D. Trotter (Madrid, 1958) and reproduced in facsimile by A. Pérez y Gómez (Valencia, 1958). J. H. Herriott in his *Towards a Critical Edition* does not consider it to be the first edition of the tragicomedia or the most accurate.

of his epic of the conquest of Chile, *La Araucana*, Rojas appears to have been far more concerned with his final role as an "honrado Bachiller" than with his youthful success as an author.

In verse, with the exception of Antonio de Obregón's version of the *Trionfi* and Hernando del Castillo's definitive *Cancionero*,[110] the holdings were moral and narrative: Juan de Mena's *Laberinto de la fortuna*, its execrable imitation, *Las docientas del castillo de la fama* (possibly written by a classmate),[111] the Marquis of Santillana's *Proverbios* (which furnished Rojas with at least one ironically misused commonplace),[112] and Fernán Pérez de Guzmán's compilation of his verses edited as *Las setecientas*. Only the last, because of the possibility that it may be a hitherto unrecognized source for *La Celestina*, needs further comment. First printed in 1492,[113] its eight-syllable quatrains were dedicated to pressing upon the reader ("Tú, hombre que estás leyendo . . .") a double mould of "sciencia y caballería."[114] But, in spite of this anti-Celestinesque intention, in the course of the lengthy Stoic argu-

[110] It is impossible, of course, to ascertain which of the many widely varying editions Rojas possessed. The earliest, proposing to include "todas las obras que de Juan de Mena acá se escrivieron," dates from 1511. Included are anti-Jewish and anti-*converso* pieces as well as others defending or bewailing the situation of the caste. The use of dialogue is prevalent, and it seems to me that, in addition to comedies in Latin and the *Corbacho*, this poetic tradition should be taken into account as a formal source for *La Celestina*.

[111] By Alfonso Albares Guerrero, "jurista," Valencia 1519. Unidentified in the *RFE*, but the facsimile edition of A. Pérez y Gómez, Valencia, 1958, reveals that it was printed together with another piece, "Las cincuentas del laberinto contra fortuna: Compuestas por el mismo autor," in "arte menor" with naïve glosses for each stanza.

[112] As noted by Castro Guisasola, "e non excludas el viejo / de tu lado" reappears in an obscene context in Act VII. It is one more striking example of Rojas' ironical conversion of moral commonplaces by juxtaposing them against living situations. A number of other possible reminiscences are listed, p. 169.

[113] Although first printed long after the death of the poet, Seville, 1492, it would appear from the introductory verses that Pérez de Guzmán, rather than a later editor, made the compilation. The Seville, 1506 edition, the first to be entitled *Las setecientas*, has been reproduced in facsimile, Cieza, 1965.

[114] In spite of his Stoic rejection of inherited nobility as against virtue, Pérez de Guzmán would have had little sympathy for later notions of peasant honor: "No digo de religiosos / ni de rústica nación / entre quien jamás question / se haze de actos famosos." *Coplas fechas por Fernán Pérez de Guzmán de vicios e virtudes, Cancionero castellano del siglo XV*, ed. R. Foulché-Delbosc, Madrid, 1912, I, 581.

ment, we hear phrases that strike us as familiar. For example at the beginning the poet-moralist comments: "E porque sin compañía / no ay alegre possessión . . ." Or again (exactly as in the first interpolation of Act XII), "El hombre apercebido / es medio combatido . . ." Even more convincing than these Senecan echoes are recommendations for coping with sudden outbursts of wrath which seem to have been made to order for Celestina.[115] Pérez de Guzmán, like other purveyors of moral commonplaces, would, of course, have been shocked at the new context of his thoughts and words. This, not only because he would have disapproved of the speakers and the perverseness of their intentions but even more because his orthodox doctrine of evil is antithetical to that of Pleberio, Rojas, and Alvaron de Montalbán:

> All misfortune is conquered by suffering
> In patience which is very pleasing
> To the Lord; not by contradicting
> His just judgements but firmly believing
> That evil for good reason our lives is afflicting . . .[116]

A final category is that of religious instruction and pious edification. Three of these tomes—the *Evangelios y Epistolas*, the *Flos Santorum*, and the *Retablo de la vida de Cristo*—are at the head of the inventory and apparently occupied a conspicuous place on the shelves. But two others—a *Confesionario* and Pérez de Chinchón's *Diálogos Christianos*—were inserted, perhaps carelessly, among the profane volumes. The only other such indications of bibliographical order are five histories and chronicles grouped not far from these and the romances of chivalry (running with two interruptions from *Amadís* to *Platir* nine tomes further on). In view of this place of honor (as well as of our previous suppositions about Rojas' skepticism), it will be necessary to attend to these

---

[115] "La fresca yra y saña / no es luego de exsecutar. / Déxala un poco amansar / después con buen tiento y maña. / / El que en si non tiene tiento / con la nueua turbación / dela tu insultación / haurá doble sentimiento; / dexa pasar el furor / si el peligro non es cercano; / despues con manso dulçor, / del enfermo farás sano" (*ibid.*, p. 596). The same word "amansar" (not used in *La Celestina*) appears in another distant resemblance: "ca non ay dolor que non canse / e que el tiempo non lo amanse : e non lo faga cesar" (p. 583).

[116] *Ibid.*, p. 604.

pious books in some detail. It is impossible to determine whether a faith that seemed at least implicitly rejected in *La Celestina* gradually took possession of its author's soul, or whether, as was the case in other *converso* families, parental lip service was maintained as an indispensable camouflage. Such is the problem posed by Rojas' ownership of these volumes. About all that can be said with certainty is that there is nothing in the library (no Old Testaments in Spanish, for example) or in *La Celestina* itself for that matter which indicates clandestine Judaism.

The *Evangelios y Epístolas*, put into "romance" by the Aragonese *converso* and lawyer, Gonzalo García de Santa María, is a glossed collection of evangelical material arranged according to specific Sundays and holidays. Translated in 1484 from the *Postilla super epistolas et evangelia* of Guillermus Parisiensis (1437), it seems to have been intended both for sermonists whose Latin was weak and for weekly reading aloud to the family circle. The translator hopes explicitly that "everyone in the privacy of home" will learn in liturgical progression the sayings ("In illo tempore dixit Jesus . . .") and deeds of his Saviour. The same temporal didacticism appears in Fray Pedro de la Vega's version of the *Flos Santorum* which seems to have been one of the most widely circulated of the several available.[117] Day by day and month by month the apprentice Christian—and not only *conversos* but all Christians are by definition apprentices—was informed of the things he must know, believe, and worship. Unlike the multitude of lower-class families of Jewish and Moorish origin whose abysmal ignorance of their new "law" preoccupied Fray Hernando de Talavera, the Rojas quite evidently made a point of comprehending their commitments. Such reading —as well as the conventional funeral arrangements and pious bequests of which we shall speak later—was a part of the price of survival.

More interesting to us than these standard compendia was the widely circulated *Retablo de la vida de Cristo* (1485)[118] of Juan de Padilla known as "el cartujano," the Carthusian. Probably inspired

---

[117] Editions bearing this title (as against *La leyenda de los sanctos: la qual se llama hystoria lonbarda*, Burgos, 1500 and Madrid, 1525) were edited in Santiago, 1483, and Madrid, 1525.

[118] J. Simon Diaz' *Bibliografía de la literatura hispánica*, vol. III, Madrid, 1953, lists nine editions during Rojas' lifetime, and it continued to be re-edited during the rest of the 16th century.

451

by a German model,[119] Padilla directs many of his "coplas de arte
mayor" to a public made up of the new *conversos* who in 1492 had
chosen baptism over exile. Explanation ("Why it was necessary for
Mary to marry?"), castigation ("You, cruel heretic, and cursed
sower of discord, / Christian outside and Jewish inside, / worse
than a pagan, you look with scorn at the Trinity's marvellous mystery"), and persuasion ("Oh incredulous blindmen who have eyes
and see not / join for salvation's sake / this great Lord who is your
enemy") successively gloss the holy biography as the preacher poet
gets carried away by his subject. In its relentless fanaticism, the
Retablo expresses the fury of its age and, in so doing, helps us comprehend the equally relentless skepticism of *La Celestina* and the
Lazarillo. In a sense, we may think of it as a kind of anti-*Celestina*,
written by a *converso* almost schizophrenic about his ancestry. In
one stanza Padilla will praise the rite of circumcision or the "just
precepts" of the Jews and in the next gloat at the diaspora and de-
mand that *all* "adversaries of our singular catholic faith" be burned
at the stake.[120] We can only guess at Rojas' reaction to such passionate excess. But it is hardly likely to have persuaded him that
Christianity was a religion of love and charity. Men such as Padilla,
as Rojas knew only too well, were the most ferocious enemies of
their kind, and it was necessary to understand them—if only for
purposes of self-defense.

The last two religious books, a *Confesionario* and the Erasmist
Bernardo Pérez de Chinchón's *Diálogos christianos contra la secta
mahomética y la pertinacia de los judíos* (Valencia, 1535)[121] are

---

[119] See *Erasmo*, I, 52.

[120] Padilla's continual transition from the evangelical past into the hate-
filled present may be illustrated by two further examples from the third
"Retablo." Those apprehended performing "cerimonias de la juderia . . .
merecen . . . yr todos ahecho a las hogueras que son temporales." Then he
lashes out at those who today, like Judas in his time, continue to betray Christ:
"Venden a Christo merchantes traperos / y los alquimistas también sobre
todos / y los echacueros con formas y modos / y mas los ypocritas y
chocarreros." "Echacueros" seems to be a corruption of "echacuervos" meaning "alcahuetes." Others mentioned are "hechiceros" and "logreros" (usurers).
All of which amounts to saying that *conversos*, identified by their typical occupations and attitudes, deserve the punishment meted out to Judas.

[121] Mistakenly identified by the editors of the *RFE* as a "catecismo de la
época," this book is described by Bataillon (*Erasmo*, I, 331) and in more detail
by Bonilla ("Erasmo en España," *RH*, XVII, 1907, pp. 466-469), since the
author was apparently a surreptitious translator of Erasmus.

quite different. The *Confesionario* is impossible to identify, but, if it was—as it might well have been—Fray Hernando de Talavera's *Breve forma de confesar*,[122] the Rojas family would have found in it useful instruction on how to behave and believe. Aimed directly at *converso* readers but with a gentle firmness which contrasts strikingly with Padilla, many of Talavera's individual *pecados* deal with such matters as arguing matters of belief,[123] consorting with Jews,[124] and (like Alvaro de Montalbán) avoiding mass at the parish church. On the other hand, in defense of those helplessly cast out from their inherited law, he states that overzealous Christian ecclesiastics are themselves guilty of sin if they baptize an adult who has not been given instruction in his new belief for a period of at least eight months. Fray Hernando, like Padilla a *converso* and fervent Christian, presented an antithetical example of humane comprehension to his intended readers.

Bernardo Pérez de Chinchón's approach to the non-believer, although equally tolerant and charitable, is less concerned with practical warnings than with precisely the kind of religious argumentation that Fray Hernando found dangerous. The *Diálogos*, of which only one copy now exists,[125] are directed against the notion

[122] This work is extant as a section of Talavera's *Breue y muy prouechosa doctrina de lo que deue saber todo christiano, con otros tratados muy prouechosos* printed before 1500 and available in the BAE, vol. xvi. However, as Haebler points out, a typographical examination indicates that the individual *tratados* were printed separately and probably so distributed. Later the printer seems to have bound his remaining stock together with a new "título y tabla común" into the form that survived.

[123] "Peca el que cree las cosas de la Santa Fé no porque Dios las dijo y las manda creer, mas por razones naturales que al su parescer convencen a creer; por manera que si las tales razones no le convenciessen, no creería." Or again, "Pecan los que delante cristianos simples, que no son por infieles o hereges temptados cerca de la fé, disputan della" (p. 4). As we saw, Pedro Serrano was punished for precisely this sin.

[124] "Pecan los no muy firmes en la fé que grande familiaridad tienen con los infieles." Writing before 1492, Fray Hernando goes on to propose rigid segregation. He condemns the presence of Christian servants and wet-nurses in Jewish homes, the use of Jewish physicians, midwives, and pharmacists, as well as mixed bathing.

[125] I can find no trace of a Valencia, 1534 edition seen by J. P. Fuster when compiling his *Biblioteca valenciana*, Valencia, 1827-30. However, I have a microfilm of a 1535 edition in the Staats-Bibliothek in Munich: *Diálogos christianos contra la secta mahomética y contra la pertinacia de los judíos compuestos por el maestro Bernardo Pérez de Chinchón: obra nueuamente*

(already mentioned as current in half-converted circles) that Moors, Jews, and Christians could "all be saved each within his own law." Based on his experience of preaching to the Morisco population of Spain's Levantine coast (he was a canon in Gandía), the author invents an eminently reasonable and dispassionate series of conversations with his "master in the Arabic language, Joseph Zumilla" in which he proves that only the way of Christ leads to salvation. The real problem is to find the path within oneself. "War and weapons" may force conversion and regulate behavior but, as Unamuno stated on a famous occasion, they can never lead to inner conviction. Only an appeal to the faculty of understanding shared "by all men"[126] can overcome the misfortune of having been brought up in an erroneous faith.[127] "God himself," Pérez de Chinchón remarks in terms that would have seemed heretical to the Inquisitors of Pedro Serrano, "wants his law examined, discussed, and probed by reason."[128] The arguments used are traditional (based for the most part on Old Testament prophecies of the Messianic biography),[129] but the attitude of tolerance and serenity

---

compuesta muy útil y prouechosa. The printer was Francisco Díaz. There is no systematic folioing.

[126] ". . . ni por parte de ser hombres nos devemos recelar el uno del otro, pues el entendimiento humano es amigable compañero desseosso de saber y amigo de la verdad, y hazer lo contrario es ser el hombre mas fiera que no hombre." This rejection of "conflictive" caste consciousness in favor of the brotherhood of reason surely awakened interesting reactions in the author of *La Celestina*, a book just as far removed from narrow-mindedness but lacking in confidence in homo sapiens. Pérez de Chinchón seems to have been a sincere *converso* who in a few remarks indicates admiration for his ancestors (the Maccabees were "martyrs") but who, at the same time, in contrast to Christian precepts, judges the Jewish way of life to be a "ley pesada."

[127] Pérez de Chinchón begins by remarking that no one should be blamed for believing what he was brought up to believe: "Cosa clara está que todo hijo naturalmente ama y sigue la doctrina y criança de su padre."

[128] "El mismo Dios quiere que su ley se examine y platique y averigüe conforme a razón. . . ." Or again: "Tanta es la excelencia de la razón humana quando esta fuera de malicia que puede juzgar de las cosas divinas."

[129] The writer feels that exponents of the new learning have lamentably abandoned the age-old task of defending the faith and confounding alien creeds: "Mueren algunos por anotar a Plinio, sudan por declarar a Virgilio, trabajan por metrificar epigramas y versos de amores, y ninguno se exercita por estirpar este error de Mahoma que tanto cunde." Only he—however unworthy—is still willing to carry on the tradition of Llull and to prove on the basis of Old Testament prophecy that Christ was indeed the Messiah. As is

displayed throughout is remarkable. Hence, perhaps, the usefulness and the appeal of the book to a person in Rojas' position. Did the author of *La Celestina,* we wonder, meditate seriously on the reason of theological unreason during his declining years? Or did he merely utilize the *Diálogos* as a source of acceptable arguments whenever he could not avoid involvement in the never ending religious discussion of his age? Once again we have been led away from the temptation to oversimplify the Spain and the mind of Fernando de Rojas.

Such then was the personal library of the author of *La Celestina,*[130] a library dedicated primarily to that consolation for the perils and annoyances of daily existence which Guevara saw as a principal function of reading. Recognizing the risks of positive judgments based on negative factors (the books that might have been listed and were not), nevertheless we discerned in it more interest in the romances of chivalry than in Erasmus, more delight in the vernacular than in the language of Humanism. A few books —notably the *Querela pacis*—reflect continuing meditation on the theme of *La Celestina.* Others represent a typical selection of the good reading (moral, exemplary, informative) and good writing available at the time. But taken as a whole, the library betrays what might be called an architectural sense of the reading experience: doors for escape (into the past, the far Orient, or the horizons of imagination) and walls of religious commonplaces and instruction behind which the skeptical mind might find repose. Rather than struggling to reshape Christianity to the measure of their tradition,

---

pointed out at the beginning, since Mohammedans accept Old Testament authority, they cannot reject such argumentation out of hand.

[130] A tome not discussed above (since it belonged to Rojas' wife) is Fray Martín de Córdoba's *Jardín de las nobles mujeres,* Valladolid, 1500, listed in the 1546 inventory. As a mirror for princesses dedicated to Isabella, when printed it became a compendium of pious and decorous advice to a public of literate young women. There Leonor Alvarez was advised on how to speak ("Mucho hablar y mucho callar . . . son vicios de la lengua), walk (". . . no sea mucho apriessa ni mucho de vagar, ni andando quebrar el paso que es una manera de loçanía y significa liviandad"), and dress ("cada una segun su estado"). If Rojas looked into it, he might have been amused at the remarks on cosmetics: ". . . no hayan en sí ningún afeite sofístico ca esto es ilícito y siempre es pecado cuando la mujer procura parescer mas hermosa de lo que es, poniendo albayalde y arrebol, açafrán y alcohol y otras posturas deshonestas." Quoted from the Toledo, 1953 facsimile.

455

Rojas and his family—we surmise—preferred to learn what was expected of them and to conform to what they learned. Once this was accomplished, they could then allow their consciousnesses and consciences to live and die in printed freedom.[131]

By way of epilogue we may note that the library as listed in the inventory did not long remain intact. In 1546 after the death of Leonor Alvarez it was divided up along with the rest of the property among the children. As for the priceless copy of *La Celestina* (valued by the assessor at 10 maravedís), it went to Alvaro the *escribano*, without discussion. The Licentiate Francisco who, as the eldest son, had first choice, passed it over, a decision which may have kept it from being included among those few of the books still in the possession of his direct descendant, don Fernando del Valle Lersundi. When, in 1580, the Licentiate died during a visit to his son, the latter brought to Valladolid the furniture and household goods that were in good condition and could be moved. This included his father's library and whatever books remained from that of his grandfather. The rest, principally the enormous *tinajas* and their contents as well as used implements and half broken furniture, was auctioned off. One cannot help but wonder what Pedro Hernández, the fisherman, did with the bookshelves ("un estante para libros") which his bid of eight reales acquired.[132]

&ℓ "Every day we see new things or hear about them"

Enclosed by the "fabric and fortress" of the city walls as well as by those of their substantial dwelling, the lives of Fernando de Rojas and his family seem singularly protected, immune to history. On the other hand, as we have remarked several times, precisely because of their veneration of order and ritual repetition, he and his contemporaries were all the more conscious of mutability and innovation. Lives that attempted to bring themselves to stasis were acutely aware "that from the first age until the hair turns white"

---

[131] The size of the library (aside from legal works, some 62 volumes are listed in the two inventories) was respectable at the time. L. Febvre and H. J. Martin in *L'Apparition du livre* mention certain men of the robe in Paris who in the 1520's owned several times as many (p. 399), but Rojas' collection seems rather ample for a Talaveran lawyer. Then, too, as suggested above, he surely had local friends with whom he could exchange books.

[132] On 22 January 1581, VLA 33.

they were engaged in battle and were subject to fortune both from within and from without. The catastrophical biological defeat to which every man is doomed found its compensation in faith or— for men without faith—in the starkness of its inevitability. But the neighborhood history that prowled outside was terrifying because it was arbitrary, unpredictable, propelled by passions and accidents in ever changing combinations. These were forces against which walls formed only the feeblest defense.

Beyond the middle distance of the neighborhood there were larger arenas for history: municipality, province, kingdom, and continent. And although not as immediately perilous as a quarrel with the family next door, the well developed sensitivity of *conversos* to their changing times created an unprecedented interest in impersonal news. Nor was this limited to their tormented caste. As Pierre Sardella brings out, a general consciousness and interest in the news seems to have spread from Italy over the rest of Europe at the end of the fifteenth and beginning of the sixteenth centuries.[133] Rojas lived at a time when current events were first becoming current, when they were beginning to intrude on daily life with all their superficiality, alarm, ostentation, and enchantment. Beyond the refuge of walls and the reassurance of schedules, in the market places and on the street corners, voices were asking each other, "Have you heard . . . ?"

Sardella is primarily concerned with the historical changes and technical developments—growth of commerce, improvements in land and sea transportation, printing—which gave unprecedented urgency and prominence to international news. He dwells at length on the effects of news on prices and living conditions and particularly on the sudden acceleration of economic activity caused by the arrival of good or bad tidings. We may think, for example, of Jacques Coeur (who had his Spanish counterparts) and his squadron of carrier pigeons. Sardella does not, however, meditate on an

---

[133] Sardella concludes: "C'est au début du XVIᵉ siècle que la nouvelle étend son pouvoir sur des domaines beaucoup plus larges et plus differenciés qu'auparavant, et acquiert un rôle beaucoup plus evident dans la vie des hommes" (*Nouvelles et spéculations à Venise au début du XVIᵉ siècle*, Paris, 1948, p. 16). Divina, the heroine of Torres Naharro's curious *Comedia Jacinta* (based on the theme of the news), appears in a posture representative of the age: "Poníase a la ventana / muchas vezes a prazer / con voluntad y con gana / de nueuas nueuas saber" (*Propalladia*, ii, 327).

aspect which is of special concern to readers of *La Celestina*: the impact of the news on the European mind as the latest and most entrancing way of being aware of mutability. My favorite example is, of course, Sempronio's speech in Act III (a fragment of which is the title of this section) representing the passage of time in an equation of local gossip and national and international news. A comparable passage in English is Lear's last speech to Cordelia in which he compares "court news" and the ins-and-outs of royal favor to the tide's "ebb and flow by th'moon," and it should not be hard to find many others. In both cases, the writer presents the news as an image of time itself and goes on to communicate a somewhat perverse pleasure in its passage. The melancholy *ubi sunt* of the preceding century was becoming a more titillating *quid novi*?

For as both Sempronio and Lear realized, news is at once fascinating and transitory—like fireworks, fascinating because so transitory. It offers an almost irresistible temptation even to a Thoreau (the much cited "Time is but a stream I go a fishing in" refers to his trudging to Concord for news) or to a Bécquer impatiently waiting for the Madrid paper by the roadside in Veruela. But to return to the sixteenth century, it is significant that in two cases, both more or less contemporary with Rojas, familiar spirits converted their masters into pundits. We have already referred to the physician Eugenio Torralba (with whom Rojas may well have been acquainted), whose supernatural contact, Zequiel, told him of the death of King Ferdinand and predicted the civil war of the Comunidades. In another trial narrated by Llorente, we find exactly the same use of occult power. A crazed nun relates having learned of the future imprisonment of Francis I, of his marriage, and also of the Comunidades from a familiar called Balbán.[134] When Peter Martyr, whose correspondence often seems to amount to a continuing newsletter, wrote that he felt "inquietude and anxiety" when cut off from the news,[135] he was expressing the mood

---

[134] *Llorente*, IV, 40.

[135] We should distinguish between news consciousness in *La Celestina* and that of a comedy such as *Volpone*. In the latter, concerned primarily with the goods of fortune, news from abroad is decisive, whereas in the former we encounter on the part of the inhabitants an equally intense but purely local concern with gossip, which is to say the news of human relationships. In both cases, however, antennae to the world without probe unceasingly and avidly.

of his times. Castile, now a part of Europe and América, no longer meditated, as it had a generation before, on the mournful passing and lasting clarity of her famous men; instead its inhabitants—*conversos* and Old Christians alike, but the former perhaps with more timorous avidity—listened to the news of their doings.

The war of the Comunidades (1520-21), predicted so unerringly by Balbán and Zequiel, was the biggest news story of the age. It was a bitter civil conflict which is usually interpreted as representing a last effort of Castilian towns and communities to defend local sovereignty against the grandiose imperial dreams and policies of the new Hapsburg dynasty. At the time, too, other more immediate causes, such as Charles V's appointment of grasping Flemish favorites to high office, were asserted. But politically speaking, the sudden and unforeseen (except by those employing supernatural help) outbreak of local violence and anarchy has been explained by historians as an effort to reverse the trend of events and to defend traditional medieval privileges and municipal autonomy against the exigencies of the crown. More recently J. A. Maravall has studied the uprising in the context of the social and economic development of Western Europe—that is to say, the growth of the bourgeoisie and the evolution of parliamentary power. The *comuneros*, Maravall believes, were, roughly speaking, Castilian counterparts of the English squires and merchants who sought a political role corresponding to their rising economic power. And their failure to prevail, the very abjectness of their total defeat, was to be Spain's historical misfortune.[136]

There is surely some truth both to the neo-medieval and proto-European interpretations of what was going on. In spite of differing emphases, they are not contradictory. However, as Américo Castro has observed (on the basis of extensive sixteenth-century documentation), behind the violence lay a tradition, not only of institutional conservatism or institutional evolution, but also of bloody inter-caste warfare. Such men as Fernando de la Torre, the *converso* rebel of Toledo, and those who belonged to the turbulent *converso* political "parties" in the time of don Alvaro de Luna were the authentic forerunners of the *comuneros*. Insofar as Old Christians (burghers angry about taxes, land poor *hidalgos*, and even

---

[136] *Las Comunidades*, Madrid, 1963.

resentful peasants) joined the ranks and wrote the platform, they did so in closely interlocked alliance with the persecuted *converso* middle class which still governed many towns and which for two generations had been preyed upon by the Holy Office. Unlike the rioters and conspirators in Toledo, Zaragoza, and Seville back in the 1480's and before, these more or less assimilated and well-established rebels had learned how to camouflage their motives and how to take advantage of the larger unrest. Advocacy of national interest, municipal rights, and the power of the "Cortes" (the Spanish parliamentary institution) now gave an attractive political aspect to hidden caste grievances. The old quarrels had found a new disguise.

It was indeed a time of disguise. As we have seen in one context after another (including that of *La Celestina*), the Spain of Fernando de Rojas was characterized by a built-in historical deceptiveness and a hypocrisy that was at once individual and social. Not only did each man wear his standardized mask but also now we find a caste pretending successfully to be a class. If Old Christian peasants converted their justified economic and political resentment into religious fanaticism and self-righteous prejudice, the *conversos* had learned how to cover their own reactions to persecution with a mantle of bourgeois patriotism and traditionalism. And, one also suspects, in many cases they learned something even more useful: how to believe it themselves.[137] But these disguises—no matter how useful and clever—can, and could be, seen through. As the comic news commentator of the epoch, "don" Francesillo de Zúñiga remarked of one encounter outside of Toledo: "In this battle many bodies were found without foreskins."[138] Himself a *converso*, Zúñiga knew how to penetrate beneath historical causes and

---

[137] In addition to *"La Celestina" como contienda*, pp. 41-67, see J. I. Gutiérrez Nieto, "Los conversos y el movimiento comunero," *Collected Studies in Honour of Américo Castro's Eightieth Year*, ed. M. P. Hornik, Oxford, 1965, pp. 199-220. In all the copiously recorded speeches and deliberations of the Inquisition-harassed burghers of Teruel (see the fascinating account given by A.C. Floriano Cumbreño, "El tribunal del Santo Oficio en Aragón," *BRAH*, LXXXVII, 1925, pp. 544-605), it is significant that they never even indirectly refer to their caste. Superficially—and perhaps in many instances profoundly—their collective self-image was that of middle-class town dwellers. But when in the course of events many of them were condemned and burnt, one wonders if the façade may not have cracked.

[138] *Crónica*, BAE, vol. XXXVI, p. 14.

self-justifications into the marrow of hatred, the aggressive and vengeful tradition, that animated the movement.

How did Rojas himself react to the news of the Comunidades? From the ironical skepticism of *La Celestina* and from the little we know about his biographical behavior, my guess would be unenthusiastically.[139] While sympathizing with the rebels, his personal alienation from history might well have led him to agree with his classmate Villalobos. The latter (who also perceived longstanding *converso* rancor at the roots of the rebellion)[140] expressed himself as follows in a 1520 letter: "I won't give you any more news, because, if I speak against the King, I would be a traitor, and, if I speak against the Comunidad I would be a *puto* (for now they don't hang anybody except by his feet),[141] and if I speak against our times, I would be a heretic, because it is a crime against the first commandment. There will be always someone to accuse me."

The town of Talavera to which Rojas had linked his life adopted a policy of neutrality which reflected a communal wariness similar to that expressed privately by Villalobos. As we remember, it received afterwards a grateful letter from the young monarch. Among those participating in municipal deliberations at this crucial moment (according to Cosme Gómez) was the same "Señor Juan de Ayala" (d. 1530)[142] whose several debts to Rojas are referred to in the inventory. This local dignitary, landholder, and great-grandson of Fernán Pérez de Guzmán,[143] was at the time the "procurador general" and apparently one of those most influential in

---

[139] There was a Fernando de Rojas "vecino de Toledo" who in 1522 was denied amnesty for his participation in the uprising (*Orígenes*, p. 247), but, as Menéndez Pelayo points out, there is no basis for asserting either identity or relationship. The name was, to say the least, not uncommon.

[140] For example, he remarks on a Flemish gentleman whose way of trying to pass for Castilian and *comunero* was to say "que no cree en Dios a cada paso" (*Algunas obras*, p. 47). Elsewhere he calls the *comuneros* directly "hereges" (p. 58). As Villalobos knew, his friend Jufre had been atrociously murdered for having called certain *comuneros* "marranos" whom he would like to execute (Introduction, p. 33).

[141] *Ibid.*, p. 48. Apparently this form of execution was meted out to homosexuals.

[142] His testament constitutes Salazar y Castro, doc. 20,889. A bequest is made to a sister, doña María de Ayala, a nun in the convent of La Madre de Dios. She is clearly the same as the original patroness mentioned by Cosme Gómez as entering the order in 1518.

[143] Salazar y Castro, docs. 20,888 and 20,889.

counselling prudence.[144] The result was that Rojas, wise in his choice of a haven from history, was probably able to reside quietly in his house during these years and to hear of the violent doings of the *comuneros* as mere items of news, intensely interesting but demanding no personal commitment.

That the war of the Comunidades rather than discoveries in America or European victories (now thought to be of far more historical importance) should have dominated the news picture indicates that from the beginning the notion of news depended on personal relevance and human interest. What is newsworthy is what I can imagine witnessing, what I can imagine taking part in, or—in line with Sardella—what might affect my situation or my affairs. Thus, the battle of Pavia itself took second place in the news to its results: the capture and imprisonment in Madrid of Francis I. And the New World precisely because it was utterly new (unimaginable and of no apparent effect on individual and community) was poor news. Balbán and Zequiel didn't bother with it.

National news interesting because of its local relevance included the 1515 passage of King Ferdinand through Talavera (Peter Martyr who was in his retinue called it a "notable city")[145] on his way to death in Madrigalejo a month later. Three years earlier the community had demonstrated its loyalty by dispatching 400 local *peones* to his wars with France.[146] In 1522 the Talaverans were even more excited by the accession and marriage of a new Duke of Estrada (the most important title in the region) and by the accompanying festivities.[147] But there was another event, surely dismissed by Rojas and his neighbors as gossip, which was to prove of far more importance to history than any of these: the birth in 1536 of a natural son to the reverend Bachelor Juan Martínez de Mariana, Dean of the Iglesia Colegial and local representative of the Inquisition.[148]

[144] Cosme Gómez gives a rather detailed description of Talaveran official prudence during those years. One of the *jurados* who counselled loyalty was a Licentiate Alonso Ortiz, who may well have been the witness of identical name present at the certification of the will.

[145] *Epistolario*, xi, 204.   [146] Jiménez de la Llave, p. 192.

[147] Salazar y Castro, doc. 27,345.

[148] This fact, unmentioned by Mariana's biographers, is recorded by Cosme Gómez. Among the father's Inquisitional duties was presiding over testimony of Talaveran witnesses and forwarding the results to Toledo. Thus in the

Aside from the two years of the Comunidades, the major source of news, news all the more fascinating because of its dolorous human interest, was the Holy Office. The secrecy and mystery which accompanied its doings had the desired effect of making them all the more exciting. Not only could one put oneself in the place of the victim ("There but for the grace of God . . ."), but also the uncertainty and rumors which accompanied individual trials and investigations gave wide scope for the collective imagination. The actual news which emerged when the charges were read and punishment inflicted in the *autos de fe* was preceded by years of apprehension, discussion, and guesswork. Unlike certain other communities, Talavera was not vengefully picked on or grievously decimated, but it did furnish a number of well-known cases still on record today. In 1486, for example, a priest from the Church of Saint Martin had been degraded and burned at the stake. The scene is described in a contemporary chronicle: he and another curate, dressed in their robes with chalices and scriptures in their hands, were "placed before the bishop who, reading their misdeeds aloud from a book, progressively stripped them of their vestments . . . down to their undergarments. Then they were turned over to the 'secular arm,' adorned with conical hats and rope nooses, and taken out of town and burned alive. So they ended."[149]

An equally newsworthy case (commented on by Lea as famous at the time) which occurred not long after Rojas' arrival was that of Bernaldino Díaz, another ecclesiastic. After being absolved of charges of heresy in 1512, he used his freedom to murder his Old Christian accuser, a rich peasant. Less because of the deed itself than because of the disrespect to its authority and the danger that future denouncers might be intimidated, the Inquisitors ordered

---

trial of Rojas' friend Diego de Oropesa we find: "En Talavera a doce dias de noviembre de mil e quinientos e diez y seis años, ante el reverendo señor bachiller Juan Martínez de Mariana, dean de la iglesia colegial de nuestra señora Santa María de la dicha villa, juez e vicario general en ella e su arcedianazgo, e en presencia de mi el notario público. . . ." In all likelihood the Dean had also been a classmate of Rojas at Salamanca, since he hardly could have achieved such a prominent position in a few years after graduation and since in a 1526 letter he describes himself as a "true son" of that university. R. Espinosa Maeso, "Una carta inédita del Licenciado Mariana," *BRAE*, xiii (1926), 285.

[149] F. Fita, "La inquisición toledana," p. 300.

rearrest. But Bernaldino Díaz evaded them, fled to Rome, secured Papal protection, and converted his case into one of the few contests of authority between Pope and Inquisition that were won by the former. In the course of the jurisdictional tug-of-war, the Inquisitors were excommunicated, Bernaldino Díaz was burned in effigy, and all his relatives were imprisoned.[150] An after-effect of the stir caused by these events was the deprivation (mentioned previously as a minimal fall of fortune) of Alonso de Arévalo, who later became Rojas' protégé and agent, of his right to exercise his profession as watchman (*guardacampos*). He had been overheard to remark approvingly of the act of revenge.[151]

Other trial records, although less sensational, serve to provide us with unexpected glimpses of Talaveran life. In that of a person baptized as Rodrigo Jiménez Herrador we learn of a curious sub-society of Morisco potters, basket weavers, and masons (there had been a mosque and a clearly defined Moorish *barrio* in Talavera as late as the 1470's)[152] shot through with messianism and superstition. Still in the 1530's these forlorn survivors of the past (far more primitive and down-trodden than most Hebrew *conversos*) would gather together secretly to practice half-forgotten rites, beginning with public washing of private parts. Then eventually, when the atmosphere was appropriately reverent and charged, one of their number would go into a trance and become possessed of an angel. The latter was reported on several occasions to have blessed the assembly, to have promised to obtain for it a Koran in Spanish, and to have predicted such encouraging news as the conquest of Venice by the Turks.[153]

Another case which probably caused amused comment because of the picturesque and public nature of the sentence was that of a young Englishman residing in Talavera. In 1524 this individual, whose name had been Hispanicized to Gaspar Guillén (Jasper Williams?) and who was apparently bilingual, was accused of having remarked in a tavern that a woodcut of the Virgin which was being hawked to the customers was so poorly executed that it wasn't fit

---

[150] See Chap. V, n. 45, and Lea, II, 123 and 550. A contemporary defender of Inquisitional secrecy pointed to this case as demonstrating its necessity (Caro Baroja, II, 311).

[151] See Chap. IV, n. 31.

[152] F. Fita, "Documentos inéditos de Talavera," *BRAE*, II (1882), 314.

[153] Inquisición de Toledo, p. 246.

to be used for wiping excrement. For this imprudent remark (self-righteously reported by several of the pious bar-flies), he was sentenced to stand all day in front of a church, stripped to the waist, gagged, and "holding in one hand an image similar to that against which he had blasphemed and beating his breast with the other. . . ."[154] As a witness of such spectacles, Fernando de Rojas' awareness of the necessity of utmost verbal caution remained sharp.

A third trial takes us out of the intoxicated imprudence of the tavern atmosphere and allows us to overhear a conversation among a group of *conversos*. At once scared, blasphemous, and jocular, it amounted to a typical interchange of news and views of the sort Rojas surely took pains to avoid. In 1535 one Francisco López Cortidor was accused by an Old Christian carpenter in his employ of pouring urine over a crucifix and pronouncing at the same time, "No creo en Dios." Of course neither the prosecutor, our old acquaintance Diego Ortiz de Angulo, nor the chief Inquisitor, the formidable Pedro de Vaguer who sentenced Juan de Lucena's daughters, were equipped with enough sensibility to perceive that the two charges were in a profound sense contradictory. So, having been arrested and informed of the accusation, the prisoner made the following statement in his defense:

This witness in order to fabricate his false testimony against me must have been inspired by an occasion on which I was talking with the Bachelor Guevara and Juan Sevilla, the clergyman, leaning on a pillar at the door of the Church of San Miguel [Rojas' parish church]. They were talking about a Jew who had lived in Badajoz and Llerena and wore a *capa de Moysén* and used to perform all sorts of stupid tricks [*bellaquerías*]. And the Bachelor Guevara said that he [the Jew] had in an attic a crucifix on which he would urinate and would put a dirty rag over the face, and would feed it excrement. And the Bachelor Montenegro[155] who was there said

---

[154] *Ibid.*, p. 146.

[155] This individual was accused of multiple and incredible blasphemies and misdeeds by the crazed *beata* mentioned previously (Chap. II, n. 58). From her testimony it would seem that he and his wife amused themselves by teasing her and allowing her to overhear outrageous dialogue. Given the serious attention initially accorded these reports, the game came close to being as dangerous as any ever played.

that all by himself he could feed the crucifix for over a week. And before they left, I had arrived and I said that I had been in Badajoz when, for the above-mentioned acts, they arrested the first man ever to be tried by the Holy Inquisition. I also said that a rich merchant named Paredes or relative of Paredes had fled the town and was in Yelves in Portugal and they had arrested his wife and he had given a Portuguese caballero 200 ducats [presumably to go to Spain to fetch her]. All this I said I had heard about, and the witness must have used the above conversation as a basis for fabricating this great calumny."[156]

The accused goes on to try to establish the prejudice of his unknown accuser and provides a list of possible enemies comparable to that of Pedro Serrano in the Puebla. However, in spite of his lack of success in this guessing game, he did manage to substantiate the above conversation and was eventually absolved.

One of the most bitterly contested cases during Rojas' Talavera years was that of Luis (Abraham) García, referred to previously on several occasions. In 1514 this bellicose bookseller and tax farmer was apprehended by a supposed friend while attempting to flee to Portugal and turned over to the Inquisition. A large number of people both in and out of prison were anxious to testify against him, and before long not less than twenty-three separate accusations had been made all of which he answered in elaborate and stubborn detail. The case is described by Caro Baroja[157] as one of extreme maladjustment. Converted by force in 1492 when he was a grown man, he spent his life regretting the choice and expressing that regret in word and deed. As a result he was shown no mercy and, according to a local Talaveran tradition, his death at the stake occurred just outside the walls in the presence of a multitude of neighbors. Part of the fuel was said to have been his store of books. A flagrantly unfaithful wife and her aggressive lover (the page of a local nobleman) who had chased him through town with a sword had contributed to the embitterment of his life, but what brought him to the flames was the apparent truth of the statement attributed to him: "I swear to God that I would rather be a swine or a pig than a convertido."[158]

---

[156] Inquisición de Toledo, p. 310.   [157] Caro Baroja, I, 434.

[158] Caro Baroja disregards the other and more complex aspects of the

Of special interest to us are two trials with which Rojas himself was personally involved. The first is that of Alvaro de Montalbán's relative and prison mate, Bartolomé Gallego mentioned in Chapter II. As summed up by Serrano y Sanz, the wandering and exile of so many of his kind had been Gallego's life-long fate:

> Among the *conversos* of the Puebla de Montalbán and undoubtedly related to Fernando de Rojas' father-in-law, there was one whose life and customs made him a perfect model for a *pícaro*. . . . Of Jewish parentage, the child was first called Menahen and afterwards Bartolomé Gallego. In 1492 he left Spain . . . and became a Christian in Sardinia. Afterwards he resided in Fez, Tlemcen, and Oran, dealing sometimes in chickpeas, oil, and linen, sometimes in rings and cheap silver jewels. There he could live as a Jew according to his pleasure or convenience. Returning to Spain he established himself in Talavera de la Reina where he became a tailor. . . .[159]

Serrano y Sanz goes on to reproduce the brief autobiography written by Gallego on 24 April 1525 for the Inquisition. In it he names his father as one Abenyule who took him at the age of six into exile and identifies his mother as a sister of Alvaro and Francisco de Montalbán. When, after his return to Spain and a year's apprenticeship as a tailor in Valencia, he arrived once more in his "clara nación," he sought help and advice from his relatives.[160] In 1522 (at the age of 36) he moved on to Talavera where after a time he was denounced for his praise of Moorish religious cleanliness as contrasted to the Christian practice "of wearing muddy boots in church." Condemned, like his Uncle Alvaro, to a *sambenito* and perpetual imprisonment, he escaped by a ruse and was afterwards

---

case that were referred to earlier. See my Chap. II, nn. 58, 84, 89; and Chap. III, n. 50.

[159] Serrano y Sanz, pp. 252-253.

[160] They were apparently living in Toledo at the time (around 1510): ". . . dende allí se vino a esta çibdad de Toledo y pasó a la Puebla de Montaluán y estuvo en casa de Carrillo xpiano nuevo de judío, y desde allí volvió a esta çibdad y habló con unos tíos suyos que se dezían los Montaluanes que biuían a la perrochia de Sant Miguel, xpianos nuevos, y que se llamavan el uno Francisco de Montaluán y el otro Alvaro de Montaluán, los quales eran hermanos de su madre deste testigo, y estuvo con ellos obra de un mes poco más o menos . . ." (Serrano y Sanz, p. 253).

burned in effigy. Of this Serrano y Sanz remarks: "If Gallego, who surely had left Spain by that time, ever learned of the *auto de fe* inflicted on his statue, the only reaction to be expected of a man of his sort was a hearty laugh. . . ." He had, in other words, played a picaresque "trick on the honorable and venerable Inquisitors."[161]

Whether or not we agree with Serrano y Sanz in equating the life of this uprooted and exposed *converso* with that of a carefree Gil Blas (for my part I imagine him shuddering rather than laughing at the fate which came so close to destroying him), there can be no doubt that he was an uncomfortable cousin for Leonor Alvarez and her husband to have on their hands in Talavera. Indeed, it would be interesting to know how the family there (not only the Rojas but also his aunt, Beatriz Alvarez) received him. Were they reluctant and withdrawn, or did they fulfill their obligations as kinsmen of the hapless Gallego? For, as Serrano y Sanz observes, the relationship is a documented fact, the only doubtful question being that of its degree.[162] In any case, whatever the extent of consanguinity and personal proximity, one thing seems certain: Gallego's arrest brought consternation to the family. What might he not confess or invent under torture? What accusations might some avaricious inquisitor induce him to make against any or all of them? Had their treatment of him annoyed him in any way? Then, when less than a month later Alvaro de Montalbán was arrested (perhaps, they might first have guessed, because of Gallego's weakness or malevolence), these feelings were multiplied many times. The year 1525 was one in which fearful and uncertain news lapped at the doorstep of the well-ordered house by the city wall.

The second trial concerned Rojas to a lesser extent. The accused, a tax farmer named Diego de Oropesa, was arrested in 1517 and charged, among other crimes, with having maintained that payment of tithes was not a "divine commandment," with wearing

---

[161] *Ibid.*, p. 255.

[162] Alvaro de Montalbán in his own interrogation does not mention the marriage of one of his sisters to an Abenyule, but, in view of the latter's departure in 1492, he may have felt that this evasion would not be discovered. It would seem from Gallego's sketchy statement that his mother chose to remain in Spain where she probably remarried as a Christian. On the other hand, it may be that Gallego was confused about his relationships to members of his long lost family. According to Alvaro (Serrano y Sanz, p. 263), he and Francisco were not brothers but cousins, so that only the latter may have been Gallego's true uncle.

468

clean shirts on Saturday, and with being reluctant to eat bacon.[163] In the course of the proceedings (the defending attorney was again the Licentiate de Bonillo), Oropesa asked a number of friends to testify in his behalf and to assure the Inquisitors that he was a good Christian. Among them was Rojas who was asked the following three questions:

Do the witnesses know that the aforesaid Diego de Oropesa lived as a faithful and Catholic Christian and that he acted as a Christian, going to Mass, listening to sermons, and other divine offices, keeping the Sabbath and Easter and all the holy days which the Holy Mother Church requires, going to confession, taking communion, and receiving the sacraments?

Do the witnesses know that the aforesaid Diego de Oropesa slaughtered hogs at his home and used to eat and still eats bacon, sausages [*morcillas y longanizas*], and suckling pigs and other dishes of pork, hare, and rabbit prohibited to Jews according to their law?

Do the witnesses know that the aforesaid Diego de Oropesa in church as elsewhere, whenever the Ave Maria was recited or the Angelus was rung, would kneel and pray with great devotion as faithful and Catholic Christians do?

Rojas' answers were transcribed as follows:

The Bachelor Fernando de Rojas, a legally sworn witness, said that he has known Diego de Oropesa for ten years here, that he is not a relative of his, that he has not been bribed or influenced. To the [first][164] question he answered that he considers him a good Christian and that he used to see him go to Mass and sermons, and that he has no more to say.

To the [second] question, he answered that he does not know.

To the [third] question, he answered that he believes [that Diego de Oropesa did so behave] but has not seen him do so.[165]

---

[163] In addition, as noted in Chap. II, n. 48, there were a number of careless remarks of the sort for which Alvaro was accused by Yñigo de Monçón.

[164] The numbering of the questions in the transcript has been rearranged for purposes of clarity.

[165] Serrano y Sanz, pp. 251-252.

More interesting than Rojas' evasive and noncommital answers (given in the same year that Luther nailed his 95 theses to the church door) are certain other features of the trial. Diego de Oropesa, "a *converso* and not of those newly converted," was denounced by two women from the village of Montearagón where he was a property owner. The instigator of the denunciation was the local priest with whose sister Oropesa had had an affair, but, aside from this specific cause, in much that is recorded we can sense the antagonism of country folk to absentee landowners, idlers, manipulators of money, slickers, and skeptics. And it is quite apparent that Diego de Oropesa's fierce and efficient efforts at defense must have enhanced rather than assuaged such feelings. For example, on learning that the denunciations were going to be made,

> he persuaded the mayor of Talavera to order the wife and the mother-in-law of the present witness to appear before him under penalty of a fine of 2,000 maravedís for disobedience. When on the day they were supposed to appear they had not come, he sent a scribe to take a declaration of their testimony and of the remarks of Diego de Oropesa which they had overheard and which they planned to report to the Inquisition. When this witness found out that the scribe was coming, he and his wife and mother-in-law hid in the vineyards . . . and the same night they came to Toledo to make their declarations. Then a police officer [*alguacil*] came from Talavera with an order for their arrest . . . and finding them absent, sequestered some of their possessions.[166]

Threats of beatings, murder, mutilation[167] and even of influencing the Cardinal Archbishop[168] against the priest were also made. But the most extraordinary act of defiance of Inquisitional power came after the arrest. Oropesa's wife and brother actually dared bring pressure on one of the accusing witnesses with the intention of learning the questions asked and answered. When the witness, a poor woman, protested that to tell would violate her oath, she was

---

[166] Inquisición de Toledo, p. 215.

[167] ". . . este declarante dijo a la dicha Mencía López que dijese a su hija que callase su lengua, si no que no sería mucho que le cruzasen la cara . . ."

[168] According to the priest's testimony, ". . . el dicho Diego de Oropesa ha dicho y publicado que ha de decir muchos males y cosas de mí al cardenal. . . .

told to go to "one of the Trinitarian friars" who would be sure to absolve her and protect her from excommunication. Not even the dreaded and sacrosanct *secreto* intimidated this family.

Although efforts to fight back probably accomplished much more harm than good (the record of the trial is incomplete), they indicate clearly the extent to which the *conversos* of Talavera could act together as a kind of local establishment. The mayor and other officers of the municipal government functioned at their bidding, and they were able (or claimed to be able) to obtain the help of friars and even of the Cardinal in Toledo. Diego de Oropesa and his friends, in other words, were not only wealthy and trained to deal in such abstractions as time, money, and law; they were also influential. At least in 1517 in Talavera, certain *conversos* still felt themselves protected by a network of relationships upon which they could call in case of need. They had not yet been driven into isolation, each into an individual hiding place, a more or less hypocritical mask, and a fabricated genealogy. Rojas with his cautious testimony (perhaps all the more cautious because of the audacity of the accused), his modest standard of living, and his careful conformity seems in this sense to have been ahead of his time. He and his kind would be the ones to survive. They had discovered that survival depended not on influencing or making the news, but on listening to it and keeping out of it.[169]

"All my property and rights of collection"

Between the modest walls of the house on the street of Gaspar Duque and the famous walls of the town, between the intimacy of family life and the publicity of news, there extended for the Bachelor Rojas an intermediate zone of activity. It was the world of business relationships and of legal negotiations, which is to say a world of human beings transformed by convention into abstract juridical and financial entities. Here was a two-dimen-

[169] Another case with which Rojas may have been concerned was that of one Diego de Vargas, an inhabitant of Talavera condemned in 1519 for unstated transgressions after a fruitless appeal to the Pope (Llorente, x, 55). Unfortunately the record has been lost since his name does not appear in the Inquisición de Toledo catalogue. In any case, a person of the same name appears on the list of "censos" in the testament: "Yten mill maravedis de censo al quitar questan sobre las casas e maxuelo de Diego de Vargas, vezino desta dicha villa, que son las casas de su morada . . ." (p. 373).

sional realm in which life was played as a serious game and in which time was measured in terms of money and money in terms of time. Lewis Mumford continues his discussion of the erosion of the medieval order by the striking of the hours as follows:

> First came a mechanical method of measuring time: then a method of measuring space: finally in money, men began more widely to apply a more abstract way of measuring power, and in money they achieved a calculus for all human activity.
>
> This financial system of measurement released the European from his old sense of social and economic limitations. No glutton can eat a hundred pheasants; no drunkard can drink a hundred bottles of wine at a sitting; and if anyone schemed to have so much food and wine brought to his table daily, he would be mad. Once he could exchange the potential pheasants and Burgundy for marks or thalers, he could direct the labor of his neighbors and achieve the place of an aristocrat without being to the manner born. Economic activity ceased to deal with the tangible realities of the medieval world —land and corn and houses and universities and cities. It was transformed into the pursuit of an abstraction—money.[170]

Economic revolution aside, these changes also represented a revolution in consciousness. When Alvaro de Montalbán, for example, took shelter from his Inquisitors behind a screen of protective commonplaces, he was really—however unintentionally—expressing this new form of evaluation: "And if he had a tiny portion of meat, he was as satisfied as another who was served twenty fowl and could only eat one." The resemblance of Alvaro's habitual meditation to Lewis Mumford's historical speculation is striking. Alvaro may have wanted to convince the Inquisitors of his Christian asceticism, but in reality these phrases dredged up from the past (phrases "he always used to say") express his commercial training. That is: he had no interest in accumulating chickens and bottles of wine precisely because he thought in monetary terms. And so it was—as readers of the last portion of the testament may observe for themselves—with his son-in-law. The modesty of the house is compensated for by the careful portfolio of investments. Alvaro's pathetic recourse to his own private variety of sententious-

[170] *The Golden Day*, p. 9.

ness illuminates ironically the extent to which he and his family were independent of outmoded forms of acquisitiveness. Not only were they liberated from the tyranny of warehouse and treasure chest but they were fully aware of their freedom and its possibilities.

On the other hand, as Gabriel Alonso de Herrera pointed out, such liberation brought with it another kind of servitude. The financial activities of the new generations of money men were beset with "toils, fears, trials, perjuries, deceits, and falsehoods," difficulties that were all the more perilous, he implies, for his fellow *conversos*. To be successful, therefore, meant being constantly alert in all interpersonal relations, professionally friendly, ever capable of winning and maintaining confidence. Jean-Paul Sartre has described these requirements with his usual burst of illumination:

The majority of French Jews belong to the petite or grande bourgeoisie. Most of them occupy themselves with what I would call *metiers d'opinion*, in the sense that their success does not depend on skill at working with materials but on other men's opinions of them. If one is a lawyer or a hatter, the clientele grows if one manages to please it. It follows accordingly that these occupations are full of ceremonies: it is necessary to seduce, capture, and hold the confidence of others; care with dress, apparent severity of conduct, honorability, all are ceremonial in nature, all a part of the thousand little dances that must be well performed in order to attract clients. Thus, the thing that counts above all is reputation; one makes the reputation from which one lives, which signifies that one is in the last analysis entirely dependent on other men—unlike the peasant who is above all concerned with his land or the artisan, with his tools and raw material. Now, the Jew is in this sense in a paradoxical situation. It is no harder for him to gain reputation of honesty than anybody else, and he does it by the same means. But it is superimposed on a prior reputation which was given to him all at once and which he cannot get rid of no matter what he does: that of being Jewish. A Jewish worker in a mine, riding a wagon, or in a foundry forgets that he is a Jew. A Jewish businessman can never forget it.[171]

[171] *Réflexions*, pp. 88-89.

In estimating the relevance of these considerations to the professional life of the Bachelor, we must not forget that many of his dealings were with other *conversos*. His appointment as mayor from the 15th of February 1538 to the 21st of March of the same year[172] in itself indicates acceptance by a courthouse gang which (as we have seen) in this as in other Castilian and Aragonese municipalities was dominated by members of his caste.[173] Rojas' local connections are confirmed by two documents in the town archives which reveal that in 1527 and 1535 he acted as its attorney. In the first instance, the municipal council ordered that he be paid a ducat for his services in "ciertas capsas."[174] Among those participating in the decision was the "Corregidor doctor Ortiz de Zárate" who ten years before had ordered Bernaldino Díaz' re-arrest and who may have been related to the "Relator" of the same last name who in Madrid recorded the accusations against Alvaro de Montalbán.[175] In the second, another payment of 340 maravedís was made to him for his participation in a lawsuit of the government against a *vecino*.[176] Others who shared the fee with him were

[172] *Orígenes*, p. 245. This particular appointment was probably made with the consent of the Archbishop, don Juan Tavera, there being no "sede bacante" at the time. During this period the town council over which Rojas presided ordered the following regulation limiting air pollution from the pottery ovens: "Dende primero de março de cada anno, asta fin de set, den fego a los fornos dende el anocheze para que ardan toda la noche; esto conformandose a las Ordenanzas antiguas y por el danno que se faze a la saluz." According to Almiro Robledo who discovered and reproduced this regulation, "La firma del bachiller Rojas es muy garabatosa ya que apenas tiene letras." Apparently, as Robledo reads it, a secretary signed for him with the abbreviation "bachiller Ferdº". Unfortunately while in Talavera I was not able to see the original myself. Almiro Robledo, "Alcalde que dejo grandiosa huella," *Municipalia,* no. 170 (1967), p. 950.

[173] See Chap. III, n. 32.

[174] As reproduced by Robledo: "Este día los sobredichos señores platicaron de como el bachiller Fernando de Rojas, bezino desta, a ayuda e ayuda sobre ciertas capsas desta dicha, como letrado y para su cuenta, y por gracia de lo que a de suplir en ello, le mandaron librar un ducado. Firma: E yo, Comes Mayordomo" (*op. cit.,* p. 950).

[175] Serrano y Sanz (p. 269) believed them to be the same, but it is hard to identify a "bachiller" who functioned as a Madrid "relator" in 1525 with the "corregidor doctor" in Talavera two years later.

[176] "Iten, que dió y pagó por otro libramiento firmado de Alonso Bernal e del dicho escribano trezientos e quarenta maravedis al dicho Francisco Verdugo, escribano, e al bachiller Alonso Martínez de Prado e al bachiller Rojas e a Iohan Fanega de las costas de un proceso que se causo contra Bartolomé

the Bachelor Alonso Martínez de Prado (possibly the same Bachelor Martínez who taught grammar to his grandson in 1549)[177] and an active local *escribano* with whom he dealt frequently, Francisco Verdugo.[178]

In addition to these documented services to the municipality, there are two other somewhat more vague recollections of Rojas' official prominence. Cosme Gómez goes beyond the few months of the mayoralty recorded in the fragmentary archives and affirms, "for several years in Talavera he held the post of *alcalde mayor*."[179] Then, too, the same Alonso Martínez who remembered the many visitors to the house mentions him and his son the Licentiate Francisco as having held other local offices and honors: "The present witness knows that they were *alcaldes de la hermandad, jurados,* and *procuradores generales* of the aforesaid town on separate occasions and always as representatives of the *hidalgos*, because it is the use and custom to give half of the aforesaid offices . . . to *hidalgos* and the other half to those who were not; and the office of *procurador general* can only be given to *hidalgos*; and he always saw the father and the grandfather [the Bachelor] of the person now engaged in litigation holding these offices as *hidalgos. . . .*"[180] Although this testimony is probably exaggerated, it cannot be dismissed out of hand. It would be reasonable to expect that a person who was eventually appointed mayor should have earlier held lesser honors. The mention of the Licentiate Francisco is also significant since, as records demonstrate, he too became mayor only a year after his father's death.[181] From all of which we may con-

---

Sanches (tachado) vecino del lugar. Su fecha a veynte y seys días del dicho mes de mayo del dicho año." From the 1535 Libro de Actas in the Archivo Municipal and first observed by Valle Lersundi. Later I obtained a photograph from which the above transcription was made.

[177] VLA 25.

[178] In the Testament he appears as the "escribano" for three "cartas de censo." He appears as an agent for the Ayalas in Salazar y Castro, doc. 23,832.

[179] *Orígenes,* p. 244. See n. 10 above.

[180] Appendix III. Also mentioned by a witness in the "probanza de Indias," VLA 32.

[181] Almiro Robledo states that he has seen documents to this effect although he does not reproduce them: "Localizamos en el Archivo Municipal que el licenciado Francisco de Rojas Alvarez tomó posesión de Alcalde Mayor en 1542, al año de morir su padre." "La Muy Noble y Leal Ciudad de Talavera de la Reina," *Municipalia,* no. 161 (1967), p. 83. Again, I was unable to see them personally.

clude that an important part of the Rojas' business and professional affairs involved dealings with a municipal in-group which was, to put it mildly, not prejudiced against his origins. At least this portion of the society with which he was involved professionally was not as hostile as that Sartre envisions surrounding a Jewish lawyer in France.

At the same time, as the list of debtors given in the inventory indicates, Rojas also had to deal with another and potentially more antagonistic clientele. Diego Díaz, Pero Martín, Juan Alonso de Castro, Juan Martin del Lomo ("neighbors of Halía"), Pero Sánchez Çaço ("neighbor of Castilblanco"), Pero González Hidalgo ("neighbor of Yllén de Vacas"), and others recorded therein are clearly peasants and small landholders of Old Christian stock. These were precisely the sort of individuals whose rancor, as in the case of Diego de Oropesa, could easily result in denunciation. Yet it is far from clear that Rojas shared the disdain of some of his fellows for their caste or that they on their part regarded him with hatred as a typical town-dwelling *converso* money lender. Not only was he not (as far as we know) denounced, but also his professional success indicates that he must have been skilled at Sartre's "thousand little ceremonial dances." The willingness of Old Christian *pecheros* (those who, not being *hidalgos*, were obliged to pay a head or "chest" tax) from the Puebla and Talavera to testify in favor of the family in two *probanzas* and the respect with which they remember the Bachelor ("a well-known *hidalgo*," "of an honorable and principal family," "a noble holder of Royal office," "of honored stock," "held to be an *hidalgo* and so esteemed and treated," etc.) are significant. As a lawyer, as a moneylender, as an *hidalgo*, and as a neighbor, he seems to have won the confidence and esteem not only of his peers but also of a wider and socially more humble circle of Old Christians.

How did Rojas achieve this reputation, a reputation essential both to his prosperity and his safety? Sartre's notion of the harmless hypocrisy inherent in "métiers d'opinion" is undoubtedly a part of the answer. To it we may add our hypothesis that the author of *La Celestina* was a master of the rigorous self-camouflage that was enforced on *conversos*. But these habits of daily deception taken by themselves tend to oversimplify the complexity and the ambivalence of the human realities with which I am attempting to deal. The Old Christians who flocked en masse to *autos de fe* and who literally worshipped the Inquisitors (Montes calls them a "miserable populacho" which "prostrates itself" before them)[182] are familiar to us. They are the same as the fanatical, violent, exalted, and unthinkingly affirmative audiences who flocked en masse in later decades to performances of *comedias*. Collectivity, however, corresponds to the realm of prejudice rather than to that of true mutual awareness. Individually—and that was the way individual *conversos* knew their neighbors—they were persons. And among persons who speak the same language affection, sympathy, and trust are in given circumstances at least as likely as envy, rancor, and suspicion.

There were, of course, many kinds of positive relationships between educated *conversos* and simple Old Christians. Amador de los Ríos describes the Zaragozan *converso* Ximeno Gordo, as a kind of Shakespearian demagogue lashing popular passions to his own political advantage. Or in the village of El Viso (on the other side of Toledo from the Puebla) there was during Rojas' boyhood a local priest and physician who gained such a reputation among his parishioners and patients that the town was still talking about his magical powers a century later.[183] And in Talavera itself, the Bachelor Alonso de Montenegro (present at the conversation recollected by López Cortidor) could not refrain from playing elaborate practical jokes on his credulous neighbors. To posture and pretend, he found, could be turned into great fun.[184]

In Rojas' case, however, it hardly seems reasonable to imagine him exploiting his intelligence and his insight into human life for the sake of political advantage, popular admiration, or tasteless laughter. Rather, I think, we should imagine him dispensing kindliness, good advice, or a loan of money to those who were in trouble—and with no overbearing efforts to collect when the borrower was temporarily unable to meet his payments. There are, in fact, overdue debts mentioned in the Inventory. As certain Inquisition trials demonstrate, such protective and affectionate relationships

---

[182] Montes, *Artes*, p. 156.

[183] In the *Relaciones* (III, 773-776) the legend of his and a companion's magic caves, familiar spirits, supernatural powers of diagnosis, etc. is recounted at such length that we can only conclude that during his tenure his simple parishioners were entirely under his spell.

[184] See n. 155.

could help save *conversos* in their hours of need. The Bachelor Sanabria (the lawyer and mayor of Almagro whose oral carelessness we compared to that of Alvaro de Montalbán), was acquitted because his clients stood up for him when called as witnesses by the Holy Office. He had lent them money, had given free advice to the harassed, and alms to the poor, and, in general, had behaved as a kind of responsible intellectual commanding officer. Similarly, the physician Juan López de Illescas, whose indiscreet remarks about the non-existence of God have also been cited, was assisted by the testimony of his grateful patients.[185]

In the record of these cases there is nothing to indicate that mutual trust and warmth of relationship resulted from a calculated policy or only from habitual performance of the proper ceremonies. Rather they seem to have developed over years of daily encounters, consultations, negotiations, greetings, and exchanges of news. What we called the two dimensional realm of business relationships can gradually be deepened, just as legal and corporate entities can on occasion express in their behavior the humanity of their directors. Sancho Panza and Sosia before him (as contrasted to Torres Naharro's grotesque and obscene "villanos") exemplify in literature the respect and affection which the simplicity, honesty, and faithfulness of Old Christian peasants could inspire in writers whose minds were far more complex and sophisticated than theirs. It is not, of course, my intention to portray the Bachelor as living in Talavera surrounded only by a congregation of faithful dependents and admirers. It takes all kinds to make up a clientele. But, on the other hand, we need not go to the opposite extreme and imagine him always walking in fear and trembling, beset constantly by hordes of self-appointed spies for the Holy Office.

We would surely know more about Rojas' legal practice, had he not retired in favor of his son at the time of his death. Unlike his grandson the Licentiate Fernando, whose executor had to collect unpaid bills from his clients, there is no indication of recent professional activity in the will and inventory.[186] Nevertheless, there

---

[185] See Chap. II, n. 44.

[186] In the "Sección de Reales Cartas Ejecutorias" of the Archivo de la Real Chancillería (Leg. 971, no. 36), Rojas' grandson Garçí Ponce, acting as executor for his dead brother, the Licentiate Fernando, obtained for the estate a favorable judgment for a debt of "diez y ocho mil maravedis por todo el

are two facts which suggest that he was retained as a lawyer and man of affairs by prominent members of local society. One was no less a personage than the secretary and canon of the Colegiata of Talavera, don Pero Martínez de Mariana. This individual (the brother of the Dean whom we saw to have been the natural father of Juan de Mariana) had his will drawn up by Rojas, the latter's copy still being in the possession of Valle Lersundi.[187] Secondly, the moneys owed to him by the estate of "el señor Joan de ayala" (some 16,000 maravedís) did not represent past loans but rather three unpaid *libramientos*. Since this means specifically orders for payment given to an administrator or financial representative, we can only conclude that at least for a time Rojas acted both as Ayala's lawyer and as his *mayordomo*. The fact of his burial in the Convento de la Madre de Dios confirms the relationship, since it had been constructed in 1517 with the patronage of a member of the family, doña María de Ayala, a nun later buried there herself.[188] Past services undoubtedly were a factor in making these arrangements, arrangements that were at once difficult and socially indispensable for a person in Rojas' position.

One probable result of such highly placed connections was Rojas' successful opposition to the confiscation by the Holy Office of half of his dowry. As we learn from the Serrano y Sanz documents,

---

tiempo que el dicho licenciado Rojas le ayudó como abogado en sus pleitos. . . ." Garcí Ponce was appointed executor in a codicil added to the Licentiate Fernando's will on the 24th of September 1594 (Archivo de Protocolos, Valladolid, Leg. 984, fos. 708-709). From the tenor of the document it appears that, unlike his grandfather, the Licentiate Fernando was aware that his imminent demise (he died two days later, as noted by Garcí Ponce in his "Libro de memorias," VLA 25) would leave him no time to straighten out his affairs. This constituted quite a task since his wealth was considerable (sufficient for the establishment of a "mayorazgo" on the 15th of September 1594, VLA 34B) and his clientele numerous and highly placed. Among those listed in the "Libro de memorias" are the Princess of Eboli, various other members of the nobility, the town of Talavera, the Archbishop of Seville, and the three major military orders. According to Valle Lersundi his substantial residence in Valladolid on the Calle de Francos (now Juan Mambrilla) is still in the possession of the family. Another last hour document also in the Archivo de Protocolos is a power of attorney from a son (Leg. 984, fos. 691-692).

[187] I have seen the document, but its importance in relation to Rojas' legal reputation was first assessed by Almiro Robledo, "Alcalde que dejó grandiosa huella," p. 947.

[188] See n. 143.

Alvaro de Montalbán on the 21st of November, 1525 (three days after his conviction) was sentenced, in addition to imprisonment, to suffer confiscation of all money and property acquired since 1480. As a result, Rojas and his brother-in-law, the *aposentador* Pedro de Montalbán (who had married Leonor's sister, Constança Núñez) were each assessed one half of their respective dowries— according to documents recently brought to light by A. Redondo.[189] The figure mentioned for Rojas, "quarenta mill maravedís de la mitad de la dote," corresponds exactly to the sum of 80,000 mentioned several times in the Valle Lersundi documents. In any case, what is surprising is not the fact of confiscation (a standard practice as we have seen) but Rojas' reaction to it. Instead of meekly handing over the money, he appealed to avoid payment, and, although his efforts met initial failure (in 1527 "the sentence was confirmed"), ultimately he either won his case or succeeded in having the sum refunded. This latter was the good fortune of Pero de Montalbán who in 1532 was reimbursed not just with the principal but also with accrued interest. As for Rojas, whose 80,000 maravedís were still intact at the time of his death, it is hard to imagine him taking such a resolute stand without the reassurance of powerful outside support.[190]

That Rojas turned over his clientele to the Licentiate Francisco (home from Salamanca with his new degree and recently married to his cousin, Catalina Alvarez de Avila) is supported by the special bequest of his "libros de derechos e leyes" to the latter. Whether living at home or not, the Licentiate seems to have carried on his father's practice in the same office for some time before and after 1541.[191] The library itself of some forty-four tomes is considered by Luis G. de Valdeavellano to be a good working collection which indicates interest not just in what the Bachelor had been taught in Salamanca but also professional development over the

[189] "Fernando de Rojas et l'Inquisition," *Mélanges de la Casa de Velázquez,* 1965, ii, 345-347.

[190] This is stated specifically by Rojas in the testament.

[191] According to the Licentiate Fernando's "Libro de memorias," his father was named judge in Llerena for the year 1546, afterwards returning to his Talaveran practice. That he was less successful professionally than either his own father (the Bachelor) or his children is indicated by the fact already noted that one of the family documents of *hidalguía* reveals his use of that status to avoid debtors' prison. See Chap. III, n. 83.

480

years. As can be seen in Appendix IV, while many of the books date from the 70's, 80's, and 90's, an appreciable number were purchased afterwards during the Talavera years. In general it compares not unfavorably to the library of the outstanding Toledan jurist (executed by fire in 1486), Doctor Alonso Cota.[192] As a collection, it in no way contradicts our surmise that Rojas was a skilled practitioner of his "facultad" and one whose professional behavior was based on the deep respect for the law (although not all lawyers) that we have observed in *La Celestina*.

Professionalism aside, there may well have been another and deeper motive for Rojas' profound esteem of his discipline. As a writer thematically concerned with time and change, he probably agreed with Peter Martyr who praised the law as reason's antidote for mutability.[193] Instead of evasion (the quiet life of well ordered domesticity in Talavera) here was a traditional form of counter-attack. That is to say, insofar as a law library could help solve the myriad problems of human coexistence, it constituted man's only effective weapon against the state of things described by Petrarch and exemplified in *La Celestina*. The battle—Rojas would have been the first to affirm—is ultimately hopeless, but that did not relieve him of the duty to engage in it with diligence and conscience. To be a competent lawyer in Talavera rather than an exile, a rebel, or a martyr involved not only prudence but its own kind of heroism.

If our knowledge of Rojas' legal practice is limited, we are partially compensated by detailed information about his investments and financial standing. At the time of his death, his total estate (or at least that part of it that was publicly accounted for) amounted to somewhat less than 400,000 maravedís,[194] and of this amount about a third (119,500) was in land mortgages. This was, of course, the most common way of investing money at the time.[195] Even the

---

[192] A. J. Battistessa, "Biblioteca de un jurisconsulto toledano," *RABM*, xlvi (1925), 342-351. Comparison of the two libraries is based on consultation with Professor Valdeavellano.

[193] See his adulatory letter to Dr. Villasandino, *Epistolario*, ix, 103-105.

[194] The "partida de bienes" among Rojas' heirs made in 1541 gives the figure of 396,510 maravedís (VLA 24). However, as we surmised previously, there may well have been hidden assets including property in the Puebla. See Chap. V, n. 126.

[195] See Carande, I, 75.

economically naïve Sancho Panza—in addition to his future *insula* —dreams of owning a portfolio of lucrative *censos*, if he can find a second sack of doubloons. The interest charged by Rojas was not usurious (invariably 8.3 or 8.4 per cent) and amounted in 1541 to some 10,572 maravedís a year. All in all, this amount combined with the proceeds of pawn brokerage,[196] rents from rural property, and fees from his practice, probably amounted to a total of 30 or 40 thousand maravedís during his peak earning years. That this provided reasonable bourgeois comfort and security (in spite of the galloping inflation of the period)[197] may be deduced from some typical salaries. In 1538 an *alguacil* (bailiff) in Salamanca earned 10,000 maravedís[198] while professors of grammar received only twice that amount.[199] In Seville in 1557 Mateo Alemán's father received a wretched 12,000 maravedís as a prison doctor,[200] a sum which may be compared to the 100,000 that was allotted to Inquisitors in 1541.[201] What do these numbers mean? As far as I can see, there is no wholly satisfactory way to translate them into modern terms,[202] but it is at least clear that the Rojas family was well to do in the sense that it earned substantially more than it needed to spend. The Bachelor was not a phenomenal success in the fashion of his grandson at the Court of Chancery, but within the more modest possibilities offered by Talavera, his accumulation of capital was eco-

---

[196] Alonso de Ercilla also engaged in this occupation on a larger scale, as we learn from Medina, p. 180. Probably the interest on such transactions was greater than for *censos*. Caro Baroja (1, 71) states that normal charges for the latter were usually 6.7 percent but could reach ten.

[197] See Carande, 1, 244-245. He estimates a rise in prices of over 50 per cent between 1518 and 1530 and notes that the curve steepens until 1540.

[198] Esperabé Arteaga, 1, 334.

[199] R. Espinosa Maeso, "El maestro Fernán Pérez de Oliva in Salamanca," *BRAE*, XIII (1926), 457. This was in 1529 when Pérez de Oliva acting as rector established two such posts.

[200] G. Alvarez, *Mateo Alemán*, Buenos Aires, 1953, p. 39.

[201] Lea, II, 251.

[202] It is possible to determine, as does E. J. Hamilton ("The History of Money and Prices in Andalusia: 1503-1660," Harvard diss., 1929) that in 1539 two pounds of beef would have cost the Rojas family some 11 maravedís, a sheepskin some 72, etc. (II, 394). But such prices must be judged in terms of the entire range of goods on the market as well as by the expectable needs and necessary expenses of a family unit at the time. It is this that makes comparisons of Rojas' financial position with, say, that of a successful lawyer in Dayton, Ohio, appear dubious.

nomically respectable. As a result, he was in a position to lend without interest to Isabel Núñez, his widowed sister-in-law, the substantial sum of 44 ducats "which he put into her hands with his."[203] And when he died he had the satisfaction not only of having succeeded in his chosen profession but also of knowing that his wife and children would not live in need.

ℛℓ "El señor bachiller Hernando de Rojas que en gloria sea"

It is ironical that we should know far more the circumstances of Rojas' death than about those of his life. The nature of his final illness cannot, of course, be determined, but from the statement in the will that it was drawn up while he was "enfermo del cuerpo y sano de la memoria," it would seem that it was of the sort that allowed him to foresee the end without undue agony, lengthy coma, or hallucination. And as he looked into the face of death on April 3, 1541 we hear an echo of that earlier self who in the Letter to his friend had looked into the face of love: "I the Bachelor Fernando de Rojas, neighbor and inhabitant that I am of the noble town of Talavera, being sick of body and sound of memory and, being, as I am, in my right and natural understanding which the Lord our God saw fit to bestow upon me, and fearing death which is a natural thing which no one can flee or escape from. . . ."[204] Here again we encounter that same self-conscious reason which so long before had observed itself ranging widely in a terrestrial and aerial search for truth. Beneath the standard phraseology we intuit the presence of a well-tempered mind.

The scene which accompanied the mortal dictation to which we have just listened is not hard to imagine. Around the dying man, as

---

[203] This act of kindness is referred to in the testament: "Yten quarenta y quatro ducados que deve la de Alonso Rodríguez de Palma, biuda, vecina de Toledo, que se los prestó el dicho señor bachiller de su mano a la suya" (p. 381). This woman is identified as his daughter by Alvaro de Montalbán: "Ysabel Núñez, muger de Alonso Rodrígues de Palma que biue en Valençia" (Serrano y Sanz, p. 263). Upon settling the estate, the heirs, apparently less charitable than the Bachelor, sent Alonso Martín, the husband of their servant, Juana de Torres (VLA 18), to Toledo to collect the debt. His wage and the expenses of the trip amounted to seven and a half *reales* (VLA 24).

[204] VL II, pp. 366-368.

around the tragicomic bedside of Alonso Quijano the Good, were gathered the family, their retainers, two *escribanos,* and the indispensable legal witnesses. It was not infrequent in the sixteenth and seventeenth century to delay preparation of the will until the last moment. Then with great solemnity, when the glories of the other world were almost in sight of the legator, he would dispose of the goods accumulated in this one. The partially mandatory division of property among members of the family under Roman law (one half to the surviving spouse, a larger fraction to the eldest son, etc.) seems to have made it unnecessary to provide ahead of time for the possibility of sudden death. Which is to say essentially that the last semi-public recording of the testament should be considered as much a rite of transition as a legal operation. Like final confession and extreme unction, both of which the Rojas surely took great pains to have administered, this was a standard part of the ceremony of leave-taking. And like all ceremonies it was performed in company. The one thing Rojas had to avoid was the desire to turn his face to the wall and surrender his spirit in solitude, according to the custom of his ancestors. In case after case, the Inquisition burned the remains and expropriated the inheritances of individuals who were seen to die in this tell-tale posture.

Aside from Leonor Alvarez, the children, and the servants, at Rojas' bedside we find a number of identifiable names: Andrés Dávyla, the *escribano* who later recorded Juan de Montemayor's renunciation of his share of the estate in return for a fixed sum prior to his departure for the Indies in 1542; Francisco Dávyla, a notary who earlier had testified in favor of Abraham García; Alonso Ortiz, who was probably one of the municipal *jurados* listed by Cosme Gómez as supporting the Royal cause against the *comuneros;*[205] and finally the Bachelor's favorite *escribano público,* Juan de Arévalo, who certified the document.[206] Two other wit-

---

[205] See n. 144.

[206] He notarized a number of the *censos* listed in the inventory, and, aside from his employment by Rojas, other records of his activity have been preserved. See, for example, Clemente Villasante, "Alcaudete de la Jara," *BRAH,* xc (1927), 157, for his inventory of goods willed to the local church. That the family had long been influential in official circles is indicated by the existence of another Juan de Arévalo who acted as *procurador* in 1476. See Fita as cited in n. 152.

nesses, Pedro Rosado and Juan Bravo, are otherwise unidentifiable. Nor do we know anything more about Gonzalo de Salzedo who, as executor and presumably a trusted professional friend, may also have been present. All of these were now prepared to certify—in case the veracity or the piety of Rojas' last public ceremony should be questioned by busybodies—that he had performed his role with irreproachable legal and religious orthodoxy.

Some attempts have naturally been made to interpret the various sanctimonious remarks and bequests as evidence that, whatever his origins, Rojas was (or had become over the years) an unquestioning believer in the "Holy Mother Church." How else to explain, it has been asked, the burial in a convent, the reiterated statements of faith ("creyendo como creo firmemente en la Santísima Trynidad . . . en la qual fee y creencia protesto de bivir e morir"), the rather expensive "ábito del señor San Francisco" which was his shroud,[207] the bequests to local monasteries and churches, or the 2,000 maravedís to be distributed as alms to "personas pobres e vergonçantes" by the *mayordomo* of the institution which offered him his ultimate asylum?

Aside from custom, two answers suggest themselves to this multiple question. The first is that certified Christian burial in a religious institution (such as that of Rojas' putative father Garcí Gonçález) was of utmost social importance to these insecure *hidalgos*. Francisco Márquez' illuminating essay on the economic background of Santa Teresa's "foundations" illustrates this fact beyond possible dispute. Much of the money was donated by *conversos* who could not buy their bodies into established crypts, chapels, convents, or churches.[208] From which we may presume that Rojas, too, in 1517 had with clear foresight contributed to the building fund of the

[207] It cost 600 maravedís and was described as "espléndido" by the examining physician of the Madrid "Laboratory of Legal Medicine" on the basis of the few fragments which were found with Rojas' remains (see n. 216). However, this sum was a small fraction of the overall funeral expenses which included a thousand maravedís to the "Cabildo" for the procession, 400 to the Cofradía de la Caridad which accompanied the bier, almost 2,000 for "hachas de cera" as well as even greater amounts for the masses requested in the testament. Uncatalogued and apparently used as a place marker, the receipt for the habit (signed on the 19th of June 1541 by one Ana López) was encountered in the Rojas archives by Valle Lersundi.

[208] "Santa Teresa y el linaje," *Espiritualidad y literatura*, pp. 141-205.

Ayalas. The second answer is that in some cases (for example, that of Ysabel Rodríguez condemned after death for a momentary indiscretion comparable to that of Alvaro de Montalbán)[209] similar testaments were used by heirs to prove the orthodoxy of their parents and so to protect their inheritances from post-mortem expropriation by the Inquisition. It is worth noting in this connection that the Licentiate Fernando also conserved the comparably worded will of his unmarried aunt, Juana, who died in 1557.[210] Apparently Leonor Alvarez had no opportunity to prepare such a safeguard for the children before her demise.

It is impossible to determine the exact date and time of Rojas' death, but presumably the funeral ceremonies were completed by the 8th of April when the inventory was begun. As for his actual tomb, we may accept Luis Careaga's opinion that, in contrast to the monumentality worshipped by his fellow Talaverans, Rojas chose a remarkably modest resting place.[211] The new convent of the Mother of God not only was without illustrious history but also was of simple and unpretentious construction suitable for the "poor and humble nuns" which it housed. Other more prominent (and less "stained") families preferred to deposit themselves in the grandiose religious edifices which abounded in town, but the Rojas scrupulously avoided external self-display. It is typical that when Juana arranged for her own sepulchre she should have ordered "the most humble one still unoccupied in the rear nave" of her parish church.

Such dispositions for death correspond to the family life which preceded them. Home was secure, comfortable, and even abundant. The linen closets were well-stocked, the *tinajas* full to the brim, the accounts in order, and the sixteen hours of the day serenely regulated. But what was clearly missing were the "ambition and presumption," the love of luxury and fine clothes, the "thirst for the inane glories and honors of the world," the "empinación y lozanía" (high growth and verdant prosperity) for

[209] See Chap. II, n. 47.   [210] VLA 18.

[211] Careaga, *Investigaciones*, cited Chap. III, n. 20. "Hacia 1541 el Monasterio de la Madre de Dios carecía de historia y de tradición, estaba habitado por monjas pobres e humildes, y seguramente presentaba poco o ningún aliciente a las familias encumbradas de la villa, como lugar destinado a recoger sus restos mortales después de la muerte . . ." (p. 4).

which Old Christians criticized their *converso* neighbors.[212] One could either seek to dominate surrounding society (like the Francos, the Escalona Rojas, or the Madrid Montalbanes with their sumptuous private chapel) or else remove oneself from its attentive eyes with protective coloration. And this latter was the Bachelor's choice.

Thus, as we envision it from the inventory, the house predicts the tomb. What was necessary was there, but the lack of lavish wardrobe for husband and wife[213] and the table service limited to seven silver spoons indicate purposeful avoidance of showiness. Most significant of all, perhaps, was Leonor Alvarez' wretched jewelry, the total value of which was only six reales and ten maravedís. Not for her to wear in public were the "little golden lantern to be hung on a lady's toque" or the "two golden rings" listed elsewhere as valuables and probably acquired through pawn brokerage.[214] So too the Bachelor took with him to his grave only the usual "medallón" on his chest and one "pequeño alfiler de oro" (gold pin). In death as in life he followed the advice given by Prudence at the end of *La visión deleitable*: "He who wishes to be prudent should not stand alone; rather let him conform to the times and to the opinion of people; for otherwise he will fall prey to gossip and he will be persecuted and abhorred; and if he cannot conform to all people, let his face conform on occasions when discussion is necessary."[215]

In his testament, Fernando de Rojas, like François Villon before him and according to the invariable custom of those times, willed his body "to the earth from which it was formed." But in the spring of 1936 this bequest was revoked by the act of exhumation. From the location and from the pitiful remnants of bone and cloth, the

---

[212] This frequently cited description is from Andrés Bernáldez' (the so-called "Cura de los Palacios") *Historia de los Reyes Católicos*, ed. M. Gómez Moreno and J. de M. Carriazo, Madrid, 1962, p. 95. He goes on to make all the usual accusations of secret Judaic practices along with the contradictory comment already cited: ". . . no eran judíos ni cristianos . . . más eran ereges e sin ley. . . ." See Chap. IV, n. 84.

[213] Only nine garments, most of them described as used, are listed for both of them.

[214] They are listed with their weight just after the "pesito de pesar oro," an essential instrument for pawn brokering.

[215] p. 388.

identity was established beyond reasonable doubt. Examination further revealed that he was a man of good stature and that, unlike Cervantes, his teeth were in perfect condition.[216]

[216] Almiro Robredo has had the kindness to provide me with a copy of "La ciencia en el descubrimiento de los restos del autor de *La Celestina*," *Aurora*, 31 May 1936. It consists of an interview by Julio Angulo with Doctors González Bernal and Aznar (no initials or Christian names are given), the professors of the "Escuela de Medicina Legal" who examined the remains. They affirm the above two statements. Rojas' height is estimated at one meter and 70 centimeters. His dental perfection, they remark, is common among Talaverans, although they cannot explain it. Natural flourides in the drinking water would seem a likely cause today.

APPENDIXES

APPENDIX I

Probanzas and *Expedientes*

Since many of the facts referred to in the preceding chapters were encountered in *probanzas de hidalguía* and *expedientes de limpieza de sangre*, it may be helpful to readers unfamiliar with such documents to include here some general remarks concerning them. Unfortunately, as far as I know, no inclusive technical studies (combining legal, sociological, and historical considerations) have been made of this almost overwhelming body of records from the Spanish past. Albert Sicroff's definitive discussion of discrimination against those of *converso* lineage provides essential knowledge concerning the human situation that was responsible for manic ancestor investigation,[1] as does Castro, above all in *De la edad conflictiva*. And F. Mendizábal in a brief article on "La Real Chancillería de Valladolid" furnishes useful explanations of the legal procedure and terminology of its collection of *probanzas*.[2] But what is missing is an overall look at the documents themselves, their several purposes, their varying techniques of information gathering, and their resultant historical reliability.

It is all very well for lineage-conscious Spaniards and Spanish Americans, the principal users of such archives today, to find therein only an unquestioned certification of their own importance. But, as we have seen, anyone who is in search of the truth about Fernando de Rojas and his family would do well to be more discriminating. Knowledge of what is going on in each suit and ability to read between the lines are essential.[3] As a student of literary texts

[1] *Les Controverses des statuts de "pureté de sang" en Espagne du XVᵉ au XVIIᵉ siècle*, Paris, 1960.

[2] *Hidalguía*, I (1953), 305-335.

[3] Even supposing that *hidalguía* required simon-pure Old Christian ancestry (which it clearly did not) it would be totally unwarranted to claim on the basis of the *probanza* that Rojas was not a *converso*—as did Cejador who had apparently seen the Valle Lersundi copy: "El bachiller Hernando de Rojas, verdadero autor de *La Celestina*," *Revista Crítica Hispano-Americana*, II (1916), 85-86. As we have already seen, perjury and falsification are built-in constituents of this as in other such documents.

and not of legal history I am surely better qualified for the former than for the latter, but I have read a fair number of these documents and come to some conclusions about them.

To begin with, it is essential to make a distinction between investigations of *hidalguía* and investigations of *limpieza*. Legal *probanzas* of the sort arranged by the Licentiate Fernando (that reproduced as Appendix III is an example) must in this sense be set apart from certification of the Old Christian blood line necessary for admission to restricted semi-official social institutions such as the military orders, residence colleges at the universities, the *cabildos* of canons in major cathedrals, the ceremonial brotherhoods called *cofradías*, and even certain guilds. Precisely because *hidalguía* was not only social but subject to legal definition (*hidalgos* were exempted from certain taxes and forms of imprisonment and given the right to hold certain offices), holders of and candidates for such status were not questioned about their blood. To identify the Spain of Fernando de Rojas with Hitler's Germany would be a gross error. It was socially reprehensible to be a *converso*, but it was not illegal.

It is true, of course (as in the case of the Francos), that an ancestry that was exclusively or preponderantly Jewish could rule out any claim to *hidalguía*. But at the same time the aim of the investigation was to establish that *hidalgo* status had been held by the family for four generations and not to prepare an exhaustive genealogy. Property holding, legal marriage, legitimacy of birth, and recognition of traditional privileges by neighbors and community were what were at stake rather than suspicion of "stains." It was not necessary to inquire into maternal lineage (frequently the most dubious), the result being that most *converso* applicants had little trouble in avoiding embarrassing disclosures. And even when these were made (as in the case of the Cepedas),[4] the applicant could still, if he was influential enough, obtain the desired *ejecutoria*. What happened to the Francos (unfortunately for them and fortunately for us) seems to have been very exceptional. We can only conclude, then, that a Pero de Montalbán, an Alonso Quijano, or those class-conscious individuals in the plays of Lope who were taunted by their caste-conscious Old Christian neighbors

[4] See Homero Serís, "Nueva genealogía de Santa Teresa," *NRFH*, x, 1956, and N. Alonso Cortés, "Pleitos de los Cepedas," BAE, 1946, p. 91.

were, in effect, *hidalgos*. Some of them may have felt shaky about their claims, particularly at the time their carefully coached witnesses made their depositions (the Licentiate Fernando's failure to push his suit through to the end may be a case in point),[5] but once the certification was made, the legal status was theirs. Testimony might have been perjured,[6] and their fortunes might have originated in part or entirely in tax farming and commerce rather than in ancestral land ownership, but they were now *hidalgos* by law as well as Sem Tob's "natura."

Not all *probanzas* were intended to provide a status which would camouflage *converso* lineage. As Spain left behind its medieval and oral past and entered into a new age of regulation and documentation it was inevitable that the legal question of whether one was an *hidalgo* or a *pechero* (as explained previously, those subject to head taxes) should be established in ink and parchment. Particularly at the beginning, many suits grew out of real disagreements. For example, inimical neighbors might incite municipal officials to enter a disagreeable *hidalgo* on the tax lists in order to annoy him, or, after moving from land poverty in the north to a new situation in a southern province or the Indies, an individual might find that his claims about his past were doubted. When such disputes occurred, legal procedures would be followed, evidence gathered by both sides, and a genuine decision made by the Court of Chancery. In other cases, however, it is clear that harassed *conversos* saw in this new legal path to status (the first recorded *probanza* was that of Pedro de la Caballería in 1447), a way of resolving their social difficulties. As we surmised, it seems to have been a stroke of genius for the Licentiate Fernando as a young lawyer to have recognized exactly this need and opportunity.

I would not, of course, presume to set up these two kinds of *probanzas* as rigidly categorical. Between such parvenus as the Francos and authentic village *hidalgos* whose presumptions might

---

[5] This was not feared in most other cases. See, for example, the *probanzas* of the Cepedas or that of the ancestors of Jorge Guillén, which I particularly enjoyed reading in the family copy. See Riva, ii, 165. The Licentiate Fernando's prudence, we may conclude, was both exceptional and justified.

[6] A case curiously parallel to that of the Rojas is provided by the *probanza* of the descendants of another famous *converso* lawyer of his time, Dr. Alonso Díaz de Montalvo, who among other things had dared to compose a strong defense of "our lineage." See Fermín Caballero, *Noticia de la vida, carga y escritos del doctor Alonso Díaz de Montalvo*, Madrid, 1873.

be questioned (such as Lazarillo's third master or don Mendo in *El alcalde de Zalamea*) there were any number of intermediate situations. And in each case the suit, if it was necessary or attempted, reveals its own particular degree and variety of authenticity. I am thinking, for example, of the *probanza* of the Cepedas, some of whose ancestors seem to have had genuine pretensions to *hidalguía*, or of the other Rojas in the Puebla who had held administrative posts congruent with elevated status in spite of suspicions about their origin. The point is that, admitting infinite shadings of possible justification for individual claims, these two motives, the one resulting from historical change and the other from social persecution, appear again and again. Taken together, they have left behind in the Chanceries of Valladolid and Granada an extraordinary quantity of historical documentation.

More searching in their questions but less expensive in their preparation were the certificates of *limpieza* required for emigration to the Indies. The great number of undoubted *conversos* who did manage to leave Spain for the new colonies indicates the relative facility of obtaining permission. The reason is simple. As in the case of that obtained by the Licentiate Fernando and his brothers, instead of opposition by a *fiscal*, the pro-forma questionnaires were usually scrutinized only by municipal officials who were likely themselves to be of suspicious stock. Such examiners would be inclined to pass over lightly hesitant or negative testimony. Nevertheless, unlike the *probanzas de hidalguía*, numerous witnesses from the applicants' places of origin were questioned about maternal lineage and specifically about Jewish ancestry. In order to escape to America, in other words, *conversos* such as Mateo Alemán,[7] Rojas' son, Juan de Montemayor, and grandsons had to request their friends and acquaintances (especially peasant Old Christians who could be bribed or otherwise influenced) to perjure themselves.

That perjury was indeed frequent[8] is testified to directly by

---

[7] See J. Gestoso y Pérez, *Nuevos datos para ilustrar las biografías del Maestro Juan de Mal Lara y de Mateo Alemán*, Seville, 1896.

[8] On the frequency of bribery and perjury, see in general (the documents used here provide enough specific examples), Caro Baroja, II, 323 ff.; Sicroff, p. 189; and Domínguez Ortiz, pp. 73 ff. The last cites the following from Roco Campofrío's contemporary discussion of the matter: "Nobility has come to depend on the oldest inhabitants of every town and village—tailors, shoe-

writers of the time and indirectly by the increasing elaborateness of the oaths that were taken. In the 1571 *expediente* of the Rojas witnesses to the provably spurious cleanliness of Inés de Avila and her husband, the physician, Juan Alvarez de San Pedro[9] were asked to swear as follows: "Before God and Saint Mary, His mother, and the words of Holy Scripture and on the cross placed in their right hands corporally, they were asked again if they had sworn truly, for, if they had, God our Lord would help them, and, if they had not, He would hold them responsible, and each one of them, accepting the strength of the oath, said: 'I do swear, Amen.'" Little wonder that in the light of such an oath one of the witnesses should answer the key question with an evasion: "The present witness held them to be good Christians and honorable people, and they were esteemed as good Christians and honorable people by every one in this town the Puebla, but, as for declaring that they were Old Christians, he cannot declare it because he does not know their lineage. The present witness does not know if they were descended from Moors or Jews, but he has never seen them to be punished by the Holy Office or heard of it either, and, if they had been, he would have known about it. . . ." It is significant that in the whole document only this one voice reveals an adverse reaction to the built-in hypocrisy of the time.[10]

---

makers, tanners, the dregs of the population, most of whom are so poor and miserable that they can be forced to say whatever is needful for four reales and a glass of wine or even through threats or caresses" (p. 237). Similar remarks are made in Diego de Hermosilla's *Diálogo de la vida de los pajes de palacio*. See J. Silverman, "Judíos y conversos en el *Libro de Chistes* de Luis de Pinedo," *Papeles de Son Armadans* (Mallorca), no. 69, 1961, p. 294. The possibility of bribery is questioned directly by an examiner in the Montalbán *probanza* (cit. Chap. III, n. 76).

[9] As we saw, their family is prominent on Cantera's list in *Judaizantes* (see Chap. II, n. 10). Caro Baroja goes so far as to call these investigations a "pura farsa económica" (II, 339).

[10] VLA 32. Another protection against influenced testimony, were the so-called "preguntas generales de la ley" to which each witness was submitted prior to interrogation. Among them was whether he was "a relative or an enemy" of the parties concerned with the litigation. Normally, as in the case of Alfonsina de Avila, a witness in the *expediente* cited above, family ties were too well known to permit perjury. Thus, she admits: "that she is a relative of the aforesaid doña Catalina but she doesn't know to what degree and also she is a relative of the aforesaid licenciate Francisco de Rojas but only a tiny bit [*poca cosa*]." On the other hand, we find Antonio de Salazar, the first witness to be called in the *probanza* reproduced as Appendix III denying any

The most expensive inquiries were those required for admittance to the exclusive orders and colleges mentioned above. In all three varieties the candidate, along with whatever bribes might be necessary, had to pay the legal costs including per diem charges and all sorts of extras to local and Chancery officials and to those proverbial gougers, the *escribanos* and their assistants. But because, as we saw in the Palavesín *expediente*, these investigations were far more exhaustive than the others, the bill could be astronomical. Again some qualifications should be made. As the case of Catalina Alvarez de Avila's brother, Francisco, indicates, it was far easier to obtain a canonry in the Cathedral of Sigüenza than in that of Toledo. As against the endless list of witnesses from numerous localities submitted to long and laboriously recorded cross examination that fill each dossier in the Toledo archives, a few witnesses briefly queried were sufficient in his case. In the same way, the order of Santiago tried to be more rigid in its demands than the others. A general rule would seem to be that the more exclusive the organization, the higher the cost. Honor was a commodity which was sold like branded merchandise, each brand priced according to its degree of prestige. In that sense a canonry in Toledo was the Rolls Royce of the time.

Even more worrisome than the expense was the danger which accompanied this third class of *expedientes*. We remember the several malicious attempts to slander Juan Francisco Palavesín because his second *apellido* was Rojas. In his case he was eventually vindicated, but there were others in which individuals of irreproachable lineage were publicly shamed by being denied admittance on the basis of anonymous testimony.[11] Since cleanliness of blood, unlike hereditary nobility was fundamentally unreal—a

---

relationship. Actually, as we learn from Palavesín testimony, he was the father-in-law of the Licentiate Fernando's brother, Garcí Ponce. See Gilman-Gonzálvez, p. 3. Also, as noted previously (Chap. I, n. 24), since he had moved to the Puebla from Esquívias, he was surely a member of Cervantes' wife's family.

[11] As a result, anyone contemplating an *expediente* was aware that he and his family were confronting a long period of social danger. Lea (ii, 301) cites a letter written by a relative to an ambitious young man advising him in the strongest possible terms to abandon such perilous pretensions. See also Castro's discussion of a sonnet of Quevedo which gloats about the hazards of investigating one's ancestors (*De la edad conflictiva*, p. 23).

social myth which was invented to justify and camouflage a hidden revolution—proof itself became more and more meaningless. *Limpieza* depended less upon facts which usually were beyond positive determination than upon *opinión*, which is to say the good will or odium of a thousand and one unknown tongues. One was who people said one was, and in extreme cases (as Domínguez Ortiz[12] and others mention) the examiners, like Calderón's more strict husbands, would refuse admittance because of rumors that they admitted knowing to be false.

On the other hand, if the risks were great so was the prize: a habit, office, or membership which was known publicly and which would provide a rebuttal to gossip. Caro Baroja discusses a number of cases in which individuals who had *converso* lineage managed to penetrate barriers of restriction,[13] but he also points out that they were effective for families whose reputation was well known. The Rojas, for example, who knew better than to ask for their *ejecutoria* would never have dared solicit a habit. About as far as Licentiate Fernando dared go was to wangle admission to a "Cofradía de los Abades" in Valladolid.[14] It was this sort of negative effectiveness that made such social organizations desirable in spite of widespread skepticism about the purity of all their members.

[12] Domínguez Ortiz, p. 193. [13] II, 350-357.
[14] See Chap. I, n. 41.

APPENDIX II

Genealogies

The first of the charts which follow is in its form a reproduction of the Franco *árbol* (see Chap. I, p. 39). Since a photograph of this sizeable document is impractical, what I have done is to set forth the schema and to reproduce separately the information it furnishes about each person listed. Contained on the original in enclosed circles, the numbering indicates where what is asserted both by the *fiscal* and by the Francos may be located below.

(1) Pedro Gonçález Notario, fue casado con Mayor Fernández su muger año de 1420. Pretende Fernán Suárez Franco, que litiga, que dexó tres hijos, Aluar Pérez que quedó en Asturias, y Garcí González de Rojas que se fue a la Puebla de Montalbán, y Pedro Franco que se fue a Toledo, y que deste deciende; y el señor Fiscal y villa de Madridejos y don Antonio de Rojas cauallero del hábito de Santiago, vezino de Toledo y delator desta causa, que deciende de Pedro Franco.[1]

(2) Aluar Pérez de Rojas, hijo mayor, sus padres solo le llaman Aluaro, pretende el actor que dexó por su hijo mayor a Aluar Pérez.

(3) Pedro Franco, arrendador y trapero, que casó con María Alvarez reconciliada, año 1485, la qual dize son sus hijos, Alonso Franco, Juan Franco, Mencía, muger de Alonso de San Pedro, y Catalina Alvarez, muger de Antonio de San Pedro, y dize fueron reconciliados en tiempo de gracia por judayzantes, que son los que tienen esta señal y fuera[2] destos lo fueron Luis Alvarez, alcayde de la casa de la moneda y Hernán Franco que no fueron reconciliados, como lo dize Alonso Franco reconciliado.

---

[1] The last sentence may have been left unfinished. It could have been concluded by the phrase "natural de Toledo" or something similar, since as it stands it seems to imply a rather unlikely agreement between the two sides as to the geographical origin of the family.

[2] Those bearing "esta señal" (a cross indicating "reconciliation") are Mencía Alvarez, Catalina Alvarez, Juan Franco, and Alonso Franco. The rest of the sentence, although somewhat obscure, may be translated: "And in addition to these, her children were Luis Alvarez and Hernán Franco who were not reconciled, as the himself reconciled Alonso Franco points out."

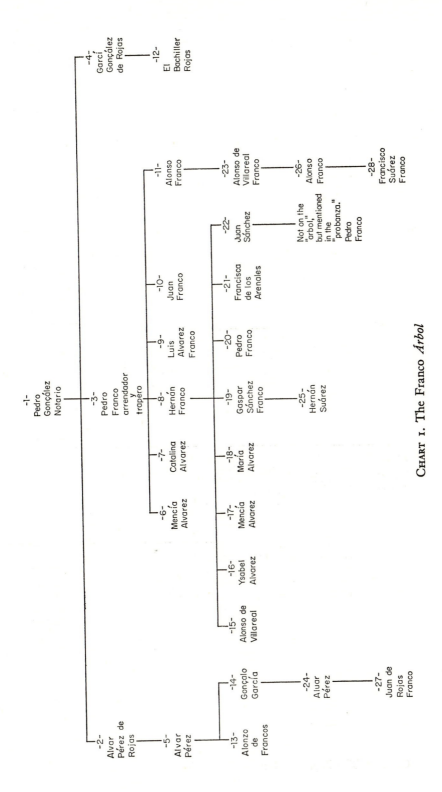

-1-
Pedro
Gonçález
Notario

-2-
Alvar
Pérez de
Rojas

-3-
Pedro
Franco
arrendador
y
trapero

-4-
Garcí
Gonçález
de Rojas

-5-
Alvar
Pérez

-6-
Mencía
Alvarez

-7-
Catalina
Alvarez

-8-
Hernán
Franco

-9-
Luis
Alvarez
Franco

-10-
Juan
Franco

-11-
Alonso
Franco

-12-
El
Bachiller
Rojas

-13-
Alonzo
de
Francos

-14-
Gonçalo
García

-15-
Alonso de
Villareal

-16-
Ysabel
Alvarez

-17-
Mencía
Alvarez

-18-
María
Alvarez

-19-
Gaspar
Sánchez
Franco

-20-
Pedro
Franco

-21-
Francisca
de los
Arenales

-22-
Juan
Sánchez

-23-
Alonso de
Villareal
Franco

-24-
Aluar
Pérez

-25-
Hernán
Suárez

-26-
Alonso
Franco

-27-
Juan de
Rojas
Franco

-28-
Francisco
Suárez
Franco

Not on the
"árbol,"
but mentioned
in the
"probanza."
Pedro
Franco

CHART I. The Franco *Árbol*

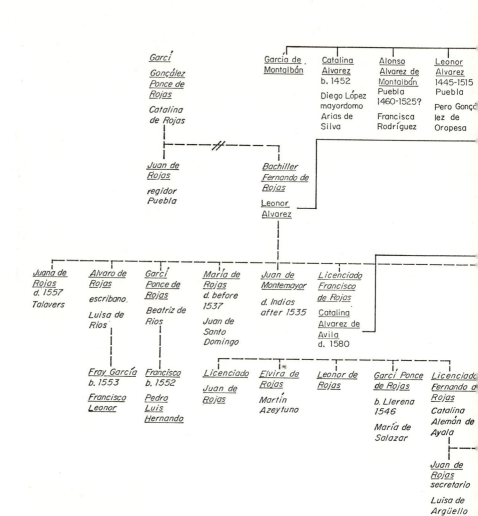

CHART 2. The Rojas and Montalbán Families

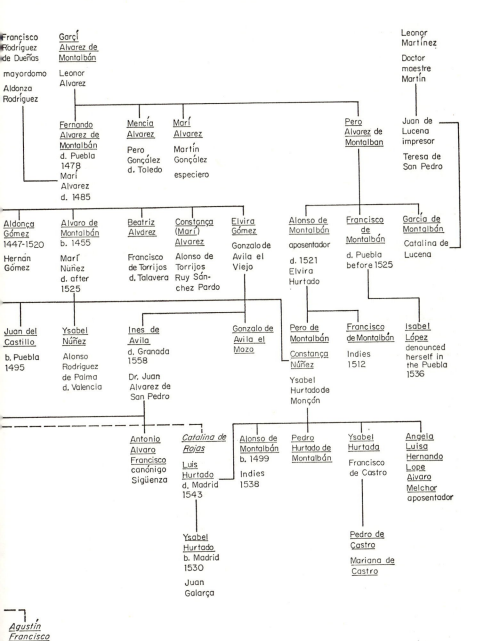

Francisco
Rodríguez
de Dueñas
mayordomo
Aldonza
Rodríguez

Garçí
Alvarez de
Montalbán
Leonor
Alvarez

Leonor
Martínez
Doctor
maestre
Martín

Fernando
Alvarez de
Montalbán
d. Puebla
1478
Marí
Alvarez
d. 1485

Mencía
Alvarez
Pero
Gonçález
d. Toledo

Marí
Alvarez
Martín
Gonçález
especiero

Pero
Alvarez de
Montalban

Juan de
Lucena
impresor
Teresa de
San Pedro

Aldonça
Gómez
1447-1520
Hernán
Gómez

Alvaro de
Montalbán
b. 1455
Marí
Núñez
d. after
1525

Beatriz
Alvdrez
Francisco
de Torrijos
d. Talavera

Constança
(Marí)
Alvarez
Alonso de
Torrijos
Ruy Sán-
chez Pardo

Elvira
Gómez
Gonzalo de
Avila el
Viejo

Alonso de
Montalbán
aposentador
d. 1521
Elvira
Hurtado

Francisco
de
Montalbán
d. Puebla
before 1525

García de
Montalbán
Catalina de
Lucena

Juan del
Castillo
b. Puebla
1495

Ysabel
Núñez
Alonso
Rodríguez
de Palma
d. Valencia

Ines de
Avila
d. Granada
1558
Dr. Juan
Alvarez de
San Pedro

Gonzalo de
Avila el
Mozo

Pero de
Montalbán
Constança
Núñez
Ysabel
Hurtado de
Monçón

Francisco
de Montalbán
Indies
1512

Isabel
López
denounced
herself in
the Puebla
1536

Antonio
Alvaro
Francisco
canónigo
Sigüenza

Catalina de
Rojas
Luis
Hurtado
d. Madrid
1543

Alonso de
Montalbán
b. 1499
Indies
1538

Pedro
Hurtado de
Montalbán

Ysabel
Hurtada
Francisco
de Castro

Angela
Luisa
Hernando
Lope
Aivaro
Melchor
aposentador

Ysabel
Hurtado
b. Madrid
1530
Juan
Galarça

Pedro de
Castro
Mariana de
Castro

Agustín
Francisco
Hernando

(4) Garcí Gonçález de Rojas, que dicen se fue a la Puebla y que tuvo por su hijo al Bachiller Rojas.

(5) Aluar Pérez, y que este tuvo por su hijo mayor a Alonso de Francos.

(6) Mencía Alvarez casó con Alonso de San Pedro mercader de paños, fueron ambos reconciliados en el término de la gracia año 1485 do dize ques su madre María Alvarez muger de Pedro Franco.

(7) Catalina Alvarez, casó con Antonio de San Pedro, trapero, fue reconciliada en el termino de gracia año 1485, do dize que es hija de Pedro Franco difunto y de María Alvarez su muger.

(8) Hernán Franco agüelo del que litiga, en el testamento que hizo año de 35 dize son sus hermanos Alonso Franco y Luis Alvarez y a Mencía Alvarez y Juan Franco que tienen esta señal;[3] casó con Catalina Alvarez, tuvieron 8 hijos.

(9) Luis Alvarez Franco, alcayde de la casa de la moneda, casó con Leonor de Villarreal, fue su hijo Juan Franco preso por judayzante, no uvo sentencia porque se volvió loco, nombra por hermanos de su padre a Hernán Franco y Alonso Franco y Mencía Alvarez.[4]

(10) Juan Franco reconciliado año de 1485, dize que es hijo de Pedro Franco, y María Alvarez su muger.

(11) Alonso Franco reconciliado año de 1485, dize que es su madre María Alvarez muger de Pedro Franco difunto y que son sus hermanos Luis Alvarez alcayde de la casa de la moneda y Hernando Franco y Mencía Alvarez muger de Alonso de San Pedro y que ambos fueron reconciliados, casó con Leonor de Villareal Cuello tuvieron por hijo a Alonso de Villarreal Franco.

(12) El Bachiller Rojas que compuso a Celestina la vieja. El señor Fiscal pretende que fue hijo de Hernando de Rojas condenado por judayzante año de 88 y que deste deciende el Licenciado Rojas abogado que fue de Valladolid letrado de Hernán Suárez para quien también pretendieron traer visaguelo de Asturias.

---

[3] Those bearing this sign (a "corazón coronado con cruz") on the *árbol* are, despite the text, Mencía Alvarez, Catalina Alvarez, Juan Franco, and Alonso Franco. Hernán Franco should be taken as the subject of the clause following "casó con Catalina Alvarez."

[4] The names of Alonso Franco and Mencía Alvarez were written in by hand.

(13) Alonso de Francos; y este no tuvo hijos y por esto vino la casa a Gonçalo García.

(14) Gonçalo García, hijo segundo del segundo Aluar Pérez, y este tuvo por hijo a Aluar Pérez.

(15) Alonso de Villareal, frayle Francisco.

(16) Ysabel Alvarez casó con Alonso Aluarez.

(17) Mencía Aluarez que casó con el licenciado Alonso Pérez de Ubeda.

(18) María Aluarez que casó con Hernán Pérez de Villareal.

(19) Gaspar Sánchez Franco, padre del que litiga, casó con doña Teresa Ortiz[5] y tuuo por hijo a Hernán Suárez.

(20) Pedro Franco, jurado.

(21) Francisca de los Arenales, monja.

(22) Juan Sánchez.[6]

(23) Alonso de Villareal Franco, que casó con doña Ynés de Cepeda; tuuo por hijo a Alonso Franco.

(24) Aluar Pérez y este tuuo por su hijo a Juan de Rojas Franco.

(25) Hernán Suárez[7] que casó con doña Ynés de Léon; tuuieron por hijos a Gaspar Suárez Franco y Hernán Suárez Franco, depositario de Toledo, y a doña Teresa Franco y Alonso Suárez Franco que fueron citados al pleito y salieron a él y están condenados en vista de la propiedad y en costas personales y procesales y puesto perpetuo silencio, año 1593.

(26) Alonso Franco, regidor que fue de Toledo, año de 1597; casó con doña Leonor Acre; tuuo por hijo a Francisco Suárez Franco.

(27) Juan de Rojas Franco, señor de la casa al tiempo que se hazía la provanza, año de 1584.

(28) Francisco Suárez Franco, regidor que es de Toledo, año 1606.

[5] The name is handwritten and accompanied by a handwritten marginal explanation: "La mujer de Gaspar Sánchez Franco se llamó doña Teresa Ortiz de quien desciende Hernán Suárez, y también fue casado con doña Ynés de Cepeda." It would appear that he married the widow of Alonso de Villareal Franco (no. 23) or perhaps the other way around.

[6] This name is erroneously listed as "Luis" in Gilman-Gonzálvez, p. 22.

[7] Another brother (or perhaps a son) was mentioned in the testimony: ". . . dijo este testigo que tubo mucha comunicación y trato con el licenciado Martín de Rojas susodicho muchos años y también con Hernán Franco y con Juan de Robles su hermano . . ." (fo. 124).

The second chart was designed to illustrate the three intermarriages of the Rojas and the Montalbanes and to put together the several sources of genealogical information about the two families. With the exception of the doubtful connection between the Bachelor and Garcí Gonçález Ponce de Rojas (indicated here by the crossed line), it tells as much of the truth about the two families as I have been able to ascertain. All patently false statements, such as the substitution of Dr. Juan Alvarez de San Pedro for Alvaro de Montalbán (see Chap. I, n. 59), are not taken into account.

The *Probanza de hidalguía* of Licentiate Fernando de Rojas

The document here reproduced is listed in the *Catálogo* of the "Sala de los hijosdalgo" (in the Archivo de la Real Chancillería in Valladolid) published by Alfredo Basanta de la Riva, Valladolid, 1922, as follows: "Rojas (Hernando de), Abogado de la Real Chanchillería—*Talavera*, 1567." This listing (to be found in vol. III, p. 238) is not accompanied by specific numbers for the *legajo* and the *expediente*, references provided by the personnel to those wishing to consult the archives. They are in this case: 1362-1.

I. Legal Depositions

The document begins with a number of legal depositions having to do with the suit. These are described in résumé by the transcriber, don Agustín Millares Carlo, as follows:

1. Solicitud de Lucas Jiménez, procurador, en nombre del licenciado Hernando de Rojas, para que se mandase hacer información sobre la condición de hijodalgo de su patrocinado. Presentada en Valladolid, ante los alcaldes de los hijosdalgo, en 9 de enero de 1567.

2. Poder del licenciado Hernando de Rojas, abogado de la Real Audiencia, a Lucas Jiménez, Alvar Pérez de Espinaredo, y Bernardino González, procuradores de dicha Audiencia, para que le representasen en el pleito que seguía con la villa de Talavera y otros lugares, y con el fiscal de su Magestad sobre su hidalguía. Valladolid, 6 de enero de 1567.

3. Presentación ante los alcaldes de hijosdalgo del anterior documento. Valladolid, 9 de enero de 1567.

4. Nueva presentación por el mismo, acusando la rebeldía de los emplazados. Valladolid, 24 de enero de 1572.

5. Notificación de la provisión real número 6 al Concejo de Talavera por el escribano Juan López. Talavera, 9 de enero de 1572.

6. Provisión real, despachada por los alcaldes de hidalguía, por

505

la cual, a petición de Lucas Jiménez, procurador del licenciado Rojas, se manda al Concejo de Talavera comparecer ante la Real Audiencia en las diligencias y probanza de la hidalguía de su patrocinado. Valladolid, 10 de enero de 1567.

7. Escrito del procurador Lucas Jiménez afirmándose en su petición. Presentado en 25 de enero de 1567.

8. Provisión real a los escribanos de hijosdalgo, Cristobal de Aulestia y Simón de Ortegón, ordenándoles dar traslado de la probanza que sobre su hidalguía habían hecho ante ellos Pedro y Alonso Franco, vecinos de Toledo, y el licenciado Rojas. Madrid, 1 de octubre de 1568.

9. Requerimiento a los interesados para que cumpliesen la provisión anterior. Valladolid, 5 de octubre de 1568.

10. Lucas Jiménez solicita se tenga el pleito por concluso. Presentada en 29 de enero de 1572.

11. Oposición del fiscal a la probanza. Valladolid, 25 de enero de 1572.

12. Ratificación en su escrito anterior del procurador Lucas Jiménez. Valladolid, 11 de Marzo de 1572.

These various items indicate that the Licentiate Fernando began the suit in 1567, and that in 1572 the *fiscal* successfully opposed the proceedings. Action was then delayed until 1584 when the Licentiate managed to present new witnesses. As noted in the Introduction, the absence of opposing testimony leads me to suppose that all that he hoped and dared to achieve out of these lengthy proceedings was a partial transcription of favorable testimony. This transcription still in the Valle Lersundi archives was that published in the *RFE* in 1925. It was apparently used by the family in lieu of a definitive *ejecutoria*. While working in Valladolid (before finding the Palavesín *expediente*) I spent days searching through uncatalogued *ejecutorias* in the hope of finding that of the Rojas but, as I should have expected, without success.

II. Transcription of the Testimony

En el margen derecho: Escribano, Aulestia

Muy poderoso señor.

El licenciado Rojas, abogado desta Real Audiencia, en el / pleito con vuestro fiscal y la villa de Talavera / e ayuntamiento desta villa de Valladolid, digo / que para en prueba de mi yntención acerca desta prouanza ad / perpetua [*sic*] presento por testigos en el dicho pleito:

Antonio de Salazar

Blas Rodríguez, Vecinos de la Puebla de Montaluán.

Por tanto a V. S. pido y suplico los aya por presentados, y se les rrequiera para el examen dellos, y para ello, etc.

El licenciado Rojas   (*Rúbrica*)

Juraron dos testigos.

En Valladolid, a veinte días del mes de / março de mill e quinientos e ochenta / e quatro años, ante los señores alcaldes / de los hijosdalgo la presentó el licenciado / Rojas, aquí contenido, y ante los dichos señores juraron dos testigos.

Por las preguntas siguientes sean preguntados los testigos que por parte / del licenciado Hernando de Rojas, hauogado en la Real Audiencia de / Valladolid son o serán presentados en el pleito que trata con el licenciado Juan / García, fiscal de su Magestad, y con el Conçejo y Ayuntamiento de la villa de Tala / uera sobre la probança que hace ad perpetuam rrey memoriam de / su hidalguía.

I. Primeramente, sean preguntados si conosçen a las dichas partes y si conosçieron al liçenciado Francisco de Rojas y al vachiller Hernando de Ro- / jas, difuntos, veçinos que fueron de la villa de Talauera, padre y ha- / buelo del dicho litigante, y si oyeron deçir a Garçí Gonçáles de Rojas, vecino / que fue de la Puebla de Montaluán, visabuelo del dicho litigante.

II. Ytem, si sauen, bieron, oyeron deçir que el dicho liçenciado Hernando de Rojas, que litiga, y los dichos sus padres, abuelo y bisabuelo y los demás sus anteçe- / ssores, todos y cada vno de ellos son y an sido ombres hijos dehalgo notorios, / de sangre y de solar conoçido, y debengar quinientos sueldos, según fuero de Hespaña, y por tales avidos y thenidos y comunmente rreputados. Digan lo que sauen.

III. Ytem, si sauen, etc., que el dicho licenciado Hernando de Rojas y los dichos / sus padres, abuelo y bisabuelo, y los demás antecessores por línea / rrecta de barón, de uno, dies, veinte, treynta, quarenta, sesenta, ochenta, cien años y más tiempo a esta parte, y de tanto tiempo acá que memoria / de hombres no es en contrario, an estado y están y siempre estubieron / en quieta y pacífica possesión de hombres hijosdalgo, no pechando / ni contribuyendo con pechos algunos rreales ni conçejales en que los bue / nos hombres pecheros suelen y acostumbran pagar, antes an sido / libres y exentos dellos y no an sido empadronados ni rrepartidos / en ellos, ansí en las dichas villas de Talauera y Puebla de Montaluán, donde an bibido y morado, como los lugares de la perrochia de Almofrague y / villa de Halía, donde han tenido bienes y haçienda y les an guardado / todas las demás honrras, franqueças y libertades que se suelen y / acostumbran guardar a los demás hijosdalgo destos rreynos, por ser ellos / tales hijosdalgo, y no por otra causa ni rraçón alguna, y lo saben / los testigos por lo auer bisto ser y pasar así en sus tiempos y oídolo deçir / a sus mayores y más ancianos, que deçían aberlo ellos bisto y oydo / a otros sus pasados, y tal era y es dello la pública boz y fama y común / opinión, sin hauer cosa en contrario. Digan lo que sauen.

IIII. Ytem, si sauen, etc., que el dicho licenciado Hermando de Rojas y los dichos sus / padre, abuelo y visabuelo, en las dichas villas y lugares donde an bi- / bido y morado y tenido bienes y haçienda, se an juntado en las juntas / y ayuntamientos de los hombres hijosdalgo y tenido los ofiçios que sola- / mente se dan y an dado a hombres hijosdalgo, por ser ellos tales hijosdal- / go y no por otra causa ni rraçón. Digan lo que sauen.

V. Ytem, si sauen, etc., ques público y notorio y pública boz y fama quel dicho Gar- / cí Gonzales de Rojas, vecino que fue de la dicha Puebla de Mon- / taluán, fue casado y velado según horden de la Santa Madre Ygle- / sia, con Catalina de Rojas, su muger, y como tales hiçieron hiçieron vida mari- / dable, y durante entre ellos el dicho matrimonio, obieron por su hijo ligítimo / y natural al vachiller Hernando de Rojas, que se fué a uibir a la / villa de Talauera, y por tales fueron avidos y tenidos y comunmente / rreputados.

VI. Ytem, si sauen, etc., quel dicho bachiller Hernando de Rojas fue ca- / sado y belado legitimamente, según orden de la Santa Madre Yglesia, con Leonor Aluares, su muger, y como tales hiçieron vida maridable, / y durante entre ellos el dicho matrimonio, obieron y proquearon en- / tre otros por su hijo ligítimo y natural al dicho licenciado Francisco de Rojas, / y como tal le tubieron y criaron y heredó sus bienes y hacienda y / por tales son y fueron abidos y tenidos y comunmente rreputados.

VII. YTEM, si sauen, etc., quel dicho licenciado Francisco de Rojas fue casado y belado / legitimamente según orden de la Santa Madre Yglesia con doña / Catalina Aluarez de Auila, su muger, y como tales hiçieron vida / maridable, y durante entre ellos el dicho matrimonio, obieron y pro- / crearon por sus hijos legitimos y naturales al dicho Hernando / de Rojas y a doña Elbira de Rojas, y por tales son y an sido auidos y / tenidos y comúnmente rreputados.

VIII. YTEM, si sauen, etc., que todo lo susodicho es pública boz y fama y público y notorio.

El licenciado Rojas   (*Rúbrica*).

El dicho Antonio de Salaçar, vecino de la Puebla de Montal- / uán, estante en esta ciudad, testigo presentado por parte / del dicho liçençiado Rojas, el qual, después de hauer / jurado en forma de derecho y siendo exsaminado en presençia del / dicho illustre señor dotor Hinojosa, alcalde de los hijosdalgo, lo que dixo y depuso fue lo siguiente:

Preguntado por las generales de la ley, dixo que es hijodalgo, / y no es pariente ni henemigo de ninguna de las partes, y es de hedad de / más de sesenta años, y que no le tocan las demás generales de la ley. [See Appendix I, n. 10.]

[I.] A la primera pregunta del dicho juramento dixo este testigo que conoce al licenciado / Hernando de Rojas, por cuya parte es presentado por testigo, de bista / y trato, abogado que es en esta Real Audiencia, e ansí mismo conos- / ció al licenciado Francisco de Rojas, padre del que litiga, por tiempo de más de doze años, biuiendo y morando con su casa poblada, bie- / nes e hazienda en la villa de Talauera, hasta que murió, / y que al licenciado Hernando de Rojas, agüelo que la pregunta llama dél que digan, no le conosció más de lo hauer oído dezir e / nombrar a honbres viejos e ançianos e que son ya difuntos, e pasados desta presente vida, en especial a Martín Alonso, que habrá que murió más de ocho años, y sería / de hedad quando murió de más de setenta años, según parecía / por su aspeto, y a otras muchas personas vecinos de la Puebla de Montaluán, que deçían hauía hecho el libro lla- mado / Celestina, y que no conosce ni oyó decir de Garçí Gonzáles de

Rojas, / bisagüelo que la pregunta llama del litigante, y tiene noticia de la villa de Talauera, con quien se litiga este pleito, y no conosçe / al fiscal de su Magestad, y esta dize de la pregunta.

[II.] A la segunda pregunta del dicho juramento dixo este testigo que lo que de la / dicha pregunta saue es que en quanto a la rreputación / del que li[ti]ga no saue cosa alguna, pero en quanto / toca a la de su padre y su agüelo dixo este testigo que oyó / decir, tratar a platicar publicamente e por cosa pública / y notoria a los biejos e ançianos que dicho tiene de la / Puebla de Montaluán como a los de Talauera, / estando este testigo en ella, en cómo el padre e aguelo del / dicho lizenciado eran notorios hijosdalgo, buenos e / prinçipales, y que por tales les tenían y hauían / tenido, acatado y estimado sus personas, y les hauían sido dados y encargados ofiçios honerosos de hijos- / dalgo, y los hauían jurado y lleuado quieta e paçifica- / mente, e por tales hijosdalgo de sangre buena e prinçipal, los susodichos e cada uno dellos se hauían / estimado y tenido, y hauían / sido comunmente rreputados / entre todas e por todas las personas vecinos / y moradores de la dicha villa de la Puebla de Montaluán como de Talauera, que dellos e de cada uno / dellos tuuieron noticia, como ellos en / sus tiempos dezían hauerla tenido, sin que jamás hu- / uiesen oydo cosa en contrario, antes dello desçían / hauer sido y ser la pública voz e fáma e común opinión / en las dichas villas oy en día, y esto cree que saue / de la pregunta, e siéndole hecha la rrepregunta de oficio, dixo / que dize lo que dicho tiene, y no saue otra cossa.

III. A la tercera pregunta del dicho juramento dixo este testigo que en quanto a la posición del que litiga no saue cosa alguna, pero en quanto a la / de su padre y agüelo dixo este testigo que oyó desir, tratar / y platicar a hombres viejos e ançianos, ansí de la / villa de Talauera como de la Puebla de Montal- / uán, que son ya difuntos e pasados desta presente vida, y en especial a su consuegro deste testigo, que se llamó Andrés de la / Carrera, vecino que fue de la villa de Talauera, que habrá que / murió siete, ocho años, al paresçer deste testigo, y sería de hedad / de más de setenta años, según paresçía por su aspetto / y vejez, en como los susodichos e cada uno dellos hauían estado en posisión muy notoria de hombres hijosdalgo / de sangre, y que como tales les hauían sido guardadas / todas las honrras, franquezas,

510

liuertades y exsen- / ciones, que se guardauan e guardaron en las / dichas villas a los caualleros hijosdalgo que bivían / en ellas, no pechando, pagando ni contribuyendo / en ninguno de los pechos rreales ni conçejales / en que pechauan, pagauan e contribuyan los / honbres buenos pecheros de las dichas villas y de cada / una dellas, y ansí mismo les oyó decir en como ellos en / sus tiempos e días lo huuieran ansí visto, sauido y entendido, / ansí en la dicha villa de Talauera / en el tiempo que hauía hauido / pechos de propios en que se hauían reconosçido los hijosdalgo / de los que no lo eran, como en la dicha Puebla de / Montaluán, sin auer sauido él en su tiempo cossa en contrario, / que ansí este testigo lo cree y tiene por cierto, porque este testigo, siendo alcalde, / rregidor y procurador general en diferentes años en la dicha villa de / la Puebla de Montaluán, a visto muchos padrones don- / de están escriptos e asentados los vecinos pecheros de la dicha villa, / y nunca en ellos vió escripto ni asentado al agüelo del dicho / litigante, por ser cosa cierta y berdadera ser tal honbre hijodalgo, / como dicho tiene, porque si fuera el susodicho pechero / y hubiera estado en tal posición, teniendo, como pareçe / por scriptura pública, que tuvo bienes y hazienda / en la dicha villa como tal vezino, de majuelos, que este testigo / los a visto y leído en procesos presentados ante este testigo, siendo alcalde, no pudiera ser menos que siendo pechero / dexara de estar escripto y asentado en los dichos padro- / nes con los demás vecinos pecheros, porque saue este testigo por / cosa muy çierta que ningún vecino de la dicha villa que no / sea muy notorio hijodalgo le dexan luego de poner / y assentar en los padrones de pecheros, por las quales / rraçones este testigo cree y tiene por cosa muy çierta, sauida y entendida, que el agüelo del dicho litigante fue honbre hijodalgo / notorio de sangre e descendiente de tales, porque / si otra cosa huuiera sido lo supiera y huuiera oído / desir, tratar e platicar, y no pudiera ser menos, por la mucha noticia que este testigo a tenido de las cosas de la dicha villa / de la Puebla de Montaluán, y ser lugar pequeño, donde / se saue y conoçe en partiqular cada uno quién es, // y porque en la dicha villa, demás y allende, de los pecheros / dichos se an rreconosçido en rrazón dello los hijosdalgo de los pecheros, en que tienen la mitad de los ofiçios honrrosos de hijosdalgo, sacado por carta executoria en la rreal chancillería / de Valladolid, y todo lo que dicho tiene y cada una cosa e parte / dello es pública vos e fama oy en día en las dichas / villas y en cada una dellas, donde de lo contenido / en la dicha pregunta se a tenido noticia, como este testigo la a tenido / y tiene, y no saue otra cosa de la pregunta, ni de la rrepregunta / que le fue hecha por su merçed del dicho señor alcalde.

A la última y final pregunta del dicho juramento dixo que todo lo / por él dicho y declarado es la verdad, público y notorio, para / el juramento que hecho tiene, y firmólo de su nombre. / Leyóse su dicho, y se rratificó en él. Encargósele el secreto, / y lo prometió, y firmólo el dicho señor alcalde.

Antonio de Salazar (*Rúbrica*).—Pasó ante mi,
Fernán Ruiz Regarbe (*Rúbrica*).

Testigo. El dicho Blas Rodríguez, vecino que dixo ser de la Puebla / de Montaluán, estante en esta Corte, testigo susodicho, / presentado por parte del licenciado Rojas / para la prueba de su yntençión, el qual después de / hauer jurado en forma de derecho, y siendo esaminado por el dicho / señor alcalde Hinojosa, y siendo preguntado por las preguntas del dicho / juramento por su parte presentado, lo que dixo fue lo siguiente:

Generales.—Preguntado por las generales de la ley, dixo que es de hedad de más de sesenta e tres años y que es pechero llano / y no es pariente ni le tocan ni enpecen ninguna de las / generales de la ley, e que Dios nuestro Señor dé la / justicia a la parte que la tuuiere. //

I. A la primera pregunta dixo este testigo que conosce al / que litiga de cinco o seis años a esta parte en esta villa / de Valladolid, abogado en ella, y saue ques natural de la / Villa de Talauera, y no le conosçe bienes rraizes en / ninguna parte, e a Francisco de Rojas, vecino que fue de Talauera, no le conosció, / pero le oyó decir muchas vezes a honbres viejos e ancianos, / y no se aquerda qué tanto a que murió, y que al bachiller / Hernando de Rojas, agüelo del litigante, padre de su padre, / le conosció por le hauer visto y hablado yendo a la villa / de la Puebla de Montaluán, donde dezían era su origen, / donde este testigo le vió y otras muchas personas, y dél te- / nían mucha noticia, por dezir que era el que hauía hecho / el libro llamado Celestina, y es público que habrä como qua- / renta años que murió poco más o menos, y que a Gar- / cí Gonzáles de Rojas, visagüelo que la pregunta llama del /

litigante no le conoçe más de le hauer oydo desir e nombrar / a muchas personas vecinas e moradores de la Puebla de Montaluán, / viejos e ançianos, que deçían hauerle conosçido biuir / y morar en la dicha villa de la Puebla, y tenido en ella / muchos bienes y haçienda, y que al fiscal de su Magestad no le conoce y tiene noticia de la villa de Talauera, y del / ayuntamiento de vecinos, y esto dize e rresponde de la pregunta.

II. A la segunda pregunta del dicho juramento, dixo este testigo que tiene / al dicho licenciado Rojas que litiga por honbre hijodalgo de / si y de su padre, agüelo y visagüelo, porque en todo / el tiempo y año que este testigo conoçió al dicho su agüelo e / oyó decir de su padre e visagüelo siempre e a la / continua oyó desir a personas viejas e ançianas, / ansí an la villa de Talauera como en la Pue- / bla de Montaluán hauer estado y estar en // rreputaçión de honbres hijosdalgo de sangre / y deçendientes de tales, y que por tales les / tratauan y comunicauan con los condes que hauían sido de la Puebla de Montaluán / y los tenían por sus deudos e parientes por / linea rrecta de varón, y en esta fama y rrepu- / tación hauían siempre estado, y es dello oy en / día la pública voz e fama, ansí en la villa / de Talauera como en la Puebla de Montal- / uán, y nunca hauía sauido ni entendido / cosa en contrario, y esto dize de la pregunta, y siéndole hecha la rrepregunta de ofiçio rrepecto / desta pregunta, dixo que dize lo que dicho tiene, y no saue otra cosa de la dicha pregunta e rrepregunta / que le fue hecha por el dicho señor alcalde.

III. A la tercera pregunta del dicho juramento, dixo este testigo que en quanto a la posición del litigante y de sus padres y agüelos no saue cosa alguna, y en quanto toca a la / posición que tuuo Garçí Gonzáles / de Rojas, bisagüelo del litigante dice lo que oyó dezir a / honbres viejos e ançianos, vecinos de la villa de / la Puebla de Montaluán que son ya difuntos / e pasados desta presente, de cuyos nombres no / tiene noticia para los poder decir e declarar que decían hauer estado en posición honbres hijos- / dalgo de sangre y descendientes de tales / por linea rreta de varón, e que como tal / sus bienes y hacienda no hauía pechado, pagado ni contribuído en ninguno de los pechos / rreales e conçejales en que hauían pechado, / pagado e contribuído los otros vecinos y mo- // radores de la dicha villa de la Puebla, pecheros llanos, y que tal dello era y hauía sido la / pública voz e fama e común opinión

513

en la dicha villa / de la Puebla y que nunca hauían visto, sauido ni / entendido cosa en contrario, y dello hauía sido y hera la pública / voz e fama e común opinión en la dicha villa. Fuéle hecha / la rrepregunta de ofiçio por su merçed del dicho señor alcalde, e / dixo que por ninguna de las causas que la fueren hechas / son por ser tales hijos dalgo, como dicho tiene, y esto dice de la pregunta.

V. A la quinta pregunta del dicho juramento dixo este testigo que lo contenido / en la dicha pregunta lo oyó decir, tratar e platicar públicamente / e por cosa pública y notoria a honbres viejos e ançianos de la villa de la Puebla de Montaluán por cosa muy çierta y de / mucha verdad, y tal dello es oy en día la pública voz / y fama e común opinión en la dicha villa, y nunca oyó cosa / en contrario, y esto dize de la pregunta y de lo en ella contenido.

VI. A la última pregunta del dicho juramento dixo este testigo que lo por el dicho / y declarado es la verdad, público y notorio, para el juramento que hecho / tiene, y leído su dicho, se rratificó en él / en presencia del dicho señor alcalde. Encargósele el secreto, y lo prometió, / y el dicho señor alcalde lo señaló. Va testado "Sánchez Lasa," no vala

Pasó ante mi, Fernán Ruiz Regarbe (*Rúbrica*).

Margen izquierdo: Presenta tres testigos. *Margen derecho*: Aulestia Muy poderoso señor:

Lucas Ximénez, en nombre del licenciado Hernando de Rojas, / en el pleito que trata con el fiscal de su Magestad y concejo / de la villa de Talauera sobre su ydal- / guía ad perpetuan rrey memorian, presentó / por testigos los siguientes:

Gaspar de Guzmán

Joan Maldonado Verdijo

Diego Hernández, vecinos de la dicha villa de / Talauera. Suplico a vuecencia mande averlos por / presentados y juren y digan sus dichos, etc.

Ximénes (*Rúbrica*) //

Juraron tres testigos

En la villa de Valladolid, a veynte días del mes de setiembre de / mill e quinientos e ochenta e quatro años, estando los señores alcaldes / de los hijosdalgo en audiencia pública, la presentó Lucas

Ximénes / en nombre de su parte ante los dichos testigos juraron dichos testigos, presente el fiscal del Rey nuestro señor.

Esaminé estos testigos. Villalobos. (*Rúbrica*)

Por las preguntas siguientes sean preguntados los testigos que por parte del liçenciado Hernando de Rojas, abo- / gado en la Real Audiencia de Valladolid son o serán presentados en el pleito que trata con el licenciado Juan / Garçía, fiscal de su Magestad, y con el Concejo y Ayuntamiento dela villa de Talauera sobre la prouança que haçe / ad perpetuam rey memoriam de su hidalguía.

I. Primeramente sean preguntados si conoçen a las dichas partes y si conocieron al liçenciado Francisco de Rojas, / padre del dicho litigante, y al bachiller Hernando de Rojas, su abuelo, vecinos que fueron de la dicha villa / de Talauera, y si oieron deçir a Garçí Gonçález Ponçe de Rojas, visabuelo que fue del que litiga, vecino que fue / de la villa de la puebla de Montaluán.

II. Yten, si sauen, vieron y oyeron deçir que el dicho licenciado Hernando de Rojas, que litiga, y los dichos sus padre y abuelo y visabuelo y los demás sus anteçessores, todos y cada uno de ellos son y an sido hombres / hijosdalgo notorios de sangre y de solar conoçido devengar quinientos sueldos, según fuero de España, y por tales auidos y tenidos y comunmente reputados.

III. Yten, si sauen, etc., que en la dicha villa de Talauera, de sesenta años y más tiempo a esta parte, no se paga / ni a pagado el pecho real ni moneda forera por repartimiento entre los pecheros, porque se ha pagado y paga / de los propios dela dicha villa de Talauera, pero antes de los dichos años se pagaba por re- partimiento y se / hacían padrones para cobrar de los buenos hombres pecheros el pecho rreal en las quales se asentauan / los buenos hombres pecheros, y no ponían ni asentauan los que eran hijosdalgo, y después que el dicho pecho no se paga por reparti- mientos, se an reconoçido los hijosdalgo de los que no lo son en la representaçión y en algunos ofiçios que se dan a hombres hijosdalgo, como son las baras de alcaldes ordinarios en tiempo / de sede vacante de los Arçobispos de Toledo, que las pone el ayuntamiento de la dicha villa, y los ofiçios de jurados y pro- curador general. Y además desto ay çierto derecho que se paga para los propios de la dicha, que se llama el portazguillo que es cierta quantidad de maravedís por cada carga de qualquiera cosa / que entra o sale de la dicha villa de algún vecino della, en el qual dicho derecho el que es pechero paga / y contribuye y ha pagado y contribuido y el que es hidalgo es libre y exempto de tal pecho y contribuçión, / y en esto se han diferençiado y diferençian, de tiempo ymmemorial a esta parte. Digan lo que sauen.

IIII. YTEN, si sauen, etc., que en las aldeas y términos de la dicha villa se pagan y han pagado de tiempo ymmemorial a esta parte pechos por repartimientos entre los pecheros, los quales an rrepartido y rreparten / entre todas las personas que tienen y an tenido bienes y hazienda en los dichos lugares, así vecinos como / forasteros, y aunque sean vecinos de la dicha villa de Talauera, y así sauen los testigos que en los lugares de la / parrochia de Almofrague y Alcaudete an enpadronado y prendado algunos vecinos de la dicha villa / por los bienes y hazienda que tenían en ella y sobre el dicho enpadronamiento y prenda han seguido sus / pleytos de hidalguía y hecho diligençias. Sobre ello digan lo que sauen.

V. YTEN, si sauen, etc., que el dicho liçenciado Hernando de Rojas y los dichos sus padres, abuelo y visabuelo / y los demás sus anteçesores por línea recta de varón, de uno, diez, veinte, treynta, quarenta, / sesenta, ochenta, çient años y más tiempo a esta parte y de tanto tienpo acá que memoria de hombres / no es en contrario, an estado y están y siempre estuvieron en quieta y pacífica posesión de hombres / hijosdalgo, no pechando ni contribuyendo en pechos algunos rreales ni conçejales en que los vuenos / hombres pecheros suelen y acostumbran pagar, antes an sido libres y exemptos dellos, y no an / sido enpadronados ni rrepartidos en ellos, así en la dicha villa de Talauera, donde an biuido / y morado, como en los lugares de la dicha parrochia de Almofrague, Alcaudete y villa de Halia, donde / an tenido vienes y hazienda y les an guardado todas las demás honrras, franquezas / y libertades que se suelen y acostumbran guardar a los demás hijosdalgo de estos rreynos, / por ser ellos tales hijosdalgo y no por otra causa ni rraçón alguna, y lo sauen los testigos / por lo hauer visto, ser y pasar ansí en sus tiempos, y oídolo deçir a sus mayores y más ançianos, que decían auerlo ellos visto ser y pasar a otros sus mayores, y tal era y es dello la pública voz / y fama y común opinión, sin auer cosa en contrario. Digan lo que sauen.

VI. YTEN, si sauen, etc., que el dicho liçenciado Hernando de Rojas y los dichos su padre y abuelo y visabuelo en las dichas villas y lugares donde an viuido y morado y tenido vienes / y hazienda, se an juntado en las juntas y ayuntamientos de los hombres hijosdalgo, y tenido ofiçios que solamente se dan y an dado a honbres hijosdalgo, y en la dicha villa de Talauera / an metido y sacado muchas bestias cargadas de huba y de otras cosas, las quales an / dexado entrar y sacar sin les llever cosa alguna por el dicho derecho del portazguillo, por ser / ellos tales hijosdalgo y no por otra causa alguna. Digan lo que sauen.

VII. Yten, si sauen, etc., que el dicho Garçí Gonçáles de Rojas fue casado y belado legitimamente, / según orden de la Santa Madre Yglesia, con doña Cathalina de Rojas, su mujer, y como tales / hicieron vida maridable, y durante entre ellos el dicho matrimonio, ouieron y procrearon por su / hijo ligítimo y natural al dicho vachiller Hernando de Rojas, y como tales marido y mujer / y hijo legítimo y natural fueron abidos y tenidos y comunmente reputados.

VIII. Yten, si sauen, etc., que el dicho bachiller Hernando de Rojas fue casado y velado legitima- / mente, según orden de la Santa Madre Yglesia, con Leonor Aluarez, su mujer, y como tales / hiçieron vida maridable, y durante entre ellos el dicho matrimonio oieron y procrearon entre / otros por su hijo ligítimo y natural al dicho liçenciado Francisco de Rojas, y como tal / le tubieron y criaron, y heredó sus bienes y hazienda, y por tales son y fueron auidos y / tenidos y comúnmente rreputados. //

IX. Yten, si sauen, etc., que el dicho liçenciado Francisco de Rojas fue casado y velado legitimamente, / según orden de la Sancta Madre Yglesia, con doña Catalina Aluarez de Auila, su mujer, y como tales hiçieron vida maridable, y durante entre ellos el dicho matrimonio, ouieron y pro- / crearon por sus hijos legitimos y naturales al dicho liçenciado Hernando de Rojas, que litiga, / y al liçenciado Juan de Rojas y a doña Eluira de Rojas y a Garci Ponçe de Rojas, y por tales son y an / sido abidos y tenidos y comúnmente reputados.

X. Yten, si sauen que todo lo susodicho es pública voz y fama y público y notorio.

El licenciado Rojas (*Rúbrica*)//

Probança ad perpetuam / del licenciado Rojas.

El dicho Diego Hernández, vezino que dixo / ser de la villa de

Talauera, que biue a la / yglesia mayor, testigo susodicho, presentado / por parte del licenciado Rojas, abogado en / esta rreal Audiençia e Chancillería, en el pleito que trata con el liçenciado Juan García, fiscal / de su Magestad, y concejo y buenos honbres de la villa / de Talavera sobre rraçón de su hidalguía e libertad que pretende ad perpetuam / rrey memoriam, e aviendo jurado e siendo / preguntado por las preguntas del / dicho ynterrogatorio, para en que fue / presentado, y por las generales, ante el / muy yllustre señor dotor Hinojosa, alcalde / de los hijosdalgo, dixo lo siguiente:

Generales. Fué preguntado por los generales, e dixo ques de hedad de setenta años, poco más / o menos, e que no es hijodalgo, pero es christiano viejo, y que no es pariente / ni henemigo del litigante ni de las partes, / ni le tocan las demás preguntas generales.

I. A la primera pregunta del dicho juramento dixo que / conoçe al dicho licenciado Rojas, por cuya parte / es presentado por testigo, desde niño chequito, / rreçién nasçido, y es natural de Talabera y rreside en la villa de Valladolid, y abrá que casó catorze o quiñze años, póco / más o menos, y no le conoçe bienes rrayzes / ningunos, y que conosçió al licenciado Francisco de // Rojas, padre deste que litiga, vezino que fué desta villa, y le conosçió mozo e casa- / do quarenta años, poco más o menos, con bienes y hazienda rraíz en Talabera, / y aurá que murió quatro años, poco más o menos, y que conosció al bachiller / Hernando de Rojas, agüelo deste que litiga, padre / de su padre, vezino que fue de Talauere, y le / conosçió casado, con bienes y hazienda / rraíz e casa poblada quinze años y más / tiempo, y abrá que murió más de quinze / años, y que a García Gonzáles Ponze de Rojas, / bisagüelo deste que litiga, no le conosçió / más de aver oydo decir de él a muchas / personas viejas e ançianas, de que al presente / no se acuerda de sus nonbres, y no se acuer- / da de dónde deçían que hera natural, / más de que syenpre oyó decir que / la deçendençia del dicho licenciado Rojas, / que litiga, / deçiende de las montañas, / e y que conoçe al concejo de Tala- / vera, y esto rresponde a la pregunta.

II. A la segunda pregunta del dicho juramento dixo que en todo el tiempo e años que dicho e declara- / do tiene en la primera pregunta que a que conosçe / al dicho licenciado Rojas, que litiga, y que a que / conosçió a los dichos licenciado Francisco / de Rojas, su padre, y al bachiller Hernando / de Rojas, su agüelo, los a tenido y tiene / por hijosdalgo notorios, porque por tales an sido y son avidos y tenidos y comúnmente rreputados en la dicha villa de Talavera por todas las personas que los an conoçido / e tratado como este testigo, y que su origen / y deçendençia es de las montañas de León, y que tanbién oyó decir a muchos / viejos e ançianos de Talavera y de / otras partes de su comarca, de que / al presente no se acuerda de sus nombres, / e quel visagüelo deste que litiga hera / hijodalgo, y dello y de lo demás que dicho tiene tal a sido y es la pública / boz y fama y común opinión, e nunca vió ni oyó deçir lo contrario, e dixo este testigo que no les a conosçido / ni conoze parientes pecheros por línea / rreta de varón, antes hijosdalgo, como heran algunos vecinos de Talabera, y otros forasteros que venían a cassa / del bachiller Rojas, agüelo deste / que litiga, que algunos dellos venían y deçían que heran mon- / tañeses e hijosdalgo y el dicho bachiller, agüelo deste que litiga, y los susodichos se tratavan como de parientes, y esto rresponde a la pregunta e rrepregunta.

III. A la tercera pregunta del dicho ynterrogatorio / dixo que de más de çincuenta e çinco / años a esta parte, que este testigo se acuerda e tiene notiçia, sabe que en la dicha villa de Talabera no se a pagado ni paga / pecho de pecheros por rrepartimiento por los buenos / honbres pecheros de la dicha villa, / los quales dichos pechos sabe que / se an pagado y pagan en dicho tiempo a esta parte de los propios de la dicha villa / de Talabera, y es público y notorio que / de sesenta años a esta parte no se / pagan los dichos pechos por el dicho / rrepartimiento por los dichos pecheros / de la dicha villa de Talavera, sino que se pagan como dicho tiene, de los propios / de la dicha villa, y también / a oído decir por público e notorio, que / antes de los dichos sesenta años se / pagavan por rrepartimiento los / dichos pechos por los vecinos pecheros / de la dicha villa, y que para ello / se hazían padrones en los quales se asentavan los pecheros y no / los hijosdalgo, lo qual es público y notorio y se rremite a los padrones; y sabe que en las dichas villas de Talavera / se an rreconosçido los hijosdalgo / de los que no lo son, de más de çinquenta // e çinco años, que se acuerda, en las varas / de alcaldes ordinarios en tiempo de sede / vacante de los arçobispos de Toledo, / las quales pone el ayuntamiento de la / dicha villa, los quales son hijosdalgo, / e ansí mismo en los ofiçios de jurados / e procuradores generales, que la mitad de los dichos / ofiçios se da a los hijosdalgo, y la otra / mitad a los que son de casta de pe- / cheros, y lo mismo en lo tocante / a los alcaldes de la Hermandad, e ansimis- / mo son rreconosçidos los hijosdalgo de / los que no lo son en çierto derecho, y no se / pasa para los propios de la dicha villa, que llaman el portazguillo, que es / çierta cantidad de maravedís que se / paga por la carga de qualquier / cossa que entra en la dicha villa, que / el concejo la arrienda, y entiende que es en poca cantidad, y esto se haze en çierta manera que el que es pechero / paga çiertos maravedís de cada carga que / entra en la dicha çibdad, y el que es hijo- / dalgo no paga nada, ansí vecinos de la / dicha villa como forasteros, lo qual sabe como vezino de la dicha villa, / y lo a visto ser y pasar desde el tiempo que dicho tiene a esta parte, y esto rresponde / a la pregunta.

IIII. A la quarta pregunta dixo que del tiempo que dicho tiene a esta parte, sabe que en las aldeas de la dicha // villa de Talabera se an pagado y pagan pechos de pecheros por / rrepartimiento por los bienes rrayzes / que tienen en los dichos pueblos, así vecinos como forasteros, siendo pecheros, aunque sean vecinos de / Talabera, y sabe este testigo que en / los lugares de la perrochia de Almofrague y Alcaudete an en - / padronado a algunos vecinos de la dicha / villa de Talabera por los bienes / que tienen en los pueblos, y sobre ello se an mobido pleitos, / e lo susodicho es público e notorio e / pública boz e fama, y esto rrespon- / de a la pregunta.

V. A la quinta pregunta dixo que en el tiempo que dicho y declarado tiene en la / primera pregunta que conosçió al licenciado Francisco de Rojas e al bachiller / Hernando de Rojas, padre y agüelo del dicho licenciado Rojas, / que litiga, bibir y morar en la dicha villa / de Talabera, donde heran vecinos, sabe / que los susodichos y cada uno delles / en su tiempo estubieron en pacifica / posesión de honbres hijosdalgo no- / torios, y como tales sabe que / en tiempo de sede bacante de los / arçobispos de Toledo fueron / nonbrados por alcaldes ordinarios // de la dicha villa cada uno dellos / en su tiempo por el ayuntamiento de / la dicha villa de Talabera, y este testigo / les vió tener y husar los dichos ofiçios / paçificamente, y si no fueran hijos- / dalgo notorios, como lo heran, no / les dieran los dichos ofiçios, e ansi- / mismo sabe que fueron alcaldes / de la Hermandad, jurados e pro- / curadores / generales de la dicha villa algunos / años ynterpolada- / mente, por el estado de los hijosdalgo, porque en la dicha villa se husa e acostumbra / que la mitad de los dichos ofiçios / de jurados e alcaldes de la Her- / mandad y fieles se dan a los / hijosdalgo, y la otra mitad a los que no lo son, y el ofiçio de procurador general syenpre se le dió a honbres / hijosdalgo, y el padre y agüelo del que litiga syenpre les vió tener y husar los dichos ofiçios por el estado de los hijosdalgo, y oyó decir por público / e notorio e pública voz e fama que / por ser tales hijosdalgo no paga- / van ni pagaron el dicho derecho del por- / tazguillo por carga de ubas / e trigo que de sus heredades y de / otras partes metían en la dicha villa / para sus casas, e ni más ni menos / oyó decir que ansimismo en los lugares // de Almofrague y Alcaudete y Halia, / y do tenían bienes y hazienda rraíz, / no pechavan ni contribuían en los / pechos de pecheros de los dichos / por los bienes rrayzes / que tenían en los dichos lugares e sus / términos, por ser hijos dalgo noto- / rios, y están en tal posición, y que si / fueran pecheros pagaran y se les / rrepartiera como a los demás vecinos / pecheros de los dichos lugares y foras- / teros que en ellos tenían bienes / rrayzes, lo qual este testigo oyó decir / por cosa pública e notoria en la dicha villa de Talavera en tiempo de los / susodichos, e dello e de lo demás / que dicho tiene tal a sido y es / la pública boz y fama y común / opinión, e nunca vió ni oyó / decir cosa en con- / trario, y en quanto a la posición del dicho licenciado Rojas, / que litiga, ordinariamente, / desde que hera muchacho a estado / ausente de Talabera, así en Salamanca / como en esta villa de Valladolid, y en / otras partes, e no sabe cossa ninguna / de su posición, y en quanto al visagüelo / dize lo que dicho tieme en la segunda pregunta deste su dicho, y esto rresponde // a la pregunta, e no sabe más della. Fuéronle hechas las rrepreguntas / de ofiçio neçesaias; dixo que / dize lo que dicho tiene.

VI. A la sesta pregunta del dicho ynterrogatorio / dixo que dize lo que dicho tiene en la pregunta / antes desta, a que se rrefiere, y esta rresponde / a la pregunta, y no sabe más della.

VII. A la sétima pregunta del dicho ynterrogatorio dixo / que dize lo que dicho tiene en la primera pregunta, / y no sabe otra cosa, y esto rresponde / de la dicha pregunta.

VIII. A la otava pregunta del dicho ynterrogatorio, dixo / que aunque no vió casar ni velar / a los contenidos en la pregunta, / los vió estar casados y hacer vida ma- / ridable en uno, como tales marido / y muger, y como tales heran avidos / e tenidos, e durante su matrimonio entre otros hijos vió que tenían por su / hijo legítimo al dicho licenciado Francisco / de Rojas, padre deste que litiga, llamán- / dole hijo y él a ellos padre e madre, e por tal su hijo legítimo fué avido / e tenido y comúnmente rreputado, y heredó sus bienes y hazienda de / los dichos su padre e madre lo que le / cupo como uno de sus hijos, e dello / es la pública boz y fama, y esto rresponde / a la pregunta.

IX. A la nobena pregunta del dicho ynterrogatorio // dixo que la sabe como en ella se contiene, / porque este testigo se halló en las bodas y ve- / laçiones de los contenidos en la pregunta / y los vió hacer vida maridable en uno, como tales marido y mujer, y durante su ma- / trimonio ovieron por sus hijos legítimos / al dicho licenciado Rojas, que litiga, y al licenciado / Juan de Rojas y a doña Elvira de / Rojas, e a García Ponze de Rojas, / llamándolos hijos y ellos a ellos / padre e madre, y por tales marido / e muger e hijos legítimos an sido / y son comúnmente rre- / putados, e dello es la pública / boz y fama, y esto rresponde a la pregunta.

A la húltima pregunta dixo que lo que dicho tiene / es verdad para el juramento que hizo, e / siéndole leído su dicho, se rratificó en él, / y le fué encargado el secreto hasta la / publicación y pro- metiólo en forma, y no lo firmó porque dixo que no sabía / escriuir, e rrubricólo el señor alcalde. Va testado lo siguiente: "porque / sabe que," y "procuradores." Pase por testado.

(*Rúbrica*)   Pasó ante mí, Juan Martín de Villalobos
(*Rúbrica*)

El dicho Juan Maldonado Verdejo, vezino / de la villa de Talabera, testigo susodicho, presentado / por parte del dicho licenciado Rojas en el dicho / pleito de hidalguía ad perpetuan / rrei memoriam, e aviendo jurado e siendo / preguntado por las preguntas del dicho ynterrogatorio / syguientes ante el dicho señor alcalde, dixo / lo siguiente:

Generales. A las generales dixo que es de hedad de se- / tenta años, poco más o menos, e que no es hijodalgo, e que no le tocan las generales.

I. A la primera pregunta dixo que conoce / al dicho licenciado Rojas, que litiga, dende / niño chiquito, el qual es natural de la / villa de Talabera, y abrá que casó / catorze años, poco más o menos / y tiene ciertas huertas y heredades / en Crespos, tierra de Escalona, que / compró después de casado, e que / conosçe al licenciado Francisco de Rojas, padre deste que litiga, / vezino que / fué de la villa de Talabera, y le conosçió / casado con sus bienes e hazienda / rrayz e casa poblada más de / treynta años, que hace que murió / tres años, poco más o menos, e también / conosçió al bachiller / Hernando de Rojas, agüelo deste que litiga, / padre de su padre, vezino que fué de / Talabera, y le conosçió casado / con bienes e hazienda rraíz e / casa poblada quinze años, poco más o menos, e abrá que murió / quarenta años, poco más o menos, y que al bisagüelo no le conosçió más de averle oído decir, y era vezino / en la Puebla de Montaluán, // e que particularmente no se / acuerda a quien oyó decillo, e di- / xo este testigo que las bienes quel dicho / licenciado Rojas tiene en Crespos, / tierra de Escalona, no sabe de çierto / sy los conpró o por qué título los ha adquirido / después de casado, y que conoze al concejo / y vecinos de la villa de Talabera, y esto rresponde a la pregunta.

II. A la segunda pregunta del dicho ynterrogatorio dixo / quel tiempo e años que dicho e declarado / tiene que a que conoze al dicho licenciado / Rojas que litiga, y en el que conoçió / a los dichos licenciados Francisco de Rojas, / su padre, y bachiller Hernando / de Rojas, su agüelo los a tenido / y tiene por hijosdalgo notorios porque por tales an sido y son / avidos e tenidos e nonbrados / e comunmente rreputados en la dicha / villa de Talabera donde an sido / vecinos, que todas las presonas / que los an conosçido y tratado / como este testigo, e por tales / hijosdalgo se preçiaron e se tuvie- / ron e trataron sus presonas, / e dello a sido y es la pública boz y fa- / ma y común opinión, e nunca vió / ni oyó decir cosa en contrario; y en quanto / al visagüelo oyó decir, como dicho / tiene, que fué vezino de la Puebla // de Montalbán, pero no oyó decir / dél otra cossa, ques la verdad, / e dixo este testigo que no le a conos- / çido ni conoze parientes pecheros por linea rreta de varón, antes les / a conosçido y conoze parientes hijos- / dalgo, y esto rresponde a la dicha pregunta / e rrepregunta.

III. A la tercera pregunta del dicho ynterrogatorio dixo / que de más de çinquenta años / a esta parte, que este testigo se acuerda, / sabe e a visto que en la dicha villa / de Talabera no se an pagado ni / pagan por los vecinos pecheros de la dicha villa pechos de pecheros / por rrepartimientos y sabe que se / pagan de los propios del concejo / de la dicha villa, e antes deste tiempo / syempre oyó decir por cosa pública / e notoria que hubo pechos de / pecheros que se pagavan por / rrepartimiento entre los vecinos de la / dicha villa, e aun este testigo a visto / algunos padrones antiguos, a los quales se rremite, y público / e notorio que de los del año de quinientos / e diez e nueve para acá no se / pagavan los dichos pechos de pecheros de la dicha villa por rrepartimiento, / syno que se pagan de los propios del concejo, como dicho tiene, y que quando / se pagavan en él ponían en los dichos / padrones los que heran pecheros, y no los que heran hijosdalgo, // lo qual es público y notorio, y como dicho tiene se rremite a los dichos padrones, pero ya que no se pagan los dichos pechos de pecheros / por rrepartimiento, sabe este testigo que ay / rreconosçimiento en ella entre los / que son hijosdalgo y los que / no lo son, que es la rreputaçión de cada uno, y en los ofiçios / del concejo de la dicha villa, que quando ay sede bacante de los arçobispos, / el ayuntamiento de la dicha villa / pone y nombra alcaldes ordinarios, los quales ofiçios syempre se han dado y dan a hombres hijos- / dalgo e prinçipales e de los prinçipales del pueblo, / y en ello se pone mucha deligen- / çia e se tiene mucho miramiento / que sean hidalgos y gente / onrrada y principal, y tan- / bién en que de tres en tres años, / o de dos en dos se hazen padrones / en la dicha villa, calle [illegible] por / honbres señalados por el ayunta- / miento de la dicha villa de los que son pecheros, e juramentados, los quales / hazen padron calle [?], y al que es / pechero le ponen por pechero, / y al que es hidalgo le ponen por hidalgo, // e ni más ni menos, y rreconosçimiento / e distinçión en que en cada un año / ay un padrón general en la dicha villa, / y en este an de ser honbres hijosdalgo. Yten, en la que toca a ofiçios de / jurados y alcaldes de la hermandad, / se dan los dichos ofiçios en cada un año, la mitad a hijosdalgo, y la otra mitad a los que son buenos honbres de / casta de pecheros, e ni más ni menos se an diferençiado los hijos- / dalgo de los que no lo son en el derecho / del portazguillo que dize la pregunta, que se paga çierto derecho de cada carga / que cada vezino mete en la dicha villa, / y el que es pechero paga el dicho derecho / y el que es hijodalgo no lo paga. Yten / ay cárçel pribada que se dize / la torre de San Pedro, a donde lleban / presos a los hijosdalgo, y otra cárçel / para los pecheros, eçepto sy el delito / fecho es muy grande, que en tal caso / se les lleban a la carçel de los pecheros, / por ser cárcel rreçia e donde ay mucha / guarda, en las quales dichas cosas / sabe este testigo que se an diferençiado / e diferençian en la dicha villa de / Talabera los hijosdalgo de los / que no lo son, y lo sabe como / vezino e natural que es de la dicha villa.

IIII. A la quarta pregunta dixo que de más de çinquenta años a esta parte que este testigo se acuerda, sabe ser verdad / y que se haze y acostumbra lo contenido en // la pregunta, segund que en ella se declara, / porque este testigo a estado en los dichos / pueblos y tiene hazienda en algunos / dellos, y lo susodicho es público e notorio / e pública boz y fama, lo qual rresponde a la pregunta.

V. A la quinta pregunta del dicho ynterrogatorio, / dixo, que en quanto a la posesión / del dicho licenciado Hernando de Rojas, / que litiga, / a oído decir por público e notorio / en el lugar de Crespos, tierra de Esca- / lona, do tiene çiertas huertas y here- / dades, que está en posiçión de hijodalgo, y que como tal no pecha en los pechos / de pecheros del dicho lugar, y este testigo lo a visto puesto por / testimonio del escriuano del dicho lugar de Crespos, y en quanto a la po- / sesión del dicho litigante no sabe / otra cossa ninguna, porque el susodicho, siendo niño, en vida / de su padre, se fué a estudiar / a Salamanca, e de allí vino a esta / villa donde se casó, y aunque / algunas vezes a ydo a Talabera, a si- / do por pocos días a ver a sus / parientes y a otros negocios, y en quanto a la posesión de los dichos / licenciado Francisco de Rojas y el / bachiller Hernando de Rojas, padre y agüelo deste que litiga, / en todo el tiempo e años que dicho e de- / clarado tiene en la primera pregunta / que los conosçió estaban casados // con bienes y hazienda rraíz e casa / poblada en la dicha villa de Ta- / labera donde fueron vecinos, y sabe que los susodichos y cada uno / dellos en su tiempo estubieron en posesión / de honbres hijosdalgo notorios, y como tales sabe que en sede / bacante de los arçobispos de Tole- / do, cuya es la dicha villa de Talabera, fueron nombrados por alcaldes ordi- / narios, e si no fueran / hijosdalgo notorios no les / dieran los dichos ofiçios, ni les / admitieran a ellos, porque, / como dicho tiene, syempre se tuvo mucha quenta e miramien- / to en que los alcaldes ordinarios / de la dicha villa, fuesen hijosdalgo y gente muy honrrada e por tal / como ellos lo heran, e tan- / bien espresó quel padre deste / que litiga fue jurado en la dicha villa un año del estado de los hijos- / dalgo, aunque desto no se / acuerda bien, más de que depone / que fue jurado un año, como dicho tiene, / del dicho estado, e sy el padre y agüelo / deste que litiga tuvieron otros ofiçios algunos del estado de los hijos- // dalgo, no tiene noticia, e que / oyó decir en Alcaudete y Almofrague, que asi mismo el padre y agüelo deste que litiga estubieron en / posesión de hijosdalgo, e que como tales / no pecharon en los pechos de pe- / cheros de los dichos lugares por / rraçón de çierta heredad que allí / tenían, que llamavan la posada del Cornicabral, lo qual, como dicho / tiene, oyó decir en los dichos lugares en el tiempo del padre y agüelo del susodicho a muchas presonas por cosa pública e notoria, e dello / e de lo demás que dicho tiene / tal a sydo y es la pública boz y fama / y común opinión, y nunca vió ni / oyó decir lo contrario, y esto rresponde / a la pregunta, y della no sabe otra cossa. Fuéronle hechas las / rrepreguntas de oficio nesçesarias, e dixo que dize lo que dicho tiene.

VI. A la sesta pregunta del dicho ynterrogatorio dixo que dize lo que dicho en la pregunta antes desta, / a que se rrefiere, y esto rresponde a esta pregunta y no sabe más della.

VII. A la setima pregunta del dicho ynterrogatorio, / dixo que dize lo que dicho tiene en las preguntas / antes desta, a que se rrefiere, y esto rresponde a la pregunta.

VIII. A la otava pregunta del dicho ynterrogatorio, / dixo que no vió casar ni velar / a los contenidos en la pregunta, los vió estar casados // y hacer vida maridable en uno como / tales marido y muger, e por tales / fueron avidos e tenidos, e de su casamiento vió que los susodichos, / entre otros hijos, tenían por su / hijo legítimo al dicho licenciado Francisco de / Rojas, padre e madre, e pareçe quel por hijo legítimo fué avido e teni- / do e por tal rreputado, y esto / rresponde a esta pregunta.

IX. A la nobena pregunta dixo que aunque no vió caer ni velar a los / contenidos en la pregunta, los / vió estar casados y hacer vida / maridable en uno, como tales marido y muger, y por tales /

fueron avidos e tenidos, e deste / su matrimonio ovieron por sus hijos / legítimos al dicho licenciado Hernando de Rojas, / que litiga, y al licenciado Juan de Rojas, / y a doña Elvira de / Rojas y a García Ponze de Rojas, llamándolos hijos, / y ellos a ellos padre e madre, criándolos e alimentándo- / los como tales e por tales sus hijos legítimos, y fueron y son avidos y tenidos e / comunmente rreputados de- / llo; es la pública boz y fama, / esto rresponde a la pregunta.

A la húltima pregunta dixo lo que / dicho tiene es verdad para el juramento / que hizo, e siéndole leído su dicho / se rratificó en él, y le fué encargado el / secreto hasta la publicación e prometiólo, e firmólo de su nombre, e rrubricólo / el señor alcalde, e firmélo yo el rreceptor.

(*Rúbrica*) Pasó ante mí, Juan Martín de Villalobos
(*Rúbrica*) Juan Maldonado Verdejo (*Rúbrica*)

III. Résumé of the Remaining Testimony

Since the witnesses who complete the document were not well acquainted with or informed about the author of *La Celestina,* only a few passages selected for their relevance to him need transcription.

1. The last witness of the above group, "Gaspar de Guzmán, vecino que dixo ser de la villa de Talavera," as a resident in Valladolid knew the Licentiate Fernando very well. But he only knew the father and grandfather in Talavera as a youth: ". . . conosció al bachiller Hernando de Rojas . . . seis o siete años, poco más o menos, . . . siendo muchacho antes que fuese a las Yndias, y no sabe si en este tiempo hera biudo o casado, y tenía bienes rrayzes en Talabera, el qual murió mientras este testigo estubo en Yndias." As far as the distinction between *hidalgos* and *pecheros* in Talavera is concerned, he adds: "Ordinariamente el tal procurador general que se nombra cada un año es hijodalgo." As an indication that the Rojas were *hidalgos* he remembers their appointment as *alcaldes*: ". . . a oído decir por público y notorio e pública boz y fama, que los susodichos y cada uno dellos en su tiempo fueron alcaldes ordinarios de la dicha villa de Talavera, nombrados por el ayuntamiento de la dicha villa, sede bacante de los arçobispos de Toledo cuya es dicha villa los quales dichos oficios no se dan syno a hijosdalgo y gente onrrada y principal."

2. The next group of three witnesses are from the Puebla de Montalbán, and it is their testimony that was transcribed for the Rojas as mentioned above. See F. del Valle Lersundi, "Documentos referentes a Fernando de Rojas," *RFE*, XII (1925), 385-396 (VL I).

3. The witness to follow is presented separately. A sixty-year-old *hidalgo*, he identified himself as: "Gerónimo de Meneses, familiar del Santo Oficio de Toledo, vezino de la villa de Talavera." He explains his acquaintance with the Rojas family as follows: ". . . conoze al lizenciado Hernando de Rojas, abogado en esta real audiencia, Corte e Chancillería, desde niño de corta hedad, y en el principio de dicho tiempo le bió y conosció en la villa de Talabera, en casa de su padre . . . y también conosció al lizenciado Francisco de Roxas, padre del dicho litigante, más de quarenta años antes que muriese, todos ellos casados, vibiendo en la dicha villa de Talavera, en la qual y en sus términos y en el lugar de Alcaudete, jurisdicción de la dicha villa, tubo bienes e hacienda rrayz de casas, tierras, biñas y colmenares, e abrá que fallesció quatro años, poco más o menos, y que también conosció al bachiller Hernando de Roxas, abuelo del que litiga, y abrá que le comenzó a conozer más de zinquenta años, e conosciole seys o siete años antes que ffaleçiese, casado y vibiendo en la dicha villa, en la qual e en sus términos tenía e tubo bienes rrayzes, y abrá que murió a su parescer deste testigo, más de quarenta e quatro años, y abrá treynta y dos años poco más o menos, que estando este testigo en la Puebla de Montalbán, en una yglesia que llaman Sant Miguel, le fue dicho e señalado el entierro del visbuelo del dicho litigante. . . ."

As far as the *hidalguía* of the three Rojas is concerned, he affirms: ". . . siempre a cada uno dellos de por si en su tiempo, este dicho testigo los tuvo e a thenido y tiene por hombres hijosdalgo porque en tal opinión, rreputaçión y fama los a visto estar, e que estubieron en la dicha villa e fuera entre sus vezinos e moradores." Then, apparently referring to Garcí González, he presents as personal knowledge the recent deception of the Licentiate Fernando: ". . . a oydo dezir a personas biexas e anzianas, cuyos nombres no tiene memoria presente para los declarar, que el susodicho hera hombre hijodalgo muy notorio e conoscido e natural de Tineo, de la casa de Roxas, la qual a visto constar por casa y solar conoscido de hombres hijosdalgo notorios de sangre. . . ."

As a proof of these assertions, he adduces his own personal inspection of the *padrones* of Talavera: ". . . porque en los padrones e rrepartimientos que antiguamente se hazía en la dicha villa de los pechos del serbicio rreal y moneda forrera que en ella se pagaban por los buenos hombres pecheros, no están puestos ni asentados el padre e abuelo del dicho litigante, porque este testigo los a visto e leído . . . y el dexar de estar en ellos hera y fue por ser hijosdalgo. . . ." He also mentions that the Licentiate Fernando did not have to pay the *pecho* tax on his possessions in Alcaudete. He knows this because ". . . fue regidor muchos años en la dicha villa de Talavera, e a estado en muchas aldeas de su jurisdicción, y especial en los lugares de Almofrague y Alcaudete y Alya."

4. The first of the next group of three Talaveran witnesses is a seventy-seven-year-old *pechero* named Francisco García. In his testimony he confirms that the family was known for its *hidalguía,* stressing their landholdings in Alía and Almofrague as well as around Talavera: ". . . rrayzes en cantidad, ansí casas como tierras y olibares y un colmenar. . . ." Of the Bachelor he says only: ". . . conosció al bachiller Hernando de Roxas . . . doze o treze años antes que falleçiese, casado vibiendo en la dicha villa de Talavera, con bienes rrayzes, y no tiene memoria quantos años abrá que fallesció." He also mentions that the Licentiate Francisco had been named *alcalde* and was exempted from paying the "portazguillo" for his "muchas cargas de bastimento."

5. The following witness, Francisco León, was also a *pechero*, and was seventy-eight years old. He confirms previous testimony, stating that no one in Alía or Almofrague had ever tried to put the Rojas on the lists of *pecheros*—as they had done in other cases, thereby occasioning lawsuits.

6. In the declaration of Nicolás de la Serna from Talavera which follows only his statement about the Bachelor seems at all relevant: "Conosció al bachiller Fernando de Rojas más de quinze o veinte años antes que muriese, vibiendo casado y con bienes rrayzes en la dicha villa de Talabera, ansí casas como holibares y heredades, e también tubo en Alya y Almofrague los vienes que dichos tiene tubo e poseyó el dicho Francisco de Rojas, so hijo."

7. The document concludes with the declaration of another Talaveran, Baltasar Sánchez, who barely knew the author of *La Celestina* and who has nothing new to say about the family.

APPENDIX IV

The Bachelor's *Libros de leyes*

The short titles enumerated here are taken directly from the inventory published by Valle Lersundi. The completed references which follow each item are Luis G. de Valdeavellano's identifications. His comments have been retained in Spanish. The short titles in Spanish for Latin works seem to be Rojas' own identifications written on the bindings. They were probably generally referred to in these abbreviations by law students.

1. EL DECRETO
   Gratianus, cum apparatu Bartholomaei Brixiensis, a Petro Albignano editum. Johannes de Deo, Hispanus: *Flosculus seu summarium totius Decreti.* Venetiis—Johannes de Colonia et Johannes Manthen, 3 enero, 1479.
   Otra edición editada por Sebastiano Brant, 1 julio 1500 (Basilea).

2. LAS DECRETALES
   Liber sextus Decretalium Bonifacii Papae VIII, cum apparatu Johannis Andreae. Johannes Andreae: Super arboribus consanguinatis et affinitatis, Venecia, Nicolaus Jenson—1476.
   Otras ediciones: Venecia. 1482, 1483, 1489, 1491 (contiene las adiciones de Clarii).
   Es más probable que sean las Decretales de Gregorio IX. *Papae libri V,* cum glossa, Venecia, 1482. Otras ediciones: Venecia, 1483, 1486.

3. EL VOLUMEN VIEJO DE TORTIS
   Tortis, Hieronymus de, *Consilium in favorem populi Florentini Papiae,* 1485.

4. LA SEGUNDA PARTE DE SALICETO
   Saliceto, Bartholomaeus de, *Lectura super IX libris Codicis,* Venecia, Johannes Herbort, 1483.
   ———, *Lectura super Digestus vetus,* Brescia, 1499.

5. Francisco de Arecio

Accolti, Francesco (llamado Francesco de Aretio o "el Aretino" (1418-1486) *Consilia, seu responsa iuris,* Pisa, 1483; Mediolani, 1483; Papiae, 1493; Venetiis, 1499.

6. Codigo

Codex Iustinianus cum glossa, Venecia, 1483, 1493-94; Lugduni, c. 1495.

7. *Yten* Alexandro de Ymola

Tartagnis, Alexander de (Imola):

Apostillae super I parte Codicis, Nápoles, 1475.

Apostillae super II parte Codicis, 1483.

Apostillae super I parte Digesti novi, 1480.

Apostillae super II parte Digesti novi, 1481.

Consilia (1477, 1480, 1484-85, 1490-92, 1499).

Lectura super I et II parte Codicis cum apostillis, Venecia, 1488.

Lectura super I parte Codicis cum apostillis, 1482.

Lectura super II parte Codicis, 1483.

Lectura super VI parte Codicis, 1476.

Lectura super I parte Digesti novi, cum apostillis, 1483.

Lectura super I parte Digesti novi, Venecia, 1488.

Lectura super II parte Digesti novi, 1481.

Lectura super I et II parte Digesti veteris, Venecia, 1488.

Lectura super I parte Digesti veteris, cum apostillis, 1481.

Lectura super I et II parte Infortiati, Venecia, 1494.

Lectura super I parte Infortiati, cum apostillis, 1482.

Lectura super II parte Infortiati, cum apostillis, 1480.

Lectura super titulo de verborum obligationibus, Venecia, 1489.

8. *Yten* la Ynstituta

Corpus Iuris Civilis (Iustinianus)

Institutiones cum glossa, c. 1481-83, Venecia (1483, 1484, 1497).

9. *Yten* Baldo sobre los feudos

Ubaldis, Baldus de (Baldo), *Commentum super usibus feudorum et super pace Constantiae,* 1483.

10. *Yten* Paulo de Castro sobre el Esforçado
    Lectura super I parte Infortiati, 1478.
    Lectura super II parte Infortiati, 1480.

11. *Yten* la primera parte de Saliceto
    Véase el número 4.

12. *Yten* Sesto y Clementinas
    Liber sextus Decretalium Bonifacii Papae VIII, cum apparatu
    Johannis Andreae. Johannes Andreae: Super arboribus
    consanguinatis et affinitatis. Venecia, Nicolaus Jenson—
    1476.
    Otras ediciones: Venecia: 1482, 1483, 1489, 1491 (contiene
    las adiciones de Clarii).
    Constitutiones Clementis Papae V, cum apparatu Johannis
    Andreae; quibus accedunt Decretales extravagantes quae
    emanarunt post Sextum, Venetiis, Nicolaus Jenson, 1476.
    Otras ediciones publicadas en Venecia:
    Baptista de Tortis, 6 nov., 1484
    Bartholomaeus de Blavis et Andreas Torresanus, 20
    abril ?, 1485
    Thomas de Blavis, 1 junio 1489
    Johannes et Gregorius de Gregoriis, 16 feb. 1489/90.

13. *Yten* el Esforçado
    Iustinianus, Corpus Iuris Civilis
    Infortiatum cum glossa, Venecia, 1484, 1491, 1494.

14. *Yten* el Digesto viejo
    Iustinianus, Corpus Juris Civilis
    Digestum vetus cum glossa, c. 1478/80; Venecia 1494.

15. *Yten* Jason sobre el Esforçado
    Ambrogio, Jason de Maino, *Commentarii super Codice,
    Digesto veteri et Infortiato*, Venecia, 1496; Pavia 1499 y sigs.
    (8 tomos).

16. *Yten* el Decreto
    Véase el número 1.

17. *Yten* Cardinalis sobre las Clementinas
    Zabarellis, Franciscus de, *Lectura super Clementinas*, Nápoles,

1477; Roma, 1487; Venecia, 1481; Turín, 1492; Venecia, 1497 y 1499.

(Se trata de los comentarios sobre las Constituciones del Papa Clemente V (= Clementinas) por el Cardenal Francesco Zabarella (†1417), frecuentemente designado como "Cardinalis florentinus".)

18. *Yten* SALICETO, SOBRE EL QUARTO Y QUINTO Y SESTO DEL CODIGO
Véase el número 4.

19. *Yten* DIGESTO NUEVO
Iustinianus, *Corpus Juris Civilis*
Digestum novum cum glossa, Venecia, 1483, 1491, 1494.

20. *Yten* ALEXANDRO SOBRE EL SESTO DEL CODIGO
Tartagnis, Alexander de (Imola), *Lectura super VI parte Codicis*, 1476.

21. *Yten* JASON SOBRE LA PRIMERA DEL DIGESTO VIEJO
Ambrogio Jason de Maino: véase el número 15.

22. *Yten* PAULO DE CASTRO SOBRE TODO EL CODIGO
Paulus de Castro, *Lectura super I, II, III, IV, VI, VII Codicis*, Mediolani, 1496.
(Paulo de Castro (*circa* 1405-*circa* 1421) fué un discípulo de Baldo.)

23. *Yten* PAULO DE CASTRO SOBRE EL DIGESTO VIEJO
Lectura super Digestus vetus, Mediolani, 1489; Venetiis, 1496.

24. *Yten* BALDO SOBRE EL ESFORÇADO
Ubaldis, Baldus de (Baldo), *Lectura super I et II parte Infortiati,* 1498.

25. *Yten* PAULO DE CASTRO SOBRE EL DIGESTO NUEVO
Paulo de Castro, *Lectura super Digestus novus,* Venetiis s.a.; Venetiis, 1494; Mediolani, 1496.

26. *Yten* TRATADO DE CEPOLA CUN CAUTELIS
Cepolla, Bartholomaeus, *De servitutibus praediorum—Cautelae.* Venecia, 1485.

27. *Yten* CINO SOBRE EL DIGESTO VIEJO
Cino da Pistoia, *Lectura Digestum vetus,* Lugduni, 1528.

28. *Yten* Petrarca en latín
    No es un libro de leyes.

29. *Yten* las leyes del Reyno
    Díaz de Montalvo, Alonso, *Recopilación de leyes, ordena-*
    mientos, y pragmáticas (llamada también *Libro de leyes*).
    Ediciones:
    > Huete, Alvaro de Castro, 11 nov. 1484.
    > Zamora, Antón de Centenero, 15 junio 1485
    > Huete, Alvaro de Castro, 23 agosto 1485
    > Salamanca, 1486
    > Burgos, Fadrique de Basilea, 24 sept. 1488
    > Zaragoza, Juan Hurus, 3 junio 1490
    > Sevilla, Ungut y Polono, 17 mayo 1492
    > Sevilla, Pegnitzer, Magno y Thomas, 4 abril 1495
    > Sevilla, 1496
    > Sevilla, Ungut y Polono, 29 marzo 1498
    > Sevilla, 1499
    > Salamanca, 29 marzo 1500

30. *Yten* prematicas del Reyno
    Las pregmáticas y capítulos que su magestad ... hizo en las
    Cortes de Valladolid (1537), Cuenca 1538.

31. *Yten* leyes de Toro glosadas
    Las leyes de toro glosadas, 1527.

32. *Yten* Ugo de Celso
    Hugo de Celso, *Repertorio de las leyes de todos los Reynos,*
    única edición encontrada: Valladolid, 1547.

33. *Yten* las Leyes de la mesta
    Copilación de todas las Leyes y Ordenanças del Honrado
    Concejo de la Mesta general de Castilla y León. Sin pié de
    imprenta ni fecha.
    (Es la primera colección impresa conocida de las Leyes de la
    Mesta. El último documento incluído en esta compilación es
    de Toledo y fechado en 1526, lo que puede orientar respecto
    de la data y lugar de publicación. La edición siguiente, o
    "Libro de Privilegios y Leyes del Ilustre y muy Honrado
    Concejo de la Mesta," Madrid, 1569, es de fecha posterior a la
    muerte de Fernando de Rojas.)

34. *Yten* Cortes de Toledo del año de veynte y cinco
    Las cortes de Toledo deste presente año de mil y quinientos y XXV años, Burgos (Alonso de Melgar) 1525, 1526, 1535.

35. Yten Cortes de Madrid del año de veynte y tres
    Debe de tratarse de un error, pues no hay noticia de que en el año 1523—ni tampoco en 1423—se reuniesen Cortes en Madrid; vid. Colección de Cortes de los antiguos Reinos de España por la Real Academia de la Historia. Catálogo, Madrid, 1855. En Madrid se celebraron Cortes, no en 1523, sino en 1528 (cf. Cortes de Madrid. Cuaderno de Leyes y pragmáticas, Alcalá de Henares, por Juan de Brocar, año de 1540. Probablemente se trata de las Cortes de Valladolid de 1523; cf. Cuaderno de Leyes y provisiones de las Cortes de Valladolid, impreso en Burgos por Juan de Junta, año 1535.)

36. *Yten* Cortes de Madrid del año de treynta y quatro, con las de Segovia
    Quadernos de las cortes que su magestad de la emperatris y reyna nra señora tuuo en la ciudad de Segouia el año de MDXXXIIII, côlas declaraciones . . . , Madrid 1534.

37. *Yten* Leyes Capitulares
    Capitula, leges et constitutiones Regni Neapolitani, Neapoli (Franciscus Tuppi ?) s.a.

38. *Yten* quadernos de las alcavalas con otras leyes menudas
    Quadernos de Alcabalas de 1484, 1490 y 1491
    ¿Burgos, Fadrique de Basilea, 1486?
    Zamora, Centenera, 1487
    Sevilla, Ungut y Polono, 1495
    ¿Salamanca, 1496?
    ¿Salamanca, ——?

39. *Yten* las notas del Relator
    Fernando Díaz de Toledo, *Notas del Relator*
    Burgos 1490; Valladolid 1493; Salamanca 1499 and 1500; Sevilla 1507.

40. *Yten* Reportorio de las leyes del Reyno de marca menor
    Gonzalo González de Bustamente, La peregrina (*Peregrina,*

535

a compilatore glossarum dicta Bonifacia, Sevilla, 1498). Según Ureña y Smenjaud esta obra es el único repertorio jurídico anterior a la obra de Montalvo; González lo escribió a fines del siglo XIV en español; fué traducido al latín e impreso en 1498. Sin embargo, es más probable que sea Hugo de Celso, *Repertorio universal de todas las leyes de estos Reinos,* 1ª ed., Alcalá de Henares, 1540.

41. *Yten* CAPITULOS DE COREGIDORES
Los capítulos . . . que han de guardar e cumplir los gouernadores, asistentes, corregidores . . . , Sevilla, 9 de junio 1500.

42. *Yten* SUMA ROSELA
Rosellis, *Tractatus,* Venedig, 1481.

43. *Yten* CINO, SOBRE EL DIGESTO VIEJO (véase el número 27).

44. *Yten* LEYES SINODALES CON OTRAS LEYES DE LA HERMANDAD E DE LA VILLA, TODO DE MANO
Quaderno de las leyes nueuas de la hermandad, existen seis ediciones del siglo XV sin indicaciones tipográficas.

INDEX

This index consists of proper names and titles of anonymous works (a topical index was essayed but found impractical) and is divided into two clearly differentiated human categories: first, the usual authorities, authors, and notabilities who are to be found in all studies of this nature; and second, a veritable "population" of individuals who exist only here and in the documentary sources. In order to distinguish one category from the other, and thereby to render the index more useful, I have appended identifying tags to those falling into the second category. The abbreviations used in these tags are as follows:

A	Alvaro de Montalbán
Carriches Rojas	Members of the aristocratic family of Martín de Rojas of Carriches identified as a relation of the Bachelor
faculty	Inconspicuous members of the faculty at Salamanca
Franco	Members of the Franco family, Rojas's cousins
Inq.	Inquisition
probanza	Those named in the *probanzas* of the Licentiate Fernando de Rojas as officials, witnesses, or informants
Puebla	Puebla de Montalbán
Puebla, other Rojas	Members of the other Rojas family in the Puebla to whom the Bachelor was probably related
R	Fernando de Rojas
Relaciones	Persons mentioned in the *Relaciones de los pueblos de España ordenadas por Felipe II*
Serrano	Puebla inhabitants named in the 1494 trial of Pedro Serrano

Tineo Rojas	Members of the *hidalgo* family of Rojas in Cangas de Tineo with whom the Licentiate Fernando claimed relationship

INDEX

556

Sigüenza, Fray José de, 228 n. 39
Siliceo, Cardinal, *see* Martínez de
  Siliceo, Juan
Silva, Arias de, 124
Silva, Feliciano de, 214 n. 15,
  217-218 n. 20, 363, 365
Silverman, J., 47 n. 56, 495 n. 8
Silvio, Aeneas, 324, 435
Simón Díaz, José, 325 n. 121, 451
Simpson, L. B., 321 n. 110
Singleton, Mack, 321 n. 110
Slote, B., 368 n. 27
Sobriqués, S., 405 n. 14, 421 n. 48
Somolinos D'Ardois, G., 133 n. 47
Sophocles, 13, 20, 339
Sorja, Martín (Toledo merchant,
  employer of A), 75, 76 n. 22
Sosia, 292 n. 50, 413, 414, 478
Spinoza, Baruch, 138, 144, 189 n. 78
Spitzer, Leo, 315, 323, 367 n. 25,
  371 n. 35
Stendhal, 6, 18, 25, 51, 60, 62, 200,
  266, 303, 319, 379
Stonequist, Everett, 136, 142, 183,
  201 n. 102
Suárez, Francisco, 118
Suárez, Hermán (Franco), 503
Suárez Franco, Alonso (Franco), 503
Suárez Franco, Francisco (Franco),
  503
Suárez Franco, Gaspar (Franco), 503
Suárez Franco, Hermán/Fernán
  (Franco), 35, 36 n. 39, 38, 39, 40,
  42, 44, 45, 46, 47, 498, 502, 503
Sylva, Pedro de (Serrano), 245

Taine, H. A., 200
Talavera, Arcipreste de, *see*
  Martínez de Toledo, Alonso
Talavera, Fray Hernando de,
  73 n. 13, 96 n. 60, 101 n. 74,
  117 n. 10, 118, 124 n. 25, 149,
  168 n. 20, 171, 175 n. 46, 184 n. 67,
  411 n. 27, 425, 427 n. 57, 429,
  451, 453
Tapia, Catalina de, 67 n. 2
Tartagnis, Alexander de (Imola),
  see Ymola, Alexander de
Tavera, don Juan (Archbishop),
  474 n. 172
Téllez Girón, Alonso/Alfonso (Lord

of Puebla), 80, 152, 173, 223, 224,
  227, 232, 242, 245, 246, 247, 248,
  249, 250, 251, 252, 253, 254, 258,
  260, 261, 262, 264, 397, 398
Téllez Girón II, Alonso, 247 n. 87
Téllez Girón, don Pedro, 263 n. 119
Téllez de Toledo, doña Juana
  (Puebla, other Rojas), 261, 262
Terciado, Diaguito (Serrano), 245
Terciado, Pedro (Serrano), 245
Terence, 58 n. 66, 297, 309 n. 86,
  312, 313 n. 93, 314, 315,
  321 n. 111, 324, 330, 361 n. 5, 431
Teresa of Avila, Saint, 27, 118, 128,
  130, 162 n. 7, 169, 187 n. 75, 201,
  438, 485, 492 n. 4
Tetzel, Gabriel, 193 n. 88
La Thebayda, 132 n. 45, 237, 362,
  363, 365, 448
Thibaudet, Albert, 57
Thomas of Aquinas, Saint, 275
Thoreau, H. D., 458
Thorndike, L., 296 n. 59
Tirso de Molina, 384
Toledo, Catalina de (Serrano), 248
Torquemada, Fray Tomás de, 118,
  167, 172
Torralba, Doctor Eugenio, 198, 458
Torre, A., de la, 148 n. 76
Torre, Alfonso de la, 195, 274 n. 12,
  314 n. 97, 325, 328, 340, 341,
  387 n. 48, 430, 447, 487
Torre, E. A. de la, 148 n. 76
Torre, Fernando de la, 124 n. 24,
  164, 169, 342, 459
Torreblanca Villalpando, Francisco,
  100 n. 69
Torrejón, Fray Andrés de, 409 n. 22,
  n. 23, 415
Torrellas, Pere, 346 n. 161
Torres, Alonso de, 133
Torres, Diego de, 350
Torres, Juana de (maidservant of
  R), 419, 424, 483 n. 203
Torres, Pedro de, 274
Torresanus, Andreas, 532
Torres Naharro, Bartolomé de
  (brother-in-law of A), 24, 182,
  217-218 n. 20, 272 n. 8, 289 n. 43,
  344 n. 154, 365, 413, 448,
  457 n. 133, 478

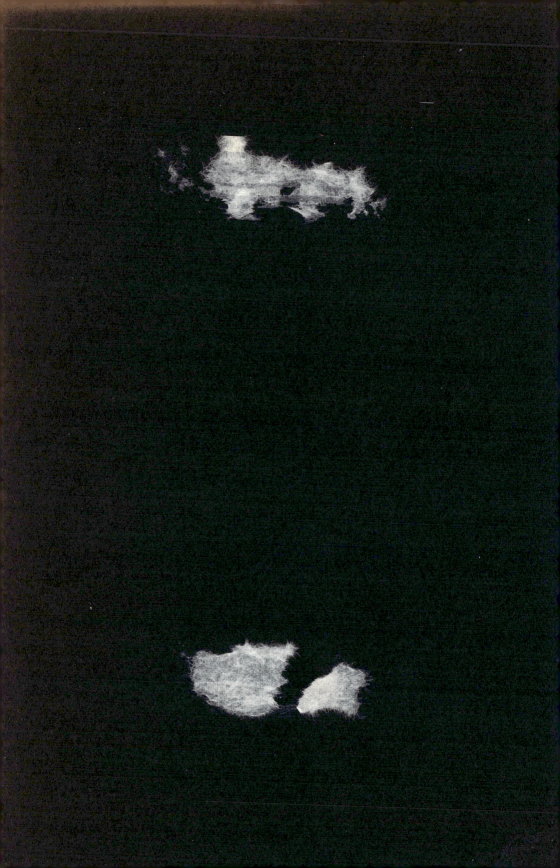